Using
Intuit® QuickBooks®
Premier 2012 for Windows®

CHRISTINE A. HEANEY

S0-CDP-973

PEARSON

Toronto

Vice-President, Editorial Director: Gary Bennett
Editor-in-Chief: Nicole Lukach
Acquisitions Editor: Megan Farrell
Sponsoring Editor: Kathleen McGill
Marketing Manager: Jenna Wulff
Supervising Developmental Editor: Suzanne Schaan
Developmental Editor: Karen Townsend
Lead Project Manager: Avinash Chandra
Project Manager: Jessica Hellen
Manufacturing Manager: Susan Johnson
Production Editor: Lila Campbell
Copy Editor: Susan Adlam
Proofreader: Leanne Rancourt
Compositor: Cenveo Publisher Services
Art Director: Julia Hall
Cover and Interior Designer: Anthony Leung
Cover Image: Antishock/Shutterstock

QuickBooks is a registered trademark of Intuit, Inc., used under license.
Windows is a trademark of Microsoft Corporation.

10 9 8 7 6 5 4 [EBM]

Library and Archives Canada Cataloguing in Publication

Heaney, Christine, 1961–
    Using QuickBooks Premier 2012
for Windows / Christine A. Heaney.

Includes bibliographical references and index.
ISBN 978-0-13-296404-3

    1. QuickBooks. 2. Small business—Accounting—Computer programs.
3. Small business—Finance—Computer programs.
4. Accounting—Computer programs. I. Title.

HF5679.H42335 2012   657'.9042028553   C2012-900361-1

ISBN 978-0-13-296404-3

CONTENTS

CD-ROM Chapters

APPENDIX   1

TAX GST, HST, & PST   1

Using QuickBooks® Premier 2012 for Windows® is the fourth edition of the QuickBooks series. This textbook is an introduction to QuickBooks, where we have covered the basic and most commonly used features of the QuickBooks program.

The biggest challenge in writing this textbook was presented by the QuickBooks program itself — the program is very flexible and offers many different ways of completing each type of transaction. Our efforts to present keystroke instructions in a simple, straightforward way meant making choices about the method we describe as the main one. In most cases, we present some alternative keystrokes when we introduce a new feature. We expect that users will choose the methods they prefer for opening forms and completing them. As long as the information entered on the form is correct, the end result is the same.

In Chapter 1, we provide an introduction and overview of the program. We have also provided a practice company data set with which you can experiment safely without damaging any other data files. This chapter also covers the basics of the Help features in the program, and we expect that you will draw on these as needed as you work through the exercises.

To teach the software, we have created 12 company simulations (Chapters 12 and 13 are found on the CD that accompanies this textbook) with realistic transactions or source documents so that as you learn the program you are also completing realistic business accounting activities. At the end of each chapter or simulation, you will be able to generate a set of meaningful business reports from these transactions.

To create meaningful reports, you must enter a variety of transactions — no business has only sales or only purchases. Therefore, we have organized topics by the features the company in the chapter might use, beginning with a very simple cash transaction business (cash sales and cash purchases) that generates basic business reports. To this we add more features in each chapter so that the chapters build progressively in both number of features and complexity of the business. Each chapter continues to use, and build on, the types of transactions introduced earlier. This approach provides practice, reinforces earlier topics, and makes the simulations more realistic.

To get you started immediately, we provide data files already set up and ready for transactions. Setting up a new company is more complex than most accounting transactions, so we introduce them later, progressing from a very simple business to a more complex setup. Even for the setup exercises, we provide data files that are ready for transactions so that you can complete the transactions for additional practice before attempting the setup of new data files.

The first time a feature is introduced in the textbook, we provide simple-to-follow, step-by-step keystroke instructions with a large number of screen shots that guide you through the transactions. Chapters that introduce new transactions also include complete instructions for generating the reports related to those transactions.

After covering the very basic cash business in Chapter 2, the second company, in Chapter 3, introduces the General Journal but still makes cash sales and cash purchases. Because of frequent requests from instructors to introduce company setups early on in the text, in Chapter 4 we show the setup for a simple non-profit organization in Winnipeg, Manitoba, that completes only cash and General Journal transactions. We also set up the taxes for the non-profit to track the 2.5% eligible GST and the 2.5% ineligible GST.

Then we add Accounts Payable (Chapter 5) and Accounts Receivable (Chapter 6) transactions. More advanced features within the areas covered up to Chapter 6 are introduced in the next two chapters — discounts , estimates, and purchase orders in Chapter 7, and banking, account reconciliation, and sales tax remittance in Chapter 8. In Chapter 9, the second setup chapter, you learn how to set up all the features that you have used in the previous chapters. Payroll, including payroll tax remittance, is covered in Chapter 10, and inventory is covered in Chapter 11. Chapter 12 (found on the CD included with the textbook) is the final keystroke setup chapter that includes setting up the payroll and inventory features. Chapter 13 (found on the CD included with the textbook) is a comprehensive practice chapter that you set up on your own. This chapter includes all the elements covered in the text for a final review. An appendix found on the CD provides an overview of sales taxes — Tax: GST, PST, and HST. Feedback from instructors has told us that this is important information.

Using This Book

The accounting applications in this textbook were prepared using QuickBooks Premier 2012 software published by Intuit Canada. You must have installed the QuickBooks Premier 2012 program that is available as a download with this textbook or another licensed copy of QuickBooks Premier to work through the applications in this textbook.

You must also have a hard disk and CD-ROM drive or a network system with Windows installed. Network users should work with their site administrator to ensure program and data access.

To review accounting principles, you should have a standard accounting text. We provide some accounting principles in the text and in the Review of Basic Accounting on the Data CD, but these are not intended to replace the breadth and depth of most standard accounting texts.

Note to Instructors
This textbook has been written for students who want to become familiar with QuickBooks 2012.

Many students are seeking to learn QuickBooks, as they are increasingly aware of the need for this skill in the employment opportunities they seek.

QuickBooks Student Edition Included
Intuit Canada has made it easy for students to study at home through the creation of a Student Edition of the software. The software is available as a download with this textbook. The information and access code can be found in the package included with the textbook.

The student edition will remain valid and accessible for 12 months after it is activated. Note that the software is non-transferable.

Step-by-Step Instruction
This textbook uses simple step-by-step instructions to take the confusion out of the learning process. Each step that the student must follow is clearly numbered.

Logical Organization
This textbook begins with simple case studies and continues with more complex case studies as the student progresses through the textbook.

Source Documents
This textbook has been changed from the original format. The source documents are incorporated within the textbook so the students do not need to flip back and forth between the source documents and the keystroke instructions. When a source document is listed in the book, a note in the side margin indicates whether there are step-by-step instructions that follow, or whether the student should enter the source document on his or her own.

Although the source documents are not listed at the beginning of each lesson, they are available in that format on the student CD if you prefer to work directly from the list of source documents.

Students' Needs
This book has been designed to make the students' learning process simple yet substantial. It has been designed so that students can work independently, at their own pace.

Instructor's Manual
Instructors can access the Instructor Solutions on the Pearson catalogue at http://catalogue.pearsoned.ca/, which includes the solution files for each chapter with all the source documents completed together with the required reports. These solution files must be accessed using QuickBooks Premier 2012 R8.

An Instructor's Manual is also available at http://catalogue. pearsoned.ca/.

The updated and improved Instructor's Manual includes:

* Multiple choice questions, short answer questions, transaction exercises, and new multi-chapter transaction exercises perfect for practice or assessment purposes in-class or for assignments

When you download the Instructor Resources from the online catalogue, the Instructor's Manual and Solutions are in separate files:

* Instructor's Resource Manual (zip)
  Compressed file contains Word, PDF, and QuickBooks files

* Textbook Solutions for Instructors (zip)
  Compressed file contains PDF and QuickBooks files

Updating QuickBooks

From time to time, Intuit releases updates for its products. Updates contain updated payroll tax tables as well as any program fixes. At the time of creating the data files on the Data CD, Release 8 was available and all company files on the CD that accompany this textbook have been created with this release. When you install the QuickBooks 2012 student edition available as a download with this textbook, Release 5 will be installed and Release 8 should automatically be downloaded after the installation. Depending on when you download the software, a later release may be available. QuickBooks is set by default to download updates automatically. If you do not have Release 8 installed, you can manually download it from the Intuit website. Instructions on how to install the automatic product update are described on page 13 in Chapter 1.

To confirm that you have the R8 or later upgrade installed, press F2 on your keyboard to display the Product Information screen. In the top left-hand corner of the screen you will see: Product QuickBooks Premier Edition 2012 Release R8P (or later). R8P was the latest release at the time of writing this textbook so you may have a higher Release number. The company files in this textbook require that the latest Release be installed.

Manually Download and Install the QuickBooks Update

Although QuickBooks should automatically download the latest release, your firewall may stop the installation. If you do not have Release 8 installed, you can manually download the latest QuickBooks product update. You will need an Internet connection to perform the download. At the time of writing this textbook the update can be downloaded and installed by performing the following steps from within QuickBooks:

a) **Click Help** from the menu

b) **Click Update QuickBooks**

c) **Select** the **Update Now tab** and **click** on the **Maintenance Releases link**

d) **Click** the **See a complete list of changes made to your QuickBooks product link**

e) Refer to the instructions on the QuickBooks support website to manually download and install the product update. Make sure you download the product update available for the QuickBooks Premier edition

What if I Don't Upgrade QuickBooks to the Latest Release?

As indicated, it is important that you upgrade your QuickBooks software to the latest release. These releases include updated payroll tax tables as well as any fixes required in the software. Some product updates contain changes to the QuickBooks database. You will receive the following message if you try to open a company file that has previously been opened in a version of QuickBooks with a later product update than the one you have installed:

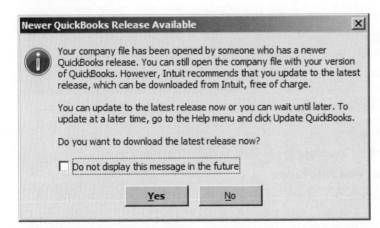

Figure Preface-1

If you receive this message, you must update QuickBooks with the latest product update before you can open the file. Refer to the instructions under the Updating the Program heading on page 13 in Chapter 1 to learn how to update QuickBooks.

INTUIT SUPPORT WEBSITE

If you have any problems while using QuickBooks, visit http://support.intuit.ca/quickbooks/ and enter the problem you are having in the search box for detailed information.

The Data CD

The data files are ready to use immediately. No passwords have been added to any of the files. You can install the data files easily because the Data CD should open automatically. The installation procedure on the CD will copy the files to your hard disk. The Data CD also includes Chapters 12 and 13 of the textbook, a Tax Appendix, the Source Document file, a ReadMe file, a PDF file of the Review of Basic Accounting, an Accounting Cycle Tutorial, and a link to the Acrobat Reader program if you do not have it installed already on your computer. You need Acrobat Reader installed in order to read PDF files.

Installing the Data Files to Your Hard Disk

1. **Insert** the **Data CD** into your CD-ROM Drive

    If the CD does not open immediately:

    a) **Choose** the **Windows Start menu**

    b) **Click Run**

    c) **Click Browse** and find the CD Drive from the Look in drop-down list

    d) **Click** the **CD drive** to open it

    e) **Click Start.exe**

    f) **Click Open** to return to the Run window (Start.exe will be displayed in the Open field)

    g) **Click OK**

2. The Data CD home page window should be displayed

    Choose to install the data files, open Chapters 12 or 13, access the Source Document file, review the Tax Appendix, view the ReadMe file, open the Review of Basic Accounting file, an Accounting Cycle Tutorial, or click the link to install Acrobat Reader from the Adobe website (required to open the Review of Basic Accounting file and the Tax Appendix).

3. To install the data files:

    a) **Click Data Files for Exercises** in the Text in the left sidebar menu

    b) **Click** the **Install Data Files button**

    The data files are copied to a Data folder and a Setup folder on your hard drive and located within a new data folder called QkBkData in Drive C. The files are ready to work with in QuickBooks.

4. **Close** the **Data CD window**

Copying Selected Data Files from the Data CD

To copy a single file or multiple files from the CD to your working folder using the Copy and Paste commands in Windows Explorer, perform the following steps. In the following steps we will select the Data folder. You can also select the Setup folder.

1. **Insert** the **Data CD** into the CD-ROM Drive

2. **Right-click** on the **Start button**

3. **Choose Explore**

4. **Click Computer** in the Folders list

5. **Click D:** (or the drive letter for your CD drive) to view the folders on the CD

6. **Click Data** to view the individual data files and folders. (Files and folders will be listed on the right side of the Folders list). You can copy the entire data set at once, or one or more files.

    To select all files for copying:

    a) **Click Bookroom**, the first file in the list to select it

    b) **Press** (shift) and **click Tours**, the last file in the list (or choose the Edit menu and click Select All)

    To select a single file for copying:

    a) **Click Chelsea.qbw** or the file you want to copy

7. Copy the selected files by performing the following steps

    a) **Choose** the **Organize menu** (Edit menu if you are using XP) and click Copy; or

    b) **Press** (ctrl) + C

    c) All selected files are copied to the Windows Clipboard

8. **Click Drive C:** and scroll through looking for the QkBkData folder

9. **Click QkBkData**, the folder created from the CD installation; or if you would prefer to create a new folder for your data files:

    a) **Right-click** the **folder or drive** where you want to create the new folder

    b) **Select New** from the menu and then Folder

    c) **Type** a **name** for the new folder

10. To paste the selected files to the QkBkData folder or your new folder:

    a) **Select** the **Organize menu** (Select the Edit menu if you're using Windows XP)

    b) **Select Paste**

    c) Replace the existing file(s) with the new one if you are asked

Setting the Computer's Date Format

The date format that you use in QuickBooks is determined by your Windows operating system and not by QuickBooks. The dates used in this textbook are in month/day/year format.

Determine which format your computer is in (you may have to do this before every session if you are working in a lab) by looking in the Regional Settings section of the Control Panel. If you begin to enter transactions without checking the date format of the computer, you may find that you have posted transactions to the wrong fiscal period.

If your computer is not set up in the month/day/year format, you have two choices:

1. You can enter the dates used in the textbook in the same format as your computer. Remember to change each date in the textbook to the format of your computer's date format or your data will not be accurate.

2. You can change your computer's date format. To change the format in Windows XP, Windows Vista, or Windows 7 do the following:

    ### Windows XP

    1. **Click** the **Start button** on the taskbar
    2. **Click** on **Control Panel**
    3. **Double click** on **Regional and Language Options**
    4. **Click** on the **Customize button**
    5. **Click** on the **Date tab**

6. **Click** on the **drop-down arrow** beside Short date format
7. **Select** one of the **styles** where the month is the first choice (**M, MM = month**)
8. **Click** on the **drop-down arrow** beside Long date format
9. **Select** one of the **styles** where the month is the first choice (**MMMM = month**)
10. **Click OK** to save the changes
11. **Click OK** to exit the Regional and Language Options window
12. **Close** the **Control Panel**

Windows Vista

1. **Click** the **Start button** on the taskbar
2. **Click** on **Control Panel**
3. **Click** on **Classic View** (if it is not already selected)
4. **Double click** on **Regional and Language Options**
5. **Click** on the **Formats tab** (this is the default tab and may already be displayed)
6. **Click** on the **Customize this format button**
7. **Click** on the **Date tab**
8. **Type mm/dd/yyyy** in the Short date field
9. **Click** on the **drop-down arrow** beside the Long date field
10. **Select** one of the **styles** where the month is the first choice (**MMMM = month**)
11. **Click OK** to save the changes
12. **Click OK** to exit the Regional and Language Options window
13. **Close** the **Control Panel**

Windows 7

1. **Click** on the **Start button** on the taskbar
2. **Click** on **Control Panel**
3. **Double click** on **Clock, Language, and Region**
4. **Click** on the **Region and Language link**
5. **Click** the **drop-down list** in the Short date field
6. **Select mm/dd/yy**
7. **Click** the **drop-down list** in the Long date field
8. **Select** one of the **styles** where the month is the first choice (MMMM = month)
9. **Click Apply** to save the changes
10. **Click OK** to exit the Region and Language window
11. **Close** the **Control Panel**

Working through the Applications

Setup applications are introduced early in the text. Advanced users should have no difficulty working through the applications in the order given and may even choose to skip some applications. However, at a minimum, we recommend working through all of the step-by-step instructions in each chapter so you become familiar with all the journals before starting the more comprehensive applications.

Order of Applications

There is an alternative order for working through the applications or chapters in the textbook. All the chapters with step-by-step instructions for transactions may be completed first and the setup chapters (Chapters 4, 9, and 12) later. Transactions for these three setup chapters may be completed before you complete the setup to provide additional practice entering transactions, to familiarize yourself with the file structure for the companies, and to make the setups easier to complete. The company files for these chapters with the setup instructions completed can be found on the CD under the Setup folder. Chapter 13 is the last chapter, and we do not provide step-by-step instructions or a setup data file for it. This chapter is intended as a challenging comprehensive practice exercise. Chapters 12 and 13 are not included in the textbook, but can be found on the CD that accompanies the textbook.

Keystroke Instruction Style

We have incorporated different paragraph styles for different kinds of statements in the text to help you identify the instructions that you must follow to complete the transactions correctly and view the screens that we present. These different styles are illustrated below:

1. **Press**   (tab) to advance to the Date field (Keystroke command line — command word is bold face and the object of the command, what you press, is in colour. Keystrokes are numbered and spaced apart.)

2. **Type**   **Spread the Word** (Command line with text you type in colour)

Regular text is presented in normal paragraphs like this one. Key words are shown in colour to make it easy to identify the topics covered in the text. The text also uses Notes and Warnings that contain information and caution. The shaded boxes contain information that you may need while working with transactions.

Source Documents

Source documents are incorporated throughout the text. Some source documents are displayed for information purposes and will be marked with a Source Docs heading. The step-by-step instructions to enter the source document follow it. Note that if you complete a source document on your own that contains step-by-step instructions, you will end up entering the source document twice and the print screens in the text will not match yours.

Other source documents are listed for you to try on your own, allowing you to have more practice entering transactions. Beside each source document or list of source documents, you will find a Source Docs for Practice heading describing what you are supposed to do.

If you have used this text in the past and would prefer to skip the step-by-step instructions and work only with a list of source documents, refer to the CD in the back of the textbook for the source documents file. You can print the complete list of source documents for the chapter you are currently working on.

Dates

Transaction Dates

When you open a QuickBooks company file, the default transaction date displayed on forms will either be your current computer date or the last entered date, depending on how your preferences are set up. When you open forms in QuickBooks, **do not compare your dates to the ones displayed in the textbook.** The dates in the textbook reflect the date the author created the print screen. Only the dates of completed transactions should match those in the textbook.

On Reports

In the top left-hand corner of most reports, you will see a date and time stamp. **Do not compare your date and time stamp to the ones shown on reports in the textbook.** The dates in the textbook reflect the date the author created the print screen.

Sample Files

Notes
The payroll information and calculations in each chapter do not reflect current payroll information. Do not use the figures calculated in the payrolls in your company file.

The data files for Chapters 10, 11, 12, and 13 have been converted to a sample file so that you can enter payroll information for dates outside of the current payroll tax table period. This is important for learning purposes. No matter what QuickBooks tax table you have installed, the payroll information in the print screens in the textbook will be the same as yours as long as you use the sample file. The sample data file is set up so that Dec. 15, 2007, is the current date displayed when entering forms. You will override this date and use dates in 2014 as you are working in each chapter.

Acknowledgements

Updating this textbook has been quite a monumental task that could not have been accomplished without a lot of help. Many thanks to Susan Adlam who did a complete and thorough job during the copy edit process and Lila Campbell, Production Editor, who provided editorial assistance and kept us all on track. Also, thank you to Karen Townsend, Developmental Editor, Avinash Chandra, Lead Project Manager, and Jessica Hellen, Project Manager for their continued support.

Many thanks to Debbie Baker-Longley from Mohawk College who works tirelessly reviewing the details in the textbook.

And finally, to my family, John, Jamie, and Mandy. Thank you again for your patience, support, and understanding.

Chris Heaney

CHAPTER ONE

Getting Started: Introduction to

QuickBooks

Objectives

After completing this chapter, you should be able to:

- **download and install** the QuickBooks program
- **use** the QuickBooks data files on the Data CD
- **access** QuickBooks data files
- **register** QuickBooks
- **update** QuickBooks
- **understand** the QuickBooks Home page
- **understand** QuickBooks Centres
- **use** QuickBooks lists
- **use** QuickBooks keyboard shortcuts
- **change** QuickBooks preference settings
- **access** Help, Live Community, and Support
- **back up** and **verify** a data file
- **restore** a data file from a backup
- **finish** a QuickBooks work session

Getting Started

Data Files

The **data files** on the Data CD were prepared using the Windows® 7 operating system and QuickBooks Premier Edition 2012 by Intuit. Subsequent versions of the software may have changes in screens or keystrokes.

The instructions in this workbook have been written for a stand-alone PC with a hard drive and a CD-ROM drive. Microsoft Windows should be correctly installed on your hard drive. Your printers should be installed and accessible through the Windows operating system. Refer to Windows Help and manuals for assistance with these procedures.

This workbook reflects the authors' approach to working with QuickBooks. There are alternative approaches to setting up company accounts and to working with QuickBooks. Refer to QuickBooks and Windows Help and manuals for further details.

Notes
The instructions in this chapter for installing the program, starting the program, and copying files refer to Windows® 7 procedures. If you are using a different version of Windows, please refer to Windows and QuickBooks Help for assistance with these procedures.

Notes
The Setup folder has data files for chapters that require you to set up the company file before working through the transactions. Three of these files — River, Darya, and Vent-data — are complete setup files that allow you to proceed with entering source document transactions.

The other two data files — Vent-start and Melody — are starter sample files that allow you to set up the data file and use the payroll features.

Notes
After you install the data files on the CD, they can be found within the C:\QkBkData folder.

Notes
The Data CD also includes a brief review of basic accounting principles and a Tax Appendix. These files are PDF documents, and you need to have Acrobat Reader installed in order to read them. If you do not have Acrobat Reader, you can install it from the Adobe website using the link on the Data CD.

Notes
No keystroke instructions are provided for Melody Music Centre in Chapter 13, which is found on the CD that accompanies this textbook.

All company files for each chapter have been set up in advance so you can begin entering transactions immediately. For chapters that require you to create the company data files from scratch, a setup company file has been created for you and can be found in a Setup folder on the CD. These data files will allow you to complete the transactions or source documents without working through the company setup, if required.

QUICKBOOKS COMPANY FILES

COMPANY NAME	FOLDER\FILENAME	CHAPTER	
Practice	Data\Practice.qbw	1	
Chelsea's Chocolates	Data\Chelsea.qbw	2	
Bob's Bookroom	Data\Bookroom.qbw	3	
River Run	Setup\River.qbw	4	See Notes
Just a Buck	Data\Buck.qbw	5	
Malin's Makeovers	Data\Malin.qbw	6	
Terrific Tours	Data\Tours.qbw	7	
Curly's Cabinets	Data\Curly.qbw	8	
Darya's Dance Studio	Setup\Darya.qbw	9	See Notes
Scotts' Total Concept	Data\Scott.qbw	10	
Sparkles	Data\Sparkles.qbw	11	
Contre le Vent	Setup\Vent-start.qbw	12	See Notes
	Setup\Vent-data.qbw	12	See Notes
Melody Music Centre	Setup\Melody.qbw	13	See Notes

OTHER FILES ON THE DATA CD

Ch. 12 Contre le Vent: Payroll & Inventory Setup
Ch. 13 Melody Music Centre: Practice Application
Appendix: Tax
Source Documents
ReadMe file
Review of Basic Accounting
Accounting Cycle Tutorial

As you work through this textbook, the businesses and the chapters become more complex, with each chapter introducing new features or setups. Each chapter also includes the features covered in previous chapters for review. This progression is shown in the following chart:

CH	COMPANY NAME	TOPIC NO.*	NEW TOPICS**	ALL TOPICS***
2	Chelsea's Chocolates	1	Cash sales and purchases	1
3	Bob's Bookroom	2	General Journal	1 + 2
4	River Run	3	Set up a cash only business	2 + 3
5	Just a Buck	4	Basic vendor transactions	2 + 4
6	Malin's Makeovers	5	Basic customer transactions	4 + 5
7	Terrific Tours	6	Advanced customer and vendor transactions	5 + 6
8	Curly's Cabinets	7	Credit cards and bank reconciliation	6 + 7
9	Darya's Dance Studio	8	Setup for complete customer and vendor transactions	7 + 8
10	Scotts' Total Concept	9	Payroll	7 + 9
11	Sparkles	10	Inventory	9 + 10
12	Contre le Vent****	11	Comprehensive setup with payroll and inventory	10 + 11
13	Melody Music Centre****	12	Comprehensive setup practice exercise	12

NOTES

*   Topic No. is the number that identifies new topics covered in a given chapter for reference in the All Topics column.

**   Step-by-step instructions are provided throughout each chapter for new topics. You are required to set up company files from scratch for River Run (Chapter 4), Darya's Dance Studio (Chapter 9), Contre le Vent (Chapter 12), and Melody Music Centre (Chapter 13). As discussed in the notes, you can use the company data files in the Setup folder for each of these companies if you prefer to work through the transactions and not complete the company setup.

***   These numbers indicate that each chapter includes the topics and features that are explained in the previous chapters, except for the company setup. For example: Scotts' Total Concept (7 + 9) introduces payroll (9) as a new topic and includes cash sales and purchases, general journal transactions, advanced customer and vendor transactions, and credit cards (all the topics in 7), but setup is not required.

**** Chapters 12 and 13 are now found on the CD that accompanies this text.

Installing QuickBooks

Notes
Skip this section if Quick-Books is already installed on your computer.

1. **Start**   your **computer** and **turn off** or **close** all other **applications** and **close** all **files**. You should be in the Windows desktop

2. Refer to the card in the inside cover of the textbook

3. If you agree with the terms and conditions and understand that opening the card means that once opened you cannot return the textbook, open the package to obtain the website information

4. As soon as you go to the QuickBooks student download website indicated on the card, you'll receive the following screen:

Notes
Step-by-step instructions are numbered and shown in highlighted text in indented paragraphs like the ones beside this note. Command words are in **bold** type; the object of the command is shown in colour. If there are multiple choices you can perform, they will be labelled with a, b, c, etc.

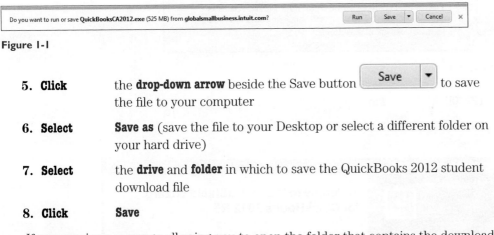

Figure 1-1

⚠ **WARNING!**
Do not download and install the QuickBooks program until you are ready to begin working on the exercises in the textbook. The program will remain valid and accessible for 12 months after you activate it.

5. **Click**   the **drop-down arrow** beside the Save button to save the file to your computer

6. **Select**   **Save as** (save the file to your Desktop or select a different folder on your hard drive)

7. **Select**   the **drive** and **folder** in which to save the QuickBooks 2012 student download file

8. **Click**   **Save**

If you receive a message allowing you to open the folder that contains the download, you can do so, or:

9. **Browse**   to the **desktop** or **folder** where you saved the QuickBooks 2012 student download file. The file will be displayed as shown:

Notes
The time it takes to download the QuickBooks program will depend on your Internet connection.

Figure 1-2

10. **Double click**   on the **QuickBooksCA2012.exe file**

11. The following Security Warning message **may** be displayed:

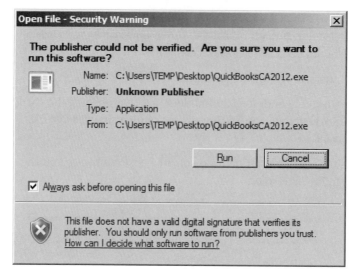

Figure 1-3

12. Click   **Run**

13. You will see the following welcome screen:

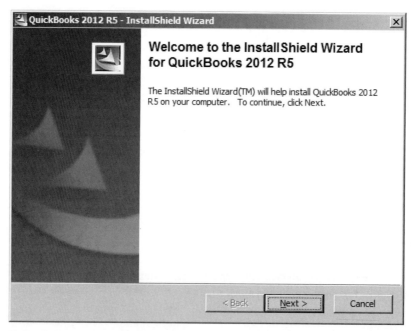

Figure 1-4

14. Click   **Next**

The InstallShield Wizard extracts the files needed to install QuickBooks 2012. This may take a few minutes. After the files are extracted, the Welcome screen indicates that it is strongly recommended that you close all open Windows programs, especially virus protection programs, before installing QuickBooks.

15. Close   all **open Windows programs** before you proceed with the QuickBooks installation

16. Click   **Next**

17. The License Agreement is displayed:

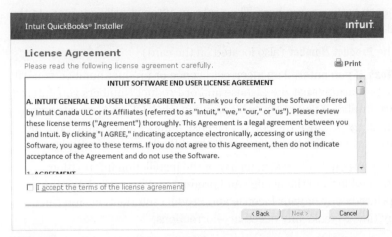

Figure 1-5

📄 **Notes**
If you do not accept the licence agreement, the installation procedure will be cancelled.

18. Read the **License Agreement** (you will have to use the scroll bar to read the entire agreement)

19. Click the **box** beside the *I accept the terms in the license agreement* option if you agree to the terms of the licence agreement

20. Click **Next** to display the Choose Installation Type screen:

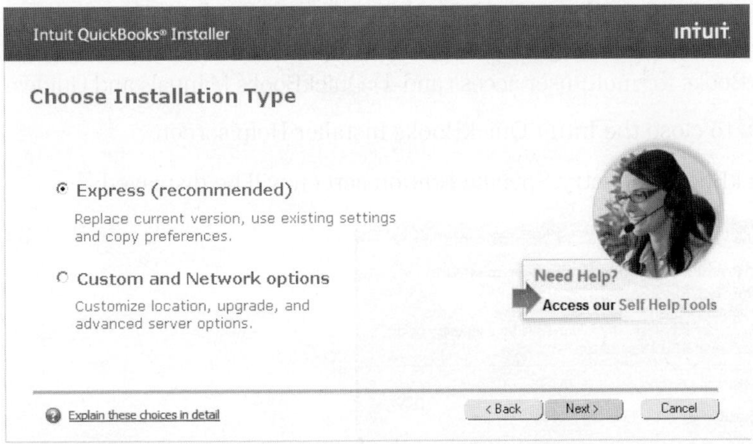

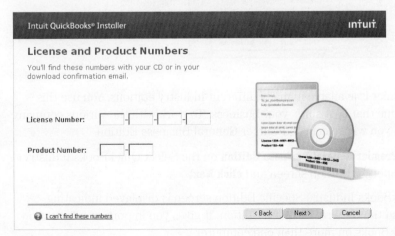

Figure 1-6

21. Accept the **Express (recommended) type** and **click Next** to display the License and Product Numbers screen:

Figure 1-7

22. Enter   the **License Number** (located on the card)

Do not enter the dash between numbers. The program automatically advances to the Product Number field.

23. Enter   the **Product Number** (also located on the card)

24. Click   **Next**. If you entered an incorrect licence or product number, you will see a warning that the License and/or Product Numbers you entered are invalid. If you receive this warning, click OK and try entering them again. Once the correct License number and Product number are entered, the Ready to Install QuickBooks screen is displayed.

The Ready to Install screen displays a summary of the installation information, including the destination folder and the licence and product numbers. Click the Print button if you want a printed copy of your License and Product information. You can use the Back button at any time to make any necessary corrections.

25. Click   the **Install button** when you're ready to begin the QuickBooks installation

QuickBooks will display various screens during the installation procedure. After the QuickBooks installation is finished, the Congratulations screen is displayed. By default, the Open QuickBooks and Help me get started options are selected. With these options selected, QuickBooks will open and a screen with information on how to get started will be displayed.

26. Click   **Finish** when the Congratulations screen is displayed

The next screen displayed is the Intuit QuickBooks Installer Help screen. This screen will help you get started with: 1) Creating a company file 2) Updating an existing company file 3) Setting up QuickBooks for multi-user access and 4) QuickBooks Manuals and Guides.

27. Click   ☒ to close the Intuit QuickBooks Installer Help screen

28. The Select QuickBooks Industry-Specific Edition screen will be displayed:

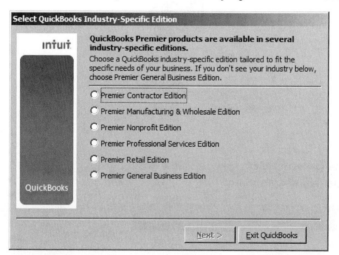

Figure 1-8

QuickBooks Premier is available in many different industry editions. You use this screen to select the one that best suits your business. To work with the various company files in this textbook, you will select the Premier General Business Edition.

29. Select   **Premier General Business Edition** on the Select QuickBooks Industry-Specific Edition screen and **click Next**

The Select QuickBooks Industry-Specific Edition screen is displayed indicating that you have selected the General Business Edition. It gives you important information about installing QuickBooks on more than one computer.

30. Click   **Finish** to configure QuickBooks to fit your industry and complete the installation

31. If a new product update is available, the following screen will be displayed:

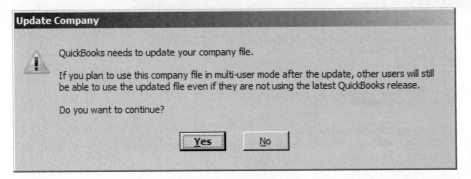

Figure 1-9

📄 **Notes**
    At the time of writing this textbook, the student edition was installed with Release 5; however, Release 8 is available.
    If Intuit updates the student download available on the website, you may not receive this message. A later release may also be available.

This screen will allow you to update your QuickBooks program with the latest product update. At the time of updating this portion of the text, the latest product update is R8. Depending on when you are installing the QuickBooks program, the product update may be higher than 8. You must upgrade your software to the latest release in order to use this textbook.

32. Click   **Yes** and the following screen will be displayed:

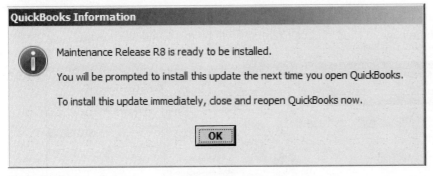

Figure 1-10

📄 **Notes**
    You must be connected to the Internet to download updates.

33. Click   **OK**

34. The following screen will be displayed:

Figure 1-11

35. Click   **Install Now**

36. Click   **OK** on the Update Complete screen which indicates that QuickBooks 2012 is now up to date

The Welcome to QuickBooks Premier Edition screen will be displayed:

Figure 1-12

Use this screen to open the Sample company file, create a new company file, or open an existing company file.

37. Click   the **icon** beside Explore QuickBooks

38. Select   **Premier Sample Company**

39. Click   **OK** on the QuickBooks Information screen that indicates this is a sample file

40. The Home page of the Practice Company will be displayed as shown:

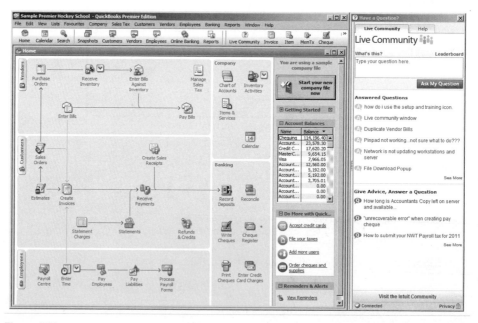

Figure 1-13

You can use the Practice Company to try various transactions without affecting your own company file.

41. Click   **File** from the menu and **click Exit** to close QuickBooks

Using the CD Data Files

Many of the chapters in this textbook begin with a QuickBooks company file that has already been created for you. These QuickBooks company files are found on the Data CD that accompanies this textbook. Before you can use these company files in QuickBooks, you must copy them from the Data CD to your hard drive. QuickBooks cannot open the files directly from the CD. If you open QuickBooks and try to select a company file directly from the CD, you will see the following warning:

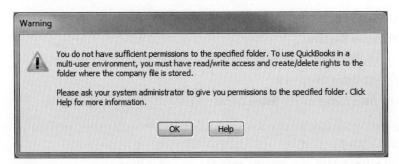

Figure 1-14

After copying the data files to your computer, store the original CD in a safe place. If you install the data files from the CD, the files will automatically be placed in the QkBkData folder below drive C.

Installing Data Files to Your Hard Drive

We have set up the Data CD so that it will open automatically. When you choose the button to install the data files, the files will be copied directly to your hard drive and the read-only attributes will be removed in a single step. To do this:

1. **Insert** the **Data CD** into your CD-ROM drive and the Data CD should open immediately (follow the instructions below if it does not open)

If the CD does not open immediately, follow these instructions if you are using Windows® 7 (ask your instructor for instructions if you are not using Windows® 7):

   a) **Open Windows Explorer** (a shortcut to open Windows Explorer is to press the Windows key + E or you can right click on the Start menu and select Open Windows Explorer)

   b) **Browse** for the **CD Drive**

   c) **Click** the **CD drive** to open it

   d) **Double click Start.exe**

When the Data CD home page is displayed, you can choose to install the data files, to view Chapters 12 (Contre le Vent Payroll & Inventory Setup) and 13 (Melody Music Centre) and the Practice file, the Appendix document entitled "Tax," the Source Document file, or the ReadMe file, to view The Accounting Cycle Tutorial, to open the Review of Basic Accounting file (in PDF format), or to install Acrobat Reader (required to open the Review of Basic Accounting file).

2. **Click**   **Data & Setup Files**

3. **Click**   **INSTALL Data & Setup Files button**

After you install the data files, they can be found on your hard drive in a new QkBkData folder in drive C. A data and setup folder will be created below the QkBkData folder. The data files in these folders are now ready to be used and can be opened directly in QuickBooks.

4. **Close**   the **Data CD window**

Copying Data Files from the CD

If a single data file becomes unreadable or if you want to start a chapter over again, you can copy a single file from the CD to your working folder.

1. **Insert**   the **Data CD** into the CD-ROM drive
2. **Open**   **Windows Explore**
3. **Browse**   for the **CD drive**
4. **Click**   the **CD drive** to open it
5. **Double click**   the **Data folder** or the **Setup folder** to view the individual data files

You can copy the entire data folder at once, or copy only one or more files in the Data or Setup folders to your hard drive.

6. **Right-click**   an **entire folder** or a **specific data file** and **click Copy**
7. **Browse**   for the **QkBkData folder** (created when you originally installed the files from the Data CD) or **select** a **different folder** if you are storing your company data files in a different folder
8. **Right-click**   the **folder** where you want to save your files and **click Paste**

Starting QuickBooks and Accessing Data Files

1. To start the QuickBooks program:

   a) **Click** the **QuickBooks Premier Edition 2012 icon** on the Desktop if you installed the shortcut; or

   Figure 1-15

   b) **Choose Start**, then **All Programs**, click **QuickBooks**, and then **click QuickBooks Premier Edition 2012**

In the following steps, you will open a company file from the CD that accompanies the textbook. When you open QuickBooks, the QuickBooks company file you used previously will automatically be displayed on the screen. We need to close it before opening a new file.

2. **Choose**   **File** from the menu, and then **click Close Company**
3. The No Company Open window is displayed:

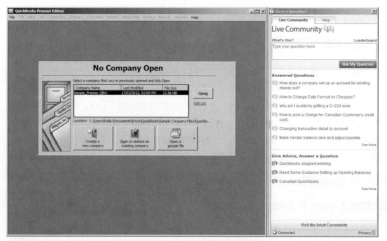

Figure 1-16

The next time you start QuickBooks, the company data file you previously worked with will open automatically (unless you choose Close Company from the File menu before exiting QuickBooks).

Open or restore an existing company

4. a) **Click** the **Open or restore an existing company button** _____; or

Figure 1-17

b) **Choose** the **File menu** and **click**
Open or Restore Company . . .

Figure 1-18

to display the Open or Restore Company screen:

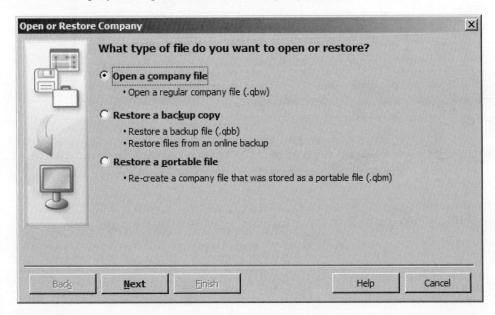

Figure 1-19

The option you select on this screen depends on how the company data file that you want to open was saved. You can determine how the file was saved by the extension of the file name:

FILE TYPE	FILE EXTENSION	SELECT
QuickBooks company file	.qbw	Open a company file
QuickBooks backup file	.qbb	Restore a backup copy
QuickBooks portable file	.qbm	Restore a portable file

5. **Select**   **Open a company file** (this should be the default) and **click Next**

Use this window to browse for the QuickBooks data that you copied onto your hard drive. If you used the install option on the CD, the data files can be found in the data or setup folder within the QkBkData folder on drive C.

6. **Click**   the **drop-down arrow** in the **Look in field** and **click Drive C**

7. **Double click**   the **QkBkData folder** and then the **data folder** to view the files in the data folder as shown:

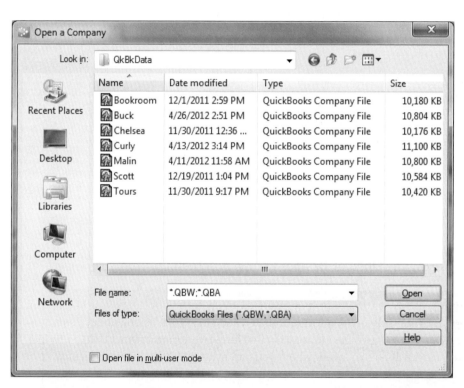

Figure 1-20

8. **Highlight**   the **company file** that you want to open and **click** the **Open button** or **double click** the **company file** to open it automatically

Program Maintenance

Registering the Program

You can use QuickBooks for 30 days before you must register it with Intuit. If you do not register QuickBooks, as you open QuickBooks company files during the 30 day period, the Registration screen will continue to be displayed.

While you are working in QuickBooks within the 30 day time period, the registration screen will be displayed:

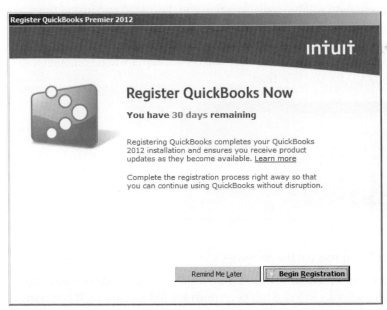

Figure 1-21

You can click the *Begin Registration* button to register immediately, or click the *Remind Me Later* button to register later. If you select the Remind Me Later button, you will receive this message each time you open QuickBooks.

You should click the Begin Registration button to register your QuickBooks program. A registration screen allowing you to select the method of registration will be displayed. Depending on the options currently available at Intuit, you will either have an option to register online, register by phone, or both.

If you select to register online, you will need to fill in the information on the Product Information form as well as the information on a second screen asking about your purchase. After you answer the information on these two forms, a QuickBooks Product Registration card will be displayed, which you can print and keep for your records.

If you select to register by phone, you need to call the toll-free number displayed on the screen to obtain a validation code. Once you enter the validation code and click OK, QuickBooks will open with the Home page displayed. In order to synchronize your licence with Intuit, you need to click Help from the menu, select Manage My License and then select Sync License Data Online.

To update the company file, you will need to select Yes to continue.

1. **Click**   **Begin Registration**

2. After following the instructions to register online or by phone, your QuickBooks program is automatically registered

To view your product and licence information at any time, choose the Help menu and click My License Information.

WARNING! The program that is available with this book includes payroll activation for 12 months after registration, but you must still download the latest updates to use the payroll features.

Updating your QuickBooks Company File

Notes
Companies using Quick-
Books payroll must be signed
up for the QuickBooks Payroll
Service with Intuit before the
payroll features in the program
can be used, unless you are
working with a QuickBooks
sample company.

If a new product update is available when you open QuickBooks, you will be prompted with a message to download it. Updates fix problems in the software, incorporate new features, and contain updated payroll taxes. You must download updates regularly if you want to use the Payroll features of the program. This ensures that you have the latest tax tables available for the program. The QuickBooks program that is available as a download with this textbook contains the Payroll Service and is available for 12 months. The Company files in this textbook require that Release 8 or later be installed; however, the most recent product update will be available when you download and install the QuickBooks program.

If a newer release is available when you install the QuickBooks student edition that accompanies this textbook, the following message will be displayed when you open a company file on the Data CD for the first time:

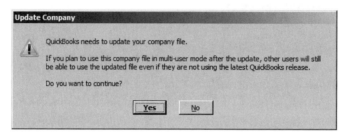

Figure 1-22

1. Click   **Yes** if you receive this message

Whenever a new product update is released from Intuit, you will receive a message indicating that a new QuickBooks Release has been downloaded and asking if you want to install it.

Refer to the "What if I don't upgrade QuickBooks to the latest release?" heading under the "Updating QuickBooks" heading on page x of the Preface.

The automatic update feature is automatically turned on when you install QuickBooks. To view this option:

2. Choose   the **Help menu** and **click Update QuickBooks**:

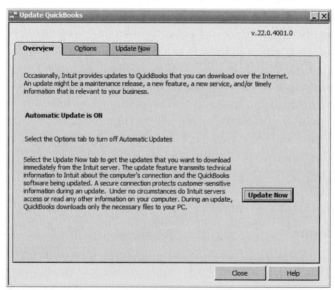

Figure 1-23

As you can see, this screen indicates that the automatic update feature is turned on. With this feature selected, QuickBooks is updated automatically without any effort on your part. If this screen indicates that the automatic option is turned off, you can select it on the Options tab and if you choose to manually update QuickBooks, you can do so from the Update Now tab.

Although QuickBooks should automatically download the latest upgrade, some software programs installed on your computer may stop the installation. If you receive an error message when updating QuickBooks using the Update QuickBooks screen, you can manually download the QuickBooks update. Follow the instructions under the "Manually download the QuickBooks update" heading found in the Preface under the "Updating QuickBooks" heading on page x.

3. **Click**   **Close** to exit the Update QuickBooks window

Notes
The program is set to download updates automatically whenever you are connected to the Internet.
To turn off the automatic updates option, choose the Options tab and click the No button beside Automatic Update. Click Yes from this same screen to turn automatic updates back on.

The QuickBooks Home Page

When you first open a company file in QuickBooks, the Home page is displayed as shown here:

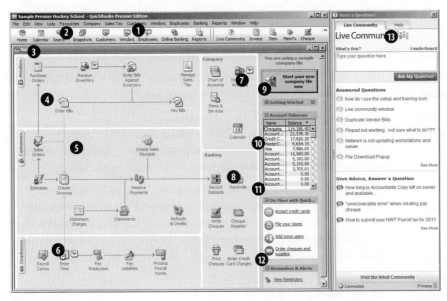

Figure 1-24

Each area on the QuickBooks Home page shown in Figure 1-23 has been numbered and is described below:

1. **QuickBooks Title Bar:**   contains the control button at the far left, displays the company name, QuickBooks edition, and the usual Windows sizing icons on the right. The ⊠ in the title bar can be used to close QuickBooks. If you click the ⊠ in the title bar, a warning will be displayed asking if you want to exit QuickBooks.

2. **Main Menu:**   is displayed directly below the title bar. Many activities in QuickBooks can be accessed from more than one location in the program, but all activities are available from the main menu. The usual Windows sizing icons are displayed on the main menu and affect the current open window. The ⊠ in the main menu can be used to close the current open window.

3. **Icon Bar:**   the Icon bar provides quick and easy access to some of the most commonly used QuickBooks activities and functions. Although QuickBooks sets the icons on the Icon bar by default, when you

Notes
Customizing the Icon bar is covered in Chapter 2.

create a new company, you can customize the Icon bar to include only the icons that represent the tasks you use on a regular basis. If the icons on the Icon bar cannot all be displayed, click the double arrow on the far right-hand side of the Icon bar to view a list of the icons that are not displayed.

4. Vendors section:	The Vendors section of the Home page shows the workflow arrows for business tasks specific to vendors. You can click on an icon to open the form, and you can click on the Vendors button on the far left-hand side of the screen to open the Vendor Centre. The Vendor Centre will be discussed in more detail in Chapter 5.
5. Customers section:	The Customers section of the Home page shows the workflow arrows for business tasks specific to customers. You can click on an icon to open the form, and you can click on the Customers button on the far left-hand side of the screen to open the Customer Centre. The Customer Centre will be discussed in more detail in Chapter 6.
6. Employees section:	The Employees section of the Home page shows the workflow arrows for business tasks specific to employees. You can click on an icon to open the form, and you can click on the Employees button on the far left-hand side of the screen to open the Employee Centre. The Employee Centre will be discussed in more detail in Chapters 10 and 12, the latter of which is found on the Student CD-ROM.
7. Company section:	The Company section of the Home page provides quick access to the Chart of Accounts and the Items list.
8. Banking section:	The Banking section of the Home page provides quick access to all banking related functions, such as recording customer deposits, reconciling accounts, writing cheques, using the cheque register, printing cheques, and entering credit card charges.
9. Getting Started:	The Getting Started section contains two buttons. The Quick Start Center button provides quick access to common tasks and includes links to reference material. The Setup and Training button provides a phone number for a free support call available with all versions of QuickBooks (except the student edition).
10. Account Balances:	This section displays each bank and credit card account and its current balance.
11. Do More with QuickBooks:	This section includes information about how to sign up for QuickBooks Merchant Services, which allows you to accept payments in QuickBooks, how to purchase the various Turbo Tax editions, how to purchase additional QuickBooks user licences, and how to order cheques, stationery, and supplies.
12. Reminders & Alerts:	Use this section to view reminders that you have set up in QuickBooks, such as a list of outstanding invoices or cheques that need to be printed. In this section, you may also find alerts that have been sent from Intuit.
13. Live Community/ Help:	This pane contains two tabs: Live Community and Help. The Live Community tab allows you to ask or answer questions in the QuickBooks community while working directly in QuickBooks. The Help tab is context-sensitive and allows you to review relevant search topics or use the search feature. You can close the Live Community/Help pane at anytime by clicking on the ☒ in the top right-hand corner. The easiest way to bring back the Live Community/Help pane, is to press F1.

QuickBooks Centres

QuickBooks organizes specific functions in Centres. There are five Centres in QuickBooks: the Customer Centre, the Vendor Centre, the Employee Centre, the Online Banking Centre, and the Report Centre. In this chapter, we will look at the Vendor Centre and the Report Centre to learn how Centres are used.

The Vendor Centre

1. **Open** the **Vendor Centre** using one of the following options:

    a) **Click** the **Vendors button** in the Vendors section of the Home page; or

    Figure 1-25

    b) **Choose** the **Vendors menu** and then **select Vendor Centre**; or

    Figure 1-26

    c) **Click** the **Vendors icon** on the Icon bar:

    Figure 1-27

2. The Vendor Centre will be displayed as shown:

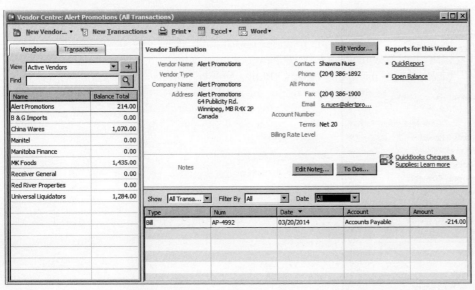

Figure 1-28

> **Notes**
> The Vendors menu contains other menu options when Inventory and Purchase Orders are enabled for a company file.

The Vendor Centre contains all the information about your vendors and their transactions. On the left-hand side of the screen, you'll see two tabs: Vendors and Transactions.

When you click the Vendors tab, the Vendors' list is displayed on the left-hand side of the screen, showing each vendor's name and balance total. You can sort the Vendors' list by vendor name or balance total and in ascending or descending order by clicking on the list headings.

When you highlight a vendor in the list (there is always a vendor highlighted by default), their vendor information is displayed in the top right portion of the screen, allowing you to quickly view the vendor address information. Click the Edit Vendor button to access the vendor record where you can make changes to it, click the QuickReport or Open Balance button to print reports for the vendor, use the Edit Notes button to add notes to the vendor record or use the To Dos button to add an item for the vendor on the To Do list. The transaction details for the vendor are listed in the bottom right portion of the screen. You can use the headings across the top of the transaction details to select which type of transaction you'd like to view and filter the transactions by a date range.

You can use the buttons across the top of the screen to add a new vendor, enter new transactions, print vendor information, export, import or paste information from and to Microsoft Excel®, or print Microsoft Word documents. The highlighted vendor will automatically be selected when you choose one of these options.

When you click on the Transactions tab, a list of transaction types is displayed down the left-hand side of the screen. When you click on one of the transaction types, a list of all transactions for all vendors will be displayed based on the criteria selected in the Filter By and Date fields.

The Report Centre

The Report Centre deals only with reports, and most QuickBooks reports are accessible from it. Although it offers most of the same reports as the Reports menu, it has the advantage of showing a sample report and a brief description of what you can learn about your company from the report.

1. **Open** the **Report Centre** using one of the following options:

   a) **Choose** the **Reports menu** and **click Report Centre**; or

Figure 1-29

b) **Click** the **Reports icon** on the Icon bar:

Figure 1-30

2. The Report Centre will be displayed as shown:

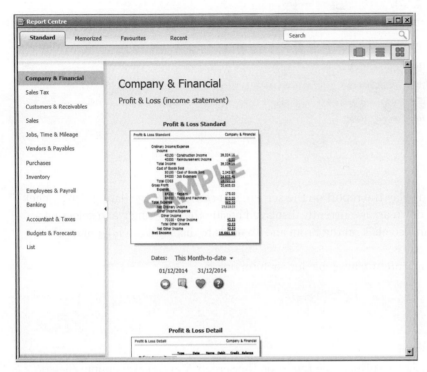

Figure 1-31

Various report categories are listed down the left-hand side of the screen. The Company & Financial category is selected by default. As you select a category, the reports for that category are displayed to the right. How the reports are displayed is dependent upon the view that is currently selected. By default, the reports are displayed in grid view when you first open the Report Centre.

There are three views that can be used to display the reports: Carousel, List, and Grid view. You can change the view by selecting the icons in the top left-hand corner of the screen as shown:

Figure 1-32

The icons that represent the views are displayed in order: Carousel, List, and Grid.

Grid View

With the reports displayed in grid view, a sample of each report is displayed on the screen. When you run your mouse over a report while in grid view, a square defines the entire report as shown:

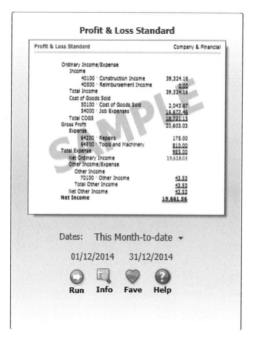

Figure 1-33

Before you display the report on the screen, you can change the date range by clicking on the drop-down arrow currently displayed beside the date range and selecting a new one. You can also click on the From and To fields to display a calendar and select the appropriate dates.

The following icons are available for each report:

Figure 1-34

Use the Run icon to display the report on the screen. You can also double click on the sample report to display it on the screen.

Figure 1-35

Use the Info icon to display a sample of the report that includes a description of the report.

Figure 1-36

Use the Fave icon to add the report to the Favourites menu for easy access.

Figure 1-37

Use the Help icon to open QuickBooks help to learn more about the report.

List View

With the reports displayed in list view, the reports are displayed in a list as shown:

Figure 1-38

As you can see, more reports are displayed on the screen at one time in list view than they are in grid view. Also, notice that a sample of each report is not displayed in this view. When you run your mouse over a report in list view, a square defines the entire report as shown:

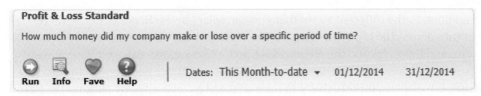

Figure 1-39

A question the report will answer is displayed under the report name. The same icons available in grid view are available in list view. You can use the Run icon to display the report on the screen or double click on the report name.

Carousel View

With the reports displayed in carousel view a sample of the current report is displayed in the middle, while a sample of the previous report is displayed to the left, and a sample of the next report is displayed to the right:

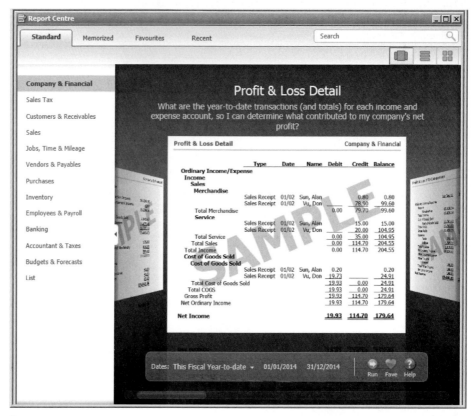

Figure 1-40

Again, you'll notice that in this view, a question the report will answer is displayed, together with all of the icons that we've seen in both list and grid view. When you click on a sample report, either to the left or right of the current sample report, it will become the current report. You can then use the icons to display the appropriate information for the report.

In addition to the different views that you can select in the Report Centre, there are four tabs across the top of the screen. The Standard tab displays the list of report categories and their reports, the Memorized tab displays reports that you have memorized (you'll learn how to memorize reports in Chapter 3, Bob's Bookroom), the Favourites tab displays reports that you have selected as favourites by clicking the Fave icon, and the Recent tab displays the reports that you have displayed in the past 30 days.

3. **Click** the **different headings** to view the reports available for each heading

4. **Change** the **view** to display the reports in carousel, list, and grid view

5. **Display** a **report** on the screen

When you open a report, you can select a pre-defined date range from the Dates drop-down list or enter a range of dates. To begin the customization of a report, you use the Customize Report button. Once you have entered your report settings, the updated report should automatically be displayed on the screen; however, you may have to press ⦅tab⦆ or click the Refresh button to update it. You can select Print to print the report, select E-mail to e-mail the report as a Microsoft Excel spreadsheet or as a pdf, or select Excel to save the report as an Excel spreadsheet or update an existing spreadsheet.

You can Modify reports by adding or omitting information, by changing font style and sizes, and by sorting and filtering the reports to reorganize or select certain criteria to include in the report. Once you have customized a report, you can memorize the report settings so that you do not have to re-enter them the next time you want to print the same report.

QuickBooks Lists

The QuickBooks Centres contain their respective lists. You will find the Customers & Jobs list in the Customer Centre, the Vendors list in the Vendor Centre, and the Employees list in the Employee Centre. There are other lists found in list windows that are also available in QuickBooks. To view the lists in list windows:

1. **Click**   the **Lists menu**:

Figure 1-41

All the list menus, other than the QuickBooks Centre lists, can be found in this menu and some of them can also be found in other related menus. Lists are central to the way QuickBooks works, and we will work with many different lists as we work through the chapters in this textbook. All QuickBooks list windows include the same three buttons with menu options relevant to the open list. Some lists contain additional buttons. To see this, let's open the Chart of Accounts.

2. **Click**   **Chart of Accounts** to view the Chart of Accounts:

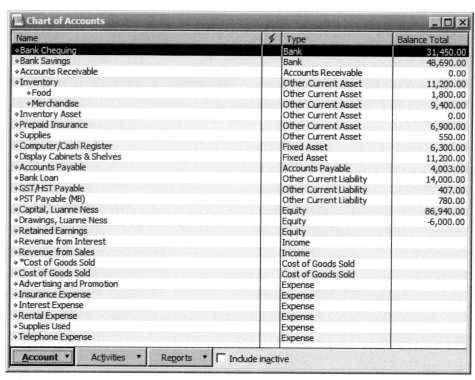

Figure 1-42

Let's review the different buttons available on the list:

3. Click   the **Account button** (this button's name is always indicative of the list) to view the menu available with this button:

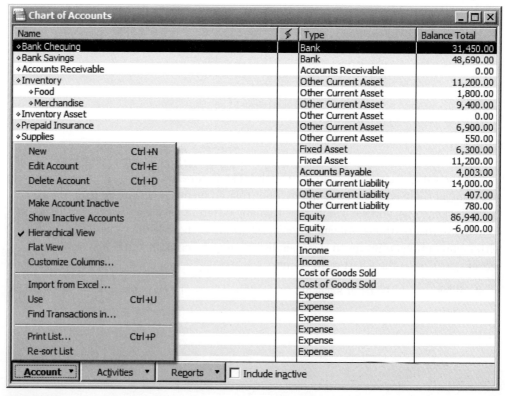

Figure 1-43

4. Click the **Activities button** (this button's name is the same in each list) to view the menu available with this button:

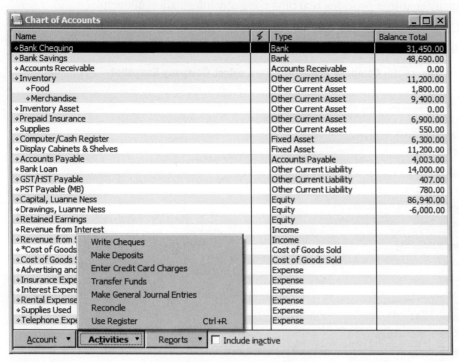

Figure 1-44

5. Click the **Reports button** (this button's name is the same in each list) to view the menu available with this button:

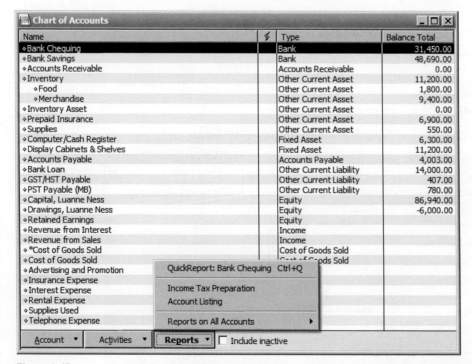

Figure 1-45

Other lists contain an Excel button, which allows you to import and export information from the list to and from Microsoft Excel.

6. Click ☒ to close the Chart of Accounts list

Company Snapshot

The company snapshot provides real time company information in one place and provides quick access to various QuickBooks tasks.

1. Display the **Company Snapshot** using one of the following options:

a) **Choose** the **Company menu** and then **select Company Snapshot**:

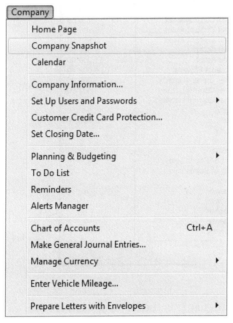

Figure 1-46

OR

b) **Click** the **Snapshots icon** on the Icon bar:

Figure 1-47

2. The Company Snapshot will be displayed as shown:

Figure 1-48

There are three tabs displayed in the top left-hand corner of the Company Snapshot: Company, Payments, and Customer. Each tab contains separate content about your company in separate panels. Depending on the content displayed, the content in a panel may be displayed as a list with links to access other information in QuickBooks, or it may be displayed in the form of a graph.

The following content can be displayed on the Company tab: account balances, previous year income comparison, income breakdown, previous year expense comparison, expense breakdown, income and expense trend, top customers by sales, best-selling items, customers who owe money, top vendors by expense, vendors to pay, and reminders.

The following content can be displayed on the Payments tab: recent transactions, receivables reports, A/R by aging period, and invoice payment status.

The following content can be displayed on the Customer tab: recent invoices, recent payments, sales history, and best-selling items.

Customizing the information displayed on each tab

You can customize the content displayed on each tab. For example, to remove a panel from a tab, simply click on the ☒ in the top right-hand corner of the panel. To add additional content, select the appropriate tab, click on the Add Content button in the top left-hand corner of the screen, and then select the additional content that you would like to add. To add additional content on the Company tab:

1. **Select**   the **Company tab** (if it is not already selected)

2. **Click**   the **Add Content button** Add Content ∨ to display the content that can be added on the tab:

📄 **Notes**
We have used the completed Just a Buck company file to generate this print screen.

Figure I-49

By selecting the Add Content button, the content that can be added on the Company tab is displayed across the top of the screen. Each topic contains either an Added button ✔Added or an Add button ➕ Add . The Added button indicates that the content is already added on the tab, and the Add button allows you to add the content to the tab by simply clicking the button.

The indicator 1-4 of 12 ⇐ ⇒ displayed below the content that can be added indicates which content panels are currently displayed and indicates the number of content items available in total. As you can see, we are currently displaying the first four content panels of a total of 12 available to be added on the Company tab. You can use the arrows to scroll through the different content boxes.

3. Click the **Add button** ⊞ Add under the Income Breakdown content

The Add button should now change to an Added button, indicating that the Income Breakdown content has been added to the Company tab.

4. Click the **Done button** Done

Clicking the Done button closes the content window and displays only the content in the tab.

If you want to restore the content displayed on a tab back to the default settings, you must select a tab and click on the Restore Default button Restore Default . The restore default button only restores the defaults for the tab currently selected. When you restore the default settings, you will receive a warning indicating that the control panels you added will be returned to the gallery, remaining panels will be returned to their original positions and dates ranges you chose will be returned to the original settings.

Using QuickBooks Keyboard Shortcuts

All Windows-based software applications are designed to be used with a mouse. However, there may be times when you would prefer to use keyboard commands to work with a program because they are faster. There are also times when you need to know the alternatives to using a mouse, especially when the mouse doesn't work. It is not necessary to memorize all the keyboard commands.

A few basic principles will help you understand how they work, and over time you will use the ones that help you work most efficiently. Some commands are common to more than one Windows-based software program. For example, ctrl + **C** (press and hold the Control key while you press the letter "c") is commonly used as the copy command and ctrl + **V** as the paste command. Any selected text or image will be copied or pasted. alt + <**F4**> is a common shortcut for closing a window or program. Many QuickBooks functions can be accessed in more than one way — from the Home page icons, QuickBooks Centres, the main menu, list menus, the icon bar, and keyboard shortcuts.

To use the keyboard shortcuts and activate the underlined letters in the main menu, press the alt key. With the underlined letters displayed, click an underlined letter in a menu item name to open the menu. Once the menu is open, use the up and down arrow keys ▲ ▼ to move up and down through the menu, or the left and right arrow keys ◀ ▶ to move back and forth to other menus. Some menu choices have direct keyboard alternatives or shortcuts. If the menu item has an underlined letter, pressing alt together with the underlined letter will access that option directly. For example, alt + **F** (press alt , and while holding down alt press the letter "**F**") accesses the File menu. Then pressing "**O**" (the underlined letter for Open) will give you the dialog box for opening a new file.

Some of the most common QuickBooks functions have their own keyboard shortcuts other than the ones discussed. For example, to open an invoice you press ctrl + **I**, to open the Customer Centre you press ctrl + **J**, and to open the Chart of Accounts you press ctrl + **A**. These shortcuts are displayed beside the items in their respective menus.

Some icons and buttons in QuickBooks have a direct keyboard shortcut. When available, these shortcuts appear as an underlined letter on the button. Press alt + the underlined letter to enter the button's command. For example, on the Invoice form, you can Save & Close the invoice by clicking the button or by pressing ⒜ + **a**, the underlined letter in Save. To choose or open a highlighted or selected item, press ⒠. To cancel the menu display, press ⒠.

When forms with input fields are displayed in QuickBooks, you can move to the next field by pressing ⒯ or to a previous field by pressing ⒮ and ⒯ together. The ⒯ key can be used as a quick way to accept input, advance the cursor to the next field, and highlight field contents for editing purposes. Using the mouse while you input information requires you to remove your hands from the keyboard, while the ⒯ key does not.

To demonstrate how to use the keyboard shortcuts:

1. From the Home page, **press** the ⒜ key (to activate the underlined letters in the menu)

Notes
The ⒜ key acts as a toggle to turn on and off the underlined letters in the menu.

Each item in the main menu should now have a letter underlined in its name. By pressing the ⒜ key, you can view which letters must be selected in order to open a menu item.

2. **Press** **u** to open the Customers menu ("u" is the underlined letter in "Customers")

Each menu item in the Customers menu also has an underlined letter in its name. Selecting a letter will open the form.

3. **Press** **y** to open the Receive Payments form (you could also have used the down arrow key to access the Receive Payments option)

The buttons on the bottom of the form also contain underlined letters. When you enter a customer payment in the Receive Payments window, you can press ⒜ + **a** to select Save & Close, or press ⒜ + **S** to select Save & New.

4. **Press** ⒠ to close the Receive Payments form

When you open a menu, some of the items in the menu also have shortcuts displayed to the right of their name. These shortcuts are usually memorized and used for quick access. Let's take a look at this.

5. **Press** ⒜ + **U** to open the Customers menu:

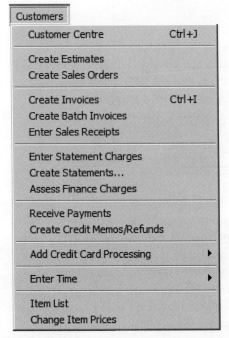

Figure 1-50

On this menu, both the Customer Centre and the Create Invoices options have specific keyboard shortcuts. To open the Customer Centre and the Create Invoices form:

6. Press   `ctrl` + **J** to open the Customer Centre

7. Press   `esc` to close the Customer Centre

8. Press   `ctrl` + **I** to open the Create Invoices form

9. Press   `esc` to close the Create Invoices form

QuickBooks Preferences

In this chapter, we will provide only an introduction to the preference settings. You won't need to change any preferences for the files we have set up, but you may want to adjust some of them. In this chapter, we will show you the preference settings that do not affect how the program works. We will cover the preferences for other modules in detail later as we use them in creating new company data files.

1. Choose   the **Edit menu** and **click Preferences**:

2. Click   the **Desktop View** heading on the left-hand side of the screen and **click** the **My Preferences tab**:

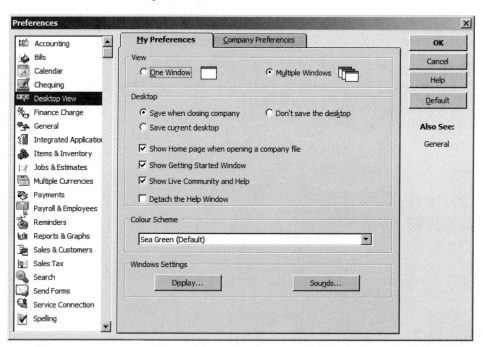

Figure 1-51

Preferences are divided into two tabs: Company preferences that can only be changed by the administrator of the company file or a user set up as an External Accountant, such as whether or not specific QuickBooks features are used; and My Preferences that influence how you work with the program and can be modified by all users to suit their own personal preferences. On the My Preferences tab for the desktop view heading, you can allow the simultaneous display of multiple open windows or just one window, save the desktop when you close the file, show the Home page when opening a company file, show the Coach window and features, show Live Community and Help, and change the colour scheme used in QuickBooks. You can also access the Windows settings for Display and Sounds. The Help button will explain each option on the Preferences window.

3. Click   the **Company Preferences tab**:

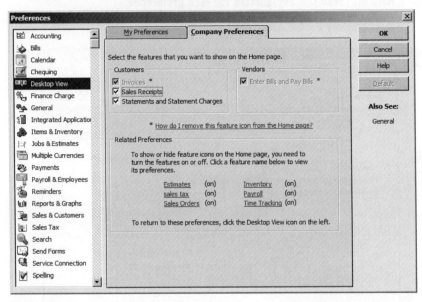

Figure 1-52

The preferences on the Company Preferences tab can only be changed by the administrator of the company file or a user set up as an External Accountant and affects all users of the system when you are working in a multi-user environment. If you are working in a single-user environment, then you will be the administrator of the company file and can make the necessary changes on the Company Preferences tab.

In the Desktop View heading, you can select the features you want to show on the Home page, such as Sales Receipts, Statements and Statement Charges, and Enter Bills and Pay Bills. If you don't use these features, you can turn them off so you don't clutter the Home page with icons you don't use. You can also use this tab to turn on or off Estimates, Sales Tax, Sales Orders, Inventory, Payroll, and Time Tracking. The Help button will explain each option on the current Preferences window.

4. Click   the **General heading** and **click** the **My Preferences tab**:

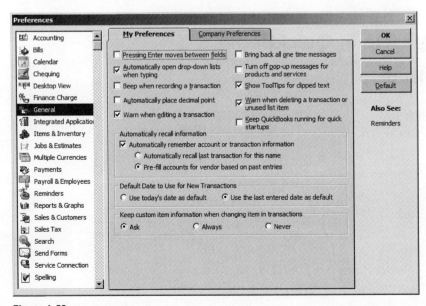

Figure 1-53

On this tab there are a number of preferences you can select, such as Beep when recording a transaction, Warn when editing a transaction, Warn when deleting a transaction or unused list item, and the Default Date to use for New Transactions.

5. **Click**   **Help** and **read** the **explanation for each preference**

6. **Click**   the **Company Preferences tab**:

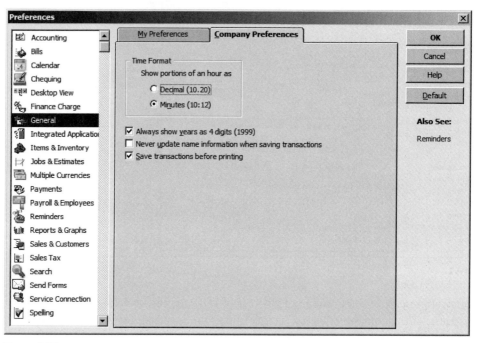

Figure 1-54

Use this tab to determine the date and time format, to indicate whether name information changed on forms should be updated in the QuickBooks record, and to save transactions before printing.

7. **Click**   **Help** and **read** the **explanation for each preference**

8. Do not save the changes you make

9. **Close**   the **Preferences window** when you have finished

Accessing Help in QuickBooks

QuickBooks Help

QuickBooks Help is displayed in its own window together with the Live Community to the right of the QuickBooks desktop. The QuickBooks Help pane is shown here:

Notes
If you make changes to the preferences and want to reset them back to the default settings, click the Default button on the right-hand side of the screen.

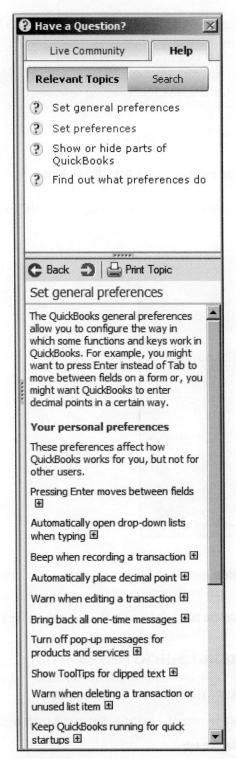

Figure 1-55

QuickBooks Help is context-sensitive, so as you move around in QuickBooks, the QuickBooks Help will automatically change to reflect the current open form. For example, when you open the QuickBooks Preferences window, Help for QuickBooks Preferences is displayed. However, as you move from one preference heading to another, you may have to click the Help button to update the information for the current preference heading.

With the Help window displayed on the screen, you can click the Relevant Topics tab in the upper section of the screen to view relevant topics for the current screen selected. Click on any of the relevant topics to view the help information in the bottom of the screen. Alternatively, you can click the Search tab and enter a help topic.

You can access Help using one of the following options:

<table>
<tr><td>Notes</td></tr>
</table>

Notes
QuickBooks Help is in the same window pane as the Live Community; therefore, Help is also displayed when you open Live Community.

a.   **Click Help**  on the Icon bar

OR

b.   **Choose** the **Help menu** and **click QuickBooks Help**

OR

c.   **Press F1** (the keyboard shortcut) to display the Help menu:

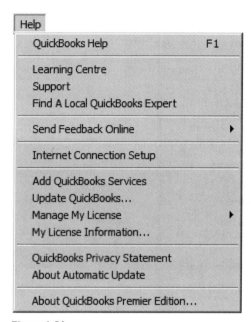

Figure 1-56

1. **Click**   the **Help icon** on the Icon bar (if the Live Community and Help pane is not currently displayed)

2. **Click**   the **Create Invoices icon** on the Customer section of the Home page to open the Create Invoices form

3. **Click**   the **Relevant Topics tab** (if necessary) to view the help topics relevant to creating invoices. Notice the topics are all about invoices because you have the Create Invoices form open

4. **Click**   a **topic** to view the information in the bottom of the Help pane

5. **Click**   the **Search tab**

6. **Type**   **Vendor Payments** and **press** (enter)

Even though you are currently on the Create Invoices form, help topics about Vendor Payments are displayed.

7. **Click**   a **topic** to view the help information

8. **Click**   ☒ to close the Help window pane

Live Community

QuickBooks Live Community is displayed in a separate tab in a window pane together with QuickBooks Help to the right of the QuickBooks desktop. The Live Community tab is shown here:

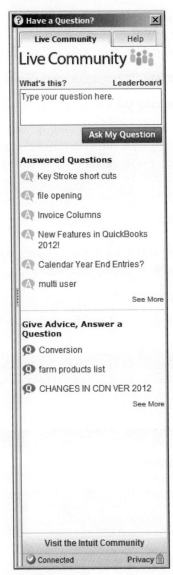

Figure 1-57

If you have an Internet connection, you can use Live Community to receive answers directly from the QuickBooks community from within QuickBooks. As you learned earlier, the Live Community is displayed in the same window as Help: Help is displayed on the screen and so is the Live Community.

To access the Live Community:

Figure 1-58

a. **Click** the **Live Community button** on the Icon bar (if it is displayed on the icon bar); or

b. **Press** any of the **options** that open QuickBooks help; or

c. **Click** the **Live Community tab** if necessary to display the Live Community pane

With the Live Community displayed, enter your question in the box and click the Ask My Question button. You can also click the Visit Intuit Community link at the bottom of the Live Community pane to access more information from the QuickBooks community.

Support

You can access QuickBooks Support from the Help menu. You need an Internet connection to use this feature. To access QuickBooks support:

1. **Choose**   **Help** from the menu

2. **Click**   **Support** to open the QuickBooks Support webpage:

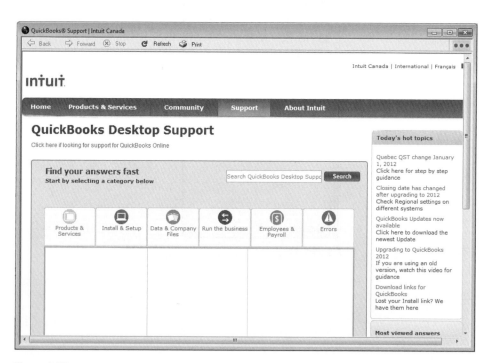

Figure 1-59

3. Take some time to review the information found on the QuickBooks Support website

The Learning Centre

The Learning Centre includes a number of resources to help you get started using QuickBooks.

To access the Learning Centre:

1. Choose	**Help** from the menu
2. Click	**Learning Centre**:

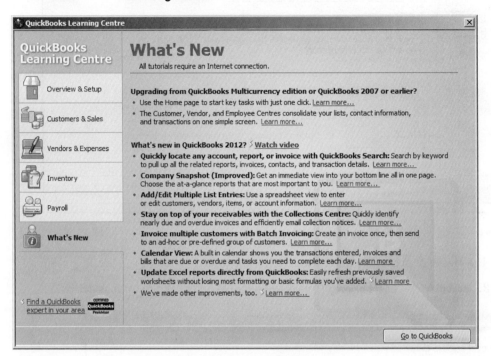

Figure 1-60

3. Click	on the **topics** down the left-hand side of the screen to view the different information available
4. Click	**What's New** to learn what's new in QuickBooks 2012
5. Click	☒ to close the Learning Centre when you're finished viewing it

Backing Up and Verifying Data Files

QuickBooks automatically saves your company file as you work in the program, but backing up your data files regularly ensures that you can continue working with your company data even if the working copy of the file becomes damaged. You should back up to a separate drive whenever possible for even greater security. We will demonstrate the backup procedure by saving the backup file onto a USB drive.

To back up the QuickBooks company file currently open:

1. Choose	**File** from the menu
2. Click	**Create Backup** to open the Create Backup screen:

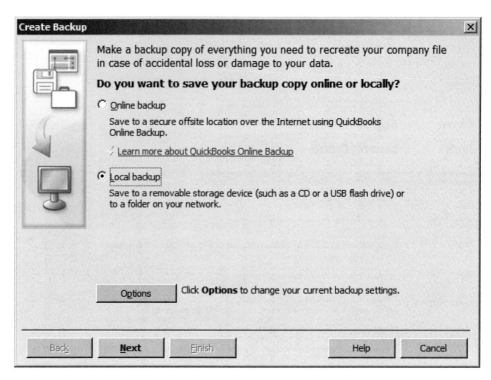

Figure 1-61

Use this screen to indicate whether you want to save your backup locally or online.

3. Accept   **Local backup** (this is the default) and **click** the **Options button**:

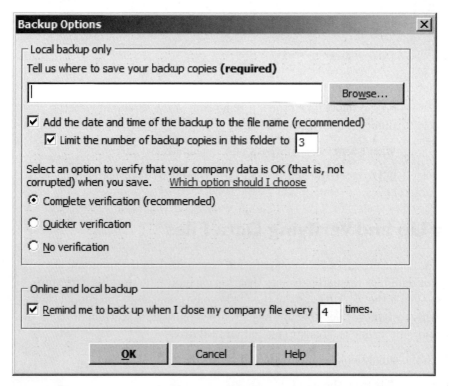

Figure 1-62

The Backup Options screen is used to set the backup options.

4. Click   **Browse** to display the Browse for Folder screen:

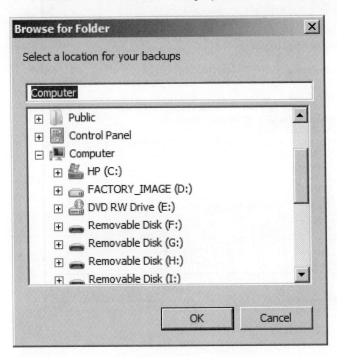

Figure 1-63

Notes
If you are using another location for your backup files, or if you are working on a network, enter the appropriate drive letter for your computer setup.

5. Select   your **USB drive** (or the drive you want to use)

6. Click   **OK** to close the Browse for Folder screen

The next time you back up this company file, this drive will automatically be displayed in the Browse field.

Add the date and time to the backup file name so it is very easy to identify when the backup file was created. When you limit the number of backups in the folder, you'll be prompted to delete the oldest backup from the folder when you reach the number entered in this field. You can decide to delete the oldest backup or choose not to.

We want to verify the data file each time we make a backup. Although this step will slow down the backup process, data file errors can be detected during this process. We can then choose to rebuild the data file to correct the errors or to restore the file from an earlier backup. We will also set the program to remind us to make a backup when the company file is closed every four times.

Notes
You can also verify your data at any time by choosing the File menu, then choosing Utilities and Verify Data. Notice that the option to Rebuild Data is located here as well.

7. Accept   **Complete Verification** as the verify option (this should be selected as the default)

8. Accept   the **default** to be reminded to back up the company file when it is closed every four times

9. Click   **OK** to close the Backup Options screen

10. Click   **Next** on the Save Copy or Backup screen to view the next backup screen:

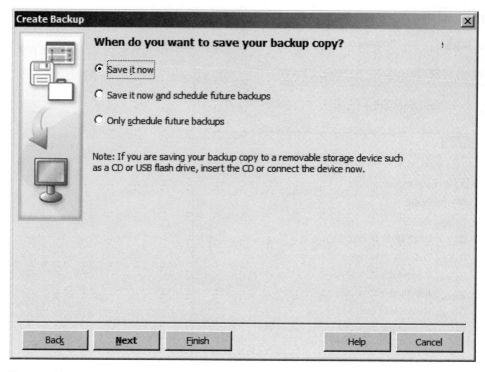

Figure 1-64

11. Click   **Finish**

When the backup is complete, you will see the following message:

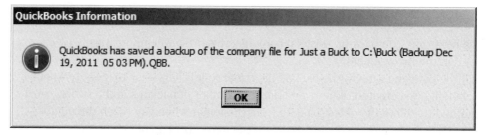

Figure 1-65

Notice that the file name contains the date and time when the backup was created and the file name ends with a QBB extension.

12. Click   **OK** to return to the company file

Scheduling Automatic Backups

QuickBooks allows you to schedule automatic backups so the data file is backed up regularly either when you close the data file, or on some other schedule.

1. Choose   the **File menu** and **click Create Backup** to open the Create Backup screen

2. Select   **Backup copy** and **click Next**

3. Select   **Local backup** and **click Next**

4. The following screen allows you to choose the backup schedule options:

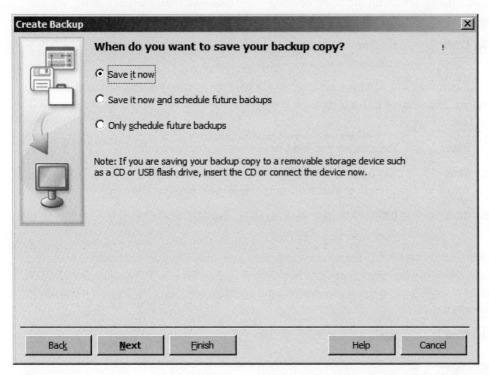

Figure 1-66

You can choose to create a backup now, create a backup now and schedule future backups, or only schedule future backups. Since we just completed a backup, we'll choose to schedule future backups.

5. Click the **Only schedule future backups** option and **click Next**:

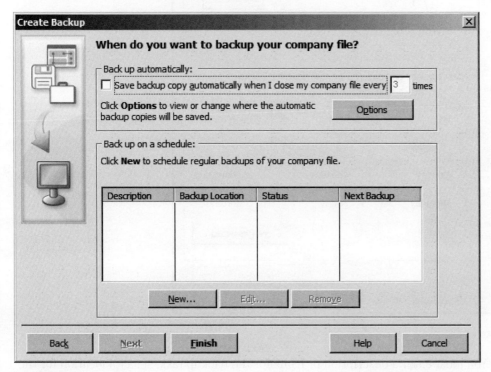

Figure 1-67

You can select to have the data file backup automatically when you close the company file by selecting the *Save backup copy automatically when I close my company file every ___ times* option and entering a number in the field.

6. **Click**   the **box** beside the *Save backup copy automatically when I close my company file every ___ times* option

The number field will become available. Every three times is entered as the default frequency. If you want to back up each time you close the file, enter 1 to replace the 3 as the default frequency.

7. **Enter**   **the number you want** in the *every ___ times* field

8. **Click**   the **Options button** and **enter** the **location** of the backup. Modify any of the other information found on this screen

9. **Click**   **OK** to close the Backup Options window after you have selected the appropriate options

You can also schedule automatic backups. Companies frequently back up their data at night when the computers are not being used by employees. To use this feature, you must, of course, leave your computer on, and the data file being backed up must not be open or in use.

10. **Click**   **New** to open the Schedule Backup screen:

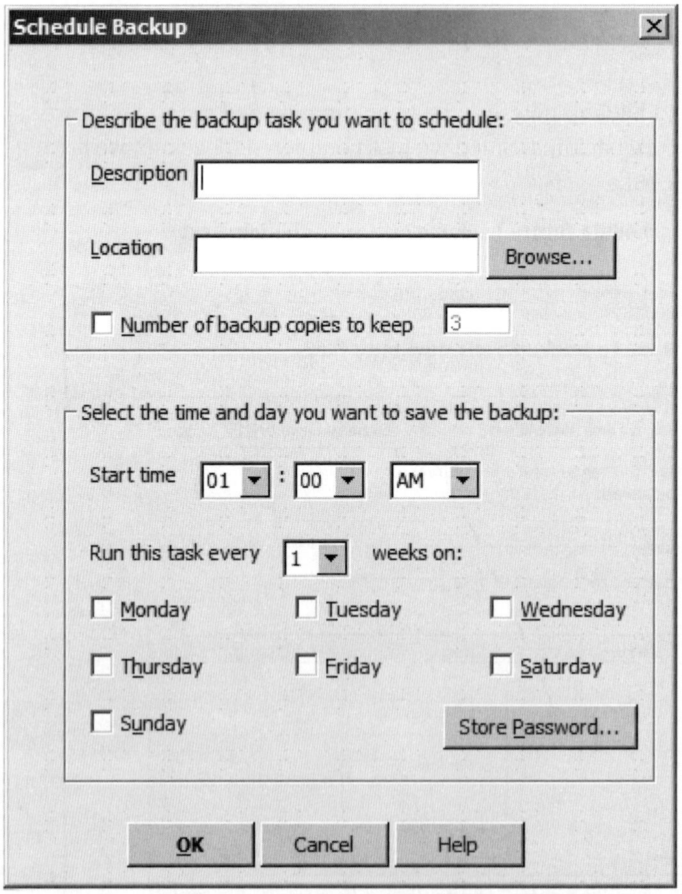

Figure 1-68

You must enter a description or name for the backup task, select a location for the backup file, enter the number of backups to keep before they are replaced by more current files, and determine how often you want to perform a backup. To back up the data file daily, you would choose 1 in the *Run this task every __ weeks on* field, and click each weekday name. You must enter the Windows password for the automatic backup to work.

11.	**Type**	**Daily Backup** in the description field
12.	**Click**	**Browse** to browse for the drive and folder you will use to save your backup file
13.	**Choose**	**1** in the *Run this task every __ weeks on* field
14.	**Click**	in the **box** beside each weekday name
15.	**Click**	**OK** to save the schedule

16. You will be prompted to enter the Windows password:

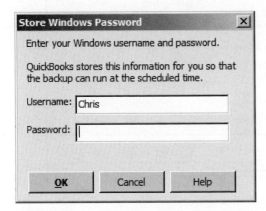

Figure 1-69

You must enter the Windows password required to unlock your computer so the QuickBooks backup can run at the scheduled time.

17.	**Click**	**OK** and you'll be returned to the Backup screen where the new backup schedule is listed:

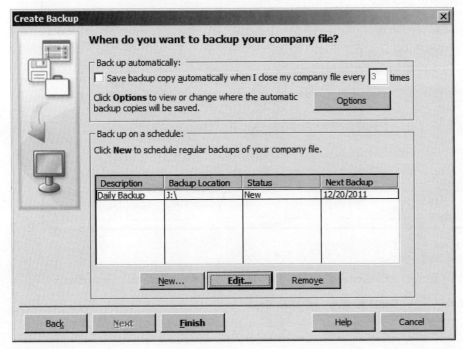

Figure 1-70

Restoring a File from a Backup

If your data files have become damaged, or if for some other reason you need to return to an earlier version of the data files, you can restore a file from its backup.

Notes
The No Company Open window also includes an Open or Restore an Existing Company button that starts the Restore Company Backup wizard.

1. **Choose** the **File menu** and **click Open or Restore Company** to open the Open or Restore Company window:

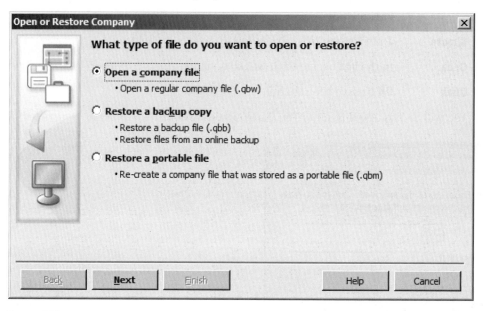

Figure 1-71

2. **Click** **Restore a backup copy** and **click Next**:

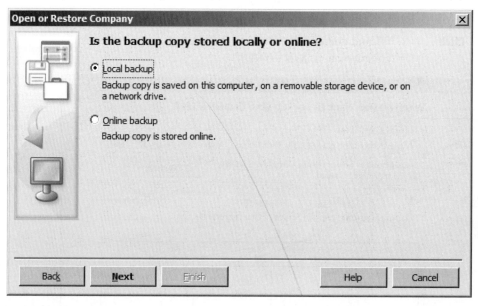

Figure 1-72

Use this screen to indicate whether your backup was saved locally or online.

3. **Click** **Local backup** and **click Next**:

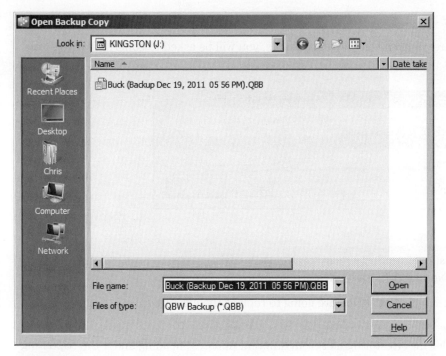

Figure 1-73

📄 **Notes**
  Your file may be
displayed differently
depending on the view you
have selected to display your
files. In Figure 1-73, files are
set to display in Detail.

4. Use   the **Look in: field** to browse for the backup file if necessary

5. Highlight   the **file** and **click Open**:

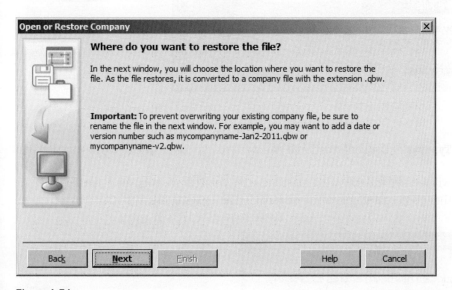

Figure 1-74

This screen indicates that you must choose the location where you want to restore your backup file and gives you information about overwriting your existing company file.

6. Click   **Next**

On this screen, select the location where you want to restore the backup file. The default is the original file name and location of the file you are restoring.

7. Click   the **drop-down arrow** in the Save in field to select the drive and folder
         where you want to restore the backup file

8. Click   Save

If you are replacing an existing data file, you will be asked to confirm that you want to replace it:

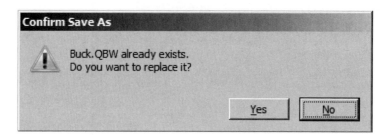

Figure 1-75

You must confirm that you are replacing the existing file. You can still make changes by clicking No to return to the Restore Company Backup window.

9. Click   Yes (if you are going to replace the existing file)

If you receive a message that this file is set to read only, please refer to page xi of the Preface under the "Restoring files from different updates" heading under the "Updating QuickBooks" heading.

If the file already exists, and is not set to read only, the following message will be displayed asking you to confirm deletion of the data file:

Notes
If you are restoring a sample company file (which is used in some of the chapters in the textbook), you will also receive a message indicating that the file is a QuickBooks Sample File and that the payroll calculations in the sample file will be incorrect.

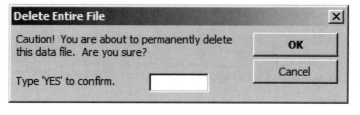

Figure 1-76

    a) **Type yes** in the confirmation if you want to permanently delete the existing file

10. You will receive the following message after you restore your file regardless of whether you created a new file or replaced an existing file:

Figure 1-77

11. Click   OK

Finishing Your Session

When you have finished entering all your accounting data in a work session, or just want to take a break, you should close the data file and the QuickBooks program. If you close the company file, you will see the No Company Open screen (page 10) the next time you start QuickBooks; otherwise, the last company data file you worked with will open automatically. You may want to close the company file if you work with many different company files so that you can choose a different company file the next time you start QuickBooks, or if you are unsure which data file you used most recently. If you work with the data for the same company each time, you won't want to close the company each time you finish your session. To close the company file:

1. **Choose** the **File menu** and **click Close Company**

2. The No Company Open window will be displayed

3. **Click** ☒ on the program title bar or **choose** the **File menu** and **click Exit** to close QuickBooks

CHAPTER TWO

Objectives

After completing this chapter, you should be able to:

- **write** cheques to vendors for purchases
- **enter** sales receipts to customers
- **customize** QuickBooks forms
- **add** an icon to the Icon bar
- **add** new vendors and customers
- **correct** cheques and receipts before recording
- **review** transaction journals after recording transactions
- **edit** sales receipts and cheques after recording
- **display** and **print** reports
- **display** and **print** graphs

Company Information

Company Profile

Notes
Chelsea's Chocolates
350 Godiva Ave.
Victoria, BC V7H 3L8
Tel: (250) 286-6199
Fax: (250) 288-6387
E-mail: ct@chelseas.com
Web: www.chelseas.com
Business No.: 448 399 844

Notes
The Business Number is the CRA (Canada Revenue Agency) number for the company that applies to all federal returns. It is also the GST/HST number for the business and, for non-profits if applicable, the charitable tax number.

Chelsea's Chocolates, located in Victoria, British Columbia, is a sole proprietorship owned and operated by Chelsea Truffles. After finishing high school in Victoria, Chelsea pursued her dream. She studied at one of Belgium's culinary schools specializing in candy and apprenticed with several famous Belgian chocolatiers to build her experience. Then she returned to Victoria to start her own business, initially selling chocolate truffles from her home, gradually expanding her business, and finally opening her own store. She has maintained several of her Belgian contacts and still imports all her chocolate and cocoa ingredients directly from Belgium.

Chelsea operates a cash business — all customers pay at the time of the sale, mostly in cash. A few customers who place large or special orders pay by cheque. All vendors who supply the store require payment immediately on receipt of merchandise, and Chelsea always pays by cheque so that she will have a complete record of her business transactions.

Her store is busiest in advance of major holiday seasons — chocolates are favourite gifts for Easter and Christmas — and she caters to special occasions for all religions. Originals, the major craft show in early April and late November, precedes some of these major holidays, and Chelsea is usually very successful at both shows, selling chocolates directly to customers and discussing special orders for future business. She has just purchased a large inventory of candy ingredients to prepare candy for the November craft show.

Over time, Chelsea acquired the capital equipment needed for her business, including the stove tops for making chocolates, refrigerators for food supplies, and customized refrigerated display shelves to keep the prepared candy fresh while on display. She keeps a minimum inventory on hand so that candy ingredients such as butter, cream, nuts, dried fruits, and marzipan are always fresh. She uses a variety of sugars to flavour the candy and also keeps these as regular inventory items. Her non-food inventory includes packaging materials, such as waxed tissue paper, paper and plastic bags, boxes in all sizes, and decorative gift tins, and supplies of plastic and vinyl gloves for serving customers.

Chelsea pays monthly rent for store space that includes heat and hydro. Her rent is higher than average for the store space to cover her above-average usage of hydro. She also pays rent for her booth at the Originals craft show.

On November 1, Chelsea's Chocolates is ready to use QuickBooks for accounting transactions after using the following information to convert the accounting records to QuickBooks:

- Chart of Accounts
- Trial Balance
- List of Vendors, Customers, and Items
- Accounting Procedures

Chart of Accounts

Chelsea's Chocolates

ASSETS
Bank
  Bank Chequing
  Bank Savings

Current Assets
  Inventory:Chocolate
  Inventory:Other Candy Ingredients
  Inventory:Packaging Material
  Supplies

Fixed Assets
  Automobile
  Candy Making Equipment
  Computer/Cash Register
  Display Cabinets & Shelves
  Range/Ovens
  Refrigerators

LIABILITIES
Current Liabilities
  GST/HST Payable

Long Term Liabilities
  Long Term Loan

EQUITY
  Capital, Chelsea Truffles
  Retained Earnings

INCOME
  Revenue from Candy Sales
  Revenue from Interest

EXPENSE
Cost of Goods Sold
  Cost of Candy Ingredients

Expenses
  Advertising
  Insurance
  Maintenance and Repairs
  Packaging Materials Used
  Rental Expense
  Supplies Expense
  Utilities

Trial Balance

Chelsea's Chocolates

AS AT OCTOBER 31, 2014

	Debits	Credits
Bank Chequing	$ 29,200.00	
Bank Savings	18,580.00	
Inventory:Chocolate	5,150.00	
Inventory:Other Candy Ingredients	3,450.00	
Inventory:Packaging Material	600.00	
Supplies	1,500.00	
Automobile	14,000.00	
Candy Making Equipment	5,000.00	
Computer/Cash Register	4,500.00	
Display Cabinets & Shelves	3,800.00	
Range/Ovens	3,300.00	
Refrigerators	26,000.00	
GST/HST Payable	$ 450.00	
Long Term Loan		$ 24,000.00
Capital, Chelsea Truffles		57,940.00
Revenue from Candy Sales		88,500.00
Revenue from Interest		2,000.00
Cost of Candy Ingredients	8,300.00	
Advertising	2,100.00	
Insurance	1,700.00	
Packaging Materials Used	3,900.00	
Rental Expense	34,000.00	
Supplies Expense	1,710.00	
Utilities	5,200.00	
	$172,440.00	$172,440.00

Vendor, Customer, and Item Lists

Chelsea's Chocolates

VENDORS

Belgian's Finest
Covers
Fournier's Fine Foods
Minister of Finance (BC)
NuTel
Originals (Craft Show)
Receiver General
Suite Properties
SuperSacs

CUSTOMERS

Craft Show Customers
Store Customers

ITEMS

Candy Sold in Store
Craft Show Sales
Special Orders

Accounting Procedures

Taxes: HST

Chelsea's Chocolates pays 12 percent HST on all goods and services that it buys except zero-rated items, including the imported products, and charges HST on all sales and services. HST collected from customers is recorded as a liability in the *GST/HST Payable* account. HST paid to vendors is recorded in the *GST/HST Payable* account as a decrease in liability to the Canada Revenue Agency. The report is filed with the Receiver General for Canada by the last day of the month for the previous quarter, either including the balance owing or requesting a refund. *GST/HST Payable* shows a debit balance because Chelsea has recently submitted a return and payment and has made a large number of purchases to prepare for the craft show.

Notes
Refer to the Tax Appendix (found on the CD that accompanies this text) for details on sales taxes.

Customer and Vendor Account Terms

Most customers pay in cash. Cash received from customers is deposited immediately and is recorded in the *Bank Chequing* account. It is not held for later deposit. Some special order customers pay for their purchases by cheque.

All vendors demand payment on receipt of merchandise. All payments are made by cheque.

Cost of Goods Sold

Most food items and supplies are used shortly after purchase so these amounts are entered directly as expenses rather than as assets. At the end of the fiscal year, adjusting entries are made for unused food inventory that is available for future periods. This amount is debited to the appropriate asset account and the expense account is reduced.

WARNING!
At the time of printing this textbook, the tax in British Columbia is HST @12% so the textbook reflects this tax in chapters where the company is in British Columbia.

In April 2013, the BC government plans to re-implement the provincial sales tax (PST). Therefore, if you are using this textbook in April 2013, the taxes in BC will be PST and GST, and not HST as reflected in the textbook.

Instructions

1. Using the Chart of Accounts, Trial Balance, and other information, record entries for the source documents for November 2014 by using QuickBooks. You will find the source documents marked with an SD beside them and listed as you work through the chapter. The procedures for entering each new type of transaction are outlined in step-by-step instructions in the chapter. Additional source documents will be provided, allowing you to have more practice entering transactions. If you have used this textbook in the past and would prefer to skip the step-by-step instructions and work only with a list of source documents, refer to the CD in the back of the textbook for the list of source documents for this chapter.

Notes
We realize that in the classroom, printing facilities may be limited. Your instructor will tell you which reports to print and which ones to display.
Instructions for reports begin on page 79.

2. After you have finished making your entries, print the reports and graphs for November 2014 indicated on the following printing form.

REPORTS FOR NOVEMBER 2014	Accountant & Taxes	GRAPHS
Company & Financial	☑ Trial Balance from Nov. 1 to Nov. 30	☑ Income and Expense
☑ Balance Sheet Standard: Nov. 30	☑ General Ledger from Nov. 1 to Nov. 30	☑ Net Worth
☑ Profit & Loss Standard (Income Statement) from Nov. 1 to Nov. 30	☑ Journal from Nov. 1 to Nov. 30	

Entering Transactions in QuickBooks

Entering transactions in QuickBooks involves entering information on different types of forms. Many of these look like the regular forms that a business uses every day — cheque registers, journal ledgers, customer invoice and vendor bills, cheques, and so on. Other than in a journal entry, you do not need to enter debit and credit amounts. QuickBooks creates the debit and credit entries for the journal behind the scene so you see them only when you look at the journal reports. In many cases, you do not even need to add the account because the account is preselected as a default for the item or transaction. Intuitive, non-accounting terms are generally used.

Command words are in bold black type; the object of the command is shown in colour.

Opening Data Files

Notes
Your computer setup may not show the file extension .qbw.

Notes
Keystroke instructions that you must use are shown in highlighted text in indented paragraphs like the one beside this note, starting with Open.

Notes
If you want to keep the Live Community and Help window open, please feel free to do so.
If you close it, you can open it again at any time by clicking Help on the Icon bar.

1. **Open**   **Chelsea.qbw** or **Chelsea**, the data file for Chelsea's Chocolates using the instructions for accessing a data file in **Chapter 1, page 8**.

2. **Click**   **No** to **close** the **Set Up an External Accountant User dialogue box** if it is displayed

3. **Click**   the **Close button** ☒ in the **Live Community** and **Help window** pane

4. **Click**   **OK** when prompted to open Live Community when starting QuickBooks

5. The QuickBooks Home page is displayed:

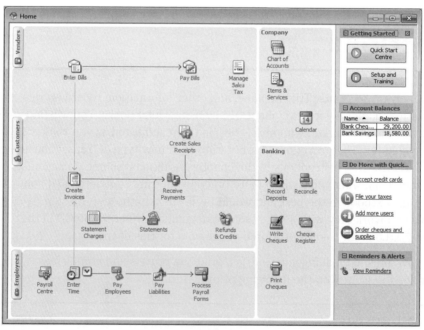

Figure 2-1

Notes
The Reminders & Alerts section will display an Alert if Intuit has sent you a message. Although our print screen does not show an Alert, your screen may show one.

Cash Purchases: Writing Cheques

The first transaction that we will enter in this company file is a purchase that was paid by cheque. Refer to the following source document as we work through the steps to enter it:

SD1: Write Cheque   **Dated November 1, 2014**

To pay cash for purchase received with Bill #BF-3367 from Belgian's Finest in the amount of $450.00 for cocoa, dark chocolate, and cocoa butter, ingredients for chocolate candy. Food is zero rated for HST. Wrote Cheque #235 to pay the bill in full.

Chelsea pays for all purchases immediately by cheque. This combines the steps of entering the bill followed by a payment.

You can access the form for writing cheques in different ways.

We will begin from the Banking section of the Home page shown below:

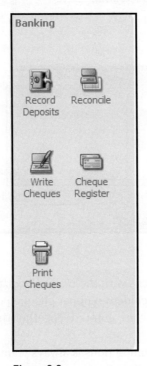

Figure 2-2

The Banking section of the Home page is the starting point for all activities involving the bank accounts. Paying for purchases that have not been entered first as vendor bills involves writing cheques.

1. **Open**   the **Write Cheques form** by using one of the following options:

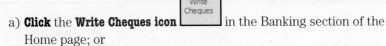

    a) **Click** the **Write Cheques icon** in the Banking section of the Home page; or

    b) **Press** `ctrl` + **W**, the keyboard shortcut; or

    c) **Choose** the **Banking menu** and **click Write Cheques**

2. The Write Cheques form will be displayed as shown:

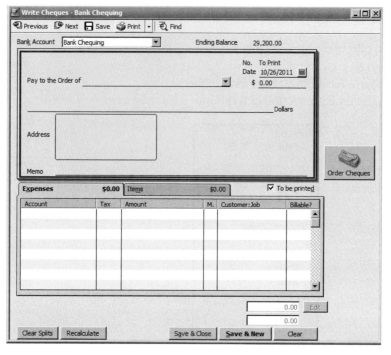

Figure 2-3

The Write Cheques form opens with the *Bank Chequing* account displayed in the Bank Account field. The form includes an upper cheque portion and a lower portion where the details of the purchase are entered. Together they provide a complete record of the purchase.

The initial default date for transactions is always your current computer date, so we need to change it for this transaction. Once you begin to enter transactions, the last date used will appear as the default until you close and re-open the company data file.

3. Press (tab) to advance to the date field

4. Type **11/01/14**

5. Click the **drop-down arrow** in the **Pay to the Order of field** to view the company's list of vendors:

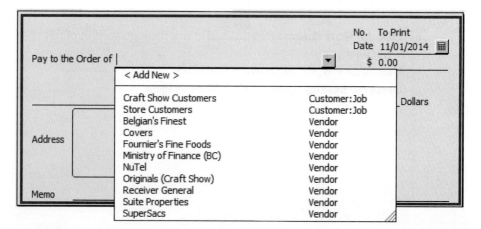

Figure 2-4

Notice that this is a list of all payees — all vendors, customers, employees, or others such as the owner and tax agencies — because you can write a cheque to any of these payees.

6. Click   **Belgian's Finest**

7. Click   the **Account field** to display the drop-down arrow

8. Click   the **drop-down arrow** in the **Account field** to view the following list of accounts:

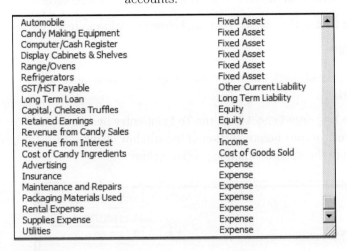

Notes
  If you need to see additional accounts, you can scroll up the list to view the asset accounts.

Figure 2-5

Accounts are listed in order by type — Income Statement accounts follow Balance Sheet accounts. Expense accounts are frequently used for vendor purchases, so the account list opens at a point where all the expense accounts are displayed. Most candy ingredients purchased are used immediately so the expenses associated with sales are entered directly as the cost of sales. Costs are not tracked separately because it is difficult to record the cost of each candy sold.

Notes
  Adjusting entries are made at the end of a business period for supplies on hand that can be carried forward to the next period.

9. Click   **Cost of Candy Ingredients**

10. Press   (tab) to advance to the Tax field

11. Click   the **drop-down arrow** in the **Tax field** to view the tax codes available for purchases:

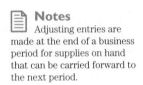

Notes
  We have increased the print screen to show the entire tax code description and taxable or non-taxable indicator. Your screen will only show each tax code with a partial description.

Figure 2-6

The tax codes available include GST Only, HST (BC) Only, PST Only, Standard Taxes (GST/PST), HST Zero Rated, and Tax Exempt.

12. Click   **Z - HST Zero Rated**

13. Press   (tab) to advance to the Amount field where you will enter the amount of the purchase before taxes

Do not type dollar signs when you enter amounts. For whole numbers, you do not need to enter the decimals.

14. **Type**   450

15. **Press**   ⎡tab⎤ to advance to the Memo field so you can enter a description for the purchase

16. **Type**   **Cocoa and other chocolate ingredients**

If additional items were purchased from the vendor, enter them on the following lines of the form by repeating the steps for the first purchase.

We still need to add the vendor's bill number to include it in the journal records.

17. **Click**   the **Memo field** in the cheque portion, below the Address text box

18. **Type**   **Inv BF-3367**

19. **Click**   the **To be printed check box** below the cheque area to remove the checkmark

When you deselect the To be printed check box, the To Print entry beside the No. field in the top right-hand corner of the cheque portion of the window changes to 1, the first cheque number as shown in the updated cheque portion below:

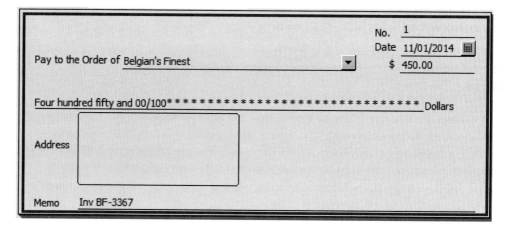

No. 1
Date 11/01/2014 🔳

Pay to the Order of Belgian's Finest   ▾ $ 450.00

Four hundred fifty and 00/100* Dollars

Address

Memo   Inv BF-3367

Figure 2-7

We need to enter a beginning cheque number to start the automatic numbering sequence for cheques. The first cheque we are writing is number 235. Once you enter a cheque number, QuickBooks will update the subsequent cheque numbers automatically.

20. **Double click**   1 in the **No. field** in the cheque portion of the window

21. **Type**   **235**

We have set up the company data files to use the *Bank Chequing* account as the default account when entering cheques in the Write Cheques form. You can select a different account by clicking the drop-down arrow in the Bank Account field in the upper left section of the window. All accounts defined as bank accounts will be available for selection. For this transaction, the default account is correct.

Your completed transaction should look like the one that follows:

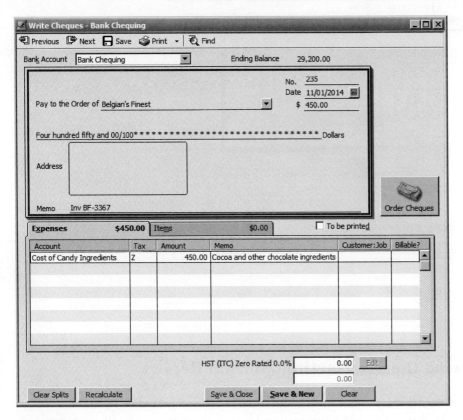

Figure 2-8

22. **Review**   the **transaction** and **make corrections** if necessary

---

CORRECTING CHEQUES OR CASH PURCHASES

Click a field to return to the error. Press ⌨(tab) to move forward from one field to the next. Highlight the incorrect information. With the incorrect information highlighted, type the correct information to replace it. After changing an amount, press ⌨(tab) and click the Recalculate button at the bottom of the form if necessary to update the amount in the cheque portion of the form.

⚠️ **WARNING!**
When you change a cheque amount, you must click the Recalculate button to update the cheque portion of the form.

   If you want to start the transaction over, you can click the **Clear button** in the lower right-hand corner of the Write Cheques form. The transaction information will be removed, leaving you with a blank Write Cheques form.

   In the next step, we will preview the transaction journal for this transaction, so leave the Write Cheques form open. The Save & Close button will save the transaction and close the form, while the Save & New button will save the transaction and leave the form open.

23. **Click**   **Save & New or press** ⌨(alt) **+ S** (the underlined letter on the Save & New button) to save the transaction and open a blank cheque form

24. As shown below, the cheque number is automatically updated to 236 and the bank account ending balance is updated after we save the transaction:

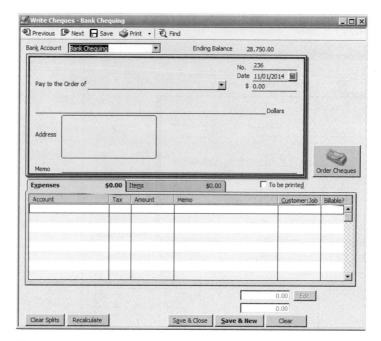

Figure 2-9

Reviewing the Transaction Journal Report

To view the journal entry created by the transaction, we can look at the Transaction Journal report. You can view the Transaction Journal report created by the transaction from the Write Cheques form after recording the transaction and displaying it back on the screen. Therefore, we need to display the transaction again before we can display the Transaction Journal report.

A blank Write Cheques form should be displayed on the screen.

1. Click the **Previous button** Previous to display Cheque #235 in the Write Cheques form:

2. Press ctrl + **Y** to display the Transaction Journal report:

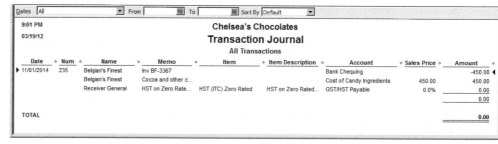

Figure 2-10

QuickBooks automatically creates a journal entry each time you complete a transaction by debiting and crediting the appropriate accounts. The *Bank Chequing* account is credited for the transaction, reducing the bank account balance, and the *Cost of Candy Ingredients* account, the expense account, has been debited or increased for the amount of the purchase. The *GST/HST Payable* amount is zero because we chose Z as the tax code (zero-rated HST 0%). When you choose tax exempt as the code, there is no amount calculated for the *GST/HST Payable* account.

Notes
In previous versions of QuickBooks, a Journal icon was available on the icon bar of a form that could be used to display the Transaction Journal report. This icon is no longer available on forms, so we must use the ctrl + **Y** shortcut to access the Transaction Journal report.

Notes
The columns in the Transaction Journal reports in this chapter have been adjusted to fit within the textbook; therefore, you will have additional columns in your reports.

Notes
Throughout the textbook, we have customized the Transaction Journal reports by hiding unused columns on the report. Refer to page 86 for more information on modifying reports.

3. **Click** ⊠ to close the Transaction Journal report

4. **Click** **No** when asked to memorize the report if you made any changes to the report

5. **Click** the **Next button** 🖙 Next on the Write Cheques icon bar or **press** ⌥ **+ N** to close the cheque for Belgian's Finest and open a blank chequing form

The second transaction that we will enter is a cheque for purchases received from Super-Sacs. Refer to the following source document as we work through the steps to enter it:

Source Docs
Refer to the following source document and then follow the step-by-step instructions to enter it.

SD2: Write Cheque   **Dated November 1, 2014**

To pay cash for purchase received with Bill #SS-1197 from SuperSacs in the amount of $540.00 plus $64.80 HST for plastic carrier bags imprinted with logos for store and Originals craft show. The total of the bill is $604.80. Wrote Cheque #236 to pay the bill in full.

6. **Click** the **drop-down arrow** in the **Pay to Order of field** to view the list of vendors

7. **Click** **SuperSacs**

8. **Type** **11/01/14** as the date

9. **Type** **Inv SS-1197** in the **Memo field**

10. **Click** the **Account field** to display the drop-down arrow

11. **Click** the **drop-down arrow** to view the list of accounts

12. **Choose** **Packaging Materials Used** as the account

13. **Choose** **Tax Code H - HST (BC) Only** as the tax code so that taxes will be automatically calculated at 12% and included on the bill total

14. **Enter** **540** as the amount

15. **Press** ⭾ to advance to the Memo field

16. **Type** **Plastic bags for store and Originals Craft Show**

17. **Click** **Save & Close** or **press** ⌥ **+ a** to close the Write Cheques form

Entering Sales Receipts

Chelsea's Chocolates is a cash business. Customers do not have accounts and always pay for purchases immediately. Most of the sales are for very small amounts that would involve a large number of transactions in QuickBooks. Therefore, we have chosen to show the sales as bi-weekly summaries of total sales for the period. The transactions for smaller individual sales would be entered in exactly the same way as the ones we show. Cash receipts are always deposited immediately to the *Bank Chequing* account.

The next transaction that we will enter is a Sales Receipt. Refer to the following source document as we work through the steps to enter it:

Source Docs
Refer to the following source document and then follow the step-by-step instructions to enter it.

SD3: Sales Receipt #2092   **Dated November 1, 2014**

To store customers, $870.00 plus $104.40 HST for chocolate sold in store in past three days. All customers paid cash for their purchases. Sales total $974.40 was deposited to the *Bank Chequing* account.

Notes
Some QuickBooks functions can be hidden on the Home page depending on the options selected in QuickBooks Preferences. We will learn how to customize Preferences in Chapter 4.

Because Chelsea accepts only immediate payment for all sales, most of the transaction functions in the Customer section of the Home page are not used. We have customized the Home page to make it more suitable for Chelsea's Chocolates. Some of the icons, such as Estimates and Sales Orders, have been removed because they are not needed. These types of transactions will be covered in later chapters.

Two icons in the Customer section of the Home page can be used to enter sales transactions: Create Invoices and Create Sales Receipts. However, because customers pay immediately and do not have accounts set up with the chocolatier, sales are entered as Sales Receipts rather than as invoices. We are bypassing the invoice entry step just as we bypassed the bill entry step for purchases.

We will enter the Sales Receipt by selecting the Create Sales Receipts icon from the Customers section of the Home page.

1. To access the Create Sales Receipts form:

   a) **Click** the **Create Sales Receipts icon** in the Customers section of the Home page as shown:

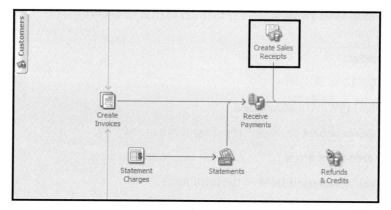

Figure 2-11

OR

   b) **Choose** the **Customers menu** and **click Enter Sales Receipts**

2. The Enter Sales Receipts form will be displayed as shown:

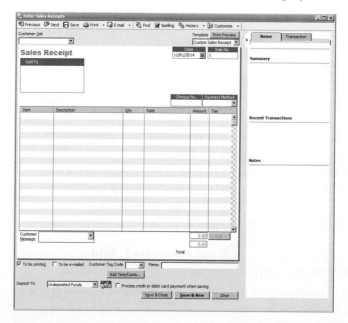

Figure 2-12

The Sales Receipts form looks just like a Sales Invoice; however, unlike an invoice, when you enter a Sales Receipt, you enter both the invoice information and the payment information together on the form. The form includes some columns that we do not need. We will customize the form after completing the sales entry.

The history tab, displayed to the right of the Sales Receipts form, will display customer and transaction information for the customer when one is selected for the transaction. This tab can be closed by clicking on the Hide history arrow in the top left-hand corner of the tab. Since Chelsea's Chocolates does not have individual customers, we will discuss the history tab in more detail in Chapters 5 and 6.

The customer name field is always named Customer:Job in QuickBooks because companies may work on more than one job at once for a customer. You may want to track these jobs separately. When you add a customer, you can also add a job name, and you can add new jobs for existing customers.

Notes
We will close the history tab before taking most transaction print screens for this textbook. You can close the history tab by clicking the Hide history arrow in the top left-hand corner of the history tab.
  If you want to open the history tab after closing it, click the Show history arrow in the top right-hand corner of the transaction screen.

3. **Click**   the **drop-down arrow** in the **Customer:Job field** to view the list of customers:

< Add New >	
Craft Show Customers	Customer:Job
Store Customers	Customer:Job

Figure 2-13

We have created two summary level customers that will separate the sales in the store from the sales at the Originals craft show.

4. **Click**   **Store Customers** to add the name to the sales receipt

For each customer, we have entered a default method of payment in their customer record. All store and craft show customers pay cash, so this is the default method of payment selected. The sale number is updated automatically by the program. Because no sales have been entered yet, 1 appears as the default starting number. We need to change it.

Notes
Although you do not need to select a customer to complete a Sales Receipt, choosing a customer allows more detailed reporting because several reports can be prepared by customer.
  Choosing a customer also allows the automatic entry of additional information for the customer, such as the method of payment and payment terms.

5. **Press**   (tab) to advance to the date field

6. **Type**   11/01/14

7. **Press**   (tab) to advance to the Sale No. field

8. **Type**   2092

9. **Click**   the **drop-down arrow** in the **Payment Method field** to view the payment method options:

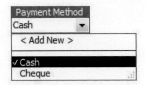

Payment Method	
Cash	▼
< Add New >	
✓ Cash	
Cheque	

Figure 2-14

Only cash and cheque, two immediate payment methods, are listed because account terms are not offered and credit cards are not accepted. Cash is selected because it is the default payment method for store customers and it was entered in the customer record. If you need to change the payment method for the Sales Receipt you can choose it from the drop-down list.

10. **Click**   **Cash**

11. **Press**   (tab) to advance to the Item field

Items in QuickBooks

Notes
We will use different kinds of items in later chapters and learn how to create items when we complete a company setup in Chapter 4.

Items are central to QuickBooks. Sales forms can be completed only by selling items. Items may be created for services, inventory that is tracked, store merchandise that is sold but not tracked as individual items, and even items that are purchased but not sold, such as regular supplies. Beginning in QuickBooks version 2008, taxes are also set up as items.

Items are linked directly to accounts — revenue accounts for items that are sold and expense or asset accounts for purchases. Tax codes are also set up as part of the item record. Prices for items may be set up in the data files as defaults, or they can be omitted from the item records and entered on invoices or sales receipts.

12.	**Click**	the **drop-down arrow** in the **Item field** to view the items created for the store:

Notes
Only the items available for sale and the HST Adjustment item are available for selection on the Sales Receipt.

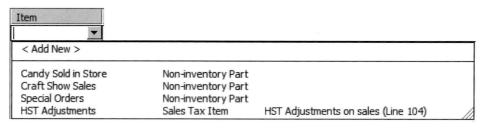

Figure 2-15

We have set up three items for the store to record sales: sales in the store, sales at the craft show, and sales from special or customized orders. Inventory is not tracked and no prices are entered because items are individually priced.

13.	**Click**	**Candy Sold in Store** to select this item
14.	**Press**	ⓣⓐⓑ to advance to the Description field

Notice that tax code H is added automatically in the last column for this item. You can select another tax code from the list by clicking on the drop-down arrow in the Tax field and selecting a different tax code if needed.

15.	**Type**	**sale of chocolates**
16.	**Double click**	**0.00** in the **Rate field** to highlight it
17.	**Type**	**870**
18.	**Press**	ⓣⓐⓑ to update the sales receipt with the tax amounts
19.	**Click**	**OK** if you receive the price level message

In QuickBooks Premier, you can add custom pricing for customers and jobs by creating price level lists. We will not be using the price level feature.

You can enter the sale of additional items on the Sales Receipt by adding more item detail lines. To do so, repeat the steps described for the first item.

Next, we will choose a comment for the Sales Receipt. Again, you can create a list of predefined comments for the company to choose from, or create a new comment when entering the transaction.

20.	**Click**	the **drop-down arrow** in the **Customer Message field** to view the list of predefined comments:

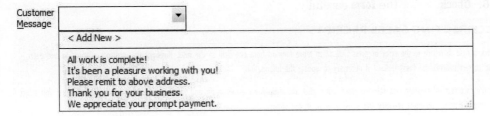

Figure 2-16

21. Click   **Thank you for your business.** to add that comment to the sales receipt

22. Click   the **To be printed check box** in the lower left-hand corner of the form
to remove the checkmark

📄 **Notes**
We assume that in most cases when you are practising, you will not want to print all the sales receipts.

If you want to print each sales receipt, leave the *To be printed* option checked. Depending on how the preferences for the QuickBooks reminders are set up, you may be reminded to print the sales receipt in the Reminders list. Printing Sales Receipts is similar to printing customer invoices. Printing invoices is covered in Chapter 6.

The final option that we need to change concerns the deposit of the Sales Receipts. The two options that control how deposits are recorded are located in the lower left-hand corner of the Enter Sales Receipts form. By default, the cash receipt will be grouped with other undeposited funds and recorded as a debit entry to the *Undeposited Funds* account. This step would be followed by a separate transaction that deposits the funds to the bank account. Instead, we will record the deposit to the bank account directly. In Chapter 6, you will learn the procedure for grouping undeposited funds and then making a deposit later.

23. Click   the **drop-down arrow** in the **Deposit To field**

24. Choose   **Bank Chequing**

The *Bank Chequing* account will remain selected as the default account to deposit funds into for future Sales Receipts so you will not have to change it again unless you need to select a different account.

25. The transaction is now complete and should look like the one that follows:

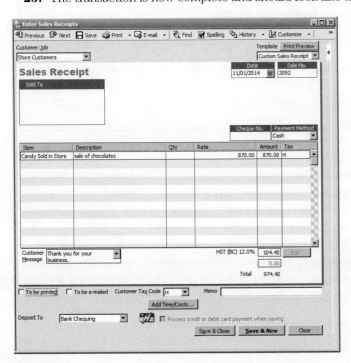

Figure 2-17

26. Check the **form** carefully

The next transaction is also a Sales Receipt so we will leave the Enter Sales Receipts form open.

27. Click **Save & New** or **press** (alt) + **S** to save the transaction and open a new blank Sales Receipt form

Before entering the next sale, however, we will review the Transaction Journal report for the sale we just completed.

Reviewing the Transaction Journal Report

The procedure for reviewing a Transaction Journal report for a Sales Receipt is the same procedure we used to display the Transaction Journal report for the cheque we entered earlier. We use the Previous button on the Sales Receipts form to display the transaction on the screen and then press (ctrl) + **Y** to view the Transaction Journal report.

1. Click the **Previous button** [Previous] on the Enter Sales Receipts icon bar

Clicking the Previous button displays the transaction you entered most recently according to the transaction date.

2. Press (ctrl) + **Y** to view the Transaction Journal report:

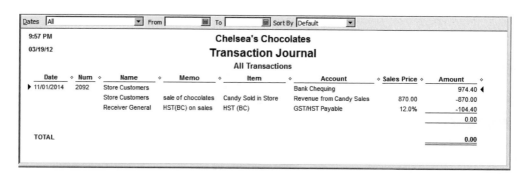

Figure 2-18

Again, QuickBooks has created the proper journal entry for the transaction behind the scenes and debited and credited all the appropriate accounts. The sale has increased the balance for the *Bank Chequing* account for the total sale amount. The sale amount net of taxes is entered as a credit to increase the *Revenue from Candy Sales* account. The tax code, H, included HST on the sale so the tax amount will increase the *GST/HST Payable* account balance. We must pay the taxes that we collect from customers to the appropriate federal and provincial tax agencies, depending on the province that we are in. The net effect of these debits and credits is a zero balance owing by customers.

3. Click [X] to close the Transaction Journal report

4. Click **No** if prompted to memorize the report

5. Click   the **Next button** 🖙 Next on the Enter Sales Receipts icon bar or **press** _(alt)_ **+ N** to close the Sales Receipt for the Store Customers and open a blank Sales Receipt form

Customizing QuickBooks Forms

We will now customize the Sales Receipt form to best reflect the items we sell to customers. We will be entering a large number of Sales Receipts so we will modify the Sales Receipt form by removing columns that we do not need and then we will add a Sales Receipts icon to the Icon bar for quick access to the Sales Receipt form.

Customizing the Sales Form

1. Click   the **Customize icon** 🖋 Customize ▾ in the Sales Receipt icon bar to open the Basic Customization window:

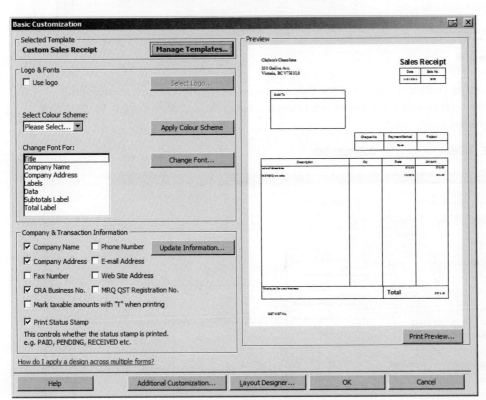

Notes
If you try to modify a default template that is supplied with QuickBooks, you will be asked to first make a copy of the template before you can modify it.

Figure 2-19

The Custom Sales Receipt is the selected template (displayed in the top left-hand corner of the window) and it is the one we want to edit.

On the Basic Customization screen, you can change the colour scheme, change the font for various headings, and add or exclude company and transaction information from the selected template.

2. Click   the **Additional Customization button** Additional Customization... to open the Additional Customization window:

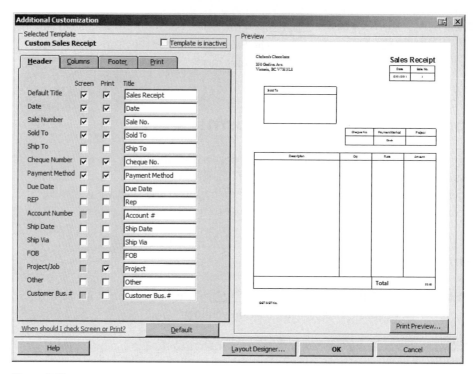

Figure 2-20

You can edit many areas of the Sales Receipt form by selecting the appropriate tab. We want to edit the form by removing the columns that do not apply to Chelsea's Chocolates.

3. Click the **Columns tab**:

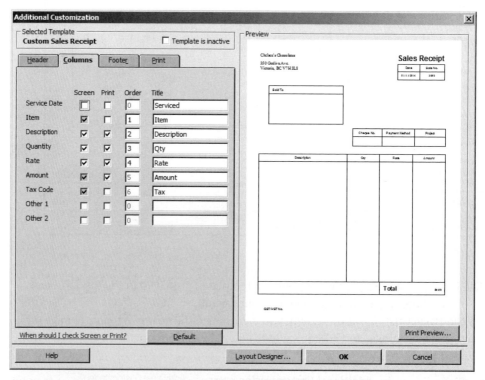

Figure 2-21

The available columns of the form are all listed. Each column can be displayed on the screen, printed on the print form, or both. A ✓ indicates the column is included. Only three columns are mandatory and must be displayed on the screen — Item, Amount, and Tax Code — and the checkmarks for these columns under the screen heading are dimmed because they cannot be changed. You can change the order of the items on the forms by entering a number in the Order field for each item and you can also change the title displayed for each item.

We do not need Rate or Quantity displayed on our screen or printed form so we will remove them.

4. Click   **Quantity** under the **Screen column** to remove the ✓

The Layout Designer screen is displayed indicating that you should use the Layout Designer to reposition overlapping fields or make other changes to the layout of your form.

5. Click   the **Do not display this message in the future option** so this message will not be displayed again

6. Click   **Rate** under the **Screen column** to remove the ✓

7. Click   **Quantity** under the **Print column** to remove the ✓

8. Click   **Rate** under the **Print column** to remove the ✓

9. Click   **OK** to save the changes

10. Click   **OK** to exit the Basic Customization screen and return to the revised form:

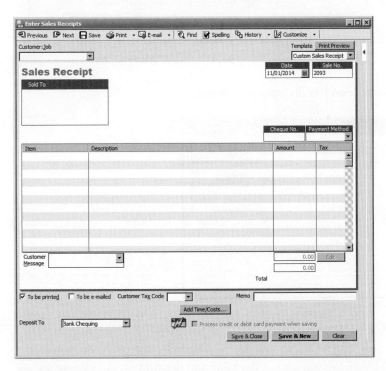

Figure 2-22

Compare the differences between the form displayed in Figure 2-22 (after the modification) with the form displayed in Figure 2-17 (before the modification). Both the quantity and rate columns have been removed in Figure 2-22.

Adding an Icon to the Icon Bar

When a form is open, you can add an icon for it directly to the Icon bar for easy access.

1. Display   the **Enter Sales Receipt form** from the previous exercise (open it if it is not displayed)

2. Choose   the **View menu** and **click Add "Enter Sales Receipts" to Icon Bar...** as shown:

Notes
You can also add an icon to the Icon bar without opening a form first by selecting the View menu, then Customize Icon bar, and then selecting the item you want to add.

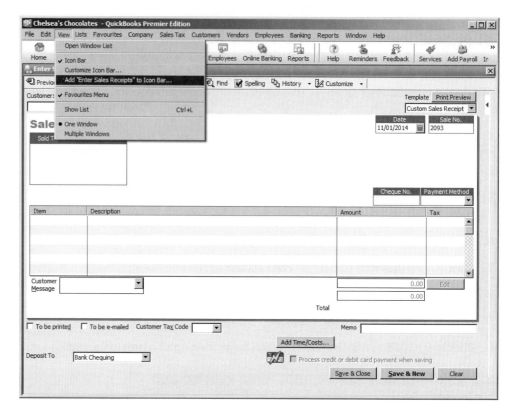

Figure 2-23

3. The Add Window to Icon Bar dialogue box opens:

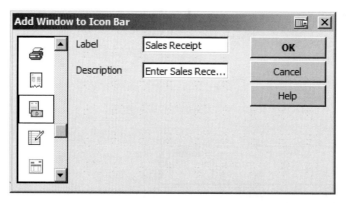

Figure 2-24

An Icon image, a Label, and a Description are suggested for the new icon. You can accept these or change them. We will accept the label and description but choose an invoice icon in a different colour from the one for invoices already displayed on the bar.

4. Click the orange/red coloured **Invoice icon**

5. Click **OK** to return to the program and you'll see that Sales Receipt has been added to the far right-hand side of the Icon bar (you may have to maximize your QuickBooks screen to view the Sales Receipt icon on the Icon bar):

> **Notes**
> You can also change the location or order of icons on the Icon bar. Choose Customize Icon Bar from the View menu to view the changes that you can make.

Figure 2-25

As you work through the remaining transactions for this company, the changes you made to the Sales Receipt form and the Icon bar will remain in effect for this company data file unless you change them again.

Source Document

Now that you have learned some of the new concepts introduced in this chapter, enter the following source document. You may need to refer to the instructions in this chapter for additional information:

SD4:   Sales Receipt #2093   **Dated November 5, 2014**

To store customers, $990.00 plus $118.80 HST for chocolate sold in the store in the past three days. All customers paid cash for their purchases. The sales total of $1,108.80 was deposited to the *Bank Chequing* account.

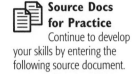

Source Docs for Practice
Continue to develop your skills by entering the following source document.

Adding New List Items

Most businesses have the need to add new records for customers, vendors, or accounts after they set up the company files. QuickBooks allows users to add these new accounts on the fly, while entering transactions.

Adding New Vendors

The next purchase is from a vendor whose name is not yet in the company data files; therefore, we must add the name. We can do this directly from the Write Cheques input form. Refer to the following source document as we work through the steps to enter it:

SD5:   Write Cheque   **Dated November 5, 2014**

To pay cash for purchase received with Bill #SW-444 from Spread the Word (use Quick Add to add the new vendor) in the amount of $980.00 plus $117.60 HST for posters to be placed in the store to advertise upcoming Originals craft show, business cards for use at craft show, and promotional flyers with discount coupons attached for craft show customers to use in the store after the craft show. The bill totalled $1,097.60. Wrote Cheque #237 to pay the bill in full.

Source Docs
Refer to the following source document and then follow the step-by-step instructions to enter it.

1. Click   the **Write Cheques icon** [Write Cheques] to open the Write Cheques form

The cheque number is correct because the program updates it automatically. If necessary, it can be changed.

The date on the blank Write Cheques form should be 11/01/14. If you have a different date, it is because you either changed it since you completed the previous cheque entry or you closed the QuickBooks data file and your current computer date is now displayed.

2. Double click   the **date field** and **type 11/05/14** if necessary

3. Click   the **Pay to the Order of** field

4. Type   **Spread the Word**

Notice that as you type the vendor name, the vendor list is displayed.

5. Press   *tab* to view the following message:

Notes
Remember that you can also open the Write Cheques form by choosing the Banking menu and clicking Write Cheques or by using the keyboard shortcut *ctrl* + **W**.

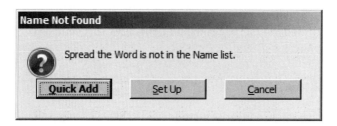

Figure 2-26

This message gives you three different options. Choosing **Quick Add** allows you to add only the vendor's name to the list of vendors. You can add the remaining vendor details later if necessary. **Set Up** allows you to create a complete record for the new vendor by opening all the vendor record fields, and **Cancel** allows you to return to the cheque without creating a record if you have typed the vendor name incorrectly or selected the wrong vendor. We will add only the vendor's name. We will set up a complete vendor record in Chapter 5.

6. **Click**   **Quick Add** or press Ⓔⁿᵗᵉʳ to display the following screen:

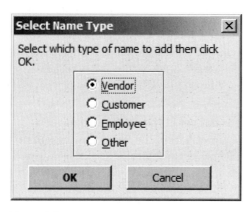

Figure 2-27

You must indicate what type of name you are creating. Remember that you can write cheques to any payee, so several name types are listed. Because this is a cheque, QuickBooks selects Vendor as the default name type and this is correct.

7. **Click**   **OK** or **press** Ⓔⁿᵗᵉʳ to proceed

8. **Click**   the **Memo field** below the vendor address box

9. **Type**   **SW-444** - the bill number

10. **Click**   the **drop-down arrow** in the **Account field** to view the account list

11. **Choose**   **Advertising** from the list of accounts

12. **Click**   the **drop-down arrow** in the **Tax field** to display the tax codes list

13. **Choose**   **H** - HST (BC) Only

14. **Click**   in the **Amount field** to highlight it

15. **Type**   **980**

16. **Press**   Ⓣᵃᵇ to advance to the Memo field

17. **Type**   **posters to advertise craft show**

18. **Review**   the **transaction** and **make corrections** if necessary before saving the entry

The next transaction is a Sales Receipt so we should close the cheque window.

19. **Click**   **Save & Close** to return to the Home page

Adding New Customers

Just as we can add vendors while entering transactions, we can add new customers on the fly from any Customer:Job field.

When you enter the next source document, Sales Receipt #2094, you will see that the customer named in the transaction is not on the customer list. We must add the customer. Refer to the following source document as we work through the steps to enter it:

SD6:   **Sales Receipt #2094**   **Dated November 5, 2014**

    To Swete Touth (use Quick Add to add the new customer) for $520.00 plus $62.40 HST for a special order of theme chocolate decorations for anniversary party. Sales total $582.40 was paid by Cheque #599 and deposited to the *Bank Chequing* account.

> **Source Docs**
> Refer to the following source document and then follow the step-by-step instructions to enter it.

1. **Click**   the **Sales Receipt icon** [💾 Sales Receipt] on the Icon bar — the icon we added in a previous exercise

2. **Enter**   **11/05/14** as the transaction date in the **Date field**

3. **Click**   the **Customer:Job field**

4. **Type**   **Swete Touth**

5. **Press**   `tab` to see the following message:

> **Notes**
> Remember that you can also access the Enter Sales Receipts form from the Customer Centre or from the Customers menu.

> **Notes**
> A colon separates a customer name from a job name and cannot be used as part of the customer name.

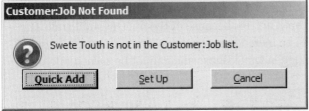

Customer:Job Not Found

Swete Touth is not in the Customer:Job list.

[Quick Add]   [Set Up]   [Cancel]

Figure 2-28

This screen gives you the same three options that we saw for vendors: choosing **Quick Add** allows you to add only the customer's name and add the other record details later if necessary, **Set Up** allows you to create a complete customer record, and **Cancel** allows you to return to the form without creating a record if you have typed the name incorrectly. For now, we will add only the customer's name. We will set up a complete customer record in Chapter 6.

6. **Click**   **Quick Add** or **press** `enter` to return to the Enter Sales Receipts form

Notice that the payment method is not selected because we did not set up a complete customer record that includes this information.

7. **Click**   the **drop-down arrow** in the **Payment Method field** and **choose Cheque**

8. **Type**   **599** in the **Cheque No. field**

9. **Enter**   the rest of the **transaction details. Choose Special Orders** as the Item, **add a description for the sale, enter 520** as the amount, **choose H** as the tax code if this is not entered as the default, and **choose** a **Customer Message**

10. **Click**   **Save & Close** to save the transaction and close the Enter Sales Receipts form

Source Document

Now that you have learned some of the new concepts introduced in this chapter, enter the following source document. You may need to refer to the instructions in this chapter for additional information:

**Source Docs
for Practice**
Continue to develop your skills by entering the following source document.

SD7: **Write Cheque**   **Dated November 6, 2014**

To pay cash for purchase received with Bill #C-784 received from Covers in the amount of $610.00 plus $73.20 HST for paper bags, foils, and boxes of various sizes for packaging chocolates purchased by customers. The bill totalled $683.20. Wrote Cheque #238 to pay the bill in full.

Correcting Entries after Recording

⚠️ **WARNING!**
The audit trail is always on while working in QuickBooks and records all business transactions for a company. Using the audit trail, an auditor can confirm which records have been modified and that records have not been altered dishonestly.

Correcting entries after saving them is very simple in QuickBooks. You can find the transaction and display it on the form on which it was entered, make any necessary corrections, and then save the transaction again. The procedure is essentially the same for correcting all kinds of transactions.

Audit Trail

📄 **Notes**
Beginning with QuickBooks version 2008, the audit trail is "always on," which means that it cannot be turned off. You will find all transactions that have been added, deleted, and modified in the audit trail. If you have users set up in your QuickBooks company file, you will be able to tell which user made the changes.

When you make changes in accounting records, you must leave a complete record of all changes so that an auditor will know that all changes were entered honestly. Pencils and erasers are not allowed in accounting. In a manual accounting system, you would make a correction by completing a reversing entry and then entering the correct entry to provide a complete audit trail. As soon as you save the changes to a transaction that you saved before, QuickBooks will save both entries because of the built-in audit trail. The original entry and the correction will be included in the Audit Trail Report. The audit trail is always on while you are working in QuickBooks and cannot be turned off.

Correcting Purchase Entries after Recording

The purchase from Spread the Word for advertising was entered with an incorrect amount so we need to correct it. The transaction was entered as a cheque, so we will open the Write Cheques form to find the cheque and correct it. Refer to the following source document as we work through the steps to enter it:

📋 **Source Docs**
Refer to the following source document and then follow the step-by-step instructions to enter it.

SD8: **Memo #1**   **Dated November 7, 2014**

From Owner: Cheque #237 to pay Bill #SW-444 from Spread the Word was entered incorrectly. The correct bill amount was $995.00 plus $119.40 HST. The bill totalled $1,114.40. Edit Cheque #237 to make the correction.

📄 **Notes**
You may use one of the other methods to open the Write Cheques form. See page 53.

1. **Press**   `ctrl` + **W** to open the Write Cheques form

There are two methods of opening the transaction that has the error. If the transaction you need was entered recently, you can use the Previous and Next icons on the forms icon bar to scroll through the transactions. Each form also has a Find tool to assist you in finding the form that you want to view or correct. If you have a large number of transactions of the same type, it is faster to use the Find tool to access the transaction you want to correct. Using the Find tool will be covered in a later chapter.

We have entered only three cheques so we can scroll through all the cheques using the Previous icon.

2. Click the **Previous button** 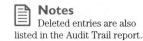 on the Write Cheques icon bar

The last cheque we entered, Cheque #238 to Covers, appears on the screen. This is not the one we need.

3. Click the **Previous button** 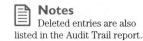 on the icon bar again. Cheque #237 to Spread the Word is displayed:

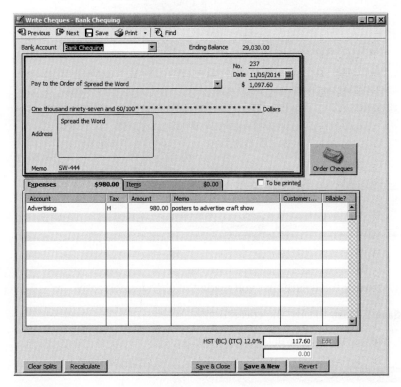

Figure 2-29

With the transaction displayed on the screen, you can modify it, delete it, or void it. The delete and void options are available from the Edit menu or on the shortcut menu displayed by right-clicking in the transaction. The menu options change to match the window that is currently open, so the menu options for this window appear as Delete Cheque and Void Cheque. Both actions will change all amounts for the transaction to zero. Voiding a cheque will leave a record of the transaction in QuickBooks while deleting it will not.

Notes
Deleted entries are also listed in the Audit Trail report.

Notice that the Clear button from the original cheque form has been replaced by Revert. If you make a change to the transaction and do not want to save it, choosing Revert will restore the recorded transaction and you can begin the edit process again or close the form.

4. Double click **980.00** in the **Amount field** to highlight it

5. Type **995**

6. Press (tab) to enter the amount and update the taxes

Notice that the amount in the cheque portion has not yet changed. Currently, it is $1,097.60.

7. Click the **Recalculate button** in the lower left-hand corner of the cheque window to complete the revision and update all amounts as shown:

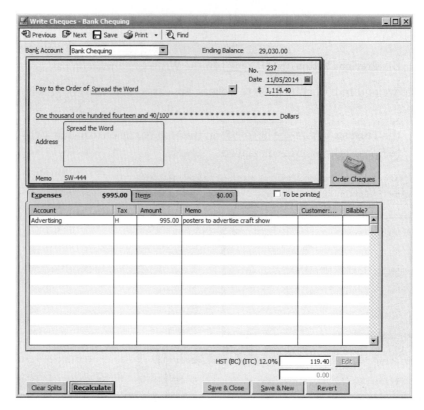

Figure 2-30

>8. **Check**   your **work** to be sure that you made the changes correctly
>
>9. **Click**   **Save & Close** to save the correction
>
>10. The following warning message will be displayed:

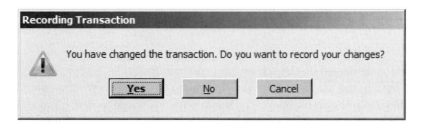

Figure 2-31

Notes
> To turn on this Quick-Books preference, select Edit from the menu and then Preferences. Select the General heading on the left-hand side of the screen. On the My Preferences tab, select the **Warn when editing a transaction** preference.

We have turned on the *Warn when editing a transaction* preference in QuickBooks preferences so that changes are not made to recorded entries accidentally. Choosing **No** will clear the form without saving the changes. Choosing **Cancel** will leave the form open for further changes. Choosing **Yes** will save the changes, and the new revised form will replace the previous one.

>11. **Click**   **Yes** to save the changes and **close** the **Write Cheques form**

Correcting Sales Receipts after Recording

Correcting Sales Receipts is similar to correcting cheques. You access the completed Sales Receipt on the Enter Sales Receipts form, make the changes, and save the revised form. There is no need to make a reversing journal entry.

For this next source document, we need to correct the amount on Sales Receipt #2092. Refer to the following source document as we work through the steps to enter it:

SD9: **Memo #2**   **Dated November 7, 2014**

Source Docs
Refer to the following source document and then follow the step-by-step instructions to enter it.

From Owner: Sales Receipt #2092 was entered incorrectly. The actual sales total amount was $910.00 plus $109.20 HST for chocolate sold in the store. Sales total led $1,019.20. Edit the Sales Receipt to make the correction.

1. **Click** the **Sales Receipt icon** Sales Receipt that you added to the Icon bar in a previous exercise

2. **Click** the **Previous button** Previous on the Sales Receipt icon bar. You should see Sales Receipt #2094

3. **Click** the **Previous button** Previous on the icon bar two more times until you reach Sales Receipt #2092

4. **Double click** **870.00** in the **Amount field** to highlight it

5. **Type** **910**

6. **Press** tab to update the taxes and total amount

Notes
Remember that you can also choose the Customers menu and click Enter Sales Receipts, or click the Create Sales Receipts icon in the Customers section of the Home page to open the Sales Receipts form.

If you make a mistake, you can click the Revert button to restore the original recorded transaction without saving any changes. You can then begin the edit process again. For practice, you can click Revert and then make the correction again.

Your corrected receipt should look like the one shown here:

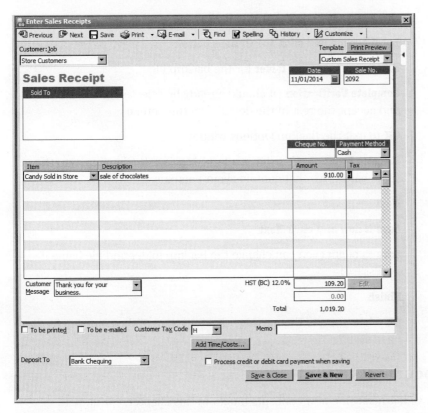

Figure 2-32

7. **Check** your **work** carefully and make additional corrections if necessary

8. **Click** **Save & Close** to record the correction and close the Enter Sales Receipts form

Because you have made changes, the program asks you to confirm that you want to save the changes:

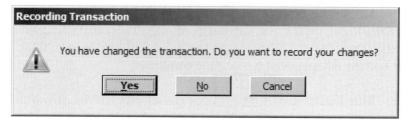

Recording Transaction

You have changed the transaction. Do you want to record your changes?

Yes   No   Cancel

Figure 2-33

9. **Click**   **Yes** to record the changed Sales Receipt and continue

Backing Up and Verifying Your Data File

Now that we have completed one week of transactions, we should back up the data file. Refer to Chapter 1, page 37 for complete instructions on backing up a data file if you need further assistance. Refer to the following source document as we work through the steps to enter it:

Refer to Chapter 1, page 37 for complete instructions on backing up a data file if you need further assistance.

Source Docs
Refer to the following source document and then follow the step-by-step instructions to enter it.

SD10: Memo # 3   **Dated November 7, 2014**

From Owner: Back up and verify the data file. Continue to back up and verify on a weekly basis.

1. **Choose**   the **File menu** and **click Create Backup**

2. **Click**   **Local backup** and **click** the **Options button**

3. **Click**   **Browse** and **choose a folder** for the backup file

4. **Click**   **Complete Verification** (it should already be selected as the default) and accept the rest of the defaults on this screen

5. **Click**   **OK** to exit the Backup Options window

Notes
It is not recommended to save your company file onto the same hard drive that contains your current QuickBooks company file.

6. **Click**   **Use this Location** if you have selected to save the backup onto the same hard drive that contains your company file

7. **Click**   **Next**

8. **Click**   **Save it now** and **click Next**

9. **Click**   **Save** to begin (you can change the backup folder and file name if necessary)

10. **Click**   **Finish**

11. **Click**   **OK** when you see the message that a backup of the company file has been saved

Source Documents

Now that you have learned some new concepts taught in this chapter, continue to develop your skills by entering the following source documents in QuickBooks. Use the information in this chapter as a guide if necessary:

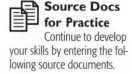

Source Docs for Practice
Continue to develop your skills by entering the following source documents.

SD11: Sales Receipt #2095   **Dated November 9, 2014**

To store customers, $960.00 plus $115.20 HST for chocolate sold in the store in the past three days. All customers paid cash for their purchases. Sales totalling $1,075.20 were deposited to the *Bank Chequing* account.

SD12: Sales Receipt #2096 Dated November 12, 2014

To store customers, $1,075.00 plus $129.00 HST for chocolate sold in the store in the past three days. All customers paid cash for their purchases. Sales totalling $1,204.00 were deposited to the *Bank Chequing* account.

SD13: Write Cheque Dated November 13, 2014

To pay cash for purchase received with Bill #SP-11-14 from Suite Properties in the amount of $3,400.00 plus $408.00 HST for monthly store rent. The bill totalled $3,808.00. Wrote Cheque #239 to pay the bill in full.

SD14: Write Cheque Dated November 15, 2014

To pay cash for purchase received with Bill #PPC-44998 from Pacific Power Corp. (use Quick Add to set up the new vendor) in the amount of $480.00 plus $57.60 HST for monthly hydro expense. The bill totalled $537.60. Wrote Cheque #240 to pay the bill in full.

SD15: Sales Receipt #2097 Dated November 15, 2014

To Originals craft show customers, $2,045.00 plus $245.40 HST for chocolate sold at Originals show in first three days. All customers paid cash for their purchases. Sales totalling $2,290.40 were deposited to the *Bank Chequing* account.

SD16: Sales Receipt #2098 Dated November 15, 2014

To store customers, $560.00 plus $67.20 HST for chocolate sold in the store in the past three days. All customers paid cash for their purchases. Sales totalling $627.20 were deposited to the *Bank Chequing* account.

SD17: Sales Receipt #2099 Dated November 18, 2014

To Originals craft show customers, $1,930.00 plus $231.60 HST for chocolate sold at Originals show in past three days of the show. All customers paid cash for their purchases. Sales totalling $2,161.60 were deposited to the *Bank Chequing* account.

SD18: Sales Receipt #2100 Dated November 19, 2014

To store customers, $995.00 plus $119.40 HST for chocolate sold in the store in the past three days. All customers paid cash for their purchases. Sales totalling $1,114.40 were deposited to the *Bank Chequing* account.

SD19: Write Cheque Dated November 20, 2014

To pay cash for purchase received with Bill #FFF-216 from Fournier's Fine Foods in the amount of $910.00 for sugar, cream, nuts, and other food ingredients for making chocolates. Food is zero rated for tax purposes. The bill totalled $910.00. Wrote Cheque #241 to pay the bill in full.

SD20: Write Cheque Dated November 21, 2014

To pay cash for purchase received with Bill #NT-9023 from NuTel for $180.00 plus $21.60 HST for telephone, cell phone, and Internet service for one month. The bill totalled $201.60. Wrote Cheque #242 to pay the bill in full. Choose the *Utilities* account.

SD21: Sales Receipt #2101 Dated November 22, 2014

To Originals craft show customers, $1,675.00 plus $201.00 HST for chocolate sold at Originals show in the past three days. All customers paid cash for their purchases. Sales totalling $1,876.00 were deposited to the *Bank Chequing* account.

SD22: Sales Receipt #2102　　　　　　　　　**Dated November 22, 2014**

To store customers, $1,180.00 plus $141.60 HST for chocolate sold in the store in the past three days. All customers paid cash for their purchases. Sales totalling $1,321.60 were deposited to the *Bank Chequing* account.

SD23: Sales Receipt #2103　　　　　　　　　**Dated November 25, 2014**

To store customers, $1,660.00 plus $199.20 HST for chocolate sold in the store in the past three days. All customers paid cash for their purchases. Sales totalling $1,859.20 were deposited to the *Bank Chequing* account.

SD24: Sales Receipt #2104　　　　　　　　　**Dated November 25, 2014**

To Originals craft show customers, $1,990.00 plus $238.80 HST for chocolate sold at Originals show in the past three days. All customers paid cash for their purchases. Sales totalling $2,228.80 were deposited to the *Bank Chequing* account.

SD25: Write Cheque　　　　　　　　　　　　**Dated November 25, 2014**

To pay cash for purchase received with Bill #GW-1649 from GlassWorks (use Quick Add to add the new vendor) for $550.00 plus $66.00 HST to replace glass and repair display cabinet frames in the store. A customer dropped a box and cracked the glass. The bill totalled $616.00. Wrote Cheque #243 to pay the bill in full.

SD26: Sales Receipt #2105　　　　　　　　　**Dated November 29, 2014**

To store customers, $1,485.00 plus $178.20 HST for chocolate sold in the store in the past three days. All customers paid cash for their purchases. Sales totalling $1,663.20 were deposited to the *Bank Chequing* account.

SD27: Sales Receipt #2106　　　　　　　　　**Dated November 30, 2014**

To Originals craft show customers, $4,350.00 plus $522.00 HST for chocolate sold at Originals show in the final three days of the show. All customers paid cash for their purchases. Sales totalling $4,872.00 were deposited to the *Bank Chequing* account.

SD28: Sales Receipt #2107　　　　　　　　　**Dated November 30, 2014**

To Birdsall Book Club (use Quick Add to add the new customer) for $1,310.00 plus $157.20 HST for special order of theme chocolate decorations for 40th anniversary celebration. Sales total of $1,467.20 was paid by Cheque #104 and deposited to the *Bank Chequing* account.

SD29: Write Cheque　　　　　　　　　　　　**Dated November 30, 2014**

To pay cash for purchase received with Bill #O-2009 from Originals (Craft Show) for $3,000.00 plus $360.00 HST for booth rental at craft show. The bill totalled $3,360.00. Wrote Cheque #244 to pay the bill in full.

SD30: Write Cheque　　　　　　　　　　　　**Dated November 30, 2014**

To pay cash for purchase received with Bill #AP-3883 from Ads Plus (use Quick Add to add the new vendor) for $1,250.00 plus $150.00 HST for advertising, posters, brochures, and business cards for store. The bill totalled $1,400.00. Wrote Cheque #245 to pay the bill in full.

SD31: Write Cheque　　　　　　　　　　　　**Dated November 30, 2014**

To pay cash for purchase received with Bill #CP-1649 from Car Protectors (use Quick Add to add the new vendor) for $185.00 plus $22.20 HST for business automobile insurance. The bill totalled $207.20. Wrote Cheque #246 to pay the bill in full.

Reports

For the last source document, you will need to learn how to print the Income Statement, verify the Sales Receipts amount, and adjust any errors. Refer to the following source document as we work through the steps to perform the various steps:

Source Docs
Refer to the following source document and then follow the step-by-step instructions to enter it.

SD32: Memo #4   **Dated November 30, 2014**

> From Owner: Display the Income Statement and verify the Sales Receipt amounts. Correct the final sales entry for craft show sales (#2106). The correct revenue amount was $2,350.00 plus $282.00 HST. Sales total of $2,632.00 was deposited to the *Bank Chequing* account.

QuickBooks offers a wide range of reports for companies. We will not cover all the reports in any one chapter. Instead, we will focus on the reports most relevant to the company in the chapter. There are many similarities in the way you display, modify, and print various reports, so once we cover the basics, you should be able to use the rest on your own. In this chapter, we will display five basic reports: the Journal, the Income Statement (Profit & Loss), the Balance Sheet, the Trial Balance, and the Audit Trail.

Reports can be accessed in a variety of ways: from the Reports menu, from the Report Centre, and from the Reports button on List windows within a list window (like the Chart of Accounts list). The list windows include only the reports that relate directly to that list. For example, from the Chart of Accounts list window, you can display reports related to the Chart of Accounts. When you click the Reports button, you can see the reports that are available. These are the QuickReport for the selected account, the Income Tax Preparation report, the Account Listing, as well as some reports that affect all accounts, like the Profit & Loss and Balance Sheet. Other list windows also have a Reports button with related reports.

The Report Centre is a useful tool for accessing reports when you are learning the program because it includes all reports and shows a sample report with a brief description of the report. To access the Report Centre,

1. Click   the **Reports icon** on the Icon bar as shown:

You can also access the Report Centre, as well as individual reports, from the Reports menu.

The Report Centre lists reports by the same categories used in the Reports menu. Generally, the reports within each category are the same as the ones on the Reports menu submenus. An advantage to using the Report Centre is the sample report that shows what your report will look like, and what the contents of the reports will show. The list of Company & Financial reports is shown initially. You can see that many of the reports in this category are variations of the Income Statement. Since the Balance Sheet is also displayed, we will begin there.

In general, to see any report or graph in any of the report categories or groupings:

a) **Choose** the **report category** from the left-hand side of the screen. While in Grid View (the default view when you open the Report Centre), a sample of each report is displayed on the screen

b) **Double click** the **sample report** or **click** on the **Run icon** [Run] to display the report on the screen

Notes
For detailed instructions on how to use the Report Centre, refer to Chapter 1, pages **18–23**.

c) **Enter** the **dates** for your report and make any other necessary modifications

Income Statement (Profit & Loss Statement)

The Income Statement shows how much income a business has earned after taking into account the expenses for a specific period. You can show the statement for any period you choose. In QuickBooks, the Income Statement is named the Profit & Loss report. You can see the report as a summary (standard), in detail with all transactions listed individually, in comparative format that shows two different income periods, for individual customers and jobs, and so on. In this chapter, we will cover the standard or summary reports. In the next chapter, we will examine other reports that deal with all accounts.

The report dates can be changed after you display the report on the screen. Your computer's calendar date is the default date used for reports. Since the company files in this textbook have been created for the year 2014, you can use the custom date filter to enter the required dates or simply enter the required dates in the From and To date fields.

Notes
Depending on your current calendar date, your default report dates will be different from the ones shown in the textbook.

2. **Click**   the **Company & Financial heading** on the left-hand side of the screen

3. **Review**   the **sample Profit & Loss Standard report** under the Profit & Loss (income statement) heading

4. **Click**   on the **Run icon** ⬤ Run to open the report

5. **Click**   on the **drop-down arrow** beside the **Dates field**

6. **Scroll down**   the **list of dates** and **select Custom**

Notes
Of course, if you complete this chapter in November 2014, you will see data for your current month and won't have to change the dates for the report.

7. **Press**   (tab) to advance to the From date field and **enter 11/01/14**

8. **Press**   (tab) to advance to the To date field and **enter 11/30/14**

9. **Press**   (tab) or **click** on the **Refresh button** to display the updated amounts:

Notes
The report dates in the upper left corner of your reports will be different from the ones shown in the textbook because your current calendar date will be different from ours.

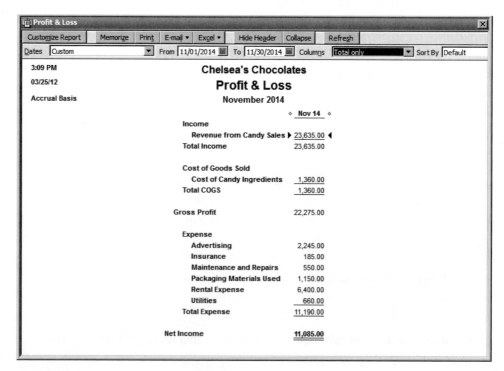

Figure 2-34

For each account, the total income or expense for the period we selected is shown. Gross Profit — total revenue minus the cost of goods sold — is reported separately from

Net Income. The revenue amount appears to be suspiciously high. We can zoom in to see the details of this amount.

The dates drop-down list shows the entry Custom because we entered our own range of dates. When you are using current calendar dates for your company, you can choose a date range from the drop-down list.

Zooming In for More Detail

The Income Statement from the previous exercise should still be open on the screen. If not, please open it.

A magnifying glass icon 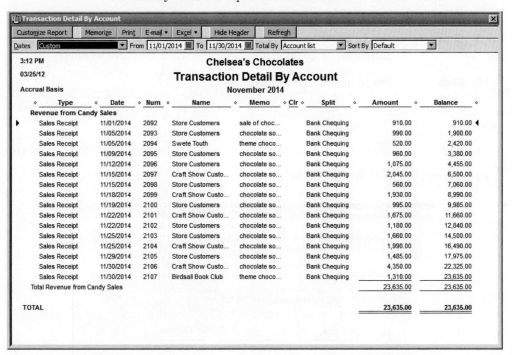 appears in reports that you display whenever you are able to drill down to view more details for an amount or a transaction. If you hold the mouse over different parts of the report the magnifying glass will appear, and double clicking will display the additional information or report.

1. **Double click** the **amount** for Revenue from Candy Sales to view the Transaction Detail By Account report for this account:

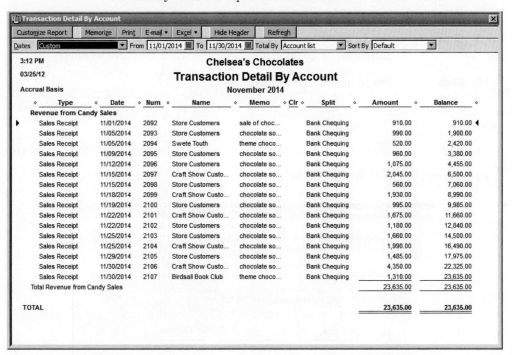

Figure 2-35

The last Sales Receipt for the craft show sales was entered incorrectly. The amount should be $2,350.00, not $4,350.00. We can drill down directly to the Sales Receipt transaction from here to make the correction.

2. **Double click** **Sales receipt #2106** (you can click anywhere on the line) to drill down to the transaction

3. **Double click** the amount **4,350.00**

4. **Type** **2350**

5. **Press** ⎯tab⎯ to update the tax amounts. The HST should now be $282.00

6. **Click** **Save & Close**

7. **Click** **Yes** when asked if you want to save the changed transaction

You will return to the Transaction Detail By Account report. Notice that the report has changed to include the correction we made.

8. Click 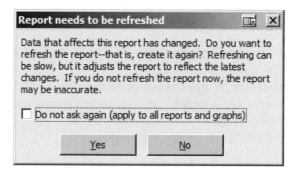 to close the Transaction Detail By Account report and return to the Profit & Loss Statement. You will see this warning message:

Figure 2-36

9. Click the **Do not ask again check box** so that all reports and graphs will be refreshed or updated automatically when we make a change

10. Click **Yes** to update the report

You will return to the Profit & Loss report. Notice that this report has also changed to include the correction we made.

11. Click 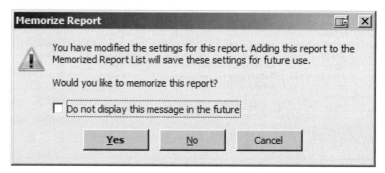 to close the Profit & Loss report and return to the Report Centre

12. You will see the following message:

Figure 2-37

Since you have modified the report settings, you can create a memorized report so you can access the report with these new settings in the future. We will learn how to create memorized reports in a later lesson.

13. Click the **Do not display this message in the future check box**

14. Click **No** when asked to create a memorized report

Displaying Profit & Loss Reports from the Reports Menu

📄 **Notes**
You cannot view a sample report when you select reports from the Report menu.

1. Choose the **Reports menu**

2. Click **Company & Financial**

3. Click **Profit & Loss Standard**

Depending on your system date, there may be no information displayed on the report because there is no data for the date range displayed by default. We need to change the dates in the report first.

In the dates field, the date range *This Month To Date* is displayed. When you are using current calendar dates for your company, you can choose a date range from the drop-down list. Because we have not used the current calendar dates, we need to customize the date range by modifying the From and the To date fields.

4. Double click	the **date** in the **From field**	
5. Type	**11/01/14**	
6. Press	(tab) to advance to the To date field	
7. Type	**11/30/14**	
8. Click	the **Refresh button** or **press** (tab) to update the report	
9. Click	[X] to close the Income Statement when you have finished viewing it	

We will access the remaining reports from the Report Centre.

Balance Sheet

The Balance Sheet is also listed with the Company & Financial reports. This report shows the financial state of the company at a particular point in time. The balances for all asset, liability, and equity accounts are shown for a selected date. In QuickBooks, you can display the Balance Sheet for any date that the company was active.

1. Click	the **Reports icon** on the Icon bar
2. Click	the **Company & Financial heading** on the left-hand side of the screen (it may already be selected because this is the default)
3. Scroll down	to the **Balance Sheet Standard report** under the Balance Sheet & Net Worth heading
4. Review	the sample **Balance Sheet report**
5. Click	the **Run icon** [Run] to display the report on the screen

The Balance Sheet will be displayed. We need to change the report date because there is no data for the current date.

6. Press	(tab) to advance to the As of date field and **enter 11/30/14**
7. Press	(tab) to refresh the report:

Notes
To display the Balance Sheet from the Reports menu, choose the Reports menu, then choose Company & Financial, and then click Balance Sheet Standard. With the Balance Sheet displayed on the screen, you can drill down to the transaction details as you did for the Profit & Loss report. You can view the Transactions by Account report when you double click an amount. When you double click a line in the Transactions by Account report you can drill down to the transaction.

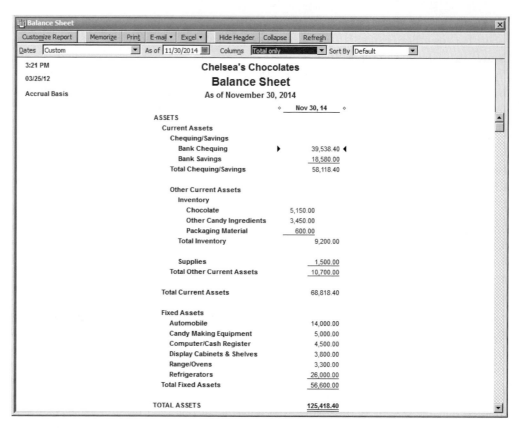

Figure 2-38

8. **Click** to close the Balance Sheet when you have finished viewing it

Trial Balance Report

The Trial Balance shows the account balances for both Balance Sheet and Income Statement accounts at a specific date in two columns of debit and credit balances.

As you have seen, you can access all reports from the Report Centre. However, the Trial Balance report is not found in the Company & Financial heading, so we need to choose a different report group. The Trial Balance and the next two reports we will look at are found within the Accountant & Taxes heading.

For the following exercise, you need to have the Report Centre open.

Notes
To access the Trial Balance from the Reports menu, choose the Reports menu, then choose Accountant & Taxes, and then click Trial Balance.

1. **Click** the **Accountant & Taxes heading** on the left-hand side of the screen to view the list of reports found in this category

2. **Scroll down** to the **Trial Balance report** under the Account Activity heading

3. **Review** the **sample Trial Balance report**

We need to change the report dates because there is no data for the current month.

4. **Click** the **Run icon** to display the report on the screen

5. **Press** (tab) to advance to the date in the From field

6. **Type** **11/01/14**

7. **Press** (tab) to advance to the date in the To field

8. **Type** **11/30/14**

9. **Press** (tab) to refresh the report:

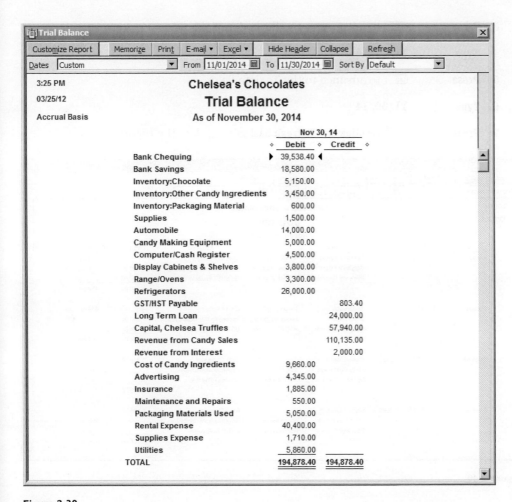

Figure 2-39

With the Trial Balance displayed on the screen, you can drill down to the transaction details as you did for the Profit & Loss report and the Balance Sheet. You can view the Transactions by Account report when you double click an amount. When you double click a line in the Transactions by Account report you can drill down to the transaction.

10. **Click** ☒ to close the Trial Balance when you have finished viewing it

Journal Report

The Journal Report shows all transactions that have taken place within the range of dates you enter for the report. Transactions are displayed in traditional accounting journal format as debit and credit entries.

We need to modify the default dates to include the dates for the transactions we entered, that is, November 1, 2014 to November 30, 2014.

For the following exercise, you need to have the Report Centre open. The Accountant & Taxes heading should still be selected in the Report Centre.

1. **Scroll down** (if necessary) to display the **Journal report** under the Account Activity heading

2. **Double click** on the sample **Journal report**

📄 **Notes**
There are also journal entries for October 31, 2014, but these entries were created for the data file setup.

📄 **Notes**
To access the Journal report from the Reports menu, choose the Reports menu, then choose Accountant & Taxes, and then click Journal.

3. Press	(tab) to advance to the From date field
4. Type	**11/01/14**
5. Press	(tab) to advance to the To date field
6. Type	**11/30/14**
7. Press	(tab) or **click** the **Refresh button** to update the report:

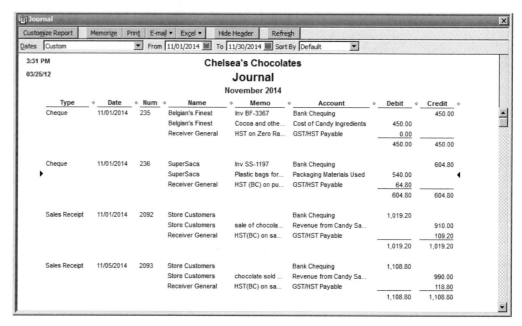

Figure 2-40

Modifying Reports

When you view a report on the screen, it may not fit the window size you are using. Frequently, a report includes columns that are empty or not needed. Resizing the columns will also help to fit the printed report on a page.

1. **Click**   the **Maximize icon** ⬜ to maximize the report on the screen

We will now modify the report so that it does not include information we do not want in the final report. We do not need the transaction number because these numbers include the historical setup transactions that you did not enter. We can drag a column heading to make the column narrower or to remove the entire column. Dragging to the right will make the column wider.

2. **Drag**   the **diamond** ◈ beside **Trans #** ▶ in the column heading to the left as far as possible

Trans # ◇
2

The column is removed (it's actually hidden) from the report. Since the Debit and Credit columns are wider than needed, and the Account column is too narrow to fit the entire account name, we will change the width of these columns.

3. **Drag**   the **column heading diamond** for both the Debit and Credit columns to the left a small amount to make the columns narrower

4. **Drag**   the **column heading diamond** for Account to the right a small amount to make this column wider

5. **Change**   the **size of other columns** that do not fit the contents or are wider than needed

6. **Close**   the **report** when you have finished modifying it

7. Do not memorize the report when prompted

Audit Trail Report

The Audit Trail report shows the journal transactions with additional information — the date that the transaction was modified most recently. Beginning in QuickBooks 2008, the audit trail is "always on," which means that it cannot be turned off. You will find all transactions that have been added, deleted, and modified in the audit trail.

The Accountant & Taxes heading should still be selected in the Report Centre.

1. **Scroll down**   to the **Audit Trail report** under the Account Activity heading

2. **Review**   the **sample report** displayed on the screen

3. **Click**   the **Run icon** to open the report

Audit Trail dates are linked to the current calendar date because they show the date and time that the entry was recorded.

4. **Click**   the **drop-down arrow** in the **Date Entered/Last Modified field**

5. **Click**   **This Fiscal Year** to display the report:

Notes
When you drag the diamond to the left as far as you can, the column disappears.

Notes
The Audit Trail report is based on the date the transactions were entered rather than the dates of the transactions. The dates in the Enter/Last Modified column will be different on your report.
Your Audit Trail may be different from the one displayed depending on the changes you have made to the transactions in your company file.

Notes
To access the report from the Reports menu, choose Accountant & Taxes, and then click Audit Trail.

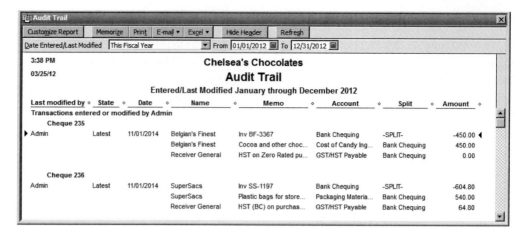

Figure 2-41

The Audit Trail report is similar to the Journal report. It shows each accounting transaction that was entered. The audit trail shows the current journal entry (marked as Latest) for a transaction as well as any previous journal entries (marked as Prior) for the same transaction. Deleted entries are marked as deleted. The calendar date and time are entered for each transaction.

6. **Close**   the **report** when you have finished viewing it

Graphs

You can also display graphs easily in QuickBooks in the same way that you display reports: from the Report Centre or from the Reports menu. Sometimes information is easier to understand when we look at it in a different format, and graphs offer this opportunity.

Income and Expense Graph

We can display the Profit & Loss report information as a graph. This graph is accessed from the Company & Financial report group.

The Report Centre should still be open from the previous exercise.

1. **Click**   the **Company & Financial heading** on the left-hand side of the screen to change the list of reports

2. **Scroll down**   to the **Income & Expense Graph** under the Income & Expenses heading

3. **Click**   the **Run icon** 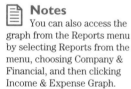 under the **Income & Expense Graph** to display it on the screen

4. **Click**   the **Dates button**

5. **Press**   (tab) to advance to the From date

6. **Type**   **11/01/14**

7. **Press**   (tab) to advance to the To date

8. **Type**   **11/30/14**

9. **Click**   **OK** to update and display the graph:

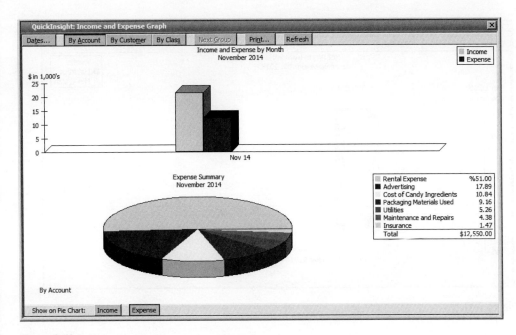

Figure 2-42

Two graphs are displayed: the bar chart of total income and expense amounts for the month and the pie chart of expenses for the month. The summary key on the right shows individual expense accounts, their percentage of total expenses, and the total amount. You can zoom in on more detail from graphs, just as you do for reports.

Double click either the Income or Expense bar of the graph to show, in a pie chart, how that single amount is broken down. Double click a part of the detail pie chart to see a bar chart for the amount. Double click the bar chart to see the transaction details. Double click a transaction detail line to drill down to the current transaction.

Double click any part of the Expense pie chart to show a bar chart for that amount. Double click the bar chart to view the transactions for that account. Double click any transaction to drill down to the current transaction.

| 10. **Click** | on the **graph** to display the information described above |
| 11. **Close** | the **graph** when you have finished viewing it to return to the Report Centre |

Net Worth Graph

The Net Worth graph is the pictorial equivalent of the Balance Sheet — it shows the financial position at a selected point in time.

1. **Click**	the **Net Worth Graph** in the Company & Financial heading under the Balance Sheet & Net Worth section. You may need to scroll down the list of reports to see this graph
2. **Click**	the **Dates button**
3. **Press**	(tab) to advance to the From date
4. **Type**	**11/01/14**
5. **Press**	(tab) to advance to the To date
6. **Type**	**11/30/14**
7. **Click**	**OK** to update and display the graph:

> **Notes**
> To access the graph from the Reports menu, choose Company & Financial and click Net Worth Graph.

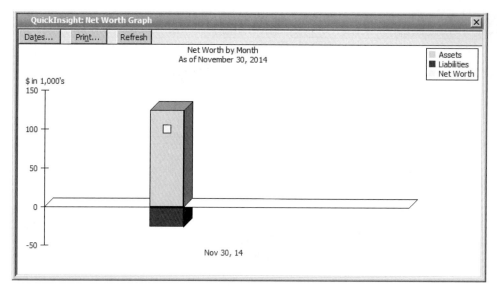

Figure 2-43

The bar graph shows assets above the line, liabilities below the line, and net worth, the difference between them, as a point on the asset portion. Again, you can zoom in on more detail from graphs.

Double click any portion of the graph to show, in a pie chart, how that single amount is broken down. Double click a part of the detail pie chart to see a bar chart for the amount and then double click that bar chart to see the transaction details. Double click a transaction detail line to drill down to the current transaction.

8. **Double click** the **graph** to display the information described above

9. **Close** the **graph** when you have finished to return to the Report Centre

Printing Reports and Graphs

Notes
We understand that in the classroom, printing facilities may be limited. Your instructor will tell you which reports to print and which ones to display.

Notes
To display the Profit & Loss Standard report from the Reports menu:
• Choose Company & Financial and click Profit & Loss Standard
• Enter 11/01/14 in the From date field and 11/30/14 in the To date field

You can print any report that you can display. The instructions that follow apply to printing any report so we will not repeat them for all reports. We will work with the Standard Profit & Loss Statement.

1. **Display** the **Profit & Loss Standard report for Nov. 1–Nov. 30, 2014**. (Refer to page 80 for instructions if necessary)

2. **Click** the **Print button** in the report window. You will see the following Print Reports dialogue box:

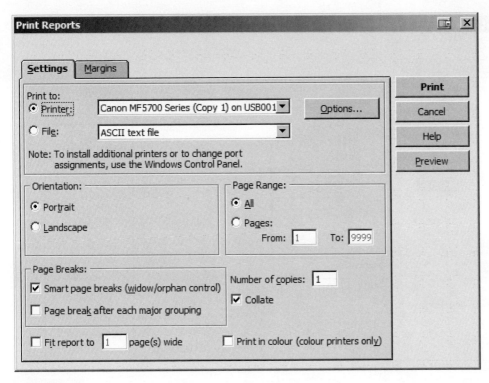

Figure 2-44

This Settings tab allows you to select the printer you are using, the number of copies you want to print, the pages you want to print, and the page orientation (portrait or landscape) — upright or sideways on the page. You can also choose whether to allow the program to apply "smart" page breaks (such as starting a new page between sections), to print in colour, or to shrink the report so that it fits on a single page. If you have a very wide report, you may prefer to print in landscape orientation.

The remaining control options are more advanced and the default settings are usually appropriate. You can access other settings by clicking the Options button and scrolling through the various tabs. You should review these settings but you do not need to change them.

3. Click   the **Margins tab** to view the options for changing the page margins:

Notes
The Options button will show printer options that are specific to your own printer.

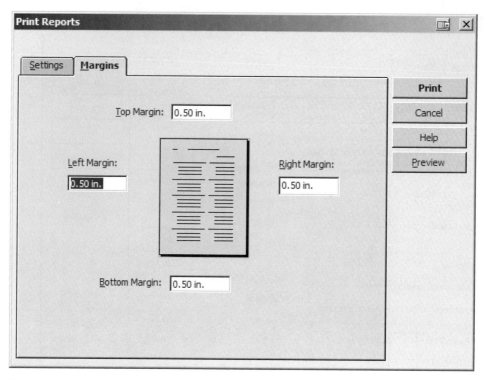

Figure 2-45

Notes
The default margins at 0.50 inches may be too small to allow for three-hole punching or binding.

From this window you can change the side, top, and bottom margins to suit your printer's capabilities or your desired report appearance. The default margins may be set for the limits of your printer.

4. Change   the **margins** to suit your printing needs

You can click Cancel to close a settings window without making any changes

Notes
You should preview the report before printing to see whether you need to make additional changes to the report options.

5. Click   the **Preview button** to view what the report will look like when you print it

6. Click   **Close** to close the preview. The Printer Settings window will open where you can make additional printer adjustments before printing

7. Click   the **Print button** to begin printing

8. Close   the **displayed report**

9. Close   the **Report Centre**

Finishing Your Session

1. Back up   the **company data file**

2. Close   the **Company file**

3. Close   the **QuickBooks program**

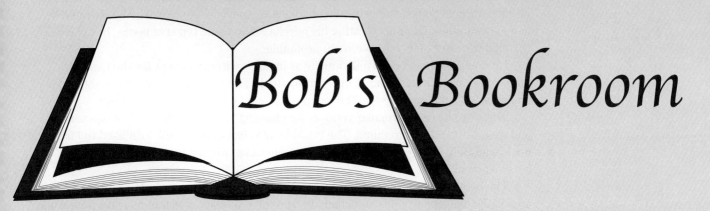

Objectives

After completing this chapter, you should be able to:

- **enter** journal transactions in the Account Register
- **enter** transactions in the General Journal
- **create** new General Ledger accounts
- **edit** General Journal entries before recording
- **review** General Journal entries after recording transactions
- **correct** General Journal entries after recording
- **use** the QuickBooks calculator in journal entries
- **display** and **print** General Ledger reports
- **modify** and **memorize** reports

Company Information

Company Profile

Bob's Bookroom, located in St. John's, Newfoundland, is a sole proprietorship owned and operated by Bob Bestseller. The store sells used books and heavyweight canvas book bags with the store name and logo. Bob encourages his customers to re-use the book bags each time they visit in order to reduce plastic waste as one small environmentally friendly step.

Bob Bestseller obtains books from various sources. He buys books back from customers and, by offering fair prices, he maintains a steady supply. He also makes the rounds of private garage sales on Saturday and Sunday mornings throughout the spring and summer, plus church and charity sales, to collect books to sell, and he buys remainders of out-of-print books from publishers. Often these are hard-cover books that have had paperback editions released.

 Notes
Bob's Bookroom
222 Dickens Rd.
St. John's, NL A1E 2B7
Tel: (709) 755-5766
Fax: (709) 755-6996
E-mail: BB@bookroom.com
Web: www.bookroom.com
Business No.: 138 745 309

Experience has taught Bob which books customers will usually buy — new books, bestsellers, cookbooks, and gardening books are especially popular. The books must be in good condition. By concentrating his purchases on these types of books, he achieves the high turnover he needs to remain profitable.

He does not track books individually as inventory items, except for the mental picture he carries in his head of his current stock. The books in the store are shelved alphabetically and organized in the categories found in most other bookstores.

The store has a few regular vendors for cleaning, office supplies, telephone service, and rent. None offers discounts. The business also has a small bank loan used to buy books and Bob will occasionally take out another loan when a good source of books becomes available.

The bookstore has very few capital or fixed assets but does include a sitting room area with comfortable sofas and chairs in front of a fireplace. Customers relax here while they browse through the books before purchasing. The store has a good supply of repeat customers who are mostly known to the owner. Most customers pay in cash, but a few regulars are allowed to pay by cheque.

The bookstore is located in a busy section of downtown St. John's in rented space. Store rent includes heat, hydro, and water service, leaving telephone service as the only additional utilities expense.

In Newfoundland, 13 percent HST is charged and paid on goods and services, except zero-rated and tax-exempt items. Books are only subject to 5% HST. Therefore, customers pay 5% HST when they buy books and 13% HST when they buy bags, and Bob pays the applicable HST amount on all purchases.

On June 1, the bookstore is ready to use QuickBooks for accounting transactions after converting all the accounting records to QuickBooks using the following:

- Chart of Accounts
- Trial Balance
- List of Vendors, Customers, and Items
- Accounting Procedures

Chart of Accounts

Bob's Bookroom

ASSETS
Bank
- Bank Chequing
- Bank Savings

Current Assets
- Book Bag Inventory
- Book Inventory
- Office Supplies
- Plastic Bags
- Prepaid Advertising
- Prepaid Insurance
- Prepaid Rent

Fixed Assets
- Automobile:Cost
- Automobile:Depreciation
- Computer Equipment:Cost
- Computer Equipment:Depreciation
- Store Furniture and Fixtures:Cost
- Store Furniture and Fixtures:Depreciation

LIABILITIES
Current Liabilities
- Bank Loan
- GST/HST Payable

Long Term Liabilities
- Long Term Loan

EQUITY
- Capital, Bob Bestseller
- Retained Earnings

INCOME
- Revenue from Interest
- Revenue from Sales

EXPENSE
Cost of Goods Sold
- Cost of Bags Sold
- Cost of Books Sold

Expense
- Advertising
- Insurance Expense
- Interest Expense
- Maintenance and Repairs
- Office Supplies Used
- Plastic Bags Used
- Rental Expense
- Telephone

Bob's Bookroom

AS AT MAY 31, 2014

	Debits	Credits
Bank Chequing	$ 14,350.00	
Bank Savings	29,580.00	
Book Bag Inventory	3,600.00	
Book Inventory	51,800.00	
Office Supplies	420.00	
Plastic Bags	380.00	
Prepaid Advertising	3,600.00	
Prepaid Insurance	2,500.00	
Prepaid Rent	3,400.00	
Automobile:Cost	18,000.00	
Automobile:Depreciation		$ 2,700.00
Computer Equipment:Cost	8,000.00	
Computer Equipment:Depreciation		1,200.00
Store Furniture and Fixtures:Cost	30,000.00	
Store Furniture and Fixtures:Depreciation		1,500.00
Bank Loan		8,500.00
GST/HST Payable		3,600.00
Long Term Loan		45,000.00
Capital, Bob Bestseller		65,660.00
Revenue from Interest		180.00
Revenue from Sales		96,800.00
Cost of Bags Sold	2,250.00	
Cost of Books Sold	41,200.00	
Advertising	790.00	
Insurance Expense	6,250.00	
Interest Expense	1,125.00	
Maintenance and Repairs	2,200.00	
Office Supplies Used	380.00	
Plastic Bags Used	205.00	
Rental Expense	4,250.00	
Telephone	860.00	
	$225,140.00	$225,140.00

Bob's Bookroom

VENDORS

Canvas Crafts
Office Essentials
Receiver General
Signal Communications
Signals

CUSTOMERS

Cash Customers

ITEMS

Book Bags
Books

Accounting Procedures

Taxes: HST

Bob's Bookroom pays 13 percent HST on all goods and services that it buys and charges 13 percent HST on most sales, except books, which are exempt from the PST portion of the HST; therefore Bob's only charges 5 percent HST on books. It uses the regular method for remittance of the tax. HST collected from customers is recorded as a liability in the *GST/HST Payable* account. HST paid to vendors is recorded in the *GST/HST Payable* account as a decrease in the liability to the Canada Revenue Agency. The report is filed with the Receiver General for Canada by the last day of the month for the previous quarter, either including the balance owing or requesting a refund.

In Newfoundland, PST is included in the 13 percent HST and is not calculated or remitted separately.

Customer and Vendor Account Terms

All customers pay in cash. Cash received from customers is deposited immediately and is recorded in the *Bank Chequing* account and not held for later deposit. Cash sales are summarized to minimize the number of individual transactions you need to enter.

All vendors demand payment on receipt of merchandise. All bills are paid by cheque.

Cost of Goods Sold

At the end of each month, the books, bags, and supplies remaining in inventory are counted to determine the cost of sales and supplies used in the month. Adjusting journal entries are completed to reduce the asset accounts and increase the relevant expense accounts.

Instructions

1. Using the Chart of Accounts, Trial Balance, and other information, you will record entries for source documents for June 2014 using QuickBooks. You will find the source documents marked with an SD beside them and listed as you work through the chapter. The procedures for entering each new type of transaction are outlined in step-by-step instructions in the chapter. Additional source documents will be provided, allowing you to have more practice entering transactions. If you have used this textbook in the past and would prefer to skip the step-by-step instructions and work only with a list of source documents, refer to the CD in the back of the textbook for the list of source documents for this chapter.

2. After you have finished making your entries, you will print the reports and graphs for June 2014 listed on the following printing form. Instructions on how to print the reports can be found in Chapter 2, page 90.

REPORTS FOR JUNE 2014

Lists
- ☑ Account Listing

Company & Financial
- ☑ Balance Sheet Detail: June 30
- ☑ Profit & Loss Detail (Income Statement) from June 1 to June 30

Accountant & Taxes
- ☑ Trial Balance from June 1 to June 30
- ☑ General Ledger from June 1 to June 30
- ☑ Journal from June 1 to June 30
- ☑ Transaction List by Date from June 1 to June 30
- ☐ Transaction Detail by Account

Other
- ☐ Custom Summary Report
- ☐ Custom Transaction Detail Report
- ☑ Transaction History
- ☑ Transaction Journal

GRAPHS
- ☐ Income and Expense
- ☐ Net Worth

---

3. **Open**   the **bookroom.qbw file** for Bob's Bookroom

Notes
Refer to the Tax Appendix (found on the CD that accompanies this text) for details on sales taxes.

General Journal Entries

Transactions that do not involve selling or buying products or services are entered in the General Journal. They do not involve customers, vendors, or employees and are often adjusting entries that must be completed at the end of a fiscal period — month, quarter, year — such as supplies used during the period, prepaid assets that have expired, adjustments for bad debts, depreciation, and so on. Bank account transactions, such as receiving a loan or making a loan payment, also are usually entered in the General Journal.

In QuickBooks, you can enter these types of transactions in the General Journal or the Accounts Register. The final journal entry will be the same for both methods, and we will demonstrate both methods in this chapter.

Notes
General Journal entries are usually entered in the Make General Journal Entries form rather than in the Account Register, but we want to illustrate both methods. We will enter the second transaction in the Make General Journal Entries form.

Entering Transactions in the Account Register

The first transaction that we need to enter is the deposit of a bank loan to the *Bank Chequing* account. This transaction is a regular General Journal entry that we will enter in the Account Register. You can use the Account Register to enter transactions for any Balance Sheet account except the *Retained Earnings* account. Refer to the following source document as we work through the steps to enter it:

SD1: **Bank Credit Memo #CM-8902**   **Dated June 1, 2014**

From Literary Credit Union, a $5,000.00 short term loan at 6 percent interest approved for a large book purchase. Amount deposited to the *Bank Chequing* account. You will use the Account Register to enter this transaction. You can access the Account Register from the Chart of Accounts.

Source Docs
Refer to the following source document and then follow the step-by-step instructions to enter it.

1. **Open**   the **Chart of Accounts** using one of the following methods:

   a) **Press** `ctrl` **+ A**; or

   b) **Choose** the **Company menu** and then **click Chart of Accounts**; or

   c) **Choose** the **Lists menu** and then **click Chart of Accounts**; or

   d) **Click** the **Chart of Accounts icon** in the Company section of the Home page

2. The Chart of Accounts will be displayed as shown here:

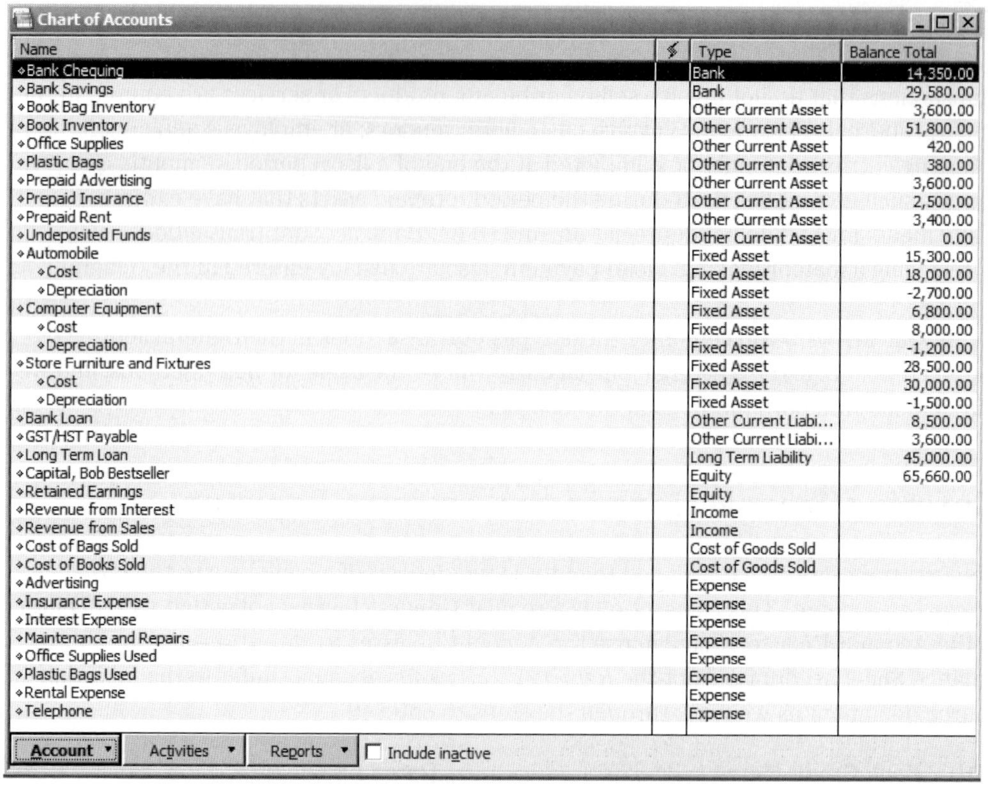

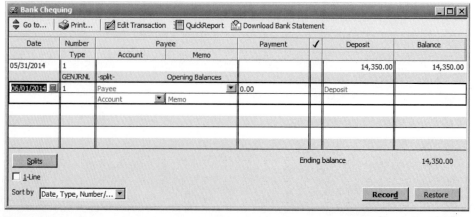

Figure 3-1

Notes
Account numbers are used in Chapter 9.

All accounts created for the company are listed in alphabetical order within their type. Bob's Bookroom does not use account numbers. First the Balance Sheet accounts are displayed (assets, liabilities, and equities), followed by Income Statement accounts (revenue followed by expenses). Balance Sheet accounts show the account balance while Income Statement accounts do not. You can enter journal transactions for the Balance Sheet accounts, except the *Retained Earnings* account, from this window. From the **Account button** menu at the bottom of the window you can add new accounts, edit accounts, and delete accounts. From the **Activities button** you can select the accounting activity you want to complete such as writing cheques, making general journal entries, and using the Register, and from the **Reports button** you can select a report related to the Chart of Accounts.

3. Double click Bank Chequing in the Chart of Accounts to open its Register:

Notes
Double clicking a Balance Sheet account (other than the *Retained Earnings* account) on the Chart of Accounts will open the Register for that account. Double clicking an Income Statement account on the Chart of Accounts will open a QuickReport for the account that lists the transactions for the selected period.

⚠ WARNING!
The date displayed in the blank transaction entry line will be your current computer date, and not the one shown in our print screen.

Figure 3-2

Accessing the Account Register

You can also access an Account Register in a number of other ways:

a. **Select** the **account** from the Chart of Accounts and then:

   i)   **Click** the **Activities button** and **click Use Register**; or

   ii) **Press** `ctrl` **+ R**; or

   iii) **Right-click** and **select Use Register**

b. From anywhere in QuickBooks:

   i)   **Choose Banking** from the menu and then **click Use Register**; or

   ii) **Press** `ctrl` **+ R**

If you use one of the methods available to access the Account Register from anywhere in QuickBooks, the Use Register window will be displayed where you need to click the drop-down arrow and select the Balance Sheet account you want to use:

Notes
If you want to use an expense account or a revenue account (Income Statement account) in a register transaction, start the transaction from the Balance Sheet account of the transaction or use the General Journal as shown in the next source document transaction.

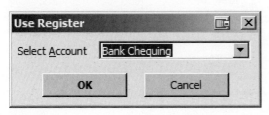

Figure 3-3

Entering the Account Register Transaction

We have selected the default option to show two lines for each transaction — the 1-Line option is not selected. The labels in the two heading lines show the contents of the field. The first line has the Date, Number, Payee, Payment amount, cleared (✓) column, Deposit amount, and Balance. Line 2 shows the Exchange Rate (if applicable), Type of Transaction, Account, and Memo.

Notes
If additional journal entry lines are required, you can choose Splits to open a journal-like window for the transaction, allowing you to enter additional lines.

The date is highlighted, with the current calendar date entered as the default. Once you begin to enter transactions, the last date used will appear as the default until you close and re-open the data file.

4. Type   06/01/14

5. Press   `tab` to advance to the Number field

6. Press   `del` to remove the default entry. (This is the next cheque number, a common choice for a bank account number entry)

Payee appears in dimmed type to indicate that this field would contain the name of an employee or vendor, if that was appropriate for the entry. There is no payee for this transaction. The Payee entry is removed when you delete the cheque number.

7. Press   `tab` to advance to the Payee field

We are making a deposit to the bank account so we must skip the Payment column and enter the amount in the Deposit column.

8. Press   `tab` to advance to the Deposit column

9. Type   5000

10. Press   `tab` to advance to the Account field (on the second line of the entry)

Notice that QuickBooks has entered DEP (deposit) as the type of transaction.

Now we must enter the second account for the transaction. The primary account for the first part of the transaction is the account whose Register we are working in — the *Bank Chequing* account.

11. Click   the **drop-down arrow** in the **Account field** to view the list of accounts:

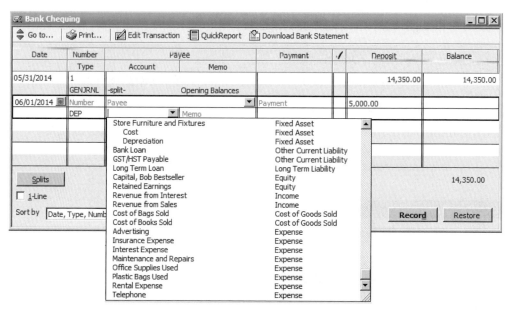

Figure 3-4

Accounts are listed in the same order as the accounts in the Chart of Accounts on page 94. *Bank Loan*, the account we need, may not be in view. Use the scroll bar to scroll up or down the list of accounts until *Bank Loan* is displayed in the list.

12. Click   **Bank Loan** and it is added to the Register

As soon as you selected the account, the entry was recognized as a transfer rather than a deposit and the transaction type is changed to TRANSFR automatically. You cannot change the transaction type.

The Memo field is used for a comment, description, or source document number that helps to identify the transaction. Use the Memo field to enter an optional note about the transaction. The memo will appear on all reports that include the transaction.

13. Press   ⎯tab⎯ to advance to the Memo field

14. Type   **Short term loan @ 6%**

You can add the Bank Credit Memo number and bank name found in the Source Document to the description in the Memo field.

15. The completed transaction is shown:

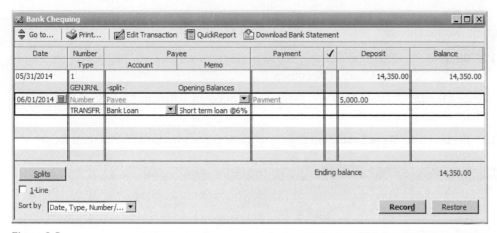

Figure 3-5

Before recording the transaction, you should review your work and make corrections if needed.

Correcting the Journal Transaction

You can make corrections on the screen before saving a transaction in QuickBooks. The concept of making corrections is the same for all journals and forms. The procedure is similar to editing text in other Windows programs.

CORRECTING REGISTER TRANSACTIONS BEFORE RECORDING

Click the field that contains the error. Press (tab) to move forward from one field to the next. Highlight the incorrect information and then type the correct information to replace it. Press (tab) if necessary to advance to the next field.

To correct an account selection, click the drop-down arrow in the Account field and select the correct account.

CORRECTING REGISTER TRANSACTIONS AFTER RECORDING

To make corrections after recording, open the Register for the account and make the necessary changes just as you did before saving the transaction. Click Record to save the changes. Click Yes when you are prompted to save the changes.

When you are certain that the information is correct, you can record the entry.

16. Click   the **Record button** to save the transaction and update the Register account balance as shown:

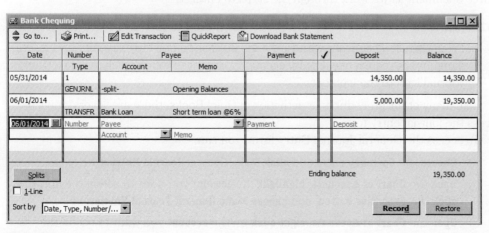

Figure 3-6

The Balance for the bank account is increased by $5,000.00; the amount of the loan deposit. Notice the bank account balance is now $19,350.00.

17. Click ☒ in the *Bank Chequing* Register window to close it and return to the Chart of Accounts

Notice the *Bank Chequing* and *Bank Loan* account balances have been updated on the Chart of Accounts by the transaction.

18. Double click Bank Loan from the Chart of Accounts to open its Account Register:

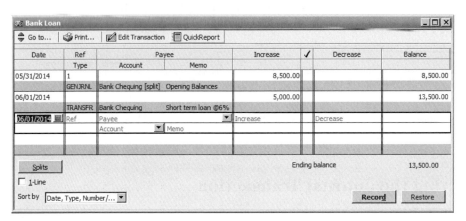

Figure 3-7

You can see that the same transaction appears in the *Bank Loan* Register. Notice that the transaction has been added automatically to this ledger as an increase in the account. To record the bank loan deposit, we could have started the transaction from the *Bank Loan* Register, entered the amount in the Increase column, and selected *Bank Chequing* as the offsetting account.

We will close both the Register window and the Chart of Accounts window; however, you can choose to keep them open if you want.

19. Click ☒ in the Bank Loan Register window

20. Click ☒ in the Chart of Accounts window to return to the Home page

Entering Transactions in the General Journal
Accessing the General Journal

We will use the General Journal to enter the next transaction. Refer to the following source document as we work through the steps to enter it:

Source Docs
Refer to the following source document and then follow the step-by-step instructions to enter it.

SD2: Memo #6-1   **Dated June 1, 2014**

From Owner: The owner withdrew $250.00 cash to buy birthday gifts for his twin daughters. Create a new Equity account: Drawings, Bob Bestseller. Add a General Journal icon to the Icon bar.

Like many other procedures or activities in QuickBooks, there are several ways to access the journal entry form.

To access the General Journal Entry form, you can:

a) **Choose** the **Company menu** and **click Make General Journal Entries**; or

b) **Open** the **Chart of Accounts**, **highlight** the **account** you want to use in the entry, **click** the **Activities button**, and **choose Make General Journal Entries**; or

Notes
There is no keyboard shortcut or icon on the Icon bar for General Journal entries. We will customize the Icon bar by adding a General Journal icon.

c) **Open** the **Chart of Accounts**, **right-click** on the **account** you want to use in the entry, and **select Make General Journal Entries**

Entering Transactions

We will open the General Journal Entry form from the Company menu.

1. Choose the **Company menu** and **click Make General Journal Entries**

You will see the following message about automatic journal entry numbers:

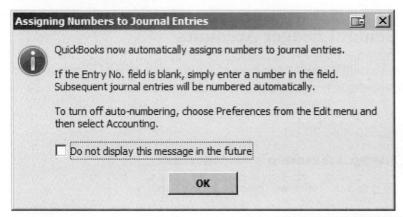

Figure 3-8

> **Notes**
> All transactions are numbered, but journal entries have a second sequence of numbers.

The numbering applies only to journal entries, not to other kinds of transactions. All transactions are assigned a transaction number, and journal entries are included in this numbering too.

2. Click the **Do not display this message in the future** check box

3. Click **OK** to close the message and open the journal entry form:

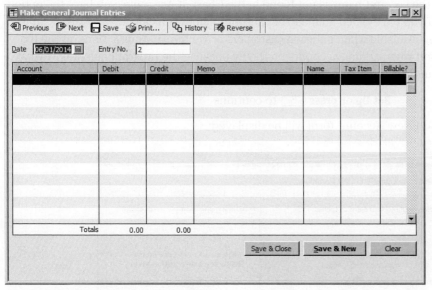

Figure 3-9

> **Notes**
> Your journal entry number and date may be different from the ones in the illustrations. The previous journal entry was used to enter opening balances and historical data for the company.

General Journal transactions are entered as traditional accounting entries with debit and credit amounts. The *Drawings, Bob Bestseller* equity account will be debited (increased) and *Bank Chequing* will be credited (decreased). Refer to "A Review of Basic Accounting" on the Data CD-ROM that accompanies this textbook if you want to review debits, credits, and accounting principles.

It is easier to complete General Journal entries by using the Make General Journal Entries form than it is to use the Register. You can complete multiple or split transactions, and you have full access to all ledger accounts.

4. **Enter**	**06/01/14** as the date if this is not the default date for the current general journal entry
5. **Click**	the **account field**
6. **Click**	the **drop-down arrow** in the **Account field** to access the account list

The account we need is not on the list so we need to create it.

Adding New General Ledger Accounts

QuickBooks allows you to add General Ledger accounts from any general ledger account field on the fly, while entering a transaction, just as it allows adding new vendors and customers.

7. **Press**	(esc) to close the account list
8. **Type**	**Drawings, Bob Bestseller** in the **Account field**
9. **Press**	(tab) and the following message is displayed:

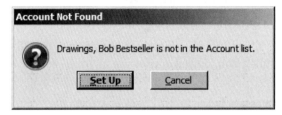

Figure 3-10

Because the account name is not found in the Chart of Accounts, you have the option to create it. If you have typed an incorrect account name, you can choose Cancel. Quick Add, an option available when entering customers or vendors in transactions on the fly, is not an option when adding accounts on the fly because the program must know what type of account is being created in order to place it correctly in the financial statements.

10. **Click**	**Set Up** or **press** (enter) to continue

11. The Add New Account form will be displayed:

Figure 3-11

On this screen, you must choose the **Account Type** for the new account. If you're not sure what Account Type to select, click each Account Type to view a list of sample accounts for that type on the right-hand side of the screen.

The account type determines the position of the account in the Chart of Accounts and on the Balance Sheet or Income Statement. The type also determines the column headings in the Account Register and whether the opening balance is a credit or debit amount.

Depending on which form you are creating the new account from, the account type may already be selected for you. The suggested **default type** will be based on the type of transaction you are entering. When entering an account from the Make General Journal Entries form, the Account Type is left blank.

Drawings is an Equity account so we need to choose Equity as the account type.

Notes
Most of the account types are self-explanatory. We will tell you what type to use when you create a new account. Account types are explained in greater detail in Chapter 4.

12. Choose   the **Equity button** as shown here:

Figure 3-12

Notes
If you create a new account while entering a purchase, Expense is the default type selected.

13. Click   **Continue** to display the second screen of the Add New Account form:

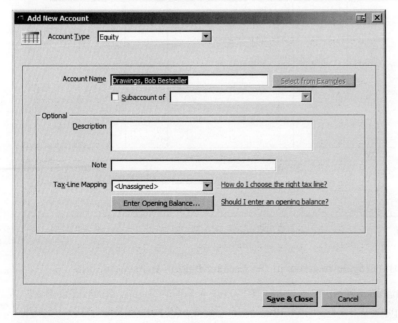

Figure 3-13

Notice the account name we originally typed in the Account field in the Make General Journal Entries window is entered in the Account Name field.

Most of the information on the Add New Account form is optional. If the account is part of a group of accounts under a subheading, you can select the account of which it is a **subaccount**. For example, you might group several bank accounts together as subaccounts under a parent account named Bank. Or you might group a capital asset with its accumulated depreciation account, as we have done for Bob's Bookroom. We used subaccounts for the fixed asset accounts. A colon in the name indicates a parent and subaccount connection, so you cannot use a colon in the account name.

The description you add will become part of the reports and could be helpful if several accounts have similar names. You can add even more information in the Note field. For Expense accounts, you can also choose a default tax code. The code can always be changed for individual transactions if it does not apply.

This is a new account, so there is no opening balance. The remaining fields are optional. We do not need them so the form is complete.

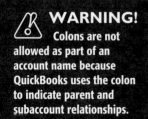
Notes

As soon as you advance to the next line of the journal, the balancing credit amount appears.

If the second line of the transaction is another debit amount, just click the Debit column and type the correct amount. The credit entry will be removed from the second line automatically and will be displayed when you move down to the third line in the transaction.

14.	**Click**	**Save & Close** or **press** (enter) to return to the General Journal Entry form. Notice the equity account you just entered is displayed on the first line in the transaction
15.	**Click**	the **Debit column**
16.	**Type**	**250**
17.	**Press**	(tab) twice to advance to the Memo field
18.	**Type**	**personal: cash for birthday gifts**
19.	**Press**	(tab) to the second journal line. As soon as you advance to the next line of the journal, the balancing credit amount appears:

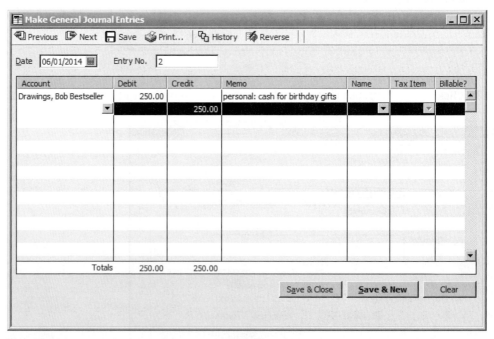

Figure 3-14

20.	**Click**	the **drop-down arrow** in the **Account field** in the second line

Notice that the balancing credit amount, $250.00, is automatically entered as the default for the next part of the transaction. If you add several journal lines, this amount changes continually to keep the transaction in balance as you add other amounts. The amount is correct and it is a credit entry, so we do not need to change it.

21.	**Click**	**Bank Chequing** to add the second account to the journal
22.	**Click**	the **Memo field**
23.	**Type**	**Memo 6-1** to replace the current memo entry

QuickBooks Premier Edition automatically adds the first memo comment to each journal line; however, you can override it as we did for this source document. We will also add Owner to the entry so that the journal report will include this information.

24.	**Press**	(tab) to advance to the Name field
25.	**Type**	**Owner**
26.	**Press**	(enter) or **press** (tab)
27.	**Choose**	**Quick Add** when prompted that Owner is not in the Name list
28.	**Choose**	**Other** as the type for the name and **click OK** to return to the completed journal, as shown:

📄 **Notes**
The Other payee type is used for payees who do not supply or buy goods and services.

📄 **Notes**
Some of the columns have been widened to display all of the information in the journal entry.

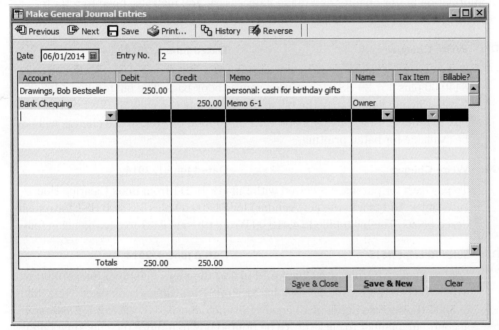

Figure 3-15

| 29. | **Review** | the **transaction** and **make corrections** if necessary |

CORRECTING JOURNAL TRANSACTIONS BEFORE RECORDING

Click in the field that contains the error. Highlight the incorrect information and then type the correct information to replace it. Press (tab) if necessary to advance to the next field.

To correct an account selection, click the drop-down arrow in the Account field and select the correct account.

To clear the transaction on the screen and begin again, click the Clear button.

Adding a General Journal Icon

Before closing the Make General Journal Entries form, we will add an icon for it on the Icon bar for easy access because we will be using this form frequently in this chapter.

1. **Choose** the **View menu** and **click "Add Make General Journal Entries" to Icon Bar**

2. **Choose** 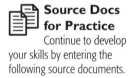 as the icon or another icon suitable for the journal. Scroll down the icon list if necessary. You can accept the default label and description

3. **Click** **OK**

4. **Click** **Save & Close** to save the Journal Entry icon and return to the Home page

A General Journal icon has now been added to the Icon bar.

📑 **Source Docs for Practice**
Continue to develop your skills by entering the following source documents.

Source Documents

Now that you have learned some of the new concepts taught in this chapter, continue to develop your skills by entering the following source documents in QuickBooks using the Sales Receipts, Write Cheques, and Make General Journal Entries forms. Use the information in this chapter as a guide if necessary. You may also need to refer to information in Chapter 2 to complete some of the source documents.

SD3: Write Cheque   **Dated June 1, 2014**

To pay cash for purchase received with Bill #CC-201 from Canvas Crafts for $440.00 plus $57.20 HST for printed canvas book bags. The bill totalled $497.20. Wrote Cheque #436 to pay the bill in full. Remember to click the To be printed box to remove the checkmark and turn this option off so that the cheque will not be available for batch printing.

📄 **Notes**
When a publisher discontinues a book, the remaining stock is often sold at a discount to bookstores as remainders. Often, hardcover books are remaindered when the paperback version is released.

SD4: Write Cheque   **Dated June 1, 2014**

To pay cash for purchase received with Bill #BCH-211 from Book Clearing House (use Quick Add to add the new vendor) for $4,200.00 plus $210.00 HST for remaindered books. The bill totalled $4,410.00 Wrote Cheque #437 to pay the bill in full.

SD5: Sales Receipt #615   **Dated June 4, 2014**

Sold to Shelley Byron (use Quick Add to add the new customer) for $270.00 plus $13.50 HST for books and $20.00 plus $2.60 HST for canvas book bags. The total of $306.10 was paid in full by Cheque #138 and deposited to the *Bank Chequing* account. Remember to click the To be printed box to remove the checkmark and turn this option off so that the sales receipt will not be available for batch printing.

SD6: Memo #6-2   **Dated June 5, 2014**

From Owner: Add the Sales Receipt icon to the Icon tool bar and customize the Sales Receipt Journal by removing the Quantity and Rate columns.

SD7: Write Cheque   **Dated June 5, 2014**

To pay cash for purchase received with Bill #S-444 from Signals for $750.00 plus $97.50 HST for designing ads to run in a local newspaper. The bill totalled $847.50. Wrote Cheque #438 to pay the bill in full.

SD8: Memo #6-3   **Dated June 5, 2014**

From Owner: Owner withdrew $150.00 cash to buy decorations and cake for daughters' birthday party.

SD9: **Sales Receipt #616**   **Dated June 7, 2014**

    Sales to cash customers in past week, $4,490.00 plus $224.50 HST for books and $260 plus $33.80 HST for book bags. All customers paid cash for their purchases. Sales totalling $5,008.30 were deposited to the *Bank Chequing* account.

Correcting General Journal Entries after Recording

Correcting General Journal entries is similar to correcting sales and cheques. After displaying the incorrect entry on the screen, you can make the changes you need and save the new transaction. QuickBooks will keep a record of the changes you have made to the original entry in the audit trail.

    Most transactions completed in the Register can also be corrected from the General Journal window because they have resulted in a normal journal entry. However, there are some exceptions. Transfers of funds, like our first loan deposit, do not appear in the General Journal so they must be corrected in the Register or in the Transfer Funds window (found in the Banking menu). For this reason, we prefer to use the Make General Journal Entries form to enter journal entries. Transactions entered in other forms can also be edited in the Register window although it is generally easier to correct a transaction in the same form you used to create the original entry.

    The entry we need to change is Memo #6-3, the one we entered most recently. Refer to the following source document as we work through the steps to enter it:

SD10: **Memo #6-4**   **Dated June 7, 2014**

    From Owner: Memo #6-3 was entered incorrectly. The amount withdrawn for personal reasons was $180.00. Edit the journal entry for Memo #6-3 to make the correction.

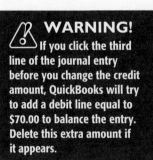

Source Docs
Refer to the following source document and then follow the step-by-step instructions to enter it.

1. **Click**   the **General Journal icon** General Journal that you added to the icon bar or **choose** the **Company menu** and **click Make General Journal Entries** to open the Make General Journal Entries form

2. **Click**   the **Previous button** ◄ Previous to view the entry for Memo #6-3 on the screen

3. **Double click**   the **Debit field** to highlight it

4. **Type**   **180**

5. **Press**   (tab). Notice that the credit amount is not changed automatically

6. **Click**   the **Credit field** and then **double click** to highlight **the amount**

7. **Type**   **180**. **Press** (tab) to enter the amount

   Click the Revert button at any time if you need to cancel the changes.

8. Review your work carefully. The corrected journal entry should be displayed as shown:

> **⚠ WARNING!**
> If you click the third line of the journal entry before you change the credit amount, QuickBooks will try to add a debit line equal to $70.00 to balance the entry. Delete this extra amount if it appears.

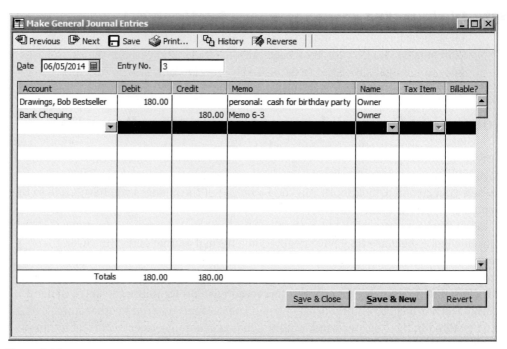

Figure 3-16

9. **Click** **Save & New** to leave the Make General Journal Entry form open for the next transaction

10. You will see the warning confirmation message that appears each time you record changes to a transaction:

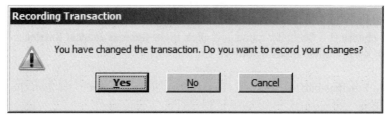

Figure 3-17

11. **Click** **Yes** to save the corrected entry

Creating New Expense Accounts

The next transaction uses a new Expense account. Each account type in QuickBooks has a different input form with fields to match the type of account. Refer to the following source document as we work through the steps to enter it:

Source Docs

Refer to the following source document and then follow the step-by-step instructions to enter it.

SD11: Bank Debit Memo #DM-3771   **Dated June 7, 2014**

  From Literary Credit Union: For monthly bank service charges, $25.00 was withdrawn from the *Bank Chequing* account. Create a new Expense account: *Bank Charges* (leave tax code blank).

1. You should still be in the Make General Journal Entries window. The date should also be correct from the previous entry

2. **Check**   that **06/07/14 is entered as the date**. Enter this date if necessary

3. **Click**   the **Account field**

4. **Type**   **Bank Charges**

5. **Press**   ⌈tab⌉

QuickBooks will try to match your entry with an existing account, so *Bank Chequing* will appear in the Account field until you type a unique sequence of letters.

6. **Click**   **Set Up** when the Add New Account message is displayed

7. **Choose**   **Expense** as the Account Type:

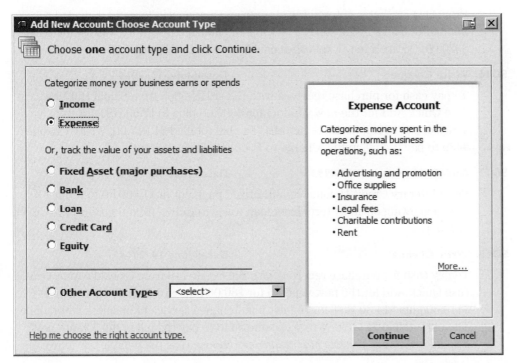

Figure 3-18

8. **Click**   **Continue**

The form is complete. We don't need to add a description because the name is unique and the Sales Tax Code field should be blank.

9. **Click**   **Save & Close** to return to the journal entry window

10. **Complete**   the **journal entry** as described in the source document, **review** it, and then **save** it

Source Documents

Continue to develop your skills by entering the following source documents in QuickBooks. Use the information in this chapter as a guide if necessary. You may also need to refer to information in Chapter 2 to complete some of the source documents.

SD12: Bank Debit Memo #DM-3779   **Dated June 7, 2014**

    From Literary Credit Union: For interest on long term loan, $180.00 was withdrawn from the *Bank Chequing* account.

📄 **Notes**
If you enter the journal entry for the bank service charges from the *Bank Chequing* Register, enter the amount in the Payment column.

Open the Chart of Accounts (press ⌈ctrl⌉ + **A**) and double click *Bank Chequing*, the asset account, to open the Register. You cannot record transactions from an expense Account Register.

Enter the debit memo number in the Number field.

📄 **Notes**
Banks use the terms *debit* and *credit* in the opposite way that accountants use the terms. A debit for the bank (the bank receives a payment for bank charges or interest from you) is a bank account credit for you (you have incurred an expense). Money deposited to your bank account, such as interest received or sales deposits (your debit), is a credit for the bank (they owe that money to you).

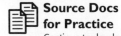 **Source Docs for Practice**
Continue to develop your skills by entering the following source documents.

SD13: Memo #6-5   **Dated June 7, 2014**

From Owner: Paid $280.00 in cash to various customers for books during the week. No HST was included in the purchase because the customers were not registered to collect HST. Use the General Journal for this transaction and choose Cash Customers in the Name field.

SD14: Sales Receipt #617   **Dated June 9, 2014**

Sold to Chaucer Shakespeare (use Quick Add for the new customer), $860.00 plus $43.00 HST for books and $40.00 for book bags plus $5.20 HST. Sales total of $948.20 was paid by Cheque #684 and deposited to the *Bank Chequing* account.

SD15: Memo #6-6   **Dated June 12, 2014**

From Owner: Water entered the store from an open window and damaged a number of books in the store. The value of damaged inventory was estimated at $620.00. Create a new Expense account: *Inventory Losses*.

SD16: Write Cheque   **Dated June 13, 2014**

To pay cash for purchase received with Bill #SHN-3095 from Signal Hill News (use Quick Add for the new vendor) for $900.00 plus $117.00 HST for weekly series of ads to run for three months. The bill totalled $1,017.00. Wrote Cheque #439 to pay the bill in full. Charge to *Prepaid Advertising*.

SD17: Bank Debit Memo #DM-4982   **Dated June 14, 2014**

From Literary Credit Union: Pre-authorized payment of $1,500.00 to reduce principal owing on short term bank loan was withdrawn from the *Bank Chequing* account.

SD18: Write Cheque   **Dated June 14, 2014**

To pay cash for purchase received with Bill #OAC-718 from Oswald's Auto Centre (use Quick Add for the new vendor) for $80.00 plus $10.40 HST for fuel and $110.00 plus $14.30 HST for regular maintenance service of business automobile. The bill totalled $214.70. Wrote Cheque #440 to pay the bill in full. Create new Expense account: *Vehicle Maintenance* (choose H as the default tax code).

SD19: Sales Receipt #618   **Dated June 14, 2014**

Sales to cash customers in past week, $6,200.00 plus $310.00 HST for books and $300.00 plus $39.00 HST for book bags. All customers paid cash for their purchases. Sales totalling $6,849.00 were deposited to the *Bank Chequing* account.

SD20: Write Cheque   **Dated June 15, 2014**

To pay cash for purchase received with Bill #SC-98998 from Signal Communications for $210.00 plus $27.30 HST for monthly telephone bill, including Internet and mobile phone charges. The bill totalled $237.30. Wrote Cheque #441 to pay the bill in full.

SD21: Memo #6-7   **Dated June 15, 2014**

From Owner: Another small batch of water-damaged books was found. The value of damaged inventory was revised to $750.00. Edit Memo #6-6 to make the correction.

SD22: Memo #6-8   **Dated June 15, 2014**

From Owner: Paid $380.00 in cash to various customers for books during the week. No HST was included in the purchases because the customers were not registered to collect HST. Use the General Journal for this transaction and choose Cash Customers in the Name field.

SD23: Sales Receipt #619   Dated June 18, 2014

Sold to Austen Bronte (use Quick Add for the new customer), $530.00 plus $26.50 HST for books and $40.00 plus $5.20 HST for canvas book bags. Sales total $601.70 paid in full by Cheque #6102 and deposited to the *Bank Chequing* account.

SD24: Write Cheque   Dated June 20, 2014

To pay cash for purchase received with Bill #OE-216 from Office Essentials for $240.00 plus $31.20 HST for printer cartridges, paper, and invoice forms. The bill totalled $271.20. Wrote Cheque #442 to pay the bill in full.

SD25: Sales Receipt #620   Dated June 21, 2014

Sales to cash customers in past week, $5,900.00 plus $295.00 HST for books and $420.00 plus $54.60 HST for book bags. All customers paid cash for their purchases. Sales totalling $6,669.60 were deposited to the *Bank Chequing* account.

SD26: Bank Debit Memo #DM-5118   Dated June 21, 2014

From Literary Credit Union: For interest on short term bank loan, $45.00 was withdrawn from the *Bank Chequing* account.

SD27: Write Cheque   Dated June 21, 2014

To pay cash for purchase received with Bill #KCMS-455 from Keep Clean Maintenance Services (use Quick Add for the new vendor) for $440.00 plus $57.20 HST for contracted store cleaning service for one month. The bill totalled $497.20. Wrote Cheque #443 to pay the bill in full.

SD28: Memo #6-9   Dated June 22, 2014

From Owner: Paid $445.00 in cash to various customers for books during the week. No HST was included in the purchase because the customers were not registered to collect HST. Use the General Journal for this transaction and choose Cash Customers in the Name field.

SD29: Sales Receipt #621   Dated June 25, 2014

Sold to Atwood Ondaatje (use Quick Add for the new customer), $380.00 plus $19.00 HST for books and $20.00 plus $2.60 HST for canvas book bag. Sales totalling $421.60 were paid in full by Cheque #249 and deposited to the *Bank Chequing* account.

SD30: Write Cheque   Dated June 26, 2014

To pay cash for purchase received with Bill #MU-1649 from Memorial University (use Quick Add for the new vendor) for $1,250.00 plus $62.50 HST for used books. The bill totalled $1,312.50. Wrote Cheque #444 to pay the bill in full.

SD31: Write Cheque   Dated June 28, 2014

To pay cash for purchase received with Bill #OAC-1020 from Oswald's Auto Centre for $70.00 plus $9.10 HST for fuel for business automobile. The bill totalled $79.10. Wrote Cheque #445 to pay the bill in full.

SD32 Sales Receipt #622   Dated June 29, 2014

Sales to cash customers in past week, $6,900.00 plus $345.00 HST for books and $360.00 plus $46.80 HST for book bags. All customers paid cash for their purchases. Sales totalling $7,651.80 were deposited to the *Bank Chequing* account.

SD33: Memo #6-10   Dated June 30, 2014

From Owner: Paid $310.00 in cash to various customers for books during the week. No HST was included in the purchase because the customers were not registered to collect HST. Use the General Journal for this transaction and choose Cash Customers in the Name field.

Compound Journal Entries

All the General Journal entries so far have involved a single debit and matching credit amount. When we complete end-of-period adjustments, we frequently need to make a compound entry, like the one in Memo #6-11. Refer to the following source document as we work through the steps to enter it:

Source Docs
Refer to the following source document and then follow the step-by-step instructions to enter it.

SD34: Memo #6-11   **Dated June 30, 2014**

Complete an adjusting entry for the following inventory and supplies used during the month:

Books	$11,900.00
Canvas Bags	500.00
Paper and Plastic Bags	245.00
Office Supplies	140.00

Notes
You can complete these adjustments as four separate journal entries if you want.

We will follow traditional accounting practice and enter all the debit amounts first.

1. **Open**   the **Make Journal Entries form** if it is not open already
2. **Enter**   **06/30/14** as the date if this date does not appear by default from the previous transaction entered
3. **Choose**   **Cost of Books Sold** as the first account
4. **Press**   (tab) to advance to the Debit field
5. **Type**   **11900**
6. **Enter**   an **appropriate comment** in the Memo field
7. **Choose**   **Cost of Bags Sold** as the second account

The amount $11,900.00 appears as the default amount in the Credit field for the account. We need to enter another debit amount for the second cost account.

8. **Press**   (tab) to advance to the Debit field
9. **Type**   **500**
10. Before you press (tab) to accept the 500.00 amount entered, amounts appear in both the Debit and Credit fields as shown:

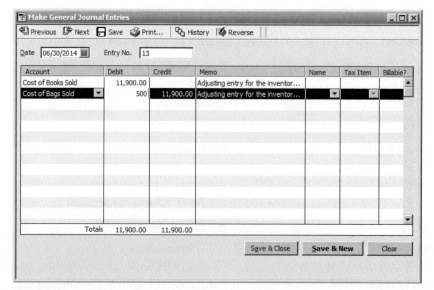

Figure 3-19

11. Press ⌨tab to enter the debit amount and remove the default credit entry

12. Choose **Plastic Bags Used** as the third account

The credit amount is updated to $12,400.00 because this amount will now balance the journal entry; however, we have more debit amounts to enter.

13. Press ⌨tab to advance to the Debit field

14. Type **245**

15. Choose **Office Supplies Used** as the fourth account

16. Press ⌨tab to advance to the Debit field

17. Type **140**

18. Choose **Book Inventory** as the fifth account

The total of all debit amounts appears as the default credit amount as shown here:

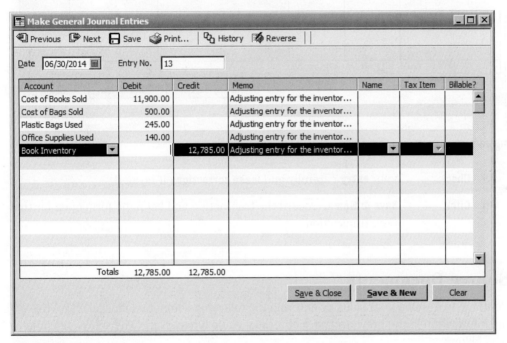

Figure 3-20

19. Press ⌨tab to advance to the Credit field to **highlight** the **default amount**

20. Type **11900**

21. Choose **Book Bag Inventory** as the sixth account

Notice that the default credit amount has been decreased by the $11,900.00 we entered for *Book Inventory*.

22. Press ⌨tab to advance to the Credit field

23. Type **500**

24. Choose **Plastic Bags** as the seventh account

The default credit amount is reduced again.

25. Press ⌨tab to advance to the Credit field

26. **Type**   **245**

27. **Choose**   **Office Supplies** as the final account

28. The remaining credit default amount of $140.00 correctly matches the entry for this account so we can accept it to complete the entry as shown:

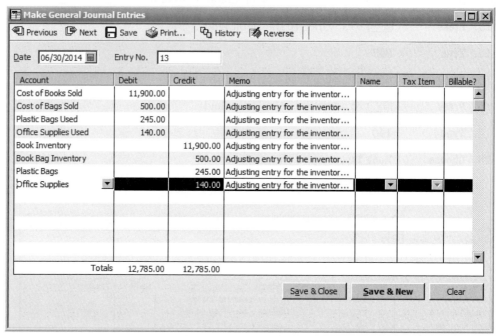

Figure 3-21

29. **Check**   your **entry** carefully and **make corrections** if needed

30. **Click**   **Save & New** to record the transaction and keep the form open for the next transaction

Source Documents

Continue to develop your skills by entering the following compound journal entry. Use the information in the previous transaction as a guide if necessary. The source document is as follows:

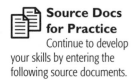
Source Docs for Practice
Continue to develop your skills by entering the following source documents.

SD35: Memo #6-12   **Dated June 30, 2014**

From Owner: Enter the adjustments for the following expired prepaid expenses:

Advertising	$1,100.00
Insurance	1,250.00
Rent	850.00

Using the Add New Account Option

The final source document in this chapter requires a new depreciation account. Refer to the following source document as we work through the steps to enter it:

From Owner: Complete an adjusting entry for six months of depreciation on fixed assets. Create a new Expense account: *Depreciation Expenses* (leave the sales tax code blank). Use the calculator to calculate the total depreciation amount.

Automobile	$2,295.00
Computer Equipment	1,020.00
Store Furniture and Fixtures	1,425.00

Although the source document requires a new depreciation account, depreciation is already used as an account name for the subaccounts for fixed assets. This will make it difficult to add the account by typing the name in the Account field, because QuickBooks will try to use the *Computer Equipment:Depreciation* account. In addition, we will enter the amount for depreciation as a single total amount for all assets, and we will use the built-in calculator to find the correct amount.

The date should be correct from the previous entry.

1. **Enter**   **06/30/14** as the date if necessary

2. **Click**   the **drop-down arrow** in the **Account field** to open the list of accounts as shown:

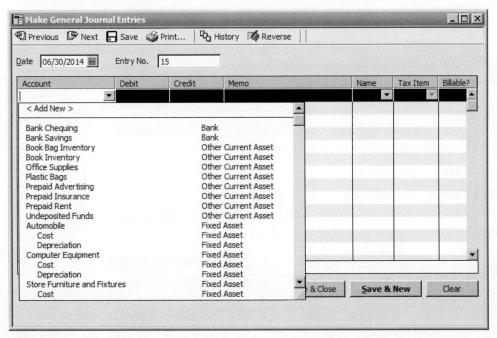

Figure 3-22

Notice that the first item on the list is the option to add a new account.

3. **Click**   **<Add New>** to open the New Account form

4. **Choose**   **Expense** as the Account Type

5. **Click**   **Continue**

6. **Type**   **Depreciation Expense** as the Account Name

7. **Click**   **Save & Close** to return to the Journal Entry form

Using the QuickBooks Calculator

Following the usual accounting practice, we will enter the debit part of the transaction first. Therefore, we must calculate the total amount for *Depreciation Expense*. We will use the built-in QuickBooks calculator to do the addition for us.

8. **Click** the **Debit field**

9. **Type** **2295**

10. **Press** + (the plus sign on the keyboard) to open the calculator tape as shown:

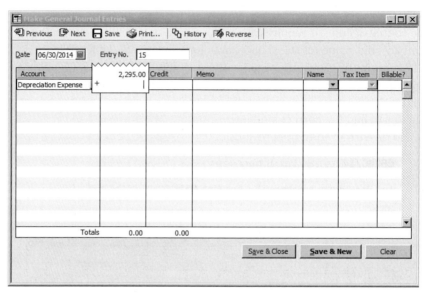

Figure 3-23

Whenever you type an arithmetic operation symbol character (+, −, *, and /) in an amount field, the calculator opens so you can complete the calculations you need without leaving the journal, or even the field you are working in.

11. **Type** **1020 +**

12. **Type** **1425**

Each number is listed with the addition sign beside it to show the operation required. The calculator tape now looks like the one below:

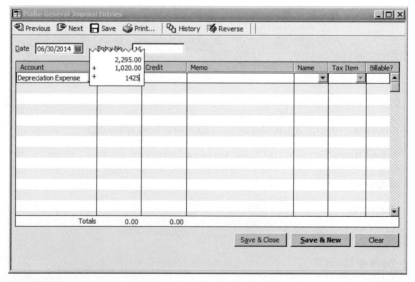

Figure 3-24

13.	**Press**	(enter) to add the total to the journal
14.	**Click**	the **Memo field** and **type total depreciation**
15.	**Enter**	the **three asset accounts, amounts, and memos for the transaction** as described in the source document. (**Choose Depreciation** under **Automobile**, **Computer Equipment**, and **Store Furniture and Fixtures** to select the correct asset accounts)
16.	**Review**	your **work** and **make corrections** if necessary
17.	**Click**	**Save & Close** to return to the QuickBooks Home page. You will see the following message:

Tracking Fixed Assets on Journal Entries

QuickBooks now uses Fixed Asset Items and Fixed Asset Listing reports to track fixed assets.

If you want to create or edit a fixed asset item to track this asset now you can do so from the Fixed Asset Item List. From the List menu, select Fixed Asset Item List, and then either select the appropriate item and edit it, or create a new one.

☐ Do not display this message in the future

OK

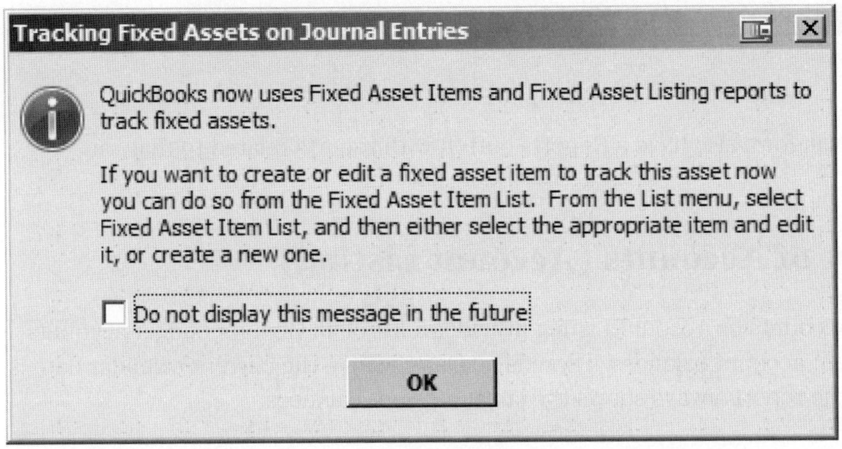

Figure 3-25

We are not using QuickBooks to track fixed assets.

18.	**Click**	the **Do not display this message in the future check box**
19.	**Click**	**OK** to continue

General Reports

QuickBooks has a large number of reports built in, and all of these can be customized or modified to suit your individual business needs. Many of the reports include similar details so you can arrive at the final report in more than one way.

In this chapter, we will show the detail version of the Profit & Loss Statement and the Balance Sheet reports. In addition, we will view the remaining reports that relate to all accounts: the General Ledger report, the Transaction Detail by Account report, and the Transaction List by Date report. We will also cover the Chart of Accounts or Account Listing and some custom and transaction reports in this chapter. We will also show how to customize these reports by changing the headers and removing and adding details.

Many reports can be accessed from the Chart of Accounts so we will start there.

| 1. | **Click** | the **Chart of Accounts icon** in the Company section of the Home page or **press** (ctrl) **+ A** to open the Chart of Accounts |

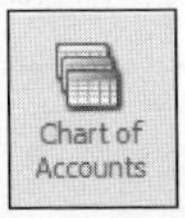

The Reports button menu in the Chart of Accounts window is shown selected:

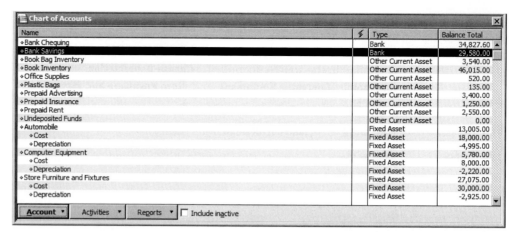

Figure 3-26

Other list windows also have a Reports button with reports related to that list.

Notes

To access the report from the Reports menu:
- Choose the Reports menu, then choose List, and click Account Listing; or
- Choose the Reports menu, then choose Accountant & Taxes, and click Account Listing

The Chart of Accounts (Account Listing)

The Chart of Accounts or Account Listing provides a list of all General Ledger accounts and their current account balances. There is no Date field — the current calendar date is shown — but the report always shows the latest account balances.

Notes

We first prepared this report on April 1, 2012, so this date is displayed in the heading of the report. The date on your reports will reflect your current computer date.

1. Choose   the **Reports button** (at the bottom of the Chart of Accounts window) and **click Account Listing** to open the report:

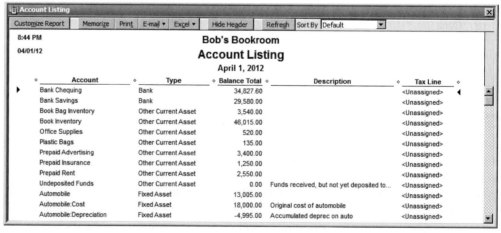

Figure 3-27

Notes

To access the Account Listing from the Report Centre:
- Click the Report Centre icon on the Icon bar, then choose the List heading on the left-hand side of the screen. Scroll down to the Account Listing report under the Listing heading and double click on the report or click on the Run icon
- Click the Reports icon on the Icon bar, then choose the Accountant & Taxes heading on the left-hand side of the screen. Scroll down to the Account Listing report under the Listing heading. Double click on the report or click on the Run icon

The report shows the current calendar date in the report heading. All accounts are included with their name, account type, description (if one was included in the record), current balance, and tax line (if one was assigned). Account balances are displayed for Balance Sheet accounts except the *Retained Earnings* account.

Modifying Reports

We have not assigned a tax line to accounts for Bob's Bookroom so we will modify the report to omit this information.

1. Click   the **Customize Report button** (in the upper left-hand corner of the Icon bar in the report window) to open the Modify Report window:

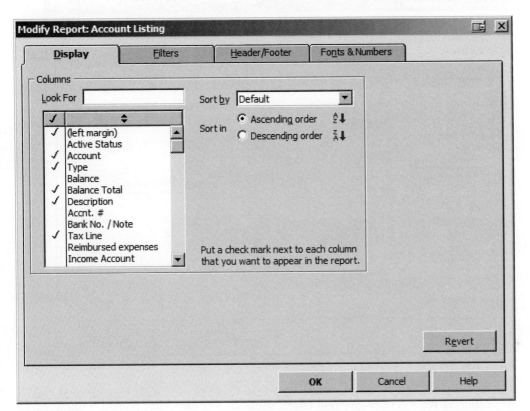

Figure 3-28

The Modify Report window opens with the Display tab shown. From this window, we can choose the details that we want to add to or remove from the report. Each detail is listed in a separate column so you can choose the columns for the report. Columns with a ✓ beside the name are on the report. Clicking any column name will add a ✓ if one is not there and remove it if it is present. From this window you can also enter sorting criteria for the report: default, account, type, balance total, description, or tax line, and you can show any of these in ascending or descending order.

We want to remove the empty Tax Line column.

2. Click   **Tax Line under the Columns heading**. The ✓ is removed

3. Click   **OK** to return to the report and view the results

4. Click   the **Customize Report button** again so that we can make further changes

Click the **Revert button** at any time to cancel your changes and to return to the default selections and format. The Revert button applies only to the changes made on the tab screen that is open.

Filtering Reports

Filtering reports involves setting criteria for what you will include in the report. For example, you might want to create a list of all Asset accounts that have balances less than $1,000.00. Or you might want to report only Expense accounts.

5. Click   the **Filters tab** to view the filters available:

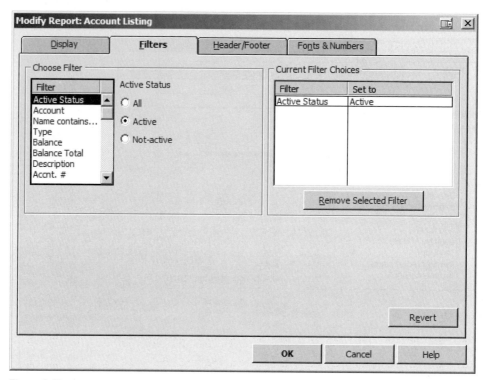

Figure 3-29

Different reports have different filters available. For each filter named, a different input field appears for entering your selections. You cannot use the same filter more than once, but you can apply more than one filter. For example, you can choose Current Asset as the Account Type for the first filter and Balance > 1,000.00 as the second filter to show only Asset accounts that have a balance greater than $1,000.00.

6. Click   **Name Contains** in the list of filters

7. Type   **Depreciation** in the text box and **press** `tab` to add the filter to the list of current filter choices

8. Click   **OK** to view the list of active accumulated depreciation asset accounts and the depreciation expense account in the Account Listing report

9. Click   the **Customize Report button** and **click** the **Filters tab** again

10. Click   **each filter** in turn and **watch** the changes to the **selection field**

11. Click   the **Revert button** to remove the filters

12. Click   **Account in the Filter list**. An Account field with a drop-down arrow is displayed

13. Click   **All Fixed Assets** in the drop-down list

Currently, the active status filter is selected and set to Active and the Account filter is set to All Fixed Assets.

Notes
You need to press `tab` to enter the Name Contains filter so that the program will know when you have finished typing the text that serves as the filter. When you select a filter from a drop-down list, the filter is added to the choices immediately.

If you want to change the report filter, click a Filter in the Current Filter Choices and click Remove Selected Filter to remove the filter from the Current Choices list, or click Revert to remove all filters.

14. **Click**   **OK** to view the list of active fixed asset accounts in the Account Listing report

15. **Click**   the **Customize Report button** and **click** the **Filters tab** again

Changing Report Headers and Footers

Headers and footers in the report affect the appearance but not the data in the report. Again, you can modify the information contained in these parts of the report. We will change the report title to Fixed Assets and Depreciation to match our revised list. We will also change the report date (subtitle) and remove the date and time prepared. Then we will add our own names to the report footer for reference.

1. **Click**   the **Header/Footer tab**:

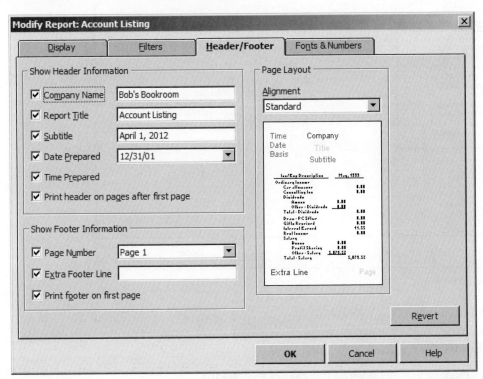

Figure 3-30

2. **Highlight**   **Account Listing** in the **Report Title text field** to select the title

3. **Type**   **Fixed Assets and Depreciation**

4. **Highlight**   the **date** in the **Subtitle field**

5. **Type**   **June 30, 2014**

6. **Click**   the **Date Prepared check box** to remove the ✓

7. **Click**   the **Time Prepared check box** to remove the ✓

8. **Click**   the **text field for the Extra Footer line**

9. **Type**   **Prepared by <add your name>**

10. **Click**   **OK** to see the revised report

Review the changes that you made to the report. The footers are not displayed on-screen; however, they are displayed when the report is printed.

Changing Report Fonts and Numbers

You can alter the appearance of the report in other ways too. You can change the font (type face or appearance of the letters) and size for different parts of the report. You can also change the way numbers are presented in the report. We will show negative numbers in red for this report.

1. Click   the **Customize Report button** again so that we can make further changes (assuming the Account Listing report is still displayed on the screen)

2. Click   the **Fonts & Numbers tab**:

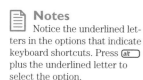
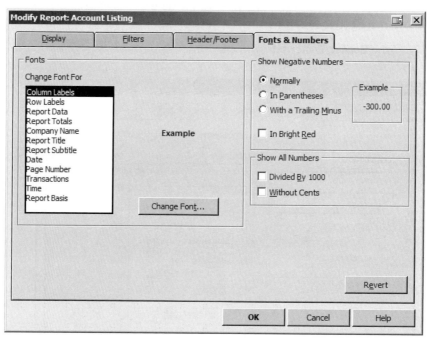

Figure 3-31

You can change the font and size for each part of the report separately. The text for the word "Example," displayed in the middle of the screen, shows you the current style selected for the highlighted option.

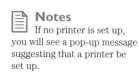
3. Click   an **entry** on the **Change Font For list**

4. Click   the **Change Font button** to open the Font dialogue box

5. Choose   the **font, style, size, effects, and colour** for the item

6. Click   **OK** to save the changes

7. Click   **No** to change all related fonts when prompted

Click the Revert button in the Font & Numbers tab screen at any time to change the style back to the default settings.

You can also choose a preferred style for numbers in the chart. Negative numbers may be displayed in black or bright red type, in parentheses (brackets), or with a minus sign before or after. All numbers may be shown as dollar amounts only, omitting the cents, or in thousands of dollars. This last feature is useful for companies that have very large amounts and want to make their summary reports more readable.

We will change the appearance of negative numbers.

8. **Click**   **In Parentheses**. The number example to the right changes to match your selection

9. **Click**   **In Bright Red** to change the number example again

10. **Click**   **OK** to view the revised report

We no longer need the account type in the report because the report includes only one type. We can remove the column from the report by selecting the appropriate option on the Display tab, as we did for the Tax Line column, or we can drag the account type column marker to the left directly on the report until the column is completely removed from the report, as we did in the previous chapter.

11. **Click**   the **Customize Report button** to open the Display tab screen

12. **Click**   **Type** in the Columns list to remove the ✓

13. **Click**   **OK** to view the final report

14. **Click**   the **Print button** and then **click** the **Preview button**. Your report should look like the one that follows:

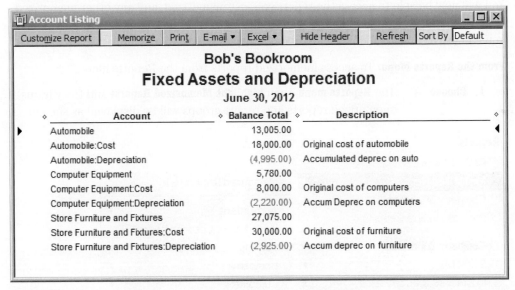

Figure 3-32

15. **Click**   **Print** to begin printing or **click** the **Close button** to return to the Print Reports dialogue box

16. **Click**   **Cancel** to close the Print Reports dialogue box and return to the Account Listing report

Memorizing Reports

We have made a number of changes to the report, so we should save the report under a new name to make it available later with the modifications.

1. **Click**   the **Memorize button** in the report display screen to open the Memorize Report dialogue box:

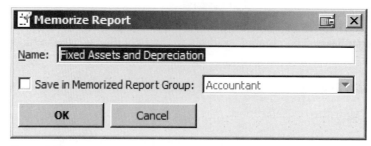

Figure 3-33

The suggested name for the report is the revised report title. You can accept this or enter a different name. The memorized report will be found on the Memorized Reports list, either within one of the existing report groups or on its own. We will accept the name. We will also place the report on its own in the list rather than in a group.

2. **Click**   **OK**

3. **Close**   the **report**

Displaying Memorized Reports

You will now be able to access the report you just memorized, and any other memorized reports, from the Reports menu or from the Memorized Report tab in the Report Centre. You can use any of the following methods to display the Memorized Report:

From the Reports Menu: To access memorized reports from the Reports menu:

1. **Choose**   the **Reports menu**, then **highlight Memorized Reports** and the various memorized reports and report groups will be displayed as shown:

Notes
The menu options, with right arrows that are displayed when Memorized Reports are highlighted, indicate a group that contains memorized reports.
The Fixed Assets and Depreciation report is displayed by itself because we did not add it to a group.

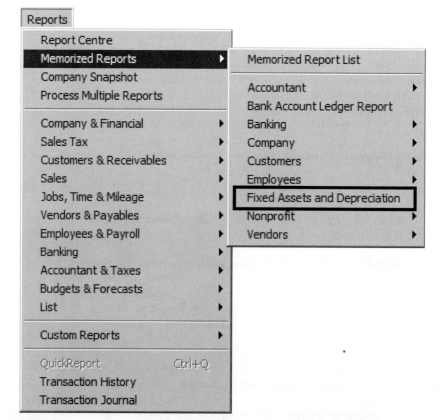

Figure 3-34

2. Click **Memorized Report List** to view the new report added to the Memorized Report List:

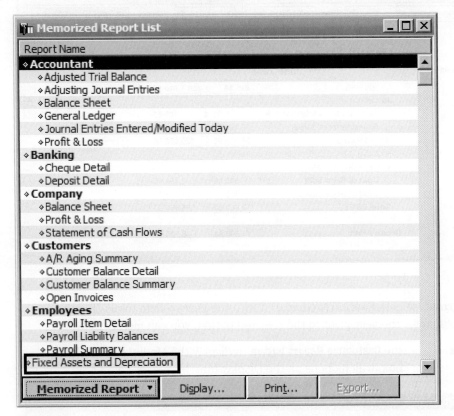

Notes
The headings displayed on the Memorized Report List represent group headings and the reports within the group are listed below each heading. The Fixed Assets and Depreciation report is displayed by itself because we did not add it to a group.

Figure 3-35

From the Report Centre: To access memorized reports from the Report Centre:

1. **Click** the **Reports icon** from the Icon bar and **click** the **Memorized tab** in the top left-hand corner of the Report Centre to display the reports included in the Memorized Transaction List as shown in Figure 3-35. The Fixed Assets and Depreciation report is displayed under the Uncategorized heading.

Profit & Loss Statement (Income Statement) YTD Comparison

This Income Statement report allows you to compare a selected period with a previous period of the same length, either in the same year or in a previous year.

To access the report from the Reports menu, see the margin notes.

1. **Click** the **Reports icon** on the Icon bar to open the Report Centre for the remaining reports

2. **Choose** the **Company & Financial heading** on the left-hand side of the screen and then **double click** on the **Profit & Loss YTD Comparison report** under the Profit & Loss (income statement) heading

3. **Enter** **06/01/14** as the From date for the report

4. **Enter** **06/30/14** as the To date

5. **Press**  or **click** the **Refresh button** to update the report:

Notes
To access the report from the Reports menu:
• Choose the Reports menu, then choose Company & Financial, and click Profit & Loss YTD Comparison to open the report
• Enter 06/01/14 as the From date for the report
• Enter 06/30/14 as the To date
• Press (tab) or click the Refresh button to update the report

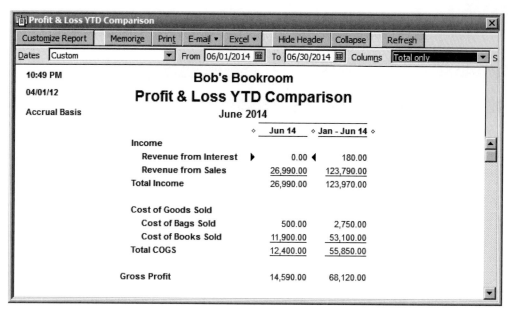

Figure 3-36

The current, selected period is compared with the year-to-date totals. To include a separate column for the year prior to the selected period, you can modify the report.

6. Click   the **Customize Report button** to display the Modify Report dialogue box, which opens on the Display tab:

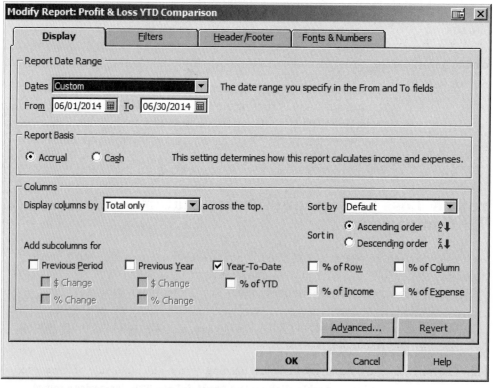

Figure 3-37

You can add columns for a previous period (of the same length as the date range you entered), for year-to-date amounts, and for amounts for the previous year, if you have them. You can also add columns for percentages of the total row, column, income, or expense amounts if you want. When you add a previous period or previous year, you can include the dollar amount or percentage change from period to period or from year to year.

Another option is to display columns by total, by day, by week, or by some other criterion you select from the Display columns by drop-down list.

We will add two columns to the report.

7.	**Click**	**Previous Period** to add a ✓
8.	**Click**	**% of YTD** under the Year-To-Date heading
9.	**Click**	**OK** to view the revised report
10.	**Close**	the **report** when you have finished reviewing it. Do not save the changes

Notes

The May column is actually the total for the period from January 1 to May 31. This total comes from the summary historical data that was entered for May 31st to set up the company files.

Detail and Transaction Reports

In the previous chapter, we saw standard reports that showed the total amounts for the selected period. We will now look at more detailed reports that include listings for individual transactions. The reports that follow show similar kinds of information for different groups of accounts.

Profit & Loss Statement (Income Statement) Detail

This report shows a Profit & Loss Statement with the individual transactions that made up the income and expenses for the selected period.

To access the report from the Reports menu, see the margin notes.

1.	**Click**	the **Reports icon** on the Icon bar to open the Report Centre
2.	**Choose**	the **Company & Financial heading** on the left-hand side of the screen and **double click** on the **Profit & Loss Detail report** under the Profit & Loss (income statement) heading

We need to set the report dates.

3.	**Enter**	**06/01/14** as the From date for the report
4.	**Enter**	**06/30/14** as the To date
5.	**Press**	⌨ tab or **click Refresh** to update the report:

Notes

To access the report from the Reports menu:
• Choose the Reports menu, then choose Company & Financial, and click Profit & Loss Detail
• Change the report dates because there is no data for the current month
• Enter 06/01/14 as the From date for the report
• Enter 06/30/14 as the To date
• Press tab or click Refresh to update the report

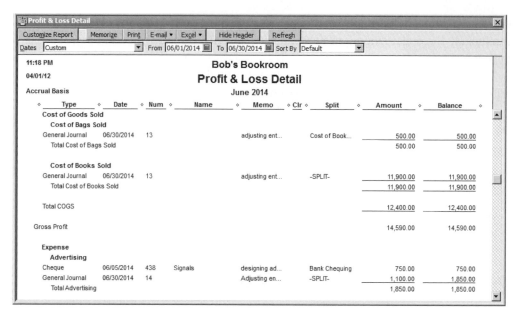

Figure 3-38

We have shown the Cost of Goods and part of the Expenses section on the Profit & Loss Detail report. The report shows each transaction for each account for the income period selected. The more detailed reports can help to identify individual items that may be unreasonably high or low for a period, and may point to errors in data entry or to the need for analysis of company costs.

Double click any part of a transaction to drill down to the original transaction entry. When you drill down to the transaction, you can make any necessary corrections. When you return to the report, it will be updated with the changes you made to the transaction. Double click a total amount in the report to view the transaction detail report for that total.

6. Close the **report** when you have finished reviewing it. Do not save the changes

Balance Sheet Detail Report

Just as the Income Statement was available in a detailed version, so is the Balance Sheet. Again the individual transactions that make up the balances for all Balance Sheet accounts are shown on the Balance Sheet Detail report.

1. Open the **Report Centre** if it is not already displayed from the previous exercise

2. Choose the **Company & Financial heading** on the left-hand side of the screen and **double click** on the **Balance Sheet Detail report** under the Balance Sheet & Net Worth heading

3. Enter **06/01/14** as the From date

4. Enter **06/30/14** as the To date

5. Press <kbd>tab</kbd> or **click Refresh** to update the report:

Notes
To access the Balance Sheet Detail report from the Reports menu:
- Choose the Reports menu, then choose Company & Financial, and click Balance Sheet Detail
  - Enter 06/01/14 as the From date
  - Enter 06/30/14 as the To date
- Press <kbd>tab</kbd> or click the Refresh button to update the report

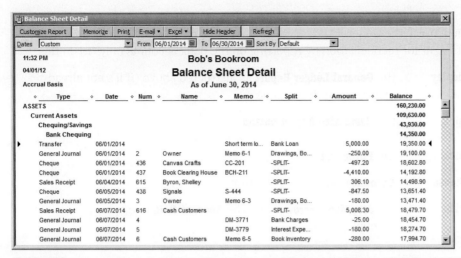

Figure 3-39

This form of the Balance Sheet shows the totals for asset subgroups (Current Assets and Chequing/Savings) at the top of each section of the report, followed by the listing of transactions for each account.

Double click any transaction detail to view the original entry. Double clicking on a General Journal entry will open the Register for the account.

6. Close   the **report** when you have finished reviewing it

General Ledger Report

The General Ledger report shows all accounting transactions for a selected period in order by accounts. All accounts will be included in the report.

1. Open   the **Report Centre** if it is not already displayed from the previous exercise

2. Choose   the **Accountant & Taxes heading** on the left-hand side of the screen and **double click** on the **General Ledger report** under the Account Activity heading

3. Enter   **06/01/14** as the From date for the report

4. Enter   **06/30/14** as the To date

5. Press   ⌧tab⌧ or **click Refresh** to update the report

Some transactions for the *Bank Chequing* account are shown here:

Notes
To access the General Ledger report from the Reports menu:
• Choose the Reports menu, then choose Accountant & Taxes, and click General Ledger to open the report
• Enter 06/01/14 as the From date for the report
• Enter 06/30/14 as the To date
• Press ⌧tab⌧ or click the Refresh button to update the report

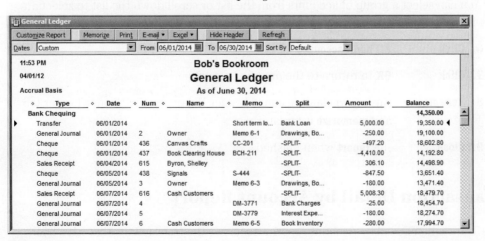

Figure 3-40

Double click any transaction detail to view the original entry.

You might use the General Ledger Report to compare the company records with a bank statement for reconciliation by reporting on the bank accounts only. To do this:

1. **Display**   the **General Ledger Report** as instructed above (if it's not already displayed on the screen)

2. **Click**   the **Customize Report button**

Notes

We modify the General Ledger report in Chapter 8 to prepare for bank reconciliation.

3. **Click**   the **Filters tab**

4. **Choose**   **Account** from the list of filters

5. **Click**   the **drop-down arrow** under the **Account field** to display the list of accounts as shown:

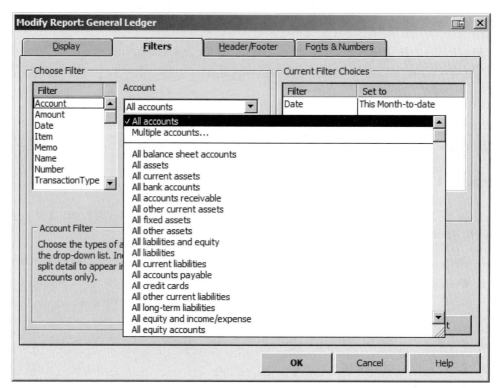

Figure 3-41

You can select a group of accounts from the list or scroll down the list to select an individual account.

6. **Click**   **All bank accounts**

7. **Click**   **OK** to return to the modified report

8. **Rename**   this **report** Bank Account Ledger Report on the Header/Footer tab and **memorize** it for later use

9. **Close**   the **report** when finished

Transaction Detail by Account Report

The Transaction Detail by Account report also shows the transactions that have been entered for each account.

1. **Open** the **Report Centre** if it is not already displayed from the previous exercise
2. **Choose** the **Accountant & Taxes heading** on the left-hand side of the screen and **double click** on the **Transaction Detail By Account report** under the Account Activity heading
3. **Click** the **Do not display this message in the future** check box if you receive the warning message about Collapsing and Expanding Transactions
4. **Click** **OK** to continue
5. **Enter** **06/01/14** as the From date for the report
6. **Enter** **06/30/14** as the To date
7. **Press** tab or **click Refresh** to update the report

> **Notes**
> To access the Transaction Detail by Account report from the Reports menu:
> - Choose the Reports menu, then choose Accountant & Taxes, and click Transaction Detail by Account
>   - Accept any warning messages
>   - Enter 06/01/14 as the From date for the report
>   - Enter 06/30/14 as the To date
> - Press tab or click the Refresh button to update the report

Using these dates, the report does not include the opening balances for the accounts that were entered on May 31, 2014, so many of the Balance Sheet accounts have negative balances. We can change the start date for the report to show the opening balances as well.

8. **Enter** **05/31/14** as the From date for the report and **press** tab twice or **click** the **Refresh button** to update the report

The transactions for the *Book Bag Inventory* and *Book Inventory* accounts are shown here:

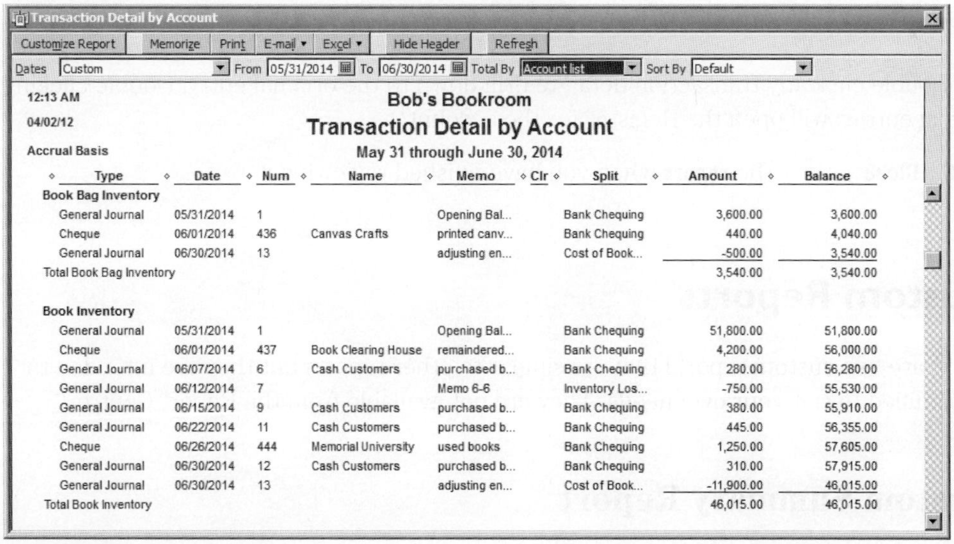

Transaction Detail by Account

Customize Report | Memorize | Print | E-mail | Excel | Hide Header | Refresh

Dates: Custom | From 05/31/2014 | To 06/30/2014 | Total By: Account list | Sort By: Default

12:13 AM
04/02/12
Accrual Basis

Bob's Bookroom
Transaction Detail by Account
May 31 through June 30, 2014

Type	Date	Num	Name	Memo	Clr	Split	Amount	Balance
Book Bag Inventory								
General Journal	05/31/2014	1		Opening Bal...		Bank Chequing	3,600.00	3,600.00
Cheque	06/01/2014	436	Canvas Crafts	printed canv...		Bank Chequing	440.00	4,040.00
General Journal	06/30/2014	13		adjusting en...		Cost of Book...	-500.00	3,540.00
Total Book Bag Inventory							3,540.00	3,540.00
Book Inventory								
General Journal	05/31/2014	1		Opening Bal...		Bank Chequing	51,800.00	51,800.00
Cheque	06/01/2014	437	Book Clearing House	remaindered...		Bank Chequing	4,200.00	56,000.00
General Journal	06/07/2014	6	Cash Customers	purchased b...		Bank Chequing	280.00	56,280.00
General Journal	06/12/2014	7		Memo 6-6		Inventory Los...	-750.00	55,530.00
General Journal	06/15/2014	9	Cash Customers	purchased b...		Bank Chequing	380.00	55,910.00
General Journal	06/22/2014	11	Cash Customers	purchased b...		Bank Chequing	445.00	56,355.00
Cheque	06/26/2014	444	Memorial University	used books		Bank Chequing	1,250.00	57,605.00
General Journal	06/30/2014	12	Cash Customers	purchased b...		Bank Chequing	310.00	57,915.00
General Journal	06/30/2014	13		adjusting en...		Cost of Book...	-11,900.00	46,015.00
Total Book Inventory							46,015.00	46,015.00

Figure 3-42

Double click any transaction detail to drill down to the original entry. Double clicking journal entries will open the Register for the account.

9. **Close** the **report** when you have finished viewing it

Transaction List by Date Report

The Transaction List by Date report also shows all transactions that have been entered during the selected periods.

📝 **Notes**
To access the Transaction List by Date report from the Reports menu:
- Choose the Reports menu, then choose Accountant & Taxes, and click Transaction List by Date to open the report
- Enter 06/01/14 as the From date for the report
- Enter 06/30/14 as the To date
- Press (tab) or click Refresh to update the report

1. **Open**   the **Report Centre** if it is not already displayed from the previous exercise

2. **Choose**   the **Accountant & Taxes heading** on the left-hand side of the screen and **double click** on the **Transaction List by Date report** under the Account Activity heading

3. **Enter**   **06/01/14** as the From date for the report

4. **Enter**   **06/30/14** as the To date

5. **Press**   (tab) or **click** the **Refresh button** to update the report:

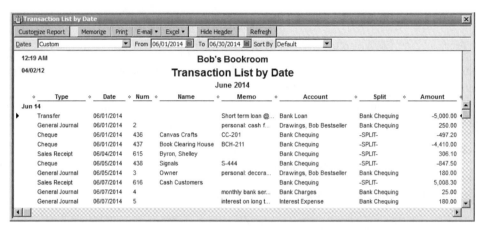

Figure 3-43

Double click any transaction detail to drill down to the original entry. Double clicking journal entries will open the Register for the account.

6. **Close**   the **report** when you have finished reviewing it

Custom Reports

There are two custom reports that are similar to other reports but they are intended to be modified to suit your own needs. They are not available from the Report Centre.

Custom Summary Report

The Custom Summary report is a standard Income Statement; however, it can be used to create customized income statements for your business.

1. **Choose**   the **Reports menu, click Custom Reports**, and then **click Summary**

The report opens in the background and the Modify Report window opens in front so that you can make your changes before viewing the report:

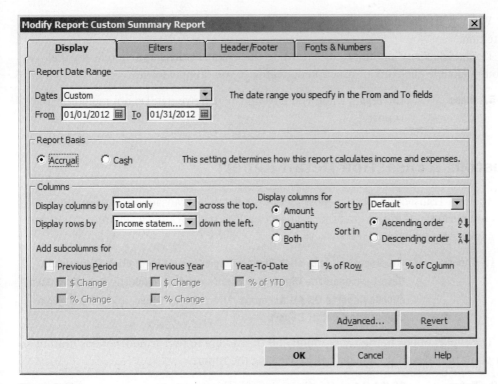

Figure 3-44

Notes
The date in the From and To fields on your screen will be different than the ones shown in Figure 3-44. The dates displayed will be based on your current computer date.

The modification options are almost the same as those for the Profit & Loss Standard report. The option to select different criteria for rows has been added, allowing you to customize an income statement to show the bottom line profitability for the item you select.

We need to enter the dates for our report because the current month-to-date setting is not appropriate.

2. **Enter**   **06/01/14** as the From date

3. **Enter**   **06/30/14** as the To date

4. **Click**   **OK** to view the report:

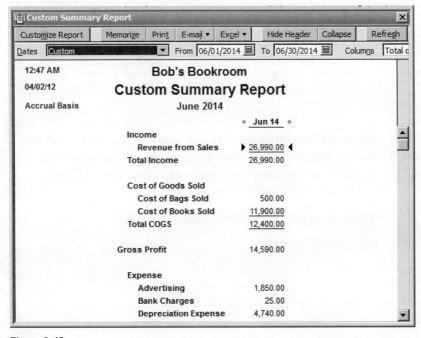

Figure 3-45

Without any modifications made on the Display tab, this report is a standard Income Statement.

Double click any amount to drill down to the original transaction details for that amount. Double click any transaction detail to see the original form.

5. Close the **report** when you have finished viewing it. Do not memorize the report

Custom Transaction Detail Report

The Custom Transaction Detail report includes a list of all transactions during the selected period. It differs from other transaction lists by providing a separate report line for each account used in the transaction.

1. Choose the **Reports menu**, **click Custom Reports**, and then **click Transaction Detail**, or **open** the **Chart of Accounts window**, **click** the **Reports button**, **choose Reports On All Accounts**, then **choose Other**, and **click Custom Transaction Detail Report**

The report opens in the background and the Modify Report window opens in front so that you can make your changes before viewing the report.

2. Enter **06/01/14** as the From date for the report

3. Enter **06/30/14** as the To date

4. Click **OK** to view the report:

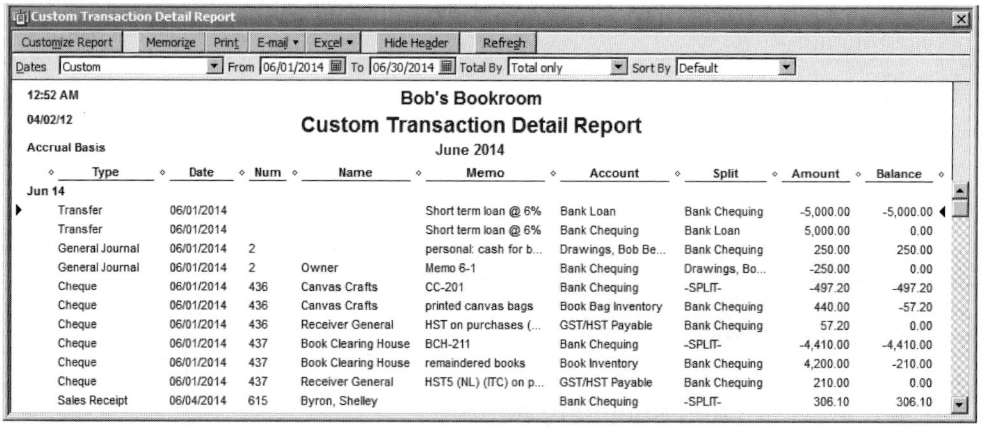

Type	Date	Num	Name	Memo	Account	Split	Amount	Balance
Jun 14								
Transfer	06/01/2014			Short term loan @ 6%	Bank Loan	Bank Chequing	-5,000.00	-5,000.00
Transfer	06/01/2014			Short term loan @ 6%	Bank Chequing	Bank Loan	5,000.00	0.00
General Journal	06/01/2014	2		personal: cash for b...	Drawings, Bob Be...	Bank Chequing	250.00	250.00
General Journal	06/01/2014	2	Owner	Memo 6-1	Bank Chequing	Drawings, Bo...	-250.00	0.00
Cheque	06/01/2014	436	Canvas Crafts	CC-201	Bank Chequing	-SPLIT-	-497.20	-497.20
Cheque	06/01/2014	436	Canvas Crafts	printed canvas bags	Book Bag Inventory	Bank Chequing	440.00	-57.20
Cheque	06/01/2014	436	Receiver General	HST on purchases (...	GST/HST Payable	Bank Chequing	57.20	0.00
Cheque	06/01/2014	437	Book Clearing House	BCH-211	Bank Chequing	-SPLIT-	-4,410.00	-4,410.00
Cheque	06/01/2014	437	Book Clearing House	remaindered books	Book Inventory	Bank Chequing	4,200.00	-210.00
Cheque	06/01/2014	437	Receiver General	HST5 (NL) (ITC) on p...	GST/HST Payable	Bank Chequing	210.00	0.00
Sales Receipt	06/04/2014	615	Byron, Shelley		Bank Chequing	-SPLIT-	306.10	306.10

Figure 3-46

This list provides more detail than other detail transaction reports. Notice that the Transfer and General Journal entries each have multiple lines, one for each account used in the transaction. The next two cheques each have three lines, one for each account.

Double click any detail to drill down to the original entry.

5. Leave the **report** open for the next two reports

Transaction Reports

The final two reports we will cover in this chapter are reports for individual transactions. To view these reports, you must first open another report that shows transaction details and select a transaction in the report. You will then be able to go to another level for the selected transaction. We will work from the Custom Transaction Detail Report that should still be open.

Transaction History Report

1. **Display** the **Custom Transaction Detail Report** for June 2014 if you have closed it. (Refer to the previous page for details on accessing this report)

The Transaction History report shows all transactions that are linked to the transaction you select. For example, if you choose an invoice, the report will show payments related to that invoice.

2. **Click** **any transaction detail line** for the Sales Receipt to Shelley Byron on the Custom Transaction Detail report to drill down to the transaction

3. **Choose** the **Reports menu** and **click Transaction History** to view the transaction history for the open transaction:

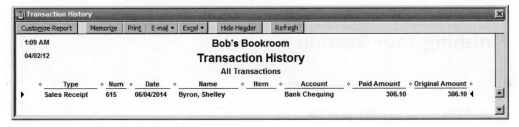

Figure 3-47

The single line for the report indicates that no other transactions are linked to this one. This is as we expected because customers do not have accounts in this company and, therefore, invoices and customer payments are not recorded separately. The original amount of the transaction is fully paid. You can modify this report just like any other report.

Double click any detail to drill down to the original transaction.

4. **Close** the **report** when you have finished viewing it to return to the Custom Transaction Detail report

Transaction Journal Report

The final report shows the journal entry for a single transaction. To use this report, you must have selected a transaction in another report to view the journal.

1. **Click** the **Sales Receipt for Shelley Byron** on the Custom Transaction Detail report to drill down to the original transaction

2. **Choose** the **Reports menu** and **click Transaction Journal** to view the journal entry for the open transaction:

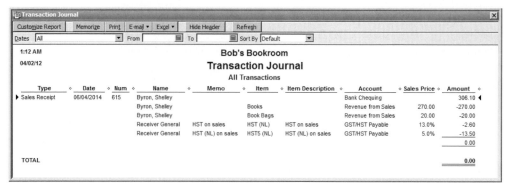

Figure 3-48

Notes
We dragged the Class and Transaction # column heading markers to the left to remove these columns and changed the size of some of the other columns so the report in Figure 3-48 would fit in the window.

The report is the same one that we see when we display a transaction on the screen and press ⌷ctrl⌷ **+ Y**. You can use the Reports menu as an alternative way of accessing this report in a transaction window. You can also double click a transaction in a report to view the original entry and then press ⌷ctrl⌷ **+ Y**. The same report shown in Figure 3-48 would be displayed by pressing ⌷ctrl⌷ **+ Y**.

3. **Close**   the **report** when you have finished viewing it

4. **Close**   the **Sales Receipt to Shelley Byron**

5. **Close**   the **Custom Transaction Detail Report**

Notes
You can close all open QuickBooks windows at one time by choosing Window from the menu and then Close All.

Finishing Your Session

1. **Back up**   the **company data file**

2. **Close**   the **Company file**

3. **Close**   the **QuickBooks program**

Objectives

After completing this chapter, you should be able to:

- **set up** new company files from manual accounting records
- **create** a Chart of Accounts
- **understand** and **use** different account types
- **enter** opening balances for accounts
- **create** customer records
- **create** vendor records
- **customize** QuickBooks preferences for a company
- **create** items
- **edit** and delete accounts
- **make** accounts and vendors inactive
- **define** a new sales tax
- **delete** default payment terms and methods
- **edit** customer messages

Company Information

Company Profile

 Notes
River Run
100 Portage Avenue
Winnipeg, MB R3C 3X2
Tel: (204) 837-4733
Fax: (204) 837-1811
E-mail: admin@riverrun.com
Web: www.riverrun.com
Business No.: 933 566 211

River Run is a charitable foundation created to raise money for environmental clean-up and restoration, focusing on rivers, waterfronts, and the surrounding parks. This run will be held for the second time in Winnipeg, Manitoba, and the foundation hopes to extend the event to other Manitoba communities in the near future.

The run covers a total distance of 20 kilometres — 10 kilometres in one direction on one side of the river and 10 kilometres return on the other side. The run begins and ends at a registration and information site in Kildonan Park on Main Street beside the Red River. Runners follow the path beside the river where possible, moving out to the street for short distances when there are breaks in the path. Emergency stations are set up at bridges to allow staff, supplies, and participants to cross over if necessary. Food and drinks are available at these stations, as well as at other points along the route. All runners receive a T-shirt and cap for sun protection at the start of the run and bottled water along the route. Spectators can buy T-shirts, caps, and snacks and beverages to help support the foundation.

Revenues are generated from participants' (runners') registration fees, from sponsors of runners, and from photos of the runners (before and after the run) sold to participants. Runners may register individually or in teams of up to four persons. Individual runners pay $25.00 to participate, and teams of up to four persons pay $80.00 per team.

The event is registered as a charity and does not charge any taxes. Like any regular business, the foundation pays 5 percent GST and 7 percent PST on taxable purchases. However, as a registered charity, the event is eligible for a rebate of 50 percent of GST paid, and it files for these refunds once a year before closing the books for the fiscal period.

A self-employed event manager, Charity Spiritus, organizes the event and is paid monthly on a contractual basis. The rest of the work is completed by a large crew of volunteers.

At the beginning of January 2014, the event manager is ready to set up the accounting records in QuickBooks by using the following:

- Chart of Accounts
- Post-closing Trial Balance
- Vendor Information
- Customer Information
- Item List
- Accounting Procedures

Chart of Accounts

River Run

ASSETS
Bank
  Bank - Chequing
  Cash on Hand
Other Current Assets
  Food Supplies
  Office & Computer Supplies
  T-shirts and Caps
Fixed Assets
  Computers/Digital Equipment:Cost
  Computers/Digital Equipment:Depreciation [S]

LIABILITIES
Other Current Liabilities
  Bank Loan
  GST/HST Payable

EQUITY
  Accumulated Surplus
  Retained Earnings

INCOME
  Revenue from Donations
  Revenue from Registrations
  Revenue from Sales

EXPENSE
Cost of Goods Sold
  Cost of Food and Drinks
  Cost of T-shirts and Caps

EXPENSES
  Depreciation Expense
  Non-refundable GST Expense
  Office & Computer Supplies Used
  Office Rent
  Printing & Copying
  Publicity & Promotion
  Telephone Expense
  Wage Contract Expenses

Post-closing Trial Balance

River Run

AS AT JANUARY 1, 2014

	Debits	Credits
Bank - Chequing	$15,540.00	
Cash on Hand	480.00	
Office & Computer Supplies	210.00	
Computers/Digital Equipment:Cost	4,500.00	
Computers/Digital Equipment:Depreciation		$ 1,820.00
Bank Loan		11,000.00
Accumulated Surplus		7,910.00
	$20,730.00	$20,730.00

Vendor Information

River Run

Vendor Name	Terms
Bell Canada	due on receipt
Receiver General	
Receiver General - Non-Taxable	
RoofOver Properties Inc.	due on receipt
Sobey's	due on receipt
Staples	due on receipt
Wear Ads	due on receipt
Winnipeg Free Press	due on receipt

Customer Information

River Run

Customer Name	Preferred Method of Payment	Terms
Donors	cash	due on receipt
Runners	cash	due on receipt

Item List

River Run

Item	Type	Price	Tax Code	Account
SERVICES ITEMS				
Photos	Service	$10.00	E	Revenue from Sales
Single Registration	Service	$25.00	E	Revenue from Registrations
Sponsorship	Service	varies	E	Revenue from Donations
Team Registration	Service	$80.00	E	Revenue from Registrations
NON-INVENTORY PART ITEMS				
Caps	Non-inventory part	$15.00	E	Revenue from Sales
Snacks and Beverages	Non-inventory part	varies	E	Revenue from Sales
T-shirts	Non-inventory part	$20.00	E	Revenue from Sales

Accounting Procedures

Taxes: GST and PST

Notes
Refer to the Tax Appendix (found on the CD that accompanies this text) for details on sales taxes.

Registered charities have two options with respect to the GST. Like regular for-profit businesses, they can register to apply the GST, charge GST on all sales and membership fees, and claim all GST paid as input tax credits to reduce the liability to the Receiver General. The second option, used by River Run, does not require registration or collection of GST but permits a partial rebate of GST paid. Periodically, the charity submits an application for refunds, listing the total of all GST paid toward its operating expenses. Fifty percent of this amount is eligible for the rebate. Therefore, River Run records GST paid on all purchases and debits these amounts to *Non-refundable GST Expense*. The rebate application is for 50 percent of this amount, leaving 50 percent as an expense. *GST Refund Receivable* is debited to record the rebate request until the refund is received and deposited.

Bank Accounts and Deposits

The proceeds from registrations and from the sale of merchandise are entered into the bank account. All cheques and cash are deposited on receipt. The *Bank - Chequing* account is used for all cheques to suppliers and to cover operating and administrative expenses and merchandise — beverages, snacks, T-shirts, caps, and supplies. During the event, the *Cash on Hand* account is used for expenses incurred by the volunteer staff. Transfers are made from the *Bank - Chequing* account to *Cash on Hand* by writing cheques to the event manager.

Cheques are hand printed at the time of the transaction and not printed through the program.

Account Terms

All customers, participants, sponsors, and spectators pay cash. All purchases are paid by cheque at the time of purchase. No accounts are set up with vendors for delayed payment.

Supplies

Supplies left at the end of the event are counted and adjusting entries are prepared. Leftovers that cannot be used for the following year's run are donated to other registered charitable organizations.

Instructions

---

1. Using the Chart of Accounts, the Trial Balance, and other information, set up the company files for River Run. Detailed instructions for the setup follow.

2. Record entries for the source documents from January to June 2014 by using QuickBooks. The source documents begin on page 207 following the instructions for setup. If you prefer to complete the source documents without setting up the company file, you can open the River company file found in the C:\QkBkData\Setup folder if you installed the data files from the CD in the back of the textbook.

3. After you have finished making your entries, print the reports and graphs for 2014 marked on the following printing form.

Creating a New Company

When you create new company files in QuickBooks, you can complete the setup step-by-step yourself, or you can complete the QuickBooks EasyStep Interview. We will choose to bypass the EasyStep Interview so that you can enter the steps separately as you work through various functions in QuickBooks. This way, you will be able to easily correct or modify settings later if needed. Although we are bypassing the EasyStep Interview, there are a few screens that must be entered in QuickBooks Setup in order to create and save the company file before you can begin working in QuickBooks.

The EasyStep Interview screens include a great deal of information that helps you make the correct choices for your business during the setup. If you use the EasyStep Interview, you should read all the screens carefully before advancing to the next screen. Frequently, they also allow you to read extra information on a specific topic.

> **Notes**
> You may want to complete the setup for River Run a second time by using the EasyStep Interview.

Setting up a new company involves the following steps:

1. Creating a QuickBooks company file
2. Adding accounts
3. Adding any required special taxes
4. Adding opening account balances
5. Creating vendor and customer records
6. Creating items
7. Choosing preferences to customize settings for all aspects of the program
8. Printing reports to check your setup data
9. Backing up your QuickBooks company file

Creating a Data File

You can create a new QuickBooks company file from the File menu when another company file is open or from the No Company Open window, which is displayed when you close the current company file, or it may be displayed when you open QuickBooks. We will close the current company file before beginning the instructions in this chapter.

1. **Start** the **QuickBooks program**. If a company file opens automatically, **choose** the **File menu** and **click Close Company**

2. The No Company Open window is displayed:

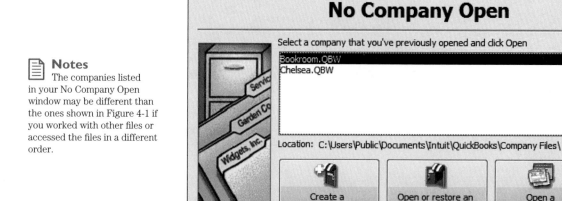

Figure 4-1

Notes
The companies listed in your No Company Open window may be different than the ones shown in Figure 4-1 if you worked with other files or accessed the files in a different order.

You will see this window when you are using the program for the first time or whenever you have closed the company you were last working with. The company files you worked with most recently are listed. You can open one of the listed files or choose another option from the buttons below the list. One of these options is to create a new company.

3. **Click** the **Create a new company button**:

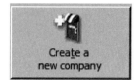

Figure 4-2

4. The QuickBooks Setup screen is displayed:

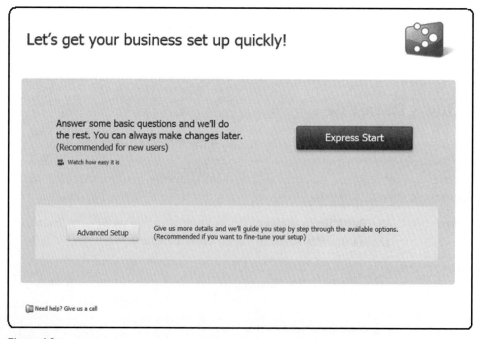

Figure 4-3

Setting up a QuickBooks company file begins on the QuickBooks Setup screen. If you choose the **Advanced Setup** button, the EasyStep Interview will open where you will go through a number of screens answering questions about your company and completing much of the required company setup. If you choose the **Express Start** button, you will be asked only a few questions about your company and you will need to enter information about your company in QuickBooks before you begin entering transactions. No matter which option you select, at any time you can click the **Back** button to go back to previous screens to change your answers and you can click the **Next** button to advance to the next screen. Some screens contain required information and you cannot advance to the next screen until you complete the required information. You should always check your answers before moving to the next screen. Some information in the EasyStep Interview cannot be changed once it is selected. When you are entering information that cannot be changed later, you will receive a message warning you of this. Check your answers very carefully if you receive a warning message.

Notes
When you select the Advanced Setup button to use the EasyStep Interview, you can leave at any time by clicking the Leave button and then enter the remaining details on your own in your QuickBooks company file. However, if you leave the EasyStep Interview before you reach the step of entering a file name, your new company file will not be created.

As mentioned, you can skip the EasyStep Interview by selecting the Express Start button on the QuickBooks Setup screen. Using this option, you will only need to complete some of the company information and then setup your QuickBooks company file from scratch. That is the approach we will use while creating the company file in this chapter. Once you have seen all the setup screens and steps this way, you will be able to easily use the EasyStep Interview on your own. It merely breaks down the setup into more steps with more instructions and screens.

We will select the Express Start button to create our company file and enter the required information to set up the company. After we create the company file, we will begin the manual setup process.

5. **Click** the **Express Start button** [Express Start] to open the company information window:

Notes
If you click the Advanced Setup button, you will receive different screens as you work through this exercise. If this happens to you, click the Back button until you return to the QuickBooks Setup screen where you can select the Express Start button.

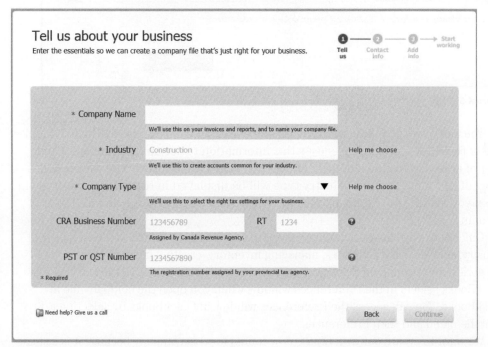

Tell us about your business
Enter the essentials so we can create a company file that's just right for your business.

1 — 2 — 3 — → Start working
Tell us   Contact info   Add info

* Company Name
We'll use this on your invoices and reports, and to name your company file.

* Industry   Construction   Help me choose
We'll use this to create accounts common for your industry.

* Company Type   ▼   Help me choose
We'll use this to select the right tax settings for your business.

CRA Business Number   123456789   RT   1234   ❓
Assigned by Canada Revenue Agency.

PST or QST Number   1234567890   ❓
The registration number assigned by your provincial tax agency.

* Required

📞 Need help? Give us a call   Back   Continue

Figure 4-4

This screen is used to enter the company name, industry, company type, CRA business number and, if your business is in Quebec, your PST or QST number. Notice that the Company Name, Industry, and Company Type fields have asterisks beside them indicating that they are required fields and must be entered before you can continue.

The cursor is in the Company Name field. The name you enter in this field is the name by which customers know you. This is also the name that will appear on your invoices and reports and will be used in the title bar of your QuickBooks desktop window.

6. **Type**   **River Run**

7. **Press**   `tab`

8. **Click**   **Help me choose** displayed at the end of the Industry field to display the list of industries set up in QuickBooks:

Figure 4-5

You can choose an industry type for the company from the list on the left-hand side of the screen. QuickBooks uses this information to set up other defaults and a set of accounts for the company file. As you select an industry type, the default Chart of Accounts for that industry type will be displayed in the column on the right. When you set up your company file, you will be able to modify the default Chart of Accounts.

QuickBooks also uses the industry type to recommend features that best suit your industry, such as using estimates, managing inventory, creating income and expense categories, and turning on Sales Orders. You can easily change any of the settings that QuickBooks selects in the Preferences window when you open the company file in QuickBooks. You can access the Preferences window in QuickBooks by selecting Edit from the menu and then Preferences.

We want to create our own Chart of Accounts for this company because it is a small set, so we will choose Other/None as the industry type.

9. **Choose**   **Other/None** from the bottom of the list of industry types and **click OK**

10.	**Click**	**Help me choose** displayed at the end of the Company Type field where you select how your company is organized:

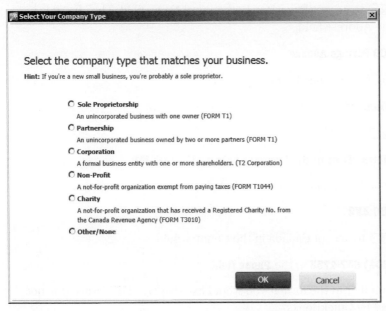

Figure 4-6

This screen asks you to select your business entity. Your selection will help QuickBooks determine which tax forms will be used to report taxes for your company. Choosing the correct form will allow you to use QuickBooks to help prepare the income tax form at the end of the year. If the business is incorporated, you should choose Corporation. If the business is a sole proprietorship that combines personal and business income tax in a single return, you should choose Sole Proprietorship. If you are uncertain, you can choose Other.

11.	**Click**	on the **radio button** beside Charity and **click OK**
12.	**Leave**	the **CRA Business Number field** and the **RT number field** blank
13.	**Click**	**Continue**

The company name that you entered on the previous screen has automatically been entered in the Legal Name field as shown:

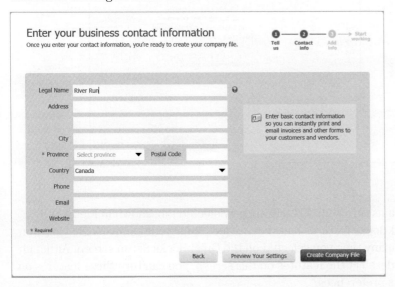

Figure 4-7

Notes
You must enter a valid CRA Business Number in these fields. Since we have made up the CRA Business Number for this company you will receive an error message if you enter it

The name you enter in the Legal Name field should be the legal name for the business.

14. Press ⬚tab⬚ to accept River Run in the Legal Name field. The cursor is in the Address field.

15. Type **100 Portage Avenue**

16. Press ⬚tab⬚ to advance to the City field

17. Type **Winnipeg**

18. Press ⬚tab⬚

19. Click the **drop-down arrow** in the **Province field** and **choose MB**

The Province is used by QuickBooks to create a default set of sales taxes.

20. Type **R3C 3X2**

21. Press ⬚tab⬚ to accept Canada in the Country field

📄 **Notes**
You can click the drop-down arrow in the Country field to select a different country.

22. Type **(204) 837-4733** in the **Phone field**

Enter the phone number in the format you would like displayed on forms. It is not automatically formatted by QuickBooks.

23. Press ⬚tab⬚ to advance to the E-mail address field

24. Type **admin@riverrun.com**

25. Press ⬚tab⬚ to advance to the Website field

26. Type **www.riverrun.com**

27. Click the **Preview Your Settings button** to display the following screen:

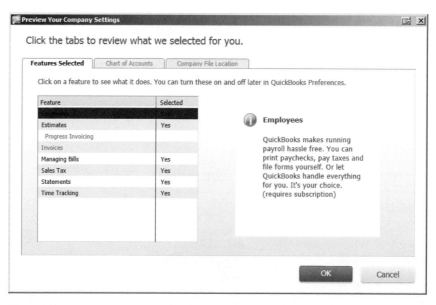

Figure 4-8

This screen contains three tabs. The Features Selected tab, shown in Figure 4-8, indicates which QuickBooks features have been selected for your company file based on the industry and company type you selected on the QuickBooks Setup screen. Although you cannot select or deselect the features on this screen, you can turn these features on and off in QuickBooks preferences.

28. Click   the **Chart of Accounts tab**

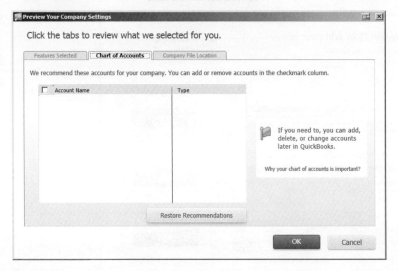

Figure 4-9

The Chart of Accounts tab displays the Chart of Accounts that QuickBooks recommends for your company. Because we selected Other/None as the industry type, this screen does not display any accounts. If you selected other industry types, you could select or deselect the accounts listed on this tab by either adding or removing the checkmark beside each account.

29. Click   the **Company File Location tab**

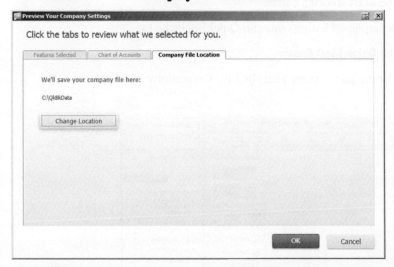

Figure 4-10

The Company File Location tab allows you to select the location of your company file. By default, the folder that contains the data file you were working with most recently is selected and the name you entered for the company is the default file name.

To change the location of your file, click on the Change Location button and select the appropriate drive and folder.

30. Click   **OK** when you have selected the location of the file

31. Click   the **Create Company File button** to create the company file

Be patient while QuickBooks creates the file based on the information you have provided. If you selected an industry type, QuickBooks will create a Chart of Accounts that may be suitable for the business. You can modify this list later if you want.

32. The following screen will be displayed when the company file is created:

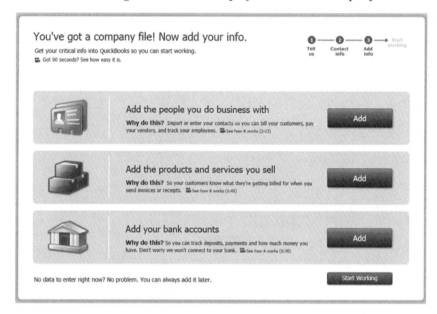

Figure 4-11

You can use this screen to add the people you do business with, the products and services you sell, and bank accounts. We are going to enter this information within QuickBooks so we'll select to start working in QuickBooks.

33. Click the **Start Working button**

Another screen is displayed listing common QuickBooks tasks.

34. Close the **Quick Start Centre**

The QuickBooks Home page opens with the Live Community and Help pane displayed to the right:

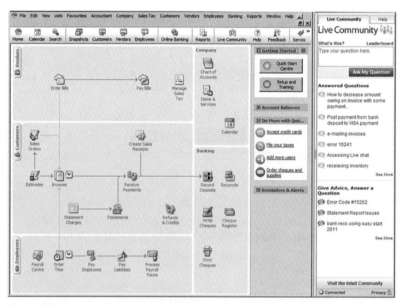

Figure 4-12

📄 **Notes**
You can open the Live Community and Help pane at any time by clicking the Help or Live Community icon on the Icon bar.

The Live Community and Help pane can be closed at any time.

35. Click the ☒ in the top right-hand corner of the Live Community and Help pane to close it

36. Click   **OK** when prompted with the message that Live Community will be opened the next time you start QuickBooks

When you create a new company file in QuickBooks, default settings and a Chart of Accounts are created based on the industry type you selected on the QuickBooks Setup screen. Tax information for the province you selected in the company address is also created. When setting up this company, we selected the Other/None industry type so very few accounts have been created on the Chart of Accounts. Before we start working in QuickBooks, we must modify the defaults or preferences to suit our business and then create the Chart of Accounts, vendor, customer, and item records. We also need to enter opening account balances to add the historical information.

Notes
You can add opening balances later when you create accounts on the fly while entering current transactions, but it is more difficult to check your work for errors.

Creating the Chart of Accounts

The first step in setting up a new company is creating new accounts. It is not necessary to create all the accounts before entering transactions in QuickBooks because they can be added to the Chart of Accounts at any time or they can be added in any account field on the fly during transaction entry when you need them. However, by creating accounts first, we can easily choose the accounts we need as defaults for other setup steps, and we can monitor the creation of the accounts in a logical order. Before we can create the new accounts, we should set some of the preferences that will influence how the accounts are set up.

Setting Preferences

Preferences in QuickBooks influence how the program works and looks. Some of the preferences are personal — you choose how you like to work with the program on the My Preferences tab screens. For example, you can define the rules for Spell Check or have the program beep when you enter transactions. Other preferences that relate to the way the company operates are located on the Company Preferences tab screens. For example, a business may or may not prepare Sales Estimates and Purchase Orders. By eliminating the unused icons, the program is easier to use. Some of these preferences should be set before you work with a module, while others can be changed at any time. Some aspects of the program have only personal preferences and some have only company preferences.

When you use the complete EasyStep Interview to set up a new company, you also set many of these preferences. However, each interview screen usually controls a single preference question and is followed by one or more input screens. When you use the Preferences screens, you can make several selections from a single input window.

We will begin by setting some general preferences for the program. We will change the preferences for individual modules later. Preferences are set from the main menu in the desktop window. This menu is always available, and preferences can be changed at any time if the needs of the business change.

General Preferences

1. Choose   the **Edit menu** and **click Preferences**

2. Click   the **General heading** on the left-hand side of the screen and, if necessary, **click** the **My Preferences tab**

The My Preferences tab for the General preferences is displayed as shown:

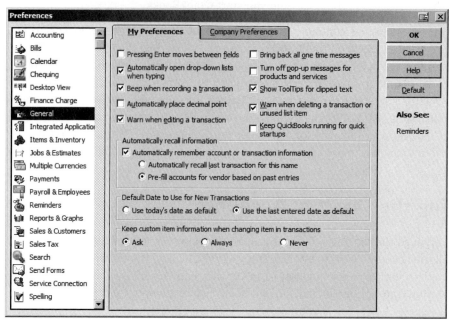

Figure 4-13

Preference headings are listed alphabetically on the left-hand side of the screen. While accessing any of the Preference windows, click the Help button on the right-hand side of the screen for more detailed information.

3. Click **Help** to view explanations of the options for each set of preferences

You can leave the Help window open until you have finished setting all preferences. Just click the Help button again after you choose the next preference heading or area to update the Help topic information.

Since the General preferences do not affect the financial aspects of the program, you should decide for yourself how you want to interact with the program and choose your settings. From this screen you can choose to:

Notes
When the cursor is in a text box field that includes more than one line, such as an address text box, pressing *enter* will automatically move the cursor to the next line in the text box regardless of whether you select the preference to press *enter* between fields.

- press *enter* to move between fields. Otherwise pressing *enter* is like choosing OK, Record, or Save & New, whichever button is highlighted
- automatically open drop-down lists when typing
- turn on or off the beep (sound) when recording transactions
- automatically add a decimal point to numbers. Thus, 4950 becomes 49.50 but 49 becomes 0.49. This option requires you to add trailing zeros for whole numbers
- warn when editing a transaction. Always leave this option selected
- bring back all one-time messages that were turned off when you selected "Do not display this message again." You can select this option later to restore the messages that you turned off
- turn off pop-up messages for products and services
- show ToolTips for clipped text
- warn when deleting a transaction or unused list item. Always leave this option selected
- keep QuickBooks running for quick startups
- automatically recall account or transaction information by selecting to recall the last transaction for the person entered on the transaction or by pre-filling accounts for vendors based on past transactions
- choose the current date or last transaction date as the default date for new transactions
- choose when to keep custom item information when changing items in transactions

WARNING!
Do not turn off the warnings for edited or deleted transactions.

To select or deselect preferences, click in the check box beside the preference to select it (which will add a ✓ indicating that the preference is selected) or click in the box that contains a checkmark (which will remove the ✓ indicating that the preference is deselected).

4. Click the **checkmark** beside Beep when recording a transaction to turn this preference off

We will use the default settings for the rest of the General preferences on the My Preferences tab.

5. Click the **Company Preferences tab**:

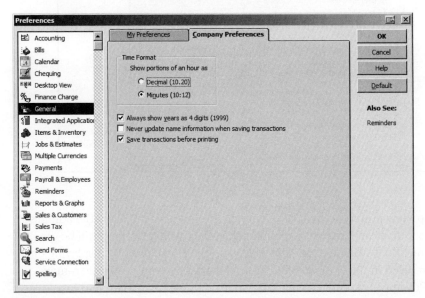

Notes
Only the administrator of the company file or a user set up as an External Accountant can change the preferences on the Company Preferences tab for all preference headings. Other users cannot change these settings. If the file has one user, that user is the administrator.

Figure 4-14

The General company preferences relate to how dates and times are entered and displayed in the program, if information updated in transactions should be updated when saving transactions, and if transactions should be saved before printing. The four-digit year format ensures that you are working with 2000 dates instead of 1900 dates. The *Never update name information when saving transactions* option is not selected, so the default setting allows you to update customer and vendor record details from invoice and form windows. The final option will save your transactions before you print them.

We will use the default settings for the General preferences on the Company Preferences tab.

Desktop View Preferences

6. Click the **Desktop View** heading on the left-hand side of the screen to view the Desktop View preferences

Because we have made changes to the General preferences, the following warning message appears as soon as you click on the Desktop View preference heading:

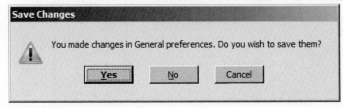

Figure 4-15

7. Click   **Yes** to save the General preferences changes

The following company preferences are displayed for the Desktop View heading:

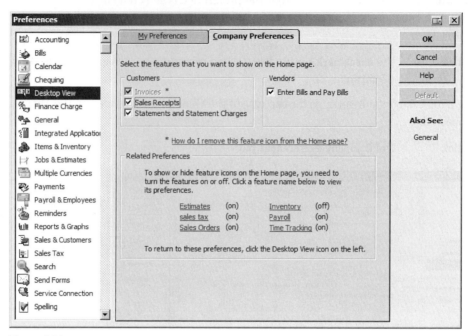

Figure 4-16

The Desktop View preferences on the Company Preferences tab allow the administrator or a user set up as an External Accountant to select which features will be displayed on the QuickBooks Home page. This cleans up the Home page by displaying only the icons that are used in the company file. From this window, you can easily remove Invoices, Sales Receipts, Statements and Statement Charges, Enter Bills, and Pay Bills icons from the Home page. You can also use this window to turn off related preferences. As you select or deselect the related preferences, the appropriate preference window will open allowing you to turn the preference on or off.

We will not be changing any of the Desktop View Company Preferences.

8. Click   the **My Preferences tab**:

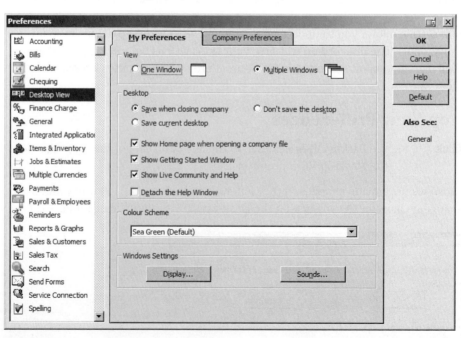

Figure 4-17

The default settings here are to open one window at a time while working in QuickBooks, to save the last desktop you worked in so that all the windows you had open when you exited the program will open the next time you open the data file, and to show the Home page, Getting Started window, and Live Community and Help when opening a company file. You can also choose the colour scheme for the forms in the program and access the Windows display and sounds settings. Most of the options are self-explanatory but the Help button provides additional information if needed.

We have not changed these default settings but you may choose to do so.

Reminders Preferences

9. Click   the **Reminders heading** on the left-hand side of the screen

If you made any changes to the Desktop View preferences, you'll need to click yes to accept them before moving to the Reminders preferences.

10. Click   **Yes** to save the Desktop View preferences if needed

The following preferences are displayed on the My Preferences tab for Reminders:

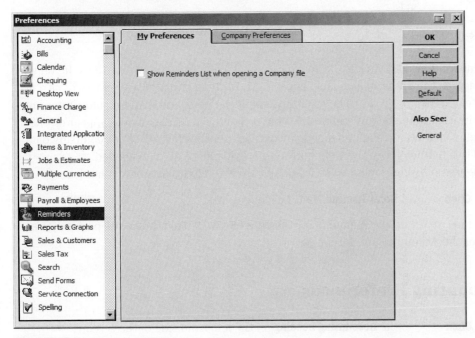

Figure 4-18

The default setting here is to not show reminders when opening the company file.

11. Click   the **Company Preferences tab**:

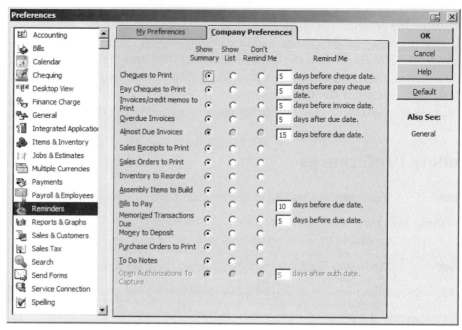

Figure 4-19

This window displays a list from which you can choose your own settings. If you use reminders in the program, you can choose to show them either as a summary or as a list, indicate whether you want to be reminded about the item, and then for some items you can indicate how many days before the item is due the reminder should appear on the Reminders list. We have not changed any of these settings for any of our company data files in this textbook. Use the Help button to provide more detail if needed.

We are not using reminders so we do not show reminder lists or summaries.

12. Click   **Don't Remind Me** for each feature

Before we set up the Accounts for the data file, we should define the preference settings for the Accounting preferences.

Accounting Preferences

13. Click   the **Accounting heading** on the left-hand side of the screen

Since you made changes to the Reminders preferences, you'll need to click yes to accept them before moving to the Accounting preferences.

14. Click   **Yes** to save the changes to the Reminder preferences

15. Click   the **My Preferences tab** for the Accounting preferences:

In the left margin:

Notes
Reminders are linked to the current calendar dates so we are not able to use them for the data files in the textbook.

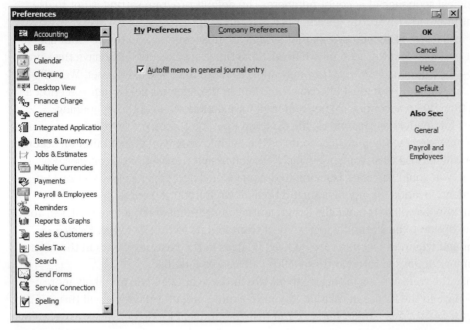

Figure 4-20

The default setting for the preference on this screen is to automatically have the memo field that you enter in the first line of a general journal entry appear automatically in subsequent lines.

We have not changed the default setting but you may choose to do so.

16. Click   the **Company Preferences tab**:

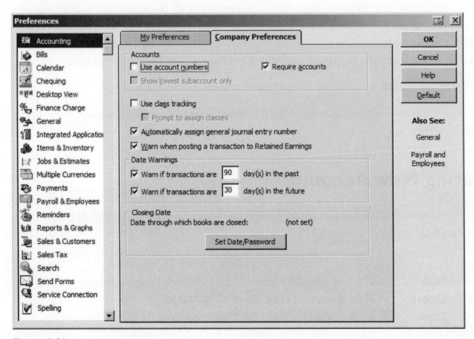

Figure 4-21

One of the preferences that affects accounts is the option to use account numbers. In the early applications in this textbook, we will not be using account numbers. When not using account numbers, accounts are listed in alphabetical order within their account type. When account numbers are used, the accounts are listed in numeric order within their account type. Although you can use any numbering system you want, it is best to use a logical sequence of account numbers. The default program setting is not to use account numbers. River Run does not use account numbers.

We will show all accounts — parent as well as subaccounts — in the account lists to make it easier to find the account we need. Sometimes subaccounts may have the same name — for example, *Depreciation* may apply to more than one fixed asset. We will also require accounts — you must choose an account in the Account field when you enter a transaction. When accounts are not required, for example when entering opening balances for vendors or customers, the program uses the *Uncategorized Income* account or the *Uncategorized Expense* account as the default when you do not enter an account.

We will not use class tracking, which lets you assign transactions to classes. For example, you could use class tracking to define income and expense transactions by department, location, or any meaningful breakdown for your business.

QuickBooks will automatically assign journal entry numbers to journal entries. You have the option to be warned when we post transactions to the *Retained Earnings* account and when transactions are entered 90 days in the past or 30 days in the future. The number of days entered in these fields can also be modified.

Since the transactions in this textbook are in the year 2014 and are likely more than 30 days in the future in relation to your current computer date, we will turn off the *Warn if transactions are 30 days in the future* option so we do not receive a warning message each time we enter a transaction. In a work environment, you should keep this option selected to ensure proper dates are entered on your transactions.

17. Click   the **check box** beside the Warn if transactions are 30 days in the future option to turn this off

In previous versions of QuickBooks, you could indicate on this screen whether you wanted QuickBooks to track all edited and deleted transactions through the audit trail. Beginning with QuickBooks 2008, the audit trail is always on and cannot be turned off. In accounting practice, you must show a complete record of all transactions, and changes must be apparent and recorded.

When we are ready to close the books, we can add the closing date and a password. The password for this field prevents unauthorized changes to historical records.

18. Click   **OK** to save the changes and return to the Home page

If you were not automatically returned to the Home page, click the Home icon on the Icon bar.

Creating New Accounts

New accounts are added from the Chart of Accounts window. The Chart of Accounts window can be accessed in a number of ways:

a) **Click**   the **Chart of Accounts icon** [Chart of Accounts] on the Home page; or
b) **Choose**   the **Lists menu** and **click Chart of Accounts**; or
c) **Press**   (ctrl) + **A**, the keyboard shortcut

1. Open   the **Chart of Accounts** by using one of the methods listed above

When you set up this company file, you selected that your company was a charity and you selected the Other/None option as the industry type. Even though you selected Other/None, QuickBooks creates the following basic accounts in the Chart of Accounts:

Notes
Journal entry numbers are not assigned to other types of transactions, although transaction numbers are assigned to all entries.

Notes
In accounting practice, pencils and erasers are not allowed because they could cover up any unauthorized changes to the data.

Figure 4-22

Notes
The accounts listed in the
Chart of Accounts were added
automatically by QuickBooks
when you selected the Other/
None industry type during
QuickBooks setup.

The *Accounts Payable* account tracks what your company owes to its vendors. The
tax accounts are set up based on the province you entered for the company address
during QuickBooks setup. The *Payroll Liabilities* account is used to track liabilities
incurred for payroll taxes and other employee deductions. The *Opening Balance Equity*
account is the net worth of a company, and this account is used as the offsetting account
when entering opening balances. The *Perm. Restricted Net Assets, Temp. Restricted Net
Assets,* and *Unrestricted Net Assets* accounts are automatically set up by QuickBooks
to record donations and contributions. The *Payroll Expense* account is automatically
added to your Chart of Accounts if payroll is turned on (it is automatically turned on in
QuickBooks Premier Student and School edition). Finally, the *Uncategorized Expenses*
account is used when you enter opening balances for your vendors.

2. **Click** the **Account button** (at the bottom of the Chart of Accounts window)
to view the pop-up menu and **click New** as shown:

Notes
You can use the keyboard
shortcut *ctrl* + **N** to open the
Add New Account window

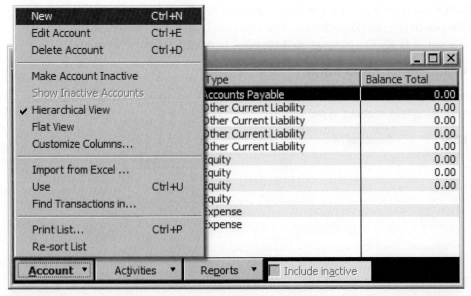

Figure 4-23

Notes
The pop-up menu may
be displayed below the Chart
of Accounts window depending on where the Chart of
Accounts window is displayed
on your screen.

Entering Bank Accounts

The Add New Account entry screen will open where you select the account type:

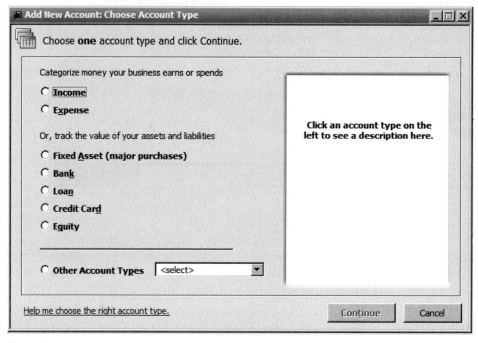

Figure 4-24

Use this screen to select the account type. You can select *Income, Expense, Fixed Asset, Bank, Loan, Credit Card,* or *Equity,* or click on the Other Account Types option and select from *Accounts Receivable, Other Current Asset, Other Asset, Accounts Payable, Other Current Liability, Long Term Liability, Cost of Goods Sold, Other Income,* and *Other Expense.*

As you select an account type, the box on the right-hand side of the screen will display examples of accounts for the selected account type.

As we saw in the previous chapter, the input fields on the New Account form vary with the account type. The first account we need to create is a bank account.

3. Click   the **Bank button**

Notice the right-hand side of the screen displays examples of accounts that can be entered by using this account type.

4. Click   **Continue** to go to the next page of the Add New Account window:

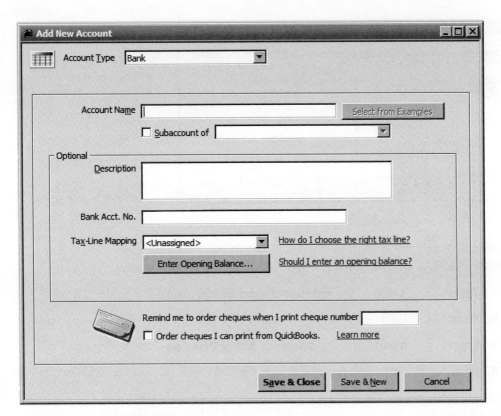

Figure 4-25

Because we chose not to use account numbers, the account name field appears without a number field. The account is not a subaccount so you can leave this field blank. We will use subaccounts for the fixed asset accounts. The description is optional. Sometimes you will want to distinguish accounts that are very similar by including the purpose of the account or a longer account name in the description field. Many of the other fields relate specifically to bank accounts. We will not be using online banking so we do not need to add the bank account number, and we will not be exporting our tax information to tax preparation software so we do not need to select a tax line mapping option. Also, we are not using pre-printed cheques so we can leave those fields blank as well.

We do need to add the opening account balance. We will enter the balance as of January 1, 2014, the day we begin to use the program for current transactions.

Name	Opening Balance	Date
Bank - Chequing	$15,540.00	January 1/14
Cash on Hand	$ 480.00	January 1/14

We need to enter two bank accounts:

5. Type **Bank - Chequing** in the **Account Name field**

6. Click the **Enter Opening Balance button** to display the Enter Opening Balance window:

Notes
When you choose to use account numbers, the Add New Account form includes a field for the account number.

Notes
Remember we cannot use colons in account names. Colons are reserved for subaccounts and are added automatically by the program.

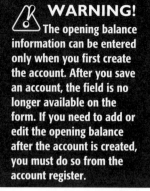
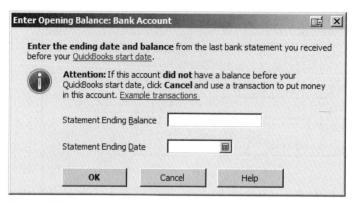

Figure 4-26

For bank accounts, you must use this screen to enter the ending date and balance from the last bank statement you received before your QuickBooks start date.

7. Type   **15540** in the **Statement Ending Balance field**

8. Press   (tab)

9. Type   **01/01/14** in the **Statement Ending Date field**

10. Press   (tab)

Because we will use the same opening balance date for all accounts, you do not have to type it each time. You can copy it and then paste it in the remaining accounts.

11. Double click   **01/01/14** in the **Statement Ending Date** and **press** (ctrl) **+ C** to copy the date to the Windows Clipboard

When you enter the next account, you can press (ctrl) **+ V** in the date field to paste the date.

12. Click   **OK** to close the Enter Opening Balance window and return to the Add New Account window

If you omit a year in the date field, the program enters the current calendar year from your computer system.

To save the new account, you can click Save & Close to save the account and close the Add New Account form or click Save & New to save the account and open a blank Add New Account form. Before creating more accounts, we will view the changes that QuickBooks has made to the file.

13. Click   **Save & Close** to save the account, close the form, and return to the Chart of Accounts

You will receive the following message asking if you want to set up online services:

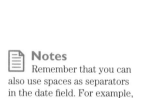

Notes

Remember that you can also use spaces as separators in the date field. For example, Type 1 1 14

Notes

Since you may be working in a different year than the one used for this company, confirm that the Add New Account screen indicates that the opening balance for this account is as of 01/01/14 before continuing.

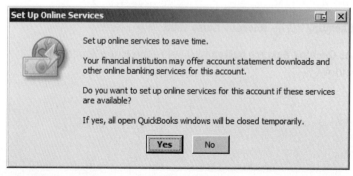

Figure 4-27

We will not be setting up Online Services for this company file.

14. Click **No** and you are returned to the Chart of Accounts:

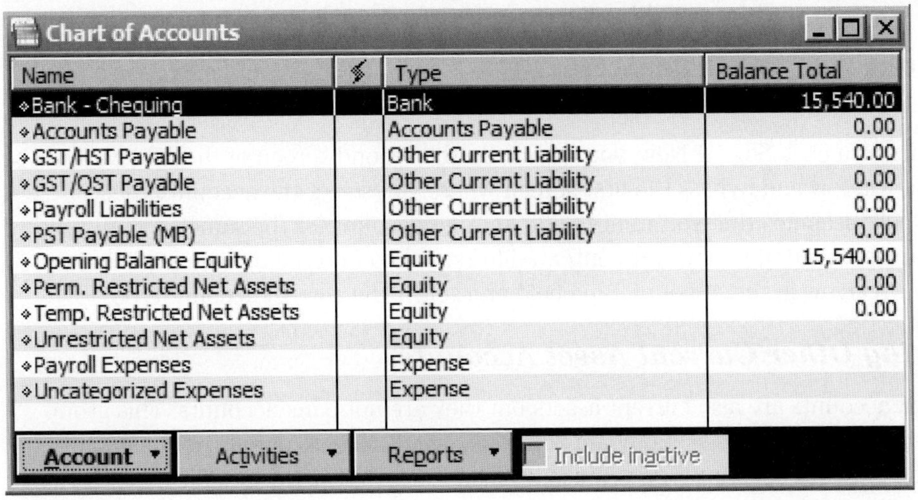

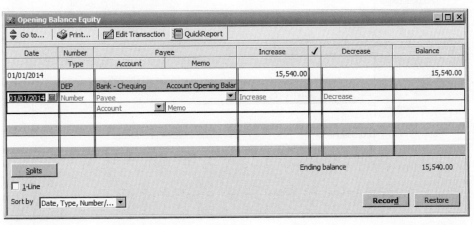

Figure 4-28

Notice that the program has added $15,540.00 to the *Bank - Chequing* account and to the *Opening Balance Equity* account. All account opening balances are treated as journal entries with the entry to *Opening Balance Equity* as the second part of the transaction. We will rename this account later.

15. Double click the **Opening Balance Equity account** to view the journal entry in the register:

Figure 4-29

16. Close the **register** to return to the Chart of Accounts

17. Press (ctrl) + **N** to open the Add New Account window to enter the next account

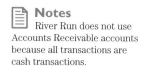

Notes
River Run does not use
Accounts Receivable accounts
because all transactions are
cash transactions.

18. Create   the **Cash on Hand account**. Refer to the Post-closing Trial Balance on page 141

19. Enter   the **account name**, **statement ending balance**, and **statement ending date** or **press** ⌈ctrl⌋ + **V** to use the date that we copied onto the clipboard

20. Click   **Save & New** or **press** ⌈alt⌋ + **N** to save the account and open a blank Add New Account form

When you click Save & New, you remain on the second screen of the Add New Account window and bypass the first screen where you select the account type. QuickBooks assumes that you want to add another account for the same account type that you just saved. If you want to enter a different account type, you must click the drop-down arrow in the Account Type field and select the correct account type.

Entering Other Current Asset Accounts

The next accounts are also current assets but they are not bank accounts. This group is named Other Current Assets. When you click Save & New to open a new account form, the previous account type you used remains selected as the default. The previous account type we used was Bank, so it is currently displayed in the Account Type field.

1. Click   the **drop-down arrow** in the **Account Type field** and **select Other Current Asset** as the type (or type o) to change the input form:

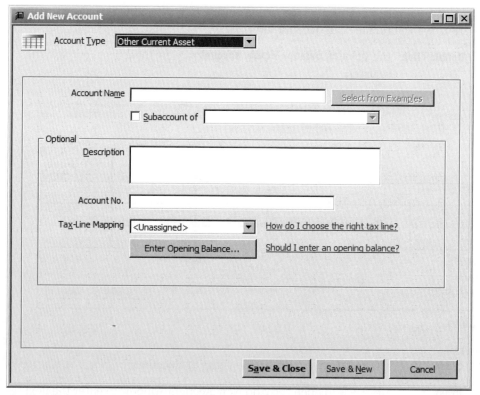

Figure 4-30

Notice that the fields that apply only to bank accounts, such as the cheque information, are not included on the input form for this account type. Notice that the Enter Opening Balance button is available. For this group of accounts you must enter the account name and enter the opening balance and date if you have historical data to enter. The remaining fields, including the description, are optional.

The three Other Current Asset accounts that we must enter are listed below:

Name	Opening Balance	Date
Office & Computer Supplies	$210.00	January 1/14
Food Supplies	0.00	January 1/14
T-shirts and Caps	0.00	January 1/14

2. Type **Office & Computer Supplies** in the **Account Name field**

3. Click the **Enter Opening Balance button** to display the Enter Opening Balance window:

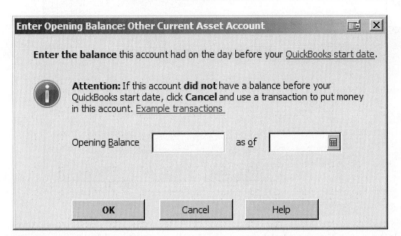

Figure 4-31

4. Type **210** in the **Opening Balance field**

5. Press 〔tab〕 to advance to the As of date field

6. Type **01/01/14** or **press** 〔ctrl〕 **+ V** if you copied the date to the clipboard

7. Click **OK** to close the Enter Opening Balance screen and return to the Add New Account window

8. Click **Save & New** or press 〔alt〕 **+ N**

For the next two accounts, the opening balance is zero so we need to enter only the account name, not the opening balance or the date.

9. Enter the two **Other Current Asset account names** shown above and then **click Save & New** or press 〔alt〕 **+ N**

Entering Fixed Asset Accounts

The next group of assets are fixed assets. These appear as the last assets on the Balance Sheet because they are the least liquid — they take the longest to be converted to cash. River Run's fixed assets are grouped into parent (heading) and subaccounts for each type of asset. This allows us to see the net asset value or subtotal (cost minus accumulated depreciation) as the parent account balance.

Notice that Other Current Asset is still selected as the account type.

1. Click the **drop-down arrow** in the **Account Type field** and **select Fixed Asset** as the type (or type f) to change the input form:

Notes
Fixed asset is the only account type that begins with F, so entering F while the drop-down list is displayed in the Account Type field will select this account type.

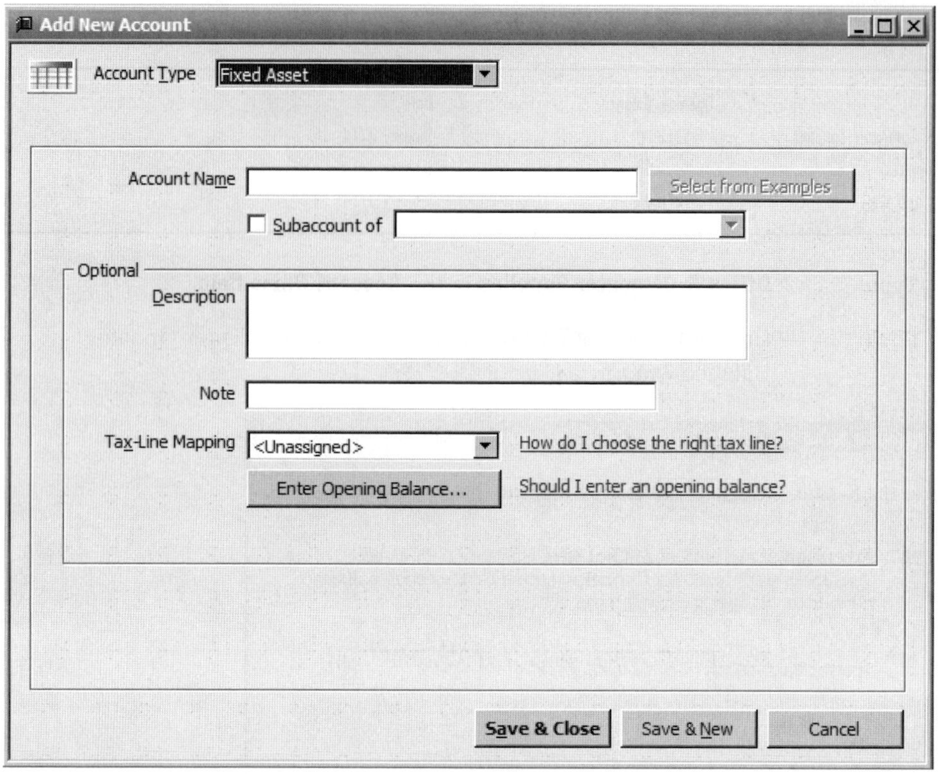

Figure 4-32

Instead of a Bank Account Number field, fixed assets allow you to add a note. Otherwise, the form is the same as that for Other Current Assets.

For parent accounts, you must enter only the account name. For subaccounts you must enter the name, the opening balance, and date if applicable; indicate that the account is a subaccount; and choose the parent account from the list. The other fields are optional. For parent accounts, the balance is calculated automatically by the program as the sum of the subaccount balances.

Depreciation accounts are contra-asset accounts. Their credit balances are entered as negative amounts, so they reduce the total asset value.

The complete list of fixed assets is presented in the following chart:

Name	Subaccount of	Description	Opening Balance	Date
Computers/Digital Equipment [Parent account]				
Cost	Computers/Digital Equipment	Original cost of computers	$4,500.00	January 1/14
Depreciation	Computers/Digital Equipment	Accum deprec on computers	$–1,820.00	January 1/14

Notes
QuickBooks has some helpful shortcuts on the Account input form too. From the Account Name field, press (tab) to advance to the Subaccount option box. Press the Space bar to select the subaccount option. Press (tab) to move to the Subaccount name field. Assuming that the parent account is already entered, you can type its first letter, in this case type C, to display the list of accounts beginning with the letter C. Computers is the first account on the Chart of Accounts beginning with the letter C so press (tab) to accept it.

2. Type   **Computers/Digital Equipment** in the **Account Name field**

You do not define an account as a parent account. QuickBooks defines it automatically when you identify a subaccount for it. QuickBooks also calculates its opening balance as the sum of all its subaccount balances.

3. Click   **Save & New** or **press** (alt) **+ N**

4. Type   **Cost** as the next Account Name

5. Click   the **Subaccount of check box**

6. Click   the **drop-down arrow** in the **Subaccount of field**

7.	Choose	**Computers/Digital Equipment**
8.	Press	(tab) to advance to the Description field
9.	Type	**Original cost of computers**
10.	Click	the **Enter Opening Balance button**
11.	Type	**4500** in the **Opening Balance field**
12.	Press	(tab)
13.	Press	(ctrl) **+ V** to paste the date (or type 01/01/14)
14.	Click	**OK**
15.	Click	**Save & New** or **press** (alt) **+ N**
16.	Type	**Depreciation** as the next Account Name
17.	Click	the **Subaccount of check box**
18.	Click	the **drop-down arrow** in the **Subaccount of field**
19.	Choose	**Computers/Digital Equipment**
20.	Press	(tab) to advance to the Description field
21.	Type	**Accum deprec on computers**
22.	Click	the **Enter Opening Balance button**

Depreciation accounts are contra-asset accounts. They have a credit balance instead of a debit balance, which is normal for asset accounts. They reduce the total asset value on the Balance Sheet. Therefore, you must enter a negative opening balance amount (add a minus sign) to create a credit balance for these accounts.

23.	Type	**–1820**
24.	Press	(tab)
25.	Press	(ctrl) **+ V** to paste the date from the clipboard (or type 01/01/14)
26.	Click	**OK**
27.	Click	**Save & New** or **press** (alt) **+ N** after adding Depreciation

River Run has no accounts of the Other Asset type.

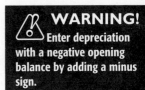

WARNING!
Enter depreciation with a negative opening balance by adding a minus sign.

Entering Other Current Liability Accounts

The next group of accounts are the liability accounts. As with assets, there are several types of liability accounts. *Accounts Payable* is the first type of QuickBooks liability account — it appears before other liability accounts on the Balance Sheet. QuickBooks automatically created an *Accounts Payable* account when the company file was originally set up. River Run has no *Accounts Payable* or *Credit Card* accounts so we will have to delete the *Accounts Payable* account later.

The next type of account we will enter is *Other Current Liability*. *Fixed Asset* is still selected as the account type since it was the last account type that was entered.

QuickBooks has already created four accounts in the Other Current Liabilities section of the Chart of Accounts — *GST/HST Payable*, *GST/QST Payable*, *Payroll Liabilities*, and *PST Payable (MB)*. The tax accounts are created automatically by QuickBooks, depending on the province selected when setting up your company file. Some of these accounts are not needed or they do not have the correct account name as used in our Chart of Accounts. Throughout this chapter, we will work with each account, either deleting it, making it inactive, or renaming it.

Notes
We do not need the *PST Payable (MB)* account or the *Accounts Payable* account, so we will delete them later. QuickBooks also created other accounts automatically that we do not need, and we will delete them or make them inactive later.

We need to make one other current liability account, the *Bank Loan* account:

1. **Click**   the **drop-down arrow** in the **Account Type field**

2. **Choose**   **Other Current Liability** as the account type (or type o until Other Current Liability is displayed)

This form has the same input fields as the Other Current Asset type. Refer to page 164 for assistance if needed.

3. **Enter**   **Bank Loan** as the account name, **11000** as the opening balance, and **01/01/14** in the As of date field

4. **Click**   **OK**

5. **Click**   **Save & New** or **press** alt + N

Entering Equity Accounts

There are no other liability accounts so we are now ready to look at the group of equity or capital accounts. QuickBooks has already created an equity account, the *Opening Balance Equity* account. We will be renaming the *Opening Balance Equity* account to *Accumulated Surplus*. We will edit this account later to match the *Equity* accounts in our Chart of Accounts on page 140.

Entering Income Accounts

After adding all the Balance Sheet accounts, we must create Income Statement accounts. River Run has only regular income accounts.

1. **Click**   the **drop-down arrow** beside Account Type and **choose Income** (or type i) to change the form:

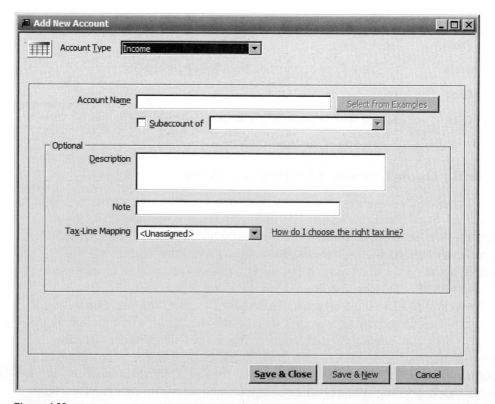

Figure 4-33

The form for income accounts has no opening balance field. The balance is generated automatically from the transactions for the account. When you have historical balances to enter, the opening balances for income accounts are added through a ledger entry for the *Opening Balance Equity* account (decreasing equity balance). All income accounts for River Run have a zero balance because the books have been closed.

Notes
Our income and expense account balances are all zero because we are entering post-closing amounts at the start of a new fiscal period.

We will enter opening income and expense account balances for Darya's Dance Studio in Chapter 9.

2. **Type**　　**Revenue from Donations**

3. **Click**　　**Save & New** or press ⌐alt⌐ + N

4. **Create**　　the **remaining two income accounts**: Revenue from Registrations and Revenue from Sales

Entering Cost of Goods Sold Accounts

QuickBooks has two types of expense accounts: Cost of Goods Sold and Expenses. Cost of Goods Sold appears separately on the Income Statement to arrive at the Gross Profit. Other expenses are then included to determine Net Income. Cost of Goods Sold applies to retail businesses that buy merchandise to resell. River Run resells T-shirts and caps as part of its fundraising campaign, so it has costs related to this merchandise. At the time of the run, food and drinks are also sold to spectators, and these related costs will also be tracked.

1. **Click**　　**Save & New** or press ⌐alt⌐ + N and **choose Cost of Goods Sold** as the account type (or type c) to change the form:

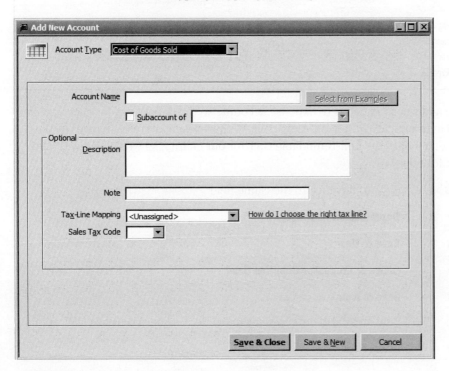

Figure 4-34

The Cost of Goods Sold account form is similar to the Income account form, but it has an additional field for the sales tax code. Many expenses are associated with taxable purchases so entering the sales tax code with the account will save some data entry time when entering transactions. Of course, you can edit the sales tax code if necessary for individual purchases.

When River Run purchases items for sale, it enters the goods as inventory. The cost of goods sold is entered later as an adjustment to the asset account so no tax code is required.

Like income accounts, the Cost of Goods Sold account opening balance is generated by the program as the sum of all transactions for the account. Our opening account balances are zero.

2. **Press**   (tab) to advance to the Account Name field

3. **Type**   **Cost of Food and Drinks**

4. **Click**   **Save & New** or **press** (alt) **+ N**

5. **Type**   **Cost of T-shirts and Caps**

6. **Click**   **Save & New** or **press** (alt) **+ N**

Entering Expense Accounts

We are now ready to enter the final group of accounts — the Expense accounts.

1. **Choose**   **Expense** as the account type (or type e) to change the form

The Expense account form is the same as the one for Cost of Goods Sold. Expense accounts for River Run are listed in the following chart:

Name	Tax Code
Depreciation Expense	(blank)
Office & Computer Supplies Used	(blank)
Office Rent	G
Printing & Copying	S
Publicity & Promotion	G
Telephone Expense	S
Wage Contract Expenses	(blank)

You can add sales tax codes to expense accounts so the default tax for each account is displayed automatically when entering a bill. We have to make some changes to the taxes to accommodate the non-refundable GST for our charity, so we will leave the tax codes blank for now.

2. **Press**   (tab) to advance to the Name field

3. **Type**   **Depreciation Expense**

4. **Click**   **Save & New**

5. **Type**   **Office & Computer Supplies Used**

6. **Click**   **Save & New**

For Office Rent, you must also enter a sales tax code. Business rent has GST applied.

7. **Type**   **Office Rent**

QuickBooks has created a default set of sales tax codes that apply to businesses in the province we selected when we set up our company file. You can assign a sales tax code to expenses and cost of goods sold accounts. When you select an account in a transaction, the sales tax code assigned to the account will automatically be displayed in the transaction. If necessary, you can change the default sales tax code during transaction entry.

River Run is a registered charity and is eligible for a rebate of 50 percent of all GST paid on purchases. The default taxes set up by QuickBooks will not work for this charity. We will set up the appropriate taxes for this company later in the chapter, so we'll leave the Sales Tax Code blank for all accounts for now.

8. Enter the **remaining expense accounts**

After adding the *Wage Contract Expenses* account:

9. Click **Save & Close** instead of Save & New to save the account and close the Add New Account form

Notes
The other account types are not used by River Run.

You will return to the Chart of Accounts. You should notice several changes. All the new accounts you created have been added with balances if you entered one for them.

There are still some accounts listed on the Chart of Accounts that we do not need, such as some of the tax accounts, the *Accounts Payable* account, and payroll accounts. We will be working with these accounts later in this chapter.

In addition, the *Opening Balance Equity* account balance has changed. Every time you entered an opening account balance, the program added an offsetting amount to the *Opening Balance Equity* account. If the account you created had a debit balance, the *Opening Balance Equity* account was credited by the same amount. If you added a credit balance, a debit amount was entered for *Opening Balance Equity*. This ensures that the Trial Balance remains balanced. The final account balance should be $7,910.00 if you entered all amounts correctly. We will rename the *Opening Balance Equity* account to *Accumulated Surplus* later in this chapter.

Notes
The balance for the *Opening Balance Equity* account may not be correct if you entered an incorrect amount for any account.

10. Compare the **Chart of Accounts** displayed on the screen with the one on page 140 and **mark** the **accounts that require corrections. Ignore** the **tax accounts** for now.

We will now make the necessary corrections to the Chart of Accounts.

Deleting Accounts

The Chart of Accounts includes the following accounts, other than the tax accounts, that are not needed (we will be working with the tax accounts later in this chapter):

> Accounts Payable
>
> Payroll Liabilities* (cannot be deleted because it is used in a payroll item)
>
> Perm. Restricted Net Assets
>
> Temp. Restricted Net Assets
>
> Unrestricted Net Assets
>
> Payroll Expenses* (cannot be deleted because it is used in a payroll item)
>
> Uncategorized Expenses

The accounts with an asterisk beside them cannot be deleted from the Chart of Accounts. Accounts cannot be deleted if they are used by other items in QuickBooks. Both the *Payroll Liabilities* and the *Payroll Expenses* accounts are used on a payroll item and cannot be deleted. In order to remove them from the Chart of Accounts, we will learn how to make them inactive or hide them later in this chapter.

Notes
You also cannot delete any account that has a balance, is used by other items in QuickBooks, or has been used in journal transactions.

1. Click **Accounts Payable** to select it

2. Press ctrl + **D** (or **choose** the **Account button** and **click Delete Account**)

You will see the following warning message:

Delete Account

? Are you sure you want to delete this account?

OK   Cancel

Figure 4-35

3. **Click**   **OK**

4. **Click**   **Perm. Restricted Net Assets** to select it

5. **Press**   `ctrl` **+ D** (or **choose** the **Account button** and **click Delete Account**)

6. **Click**   **OK**

7. **Continue deleting**   the **rest of the accounts** in the list (other than the ones with an asterisk beside their name)

8. **Click**   **OK** to return to the Chart of Accounts when you have finished deleting the accounts

Making Accounts Inactive

There may be accounts that you don't need in the Chart of Accounts but they cannot be deleted. For example, you cannot delete accounts that are linked to other items, have balances, or have been used in transactions. If an account meets any one of these criteria, then the account must be made inactive (or hidden).

The Chart of Accounts includes the following accounts that we do not need but cannot be deleted:

> Payroll Liabilities
> Payroll Expenses
> GST/QST Payable
> PST Payable (MB)

We'll try to delete the first account so you can see the type of message displayed when an account cannot be deleted:

1. **Click**   **Payroll Liabilities** and **press** `ctrl` **+ D**

2. The following warning is displayed:

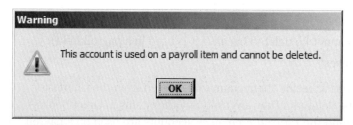

Figure 4-36

The account is used on a payroll item and cannot be deleted. You could delete the payroll item for which the account is used and then delete the account, or just make the account inactive (or hide it), which will allow you to make it active again in the future if you find you need to use it.

3. **Click**   **OK**

4. **Right-click**   **Payroll Liabilities** and **click Make Account Inactive**

The account is removed from the Chart of Accounts.

5. **Make**   the **Payroll Expenses**, **GST/QST Payable**, and **PST Payable (MB) accounts** inactive

Editing Accounts

When you review the Chart of Accounts, you may find that some of the accounts were entered incorrectly. You can easily correct an account number (if you use them) or name at this stage by opening the account record. To correct an opening balance or date, you must change the amount in the register for the account. As soon as you save a new account, the Opening Balance button is no longer available in the record; however, it is replaced with a Change Opening Balance button that will open the account register, allowing you to make changes to the opening balance.

Editing Account Names

The following account automatically created by QuickBooks does not match our Chart of Accounts. We need to edit the account name as shown in the following chart:

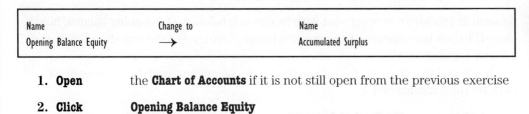

Name	Change to	Name
Opening Balance Equity	$\longrightarrow$	Accumulated Surplus

WARNING!
Do not double click the account as this will open the register for the account, not the account form.

1. **Open**   the **Chart of Accounts** if it is not still open from the previous exercise

2. **Click**   **Opening Balance Equity**

3. **Press**   *ctrl* + **E** (or **choose** the **Account button** and **click Edit Account**)

The Edit Account form appears for the selected account:

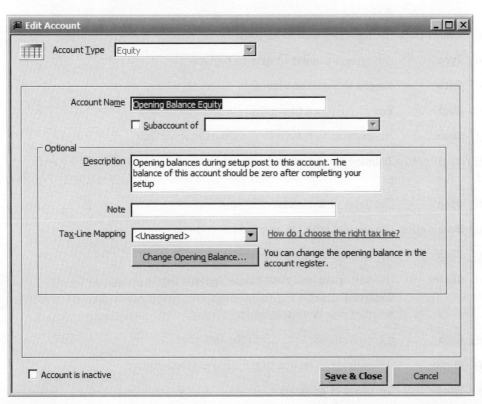

Figure 4-37

Notice that the Opening Balance button has been replaced with the Change Opening Balance button. Clicking on this button would open the account register where you can update the balances entered for the Opening Balance Equity account. Since this account is the offsetting account for all opening balances entered, you would have to change the individual transactions in the register.

The account type is dimmed. You cannot change the type if the account has been used in journal entries or if the account is linked to another function. The *Opening Balance Equity* account has been used in several journal transactions — one for each account opening balance we added — so its type cannot be changed. The account name is highlighted so we can change it.

4. **Type**   **Accumulated Surplus** to replace Opening Balance Equity as the Account Name

5. **Click**   **Save & Close** to save the changes and return to the Chart of Accounts

6. **Close**   out of the **Chart of Accounts** to return to the Home page

Editing Opening Balances and Dates

Notes
Opening balances and dates can be edited for an account directly from its register. Only Balance Sheet accounts have registers, with the exception of the *Retained Earnings* account.

As soon as you save a new account with its opening balance, the opening balance field is closed. To edit the balance, or the opening balance date, you must edit the entry in the account register.

If you find that you entered an incorrect opening amount or date for an account perform the following steps:

a) **Open**   the **Chart of Accounts**

b) **Double click** the **account with the error** to open the account's register (this is only available for Balance Sheet accounts except the *Retained Earnings* account)

c) **Double click** the **incorrect date** or **amount**

d) **Type**   the **correct amount** or **date** to replace it

e) **Click**   **Record** to save the change

f) **Click**   **Yes** when asked to confirm the change

g) **Close**   the **register** to return to the Chart of Accounts

If you entered a balance for the wrong account, you can delete the entry by performing the following steps:

a) **Open**   the **Chart of Accounts**

b) **Double click** the **account with the error** to open the account's register

c) **Click**   the **transaction that is incorrect** to select it

d) **Choose**   the **Edit menu** and **click Delete Deposit**, **Delete Cheque**, or **Delete General Journal**. (The menu item will change according to the type of account you have selected)

e) **Click**   **OK** when asked to confirm the deletion

f) **Close**   the **register** to return to the Chart of Accounts

g) **Close**   the **Chart of Accounts**

Sales Taxes

Changing Tax Preferences

The settings for sales taxes can be found on the Company Preferences tab of the Sales Tax heading in QuickBooks preferences.

1. **Choose**	the **Edit menu** and **click Preferences**
2. **Click**	the **Sales Tax heading** on the left-hand side of the screen. There are no personal preferences on the My Preferences tab for sales taxes
3. **Click**	the **Company Preferences tab** to view the screen we need:

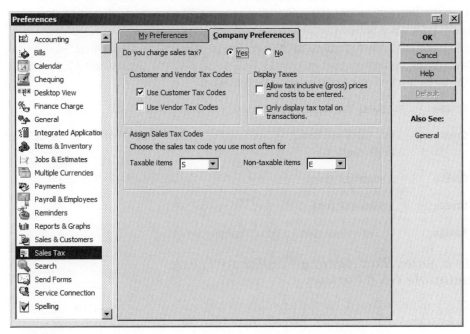

Figure 4-38

The first question on the form — Do you charge sales tax? — is preset to Yes. If no taxes are charged or tracked, you can choose No and the remaining options will be dimmed and unavailable. All prices can be recorded with taxes included.

Use this screen to determine if you want QuickBooks to use the sales tax codes entered in customer and vendor records instead of the sales tax codes assigned to items when entering transactions. You can also determine how sales taxes will be displayed on forms. You can select to display the amount on forms to include tax and/or you can select to display only one sales tax total on forms instead of separate provincial and federal tax amounts. You can save time when entering items by selecting the default tax code to be used for new taxable and non-taxable items.

River Run is not registered for GST or PST. As a registered charity, however, River Run is eligible for a rebate of 50 percent of all GST paid on purchases. Therefore, we do need to set up the GST so that GST paid can be tracked. The request for a rebate is filed annually.

4. **Click**	**Yes** beside the question **Do you charge sales tax?**
5. **Click**	**OK** to close the Company Preferences window and return to the Home page

Defining a New Sales Tax

When you set up a company file, QuickBooks automatically sets up a list of common sales tax codes, sales tax agencies, and sales tax liability accounts based on the province selected for your company. If your company charges the standard taxes for your province, then you can use these tax codes without making changes. However, if you have other taxes that you need to set up, such as a tire tax or a hotel tax, or if you have a variation on the standard taxes, you need to manually add additional vendors, tax items, tax groups, and tax codes.

River Run does not require registration or collection of GST but receives a partial rebate of GST paid. The charity submits an application for refunds annually, listing the total of all GST paid toward its operating expenses. Fifty percent of this amount is eligible for the rebate. Therefore, River Run records GST paid on all purchases and debits these amounts to the *Non-refundable GST Expense* account. The rebate application is for 50 percent of this amount, leaving 50 percent as an expense. *GST Refund Receivable* is debited to record the rebate request until the refund is received and deposited.

When setting up new a new tax to track GST at 2.5 percent eligible and 2.5 percent ineligible, there are five steps that need to be followed:

1.	**Create**	a **Sales Tax Agency vendor** to track the ineligible GST portion
2.	**Create**	**two sales tax items** — one for GST @ 2.5% eligible and one for GST @ 2.5% ineligible
3.	**Create**	a **sales tax group**
4.	**Create**	a **sales tax code**
5.	**Assign**	the **sales tax code** to your expense accounts

Create a Sales Tax Agency Vendor to Track the Ineligible GST Portion

The GST is remitted to the Receiver General, which is automatically set up by QuickBooks at the current rate of 5 percent. In order to set up the GST to keep track of the GST rate of 2.5 percent refundable and 2.5 percent non-refundable, we must first set up a sales tax agency vendor to track the non-refundable GST that cannot be claimed as an input tax credit on your GST return.

1.	**Click**	the **Vendors icon** on the Icon bar

Notice that there is a vendor called Receiver General. This vendor was set up by QuickBooks when you created the company file and keeps track of the 5 percent GST that can be claimed as an input tax credit on your GST return.

2.	**Click**	the **New Vendor button** and **click New Vendor**
3.	**Click**	the **check box** beside **Do not display this message in the future** on the Add/Edit Multiple List Entries window
4.	**Click**	**OK**
5.	**Type**	**Receiver General Non-Taxable** in the **Vendor Name field**
6.	**Click**	the **Vendor is a Sales Tax Agency check box** on the right-hand side of the screen
7.	**Click**	the **Tax Agency Info tab**
8.	**Click**	on the **drop-down arrow** beside the **Tax Return field**
9.	**Select**	**GST/HST Return**

📄 **Notes**
We are only entering one new vendor, so we will not be using this new feature in QuickBooks 2012.

10.	**Type**	**GST Non-refundable** in the **Tax Label field**
11.	**Click**	the **Track tax on purchases separately to check box** and press (tab)
12.	**Type**	**Non-refundable GST Expense** in the **Account field** and **press** (enter)
13.	**Click**	the **Set Up button** in the **Account Not Found message**
14.	**Click**	the **drop-down arrow** in the **Account Type field**
15.	**Select**	**Expense**
16.	**Click**	**Save & Close**

17. The Tax Agency Info tab for the vendor should contain the following information:

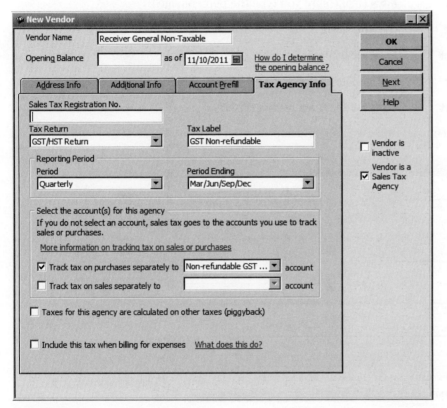

Figure 4-39

18. **Click**   **OK**

The Receiver General Non-Taxable should now be displayed on the Vendors list.

19. **Close**   the **Vendor Centre**

Create Sales Tax Items

Next, we have to create two sales tax items that make up the 5 percent GST tax rate. One item will track the GST @ 2.5 percent that is claimable on the GST Return, while the other will track the portion of GST @ 2.5 percent that is not claimable on the GST Return.

1. **Choose**   **Lists** and **click Item List**

The items that are currently listed on the item list are tax items that were set up automatically by QuickBooks when you set up the company file. You also use the item list to add items that you buy and sell. Later in the chapter, we'll add items that we sell.

First, we'll enter the tax item that will track the 2.5 percent of GST that is claimable on the GST Return.

2.	**Click**	the **Item button** and **click New**
3.	**Choose**	**Sales Tax Item** as the Type (we'll talk more about item types later)
4.	**Type**	**GST Eligible 2.5%** in the **Sales Tax Name field**
5.	**Press**	(tab)

The sales tax name is automatically entered in the description field.

6.	**Press**	(tab) to advance to the Tax Rate (%) or Amt field
7.	**Type**	**2.5%** (make sure you type the percent sign)
8.	**Click**	the **drop-down arrow** under the **Tax Agency field**
9.	**Select**	**Receiver General**
10.	**Click**	the **drop-down arrow** beside the Sales Tax Return Line
11.	**Select**	**Line 106 Input tax credits (ITCs)**
12.	The completed tax item should appear as shown:	

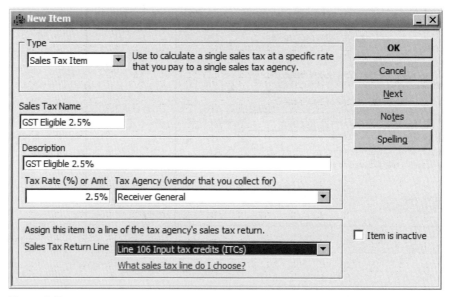

Figure 4-40

📄 **Notes**

To turn off the spell check feature, choose Edit and click Preferences. Click on the Spelling heading on the left-hand side of the screen and uncheck the box for the *Always check spelling before printing, saving, or sending supported forms* option.

13.	**Click**	**OK**

If the Spell Check window is displayed, use it to check your work.

Next, we'll enter the tax item that will track the 2.5 percent of GST that is not claimable on the GST Return.

1.	**Click**	the **Item button** and **click New**
2.	**Choose**	**Sales Tax Item** as the Type
3.	**Type**	**GST Ineligible 2.5%** in the **Sales Tax Name field**
4.	**Press**	(tab)

The sales tax name is automatically entered in the description field.

5.	**Press**	(tab) to advance to the Tax Rate (%) or Amt field

6.	**Type**	**2.5%** (make sure you type the percent sign)
7.	**Click**	the **drop-down arrow** under the **Tax Agency field**

The following selection is very important and is what differentiates the GST from being eligible or ineligible.

8.	**Select**	**Receiver General Non-Taxable**
9.	**Click**	the **drop-down arrow** beside the Sales Tax Return Line
10.	**Select**	**Line 106 Input tax credits (ITCs)**
11.		The completed tax item should appear as shown:

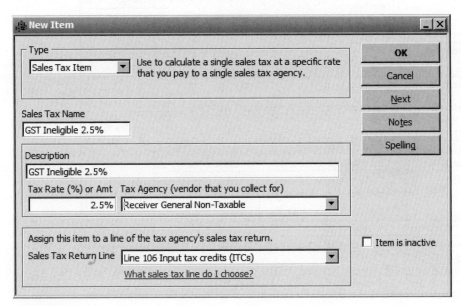

Figure 4-41

12.	**Click**	**OK**

If the Spell Check window is displayed, use it to check your work.

Create a Sales Tax Group

Sales tax groups are used to group sales tax items that are needed on individual sales or purchase transactions. A sales tax group must be created that contains the two GST tax items that you just added.

After you create a sales tax group, you assign it to a sales tax code. When you enter a bill from a vendor that contains GST only, you will select the sales tax code that represents the two GST tax codes to use on the bill.

1.	**Choose**	**Lists** and **click Item List** if you are not already on the Item list from the previous exercise
2.	**Click**	the **Item button** and **click New**
3.	**Choose**	**Sales Tax Group** as the Type
4.	**Type**	**GST Eligible/Ineligible** in the **Group Name/Number field**
5.	**Press**	(tab) to advance to the Tax Item column
6.	**Click**	the **drop-down arrow** in the **Tax Item field**
7.	**Select**	**GST Eligible 2.5%**

📄 **Notes**
Enter an easily identifiable name as the group name.

Notice the information entered on the screen. You can view the Rate, Tax Agency, and Description for the selected Tax Item.

8.	**Click**	the **drop-down arrow** on the second line under the **Tax Item field**
9.	**Select**	**GST Ineligible 2.5%**

10. The Sales Tax Group should be displayed as shown:

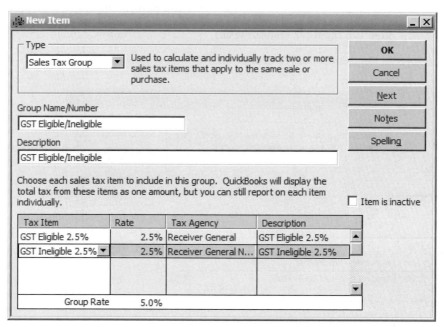

Figure 4-42

11.	**Click**	**OK** if the Spell Check window is displayed

River Run also purchases items from vendors that contain both GST (2.5 percent eligible and 2.5 percent ineligible) and PST. Therefore, we need to create one more sales tax group that will contain all three taxes.

The Item list must be open to perform the following steps:

1.	**Click**	the **Item button** and **click New**
2.	**Choose**	**Sales Tax Group** as the Type
3.	**Type**	**GST Eligible/Ineligible & PST** in the **Group Name/Number field**
4.	**Press**	⌨(tab) to advance to the Tax Item column
5.	**Click**	the **drop-down arrow** in the **Tax Item field**
6.	**Select**	**GST Eligible 2.5%** as the first tax item
7.	**Select**	**GST Ineligible 2.5%** as the second tax item
8.	**Select**	**PST (MB) on purchases** as the third tax item

9. The Sales Tax Group should be displayed as shown:

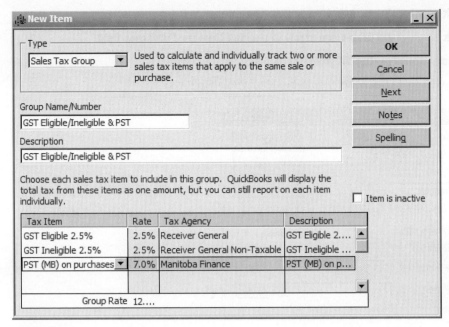

Figure 4-43

10. **Click**   **OK** to save the new Sales Tax Group and return to the Item list

11. **Close**   the **Item list**

Create a Sales Tax Code

Next, we have to add sales tax codes and assign the sales tax groups we just created to them.

1. **Choose**   **Lists** and **click Sales Tax Code List** to display the Sales Tax Code List:

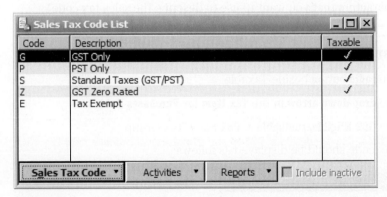

Figure 4-44

These are the default sales tax codes that were automatically created by QuickBooks when you set up the company file. Sales Tax Codes are used to determine the taxes calculated when entering customer sales transactions and vendor bills.

2. **Click**   the **Sales Tax Code button** and **click New**

3. **Type**   **GEI** in the **Sales Tax Code field** (this can be a maximum of any three characters that you want to use to describe the sales tax code)

4. **Press**   ⌨ *tab* to advance to the description field

5. **Type**   **GST Eligible/Ineligible**

> **Notes**
> You can use any three characters you want to create your sales tax code. We used GEI to represent GST Eligible/ Ineligible.

6. **Click**   the **radio button** beside Taxable

7. **Click**   the **drop-down arrow** in the **Tax Item for Purchases field**

8. **Select**   the **GST Eligible/Ineligible** Sales Tax Group

9. The GEI sales tax code should be displayed as follows:

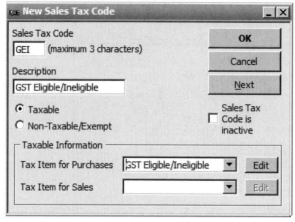

Figure 4-45

10. **Click OK**

11. **Click** the **Sales Tax Code button** and **click New**

We need to create another sales tax code that not only includes the eligible and ineligible GST but must also include PST. Consider a bill from a vendor that contains both GST and PST. We want to track the GST correctly (2.5 percent eligible and 2.5 percent ineligible), but we also need to include PST. The only way to do this is to create another sales tax code that includes all three sales tax items.

12. **Type**   **GP** in the **Sales Tax Code field** (this can be a maximum of any three characters that you want to use to describe the sales tax code)

13. **Press**   (tab) to advance to the Description field

14. **Type**   **GST Eligible/Inelible and PST**

15. **Click**   the **radio button** beside Taxable

16. **Click**   the **drop-down arrow** in the **Tax Item for Purchases field**

17. **Click**   the **GST Eligible/Ineligible & PST** Sales Tax Group

18. The GP sales tax code should be displayed as follows:

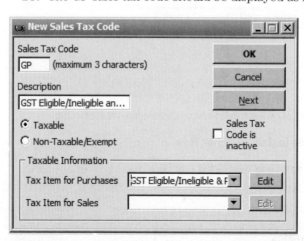

Figure 4-46

| 19. | Click | OK |
| 20. | Close | the **Sales Tax Code list** |

Assigning Sales Tax Codes to Expense Accounts

The last step when setting up taxes is to assign sales tax codes to accounts. When we set up the expense accounts earlier, if the sales tax codes were set up correctly, we could have assigned the sales tax codes at that time. Now that the sales tax codes have been set up correctly, we will go back and assign the sales tax codes to the expense accounts.

We will edit the accounts from the Chart of Accounts window.

1.	Choose	**Company** and then **click Chart of Accounts**
2.	Right-click	**Office Rent** and **click Edit Account**
3.	Click	the **drop-down arrow** in the **Sales Tax Code field**
4.	Click	**GEI**

When we receive a bill for rent, we are charged GST only. We will use the GEI sales tax code because it has been set up to track 2.5 percent of the GST as eligible and the other 2.5 percent of the GST as ineligible.

| 5. | Click | **Save & Close** or ⌐alt⌐ + **A** |
| 6. | Add | the following sales tax codes to the following accounts: |

Name	Tax Code
Printing & Copying	GP
Publicity & Promotion	GEI
Telephone Expense	GP

| 7. | Close | the **Chart of Accounts** |

Notes
The G sales tax code has been set up automatically by QuickBooks to track 5 percent of the GST as eligible.

Notes
The GEI sales tax code has been set up to track 2.5 percent of the GST as eligible and the other 2.5 percent as ineligible.

Notes
The GP sales tax code has been set up to track 2.5 percent of the GST as eligible and the other 2.5 percent ineligible and includes 7 percent PST

Notes
The S code is set up automatically by QuickBooks to track 5 percent of the GST as eligible and includes 7 percent PST

Creating Customer Accounts

As we have seen in earlier chapters, customer records can be entered from any customer field in the program. Although we could use this approach to add customers as needed, it is more efficient to start with a list of existing customers. Even though we will create only skeletal customer records, we will create the records at the start so that we can add the payment terms and method of payment as defaults.

As with many other activities in QuickBooks, customers can be added in many ways. Other than starting in a Customer:Job field on a form, all other methods begin from the Customers & Jobs list. This list can be viewed in the Customer Centre, which can be accessed in several ways:

| a) | Click | the **Customers icon** on the Icon bar: |

Figure 4-47

OR

b) **Click** the **Customers icon** in the Customers section of the Home page:

Figure 4-48

OR

c) **Click** the **Customers menu** and **select Customer Centre**:

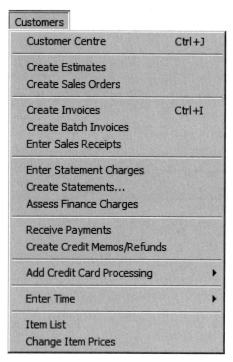

Figure 4-49

OR

d) **Press** (ctrl) + **J**

1. **Open** the **Customers & Jobs list** by using one of the options listed above

You will notice that there are no customers on the Customers & Jobs list because we have not yet created them.

2. **Click** the **New Customer & Job button** to display the menu and **click New Customer** as shown here or **press** (ctrl) + **N**:

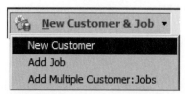

Figure 4-50

Pressing (ctrl) + **N** will open a new form in the current list once the list is displayed on the screen. The other keyboard shortcuts are also the same from one list to another. To edit a record, click (ctrl) + **E**; and to delete a record, click (ctrl) + **D**.

A blank New Customer form is displayed:

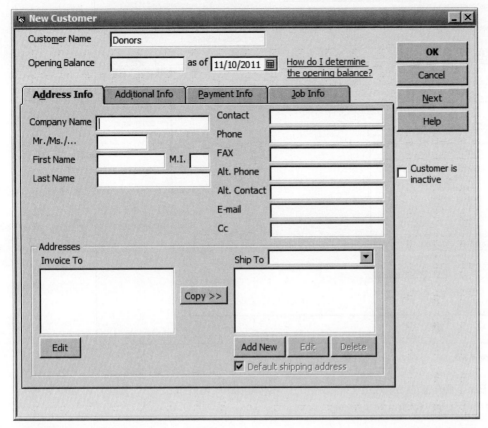

Figure 4-51

Notes
The date displayed in the as of field on this screen will be your current computer date and will not be the same as the one shown in Figure 4-51.

The cursor is in the Customer Name field where you add the customer's name.

3. Type   **Donors**

The date in the *as of* field on this form applies only to customers with outstanding invoices, so you do not need to change it.

Since this customer record will be used for all donors and not a specific donor, the address and contact information will be left blank.

4. Click   the **Additional Info tab** to access the fields on this tab

On this tab we need to add only the customer terms.

5. Click   the **drop-down arrow** in the **Terms field** to view the default payment terms:

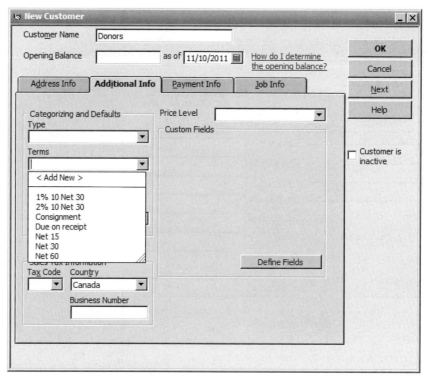

Figure 4-52

River Run accepts only cash from its participants and sponsors. Later, we will delete the terms that we do not use.

6. Click   **Due on receipt** to add the term to the customer record

7. Click   the **Payment Info tab** to access the fields on this tab

8. Click   the **drop-down arrow** in the **Preferred Payment Method field** to view the payment methods:

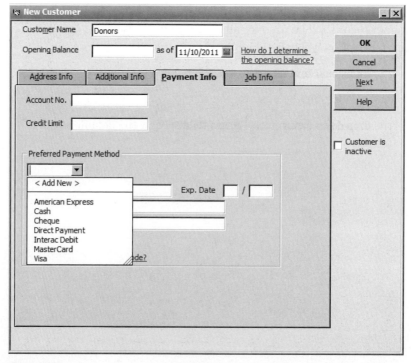

Figure 4-53

Again, these payment methods were created automatically by the program, and we will edit the list later. All customers pay cash.

9. **Click**   **Cash**

The fourth tab, Job Info, allows you to organize the work done for customers according to specific jobs. This allows you to track the work done for customers in a more detailed way. When jobs are set up, you can choose the Customer and Job from the Customers & Jobs list. Customer jobs do not apply to River Run.

CORRECTING CUSTOMER RECORDS

Before Saving the Record

To correct a record while you are creating it, just return to the field that has the error, highlight the incorrect details, and type the correction. Click the Address Info tab and Additional Info tab to return to those tabs to check your work. If the terms code is incorrect, select the correct terms code from the list to replace the incorrect one selected.

After Saving the Record

If you need to make corrections or changes later, open the Customers & Jobs List. Click the customer name to select it. With the customer selected, there are a number of ways to open the customer record for editing. You can right click the customer name and select Edit Customer:Job, you can double click the customer name, you can select Edit from the menu and then select Edit Customer:Job, or you can use the keyboard shortcut ⌈ctrl⌉ + E. With the customer record open, find the incorrect details and make the correction. Click OK to save the changes and return to the Customer:Job List.

---

10. **Check**   **your work** carefully

11. **Click**   ⌈alt⌉ + **N** or **click Next** to save the record and display a blank customer record form

12. **Enter**   the **name**, **terms**, and **method of payment** for Runners, the second customer record. Refer to page 141 for details

13. **Click**   **OK** to save the last customer record and return to the Customer Centre

Your new customers are displayed in the Customers & Jobs list on the left-hand side of the screen in the Customer Centre.

14. **Close**   the **Customer Centre**

Creating Vendor Records

As with many other activities in QuickBooks, vendors can be added in many ways. Other than starting in a Vendor field on a form, all other methods begin from the Vendors list found in the Vendor Centre. This list can only be viewed in the Vendor Centre, which can be accessed in several ways:

a)   **Click**   the **Vendors icon** on the Icon bar:

Figure 4-54

OR

b)   **Click**   the **Vendors icon** in the Vendors section of the Home page:

Figure 4-55

OR

c) **Click** the **Vendors menu** and **select Vendor Centre**:

Figure 4-56

The Vendors section of the Home page has the minimum number of icons displayed for River Run because we have not indicated that we want to use inventory and Purchase Orders:

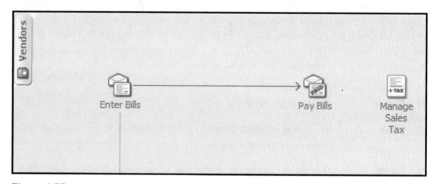

Figure 4-57

We will examine the preferences later to see if any others need to be changed. They do not affect the entry of new vendor records.

1. Open the **Vendors list** by using one of the options listed above

QuickBooks has created records for Manitoba Finance, Ministère du Revenu, and the Receiver General, the tax agencies for the collection of sales taxes. You cannot remove these records, even if you do not collect taxes. We will make the Ministère du Revenu and Manitoba Finance records inactive so they will not appear on our lists.

Notes
The keyboard shortcuts that apply to the Customers & Jobs List also apply to the Vendors List.

2. Click the **New Vendor button** and **click New Vendor** or **press** ⌃ctrl + **N**:

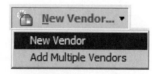

Figure 4-58

A blank New Vendor form is displayed:

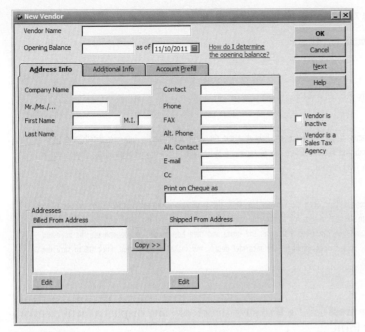

Figure 4-59

📄 **Notes**
The date displayed in the as of field on this screen will be your current computer date and will not be the same as the one shown in Figure 4-59.

All vendors require immediate payment, so we will create only partial records for vendors that contain names and payment terms.

The cursor is in the Vendor Name field where you add the vendor's name.

3. Type   Bell Canada

As in customer records, the date in the *as of* field on the vendor form applies only to vendors with outstanding bills, so you do not need to change it.

4. Click   the Additional Info tab to view the fields on that tab

5. Click   the drop-down arrow in the **Terms field** to view the predefined list of terms:

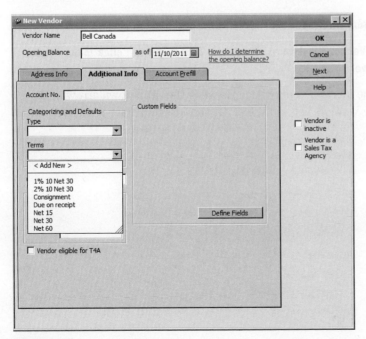

Figure 4-60

All vendors demand payment upon receipt of goods or invoice.

6. **Click**   **Due on receipt**

7. **Check**   your **work** carefully

CORRECTING VENDOR RECORDS

Before Saving the Record

To correct a record while you are creating it, just return to the field that has the error, highlight the incorrect details, and type the correction. Click the Address Info tab and Additional Info tab to return to those tabs to check your work. If the terms code is incorrect, select the correct terms code from the list.

After Saving the Record

If you need to make corrections or changes later, open the Vendors List. Click the vendor name to select it. With the vendor selected, there are a number of ways to open the vendor record for editing. You can right click on the vendor name and select Edit Vendor, you can double click on the vendor name, you can select Edit from the menu and then Edit Vendor, or you can use the keyboard shortcut (ctrl) + E. With the vendor record open, highlight the incorrect details and make the correction. Click OK to save the changes and return to the Vendors List.

---

8. **Click**   **Next** or **press** (alt) + **N** to save the record and display a blank vendor record form

9. **Enter**   the **remaining vendor records** on page 141. **Enter** the **name** and **choose Due on receipt** as the term for each vendor

10. **Click**   **OK** to save the last new vendor and return to the Vendors List (**Click Cancel** if you have a blank vendor form open)

Making a Vendor Record Inactive

The Ministère du Revenu and the Manitoba Finance records are not used by River Run, but we cannot delete them because they are tax agencies. We can, however, make the records inactive so they will not be displayed on the Vendors list for selection when we are writing cheques.

1. **Right-click**   **Ministère du Revenu** on the Vendors List

2. **Click**   **Make Vendor Inactive** or **choose** the **Edit menu** and **click Make Vendor Inactive**

If you need to show the inactive vendor records, click the drop-down arrow in the View field at the top of the Vendors list and select All Vendors to display all active and inactive vendors.

Notes
Before you can make a record active again, it must be displayed in the Vendors list.

The inactive vendor records have an X beside them as shown:

Figure 4-61

Once inactive records are displayed in the list, you can select a record and make it active. One way to do this is to highlight the vendor name in the Vendors list and then right-click and select Make Vendor Active, or choose the Edit menu and click Make Vendor Active. Alternatively, when all vendors are displayed, clicking on the "X" in the inactive column to the left of the vendor name will make the vendor active. If there is no "X" in the inactive column, clicking in the column will add an "X" and make the record inactive.

3. Click   the **inactive column beside Manitoba Finance** to add an "X" in the column and make the vendor inactive

4. Close   the **Vendor Centre**

Creating Items

📄 **Notes**
   The only alternative to using items for sales is to enter all sales transactions as General Journal entries. However, doing so requires you to make compound entries for each sale and calculate all sales tax amounts.

We have seen that QuickBooks processes all sales by selling items. Revenue accounts are linked to items. Therefore, you must create items to use the program. You cannot access revenue accounts from any of the customer sales forms.

Perhaps because items are central to the way the program operates, you can add records for items from many different places. Just like customers and vendors, you can add items on the fly from any Item field in a form. You can also set up records for items from the Item List that you can access in several ways. To open the Item List:

a)   **Choose** the **Lists menu** and **click Item List**:

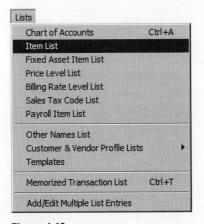

Figure 4-62

OR

b)   **Choose**   the **Sales Tax menu** and **click Item List**:

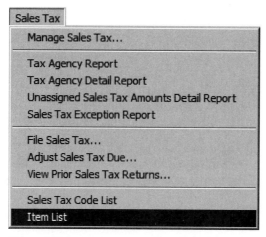

Figure 4-63

OR

c)   **Choose**   the **Customers menu** and **click Item List**:

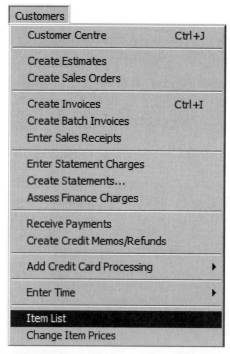

Figure 4-64

OR

d)   **Choose**   the **Vendors menu** and **click Item List**:

Figure 4-65

OR

e) **Choose** the **Items and Services icon** on the Home page:

Items &
Services

Figure 4-66

1. Open the **Item List** by using one of the options listed above:

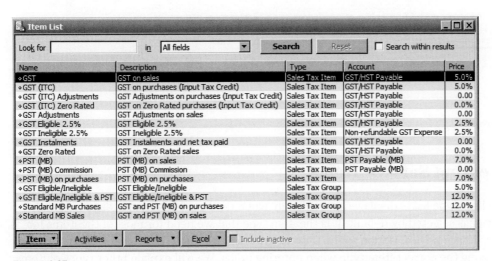

Figure 4-67

2. Click the **Item button** and **click New** as shown, or **press** (ctrl) + **N**:

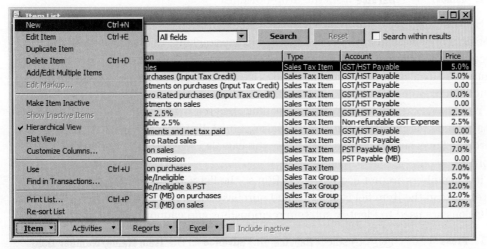

Figure 4-68

📄 **Notes**
Again, we can use the
same keyboard shortcuts for
the Item List as we did for the
Customers & Jobs List and the
Vendors List.

📄 **Notes**
The pop-up menu may
be displayed below the Item
List window depending on
where the Item List window is
displayed on your screen.

A blank New Item form is displayed:

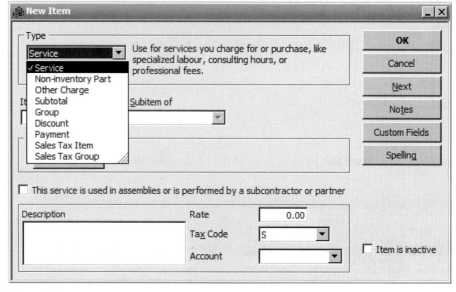

Figure 4-69

Creating Service Items

The item type list is displayed immediately when the New Item form is displayed and Service is selected by default. It is the item type that we need for most of the items for River Run. The description to the right of the selected item type appears to assist you in selecting the correct item type when entering items. We will explain other types of items when we use them.

> **3. Click**   **each type** in turn and **read** the **description**
>
> **4. Select**   **Service** from the drop-down list

Service items are not purchased, held in stock, or tracked as inventory. They are associated only with an income account for income tracking. For each service, you can indicate the item name and/or number, description, default price (rate), tax code, and account. You can change the tax code and price for individual sales, but you cannot change the income account.

You can also set up services under headings by creating a parent item with subitems, just as you do for accounts, but this setup is optional. If the service is used in assemblies or provided by a subcontractor or partner, you can also select that option in the item record.

Item numbers are not used by River Run so the list will appear in alphabetical order on item lists in the Item fields on sales and purchase forms.

Colons are used to identify subitem relationships and cannot be used in item names.

> **5. Press**   (tab) to select **Service** and **advance** to the **Item Name/Number field**
>
> **6. Type**   **Photos**
>
> **7. Double click**   **0.00** in the **Rate field**
>
> **8. Type**   **10**
>
> **9. Press**   (tab) to advance to the Tax Code field

River Run does not apply taxes so the correct option is to leave this field blank.

10. **Highlight**   the **Tax Code field** and **press** (del)

11. **Press**   (tab) to advance to the Account field

12. **Click**   the **drop-down arrow** in the **Account field**

13. **Select**   **Revenue from Sales**

If the account is not on the list, type the account name in the account field and press (tab) to set up the new account. Click Set Up to display the New Account form. Income will be selected correctly as the account type for the new revenue account.

CORRECTING ITEM RECORDS

Before Saving the Record

To correct a record while you are creating it, return to the field that has the error, highlight the incorrect details, and make the correction.

After Saving the Record

If you need to make corrections or changes later, open the Item List. Click the item name to highlight it, then click the Item button and choose Edit Item to open the record for editing. Highlight the incorrect details and make the correction. Click OK to save the changes and return to the Item List.

---

14. **Click**   **Next** or **press** (alt) + **N** to save the item and open a blank New Item form

Notice that the tax code and account number selected in the previous entry are the defaults for this new item (this only applies if you selected the Next button on the screen and did not close the item window and then opened a new window).

15. **Enter**   the **remaining service items** on page 141

16. **Leave**   the **Rate field** blank for Sponsorships

17. **Click**   **Next** after entering Team Registration

Notes
You can choose Service as the type for all items for River Run because it has all the fields we need: name, account, and tax code.

Creating Non-inventory Part Items

The remaining items are inventory items that we do not track individually.

1. **Click**   the **drop-down arrow** in the **Type field**

2. **Choose**   **Non-inventory Part** from the item type list to modify the form:

Notes
Even though food, T-shirts, and caps are inventory items, they are not tracked individually so we enter them as Non-inventory part items.

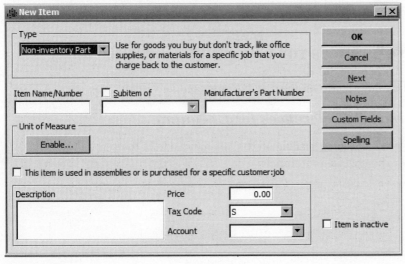

Figure 4-70

3. Read the **Non-inventory Part description** displayed on the form

This type is used for inventory that is not tracked — either items that you sell, items that you make and sell, or items that you buy as supplies. It is also used for items that are reserved for specific customer jobs and charged back to the customer. It has the fields that we need and the same ones we used for service items: item name, price, tax code, and account. We need to delete the default tax code and add the name, price, and account.

4.	**Press**	⌨ tab to advance to the Item Name/Number field
5.	**Type**	**Caps**
6.	**Double click**	**0.00** in the **Price field**
7.	**Type**	**15**
8.	**Remove**	the **tax code** in the **Tax Code field**
9.	**Click**	the **drop-down arrow** in the **Account field**
10.	**Select**	**Revenue from Sales**
11.	**Click**	**Next**

Notice that the Non-inventory Part remains selected as the Item type.

12.	**Enter**	the **remaining two items** on page 141. **Enter** the **Price for T-shirts**. **Leave the Price field for Snacks and Beverages** and **the tax code field** blank, and **choose Revenue from Sales** in the **Account field** for both items
13.	**Click**	**OK** to save the item and **close** the **New Item form**
14.	**Close**	the **Item List**

Changing Preferences

We are now ready to change the remaining QuickBooks preference settings. This involves setting some more defaults and turning off features that we are not using in our company file in order to streamline the appearance of the Home page.

1.	**Click**	the **Edit menu** and **click Preferences** to open the preference window you worked with previously

Changing Preferences for Chequing

Preferences for chequing can be set for personal and company details.

Changing Personal Preferences for Chequing

2.	**Click**	the **Chequing heading** on the left-hand side of the screen to display the cheque preferences

3. Click the **My Preferences tab** if necessary:

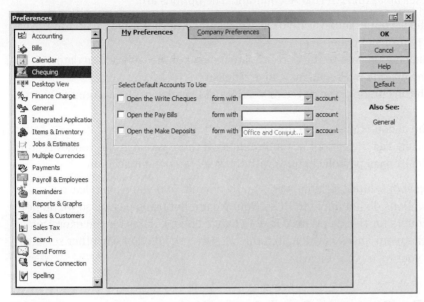

Figure 4-71

From this screen you can choose a default account for writing cheques, paying bills, and making deposits. River Run uses the *Bank - Chequing* account for all these purposes. You must indicate that you want to set a default account for each action, and then choose the account. You can change these defaults at any time.

4. Click **Open the Write Cheques** or its check box to add a ✓

5. Choose **Bank - Chequing** from the account drop-down list

6. Click the **check box** for **Open the Pay Bills** and **Open the Make Deposits Preferences** and **choose Bank - Chequing** as the default account for both

Changing Company Preferences for Chequing

1. Click the **Company Preferences tab**:

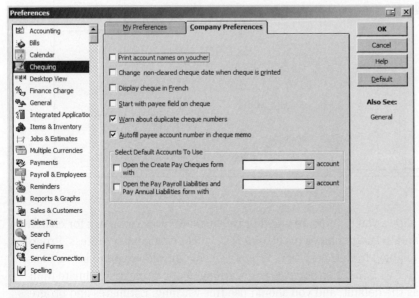

Figure 4-72

The company preferences affect all users and can be changed only by the administrator or a user set up as an External Accountant. The options are:

- **include** the account name (or item) as well as the other information on the voucher part of a cheque
- **change** the cheque date to the current date instead of the transaction date
- **display** the cheque in French instead of English
- **start** with the cursor in the payee or vendor field instead of the account field on forms
- **warn** if the cheque number is a duplicate
- automatically **add** the vendor account number if there is one in the vendor record
- automatically **open** payroll cheques with the selected default account

The warning about duplicate numbers is on by default, and you should leave it on. The remaining options do not apply to River Run. We are not using payroll so we do not need to add accounts for these options. Do not change cheque dates for the exercises in this book so that your answers will match the ones we provide. For the other settings you can choose your own preferences.

Changing Preferences for Jobs & Estimates

River Run does not give estimates, so we can turn off this feature.

1. Click the **Jobs & Estimates** heading on the left-hand side of the screen and **click Yes** to save the previous changes. The company preferences tab is displayed:

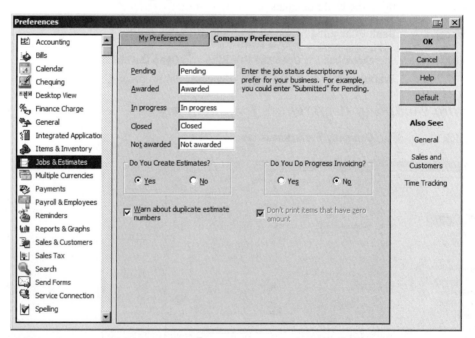

Figure 4-73

This screen allows you to indicate whether the business uses estimates for customer jobs or services and to assign names to the different stages of a job in progress. Progress invoicing is also enabled from this screen. Progress invoicing allows you to invoice customers regularly for work in progress. Again, a warning about duplicate estimate numbers is selected as the default, and you should use this warning. Estimates and progress invoicing do not apply to River Run.

Estimates and progress invoicing appear as questions on the form. We will answer No to the question Do You Create Estimates? This will remove the Estimates icon from the Customers section of the Home page. The option for progress invoicing will become unavailable because it no longer applies.

2. Click   **No** for the question **Do You Create Estimates?**

There are no personal preferences for the Jobs & Estimates preferences.

Changing Preferences for Reports & Graphs

Report preferences can be set for individual and company levels.

1. Click   the **Reports & Graphs** heading on the left-hand side of the screen and **click Yes** to save the previous changes

2. Click   **OK** when told that QuickBooks must close all open windows to apply the change

The company preferences tab for Reports & Graphs is displayed:

Notes
QuickBooks will close all QuickBooks windows that you have open in the background before it can make the changes to the Jobs & Estimates settings.

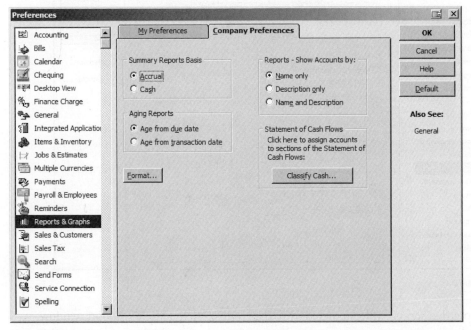

Figure 4-74

River Run uses the accrual basis for summary reports so this setting is correct. We want to use account names only in reports because we have not used descriptions for all accounts. If you want, you can add both name and descriptions to reports. Aging periods do not apply because all transactions are cash and no account terms are offered. In other data files, we age reports from the transaction date.

The Format button allows us to choose a standard format for reports — what headings to include, date format, fonts, etc., and the Classify Cash button allows us to decide how accounts should be classified for cash flow reports.

We will change the report format from this window so that the changes will apply to all our reports. Later, you can still modify individual reports if you want. We will add our own name to the report, remove the time from the report, and remove the basis because all reports are accrual based. We will change the format for negative numbers.

3. Click   the **Format button** to open the Report Format Preferences screen

4.	**Click**	the **Time Prepared** and **Report Basis options** to remove the ✓
5.	**Click**	in the **Subtitle field**
6.	**Type**	**Report prepared by {your name}**
7.	**Click**	the **Fonts & Numbers tab**
8.	**Click**	the **In Parentheses** and **In Bright Red** for **Show Negative Numbers options**
9.	**Choose**	**other standard format settings** for the report if you want
10.	**Click**	**OK** to save the format changes

Changing Personal Preferences for Reports & Graphs

1.	**Click**	the **My Preferences tab** to view the personal preferences screen:

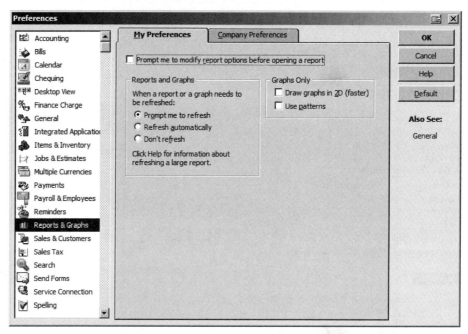

Figure 4-75

From this screen, you can decide whether to display the Modify Report window automatically when you open a report. You can also choose whether reports should be refreshed automatically when you make a change to any of the settings. Graphs can be drawn in two or three dimensions and with or without patterns.

2.	**Click**	**Refresh automatically** under the Reports & Graphs heading
3.	**Change**	**other settings** to suit the way you want to work with the program

Changing Preferences for Sales & Customers

Some of the options for Sales & Customers relate to features that we do not need. They are initially turned on by default.

1.	**Click**	the **Sales & Customers heading** on the left-hand side of the screen to open the Sales & Customers preferences
2.	**Click**	**Yes** to save the changes to the Reports & Graphs preferences

3. The My Preferences tab for the Sales & Customers preferences is displayed:

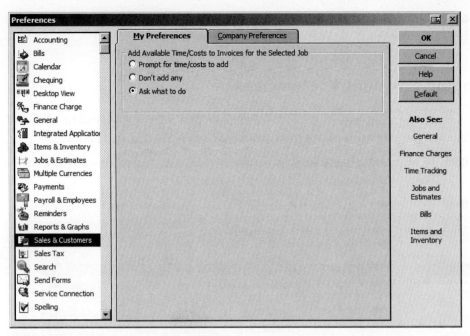

Figure 4-76

River Run does not bill customers for time and costs, so you can leave the Ask what to do option selected.

4. Click   the **Company Preferences tab**:

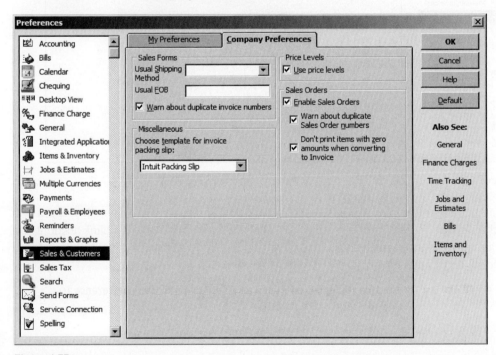

Figure 4-77

Many of these preferences refer to businesses that sell inventory, so most of these preferences do not apply to River Run. Shipping does not apply to River Run, nor do pricing levels; however, duplicate invoice numbers should display a warning. Sales Orders should be turned off, which will remove the Sales Orders icon from the Home page.

5. **Click**	the **Use Price Levels** preference to remove the ✓
6. **Click**	the **Enable Sales Orders** preference to remove the ✓ and dim its related options

Changing Payment Preferences

The preferences on the Company tab of the Payments preferences allow you to determine which payments received from customers are handled in QuickBooks.

1. **Click**	the **Payments heading** on the left-hand side of the screen to open the Payments preferences
2. **Click**	**Yes** to save the changes for the Sales & Customers preferences

3. The company preferences tab is displayed:

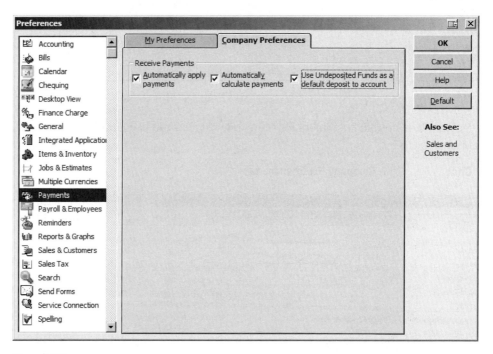

Figure 4-78

Since River Run only accepts cash, we need to be able to select the bank account in the Deposit To field when entering sales receipts. In order to enter a bank account on a sales receipt, we must turn off the Use Undeposited Funds as a default deposit to account on this screen.

📄 **Notes**
You will learn more about Undeposited Funds in Chapter 6.

4. **Click**	the **Use Undeposited Funds as a default to account preference** to remove the ✓

There are no personal preferences for the Payments preferences.

Changing Time Tracking Preferences

QuickBooks allows you to keep track of the time that employees spend on specific jobs for specific customers. River Run does not use time tracking so we should turn it off.

1. Click   the **Time & Expenses heading** on the left-hand side of the screen to access the Time & Expenses preferences (you may have to scroll down the preference heading list to view the Time & Expenses heading)

2. Click   **Yes** to save the changes for the Payments preferences

3. The company preferences tab is displayed:

📄 **Notes**
     If other QuickBooks windows are open, you will be told that QuickBooks must close them to apply the Sales & Customers changes (or the Payments or Time & Expenses changes below). Click OK to accept the warning. If the windows are still closed from a previous change you made, you will not see the message.

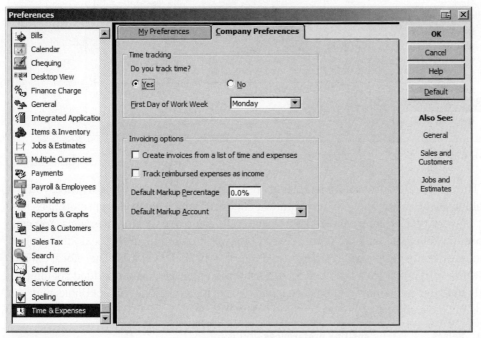

Figure 4-79

4. Click   **No** for the question **Do you track time?**

Changing Spelling Preferences

The final preferences we will examine relate to the QuickBooks spell checking feature.

1. Click   the **Spelling heading** on the left-hand side of the screen

2. Click   **Yes** to save the changes made to the Time & Expenses preferences

There are no Company Preferences for Spelling.

3. Click the **My Preferences tab**:

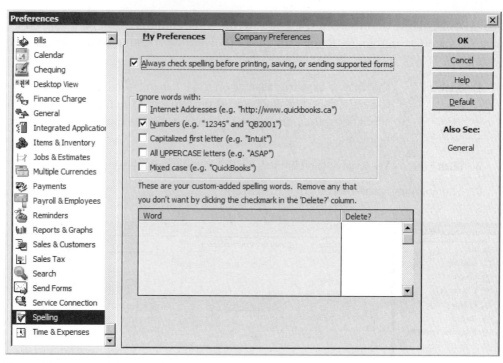

Figure 4-80

The spelling feature is initially turned on. When you use the spelling feature, you should limit the words that the program will check for you. The spelling preferences has a list of word types that are most likely to generate incorrect spelling messages. You can choose to exclude all or some of these word types. For example, in this text and in most businesses, many names will be considered incorrectly spelled words. Therefore, excluding words with initial caps is a good idea. This screen also lists custom-added spelling words that you can add as you perform spell checks in QuickBooks. QuickBooks and TurboTax have automatically been added to the list.

4. Select the **spelling preferences** you want

5. Click **OK** to save all your changes

Other Preferences

The initial default settings for the remaining preferences are correct so we do not need to change any of the settings for them. We will modify some of these preferences in later setup applications.

Editing Lists

When we chose terms and payment methods for vendors and customers, we saw that QuickBooks created a number of list entries automatically. River Run does not need all of these list entries so we should delete the extra ones so they are not accidentally selected during transaction entry.

Editing Terms

1. **Choose**   the **Lists menu**, then **choose Customer & Vendor Profile Lists**, and **click Terms List**

The Terms List is displayed:

Figure 4-81

This list is just like any other list in QuickBooks. From this window, you can create new terms, edit or delete terms, make terms inactive, display a number of reports, etc. The keyboard shortcut commands are the same as for other lists.

Most of these terms are not needed so we will delete them. The only one we need to keep is Due on receipt, the term that applies to cash transactions.

2. **Click**   **1% 10 Net 30** if this is not already selected

3. **Click**   the **Terms button** and **click Delete Terms** or **press** ⌃ `ctrl` **+ D** or **choose** the **Edit menu** and **click Delete Terms** to view the warning message

4. **Click**   **OK** to authorize the deletion

5. **Delete**   the **remaining terms except Due on receipt**

6. **Close**   the **Terms List**

Editing Payment Methods

1. **Choose**   the **Lists menu**, then **choose Customer & Vendor Profile Lists**, and **click Payment Method List**

The Payment Method List is displayed:

Figure 4-82

We can delete most of the payment methods on the list. We want to keep Cash and Cheque.

Notes
All QuickBooks List windows are available from the Lists menu. The only lists that are not available from this menu are the Customers & Jobs List, the Vendors List, and the Employees List. These are available in their respective QuickBooks Centres.

Notes
In other business settings you may want to keep the set of default terms so that you won't need to add them later when new vendors offer different terms from the ones you have entered in QuickBooks.

Notes
The warning message is displayed because the *Warn when deleting a transaction or unused list item* preference is enabled in the General preferences.

Notes
QuickBooks will not allow you to delete the Due on receipt term because we previously applied it to vendor and customer records.

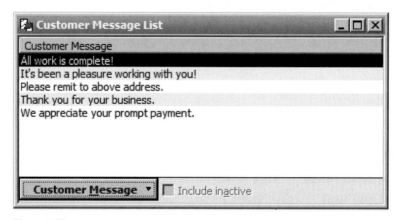

2. Click	**American Express**
3. Click	the **Payment Method button** and **click Delete Payment Method** or **press** `ctrl` **+ D** to view the warning message
4. Click	**OK** to authorize the deletion
5. Repeat	the **above steps** to **delete MasterCard**, **Visa**, **Direct Payment**, and **Interac Debit**
6. Close	the **Payment Method List**

Editing Customer Messages

1. Choose	the **Lists menu**, then **choose Customer & Vendor Profile Lists**, and **click Customer Message List**

The Customer Message List will be displayed:

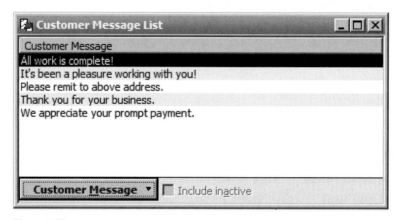

Figure 4-83

We can delete most of the messages on this list because they are not appropriate for River Run. We will keep one message: "Thank you for your business," and edit it to make it suitable for the charity.

2. Click	**Thank you for your business**
3. Click	the **Customer Message button** and **click Edit Customer Message** or **press** `ctrl` **+ E** to open the Edit Customer Message screen:

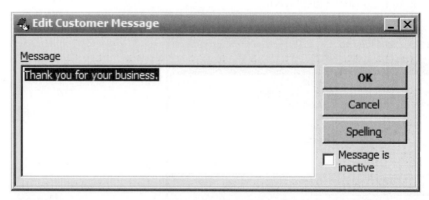

Figure 4-84

The message appears and is highlighted for editing. We will modify the message to "Thank you for your donation. Ask to be placed on our mailing list."

4. **Double click** **business** the last word in the current message

5. **Type** **donation. Ask to be placed on our mailing list.**

6. **Click** **OK** to save the revised message and return to the list

7. **Click** **All work is complete!**

8. **Click** the **Customer Message button** and **click Delete Customer Message** or **press** (ctrl) **+ D** to view the warning message

9. **Click** **OK** to authorize the deletion

10. **Delete** **all other customer messages except the one we changed**

11. **Close** the **Customer Message List**

> **Notes**
> You can also delete the customer message by selecting the Edit menu and then Delete Customer Message.

Checking the Setup

The final step before entering transactions is to make a final check of all the information you entered to verify the accuracy of your work. Although you can make corrections at any time, you should attempt to have a company file that is error free.

1. **Print or display** the **Account Listing** and **Trial Balance dated January 1, 2014**

2. **Review** the **Customer List**, **Vendor List**, and **Item List**

Your reports and lists should match the ones on pages 140–141.

> **Notes**
> Refer to page 84 for help with displaying the Trial Balance and page 120 for help with displaying the Account Listing.

Source Documents

Now that you have set up the company, you are ready to begin entering source documents. You may need to refer to previous chapters for additional information.

When entering the following source documents, be sure to use the sales tax codes that we set up earlier in this chapter to track 2.5 percent of GST as eligible and 2.5 percent of GST as ineligible.

January 1 – January 31, 2014

SD1: **Write Cheque** Dated January 2, 2014

To pay cash for purchase received with Bill #ROP-14-01 from RoofOver Properties for $1,800.00 plus $90.00 GST for office rent for six months. Bill total of $1,890.00 was paid by Cheque #188. Create a new Other Current Asset account: *Prepaid Rent*. Remember to click the To be printed option to turn this option off.

SD2: **Write Cheque** Dated January 10, 2014

To pay cash for purchase received with Bill #WFP-2252 from the Winnipeg Free Press for $1,500.00 plus $75.00 GST for weekly ads publicizing the event to appear in the local newspaper for five months. The bill total of $1,575.00 was paid by Cheque #189. Create a new Other Current Asset account: *Prepaid Advertising*.

SD3: **Write Cheque** Dated January 15, 2014

To pay cash for purchase received with Bill #S-9976 from Staples for $160.00 plus $8.00 GST and $11.20 PST for printing registration and sponsorship pledge forms for participants and sponsors. The bill total of $179.20 was paid by Cheque #190.

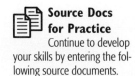

> **Source Docs for Practice**
> Continue to develop your skills by entering the following source documents.

SD4: **Write Cheque**   **Dated January 20, 2014**

To pay cash for purchase received with Bill #BC-10116 from Bell Canada for $50.00 plus $2.50 GST and $3.50 PST for telephone service for one month. The bill total of $56.00 was paid by Cheque #191.

SD5: **Memo #1**   **Dated January 28, 2014**

Pay Charity Spiritus, the event manager (use Quick Add and choose Other as the type of payee), $2,000.00 monthly contract wages. Issue Cheque #192 in full payment. Use the Write Cheques form to pay the event manager contract fee.

February 1 – March 31, 2014

📄 **Notes**
Enter funds raised as Sales Receipts. Remember: you can add a Sales Receipt icon to the Icon bar for easy access to the Sales Receipt form.

SD6: **Funds Raised Form #1**   **Dated February 6, 2014**

Cash received for early registrations from runners.

16 Single registrations @ $25.00 $400.00
11 Team registrations @ $80.00 $880.00

Total $1,280.00 deposited to the *Bank - Chequing* account.

Remember to click the To be printed option to turn this option off and select the appropriate account in the Deposit To field. Add a Sales Receipt icon to the Icon bar.

SD7: **Memo #2**   **Dated February 28, 2014**

Pay Charity Spiritus, the event manager, $2,000.00 monthly wages as per contract. Issue Cheque #193 in full payment. Use the Write Cheques form to pay the event manager contract fee.

SD8: **Funds Raised Form #2**   **Dated March 15, 2014**

Cash and cheques received for early registrations from runners.

28 Single registrations @ $25.00 $700.00
8 Team registrations @ $80.00 $640.00

Total $1,340.00 deposited to *Bank - Chequing* account.

SD9: **Write Cheque**   **Dated March 20, 2014**

To pay cash for Bill #BC-17910 from Bell Canada for $90.00 plus $4.50 GST and $6.30 PST for telephone service for two months. The bill total of $100.80 was paid by Cheque #194.

SD10: **Memo #3**   **Dated March 31, 2014**

Pay Charity Spiritus $2,000.00 monthly wages as per contract. Issue Cheque #195 in full payment.

April 1 – April 30, 2014

SD11: **Funds Raised Form #3**   **Dated April 6, 2014**

Cash and cheques received for early registrations from runners.

38 Single registrations @ $25.00 $950.00
16 Team registrations @ $80.00 $1,280.00

Total $2,230.00 deposited to *Bank - Chequing* account.

SD12: **Write Cheque**   **Dated April 14, 2014**

To pay cash for purchase received with Bill #WA-4200 from Wear Ads for $2,500.00 plus $125.00 GST and $175.00 PST for T-shirts for participants, volunteers, and fundraising. T-shirts are printed with event and sponsor logos. The bill total of $2,800.00 was paid by Cheque #196.

SD13: Write Cheque   **Dated April 15, 2014**

To pay cash for purchase received with Bill #KP-5306 from Kopy Plus (use Quick Add for the new Vendor) for $500.00 plus $25.00 GST and $35.00 PST for printing environmental conservation information leaflets for participants and spectators. The bill total of $560.00 was paid by Cheque #197.

SD14: Write Cheque   **Dated April 24, 2014**

To pay cash for purchase received with Bill #WA-4232 from Wear Ads for $2,400.00 plus $120.00 GST and $168.00 PST for printed caps for participants, volunteers, and fundraising. The bill total of $2,688.00 was paid by Cheque #198.

SD15: Memo #4   **Dated April 30, 2014**

Pay Charity Spiritus $2,000.00 monthly wages as per contract. Issue Cheque #199 in full payment.

May 1 – May 31, 2014

SD16: Write Cheque   **Dated May 1, 2014**

To pay cash for purchase received with Bill #S-18299 from Stitsky's (use Quick Add for new vendor) for $40.00 plus $2.00 GST and $2.80 PST for safety pins to pin number tags on runner participants for identification. The bill total of $44.80 was paid from *Cash on Hand*. (Use *Office & Computer Supplies* account.)

SD17: Funds Raised Form #4   **Dated May 2, 2014**

Cash and cheques received from runners.

52	Single registrations @ $25.00	$1,300.00
22	Team registrations @ $80.00	$1,760.00

Total $3,060.00 deposited to *Bank - Chequing* account.

SD18: Funds Raised Form #5   **Dated May 2, 2014**

Cash and cheques received from donors deposited to *Bank - Chequing* account. Sponsorships $4,800.00.

SD19: Write Cheque   **Dated May 3, 2014**

To pay cash for purchase received with Bill #S-14322 from Staples for $250.00 plus $12.50 GST and $17.50 PST for photo paper and colour printer cartridges. The bill total of $280.00 was paid by Cheque #200.

SD20: Write Cheque   **Dated May 3, 2014**

To pay cash for purchase received with Bill #QAS-4632 from Quarts Arts Supplies (use Quick Add for new vendor) for $190.00 plus $9.50 GST and $13.30 PST for bristol board and paint supplies to make signs to place along running route. The bill total of $212.80 was paid by Cheque #201. (Use the *Office & Computer Supplies* account.)

SD21: Write Cheque   **Dated May 12, 2014**

To pay cash for purchase received with Bill #SFM-3990 from Sobey's for $1,800.00 for zero-rated food and beverages for participants and spectators during event, and $800.00 plus $40.00 GST and $56.00 PST for taxable snack foods. The bill total of $2,696.00 was paid by Cheque #202.

SD22: Memo #5   **Dated May 18, 2014**

From Event Manager: Issue Cheque #203 for $1,500.00 to Charity Spiritus to transfer funds to *Cash on Hand* for miscellaneous expenses during event.

Notes
Choose *Cash on Hand* as the bank account for the purchase from Stitsky's.

Notes

Remember that you can add a General Journal icon to the Icon bar.

SD23: Memo #6   **Dated May 18, 2014**

From Event Manager: Give T-shirt and cap to each volunteer. The cost of T-shirts given out is $240.00. The cost of caps is $210.00. Reduce the *T-shirts and Caps* asset account and increase the *Cost of T-shirts and Caps* expense account.

SD24: Funds Raised Form #6   **Dated May 20, 2014**

Cash and cheques received from runners on day of event.

64	Single registrations @ $25.00	$1,600.00
14	Team registrations @ $80.00	$1,120.00
730	Photos sold to participants	$7,300.00

Total $10,020.00 deposited to the *Bank - Chequing* account.

SD25: Funds Raised Form #7   **Dated May 20, 2014**

Cash and cheques received from donors deposited to *Bank - Chequing* account.
Sponsorships $8,200.00

SD26: Write Cheque   **Dated May 20, 2014**

To pay cash for purchase received with Bill #SFM-4821 from Sobey's for $400.00 for zero-rated food and beverages for participants and spectators during event, and $200.00 plus $10.00 GST and $14.00 PST for taxable food items. The bill total of $624.00 was paid from *Cash on Hand*.

SD27: Memo #7   **Dated May 20, 2014**

From Event Manager: Give T-shirt and cap to each participant. The cost of T-shirts given out is $880.00. The cost of caps is $835.00. Reduce the *T-shirts and Caps* asset account and increase the *Cost of T-shirts and Caps* expense account.

SD28: Funds Raised Form #8   **Dated May 20, 2014**

Cash and cheques received from event spectators. Use Quick Add to add the new customer — Spectators.

180	T-shirts @ $20.00 sold to spectators	$3,600.00
186	Caps @ $15.00 sold to spectators	$2,790.00
	Snacks and beverages sold to spectators	$5,280.00

Total $11,670.00 deposited to *Bank - Chequing* account.

SD29: Write Cheque   **Dated May 20, 2014**

To pay cash for purchase received with Bill #PPH-34982 from Papa's Pizza House (use Quick Add to add the new Vendor) for $270.00 plus $13.50 GST and $18.90 PST for pizza and soft drinks for volunteers. The bill total is $302.40. Paid from *Cash on Hand*. Create new Expense account: *General Expenses*. Choose GP as the tax code.

SD30: Write Cheque   **Dated May 20, 2014**

To pay cash for Bill #BC-30837 from Bell Canada for $90.00 plus $4.50 GST and $6.30 PST for telephone service for two months. The bill total of $100.80 was paid by Cheque #204.

SD31: Write Cheque   **Dated May 30, 2014**

To pay cash for purchase received with Bill #S-21110 from Staples for $140.00 plus $7.00 GST and $9.80 PST for printing receipt forms for participants and sponsors. The bill total of $156.80 was paid by Cheque #205.

SD32: Memo #8   **Dated May 31, 2014**

Pay Charity Spiritus $2,000.00 monthly wages as per contract. Issue Cheque #206 in full payment.

June 1 – June 30, 2014

SD33: Funds Raised Form #9   **Dated June 2, 2014**

Cash and cheques received from sponsors.
Sponsorships $45,460.00
Total $45,460.00 deposited to the *Bank - Chequing* account.

SD34: Funds Raised Form #10   **Dated June 9, 2014**

Cash and cheques received from sponsors.
Sponsorships $9,560.00
Total $9,560.00 deposited to *Bank - Chequing* account.

SD35: Memo #9   **Dated June 13, 2014**

From Event Manager: Issue Cheque #207 for $500.00 to Charity Spiritus to transfer funds to *Cash on Hand* to purchase postage for mailing charitable donation receipts.

SD36: Write Cheque   **Dated June 15, 2014**

To pay cash for purchase received with Bill #CP-2 from Canada Post (use Quick Add to add the new Vendor) for $500.00 plus $25.00 GST for postage to mail receipts. The bill total of $525.00 was paid from *Cash on Hand*. Create new Expense account: *Postage*. Use tax code GEI.

SD37: Memo #10   **Dated June 15, 2014**

From Event Manager: Display the Trial Balance to determine amounts for the GST rebate and adjusting entries. Apply for GST rebate of $287.00. Create a new Other Current Asset account: *GST Refund Receivable*.

Notes
Use the General Journal to record the GST rebate application.

SD38: Bank Debit Memo #TDCT-5218   **Dated June 20, 2014**

From TD-Canada Trust, withdraw $11,330.00 from chequing account to repay loan for $11,000.00 plus $330.00 interest. Create a new Expense account: *Interest Expense*.

SD39: Write Cheque   **Dated June 20, 2014**

To pay cash for Bill #BC-36464 from Bell Canada for $50.00 plus $2.50 GST and $3.50 PST for final month of telephone service. The bill total of $56.00 was paid by Cheque #208.

SD40: Memo #11   **Dated June 30, 2014**

Pay Charity Spiritus $2,000.00 monthly wages as per contract. Issue Cheque #209 in full payment.

SD41: Bank Debit Memo #TDCT-5881   **Dated June 30, 2014**

From TD-Canada Trust, $42.50 in accumulated bank charges for cheques and statement preparation. Create a new Expense account: *Bank Charges*.

SD42: Memo #12   **Dated June 30, 2014**

From Event Manager: Transfer $983.80, balance of *Cash on Hand*, to *Bank - Chequing* account.

Notes
Use the General Journal to record the deposit of balance of *Cash on Hand*. You can also use the Transfer Funds form in the Banking menu, but we have not yet covered it in this text.

SD43: Memo #13   **Dated June 30, 2014**

From Event Manager: Small quantities of supplies were left at the end of the tournament. Leftover food supplies and T-shirts have been donated to women's shelters; craft and some office supplies have been donated to the University's daycare centre. Reduce the following asset accounts and increase the corresponding expense accounts to reflect supplies used during tournament:

Reduce *T-shirts and Caps* and increase *Cost of T-shirts and Caps* by $3,078.00.
Reduce *Food Supplies* and increase *Cost of Food and Snacks* by $3,270.00.
Reduce *Office & Computer Supplies* and increase *Office & Computer Supplies Used* by $503.00.

SD44: Memo #14   **Dated June 30, 2014**

From Event Manager: Enter adjustment for prepaid expenses:
Charge $1,800.00 to *Office Rent* for expired prepaid rent.
Charge $1,500.00 to *Publicity & Promotion* for expired prepaid advertising.

SD45: Memo #15   **Dated June 30, 2014**

From Event Manager: Enter $800.00 as depreciation on computer equipment.
(Click OK to close the message about fixed assets.)

SD46: Memo #16   **Dated June 30, 2014**

Received Cheque #488129 for $287.00 from the Receiver General for GST rebate.
Enter the receipt in the General Journal and deposit the refund to *Bank - Chequing* account.

Finishing Your Session

1. **Back up**   the **company data file**

2. **Close**   the **Company file**

3. **Close**   the **QuickBooks program**

CHAPTER FIVE

$1 Just a Buck

Objectives

After completing this chapter, you should be able to:

- **enter** bills from vendors for purchases
- **enter** payments to vendors
- **edit** vendor transactions before recording
- **create** complete new vendor records
- **review** vendor transactions after recording transactions
- **memorize** recurring transactions
- **find** previously recorded transactions
- **use** memorized transactions
- **edit** memorized transactions
- **enter** receipts for multiple items
- **correct** bills after recording
- **correct** payments after recording
- **print** cheques
- **display** and **print** vendor reports and graphs

Company Information

Company Profile

Just a Buck, located in a busy suburban mall in Winnipeg, Manitoba, is a typical dollar store in terms of the products it sells. However, Luanne (Lu) Nees, the owner, made a decision when starting the business that no item would ever cost more than one dollar. Items that cost less than one dollar are even sold in packages so that the total is always one dollar. This pricing decision makes Just a Buck different from some dollar stores that carry a wider price range of low-cost merchandise.

Notes
Just a Buck
Store 3499, Red Deer Mall
Winnipeg, MB R4T 6C4
Tel: (204) 453-4992
Fax: (204) 453-5882
E-mail: ln@justabuck.com
Web: www.justabuck.com
Business No.: 586 566 490

The store accepts only cash from customers; cheques, credit cards, and debit cards are not accepted, making the sale transactions straightforward.

Nees has accounts set up with vendors, and she writes cheques to pay for the goods she buys. Bills arrive with the merchandise and payment terms vary. Currently, no vendors offer discounts for early payments.

Just a Buck sells both taxable and non-taxable items. The store sells a few canned goods and dried and packaged foods that are non-perishable — these food items are non-taxable. All other store merchandise is taxable and both PST and GST apply. Taxable merchandise includes foods such as candy, chocolate bars, and soft drinks. All non-food items sold in the store, the largest portion of the store's inventory, are taxable. The products are quite varied, including house and kitchenware items (dinnerware, mugs, glasses, cutlery, glass and plastic storage containers, vases) paper products (cards, stationery, wrapping paper, gift bags, decorations), toys (balloons, party favours, small games, toys), and office supplies (pens, paper clips, staplers, tape, sticky note pads, paper, envelopes, glue).

To facilitate tax reporting and entering merchandise sales, the inventory is divided into taxable and non-taxable food items, and other taxable merchandise. Just a Buck pays only GST on its taxable inventory purchases — items that it will sell — because these items are resold and only the final customer pays PST. However, the store pays both GST and PST on other business-related purchases.

The store has very few non-inventory assets other than some store display shelves and computer equipment. The monthly rent for the store includes all utilities except telephone.

At the end of March 2014 Luanne Nees converted her accounting records to QuickBooks. On April 1, the files are ready for data entry in QuickBooks. To convert the records, Nees used the following information:

- Chart of Accounts
- Trial Balance
- Vendor Information
- List of Customers and Items
- Accounting Procedures

Chart of Accounts

Just a Buck

ASSETS
Bank
    Bank Chequing
    Bank Savings

Other Current Assets
    Inventory:Food
    Inventory:Merchandise
    Prepaid Insurance
    Supplies

Fixed Assets
    Computer/Cash Register
    Display Cabinets & Shelves

LIABILITIES
Accounts Payable
    Accounts Payable

Other Current Liabilities
    Bank Loan
    GST/HST Payable
    PST Payable (MB)

EQUITY
    Capital, Luanne Nees
    Drawings, Luanne Nees
    Retained Earnings

INCOME
    Revenue from Interest
    Revenue from Sales

EXPENSE
Cost of Goods Sold
    Cost of Goods Sold

Expense
    Advertising and Promotion
    Insurance Expense
    Interest Expense
    Rental Expense
    Supplies Used
    Telephone Expense

Trial Balance

Just a Buck

AS AT MARCH 31, 2014

	Debits	Credits
Bank Chequing	$ 31,450.00	
Bank Savings	48,690.00	
Inventory:Food	1,800.00	
Inventory:Merchandise	9,400.00	
Prepaid Insurance	6,900.00	
Supplies	550.00	
Computer/Cash Register	6,300.00	
Display Cabinets & Shelves	11,200.00	
Accounts Payable		$ 4,003.00
Bank Loan		14,000.00
GST/HST Payable		407.00
PST Payable (MB)		780.00
Capital, Luanne Nees		86,940.00
Drawings, Luanne Nees	6,000.00	
Revenue from Interest		420.00
Revenue from Sales		41,900.00
Cost of Goods Sold	7,800.00	
Advertising and Promotion	1,500.00	
Insurance Expense	6,900.00	
Interest Expense	420.00	
Rental Expense	9,000.00	
Supplies Used	180.00	
Telephone Expense	360.00	
	$148,450.00	$148,450.00

Vendor Information

Just a Buck

Vendor Name (Contact)	Address	Phone No. Fax No.	E-mail Business No.	Terms Credit Limit
Alert Promotions (Shawna Nues)	64 Publicity Rd. Winnipeg, MB R4X 2P8	Tel: (204) 386-1892 Fax: (204) 386-1900	s.nues@alertpromo.com 453 774 883	net 20 $6,000.00
B & G Imports	450 Red Deer Path Winnipeg, MB R3B 8G6	Tel: (204) 577-6875 Fax: (204) 577-9012	bg@bgimports.com 126 355 472	net 15 $5,000.00
China Wares (Crystal Bowles)	510 Corelle Blvd. Winnipeg, MB R2L 7V4	Tel: (204) 386-3377 Fax: (204) 386-8100	CBowles@chinawares.com 823 453 591	net 20 $5,000.00
Manitel (Oral Speaker)	19 Converse Ave. Winnipeg, MB R2P 6R1	Tel: (204) 577-3481 Fax: (204) 577-3927		net 10 $500.00
Manitoba Finance	125 Fiscal Way Winnipeg, MB R3J 6M9	Tel: (204) 577-0811 Fax: (204) 577-0283		end of month
MK Foods (Mario Kapinski)	1500 Caloric Rd. Winnipeg, MB R4F 6G1	Tel: (204) 387-4500 Fax: (204) 387-5003	MKapinski@mkfoods.ca 488 181 503	net 30 $4,000.00
Receiver General	200 Governors Rd. Winnipeg, MB R2K 8B2	Tel: (204) 384-6186 Fax: (204) 384-5813		end of month
Red River Properties (Red Rivers)	999 Towers Rd. Winnipeg, MB R3C 4D6	Tel: (204) 578-4880 Fax: (204) 578-2833	rr@rrp.com 723 456 199	due on receipt
Universal Liquidators (Leff Tovers)	900 Algone Ave. Winnipeg, MB R3N 8F3	Tel: (204) 386-1990 Fax: (204) 386-2736	lt@getridofit.com 725 912 273	net 10 $4,000.00

Just a Buck

Vendor Name	Date	Terms	Due Date	Bill No./ Cheque No.	Amount	Balance Owing
Alert Promotions	03/20/14	net 20	04/9/14	AP-4992	$ 214.00	$ 214.00
China Wares	03/26/14	net 20	04/15/14	CW-3400	$1,070.00	$1,070.00
MK Foods	03/5/14	net 30	04/4/14	MKF-59902	$ 935.00	
	03/25/14	net 30	04/24/14	MKF-68230	500.00	$1,435.00
Universal Liquidators	03/27/14	net 10	04/6/14	UL-4002	$1,284.00	$1,284.00
				Grand Total		$4,003.00

Customer and Item Lists

Just a Buck

CUSTOMERS

Cash Customers

ITEMS

Food - Non-taxable
Food - Taxable
Merchandise

Accounting Procedures

Taxes: GST and PST

Notes
Refer to the Tax Appendix (found on the CD that accompanies this text) for details on sales taxes.

Just a Buck pays GST on all goods and services that it buys, except the food items that are zero rated. The store charges GST and PST on the sale of all items except the food items that are zero rated. It uses the regular method for remittance of the GST. GST collected from customers is recorded as a liability in the *GST/HST Payable* account. GST paid to vendors is recorded in the *GST/HST Payable* account as a decrease in the liability to the Canada Revenue Agency. The report is filed with the Receiver General for Canada by the last day of the month for the previous quarter, either including the balance owing or requesting a refund.

In Manitoba, PST at the rate of 7 percent is calculated on the base amount of the invoice, which does not include the GST. In this application, PST is applied to all taxable food and merchandise sold by Just a Buck.

Account Terms

All customers pay cash at the time of the sale. Cash received from customers is deposited to the *Bank Chequing* account immediately; it is not held for later deposit.

Accounts are set up with some vendors, and payment terms range from net 30 days to payment due on receipt of goods. However, presently, no vendors offer discounts. All payments are made by cheque.

Items Sold in Store

Separate items were created for taxable and non-taxable food items because they have different tax codes. When food items are purchased, they are combined in the

Inventory:Food asset account. All other items are grouped as Merchandise items for both sales and purchases.

Cost of Goods Sold

The owner counts inventory on a monthly basis to determine the cost of goods sold, and adjusting entries for this inventory are completed at the end of each month.

Instructions

1. Using the Chart of Accounts, the Trial Balance, and other information, you will record entries for source documents for April 2014 by using QuickBooks. You will find the source documents marked with an SD beside them and listed as you work through the chapter. The procedures for entering each new type of transaction are outlined in step-by-step instructions in the chapter. Additional source documents will be provided, allowing you to have more practice entering transactions. If you have used this textbook in the past and would prefer to skip the step-by-step instructions and work only with a list of source documents, refer to the CD in the back of the textbook for the list of source documents for this chapter.

Notes
Instructions for printing Vendors and Payables reports begin on page 255.

2. After you have finished making your entries, print the reports and graphs for April 2014 as indicated on the following printing form.

REPORTS FOR APRIL 2014

Lists
- ☐ Account Listing
- ☐ Vendor Phone List
- ☐ Vendor Contact List

Company & Financial
- ☑ Balance Sheet Standard at Apr. 30
- ☑ Profit & Loss Standard (Income Statement) from Apr. 1 to Apr. 30
- ☐ Expenses by Vendor

Accountant & Taxes
- ☑ Trial Balance from Apr. 1 to Apr. 30
- ☐ General Ledger
- ☑ Journal from Apr. 1 to Apr. 30
- ☐ Transaction List by Date
- ☐ Transaction Detail by Account

Other
- ☐ Custom Summary Report
- ☐ Custom Transaction Detail Report
- ☐ Transaction History
- ☐ Transaction Journal

Vendor
- ☑ Accounts Payable Aging at Apr. 30
- ☑ Vendor Balance
- ☑ Unpaid Bills at Apr. 30
- ☑ Transaction List by Vendor — Apr. 1 to Apr. 30

GRAPHS
- ☐ Income and Expense
- ☐ Net Worth
- ☑ Accounts Payable at Apr. 30

---

3. **Open** the **Buck.qbw** file for Just a Buck

Entering a Bill for Purchases

Entering bills for merchandise purchased on account is similar to entering cheques for cash purchases. However, instead of entering cash purchases and paying the vendors as soon as you purchase the item using the Write Cheques feature as you learned in Chapter 2, you enter the bill and then pay the bill at a later time, thus creating two transactions in QuickBooks.

The first transaction we'll enter is a purchase invoice (referred to as a Bill in QuickBooks). Refer to the following source document as we work through the steps to enter it:

Notes
Vendor invoices are referred to as Bills in QuickBooks. Bills are used primarily throughout this chapter to reflect the terms used in QuickBooks.

SD1: Bill   **Dated April 2, 2014**

Bill #BGI-2118 received from B & G Imports, $825.40 plus $41.27 GST for paper products (merchandise inventory). The bill totals $866.67. Terms: Net 15.

Source Docs
Refer to the following source document and then follow the step-by-step instructions to enter it.

Vendor transactions can be entered from three different areas in QuickBooks:

a. The Vendors section of the Home page:

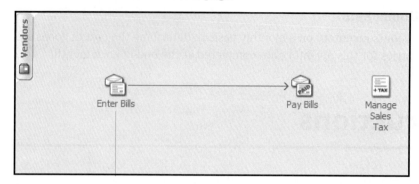

Figure 5-1

Notes
We have hidden the icons for vendor functions that are not used by Just a Buck in the Items & Inventory heading of QuickBooks preferences. These functions will be used in later chapters.
    To access the Items & Inventory preferences, choose the Edit menu, click Preferences, and then click the Items & Inventory icon.

The Vendors section of the Home page is organized like a flow chart that indicates the usual sequence of transactions. For example, after entering bills, the next step is to pay them. We have turned off the items and inventory features that are not used by Just a Buck, so the icons for them are removed from this company file.

From this window, you can also pay sales taxes by using the Manage Sales Tax icon (the Receiver General and Manitoba Finance are listed as vendors for the company), and access the Vendor Centre by clicking on the Vendors icon.

b. The Vendors menu:

Figure 5-2

You can use the Vendors menu to access the Vendor Centre, enter bills, pay bills, use vendor forms, and access the item list.

c. The Vendor Centre:

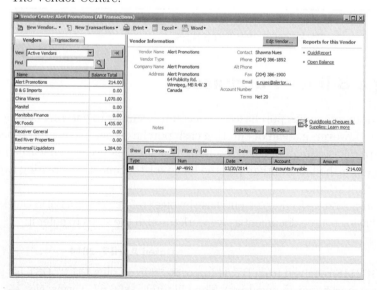

Figure 5-3

The Vendor Centre contains more information and it requires more explanation. On the left-hand side of the screen, you'll see two tabs: a Vendors and a Transactions tab.

When you click on the Vendors tab, the Vendors list is displayed on the left-hand side of the screen, which shows each vendor's name and the total outstanding balance. You can sort the Vendors list by vendor name or balance total and by ascending or descending order by clicking on the list headings.

When you highlight a vendor in the list, the vendor information is displayed in the top right portion of the screen, allowing you to quickly view the vendor address information, click on the Edit Vendor button to access the vendor record where you can make changes to it, click on the QuickReport or Open Balance button to print reports for the vendor, use the Edit Notes button to add notes to the vendor record, or use the To Dos button to add an item on the To Do list for the vendor. The transaction details for the vendor are listed in the bottom right portion of the screen. You can use the headings across the top of the transaction details to select which type of transactions you'd like to view and filter them by a date range.

You can use the buttons across the top of the screen to add a new vendor, enter new transactions, print vendor information, export information to Excel, or print Word documents. The highlighted vendor will automatically be selected when you choose one of these options.

When you click on the Transactions tab, a list of transaction types is displayed. When you click on one of the transaction types, a list of all transactions for all vendors will be displayed based on the criteria selected in the Filter By and Date fields.

As we work through this chapter, we will use various methods to access the vendor transactions.

1. **Click** the **Enter Bills icon** to open the Enter Bills form:

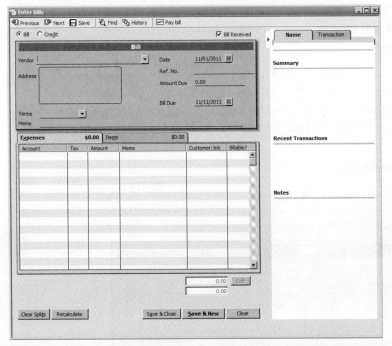

Figure 5-4

Notes
The date displayed on the Enter Bills form when you first open it will reflect your computer's current date.

Notes
We will close the history tab before taking most transaction print screens for this textbook. You can close the history tab by clicking the Hide history arrow in the top left-hand corner of the history tab.

If you want to open the history tab after closing it, click the Show history arrow in the top right-hand corner of the transaction screen.

Notice that this bill form resembles the Write Cheques form, but the cheque details are missing. Completing the bill is also similar to writing cheques for cash purchases. The selection box for Bill Received is checked, and in this example this setting is correct.

The history tab, displayed to the right of the bills form, will display vendor and transaction information for the vendor when one is selected for the transaction. This tab can be closed by clicking on the Hide history arrow in the top left-hand corner of the tab.

2. **Click**   the **drop-down arrow** in the **Vendor field** to view the list of vendors in the Vendors list:

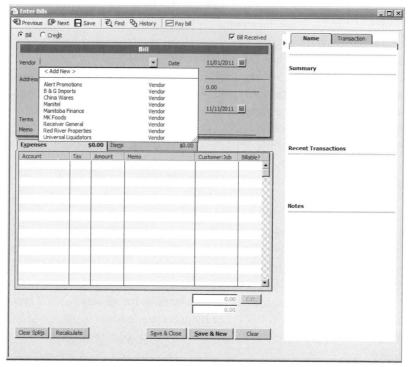

Figure 5-5

 Notes
  If merchandise arrives before the bill, you can uncheck the Bill Received box to receive only the items into QuickBooks. You can receive the bill against the items received at a later time. You'll learn more about this in Chapter 7.

Unlike the Write Cheques Pay to the Order of list that includes all possible payees, the Enter Bills form shows only vendors entered in the Vendors list.

3. **Click**   **B & G Imports**

4. **Press**   `tab`

The vendor's payment terms, net 15 days, are added to the form, and the due date has changed to reflect these terms. The date is highlighted with the current calendar date entered as the default. As in the previous chapter, once we enter transactions, the last date used will appear as the default until the current calendar date changes or you close the company data file.

Notes
  When you press `tab` to enter the vendor on the bill, the vendor information and recent transactions are displayed in the history tab.

5. **Type**   **04/02/14**

6. **Press**   `tab` to enter the transaction date and revise the due date. It is now 15 days past the transaction date as shown in the following cheque portion of the form:

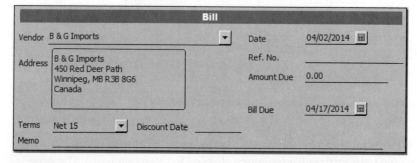

Figure 5-6

Notes
  The Amount Due field in the cheque portion of the form will be updated when we enter expense accounts in the account portion of the form.

The next steps are the same as they are when writing cheques. We need to add the bill number from the vendor so that it will be added to the journal records. Then we will enter the account, tax code, and memo.

7.	**Type**	**BGI-2118** in the **Ref. No. field**
8.	**Click**	the **Account field** to display the drop-down arrow
9.	**Click**	the **drop-down arrow** in the **Account field** to view the list of accounts available in the Chart of Accounts

As usual for purchases, the list displays all the expense accounts. If you have a lot of expense accounts, the list begins at the expense accounts. If you have a small number of expense accounts, the list displays other accounts together with the expense accounts. We need to choose an asset account for the purchase.

10.	**Click**	the **up scroll arrow** ▲ to view the asset accounts
11.	**Click**	**Merchandise** under the Inventory subheading to select the account
12.	**Press**	⎡tab⎤ to advance to the Tax field
13.	**Click**	the **drop-down arrow** in the **Tax field** to view the tax codes available for purchases

Businesses do not pay PST on items that are purchased for resale. Only GST applies to these purchases, so the tax code G (GST Only) is needed.

14.	**Click**	**G (GST Only)** to select the code
15.	**Press**	⎡tab⎤ to advance to the Amount field — the amount of the purchase before taxes
16.	**Type**	**825.40**
17.	**Press**	⎡tab⎤ to advance to the Memo field so you can enter a description for the purchase
18.	**Type**	**assorted paper inventory products**

Notice that the total amount of the bill is updated in the Amount Due field in the cheque portion of the form.

Enter additional items, if there are any, in the same way. Click the account field on the second line, choose the account, enter the tax, amount, memo, and so on.

19. Your completed transaction should look like the one shown here:

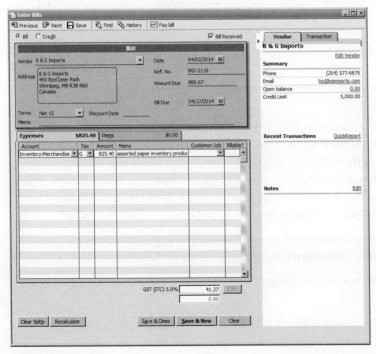

Figure 5-7

Notes
If you discover an error in the transaction later, you can still make corrections. See page 242.

20. **Check** your **work** carefully before recording the purchase so you won't need to make corrections later

We want to review the transaction journal, so we should save the entry without closing the Enter Bills form.

21. **Click** **Save & New** or **press** `alt` + **S** to save the transaction

Reviewing the Transaction

To begin this exercise, a blank Bill should be displayed on the Enter Bills form from the previous exercise.

1. **Click** the **Previous button** [⬅ Previous] or **press** `alt` + **P** to view the bill we just completed

2. **Press** `ctrl` + **Y** to view the Transaction Journal report:

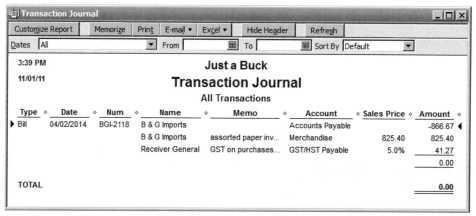

Notes
We have deleted the transaction number, class and item, and item description, columns from the transaction journal report and re-sized some of the other columns by dragging the column heading markers to the desired location in order to display all the important details on the screen. Most of the Transaction Journal reports throughout the textbook have been modified to fit on the page.

Figure 5-8

The only account we entered on the Bills form was the *Inventory:Merchandise* account. QuickBooks has debited this account for the purchase. In addition, QuickBooks has automatically debited the *GST/HST Payable* account to reduce the liability to the Receiver General and increased (credited) the *Accounts Payable* account for the full amount of the purchase. The account for the vendor, B & G Imports, has also been increased as we will see when we display the vendor reports later in the chapter.

3. **Click** [X] when you have finished viewing the report to close the Transaction Journal report and return to the Bill from B & G Imports

The next transaction that we are going to enter is a bill payment, so we should close the Enter Bills form.

4. **Click** [X] to close the Enter Bills form and return to the QuickBooks Home page

Paying Bills

The second transaction that we are going to enter is a cheque paid to MK Foods for items purchased before the date we converted our accounting records to QuickBooks. Refer to the following source document as we work through the steps to enter it:

Source Docs
Refer to the following source document and then follow the step-by-step instructions to enter it.

SD2:   Pay Bill   **Dated April 2, 2014**

> Cheque #197 paid to MK Foods, $1,035.00 in payment of account. Reference Bill numbers MKF-59902 and MKF-68230.

In this transaction, two bills are being paid with one cheque. The first bill is fully paid and the second one is partially paid. Bill payments are entered after bills are recorded.

QuickBooks distinguishes between paying a bill listed as an Accounts Payable and paying for a cash purchase. When you are paying an outstanding Accounts Payable bill —working with vendor accounts — you are "paying bills." When you make cash purchases that are paid by cheque you are "writing cheques."

If you try to pay outstanding vendor bills from the Write Cheques window, you will see the following warning when you choose the vendor:

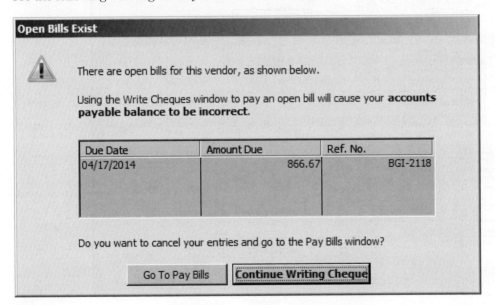

Figure 5-9

The Write Cheques form should be used only for cash purchases — when items are received and paid for immediately. If you select the Write Cheques icon, select a vendor and the Open Bills Exist window is displayed as shown above, click [Go To Pay Bills] to open the Pay Bills window where you can enter the payment to the vendor. Alternatively, you can click [Continue Writing Cheque] to continue writing a cheque to the vendor in the Write Cheques window — ignoring the warning message. You should only ignore the warning message if you are paying a bill that has not been entered in QuickBooks.

Vendor bills are paid on the Pay Bills window, which can be accessed through the Vendor section of the Home page, the Vendors menu, or the Vendor Centre.

The Vendor section of the Home page shows the flow of business activities and in which order they should be performed. As you can see, the Vendors section of the Home page indicates that Vendor bills are paid after the Vendor bills have been entered:

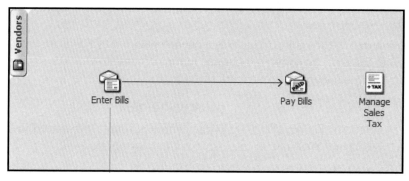

Figure 5-10

Notes
You can add the Pay Bills icon to the Icon bar for quick and easy access to the Pay Bills window.

1. **Click** the **Pay Bills icon** to open this window, or **choose** the **Vendors menu** and **click Pay Bills**:

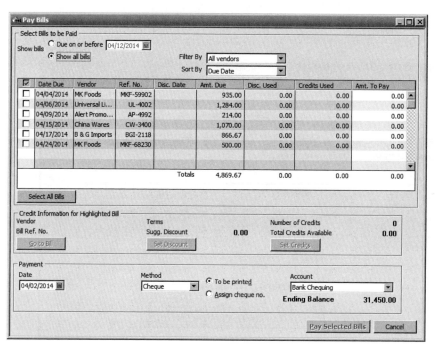

Figure 5-11

The default setting for selecting bills to be paid is to show all bills. With this option selected, all outstanding vendor bills are displayed. Notice that the total amount due displayed at the bottom of the Amt. Due column is $4,869.67. You can also select bills to be paid that are due on or before a specific date. To demonstrate this:

2. **Click** the **button** beside the **Due on or before field**

3. **Type** **04/12/14** in the **Date field** (if necessary)

Notice that some of the vendor bills have been removed from the list. With this option selected, notice the total amount due has changed to $2,433.00. The bills displayed have a due date of April 12, 2014 or earlier.

To show bills due within a shorter period, type an earlier date in the Select Bills to be Paid Due on or before date field. To show more bills, enter a later date in this date field or leave the Show all bills option selected.

We are making a payment toward both bills from MK Foods. Currently, only one of these bills is displayed on the screen based on the date entered in the Due on or before date field.

4. **Click** the **button** beside **Show all bills**

Both bills from MK Foods are now included on the list as the first and last entries. You will have to scroll down the list to view the second bill. You can filter the list to show only bills from MK Foods by selecting them in the Filter By field, or you can change the order of the bills on the screen by selecting a different option in the Sort By field. The default order is by the date that bills are due, a logical choice because bills due first are generally paid before those due later.

5. Click   the **drop-down arrow** in the **Sort By field** to view the sort options:

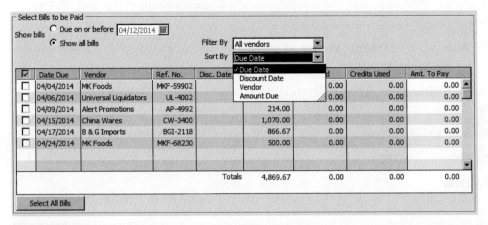

Figure 5-12

6. Click   **Vendor**

Sorting the list by Vendor will place the bills in alphabetic order by vendor name. Bills for the same vendor will appear together on the list. When you are paying several bills for one vendor at the same time, you may prefer to sort the bills by vendor. The two MK Foods bills now appear together in the list.

If you want to view invoices for only one vendor, you can use the Filter By field to select only that vendor.

Notes
If you change the order in the Sort By field, your new selection becomes the default the next time you open the Pay Bills form.

7. Click   the **drop-down arrow** in the **Filter By field** to view the list of vendors:

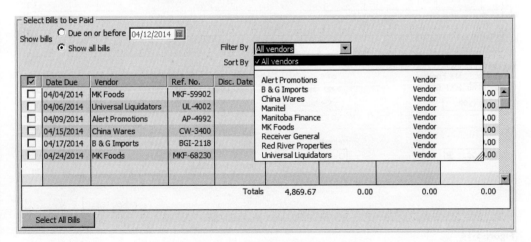

Figure 5-13

Filtering the list for a specific vendor will display only the invoices for the vendor selected.

8. Click   **MK Foods**

Only the two invoices for MK Foods, sorted by Due Date, are displayed on the Pay Bills form.

9. **Click**   the **box** to the left of the first bill from MK Foods to select it for payment

A ✓ (checkmark) is now displayed in the box indicating that it has been selected for payment.

The full amount of the bill is automatically entered in the Amt. To Pay column. You can accept this amount or enter a smaller amount if you want to make a partial payment. We can accept the full amount because this bill is being paid in full.

The payment cheque includes $100.00 as a partial payment for the second bill so we need to select this bill as well and then change the default amount in the Amt. To Pay column.

10. **Click**   the **box** to the left of the second bill from MK Foods to select it for payment

A ✓ (checkmark) will be displayed in the box indicating that it has been selected for payment.

11. **Double click 500.00** in the Amt. To Pay column to select the amount

12. **Type   100** to enter a partial payment

13. **Press**   ⌈tab⌉ to update the totals as shown:

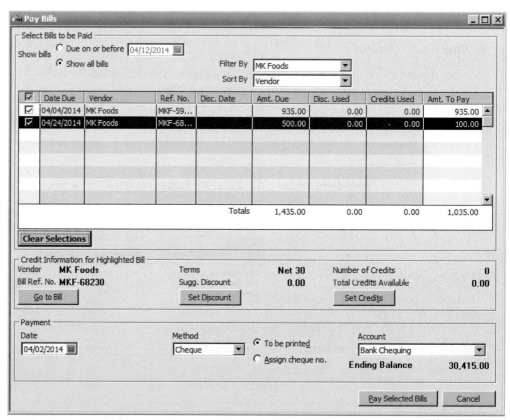

Figure 5-14

Notice that the Ending Balance for *Bank Chequing* is updated to include the payment you are entering.

We are now ready to make the necessary selections on the bottom portion of the screen. The Payment Date should be correct from the previous transaction, unless you have closed the program.

14. Confirm	that the **date** in the **Payment Date field** at the bottom of the form is 04/02/14. **Type 04/02/14** in the Payment Date field if necessary

Cheque is correctly selected as the method of payment, and the default bank account for the payment is correct. These selections are set as default Chequing Preferences for the company data file. If you need to select a different account, you can click on the drop-down arrow in the account field and choose from the list of Bank accounts.

Writing Cheques Manually

We want to prepare the cheque manually and assign the cheque number. If we do not uncheck the To be printed option, the cheque will be added to the list of cheques to be printed (see page 236). You can assign cheque numbers when you print the cheques.

1. Click	the **button** beside the **Assign cheque no.** option

The To be printed option is no longer selected.

2. Click	**Pay Selected Bills** or **press** ⒜ + **P** to continue. The Assign Cheque Numbers screen is displayed:

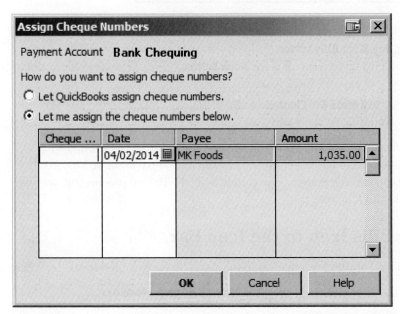

Figure 5-15

Numbers are assigned automatically during printing or manually, based on the selection on this screen. You can accept the next default cheque number and allow QuickBooks to assign it automatically, or you can manually enter cheque numbers for each cheque in the list. When you are paying bills from several vendors at once, you might need to change the numbering sequence to match the numbers on the cheques because you may not have prepared the cheques in the same order as the list in this window.

We need to enter the first cheque number to begin the automatic numbering sequence. Even though we are preparing the cheques manually, we want the numbers to match the ones in the QuickBooks file.

3. Click	the **Cheque No. field**
4. Type	197

If you are not ready to assign cheque numbers yet, you can choose Cancel to return to the Pay Bills window.

5. Click   **OK** to display the Payment Summary screen:

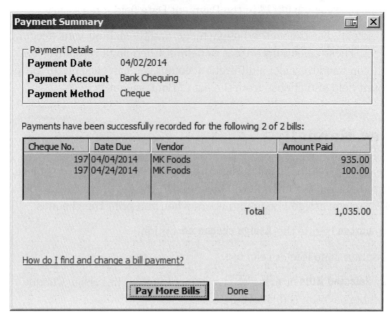

Figure 5-16

You can click the **Pay More Bills button** Pay More Bills to return to the Pay Bills window and pay more bills or you can click the **Done button** Done to close the window.

6. Click   the **Pay More Bills button** Pay More Bills to return to the Pay Bills window

Notice that the first bill from MK Foods has been removed from the list and the amount due for the second bill has been reduced by the partial payment of $100.00. The original bill was $500.00 and the amount due is now $400.00. Before proceeding, we will add a Pay Bills icon to the Icon bar.

Adding a Pay Bills Icon to the Icon Bar

When a form is displayed on the screen, an icon for it can be easily added to the Icon bar.

1. Choose   the **View menu** and **click Add "Pay Bills" to the Icon Bar ...**

Select a new icon to be placed on the Icon bar and accept the default label and description. (We chose the icon that resembles a dollar bill.)

2. Click   **OK** to return to the Pay Bills form

The Pay Bills icon is added to the end of the Icon Bar.

Reviewing the Transaction

We have already saved the payment entry, but we want to review the Transaction Journal report. The Pay Bills form does not have a tool bar. Once a cheque has been written, it must be viewed from the Write Cheques form, just like the cheques we entered for Chelsea's Chocolates in Chapter 2.

1. Click   ☒ to close the Pay Bills form

2. Click   the **Cheque icon** Cheque on the Icon bar to open the Write Cheques form, or **choose** the **Banking menu** and **click Write Cheques**, or **click** the

Write Cheques icon in the Banking section of the Home page

3. **Click** the **Previous button** Previous or **press** _alt_ + **P** to view the cheque we just wrote:

Bill Payments(Cheque) - Bank Chequing

◄ Previous   ▷ Next   💾 Save   🖨 Print ▾   🔍 Find   🗐 History

Bank Account [Bank Chequing ▾]   Ending Balance   30,415.00

No. 197
Date 04/02/2014

Pay to the Order of MK Foods $ 1,035.00

One thousand thirty-five and 00/100* *Dollars

Address
MK Foods
1500 Caloric Rd.
Winnipeg, MB R4F 6G1
Canada

Memo

Order Cheques

Bills paid in this transaction: ☐ To be printed

P...	Date Due	Vendor	Ref. No.	Bill Amt.	Amt. ...	Disc. Date	Amt. Paid
✓	04/04/2014	MK Foods	MKF-59902	935.00	935.00		935.00
✓	04/24/2014	MK Foods	MKF-68230	500.00	500.00		100.00

[Clear Splits] [Recalculate] [Discounts]   [Save & Close] [Revert]

Figure 5-17

This cheque form is different from the ones we saw for Chelsea's Chocolates because this cheque was issued to pay vendor bills. Therefore, the reference or stub portion of the form includes the bills paid by the cheque instead of the account and item purchased with the cheque. Those items appear on the bill and were entered on the Enter Bills form.

4. **Press** _ctrl_ + **Y** to view the Transaction Journal report:

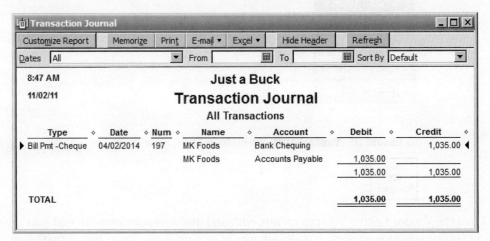

Transaction Journal

[Customize Report] [Memorize] [Print] [E-mail ▾] [Excel ▾] [Hide Header] [Refresh]

Dates [All ▾] From [   ] To [   ] Sort By [Default ▾]

8:47 AM
11/02/11

Just a Buck
Transaction Journal
All Transactions

Type	Date	Num	Name	Account	Debit	Credit
Bill Pmt -Cheque	04/02/2014	197	MK Foods	Bank Chequing		1,035.00
			MK Foods	Accounts Payable	1,035.00	
					1,035.00	1,035.00
TOTAL					**1,035.00**	**1,035.00**

Figure 5-18

Although we did not enter any accounts for the bill payment, QuickBooks created a complete journal entry for the transaction. The *Accounts Payable* account has been debited to reduce the total amount owing to the vendor and the *Bank Chequing* account has been credited or reduced by the amount of the payment. The account for the vendor, MK Foods, has also been reduced as we will see when we display the vendor reports later in the chapter.

5. **Click** to close the Journal Transaction report and return to the Cheque for MK Foods

6. **Click** to close the Bill Payments (Cheque) window

Adding a Complete Vendor Record

For the next transaction, we will be setting up a new vendor and entering a bill. Refer to the following source document as we work through the steps to enter it:

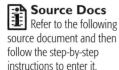
Notes
Bulk Bargains
Contact: Max Cheipe
500 Risquer Blvd.
Winnipeg, MB R3R 7H8
Phone: (204) 459-4990
Fax: (204) 459-6889
Alt. Contact: Asst. Manager
E-mail: mc@bbargains.com
Terms: Net 25
Credit Limit: $3,000.00
Business No.: 345 668 299

SD3: Bill   **Dated April 2, 2014**

Bill #BB-451 received from Bulk Bargains (set up the new vendor), $600.00 plus $30.00 GST for inventory merchandise to be sold in store. The bill totals $630.00. Terms: Net 25 days.

In previous chapters, we added new vendor records by choosing Quick Add after typing a new name on a form. From the Vendor field in the Enter Bills or Write Cheques form, we can also add complete vendor details by choosing Set Up when prompted instead of Quick Add. Choosing the Set Up option allows us to include address details and payment terms so that this information will appear on cheques or bills. You can also add vendors directly from the Vendors List, as we did for River Run in Chapter 4.

The Vendors List can only be accessed from the Vendor Centre.

1. **Select**   **one of the following methods** to open the Vendor Centre:

a) **Click** the **Vendors icon** in the Vendors section of the Home page:

OR

b) **Choose** the **Vendors menu** and **click Vendor Centre**:

OR

c) **Choose** the **Vendors icon** on the Icon bar:

From the Vendor Centre, you can create, edit, and delete vendor records; make an unused vendor record inactive so it does not appear in vendor lists or on forms; find transactions involving a vendor; print lists; and so on.

2.	**Click**	the **New Vendor button** at the top of the Vendor List and **click New Vendor** or **right-click** in the **Vendor list** and **click New Vendor**, or **press** (*ctrl*) **+ N** to open the New Vendor form
3.	**Click**	⊠ to close the Add/Edit Multiple List Entries window
4.	The New Vendor form is displayed as shown:	

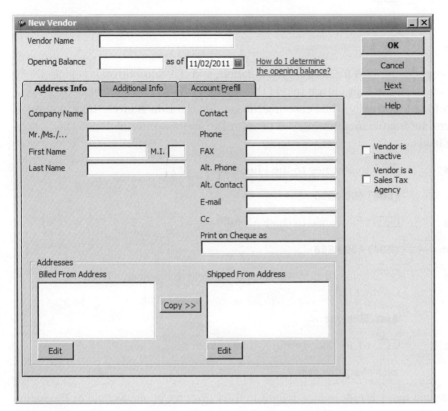

Figure 5-19

The cursor is in the Vendor Name field where you add the name of the vendor.

5.	**Type**	**Bulk Bargains**

There is no opening balance because this is a new vendor. The current date displayed on this form will be the current system date on your computer and will not be the same as the one shown in this print screen. The Opening Balance field and as of fields apply only to historical or opening balance bills.

6.	**Click**	the **Company Name field**
7.	**Type**	**Bulk Bargains**
8.	**Press**	(*tab*) twice to advance to the First Name field
9.	**Type**	**Max**
10.	**Press**	(*tab*) twice to advance to the Last Name field
11.	**Type**	**Cheipe**
12.	**Press**	(*tab*)

The company name and contact name appear in the Billed From Address text area and the name we entered is added in the Contact field. You can enter a different name in the Contact field if necessary. The cursor has advanced to the Billed From Address text box.

Notes
QuickBooks allows you to add historical transactions (transactions that occurred before the date you started using QuickBooks) after you start using the program.

We entered all historical data before entering the current transactions because it is easier to find and correct errors.

Notes
You might want to remove the contact name from the Address field if the name should not appear on address labels.

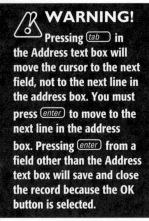
13.	**Press**	(enter) to move to the blank line below Max Cheipe
14.	**Type**	**500 Risquer Blvd.**
15.	**Press**	(enter)
16.	**Type**	**Winnipeg, MB**
17.	**Press**	(enter)
18.	**Type**	**R3R 7H8**
19.	**Press**	(tab)

There are no more lines for address information, and the Edit button is selected. You could have used the Edit button to add the vendor address into specific fields. If you enter the address incorrectly while entering the vendor, the Edit Address Information window opens automatically, allowing you to enter the address information in the appropriate fields.

20.	**Press**	(tab) to advance to the Phone field
21.	**Type**	**(204) 459-4990**
22.	**Press**	(tab) to advance to the FAX field
23.	**Type**	**(204) 459-6889**
24.	**Press**	(tab) twice to skip the Alt. Phone field and advance to the Alt. Contact field
25.	**Type**	**Asst. Manager**
26.	**Press**	(tab) to advance to the E-mail field
27.	**Type**	**mc@bbargains.com**

The company name is entered by default in the Print on Cheque as field as the name that will be printed on cheques. You can edit this name if necessary.

28.	**Click**	the **Edit button** to open the Edit Address Information window:

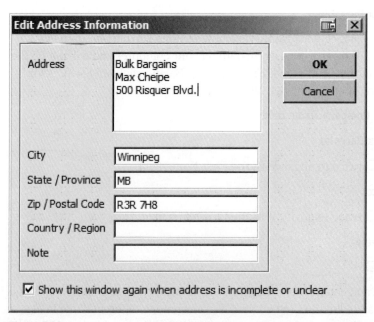

Notes
QuickBooks uses the two-letter abbreviation or code for provinces. The code for Manitoba is MB.

Figure 5-20

This screen has separated the address fields for easier editing. If you need to make changes to the address details later, it is easier to do so from this screen. The address information has been entered in the correct fields but the country is missing.

29.	**Click**	the **Country/Region field**
30.	**Type**	**Canada**
31.	**Press**	$\boxed{tab}$ to advance to the Note field. This note will be added to address labels so it should be used only for address clarification details
32.	**Click**	**OK** to return to the New Vendor form. The address is now complete
33.	**Click**	the **Additional Info tab**:

📄 **Notes**
If you want to add a general note for the vendor, save the record and then open it for editing. A Notes button will be available in the vendor record so you can add a note to the vendor record.

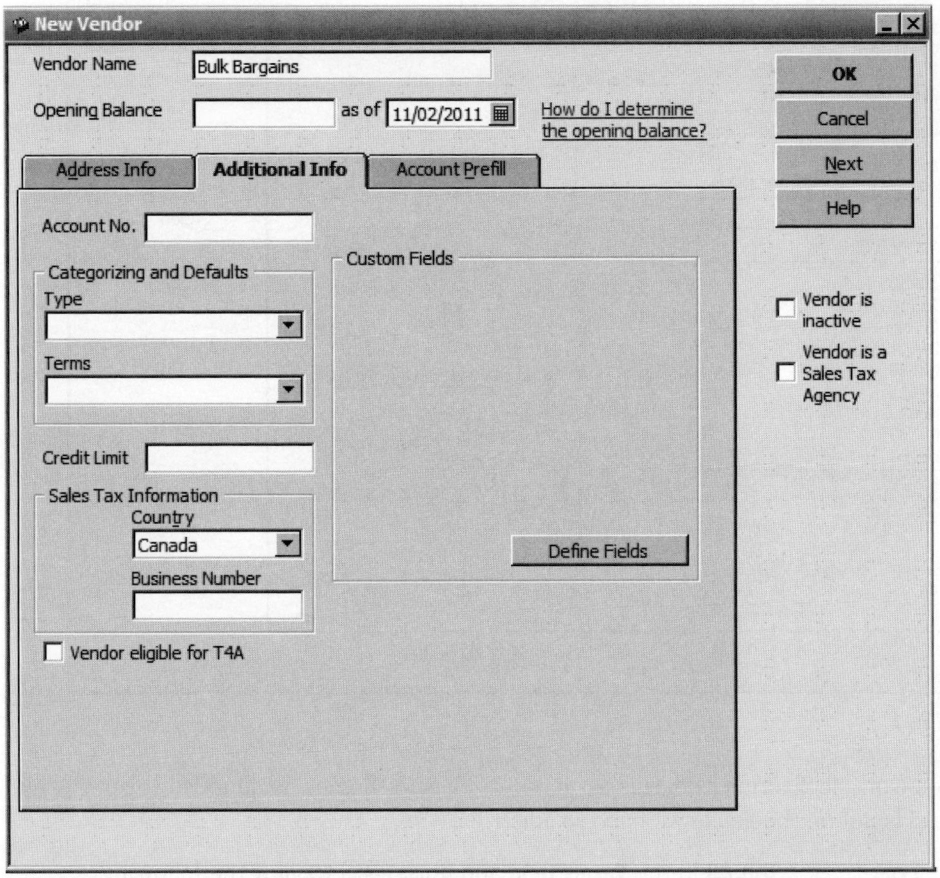

Figure 5-21

Some companies assign unique account numbers to each customer and personnel numbers to employees. The account number you enter on this vendor form is the number assigned by Bulk Bargains to Just a Buck. Vendors can also be grouped by types such as region or type of business for targeted business contacts. For example, information about items needed for special contracts may be sent only to the businesses that supply those kinds of products. Account numbers and types are not used by Just a Buck so we can skip these fields.

Most businesses place limits on the amounts that a customer is allowed to purchase on credit. Once the credit limit is reached, the customer may be asked for a down payment or may be granted a limit increase. The program warns when a credit limit is exceeded by a purchase or sale. Just a Buck is allowed to make purchases on account from Bulk Bargains up to $3,000.00.

Business numbers are also frequently added to invoices for tax purposes when taxes are charged by a business. The T4A field will be checked for businesses that provide subcontracting labour and need the T4A income tax form, and the T5018 field will be checked for construction businesses to report construction subcontractor payments.

34. Click the **drop-down arrow** in the **Terms field** to view the payment terms already set up in the Terms list:

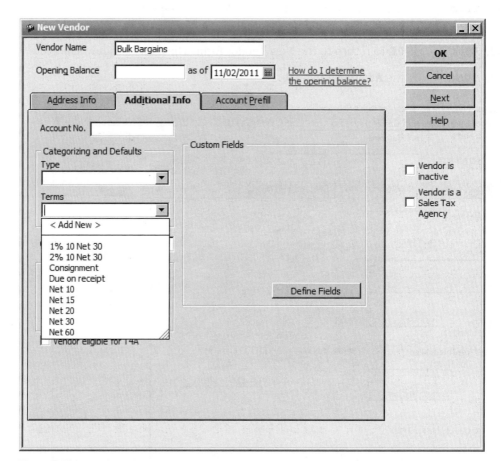

Figure 5-22

You can select terms from this list if one applies to the new vendor. However, the one we need is not on the list so we need to add it.

35. Type **Net 25** in the **Terms field** and **press** ⌨tab to view the following message screen:

Figure 5-23

36. Click **Set Up** to enter the new term information. The New Terms screen opens:

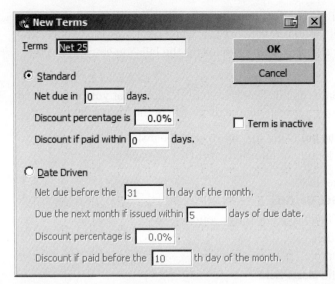

Figure 5-24

There are no discounts so we need only to enter the number of days in which net payment is due. QuickBooks uses this number to calculate the due date for bills.

37.	**Double click**	the **Net due in ___ days field**
38.	**Type**	**25**
39.	**Click**	**OK** or **press** `enter` to save the terms code and return to the Additional Info tab
40.	**Type**	**3000** in the **Credit Limit field** and **press** `tab` to format it
41.	**Click**	the **Business Number field**
42.	**Type**	**345 668 299**
43.	**Click**	**OK** to save the vendor record and return to the Vendors list

> **Notes**
> Business numbers do not usually have spaces. We have added spaces to make the numbers easier to read.

CORRECTING VENDOR RECORDS

Click a field to return to the error. Press `tab` to move forward from one field to the next. Highlight the incorrect information and type the correct information in the field. Press `tab` if necessary to update the information.

Click the Address Info tab or the Edit button to return to those screens to check your work before saving the vendor record. If you need to make corrections or changes later, select the vendor name in the Vendors List, then right-click and choose Edit Vendor or press `ctrl` + E to open the record for editing. Click OK to save the record and return to the Vendors List.

Entering Bills from the Vendors List

We will open the Enter Bills form from the Vendors list.

| 1. | **Highlight** | **Bulk Bargains** in the Vendors list, if necessary. (Bulk Bargains should already be selected from the previous exercise) |
| 2. | **Click** | the **New Transactions button** and **select Enter Bills**: |

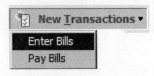

Figure 5-25

The Enter Bills form opens with Bulk Bargains automatically entered in the Vendor field. Because Bulk Bargains was selected in the Vendors List when the Enter Bills option was selected, they are automatically selected as the vendor for the bill. You can select a different vendor if needed.

3. **Press**   ⌨ *tab* to update the bill. The Net 25 terms code that you just entered in the vendor record should be displayed in the Terms field

4. **Complete**   the **rest of the bill** using the information below (you can also refer to the source document information (SD3) on page 230):

    a)   **Enter 04/02/14** as the date
    b)   **Enter BB-451** in the **Ref. No. field**
    c)   **Choose Merchandise** (Inventory) as the account
    d)   **Enter G** as the tax code
    e)   **Enter 600** as the amount
    f)   **Add** a **description** in the **Memo field**

5. **Click**   **Save & New**

Source Documents

Now that you have learned how to enter a bill, continue to develop your skills by entering the following source document in QuickBooks on the Enter Bills form. Use the information in this chapter as a guide if necessary.

Source Docs for Practice
Continue to develop your skills by entering the following source document.

SD4:   **Bill**   **Dated April 3, 2014**

Bill #MKF-72236 received from MK Foods, $200.00 for zero-rated food inventory items and $300.00 plus $15.00 GST for taxable food inventory to be sold in the store. The bill totals $515.00. Terms: Net 30 days.

Be sure to delete the *Uncategorized Expense* account on the Expenses tab of the bill. This expense account is displayed on the Expenses tab of this bill by default for two reasons: 1) this account was used to set up the vendor's opening balance when we originally created the QuickBooks company file and 2) the Pre-fill accounts for vendor based on past entries preference is enabled in the General preferences.

Printing Cheques through the Computer

Notes
If you are working in a classroom with a shared printer, ask your instructor if you should print the cheques.

We will use the computer to generate the next two cheques. Using the information in the following three source documents, we will work through the procedures to pay the vendor bills and then print the cheques:

Source Docs
Refer to the following source documents and then follow the step-by-step instructions to enter them.

SD5:   **Pay Bill**   **Dated April 3, 2014**

Cheque #198 to Universal Liquidators, $1,284.00 in payment of account. Reference Bill #UL-4002. Cheque will be printed later (choose: To be printed).

SD6:   **Pay Bill**   **Dated April 4, 2014**

Cheque #199 paid to Alert Promotions, $214.00 in payment of account. Reference Bill #AP-4992. Cheque will be printed later.

SD7:   **Memo #1**   **Dated April 4, 2014**

From Owner: Print Cheques #198 and 199.

For both vendor bills, the full amount is being paid.

1.	**Click**	the **Pay Bills icon** `Pay Bills` on the Icon bar or the Pay Bills Icon `Pay Bills` in the Vendors section of the Home page to open the Pay Bills form	**Notes** The first icon is the Pay Bills icon we added to the Icon bar in a previous exercise.
2.	**Accept**	**Show all bills** (this is the default for this option) to show all outstanding bills	
3.	**Click**	the **drop-down arrow** beside the **Sort By field**	**Notes** Vendor was last selected in the Sort By field and should have been selected when you first opened the Pay Bills form. We will select Due Date in order to view all bills that are being paid.
4.	**Select**	**Due Date** (this is the default for this field)	
5.	**Click**	the **box beside the Universal Liquidators bill** to select it for payment. A ✓ (checkmark) will be added to the box	

6. The Payment Date, in the lower left-hand corner of the screen, should be correct from the previous transaction. **Enter 04/03/14** if necessary

7.	**Click**	the **To be printed** option to select it. The Pay Bills form should look like the one shown here:

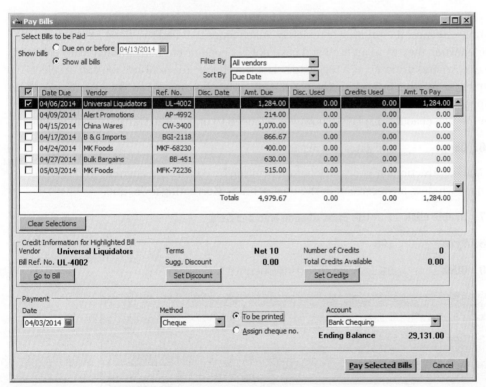

Figure 5-26

8.	**Click**	the **Pay Selected Bills button** to complete the payment
9.	**Review**	the **Payment Summary** screen and **click** the **Pay More Bills button** to return to the Pay Bills form to enter the next payment
10.	**Click**	the **box beside the Alert Promotions bill** to select it for payment. A ✓ (checkmark) will be added to the box
11.	**Type**	**04/04/14** in the **Payment Date field**

Notes
We could not enter both bill payments on the same Pay Bills screen because the Payment Date is different.

The To be printed option should still be selected from our previous changes.

12.	**Click**	the **Pay Selected Bills button** to complete the payment

13. Review   the **Payment Summary screen** and **click Done**

14. Choose   the **File menu**, then **choose Print Forms** and **click Cheques**

15. The Select Cheques to Print dialogue box opens:

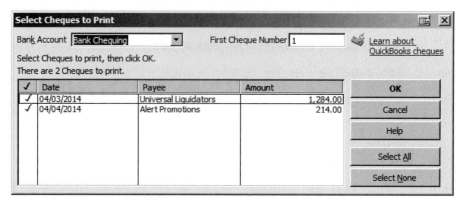

Figure 5-27

On this screen, you can edit the first cheque number, select one or more cheques for printing, or cancel the printing completely. All cheques that had the *To be printed* option selected when they were entered and have not yet been printed are automatically selected. The checkmarks are used as a toggle to select the cheque for printing. You can deselect cheques for printing by clicking the checkmark or by choosing the Select All or Select None buttons to start with the best option and toggle cheques on or off as needed. We want to print the two cheques displayed; however, we need to update the starting cheque number.

16. Check   the **dates and amounts**

Make corrections if necessary before printing by editing the cheques in the Write Cheques window, as described in the next section, Correcting a Cheque.

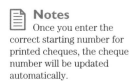

Notes
Once you enter the correct starting number for printed cheques, the cheque number will be updated automatically.

17. Double click   1 in the **First Cheque Number field**

18. Type   **198**

19. Click   **OK** to open the Print Cheques form:

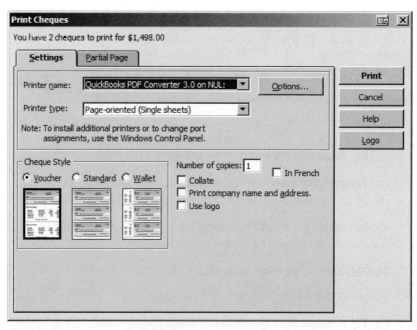

Figure 5-28

20. **Choose**   the **cheque style** you want

21. **Click**   **Print** to print the cheques

22. The following confirmation screen will be displayed after the cheques have printed:

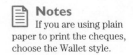

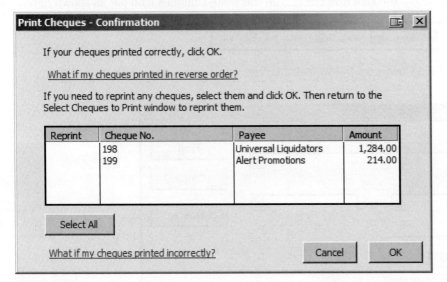

Print Cheques - Confirmation

If your cheques printed correctly, click OK.

What if my cheques printed in reverse order?

If you need to reprint any cheques, select them and click OK. Then return to the Select Cheques to Print window to reprint them.

Reprint	Cheque No.	Payee	Amount
	198	Universal Liquidators	1,284.00
	199	Alert Promotions	214.00

Select All

What if my cheques printed incorrectly?   Cancel   OK

Figure 5-29

If any of the cheques did not print correctly, click on the first cheque that was not correct. A ✓ (checkmark) will be entered under the Reprint column for that cheque. Continue selecting all cheques that did not print correctly. You can use the Select All button if all the cheques did not print correctly. When you click OK, the cheques will have the To be printed option selected and must be reprinted from the Select Cheques to Print dialogue box.

Notes
If you are using plain paper to print the cheques, choose the Wallet style.

Notes
Cheques that are selected for reprinting are not automatically printed from the Print Cheques confirmation screen. You must re-select them on the Select Cheques to Print dialogue box.

23. **Click**   **OK** if the cheques printed correctly

Correcting a Cheque

Just as we corrected Sales Receipts, cheques, and General Journal entries, we can correct bill payments in QuickBooks. Cheques written in payment of Vendor bills in the Pay Bills form can be corrected from the Write Cheques form, just like other cheques. We will correct the amount paid on the cheque to MK Foods. Refer to the following source document as we work through the steps to enter it:

SD8: **Memo #2**   **Dated April 4, 2014**

From Owner: Cheque #197 to MK Foods was entered incorrectly. The actual amount paid on the cheque was $1,045.00. Edit the cheque to make the correction.

Source Docs
Refer to the following source document and then follow the step-by-step instructions to enter it.

1. **Open** the Write Cheques form using one of the following options:

a) **Click** the **Write Cheques icon** [Write Cheques] in the Banking section of the Home page; or

b) **Click** the **Cheque icon** [Cheque] on the Icon bar (this icon will only be available if it has been added to the Icon bar); or

c) **Press** (*ctrl*) + **W**; or

d) **Choose** the **Banking menu** and **click Write Cheques**

Finding a Recorded Transaction

To find the cheque we need, we could use the Previous button, as we did in earlier chapters, or we can use the QuickBooks Find feature to locate the transaction we want.

2. Click   the **Find icon**  on the Write Cheques Icon bar as shown here:

3.   The Find Cheques window is displayed:

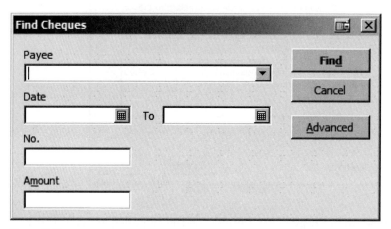

Figure 5-30

From this window you can enter search parameters. You can choose the payee for the cheque, enter a range of dates, enter the cheque number, or enter the exact amount of the cheque to open the one you want. If there is more than one cheque for the payee or the range of dates, you can choose the one you need from the list provided from the search criteria entered.

We know that the cheque was made out to MK Foods so we will search by payee.

4. Click   the **drop-down arrow** in the **Payee field** to view the list of payees:

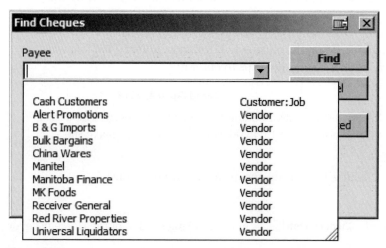

Figure 5-31

5. Click   **MK Foods** as the payee

6. Click   the **Find Button** to open the cheque that we entered to MK Foods:

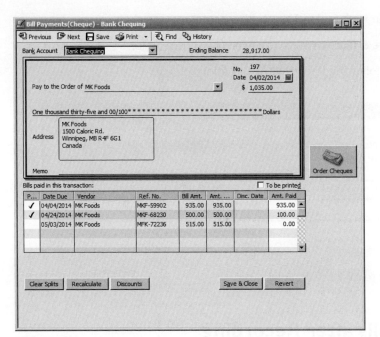

Figure 5-32

Notes
Notice that the form is renamed Bill Payments (Cheque)

Because only one payment was made to MK Foods, the cheque we need opens immediately in the Write Cheques form.

With the payment displayed on the screen, you can make any necessary corrections, including adding additional bills or removing bills from the payment. For this source document, all we need to do is edit the Amt. Paid entry on the second line.

Notes
If there is more than one cheque for the payee, a list of cheques will open so you can select one. This secondary selection screen is similar to the one for bills in Figure 5-36 on page 243.

7. **Double click**   **100.00**

8. **Type**   **110**

9. **Press**   ⌨ tab ⌨ to update the amount

10. **Click**   the **Recalculate button** at the bottom of the form to update the cheque amount if necessary

11. The completed and corrected cheque is shown below:

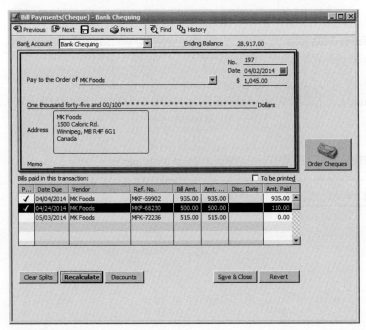

Figure 5-33

12. **Check** your **work** and **make** any other **necessary corrections**

13. **Click** **Save & Close** to record the corrected transaction

14. You will see the following Recording Transaction screen:

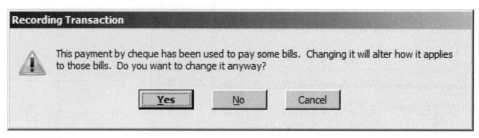

Figure 5-34

15. **Click** **Yes** to save the changes

Correcting Bills after Recording

We can make corrections to bills we entered in the same way that we make other corrections in QuickBooks. These corrections are made on the Enter Bills form. We will make a correction on a bill entered from MK Foods. After we make the correction, we will memorize the transaction for future use so that we can enter it over and over again without having to re-enter it from scratch. Refer to the following source document as we work through the steps to enter it:

Source Docs
Refer to the following source document and then follow the step-by-step instructions to enter it.

SD9: Memo #3   **Dated April 5, 2014**

From Owner: Bill #MKF-72236 from MK Foods was entered incorrectly. Zero-rated food items purchased cost $250.00. Taxable food items were correctly entered. The revised bill totalled $565.00. Terms: Net 30 days. Correct the transaction and then memorize the changed transaction because Just a Buck will be making this purchase every week beginning April 10, 2014.

1. **Click** the **Enter Bills icon** in the Vendors section of the Home page to open the Enter Bills form

You can look for bills by clicking the Previous button as we did in the previous chapter, or you can use the Find tool to search for specific criteria as we did for cheques in the previous transaction. The Find tool is located on the Icon bar of the Enter Bills form.

2. **Click** the **Find icon** on the Enter Bills Icon bar:

3. The Find Bills window is shown here:

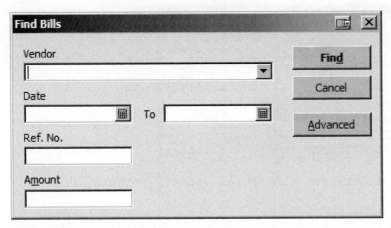

Figure 5-35

Although the name of the window has changed to match the type of transaction we are searching for — based on the form from which we started the search — it operates the same way for all forms.

4. Click the **drop-down arrow** in the **Vendor field** to view the list of vendors

5. Click **MK Foods**

6. Click the **Find button** or **press** ⟨alt⟩ + **D**

📄 **Notes**
  D is the underlined letter on the Find button.

7. A list of bills from this vendor is displayed:

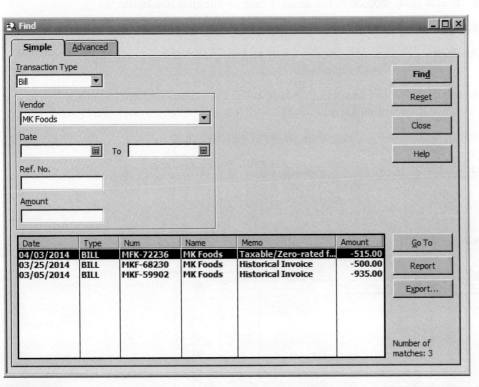

Figure 5-36

📄 **Notes**
  A list of purchases is displayed because there is more than one bill from MK Foods that meets the criteria we entered in the Find dialogue box. To find the exact bill you are looking for, you need to enter specific criteria.

8. Click the **first bill listed** because it is the one we need to edit

The other two bills are historical bills that precede the date we started using QuickBooks.

Notes
The Vendor and Transaction tabs to the right of the bill are used to view vendor and transaction information.

The Vendor tab displays summary information about the vendor, recent vendor transactions, and notes that have been entered in the vendor record.

The Transaction tab displays information about the transaction, including when it was created, last edited, and by whom. It also displays related transactions and allows you to enter notes specific to the transaction.

To close the Vendor and Transaction tabs, click on the arrow in the top left-hand corner of the tab. To reopen the tab, click the arrow in the top right-hand corner of the bill.

9. **Click** the **Go To button** to access the bill:

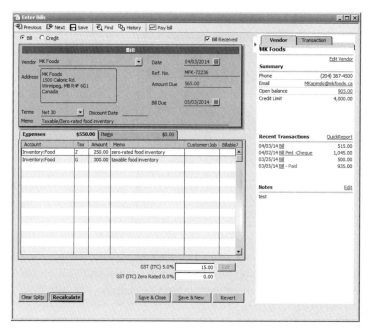

Figure 5-37

Notes
If you want to view the information on the Vendor and Transaction tabs, click the left arrow ◄ in the top right-hand corner of the screen.

You can now make corrections to any part of the bill.

10. **Click** the **right arrow** ▶ to the left of the Vendor tab to close the Vendor and Transaction tabs

11. **Double click** **200.00** in the **Amount field** on the first line of the bill

12. **Type** **250**

13. **Press** (tab) to update the total. Notice that the amount of the cheque has not yet changed

14. **Click** the **Recalculate button** at the bottom of the form to update the cheque amount and complete the bill as shown here:

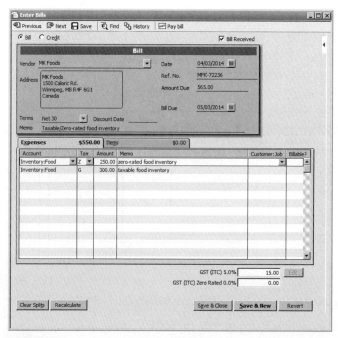

Figure 5-38

Memorizing an Unrecorded Transaction

Businesses frequently have scheduled transactions — bills that arrive on a regular basis. Supplies may be received from the same vendor every month; inventory may be purchased on a regular cycle; utility bills and rent payments are usually due at the same time each month; and insurance, loan, and mortgage payments are usually made on the same day each month. To avoid entering the same details for the bill each time it occurs, you can enter the transaction once and memorize it, and then use the memorized transaction when it is needed.

We will memorize Bill #MKF-72236 from MK Foods because Just a Buck places the same order with them every week.

1. With Bill #MKF-72236 MK Foods displayed from the previous exercise,
   press (ctrl) **+ M**, the keyboard shortcut used to memorize transactions, or **choose** the **Edit menu** and **click Memorize Bill**

2. The Memorize Transaction window is displayed:

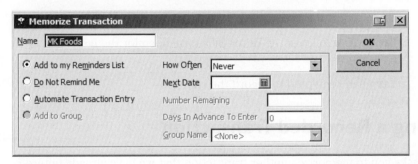

Figure 5-39

You can ask QuickBooks to add the transaction to the Reminders List, do nothing, automate the transaction, or enter it in a group. After you choose an option and then select a frequency, the transaction will appear on the Memorized Transactions List with the next date that it is due to be entered.

3. **Accept**   the **Add to my Reminders List option** (the default)

4. **Click**   the **drop-down arrow** in the **How Often field** to view the frequencies available:

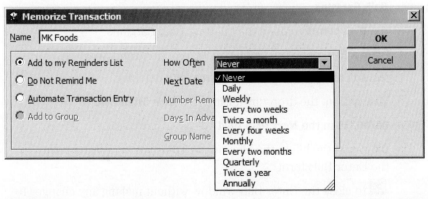

Figure 5-40

You can choose to have the transaction repeated never, daily, weekly, every two weeks, twice a month, every four weeks, monthly, every two months, quarterly, twice a year, or annually.

When you choose a frequency, the Next Date field opens, and you should type in the next date on which you want to enter the transaction again.

> **Notes**
> These frequencies are available when you select the Add to my Reminders List or the Automate Transaction Entry option.

Notes
The memorized transaction will also appear on the Reminders list before the transaction is due if you have set the Memorized Transactions preference to display memorized transactions on the Reminders List a certain number of days before they are due. Because the Reminders list is linked to your computer system and we don't know your current computer date, we cannot use the Reminders list for these recurring transactions because it will not be the same for everyone.

You can also set the program to enter a memorized transaction automatically according to the frequency you enter by selecting the Automate Transaction Entry option. When the computer date passes the next date for the memorized transaction, an Enter Memorized Transactions screen will be displayed when you open QuickBooks. This screen lists the memorized transactions that are due to be entered and allows you to select the ones you want to enter. When you click on the Enter Checked Now button, all selected memorized transactions will be entered automatically. Of course, you can still edit the transactions that are entered at any time.

5.	**Choose**	**Weekly** as the frequency
6.	**Press**	(tab) to advance to the Next Date field. Your current computer system date will appear as the default date
7.	**Type**	**04/10/14**

If you choose Never as the frequency, you can still memorize the transaction and enter your own date each time you use the memorized transaction. You might use this option when the cycle is not a regular one.

8.	**Click**	**OK** to return to the Enter Bills form
9.	**Click**	**Save & New** to leave the Enter Bills form open for the next transaction
10.	**Click**	**Yes** when prompted to record the changes

Memorizing a Recorded Transaction

The next memo asks you to memorize another transaction that we have already entered. The Enter Bills form should still be open. Refer to the following source document as we work through the steps to enter it:

Source Docs
Refer to the following source document and then follow the step-by-step instructions to enter it.

SD10: Memo #4   **Dated April 5, 2014**

From Owner: Find the bill from Bulk Bargains and memorize the transaction with weekly reminders starting April 9, 2014. Close the transaction form.

1.	**Click**	the **Find icon** [🔍 Find] on the Enter Bills Icon bar
2.	**Click**	the **drop-down arrow** in the Vendor field
3.	**Choose**	**Bulk Bargains**
4.	**Click**	the **Find button** to open the bill from Bulk Bargains
5.	**Press**	(ctrl) + **M** to open the Memorize Transaction window
6.	**Accept**	the **Add to my Reminders List option** (the default)
7.	**Choose**	**Weekly** from the drop-down list in the **How Often field**
8.	**Type**	**04/09/14** in the **Next Date field**
9.	**Click**	**OK** to add the bill to the Memorized Transaction List and return to the Enter Bills form
10.	**Click**	[X] to close the Enter Bills window without making any changes to the original transaction

⚠️ **WARNING!**
If you do not change the original bill, you will not be prompted to record the changes. If you are prompted to record the changes and you did not intend to change the original bill, choose No so you do not record the changes.

Source Docs for Practice
Continue to develop your skills by entering the following source documents.

Source Documents

Now that you have learned some more of the new concepts taught in this chapter, continue to develop your skills by entering the following source documents in QuickBooks. Use the information in this chapter as a guide if necessary.

SD11: Write Cheque   **Dated April 5, 2014**

To pay cash for purchase received with Bill #HAC-6733 from Hold All Containers (use Quick Add to add the new vendor) for $85.00 plus $4.25 GST and $5.95 PST for supply of bags for customer purchases. The bill totals $95.20. Cheque #200 will be printed later to pay the bill in full. Memorize the transaction with reminders every two weeks beginning April 19, 2014.

SD12: Write Cheque   **Dated April 5, 2014**

To pay cash for purchase received with Bill #RDP-4-14 from Red River Properties for $3,000.00 plus $150.00 GST for monthly rent. The bill totals $3,150.00. Cheque #201 will be printed later to pay the bill in full. Memorize the transaction. Choose to be reminded monthly starting May 5, 2014.

⚠ WARNING!
Use the Write Cheques form for cash purchases.
Do not change the default selection for the To be printed option in the Write Cheques form for the cash purchases from Hold All Containers and Red River Properties.

Memorizing Sales Receipts

We have created a customer called Cash Sales to record Sales Receipts. In addition, to avoid entering a very large number of small sales, we record weekly summaries for sales. The summary cash sales involve the sale of more than one type of item to the customer. In addition, we want to memorize the receipt because each week the transaction is the same, except for the amounts. We can edit the amounts each time we use the transaction and still save some data entry time. Refer to the following source document as we work through the steps to enter it:

SD13: Sales Summary Receipt #234   **Dated April 7, 2014**

To Cash Sales customers:

Food - Taxable	$ 500.00
Food - Non-taxable	220.00
Other merchandise	4,380.00
GST	244.00
PST	341.60
Total deposited to the *Bank Chequing* account:	$5,685.60

Do not print the receipt. Memorize the transaction with weekly reminders beginning April 14, 2014.

1.	**Choose**	the **Customers menu** and **click Enter Sales Receipts**
2.	**Choose**	**Cash Customers** as the customer
3.	**Enter**	**04/07/14** as the Date
4.	**Press**	(tab) to advance to the Sale No. field
5.	**Type**	**234**
6.	**Choose**	**Food - Taxable** as the first item
7.	**Enter**	**500** in the **Amount field**
8.	**Press**	(tab) to advance to the Tax field
9.	**Accept**	**S** (both PST and GST are charged on this item) as the tax code for this item
10.	**Click**	the **second detail line**
11.	**Choose**	**Food - Non-taxable** as the second item and **enter 220** in the **Amount field**

Source Docs
Refer to the following source document and then follow the step-by-step instructions to enter it.

Notes
Although the sales amounts will change, the remainder of the receipt will be the same each week.

Notes
The S (Standard) tax code was entered in the Food - Taxable item record and will be displayed by default on all forms when this item is selected.

12.	**Press**	(tab) to advance to the Tax field

13. **Accept** **E** (no taxes are charged on this item) as the tax code for this item

14. **Click** the **third detail line**

15. **Choose** **Merchandise** (Inventory) as the item and **enter 4380** in the **Amount field**

16. **Press** (tab) to advance to the Tax field

17. **Accept** **S** (both PST and GST are charged on this item) as the tax code for this item

18. **Click** **To be printed** to remove the ✓

19. **Click** the **drop-down arrow** in the **Deposit To field**

20. **Click** **Bank Chequing** (it should be the default)

21. **Press** (ctrl) + **M** to memorize the transaction

22. **Accept** the **Add to my Reminders List option** (the default)

23. **Choose** **Weekly** as the frequency and **enter 04/14/14** in the **Next Date field**

24. **Click** **OK** to return to the Sales Receipt

25. **Click** **Save & Close** or **press** (alt) + **a** to save the receipt and close the form

Source Documents

Continue to develop your skills by entering the following source documents in QuickBooks. Use the information in this chapter as a guide if necessary.

SD14: Memo #5   **Dated April 7, 2014**

From Owner: Print Cheques #200 and #201 to Hold All Containers and Red River Properties. (The first cheque number should be correctly entered as the default.)

SD15: Bill   **Dated April 9, 2014**

Bill #CW-4101 received from China Wares, $520 plus $26.00 GST for houseware items (merchandise inventory) to be sold in the store. Delete the *Uncategorized Expenses* account on the Expenses tab of the bill. The bill totalled $546.00. Terms: Net 20 days.

Using a Memorized Transaction

When we use a memorized transaction we do not need to re-enter all the transaction details. QuickBooks adds the memorized transactions created from all forms to a single list so you can see all the memorized transactions at the same time. You can access the form for any one of these transactions directly from the list. You do not need to open the form before choosing the memorized transaction. We will enter a bill using the bill that we memorized earlier from Bulk Bargains. Refer to the following source document as we work through the steps to enter it:

SD16: Bill   **Dated April 9, 2014**

Bill #BB-611 received from Bulk Bargains, $600.00 plus $30.00 GST for merchandise inventory to be sold in the store. The bill totalled $630.00. Terms: Net 25 days. Use the memorized transaction.

1. Use one of the following options to access the Memorized Transaction List:
   a) **Choose** the **Lists menu** and **click Memorized Transaction List**, or
   b) **Press** ⌐ctrl⌐ + **T**

2. The list of all the transactions we have memorized will be displayed:

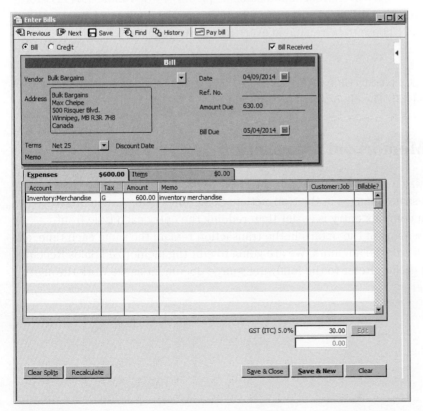

Memorized Transaction List

Transaction Name	Type	Source Account	Amount	Frequency	Auto	Next Date
◈ Bulk Bargains	Bill	Accounts Payable	630.00	Weekly		04/09/2014
◈ Cash Customers	Sales Receipt	Bank Chequing	5,685.60	Weekly		04/14/2014
◈ Hold All Containers	Cheque	Bank Chequing	95.20	Every two weeks		04/19/2014
◈ MK Foods	Bill	Accounts Payable	565.00	Weekly		04/10/2014
◈ Red River Properties	Cheque	Bank Chequing	3,150.00	Monthly		05/05/2014

Memorized Transaction ▾   Enter Transaction

Figure 5-41

Notes
Once you open the Memorized Transaction List, you may want to leave it open for easy access for later transactions. Simply click the Memorized Transaction List from the Open Window List or the Window menu the next time you need it.

Initially, the list is sorted alphabetically by transaction name. To change the order of transactions, click on any of the column headings to sort by that criterion. For example, to sort by next date, you would click the Next Date column heading. Bulk Bargains is selected because it is first on the list. It is the transaction we need so we can proceed.

To create a transaction from a memorized transaction, you can double click on the transaction or click on the Enter Transaction button.

Notes
Click the Next Date column to change the order of the memorized transactions.

3. **Highlight** the **Bulk Bargains transaction**

4. **Click** the **Enter Transaction button** at the bottom of the Memorized Transaction List to open the Enter Bills form:

Notes
After changing the order of the memorized transactions, you can restore the initial order by choosing the Memorized Transaction button and clicking Re-sort List. Click OK to confirm the change.

Notes
To select the memorized transaction you want, click anywhere on the line to select it.

Enter Bills

⏪ Previous ⏩ Next 💾 Save 🔍 Find ⟳ History Pay bill

⦿ Bill ◯ Credit   ☑ Bill Received

Bill

Vendor Bulk Bargains ▾   Date   04/09/2014

Address Bulk Bargains   Ref. No.
         Max Cheipe
         500 Risquer Blvd.   Amount Due 630.00
         Winnipeg, MB R3R 7H8
         Canada

                               Bill Due 05/04/2014

Terms Net 25 ▾   Discount Date
Memo

Expenses	$600.00	Items	$0.00			
Account	Tax	Amount	Memo		Customer:Job	Billable?
Inventory:Merchandise	G	600.00	inventory merchandise			

GST (ITC) 5.0%   30.00 Edit
                  0.00

Clear Splits Recalculate   Save & Close Save & New Clear

Figure 5-42

The bill is almost complete. The bill and due dates have been updated based on the information we entered when we memorized the transaction. All we need to do is add the reference number. Because this number cannot be duplicated, its field remains blank on the form.

5. **Click**   the **Ref. No. field**

6. **Type**   **BB-611**

7. **Click**   **Save & Close** to return to the Memorized Transaction List

8. **Click**   the **Next Date** column heading to sort the list by the next date. This places the transaction we need next at the top of the list (**click** the **Next Date** column heading until the purchase from MK Foods is displayed at the top of the list)

Another bill from MK Foods has arrived so use the transaction you memorized earlier to record it. The source document is as follows:

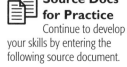

Source Docs for Practice

Continue to develop your skills by entering the following source document.

SD17: Bill   Dated April 10, 2014

Bill #MKF-83100 received from MK Foods, $250.00 for zero-rated food inventory items and $300.00 plus $15.00 GST for taxable food inventory to be sold in the store. The bill totalled $565.00. Terms: Net 30 days. Use the memorized transaction.

Source Documents

Now that you have learned more of the new concepts taught in this chapter, continue to develop your skills by entering the following source documents. Use the information in this chapter as a guide if necessary.

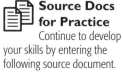

Source Docs for Practice

Continue to develop your skills by entering the following source documents.

SD18: Bill   Dated April 12, 2014

Bill #MT-40101 received from Manitel, $62.00 plus $3.10 GST and $4.34 PST for the store telephone. The bill totalled $69.44. Terms: Net 10 days. Memorize the transaction. Choose to be reminded every month starting May 12, 2014.

SD19: Pay Bill   Dated April 13, 2014

Cheque #202 paid to China Wares, $1,070.00 in payment of account. Reference Bill #CW-3400. The cheque will be printed later.

Editing a Memorized Transaction

Once we memorize a transaction, we can use it exactly as it was entered or edit it to reflect necessary changes in the transaction. Sometimes using a memorized transaction for a complex entry is easier than redoing the entry each time from scratch. Because many of the details in the transaction remain the same each time, all you need to do is edit the amounts. We are going to edit the memorized Sales Receipt that we entered earlier. Refer to the following source document as we work through the steps to enter it:

SD20: Sales Receipt   **Dated April 14, 2014**

To Cash Sales customers:

Food - Taxable	$ 400.00
Food - Non-taxable	190.00
Other merchandise	3,990.00
GST	219.50
PST	307.30
Total deposited to the *Bank Chequing* account:	$5,106.80

Use the memorized transaction to create Sales Summary Receipt #235 and edit the amounts.

1. **Press** (ctrl) **+ T** to open the Memorized Transaction list (or **use a method of your choice**)

2. **Click** **Cash Customers** to select the memorized transaction

3. **Click** the **Enter Transaction button** at the bottom of the list window or **press** (alt) **+ T** to open the Cash Sales Receipt transaction. You can now edit the amounts before saving the transaction.

4. **Double click** **500.00** in the Rate column for the Food - Taxable item

5. **Type** **400**

6. **Press** the **down arrow key** ▼ to highlight 220.00

7. **Type** **190**

8. **Press** the **down arrow key** ▼ to highlight 4,380.00

9. **Type** **3990**

10. **Press** (tab) to update the Sales Receipt totals and taxes

The date and Sales No. field should be correct. The date is determined by the frequency of the memorized transaction and the Sales No. field is automatically updated to the next sequential number. The Sales No. should be 235.

11. **Click** **Save & Close** to save the transaction and return to the Memorized Transaction List

Source Documents

Now that you have learned more of the new concepts taught in this chapter, continue to develop your skills by entering the following source documents in QuickBooks. Use the information in this chapter as a guide if necessary.

SD21: Memo #6   **Dated April 14, 2014**

From Owner: Print Cheque #202 to China Wares.

SD22: Bill   **Dated April 15, 2014**

Bill #UL-5184 received from Universal Liquidators, $1,100.00 plus $55.00 GST for small toys and party favours from a bankruptcy sale (merchandise inventory to be sold in store). Delete the *Uncategorized Expenses* account on the Expenses tab of the bill. The bill totalled $1,155.00. Terms: Net 10 days.

SD23: Bill Dated April 16, 2014

Bill #BB-883 received from Bulk Bargains, $600.00 plus $30.00 GST for merchandise inventory to be sold. The bill totalled $630.00. Terms: Net 25 days. Use the memorized transaction.

Notes
Continue to select the To be printed option for all cheques.

SD24: Pay Bill Dated April 16, 2014

Cheque #203 paid to B & G Imports, $866.67 in payment of account. Reference Bill #BGI-2118.

SD25: Bill Dated April 17, 2014

Bill #MKF-96123 received from MK Foods, $250.00 for zero-rated food inventory items and $300.00 plus $15.00 GST for taxable food inventory to be sold in the store. The bill totalled $565.00. Terms: Net 30 days. Use the memorized transaction.

Changing the Frequency or Next Date

Sometimes we need to change the details of a memorized transaction, such as the frequency or the next due date. We can edit these details by editing the memorized transaction from the Memorized Transaction List. We need to change the frequency of the purchase from Hold All Containers and its next due date. Refer to the following source document as we work through the steps to enter it:

Source Docs
Refer to the following source document and then follow the step-by-step instructions to enter it.

SD26: Memo #7 Dated April 18, 2014

The purchase from Hold All Containers will be repeated every four weeks rather than bi-weekly. Edit the memorized transaction details to change the frequency.

1. **Open** the **Memorized Transaction List** by using an option of your choice

2. **Click** **Hold All Containers** to select the memorized transaction for that vendor

Notes
Once the transaction is selected in the list, you can also choose the Edit menu and click Edit Memorized Transaction.

Notes
Pressing *ctrl* + **E** will open the edit screen for a selected entry in any type of list in QuickBooks.

3. **Click** the **Memorized Transaction button** and **choose Edit Memorized Transaction** or **press** *ctrl* + **E** to open the details of the memorized transaction:

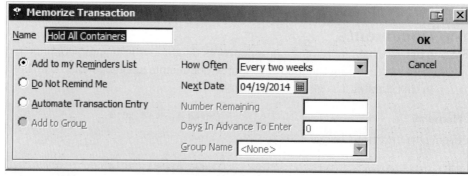

Figure 5-43

We can now edit any information about the transaction.

4. **Click** the **drop-down arrow** in the **How Often field**

5. **Choose** **Every Four Weeks**

6. **Press** *tab* to advance to the Next Date field

7. **Type**   05/03/14

8. **Click**   **OK** to save the changes and close the form. You will return to the
Memorized Transaction List

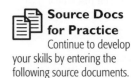

Notes
Depending on how the list of memorized transactions is sorted, the item may have moved up or down in the list.

Source Documents

Using the information you have learned in this chapter and others, continue entering the following source documents in QuickBooks:

Source Docs for Practice
Continue to develop your skills by entering the following source documents.

SD27: Pay Bill   **Dated April 20, 2014**

Cheque #204 paid to Manitel, $69.44 in payment of account. Reference Bill #MT-40101.

SD28: Sales Receipt   **Dated April 21, 2014**

To Cash Sales customers:

Food - Taxable	$ 410.00
Food - Non-taxable	210.00
Other merchandise	5,110.00
GST	276.00
PST	386.40
Total deposited to the *Bank Chequing* account:	$6,392.40

Use the transaction in the memorized transactions list to create Sales Summary Receipt #236 and edit the amounts.

SD29: Memo #8   **Dated April 21, 2014**

From Owner: Print Cheques #203 and #204 to B & G Imports and Manitel.

SD30: Pay Bill   **Dated April 22, 2014**

Cheque #205 paid to MK Foods, $955.00 in payment of account. Reference Bills MKF-68230 and MKF-72236.

SD31: Bill   **Dated April 22, 2014**

Bill #CL-719 received from Cards for Less (Set up the new vendor), $450.00 plus $22.50 GST for greeting cards and note cards to be sold in the store (merchandise inventory). The bill totalled $472.50. Terms: Net 15 days.

Notes
Cards for Less
Contact: Trite Sayers
1200 Bavarder Ave., Suite 5A
Winnipeg, MB R2P 7F4
Canada
Phone: (204) 698-2301
Fax: (204) 698-3923
E-mail: ts@cardsforless.com
Terms: Net 15
Credit Limit: $2,000.00
Business No.: 488 566 302

SD32: Bill   **Dated April 23, 2014**

Bill #BB-1299 received from Bulk Bargains, $600.00 plus $30.00 GST for inventory merchandise to be sold in the store. The bill totalled $630.00. Terms: Net 25 days. Use the memorized transaction.

SD33: Bill   **Dated April 24, 2014**

Bill #MKF-99011 received from MK Foods, $250.00 for zero-rated food inventory items and $300.00 plus $15.00 GST for taxable food inventory to be sold in the store. The bill totalled $565.00. Terms: Net 30 days. Use the memorized transaction.

SD34: Pay Bill   **Dated April 25, 2014**

Cheque #206 paid to Universal Liquidators, $1,155.00 in payment of account. Reference Bill #UL-5184.

SD35: Bill   **Dated April 26, 2014**

Bill #AP-5622 received from Alert Promotions, $800.00 plus $40.00 GST and $56.00 PST for business cards for owner and promotional flyers to distribute in the mall. Delete the *Uncategorized Expenses* account on the Expenses tab of the bill. The bill totalled $896.00. Terms: Net 20 days.

Deleting a Memorized Transaction

When a memorized transaction is no longer needed, the transaction should be deleted from the list. These unneeded transactions can make it harder to find the entry we need and might be used in error. Just a Buck will not be making additional purchases from Hold All Containers, so we can delete the memorized bill from the Memorized Transaction List. Refer to the following source document as we work through the steps to enter it:

SD36: Memo #9   **Dated April 28, 2014**

From Owner: Delete the memorized bill for Hold All Containers from the Memorized Transactions List because it is no longer needed. Another supplier was found.

1. **Open**   the **Memorized Transaction List** using one of the options you've learned in this chapter

2. **Click**   **Hold All Containers** to select the memorized bill

3. **Click**   the **Memorized Transaction button** and **choose Delete Memorized Transaction** or **press** ⌃ *ctrl* + **D** to view the Delete Memorized Transaction screen:

Notes
When a transaction is selected on the Memorized Transaction List, you can choose the Edit menu and click Delete Memorized Transaction to remove the entry.
Pressing ⌃ *ctrl* + **D** will also delete the selected entry on any type of list in QuickBooks.

Figure 5-44

4. **Click**   **OK** to confirm the deletion

You will return to the Memorized Transaction List. You should see that the memorized bill for Hold All Containers has been removed from the Memorized Transaction List.

Source Documents

Using the information you have learned in this chapter and other chapters, continue entering the following source documents in QuickBooks:

SD37: Sales Receipt   **Dated April 28, 2014**

To Cash Sales customers:

Food - Taxable	$ 470.00
Food - Non-taxable	180.00
Other merchandise	5,330.00
GST	290.00
PST	406.00
Total deposited to the *Bank Chequing* account:	$6,676.00

Use the transaction in the Memorized Transaction List to create Sales Summary Receipt #237 and edit the amounts.

SD38: Memo #10   Dated April 28, 2014

From Owner: Print Cheques #205 and #206 to MK Foods and Universal Liquidators.

SD39: Bill   Dated April 30, 2014

Bill #BB-1624 received from Bulk Bargains, $600.00 plus $30.00 GST for inventory merchandise to be sold in the store. The bill totals $630.00. Terms: Net 25 days. Use the memorized transaction. Allow the transaction to exceed the credit limit. A payment will be made immediately.

SD40: Pay Bill   Dated April 30, 2014

Cheque #207 was paid to Bulk Bargains, $630.00 in payment of account. Reference Bill #BB-451. Print the cheque.

SD41: Memo #11   Dated April 30, 2014

From Owner: Complete adjusting entries for inventory sold during month.
Food inventory $1,600.00
Merchandise inventory   8,200.00
Supplies (cleaning, office supplies, plastic bags)   285.00

SD42: Memo #12   Dated April 30, 2014

From Owner: Complete adjusting entry for $2,300.00 of expired prepaid insurance.

SD43: Bank Debit Memo DM-56621   Dated April 30, 2014

From MidWest Bank: Loan payment $1,140.00, consisting of $140.00 interest and $1,000.00 principal, was withdrawn from the *Bank Chequing* account.

Vendors and Payables Reports

Vendor reports and graphs can be accessed from the Reports menu or from the Report Centre. Each report can be modified by adding or removing columns; by sorting and filtering to select only parts of the data for the report; and by changing headers, footers, fonts, and number formats. The principles for modifying and customizing vendor reports are the same as they are for the reports discussed in Chapter 3.

You can also memorize the report after modifying it, rename it, and add it to your list of memorized reports.

1. **Choose**   the **Reports menu**, then **choose Vendors & Payables** as shown here to view the list of all vendor and payables reports:

Notes
The T4A Detail report will be covered in later chapters.

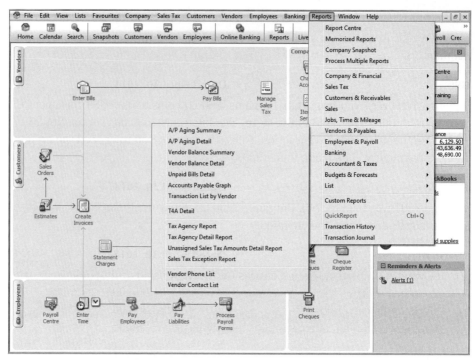

Figure 5-45

We will print reports from the Report Centre rather than selecting them from the Reports menu.

Notes
Refer to Chapter 1, page 19–23, to learn more about the various views available in the Report Centre.

2. **Click** the **Reports icon** on the Icon bar to open the Report Centre

3. **Click** the **Vendors & Payables heading** on the left-hand side of the screen

and **click** on the **List View icon** 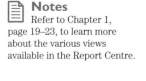 to view the list of Vendors & Payables reports:

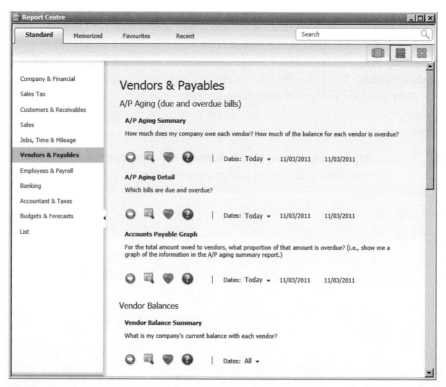

Figure 5-46

Accounts Payable Aging Reports

The Accounts Payable Aging reports show the outstanding amounts you owe your vendors aged according to the current and previous billing periods. The default is to display the report in 30-day intervals. You can view the report in Summary form, with only the total amount owing to each vendor in each billing period, and in Detail form, showing the transaction details for each bill that is outstanding in each billing period. From these reports, you can see if any bills are overdue or plan a payment schedule.

The Accounts Payable Aging Summary Report

1. **Click**   the **Run icon** [Run] under the **A/P Aging Summary report** to open the report on the screen

2. **Double click** in the **Date field**

3. **Type**   **04/30/14**

4. **Click**   the **Refresh button** or **press** (tab) to update the report:

Notes
To access the report from the Reports menu:
- Choose the Reports menu, then choose Vendors & Payables, and click A/P Aging Summary to open the report
- Enter 04/30/14 in the Date field
- Press (tab) or click Refresh to update the report

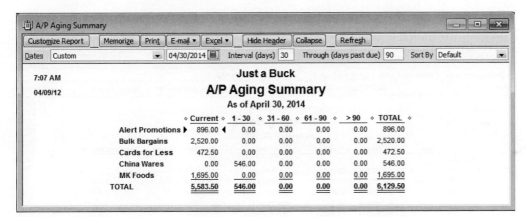

Figure 5-47

The A/P Aging Summary report shows the total amount owing to each vendor. The columns on the report include how much your company owes to each vendor in the current billing period and how much it owes from previous billing periods. For example, all current bills are dated within the last 30 days and are displayed in the current column, while amounts that are between 31 and 60 days overdue are displayed in the 31–60 column, amounts that are between 61 and 90 days overdue are displayed in the 61–90 column, etc. By default, vendors without outstanding balances are included in the report. You can sort the report by total amount or vendor (the default) from the Sort By field list. By default, the report shows overdue billing periods to 90 days, but you can include more periods (columns) by entering a different number in the Through (Past Days Due) field. For example, if some of your accounts are more than 120 days overdue, you can extend the reporting detail to show the overdue balances that are beyond 120 days by entering 120 in the Through (days past due) field.

To change the length of billing periods in the column heading, we can enter a different number in the Interval (Days) field. We will modify the report to show 15-day billing periods instead of 30 because some vendors request payment in less than 30 days.

5. **Double click** **30** in the Interval (days) field

6. **Type**   **15**

7. Click   **Refresh** to change the column headings to Current, 1–15, 16–30, and so on

You can also drill down on the report to view more transaction details.

8. Double click   an **amount** or a total for a vendor to view the transaction details for that amount. **Double click** the **transaction detail line** to view the transaction

9. Close   the **report** when you have finished, unless you want to print it first

10. Click   **No** to indicate that you do not want to memorize the report

The Accounts Payable Aging Detail Report

Notes
To access the report from the Reports menu:
• Choose the Reports menu, then choose Vendors & Payables, and click A/P Aging Detail to open the report
• Enter 04/30/14 in the Date field
• Press ⟨tab⟩ or click the Refresh button to update the report

1. Click the **Run icon** [Run] under the **A/P Aging Detail report** under the A/P Aging (due and overdue bills) heading to open the report

2. Double click   the **Date field**

3. Type   **04/30/14**

4. Click   the **Refresh button** or press ⟨tab⟩ to update the report:

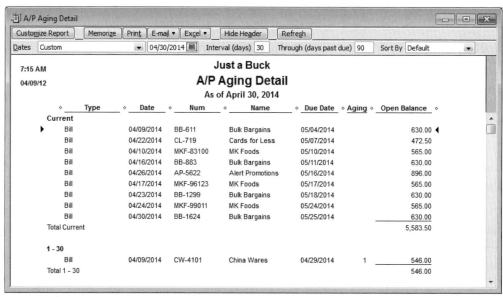

Figure 5-48

The A/P Aging Detail report has a separate line for each transaction by vendor within each period and the due date is displayed for each bill. If a bill is overdue, the Aging column in the report shows the number of days the bill is past due.

You can modify the detail report as you can the summary report. You can change the aging intervals, change the reporting through period, sort by vendor or total, and drill down to view more detail.

Notes
Double clicking a total amount in the A/P Aging Detail report will open the individual transaction.

5. Double click   a **transaction line** to drill down to the transaction

6. Close   the **report** when you have finished, unless you want to print it first

7. Click   **No** to indicate that you do not want to memorize the report, if you changed the report default settings

Vendor Balance Reports

The Vendor Balance Reports show the amounts currently owed to each vendor. The summary report shows only the total amount, while the detail report shows individual transactions, both bills and payments.

The Vendor Balance Summary Report

Notes
To access the report from the Reports menu:
- Choose the Reports menu, then choose Vendors & Payables, and click Vendor Balance Summary to open the report

1. **Click** the **Run icon** under the **Vendor Balance Summary report** under the Vendor Balances heading to open the report:

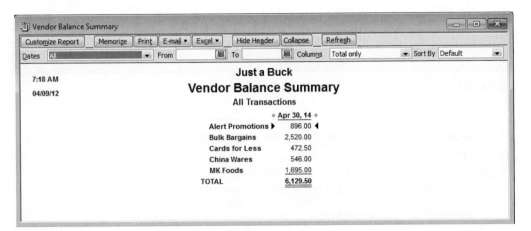

Figure 5-49

The date for this report is entered automatically by the program as the date of the latest transaction. Totals for each vendor are shown as the default but you can add columns for different intervals, such as weeks or months, by choosing from the Columns drop-down list. You can sort the report by total amount instead of the default, by vendor.

2. **Double click** an **amount** or total for a vendor to view the transaction details for that amount

3. **Double click** a **transaction detail line** to view the original bill or payment

4. **Close** the **report** when finished, unless you want to print it first

5. **Click** **No** to indicate that you do not want to memorize the report, if you changed the report default settings

The Vendor Balance Detail Report

Notes
To access the report from the Reports menu:
- Choose the Reports menu, then choose Vendors & Payables, and click Vendor Balance Detail to open the report

1. **Click** the **Run icon** under the **Vendor Balance Detail report** under the Vendor Balances heading to open the report:

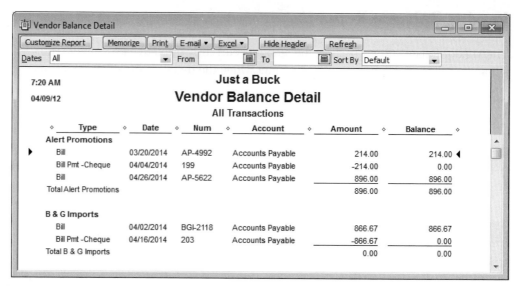

Figure 5-50

The report is organized by vendor, with a line for each bill and payment. All dates are included initially, but you can change the date range for the report in the From and To date fields.

You can sort the report by any of the column headings — Type, Date, Number, Account, and Amount — in either ascending or descending order.

2. **Double click** a **transaction line** to drill down to the transaction

3. **Close** the **report** when finished unless you want to print it first

4. **Click** **No** to indicate that you do not want to memorize the report if you changed the report default settings

The Unpaid Bills Detail Report

The Unpaid Bills Detail report shows which bills have not been paid by a specific date, the due dates, and the age of the bills (number of days). Individual bills are listed.

Notes
To access the report from the Reports menu:
- Choose the Reports menu, then choose Vendors & Payables, and click Unpaid Bills Detail to open the report
- Enter 04/30/14 in the Date field

1. **Click** the **Run icon** ![Run] under the **Unpaid Bills Detail report** under the Vendor Balances heading to open the report

2. **Double click** the **Date field**

3. **Type** **04/30/14**

4. The following report will be displayed:

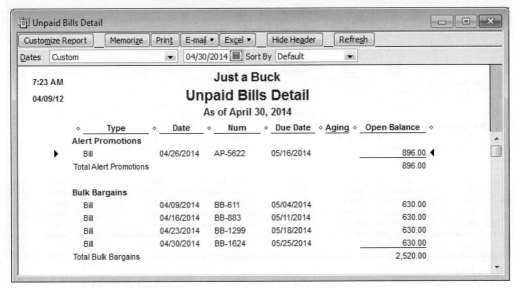

Figure 5-51

The aging column shows the number of days since the bill was entered. You can sort the report by any of the column headings, Type, Date, Number, Due Date, Aging, or Open Balance amount, in either ascending or descending order. Sorting is done within the transactions for each vendor. You can also zoom in to more detail.

5. Double click a **transaction line** to drill down to the bill

6. Close the **report** when finished unless you want to print it first

7. Click **No** to indicate that you do not want to memorize the report if you changed the report default settings

The Transaction List by Vendor Report

This is another report that shows individual transactions for all vendors for the selected report period.

1. Click the **Run icon** under the **Transaction List by Vendor report** under the Vendor Balances heading to open the report

2. Double click the **From date field**

3. Type **04/01/14**

4. Double click the **To date field**

5. Type **04/30/14**

6. Press ⌨tab⌨ or **click** the **Refresh button** to update the report:

Notes
To access the report from the Reports menu:
- Choose the Reports menu, then choose Vendors & Payables, and click Transaction List by Vendor to open the report
- Enter 04/01/14 as the From date
- Enter 04/30/14 as the To date
- Press ⌨tab⌨ or click the Refresh button to update the report

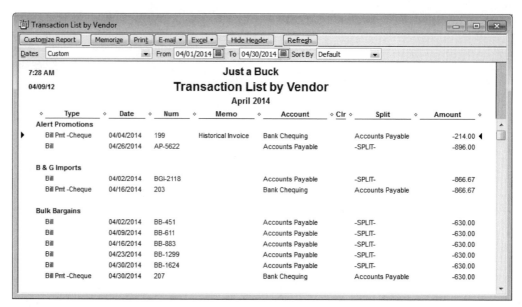

Figure 5-52

Notes

If - SPLIT - appears in the Split column, it indicates that more than one account was used in the transaction.

The Transaction List by Vendor report includes all accounts involved in a transaction. You can sort this report by any of the column headings and show the transactions in ascending or descending order. Sorting is done within the transactions for each vendor.

7. **Double click** a **transaction line** to drill down to the transaction

8. **Close** the **report** when finished

9. **Click** **No** to indicate that you do not want to memorize the report, if you changed the report default settings

Vendor Lists

Notes

To access the report from the Reports menu:
- Choose the Reports menu, then choose Vendors & Payables, and click Vendor Phone List; or
- Choose the Reports menu, then choose List, and click Vendor Phone List

QuickBooks offers two lists for vendors: the phone list and the contact list. These lists allow you to check for missing details.

The Vendor Phone List

The Vendor phone list includes only the vendor's name and phone number.

1. **Click** the **Run icon** under the **Vendor Phone List report** under the Lists heading to open the report:

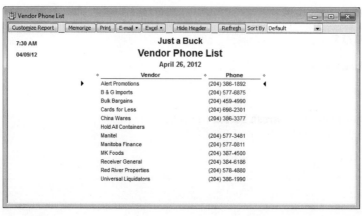

Figure 5-53

You can sort the list by vendor name or by phone number. Sorting by phone number might be useful if you have different vendors with different area codes and want to phone all the vendors in one region.

2. **Close**   the **report** when finished

3. **Click**   **No** to indicate that you do not want to memorize the report, if you changed the report default settings

The Vendor Contact List

The contact list has the vendor's name, account number, address, contact name, phone and fax numbers, and balance owing as at the latest transaction date.

1. **Click** the **Run icon**  under the **Vendor Contact List report** under the Lists heading to open the report:

Figure 5-54

Notes
To access the report from the Reports menu:
- Choose the Reports menu, then choose Vendors & Payables, and click Vendor Contact List; or
- Choose the Reports menu, then choose List, and click Vendor Contact List

You can sort this report by any of the column headings and show the report lines in ascending or descending order.

You can double click on a vendor on the report to open the vendor record and make any necessary changes.

2. **Close**   the **report** when finished

3. **Click**   **No** to indicate that you do not want to memorize the report if you changed the report default settings

Notes
If you double click on a vendor on the report and the Add/Edit Multiple List Entries screen is displayed, close it to open the vendor record.

The Accounts Payable Graph

The final report for vendors is presented as a graph. It shows aging information, as well as the total amount owing to individual vendors.

1. **Click** the **Run icon** under the **Accounts Payable Graph** under the A/P Aging (due and overdue bills) heading to open the graph

2. **Click**   the **Dates button**

3. **Type**   **04/30/14** in the **Show Aging as of field**

4. **Click**   **OK** to view the graph:

Notes
To access the graph from the Reports menu:
- Choose the Reports menu, then choose Vendors & Payables, and click Accounts Payable Graph to open the graph
- Click the Dates button to set the date
- Enter 04/30/14 in the Show Aging as of field
- Click OK to view the report

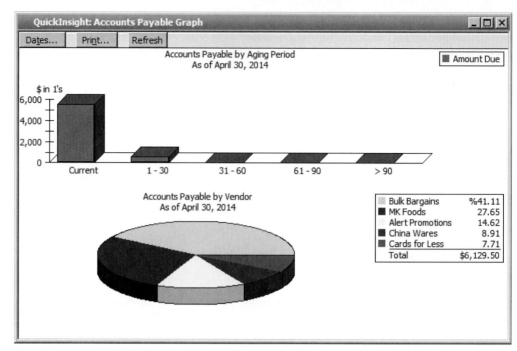

Figure 5-55

The graph has two sections: a bar graph in the upper section that shows the total amount owing for each aging interval, and a pie chart in the lower section that shows the total owing to each vendor. You can zoom down to several other reports and graphs from both sections of the graph.

Double click a bar in the bar chart in the upper section of the graph to view the pie chart breakdown of vendor amounts that make up its total. Then, double click a section of this pie chart to view the A/P Aging report for the vendor selected. Double click a transaction listed in the A/P Aging report to drill down to the transaction.

Double click a pie section in the pie chart in the lower section of the graph to view an aging bar chart for that vendor with separate bars for the total in each aging period. Then, double click a bar in this chart to view the A/P Aging report for the vendor selected. Double click a transaction listed in the A/P Aging report to drill down to the transaction.

5. **Close**   the **report** when finished

6. **Click**   **No** to indicate that you do not want to memorize the report if you changed the report default settings

Finishing Your Session

1. **Back up**   your **company data file**

2. **Close**   the **company file**

3. **Close**   the **QuickBooks program**

Objectives

After completing this chapter, you should be able to:

- *enter* invoices for customer sales

- *enter* customer payments

- *add* complete new customer records

- *deposit* customer payments in a bank account

- *print* sales invoices

- *print* mailing labels

- *enter* NSF cheques from customers

- *correct* sales invoices after recording

- *correct* receipts after recording

- *display* and *print* customer and sales reports and the sales graph

Company Information

Company Profile

Malin's Makeovers, located in Ottawa, Ontario, is owned and operated by Malin
Andersson as a partnership. After studying hairdressing and cosmetology in
Stockholm, Malin Andersson immigrated to Canada. For the next few years, she worked
in some excellent salons, building her reputation and skills. Before launching her own
business, she completed additional courses in colour and design and in business studies.
After working on her own for three years, the demand for her services led her to bring in
two classmates from her course as partners, Kiera O'Sullivan and Dhaibhen Mehta. She
has been operating her salon now for several years. The salon has three booth areas so
that the clients always have privacy during their consultations.

The consultants, affectionately known as "change artists," offer complete makeover
consultations, from changes in hair styles and makeup, to dress, colour, and fashion advice.

Notes
Malin's Makeovers
515 Sparks Street
Ottawa, ON K2C 8J9
Tel: (613) 753-9219
Fax: (613) 753-8003
E-mail: mm@makeover.com
Web: www.makeover.com
Business No.: 277 544 732

They use computer imaging, a digital camera, and specialized software to place the client in photographs with alternate styles, designs, and colours to illustrate how a change in design can be more or less flattering. The partners also advise professionals on dressing or changing their image for a new career or a special occasion. Assistance with wardrobe shopping is also available. Malin's Makeovers has helped some local politicians prepare for increased media exposure. For corporate groups, the team offers training seminars, as well as individual follow-up consultation. Clients can order personalized reports after a consultation.

January and February are busy months for the salon because the consultation sessions are popular gifts for holidays and for Valentine's Day, so the salon is open 7 days a week during these months.

Individual customers pay for their services immediately, while corporate customers have accounts set up with Malin's Makeovers and carry account balances. All customers pay 13 percent HST on services in the salon, and accounts are to be settled within 15 days with no discounts for early payment. Customer cheques and cash are deposited weekly. The salon does not sell any products directly to customers.

The partners use their own vehicles for business travel and always carry their cell phones and laptop computers. In this way, they can contact each other or give client demonstrations at any time. They are reimbursed for expenses. The partners clean the salon themselves daily, but rely on professional cleaners for a thorough weekly service.

Accounts are set up with regular vendors who provide salon supplies, such as cosmetics and hair care products, customized salon chairs, and hair dryers. None of these vendors offers discounts for early payment. Malin's Makeovers pays 13 percent HST on business-related purchases. Invoices are received with merchandise and paid later. Some bills are paid immediately by manually prepared cheques.

At the end of January 2014, the business converted the accounting records to QuickBooks, using the following documents:

- Chart of Accounts
- Trial Balance
- Vendor Information
- Customer Information
- Item List
- Accounting Procedures

Chart of Accounts

Malin's Makeovers

ASSETS
Bank
    Bank Chequing
    Bank Savings

Accounts Receivable
    Accounts Receivable

Other Current Assets
    Cosmetics Supplies
    Hair Care Supplies
    Imaging Software
    Office and Computer Supplies
    Prepaid Insurance

FIXED ASSETS
    Computer Equipment:Cost
    Computer Equipment:Depreciation
    Computer Equipment:Other

Salon:Cost
Salon:Depreciation
Salon Equipment:Cost
Salon Equipment:Depreciation
Salon Furniture:Cost
Salon Furniture:Depreciation

LIABILITIES
Accounts Payable
    Accounts Payable

Other Current Liabilities
    Bank Loan
    GST/HST Payable

Long Term Liabilities
    Long Term Loan
    Mortgage Payable

EQUITY
    Capital, Dhaibhen Mehta
    Capital, Kiera O'Sullivan
    Capital, Malin Andersson
    Drawings, Dhaibhen Mehta
    Drawings, Kiera O'Sullivan
    Drawings, Malin Andersson
    Retained Earnings

INCOME
    Other Revenue
    Revenue from Interest
    Revenue from Services

EXPENSE
    Advertising and Promotion
    Depreciation Expense
    General Expense
    Insurance Expense
    Interest Expense
    Maintenance and Cleaning
    Other Supplies Used
    Salon Supplies Used
    Telephone Expense
    Travel/Vehicle Expenses

Malin's Makeovers

AS AT JANUARY 31, 2014

	Debits	Credits		Debits	Credits
Bank Chequing	$ 8,995.00		Mortgage Payable		120,000.00
Bank Savings	35,460.00		Capital, Dhaibhen Mehta		27,393.56
Accounts Receivable	5,370.70		Capital, Kiera O'Sullivan		27,393.57
Cosmetics Supplies	1,256.00		Capital, Malin Andersson		27,393.57
Hair Care Supplies	980.00		Drawings, Dhaibhen Mehta	2,000.00	
Imaging Software	4,000.00		Drawings, Kiera O'Sullivan	2,000.00	
Office and Computer Supplies	590.00		Drawings, Malin Andersson	2,000.00	
Prepaid Insurance	4,200.00		Revenue from Interest		55.00
Computer Equipment:Cost	12,000.00		Revenue from Services		27,410.00
Computer Equipment:Depreciation		$ 300.00	Advertising and Promotion	1,400.00	
Salon:Cost	180,000.00		Depreciation Expense	1,220.00	
Salon:Depreciation		750.00	General Expense	245.00	
Salon Equipment:Cost	1,400.00		Insurance Expense	2,100.00	
Salon Equipment:Depreciation		20.00	Interest Expense	1,940.00	
Salon Furniture:Cost	18,000.00		Maintenance and Cleaning	600.00	
Salon Furniture:Depreciation		150.00	Other Supplies Used	110.00	
Accounts Payable		2,506.00	Salon Supplies Used	195.00	
Bank Loan		8,000.00	Telephone Expense	285.00	
GST/HST Payable		1,325.00	Travel/Vehicle Expenses	1,350.00	
Long Term Loan		45,000.00		$287,696.70	$287,696.70

Vendor Information

Malin's Makeovers

Vendor Name (Contact)	Address	Phone No. Fax No.	E-mail Business No.	Terms Credit Limit
Crystal Wireless Communications (Kia Noe)	399 Mobility Ave. Kanata, ON K5C 1Y5	Tel: (613) 462-3918 Fax: (613) 462-7322	kia.noe@cwc.com	net 10 $500.00
Faces Inc. (Klier Visages)	8 Foundation St. Ottawa, ON K3B 5D6	Tel: (613) 776-2938 Fax: (613) 776-2199	kv@facesinc.com 384 674 288	net 30 $3,000.00
Keep It Clean (Mollie Maydes)	25 Sanitizing St. Ottawa, ON K4B 7J1	Tel: (613) 288-1725		net 15 $1,000.00
Ministry of Finance (ON)				
Office Outfitters (Daye Tymer)	210 Stationery Rd. Ottawa, ON K3J 7V2	Tel: (613) 622-3456 Fax: (613) 622-3917	273 911 720	net 20 $2,000.00
Receiver General				due quarterly

Outstanding Vendor Transactions

Malin's Makeovers

Vendor Name	Date	Terms	Due Date	Invoice No.	Amount	Total Owing
Faces Inc.	01/06/2014	net 30	02/05/2014	F-4910	$805.00	$805.00
Keep It Clean	01/20/2014	net 15	02/04/2014	KC-662	$160.50	
	01/27/2014	net 15	02/11/2014	KC-688	$160.50	$321.00
Office Outfitters	01/24/2014	net 20	02/13/2014	00-500	$1,380.00	$1,380.00
				Grand Total		$2,506.00

Malin's Makeovers

Customer Name (Contact)	Address	Phone No. Fax No.	E-mail Tax Code	Terms Credit Limit
AIM International (Purdey Lookes)	5180 Richmond St. Ottawa, ON K2H 8B4	Tel: (613) 688-3613 Fax: (613) 688-1928	plookes@AIM.com H	net 15 $5,000.00
Cash Sales			H	due on receipt
Jammers (Harde Rock)	69 Swingers Ave. Ottawa, ON K4P 1M8	Tel: (613) 527-5223 Fax: (613) 527-3813	rocke@jammers.com H	net 15 $3,000.00
ODSB (Sloe Lerner)	450 Fastrak Rd. Ottawa, ON K4B 2B6	Tel: (613) 725-4611 Fax: (613) 725-9124	slerner@odsb.on.ca H	net 15 $5,000.00
OTV News (Vanna Taye)	13 Broadcast Ave. Ottawa, ON K7G 3P8	Tel: (613) 286-3977 Fax: (613) 286-0971	vanna@otv.com H	net 15 $5,000.00

Malin's Makeovers

Customer Name	Date	Terms	Due Date	Invoice No.	Amount	Total Owing
AIM International	01/18/2014	net 15	02/02/2014	3084	$ 588.50	
	01/28/2014	net 15	02/12/2014	3118	$1,177.00	$1,765.50
Jammers	01/19/2014	net 15	02/03/2014	3092	$ 609.90	$ 609.90
ODSB	01/24/2014	net 15	02/08/2014	3101	$ 856.00	$ 856.00
OTV News	01/21/2014	net 15	02/05/2014	3097	$2,139.30	$2,139.30
					Grand Total	$5,370.70

Malin's Makeovers

Item	Description	Price	Tax Code	Revenue Account
Clothing style consultation	Consultation on suitable clothing styles and colours	$190.00	H	Revenue from Services
Customized seminar/training	Customized training seminars and presentations	custom pricing	H	Revenue from Services
General consultation	General consultation charged on hourly basis	$110.00/hour	H	Revenue from Services
Hair consultation	Hair style consultation and cut	$150.00	H	Revenue from Services
Makeover	Complete makeover consultation: hair, makeup, and clothing	$390.00	H	Revenue from Services
Makeup consultation	Consultation and demonstration of makeup techniques	$120.00	H	Revenue from Services
Report	Personalized makeover report following consultation	$90.00	H	Revenue from Services
NSF Charges	Service fee for NSF cheque	$25.00	Not Used	Other Revenue
NSF Cheque	Amount of NSF cheque	cheque amount	Not Used	Bank Chequing

Accounting Procedures

Taxes: HST

📄 **Notes**
Refer to the Tax Appendix (found on the CD that accompanies this text) for details on sales taxes.

Malin's Makeovers pays HST on all goods and services that it buys and charges HST on all services it provides. It uses the regular method for remittance of the HST. HST collected from customers is recorded as a liability in the *GST/HST Payable* account. HST paid to vendors is recorded in the *GST/HST Payable* account as a decrease in liability to the Canada Revenue Agency. The report is filed with the Receiver General for Canada every quarter, remitting the balance owing or requesting a refund.

Account Terms

Most customers have set up accounts with Malin and are expected to settle these accounts by cheque within 15 days. One-time customers who do not order customized services pay by cash immediately at the time of the service. These cash sales are summarized and entered on a weekly basis as total sales for the week.

All cash and cheques are held in the on-site safe until they are deposited to the bank account. Bank deposits are made weekly.

Accounts are also set up with most vendors, although none presently offers discounts for early payment. Malin pays for business purchases by cheque.

Supplies

The partners count the supplies left in the salon on a monthly basis to determine the cost of materials and supplies used. Adjusting entries are then made.

Partner Expenses and Drawings

Each partner draws $2,000.00 per month in lieu of a salary. Partners are also reimbursed for their travel expenses at a rate of $0.50 per kilometre when they use their personal vehicles for business. Reimbursement is made at the end of each month.

Instructions

1. Using the Chart of Accounts, the Trial Balance, and other information, you will record entries for source documents for February 2014, using QuickBooks. You will find the source documents marked with an SD beside them and listed as you work through the chapter. The procedures for entering each new type of transaction introduced in this chapter are outlined in step-by-step instructions. Additional source documents will be provided, allowing you to have more practice entering transactions. If you have used this textbook in the past and would prefer to skip the step-by-step instructions and work only with a list of source documents, refer to the CD in the back of the textbook for the list of source documents for this chapter.

📄 **Notes**
Instructions for printing Customer and Sales reports begin on page 313.

2. After you have finished making your entries, print the reports and graphs for February 2014 as indicated on the following printing form:

REPORTS FOR FEBRUARY 2014

Lists
- ☐ Account Listing
- ☐ Customer Phone List
- ☐ Customer Contact List
- ☐ Vendor Phone List
- ☐ Vendor Contact List
- ☐ Item Listing
- ☐ Item Price List

Company & Financial
- ☑ Balance Sheet Standard at Feb. 28
- ☑ Profit & Loss Standard from Feb. 1 to Feb. 28
- ☐ Expenses by Vendor
- ☐ Income by Customer

Accountant & Taxes
- ☑ Trial Balance at Feb. 28
- ☐ General Ledger
- ☑ Journal from Feb. 1 to Feb. 28
- ☐ Transaction List by Date
- ☐ Transaction Detail by Account

Other
- ☐ Custom Summary Report
- ☐ Custom Transaction Detail Report
- ☐ Transaction History
- ☐ Transaction Journal

Vendor
- ☑ A/P Aging at Feb. 28
- ☐ Vendor Balance
- ☐ Unpaid Bills
- ☐ Transaction List by Vendor

Customer
- ☑ A/R Aging at Feb. 28
- ☑ Customer Balance
- ☐ Open Invoices
- ☐ Collections Report
- ☐ Transaction List by Customer

Sales
- ☑ Sales by Customer from Feb. 1 to Feb. 28
- ☐ Sales by Item

GRAPHS
- ☐ Income and Expense
- ☐ Net Worth
- ☐ Accounts Payable
- ☑ Accounts Receivable at Feb. 28
- ☑ Sales from Feb. 1 to Feb. 28

---

3. Open Malin.qbw, the data file for Malin's Makeovers

Entering Sales Invoices

Entering sales transactions for merchandise purchased by your customers on account is similar to entering Sales Receipts. However, instead of entering cash sales where the payment is made by the customer at the time of invoice entry using the Enter Sales Receipts form, as you learned in Chapter 2, you enter the customer invoice, the customer pays you at a later time, and the payment must be deposited in the bank. Depending on whether the deposit is sent directly to the bank, this could result in two or three transactions in QuickBooks.

The first transaction that we will enter is an invoice sent to our customer, AIM International. Refer to the following source document as we work through the steps to enter it:

Source Docs
Refer to the following source document and then follow the step-by-step instructions to enter it.

SD1: Invoice   **Dated February 1, 2014**

Invoice #3125 to AIM International, $3,150.00 plus $409.50 HST for customized seminars on international dress standards to prepare employees for overseas assignments. Invoice total: $3,559.50. Terms: Net 15 days.

Customer transactions can be entered from three different areas in QuickBooks:

a. The Customers section of the Home page:

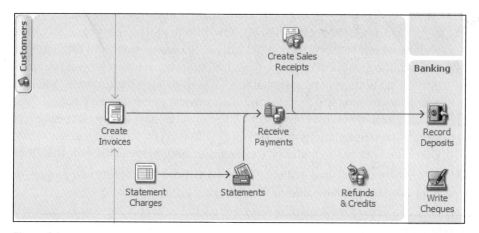

Figure 6-1

The Customers section of the Home page is organized like a flow chart that indicates the usual sequence of transactions. A portion of the Banking section has been included to show the Record Deposits icon.

For example, after entering customer invoices, the next step is to receive payments and then record the deposits. Finance charges, customer statements, and credits or refunds may occur before payments are received. Finance charges and credits will be covered in a later chapter. We have turned off the Sales Orders and Estimates options because they are not used by Malin's Makeovers, so the icons for them have been removed from this company file.

b. The Customers menu:

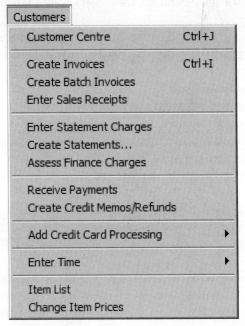

Figure 6-2

You can use the Customers menu to access the Customer Centre, enter customer transactions, and access the item list.

c. The Customer Centre:

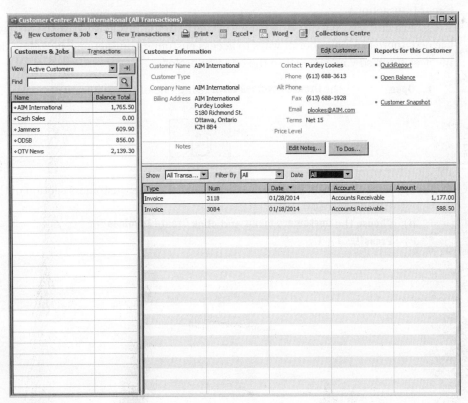

Figure 6-3

The Customer Centre contains more information and it requires more explanation. On the left-hand side of the screen, you'll see two tabs: a Customers & Jobs tab and a Transactions tab.

When you click on the Customers & Jobs tab, the customer list is displayed on the left-hand side of the screen, which displays each customer's name and total balance. You can sort the customer & jobs list by customer name or total balance and by ascending or descending order by clicking on the list headings.

When you highlight a customer in the list, their customer information is displayed in the top right portion of the screen, allowing you to quickly view the customer address information, click on the Edit Customer button to access the customer record where you can make changes to it, click on the QuickReport or Open Balance button to print reports for the customer, use the Edit Notes button to add notes to the customer record, or use the To Dos button to add an item on the To Do list for the customer. The transaction details for the customer are listed in the bottom right portion of the screen. You can use the headings across the top of the transaction details to select which type of transactions you'd like to view and filter them by a date range.

You can use the buttons across the top of the screen to add a new customer & job, enter new transactions, print customer information, export information to Microsoft Excel, or print Microsoft Word documents. The customer highlighted in the customers & jobs list will automatically be selected when you choose one of these options.

When you click on the Transactions tab, a list of transaction types is displayed on the left-hand side of the screen. When you click on one of the transaction types, a list of all transactions for all customers will be displayed based on the criteria selected in the Filter By and Date fields.

As we work through this chapter, we will use various methods to access the customer transactions.

In this first transaction, we will be working with the Invoices form. As you have learned, there are a number of ways to access customer transactions, including the Invoices form, so you can choose the one you prefer.

1. **Open** the **Create Invoices form** using one of the following options:

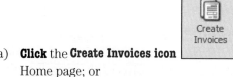

Create
Invoices

a) **Click** the **Create Invoices icon** in the Customers section of the Home page; or
b) **Choose** the **Customers menu** and **click Create Invoices**; or
c) **Press** ⌨ctrl + **I**

2. The Create Invoices form is displayed as shown:

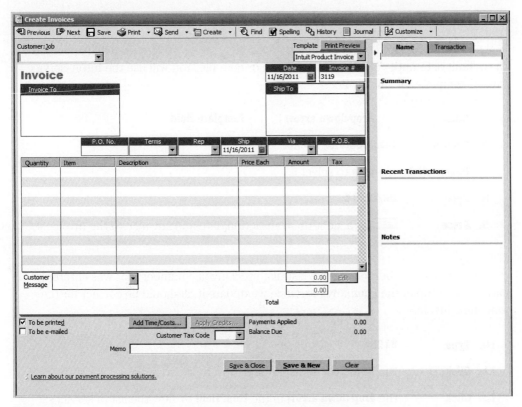

Figure 6-4

Notice that this form resembles the Sales Receipt form, but the deposit and payment method details are missing because the payments are made later. Completing the invoice is also similar to entering Sales Receipts.

The history tab, displayed to the right of the invoice form, will display customer and transaction information for the customer when one is selected for the transaction. This tab can be closed by clicking on the Hide history arrow in the top left-hand corner of the tab.

3. Click the **drop-down arrow** in the **Customer: Job field** to view the list of customers on file:

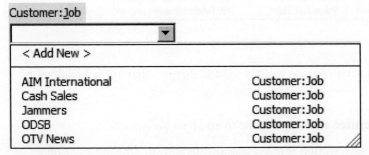

Figure 6-5

> **Notes**
> We will close the history tab before taking most transaction print screens for this textbook. You can close the history tab by clicking the Hide history arrow in the top left-hand corner of the history tab.
> If you want to open the history tab after closing it, click the Show history arrow in the top right-hand corner of the transaction screen.

4. Click   **AIM International**

The customer address and payment terms (net 15 days) are added to the form from the customer record. The current calendar date is entered as the default date. As in the previous chapter, once you enter transactions, the last date used will appear as the default date until you close the program or data file. You will use the Intuit Service Invoice template for this invoice.

5. Click   the **drop-down arrow** in the **Template field**

6. Choose   **Intuit Service Invoice**

7. Double click   the **date** to select it

8. Type   **02/01/14**

9. Press   ⎡tab⎤ to accept the transaction date and advance to the Invoice # field

The invoice number follows the last historical invoice number that was entered as part of the setup of the company file. Once we update it, it should be correct for the remaining invoices.

10. Type   **3125**

11. Click   the **Item field** to display the drop-down arrow

12. Click   the **drop-down arrow** in the **Item field** to view the list of services available for selection:

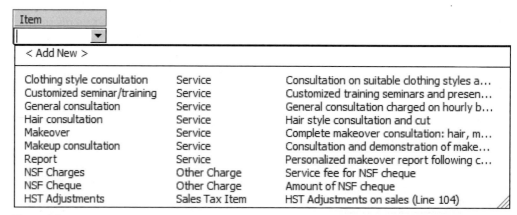

Figure 6-6

Notice the list includes two entries related to NSF cheques that are not customer services for regular sale. These will be used later in the chapter.

13. Click   **Customized seminar/training** to add it to the invoice

Notice that the item description is automatically displayed. This information is coming from the item record.

14. Press   ⎡tab⎤ to advance to the Quantity field (Qty)

For customized work, the quantity is one and the price is negotiated before the work is started.

15.	**Type**	**1**
16.	**Press**	(tab) to skip the Description field and advance to the Rate field
17.	**Type**	**3150**
18.	**Press**	(tab) to update the Amount and taxes
19.	**Click**	the **drop-down arrow** in the **Customer Message field**
20.	**Choose**	**It's been a pleasure working with you!**

We will print the invoices in batches later so the invoice is now complete as shown:

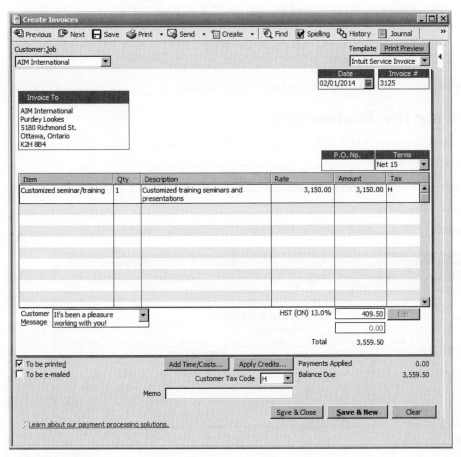

Figure 6-7

21.	**Check**	your **work** carefully before recording the invoice so you won't need to make corrections later

CORRECTING SALES INVOICES

Click the field that contains the error. You can press (tab) to move forward from one field to the next. Highlight the incorrect information and type the correct information in the field. Press (tab) if necessary to update the information.

If the incorrect information was selected from a list, click the drop-down arrow again and select the correct item. If you select a different item, you must re-enter the quantity and/or the amount. If you change the amount, press (tab) to update the taxes and totals.

Click the Clear button to start again.

We want to review the journal entry created from this transaction, so we need to save the invoice and keep the Create Invoices form open on the screen.

22.	**Click**	**Save & New** or **press** (alt) **+ S** to record the invoice and leave the Create Invoices form open. You will see the following warning:

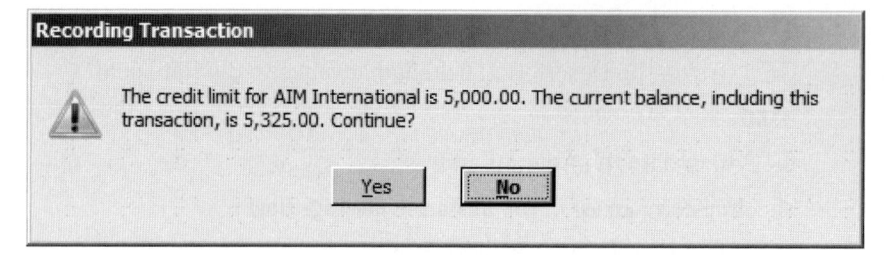

Figure 6-8

AIM International has a credit limit of $5,000.00 and an outstanding balance. The current invoice will cause them to exceed this credit limit so you must choose what to do next. You can proceed with the sale or contact the customer and request a deposit or payment before continuing. We will proceed with the sale because the company has always paid its account on time.

23. Click   **Yes** to continue and record the invoice

Reviewing the Transaction

To begin this exercise, a blank invoice should be displayed on the Create Invoices form from the previous exercise.

1. Click   the **Previous button** [Previous] or **press** (alt) + **P** to view the invoice we just completed

2. Press   (ctrl) + **Y** to view the Transaction Journal report:

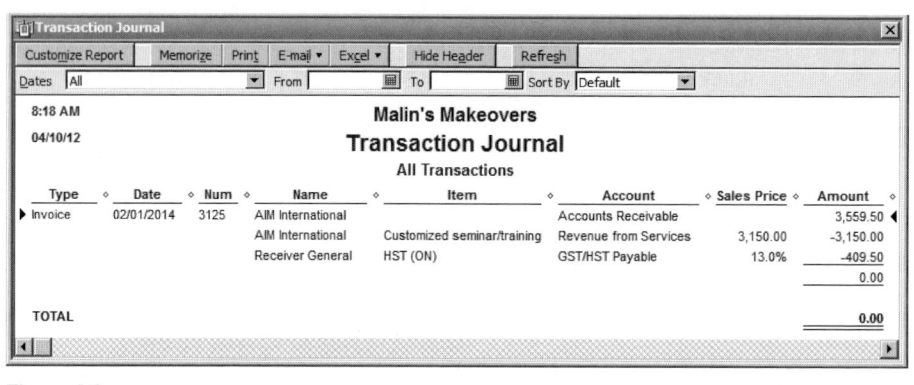

Figure 6-9

The complete journal entry is included, with all accounts properly debited and credited. Credit amounts contain a minus sign. QuickBooks has made the entry in the background by increasing the *Accounts Receivable* balance. The *Accounts Receivable* debit entry is matched by the credit entries for *Revenue from Services* and *GST/HST Payable*. The customer's account balance — amount owing — has also increased by the total amount of the sale.

3. Click   [X] when you have finished viewing the journal entry to close the Transaction Journal report and return to the Invoice for AIM International

The next transaction that we are going to enter is a cash receipt so we will close the Create Invoices form.

4. Click   **No** to indicate that you do not want to memorize the report if you changed the default report settings

5. Click   [X] to close the Create Invoices form and return to the QuickBooks Home page

Entering Customer Payments

The second transaction that we are going to enter is a cheque from AIM International that should be applied to historical invoices. Historical invoices are invoices that were outstanding before the accounting records were converted to QuickBooks. Refer to the following source document as we work through the steps to enter it:

SD2: Customer Payment   **Dated February 2, 2014**

> From AIM International, Cheque #1285 for $1,100.00 in payment of account. Reference Invoices #3084 and #3118. Cheque held for deposit.

In this transaction, one cheque has been received to partially pay the account. The first invoice is fully paid and the second invoice is partially paid. Customer payments are entered after the invoices are recorded in the Receive Payments form.

You cannot enter customer payments received for payment of invoices on the Sales Receipts form. The Sales Receipts form is used only for cash sales — sales that are accompanied by a payment.

Source Docs
Refer to the following source document and then follow the step-by-step instructions to enter it.

⚠ WARNING!
Do not attempt to use the Sales Receipts form for payments on account. This form is used only for cash sales – sales that are accompanied by payment.

1. **Click**   the **Receive Payments icon** in the Customers section of the Home page, or **choose** the **Customers menu** and **click Receive Payments** to open the Receive Payments form:

Notes
The Icon bar does not include an icon to access the Receive Payments form directly. You can access the form from the Customers menu. We will add an icon for it on the Icon bar after entering the receipt.

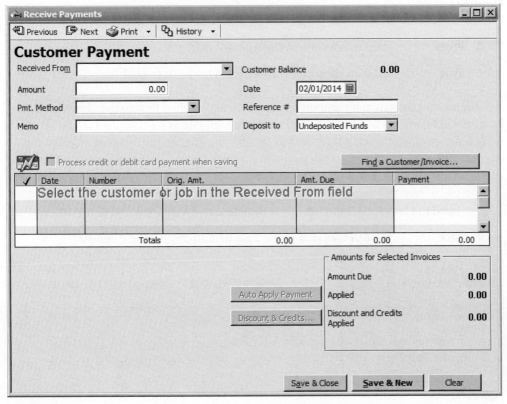

Figure 6-10

2. **Click**   the **drop-down arrow** in the **Received From field** to access the list of customers

3. **Choose**   **AIM International**

4. All outstanding invoices for AIM International are displayed in the Receive Payments form as shown:

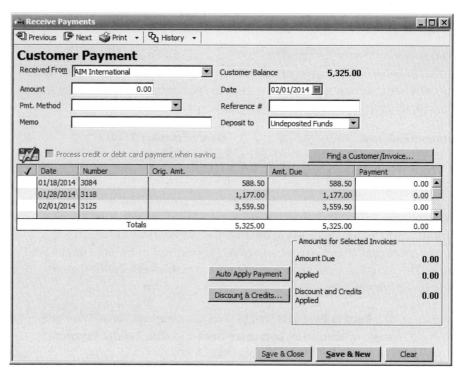

Figure 6-11

5. Press `tab` to advance to the Amount field

6. Type **1100** and **press** `tab` to advance to the date field

Notice that the payment amount is automatically applied first to the oldest invoice, Invoice #3084, until it is fully paid. The remaining amount is then applied to the second oldest invoice, Invoice #3118, and so on. You can change the invoices selected for payment if needed by entering the payment for each invoice in the Payment field in its corresponding invoice line.

We will accept the invoices and amounts selected for payment.

We need to change the date for this transaction to February 2, 2014.

7. Click the **calendar icon** in the **Date field** to display the calendar:

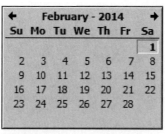

Figure 6-12

8. Click **2** on the February 2014 calendar

If you closed the data file before opening the Receive Payments form, the current date will be displayed in the date field and depending on the current year, you may have to scroll through a number of months to reach the one you want. In that case, it would be easier to manually type 02/02/14 in the Date field.

9. Press `tab` to advance to the Pmt. Method field

> ⚠️ **WARNING!**
> If the current date appears in the Date field, the calendar will show the current month. When you display the calendar, you can click the right arrow at the top of the calendar to advance through consecutive months or the left arrow to move through previous months until you find the month you need.

10.	**Click**	the **drop-down arrow** to display the payment methods available on the payment method list:

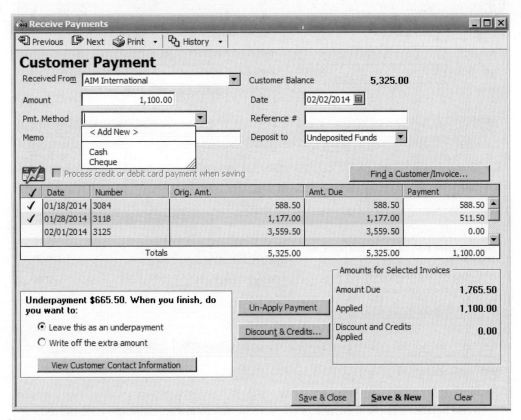

Figure 6-13

You can select a payment method in the list or create a new payment method by selecting the <Add New> option.

11.	**Select**	**Cheque** and **press** (tab)
12.	**Type**	**1285** in the **Cheque # field**
13.	**Press**	(tab) until you reach the Deposit to field

The final option that we have to select is whether the cheque is held for later deposit or deposited immediately to the bank account. In previous chapters, we deposited receipts immediately to the bank account. Malin's Makeovers holds the cheques and makes weekly deposits. Thus the Undeposited Funds account is the account to which we want to deposit this receipt.

14.	**Accept**	the **Undeposited Funds account** (select it if necessary)
15.	The completed customer payment is displayed in the Receive Payments form as shown:

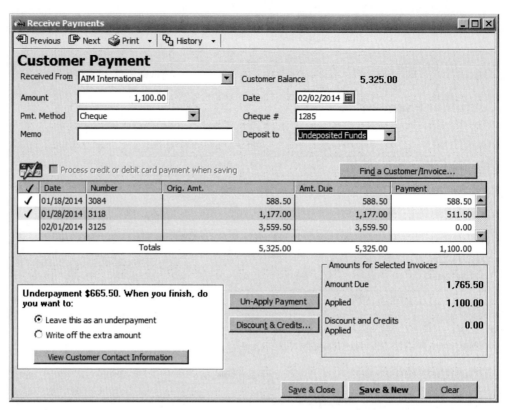

Figure 6-14

In the bottom left-hand corner of the screen, the following message is displayed:

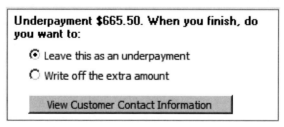

Figure 6-15

This message indicates that there is an underpayment of $665.50 and asks whether you want to leave the amount as an underpayment or write off the extra amount. This message is displayed because a partial payment has been made on Invoice #3118. AIM International still owes you the balance of $665.50 on this invoice, so you will accept the default option to leave the amount as an underpayment.

16. Check   your **work** carefully before recording the sale so you won't have to make corrections later

> **CORRECTING CUSTOMER PAYMENTS**
>
> Click the field that contains the error. Press `tab` to move forward from one field to the next. Highlight the incorrect information and type the correct information in the field. Press `tab` if necessary to update the information.
>
> You can also start the transaction again by clicking the Clear button.

17. Click   **Save & New** or **press** `alt` **+ S** to record the customer payment

Reviewing the Transaction

In this exercise, we will review the journal entry that was created by the customer payment. But before we do, let's review the updated outstanding payments for AIM International.

With a blank Receive Payments form displayed on the screen:

1. Click   the **drop-down arrow** in the **Received From field** and **select Aim International**

2. You will see that the list of outstanding invoices for AIM International has been updated:

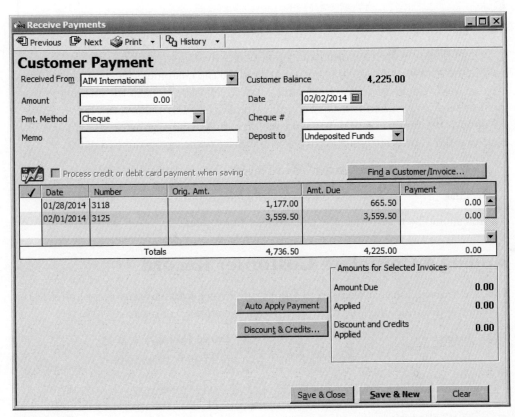

Figure 6-16

Notice Invoice #3084 is no longer displayed in the list, the amount due for the next invoice has been reduced by the partial payment of $511.50, and the amount due is $665.50; the amount you saw in Figure 6-15.

We will now look at the journal entry for the customer payment we entered in the previous exercise.

3. Click   the **Clear button** at the bottom of the form to clear the form

4. Click   the **Previous button** Previous to view the completed customer payment

5. Press ⌨`ctrl` **+ Y** to view the Transaction Journal report:

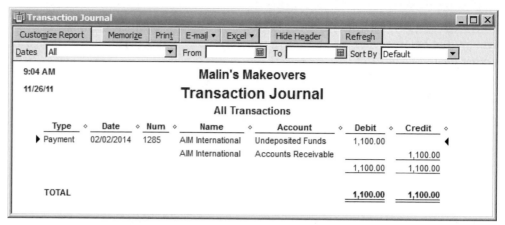

Figure 6-17

QuickBooks created a journal entry that debits the *Undeposited Funds* account and credits the *Accounts Receivable* account to reduce the customer's balance. QuickBooks created the *Undeposited Funds* account when we chose to deposit the customer payment to the *Undeposited Funds* account on the Receive Payments form. Later, when we deposit the funds in the Make Deposits form, they will be transferred from the *Undeposited Funds* account (credit) to the *Bank Chequing* account (debit).

6. Close the **Transaction Journal report**

7. Click ☒ to close the Receive Payments form

You should be returned to the QuickBooks Home page.

Adding a Complete Customer Record

The next transaction that we need to enter is an invoice for a new customer. Refer to the following source document as we work through the steps to enter it:

 Source Docs
Refer to the following source document and then follow the step-by-step instructions to enter it.

SD3: Invoice   **Dated February 3, 2014**

Invoice #3126 to Amore Bridal Party (Set up the new customer)

3	Clothing style consultations	$190.00 each	$ 570.00
5	General consultations	110.00 each	550.00
3	Reports	90.00 each	270.00
	HST 13%		180.70
	Invoice total		$1,570.70
	Terms: Net 15 days		

Notes
Amore Bridal Party
Contact: Ms Lisa Amore
250 Busquer St.
Ottawa, ON K3R 2P8
Canada
Phone: (613) 769-4180
Fax: (613) 769-3829
Alt. Phone: (613) 534-9418
E-mail: l.amore@romanza.ca
Tax Code: HST
Terms: Net 15
Credit Limit: $3,000.00
Pay by: Cheque

You can add new customer records from several locations in QuickBooks. In previous chapters, we added customer names only by choosing Quick Add when we typed a new name in a Customer:Job field in a transaction form. We can also add complete customer details when entering a new name in a Customer:Job field in a transaction form by choosing Set Up instead of Quick Add when prompted.

When you type a new name in the Customer:Job field on a sales transaction form and press ⌨`tab`, the following Customer:Job Not Found message containing the customer name you entered is displayed:

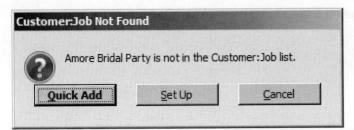

Customer:Job Not Found

Amore Bridal Party is not in the Customer:Job list.

[**Quick Add**]   [Set Up]   [Cancel]

Figure 6-18

Choosing Set Up opens the Customer record where you can enter detailed customer information, such as address details and payment terms. When you click OK after entering the customer information, you will be returned to the sales transaction form with the record details — terms and address information — added to the transaction.

You can also add customers directly on the Customers & Jobs list found in the Customer Centre. To access the Customer Centre:

1. **Click** the **Customers icon** [Customers] on the Icon bar to open the Customer Centre:

Notes
You can also open the Customer Centre from the Customers menu, clicking on the Customers icon in the Customer section of the Home page or by pressing `ctrl` + **J**.

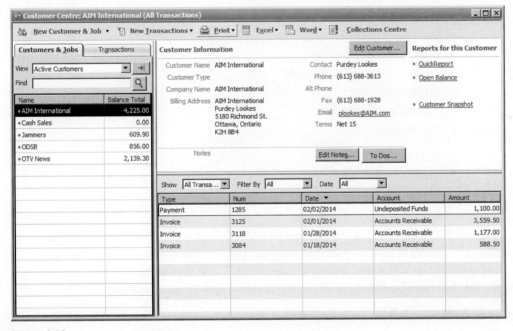

Figure 6-19

The following methods can be used to add a new customer in the Customer Centre:

a) **Click** the **New Customer & Job button** at the top of the screen to add a new customer or job as shown:

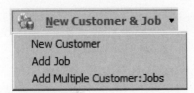

New Customer
Add Job
Add Multiple Customer:Jobs

Figure 6-20

b) **Right-click** the **Customers & Jobs** list to display the following menu:

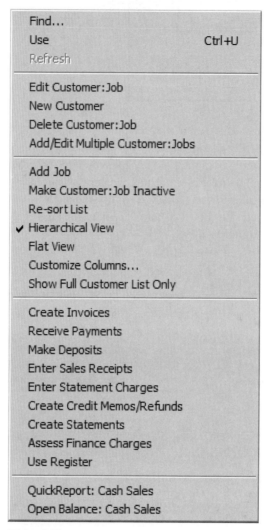

Find...	
Use	Ctrl+U
Refresh	

Edit Customer:Job
New Customer
Delete Customer:Job
Add/Edit Multiple Customer:Jobs

Add Job
Make Customer:Job Inactive
Re-sort List
✓ Hierarchical View
Flat View
Customize Columns...
Show Full Customer List Only

Create Invoices
Receive Payments
Make Deposits
Enter Sales Receipts
Enter Statement Charges
Create Credit Memos/Refunds
Create Statements
Assess Finance Charges
Use Register

QuickReport: Cash Sales
Open Balance: Cash Sales

Figure 6-21

From this menu you can create new customers, edit existing customer records, delete a customer record, or make an unused customer record inactive if it does not meet the deletion criteria so it does not appear in forms that access the Customers & Jobs list. You can also enter customer transactions directly from this menu.

Notes
The keyboard shortcut *ctrl* + **N** can be used in all lists to open a new form.

c) **Press** *ctrl* + **N** the New keyboard shortcut

2. Click   the **New Customer & Job button** and **click New Customer** or **press** `ctrl` + **N** to open a blank New Customer form:

3. Click   in the **box** beside Do not display this message in the future on the Add/Edit Multiple List Entries window and **click OK**

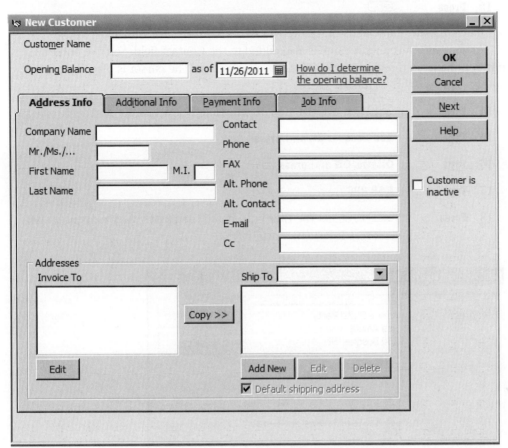

Figure 6-22

The cursor is in the Customer Name field, where you add the name of the customer.

4. Type   **Amore Bridal Party**

The historical transactions were already entered in the company file before you began entering transactions.

There is no opening balance to enter for this customer because this is a new customer. If there were an opening balance, you would enter the opening balance in the as of field so that the opening balance could be aged correctly, according to the payment terms.

The date displayed in the as of field will be the current system date on your computer.

5. Click   the **Company Name field**

6. Type   **Amore Bridal Party**

7. Press   `tab` to move to the title (Mr./Ms.) field

8. Type   **Ms**

9. Press   `tab` to move to the First Name field

10. **Type**	Lisa
11. **Press**	(tab) twice to move to the Last Name field
12. **Type**	Amore
13. **Press**	(tab)

The company name and contact appear in the Address area under the Invoice To section, and the contact name is also added to the Contact field. You can enter a different name in the Contact field if this is appropriate. The cursor is placed after the contact name in the Address text area.

14. **Press**	(enter) to move the cursor to the line below Lisa Amore
15. **Type**	**250 Busquer St.** and **press** (enter)
16. **Type**	**Ottawa, ON** and **press** (enter)
17. **Type**	**K3R 2P8**
18. **Press**	(tab) to select the Edit button and then **press** (enter) to open the Edit Address Information window:

WARNING!

Pressing (tab) in the Address text box will take the cursor out of the address area and select the Edit button.

Pressing (enter) in the Address text box will allow you to enter each address line; however, pressing (enter) in a field other than the Address text box will save and close the record because the OK button is selected by default.

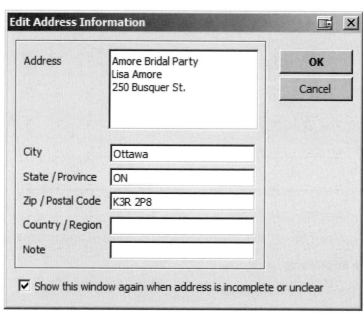

Figure 6-23

You can enter additional lines of address information on the Edit Address Information screen and correct the address details if needed. Alternatively, you could have opened the Edit Address Information screen and entered the details in here first. We will add the country information on this screen. This screen also has a field for an address note.

Notes
The note entered on the Edit Address Information screen will be displayed below the customer address. To add a general note for the customer record, you must save the customer record and then edit the record and add a note. The Notes button appears after you create the customer record.

19. **Correct**	the **address details** if needed
20. **Click**	the **Country/Region field**
21. **Type**	**Canada**
22. **Click**	**OK** to return to the Customer Record
23. **Click**	the **Copy button** Copy >> to copy the invoice address to the ship to address box

24. The Add Shipping Address Information screen is displayed:

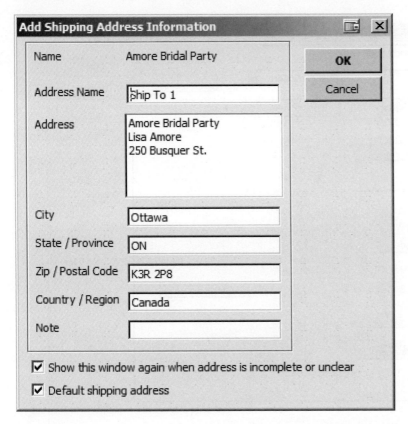

Add Shipping Address Information

Name	Amore Bridal Party	**OK**
Address Name	Ship To 1	Cancel
Address	Amore Bridal Party Lisa Amore 250 Busquer St.	
City	Ottawa	
State / Province	ON	
Zip / Postal Code	K3R 2P8	
Country / Region	Canada	
Note		

☑ Show this window again when address is incomplete or unclear

☑ Default shipping address

Figure 6-24

The ship to address is automatically given the name *Ship To 1*. If a checkmark is displayed beside the Default shipping address option, this address will be the default ship to address on sales forms. If the customer has merchandise shipped to different locations, you can enter multiple ship to addresses by clicking on the Add New button below the Ship To address text box on the customer record. Each ship to address will be given a unique name and that name can be selected on customer transactions if a template allowing ship to addresses is selected.

25.	**Click**	**OK** to accept the ship to address information
26.	**Click**	the **Phone field**
27.	**Type**	**(613) 769-4180**
28.	**Press**	⌨ tab to advance to the FAX field
29.	**Type**	**(613) 769-3829**
30.	**Press**	⌨ tab to advance to the Alt. Phone field. Amore has given her home number as an alternate
31.	**Type**	**(613) 534-9418**
32.	**Press**	⌨ tab to skip the Alt. Contact field and advance to the E-mail field
33.	**Type**	**l.amore@romanza.ca**

📄 **Notes**
Phone numbers are not automatically formatted by QuickBooks. You must manually format each phone number.

34. Click   the **Additional Info tab**:

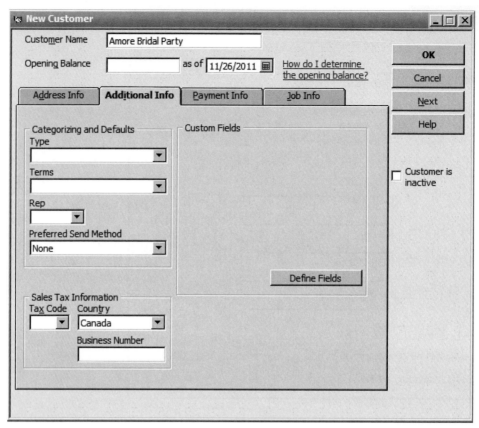

Figure 6-25

Malin's Makeovers does not use customer types, such as region, or type of business to organize their customer records. It also does not keep track of customer and vendor business numbers.

The Rep field may be used to select an employee from a list if one is usually assigned to the customer. Malin's Makeovers does not have employees so we will not be selecting a Rep for each customer.

35. Click   the **drop-down arrow** in the **Terms field** to view the payment terms already set up

36. Click   **Net 15** to add the term to the customer record

37. Click   the **drop-down arrow** in the **Tax Code field**

The default code is H; HST at 13 percent is applied to services.

38. Click   **H**

The H tax code will now be added to invoices for this customer automatically but can, of course, be changed for individual items if necessary.

39. Click   the **Payment Info tab**:

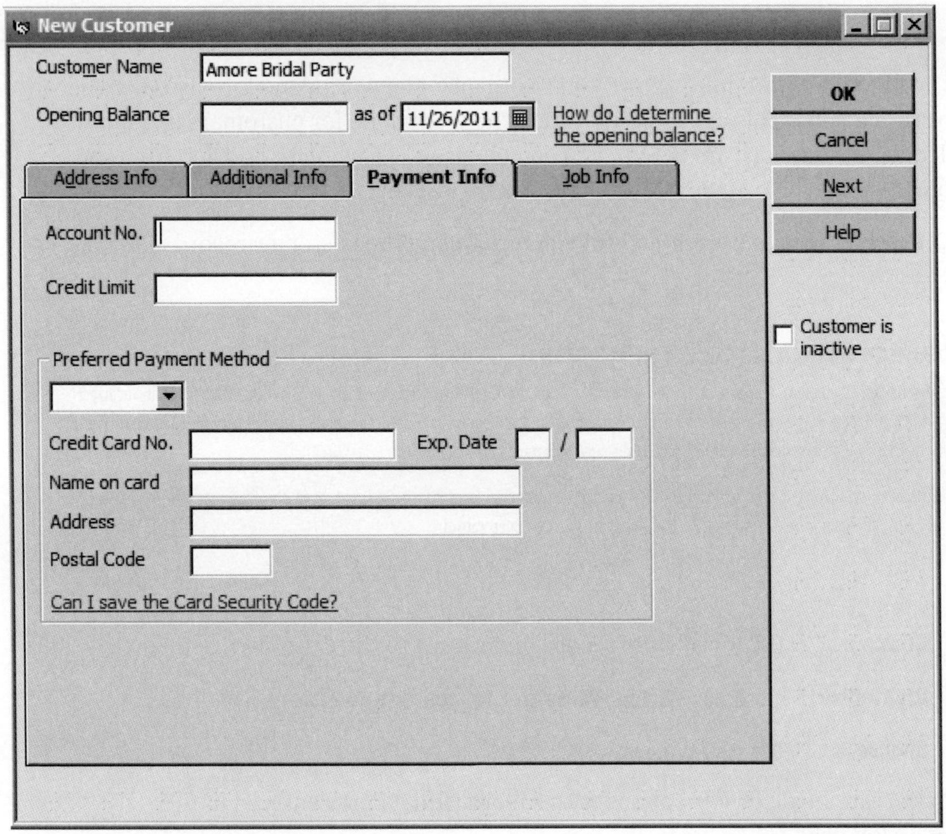

![New Customer dialog box showing the Payment Info tab. Customer Name: Amore Bridal Party. Opening Balance field, as of 11/26/2011. Tabs: Address Info, Additional Info, Payment Info, Job Info. Account No. and Credit Limit fields. Preferred Payment Method section with drop-down, Credit Card No., Exp. Date, Name on card, Address, Postal Code fields. Buttons: OK, Cancel, Next, Help. Checkbox: Customer is inactive.]

Figure 6-26

Most businesses place limits on the amount that a customer is allowed to purchase on credit. Once the credit limit is reached, the customer may be asked for a down payment or may be granted a credit limit increase. Customer credit limits should be reviewed regularly with reference to a customer's buying and payment patterns to determine whether the limits should be raised or lowered for individual customers. As we saw on page 276, the program warns when a sale to a customer will exceed the customer's credit limit. The limit for Amore Bridal Party is $3,000.00.

40. Click   the **Credit Limit field**

41. Type   **3000**

42. Click   the **drop-down arrow** in the Preferred Payment Method list to view the payment methods available:

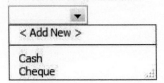

Preferred Payment Method

< Add New >

Cash
Cheque

Figure 6-27

Malin's Makeovers accepts only cash and cheques in payment for services, so these are the only payment methods available.

43. Click   **Cheque**

The fourth tab, Job Info, allows you to organize the work done for customers according to specific jobs. This allows you to track the work done for customers in a more detailed way. When jobs are set up, you can choose the Customer and Job from the Customers & Jobs list. Malin's Makeovers has not set up customer jobs.

44. Check   your **work** carefully before saving the customer record

---

CORRECTING CUSTOMER RECORDS

Click the field that contains the error. You can press (tab) to move forward from one field to the next. Highlight the incorrect information and type the correct information in the field. Click the Address Info tab, Additional Info tab, and Payment Info tab to return to those tabs to review your work and make any necessary corrections.

If you need to make corrections or changes later after the customer record has been saved, open the Customer Centre and double click the customer name or press (ctrl) + E to open the customer record.

---

45. Click   **OK** to save the record and return to the Customer Centre

46. Right-click   on **Amore Bridal Party** in the Customers & Jobs list

47. Choose   **Create Invoices**

The Create Invoices form opens with Amore Bridal Party entered in the Customer:Job field.

48. Press   (tab) to add the customer's address, terms, and tax code to the invoice

49. Enter   **02/03/14** as the date

50. Click   the **drop-down arrow** in the **Item list field** and **click Clothing style consultation**

51. Press   (tab) to advance to the Qty (quantity) field

The item description, rate, and tax code are entered automatically from the item record.

52. Type   **3** and **press** (tab) to update the Amount field

53. Press   (tab) repeatedly to advance to the Item field on the second line, or **click** the **Item field** on the second line

54. Click   the **drop-down arrow** in the **Item list field** and **click General consultation**

55. Press   (tab)

56. Type   **5** and **press** (tab) to update the Amount

57. Click   the **Item field** on the third line

58. Click   the **drop-down arrow** in the **Item list field** and **click Report. Press** (tab)

59. Type   **3**

60. Press   [tab] to update the Amount. Your completed invoice should look like the one shown here:

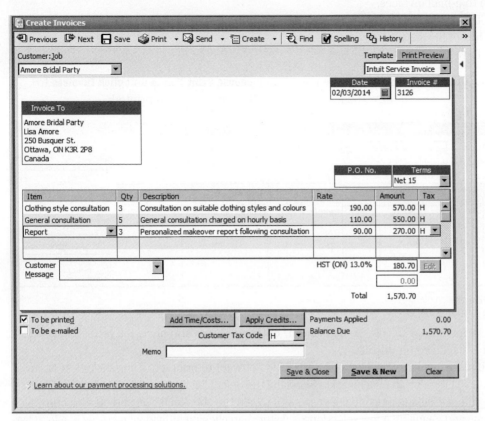

Figure 6-28

61. Check   your **work** and **make corrections** if needed

62. Click   **Save & Close** or **press** [alt] + **a** to save the invoice and return to the Customer Centre

63. Click   ☒ to close the Customer Centre

Printing Customer Invoices

The next source document refers to printing customer invoices. Refer to the following source document as we work through the steps to print the customer invoices:

SD4:   **Memo #1**   **Dated February 3, 2014**

     From Partners: Print customer Invoices #3125 and #3126.

     Even if you do not print the invoices and labels, you may want to work through the printing procedure in order to preview the final printed documents.

     You can print or e-mail invoices individually when you enter the transaction or you can print them in batches later for mailing to customers. Sometimes customers are invoiced regularly for services delivered over a period of time, items ordered for delivery, or services provided at the customer's location, such as telephone or security services.

📑 Source Docs
Refer to the following source document and then follow the step-by-step instructions to enter it.

Invoices for construction or contracting work also may be sent later. The Create Invoices form window includes both a Print button and a Send button that is used to e-mail invoices.

These buttons allow you to print or e-mail individual invoices or print or e-mail batches of invoices.

To print a batch of invoices:

Notes
You can also print a batch of invoices from the Create Invoices form by selecting the drop-down arrow in the print button and selecting Print Batch. The same screen that you see in Figure 6-29 will be displayed.

1. **Choose** **File** from the menu, then **choose Print Forms** and **click Invoices** to view the list of invoices that have not been printed:

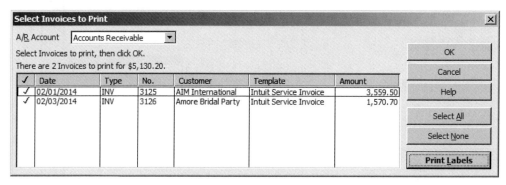

Figure 6-29

All invoices with the "To be printed" option selected and have not yet been printed will be displayed on this list.

If some invoices are selected that you do not want to print, choosing the Select None button will remove all checkmarks. Choosing the Select All button will include all invoices for printing. Clicking individual invoices will toggle the checkmark on and off. Selecting all or none and changing a few selections is faster than clicking individual invoices in a long list.

The two invoices that we need to print are already selected so we can proceed.

From the Select Invoices to Print dialogue box, you can also print mailing labels for the invoices to be printed and mailed to customers.

2. **Click** **Print Labels** to access the Select Labels to Print dialogue box:

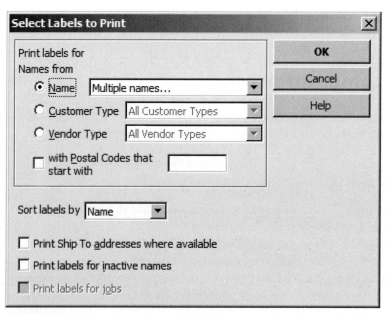

Figure 6-30

You can select the labels you need to print from various lists.

3. Click   the **drop-down arrow** beside the **Name field** to view the choices from which you can select:

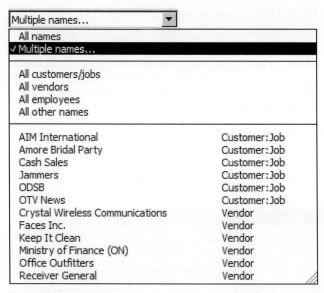

Figure 6-31

You can create labels for all names in your QuickBooks company file, for all customers and jobs, for all vendors, for all employees, or for all other names. You can also print the label for an individual by choosing a name from the list. You can print labels for some of the names on the list by using the sorting features available on the Select Labels to Print dialogue box to further define the list of names you want.

The names on the invoices to be printed are preselected initially. You can click individual names to add them to the list of labels.

4. Click   **Multiple names** to view the list of preselected names based on the invoices that have been selected to be printed in the batch:

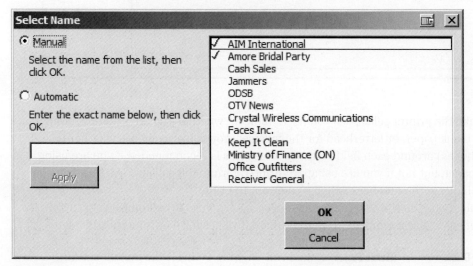

Figure 6-32

Notice that the two names selected are AIM International and Amore Bridal Party, the names of the customers for whom the invoices are going to be printed in the batch.

5. Click   **OK** to return to the Select Labels to Print dialogue box

6. Click   **OK** again to open the Print Labels dialogue box

7. Click   **Preview** to see what the printed labels will look like

Notes
Printing from a Preview window will close the preview.

8. Click   **Close** to return to the Print Labels dialogue box. Make changes to the printing options if needed

If you do not want to print the labels, click Cancel to return to the Select Labels to Print dialogue box. Click Cancel again to return to the Select Invoices to Print dialogue box.

If you want to print labels, be sure that you have label forms in your printer and that the correct label format is selected in the Print Labels dialgoue box.

9. Click   **Print** to begin printing labels (or click Cancel twice to return to the Select Invoices to Print dialogue box)

If you printed the labels to the printer, return to the Select Invoices to Print dialogue box.

10. Click   **OK** to view the Print Invoices printer control screen:

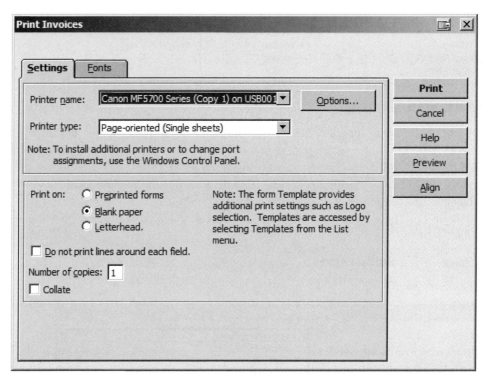

Figure 6-33

Make the printer selections you need. Indicate whether you are using pre-printed forms, blank paper, or letterhead for the invoices. You can also choose whether to add lines (boxes) around each field on the invoice. This is recommended if you are using blank paper, but not if you are using pre-printed forms. You can also use this dialogue box to indicate the number of copies you want to print.

QuickBooks also provides Templates that you can use to customize your invoices. You can customize a template from the Create Invoices form or from the Templates list.

11. Click   **Blank Paper** as the Print on option (this is the default setting)

12. Click   **Preview** to see what the first printed invoice will look like. You can print directly from the Preview screen by clicking the Print button

13. Click   **Close** to return to the Print Invoices dialogue box. Make changes to the printing options if needed

14. Click   **Print** to start printing. QuickBooks will ask you whether the forms printed correctly:

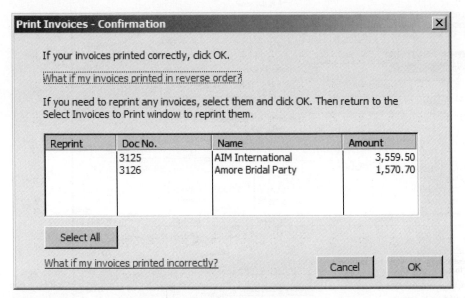

Print Invoices - Confirmation ☒

If your invoices printed correctly, click OK.

What if my invoices printed in reverse order?

If you need to reprint any invoices, select them and click OK. Then return to the Select Invoices to Print window to reprint them.

Reprint	Doc No.	Name	Amount
	3125	AIM International	3,559.50
	3126	Amore Bridal Party	1,570.70

Select All

What if my invoices printed incorrectly?   Cancel   OK

Figure 6-34

For any invoices that did not print correctly, click in the box beside it under the Reprint column. A ✓ will be displayed, indicating that the invoice needs to be printed again. You have to return to the Select Invoices to Print dialogue box to reprint the invoices that you indicated did not print correctly.

We'll assume that our invoices have printed correctly.

15. Click   **OK** to continue

Correcting a Previously Recorded Customer Payment

The next source document that we must enter is a memo from the partners indicating that the cheque from AIM International was entered incorrectly. Refer to the following source document as we work through the steps to make the corrections to the cheque:

SD5:   Memo #2   **Dated February 3, 2014**

> From Partners: Cheque #1285 received from AIM International was entered incorrectly. The actual cheque amount was $1,200.00. Edit the customer payment to make the correction.

Source Docs
Refer to the following source document and then follow the step-by-step instructions to enter it.

Just as you can correct sales receipts, bills, and cheques after recording, you can correct customer payments and sales invoices. The procedure is the same for all forms — display the completed form on the screen, edit it, and save the changed form.

1. Click   the **Receive Payments icon** [Receive Payments] in the Customers section of the Home page to open the Receive Payments form

The Receive Payments form does not have a Find icon, so we need to use the Previous button to scroll back through payments previously entered to find the one we need to edit.

2. Click   the **Previous button** [Previous]

3. The customer payment entered most recently is displayed on the screen. It is the one from AIM International that we want to edit:

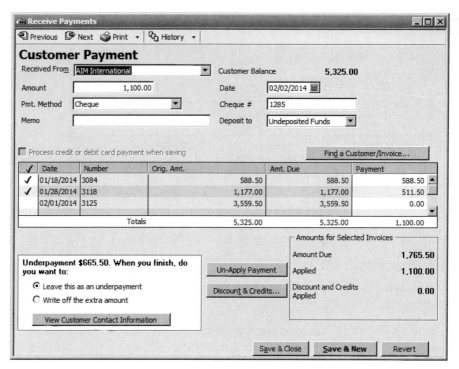

Figure 6-35

4. **Double click**   **1,100.00** in the **Amount field** of the cheque portion to select it

5. **Type**   **1200** and **press** (tab) to update the receipt form:

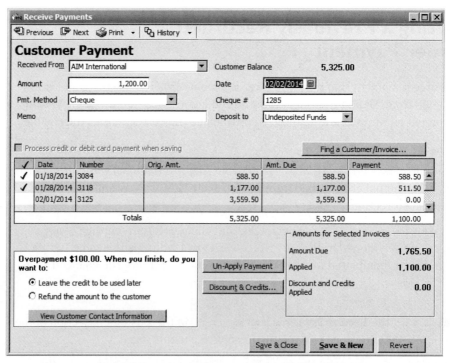

Figure 6-36

The revised amount has not been reallocated to invoices. In the bottom left-hand corner, you can see that QuickBooks now thinks there is a $100.00 overpayment. We need to change the amount applied to Invoice #3118.

6. **Click**   the **Un-Apply Payment button** to remove the ✓s beside all selected invoices

Notes
You can also click the ✓ for Invoice #3118 and then click the ✓ column again. This will remove the original payment amount and update the payment amount to reflect the updated amount entered in the Amount field.

Or, you can double click 511.50, the Payment field amount for the invoice line, and type the amount that should be applied to this invoice, 611.50.

Notice that the Un-Apply Payment button has changed to Auto Apply Payment. Clicking this button will allow QuickBooks to allocate the payment amount to the invoices.

7. Click the **Auto Apply Payment button** to reapply the payment and update the customer payment:

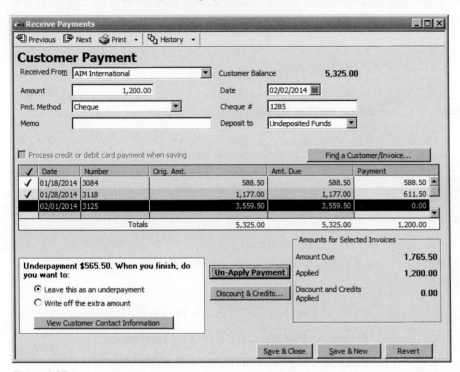

Figure 6-37

8. Click **Save & Close** or **press** (alt) **+ a** to view the following confirmation message:

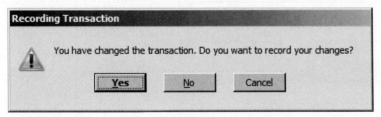

Figure 6-38

9. Click **Yes** to indicate that you want to record the changed transaction. It will replace the original transaction

Correcting Sales Invoices

The next source document that we must enter is a memo from the partners indicating that Sales Invoice #3126 sent to Amore Bridal Party was entered incorrectly. Refer to the following source document as we work through the steps to make the corrections to the Sales Invoice:

SD6: Memo #3   **Dated February 3, 2014**

From Partners: Invoice #3126 was entered incorrectly. The Amore party had 3 hours of consultation and not 5, as originally entered on the invoice. The revised invoice total is $1,322.10. Edit the invoice to make the correction and then print the corrected invoice.

Source Docs
Refer to the following source document and then follow the step-by-step instructions to enter it.

Like other transactions in QuickBooks, Sales Invoices can be edited by displaying the recorded transaction on the screen. Use the Previous and Next buttons until the invoice you want to correct is displayed on the screen. You can also use the Find icon on the invoice form to locate the invoice. For the next correction, we will use the Find icon to locate the transaction that was recorded incorrectly. After correcting the invoice, we will print it in order to mail the revised copy to our customer.

Notes
You can also open the Create Invoices form directly from the Customers menu or from the shortcut menu in the Customers & Jobs list.

1. **Click** the **Create Invoices button**  or **press** ⌃ctrl + **I** to open the Create Invoices form

The Find icon is located on the Create Invoices Icon bar as shown here:

Figure 6-39

There are three ways to open the Find window when a QuickBooks invoice is displayed on the screen:

Notes
Because the Invoices form is open, the Edit menu will have Find Invoices as its Find option, and ⌃ctrl + **F** will open the Find Invoices form directly.

a) **Click** the **Find icon** [Find] in the Create Invoices form; or

b) **Choose** the **Edit Menu** and **click Find Invoices**; or

c) **Press** ⌃ctrl + **F** to open the Find Invoices window:

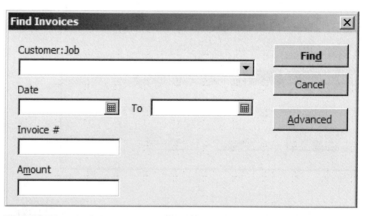

Figure 6-40

When you want to find an invoice but the invoice form is not displayed on the screen, choose the Edit menu and click Find. Click the Simple tab, choose Invoice as the transaction type, and enter the rest of the search criteria. The Advanced tab has even more search options.

You can find all invoices for a single customer, all invoices that fall within a given range of dates, or a specific invoice. When more than one invoice results from the search, you will see a list of invoices to select from. We will enter the invoice number because we know which one we need.

2. **Click** the **Invoice # field**

3. **Type** 3126

4. **Click** the **Find button** 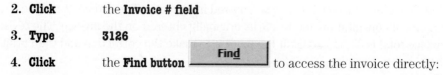 to access the invoice directly:

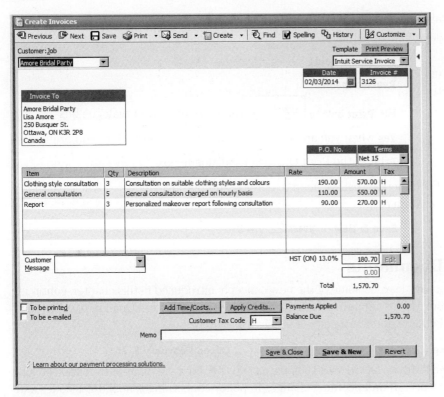

Figure 6-41

Notice that the To be printed box is not checked because we already printed this invoice in a previous exercise.

5. **Double click** **5** in the **Qty field** for General consultation on the second invoice line

6. **Type** **3**

7. **Press** ⌈ tab ⌉ to update the tax and total amounts as shown:

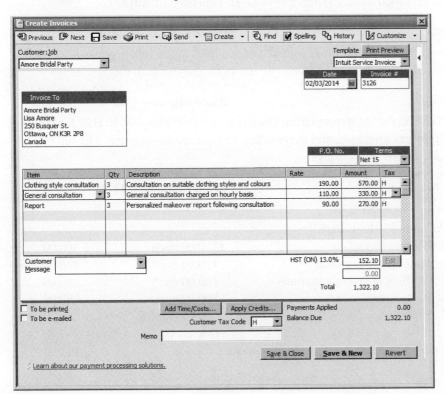

Figure 6-42

> **Notes**
> If you didn't print the invoices as outlined in SD4, the To be printed option will still be selected on the invoice.

We will also add a note in the Memo field and reprint the invoice so that we can send the revised copy to the customer.

8. **Click**   the **Memo field**

9. **Type**   **Revised invoice**

10. **Click**   the **Print button** to open the printer dialogue box

11. **Click**   **Yes** when you are asked to record the changes before you print

12. **Click**   **Print** in the Print One Invoice dialogue box

The next transaction that we need to enter is another invoice, so we will leave the Create Invoices form open.

13. **Click**   **Save & New** or **press** (alt) + **S**

Source Documents

Now that you have learned some of the new concepts introduced in this chapter, continue to develop your skills by entering the following source documents in QuickBooks. Use the information in this chapter as a guide if necessary.

Source Docs for Practice
Continue to develop your skills by entering the following source documents.

SD7:   Invoice   **Dated February 5, 2014**

Invoice #3127 to ODSB, $185.00 plus $24.05 HST for a one-hour customized seminar for school staff on upcoming changes in policy concerning school dress codes and how to reinforce them in a positive manner with students. Invoice totals $209.05. Terms: Net 15 days. The seminar will be repeated in all schools over the coming months. Memorize the transaction with weekly reminders to begin February 12, 2014.

SD8:   Bill   **Dated February 5, 2014**

Bill #KC-724 received from Keep It Clean, $150.00 plus $19.50 HST for a weekly cleaning of the salon. The bill totals $169.50. Terms: Net 15 days. Memorize the transaction with weekly reminders to begin February 12, 2014.

Notes
When entering the bill from Keep It Clean, the *Uncategorized Expense* account will be displayed on the bill by default. This account was used in a historical transaction, and QuickBooks remembers the account last used for each Vendor and displays it on forms by default.

SD9:   Pay Bill   **Dated February 5, 2014**

To Keep It Clean, $321.00 in payment of account. Reference Invoices #KC-662 and KC-688. Assign Cheque #388 (do not print the cheque).

SD10: Bill   **Dated February 6, 2014**

Bill #OO-692 received from Office Outfitters, $180.00 plus $23.40 HST for paper, CDs, printer cartridges, and other office and computer supplies. The bill totals $203.40. Terms: Net 20 days.

Notes
To begin the sequential numbering of Sales Receipts, enter 5 in the Sale No. field.

SD11: Sales Receipt #5   **Dated February 6, 2014**

To Cash Sales customers

Payment Method: Cash

2	Hair consultations	$150.00 each	$ 300.00
1	Makeup consultation	120.00 each	120.00
2	Clothing style consultations	190.00 each	380.00
2	Makeovers	390.00 each	780.00
4	Reports	90.00 each	360.00
	HST	13%	252.20
	Sales Receipt total cash held for deposit		$2,192.20

Notes
For the Sales Receipt, accept the default to deposit to the *Undeposited Funds* account so the deposit can be made later.

Memorize the transaction with weekly reminders beginning February 13, 2014. The summary will be entered each week with different sales amounts.

SD12: Customer Payment   **Dated February 6, 2014**

From OTV News, Cheque #4663 for $2,139.30 in payment of account. Reference Invoice #3097. Cheque held for deposit.

Making Deposits to a Bank Account

Our next source document involves depositing all cheques and cash held for weekly deposit to the *Bank Chequing* account. Refer to the following source document as we work through the steps to enter it:

SD13: Memo #4   **Dated February 6, 2014**

From Partners: Deposit all cheques and cash held for weekly deposit to the *Bank Chequing* account. Total deposit is $5,531.50.

When cheques and cash are received from customers, they can be held for later deposit. QuickBooks records these items as debits in the *Undeposited Funds* account. Later, when deposits are entered, the funds from the *Undeposited Funds* account are transferred to the selected bank account.

When there is money in the *Undeposited Funds* account, it is ready to be deposited into a bank account. You can use the Reminders list to view various functions to be performed in QuickBooks. One of the reminders you can set is to show when money is available to be deposited. To view the Reminders list on a regular basis, you can set the Reminders list to display when you open a company file.

Source Docs
Refer to the following source document and then follow the step-by-step instructions to enter it.

1. **Select**   **Company** from the menu and **click Reminders:**

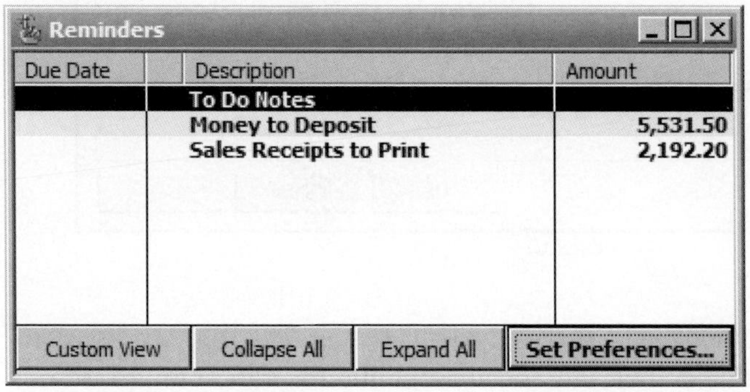

Due Date	Description	Amount
	To Do Notes	
	Money to Deposit	5,531.50
	Sales Receipts to Print	2,192.20

Custom View	Collapse All	Expand All	Set Preferences...

Figure 6-43

The total amount of $5,531.50 held for deposit is displayed beside the Money to Deposit heading. We will expand the list to view the details.

2. **Double click**   the **Money to Deposit** heading in the Reminders list to expand the list and show the details:

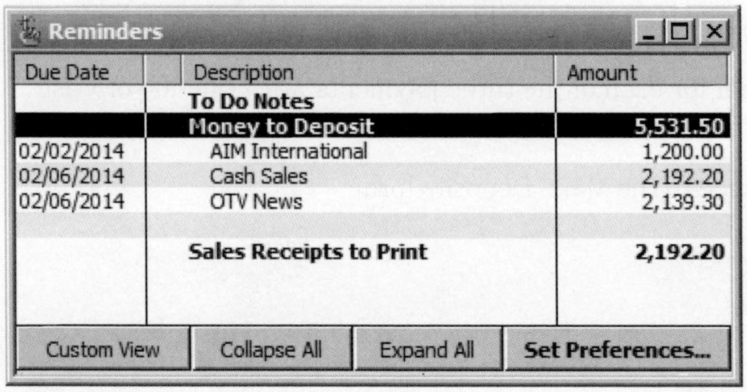

Due Date	Description	Amount
	To Do Notes	
	Money to Deposit	**5,531.50**
02/02/2014	AIM International	1,200.00
02/06/2014	Cash Sales	2,192.20
02/06/2014	OTV News	2,139.30
	Sales Receipts to Print	**2,192.20**

Custom View	Collapse All	Expand All	Set Preferences...

Figure 6-44

Notes
If you do not see the deposits listed, check whether you deposited the receipts directly to the *Bank Chequing* account instead of the *Undeposited Funds* account in the original transactions. If they were deposited to the *Bank Chequing* account, you will have to correct the transaction and select the *Undeposited Funds* account.

3. Open the **Payments to Deposit form** using one of the following options:

a) **Click** the **Record Deposits icon** 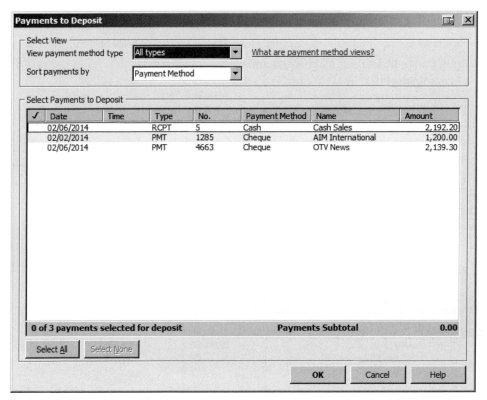 in the Banking section of the Home page; or

b) **Choose Banking** from the menu and then **click Make Deposits**

4. The Payments to Deposit form will be displayed as shown:

Figure 6-45

The Payments to Deposit form lists the three payments that are ready to be deposited. The details for the payments include not only the amount and the date, but also the payment method. Many companies have more than one bank account — credit card bank accounts are usually separate from the chequing bank accounts.

You can select a payment method by choosing a type in the View payment method type field. By selecting a payment type from the list, one payment method can be selected for a deposit. This list makes it easy to select the payments that should be deposited to each account. By default, all payments are listed, and this is the correct selection in our case. We will deposit all the cheques and cash to the *Bank Chequing* account. In Chapter 8, we will use multiple bank accounts for deposits.

📄 **Notes**
You can click anywhere on the payment line to add a ✓ for the line.

5. Click the ✓ **column** for each of the three payments, with Cheque or Cash as the payment method, or **click** the **Select All button**

6. Click **OK** to advance to the Make Deposits form:

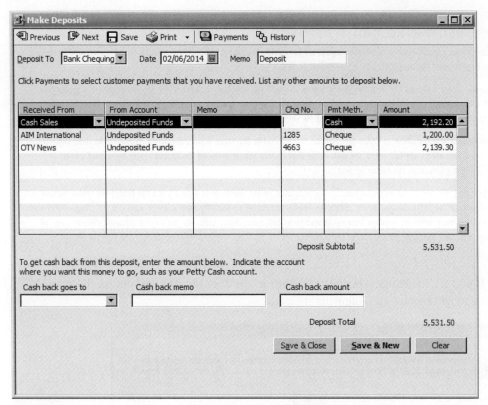

Figure 6-46

If you made an error when selecting the payments on the Payments to Deposit form, click the Payments icon [🖳 Payments] to return to the Payments to Deposit form and select or deselect the payments as necessary. When you're finished making the changes, click OK to return to the Make Deposits form.

The transactions we selected on the Payments to Deposit form are listed on the Make Deposits form and the total deposit amount is shown at the bottom of the form. *Bank Chequing* should be selected in the Deposit To field at the top of the form. If you are depositing the funds into a different account, click the drop-down arrow in the Deposit To field and select the appropriate account.

The fields at the bottom of the form allow you to record a cash withdrawal from the deposit. If part of the total payment amount is taken in the form of cash at the time of the deposit, you should complete these fields by entering the Cash back amount, a memo or explanation of the use of the funds, and selecting the account that the cash should be debited to — often a *Petty Cash* account in the Cash back goes to field. No cash is withdrawn at this time. We should also print the deposit summary for reference.

7. **Verify**   that **Bank Chequing is selected** as the account in the Deposit To field

8. **Enter**   **02/06/14** as the date of the deposit if this is not the date already shown

9. **Check**   the **form carefully** before proceeding and **make** any **necessary corrections**

Notes

If a cheque number or Payment Method is missing on the Make Deposits form, you can enter it in the appropriate columns. Since you are changing the original transaction, select Yes when prompted to record the changes.

CORRECTING RECORDED DEPOSITS

The changes you can make to a recorded deposit are limited. You can change the date and you can correct the account for deposit. To do this, select the correct account in the Deposit To field.

You can delete a deposit line from the deposit form if it should not have been included in the deposit. To remove a deposit line, click the payment that you want to remove. Then choose the Edit menu and click Delete Line. After saving the deposit, repeat the deposit process to deposit the deleted payment to the correct account.

Alternatively, you can delete an entire deposit if necessary. To delete the entire deposit, display the deposit in the Make Deposits window. Then choose the Edit menu and click Delete Deposit. After you have deleted the deposit, repeat the deposit process to deposit the payments to the correct account.

You cannot edit a customer name, account, or deposit amount on the deposit form. Although you can change the cheque number and payment method, these changes do not update the original transaction, so changing them is not a good idea. To change any of these items, you must delete the payment from the deposit form (Edit menu, Delete Line), edit the original customer payment (refer to page 295), and then redo the deposit for the payment.

If you try to change a customer name, account, or deposit amount on the deposit form you will receive the following message:

Figure 6-47

10. Click   **OK** to return to the Make Deposit form

When the deposit form is correct, you can print the deposit slip and deposit summary. These reports are both printed from the Print button; however, how you click the Print button will depend on which menu is displayed:

a) **Click** the **drop-down arrow** beside the Print button to view the print options available:

Figure 6-48

b) **Click** the **Print button** and you will see the following message:

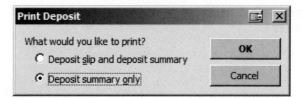

Figure 6-49

Depending on the print option you select, you can choose to print a deposit slip, a deposit summary, or both.

The deposit slip is printed and taken to the bank with the deposit. To print the deposit slip, you should use the proper form so that the amounts will be aligned in the correct deposit slip boxes with their labels.

The summary includes cheque numbers, payment method, customer name, memo, and amounts in columns with totals. The deposit summary can be printed on plain paper because column headings are included.

11.	**Click**	the **Print button** 🖨 Print and **select Deposit slip and deposit summary** to print both reports
12.	**Click**	**OK**
13.	**Click**	**Print**
14.	**Click**	**Save & New** to save the deposit and leave the Deposits window open so you can review the journal entry created from the deposit transaction in the next exercise

📄 **Notes**
You can preview both the summary and the deposit slips before printing.

Reviewing the Transaction

With a blank Make Deposits form displayed on the screen:

| 1. | **Click** | the **Previous button** 🔁 Previous to view the deposit that we just entered and then **click** ⌃ + **Y** to view the Transaction Journal report: |

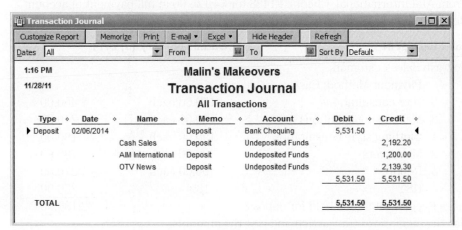

📄 **Notes**
We have removed the Transaction, Number, and Class columns from this Transaction Journal report.

Figure 6-50

The *Bank Chequing* account is debited for the full deposit amount of $5,531.50. All individual transactions that were deposited to the *Undeposited Funds* account are credited to reverse the original entries, and customer names are included so that the journal records of the transactions are complete.

| 2. | **Close** | the **Transaction Journal report** |
| 3. | **Click** | ✕ to close the Make Deposits form |

Source Documents

Now that you have learned more of the new concepts introduced in this chapter, continue to develop your skills by entering the following source documents in QuickBooks. Use the information in this chapter as a guide if necessary.

SD14: Pay Bill   **Dated February 7, 2014**

To Faces Inc., $805.00 in payment of account. Reference Invoice #F-4910. Automatically assign Cheque #389.

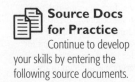

📑 **Source Docs for Practice**
Continue to develop your skills by entering the following source documents.

SD15: Customer Payment   **Dated February 9, 2014**

From ODSB, Cheque #10034 for $856.00 in payment of account. Reference Invoice #3101. Cheque held for deposit.

SD16: Customer Payment   **Dated February 10, 2014**

From Jammers, Cheque #102 for $300.00 in partial payment of account. Reference Invoice #3092. Cheque held for deposit.

SD17: Invoice   **Dated February 12, 2014**

Invoice #3128 to ODSB, $185.00 plus $24.05 HST for a one hour customized seminar for school staff on dress code policy. Invoice totals $209.05. Terms: Net 15 days. Use the memorized transaction.

SD18: Bill   **Dated February 12, 2014**

Bill #KC-779 received from Keep It Clean, $150.00 plus $19.50 HST for weekly cleaning of salon. The bill totals $169.50. Terms: Net 15 days. Use the memorized transaction.

SD19: Invoice   **Dated February 13, 2014**

Invoice #3129 to OTV News, $780.00 plus $101.40 HST for two complete make-over consultations for newly hired news broadcasters to prepare them for regular television appearances. Invoice totals $881.40. Terms: Net 15 days.

SD20: Customer Payment   **Dated February 13, 2014**

From AIM International, Cheque #1428 for $4,125.00 in full payment of account. Reference Invoices #3118 and #3125. Cheque held for deposit.

SD21: Sales Receipt #6   **Dated February 13, 2014**

To Cash Sales customers

Payment Method: Cash

3	Hair consultations	$150.00 each	$ 450.00
2	Makeup consultations	120.00 each	240.00
1	Clothing style consultation	190.00 each	190.00
2	Makeovers	390.00 each	780.00
3	Reports	90.00 each	270.00
	HST	13%	250.90

Sales Receipt total cash held for deposit $2,180.90

Use the memorized transaction and edit the amounts.

SD22: Memo #5   **Dated February 13, 2014**

From Partners: Deposit all cheques and cash held for weekly deposit to the *Bank Chequing* account. Total deposit is $7,461.90.

SD23: Pay Bill   **Dated February 13, 2014**

To Office Outfitters, $1,380.00 in payment of account. Reference Invoice #OO-500. Automatically assign Cheque #390.

SD24: Bill   **Dated February 14, 2014**

Bill #F-5723 received from Faces Inc., $120.00 plus $15.60 HST for makeup and cosmetics supplies. Be sure to delete the *Uncategorized Expense* account on the Expenses tab of the bill. The bill totals $135.60. Terms: Net 30 days.

SD25: Write Cheque   **Dated February 15, 2014**

To pay for cash purchase received with Bill #H-388 from Heads Up (use Quick Add to add the new vendor) for $140.00 plus $18.20 HST for hair care products for use in salon. The bill total of $158.20 is paid in full with Cheque #391.

Notes

The *Uncategorized Expense* account is displayed on the Expenses tab of this bill by default for two reasons: 1) this account was used to set up the vendor's opening balance when we originally created the QuickBooks company file and 2) the Pre-fill accounts for vendor based on past entries preference is enabled in the General preferences.

Recording NSF Cheques

For the next transaction, a cheque received from Jammers was returned by the bank as NSF. We will record the returned cheque and NSF charges. Refer to the following source document as we work through the steps to enter it:

SD26: Bank Debit Memo #CB-5338   **Dated February 15, 2014**

Source Docs
Refer to the following source document and then follow the step-by-step instructions to enter it.

> From Capital Bank: Cheque #102 for $300.00 from Jammers for Invoice #3092 was returned as NSF. The bank charged $25.00 as the NSF fee. Create Invoice #3130 to record the returned cheque and NSF charges to restore the customer's account balance. No taxes are charged on these amounts. Invoice totals $325.00.
>
> Terms: Due on receipt.

Sometimes a cheque is drawn on an account that does not have sufficient funds to cover the amount of the cheque. When this happens, the bank will return the cheque as NSF (non-sufficient funds). Normally, the bank will charge for this service, and a business may choose to pass this cost on to its customers. Customers should be notified immediately of any outstanding amounts so that they can replace the bad cheque.

Malin has created two Other Charge items to handle the NSF cheques: one to enter the amount of the cheque and one for the administration or handling fees charged by the bank. Malin's Makeovers passes the bank charges on to the customer. NSF cheques are entered as Sales Invoices — selecting these special items for the sale.

1. **Click**   the **Create Invoices icon** ⬚ from the Customers section of the Home page to open the Create Invoices form

2. **Choose**   **Jammers** in the **Customer:Job field**

3. **Enter**   **02/15/14** as the date if this date does not appear already

Several defaults for the customer are entered automatically.

4. **Choose**   **NSF Cheque** as the first item

5. The following Sales Tax Codes message is displayed:

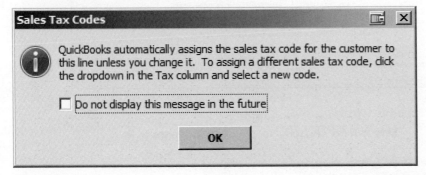

Sales Tax Codes

ⓘ QuickBooks automatically assigns the sales tax code for the customer to this line unless you change it. To assign a different sales tax code, click the dropdown in the Tax column and select a new code.

☐ Do not display this message in the future

OK

Figure 6-51

This message indicates that the customer's tax code is entered as the tax code for this line and overrides the non-taxable code for the item so we must change it.

6. **Click**   the **Do not display this message in the future option**

7. **Click**   **OK** to continue

8. **Enter**   **1** as the quantity and **300** as the amount

<table>
<tr><td>9.</td><td>**Select**</td><td>**E - Tax Exempt** as the tax code</td></tr>
<tr><td>10.</td><td>**Choose**</td><td>**NSF Charges** as the second item</td></tr>
</table>

The price and amount are entered automatically because they remain the same for all customers; however, you can override it if necessary.

<table>
<tr><td>11.</td><td>**Enter**</td><td>**1** as the quantity and **select E - Tax Exempt** as the tax code</td></tr>
</table>

We need to change some of the other defaults for the customer. The terms for this invoice should be set to Due on receipt, and we should add the customer's cheque number for reference as a memo for the invoice.

<table>
<tr><td>12.</td><td>**Click**</td><td>the **drop-down arrow** in the **Terms field** and **select Due on receipt**</td></tr>
<tr><td>13.</td><td>**Click**</td><td>the **Memo field**</td></tr>
<tr><td>14.</td><td>**Type**</td><td>**Re: NSF Cheque #102 Re: Invoice #3092**</td></tr>
<tr><td>15.</td><td>**Choose**</td><td>**Please remit to above address** in the **Customer Message field**</td></tr>
<tr><td>16.</td><td colspan="2">The completed invoice will be displayed as shown:</td></tr>
</table>

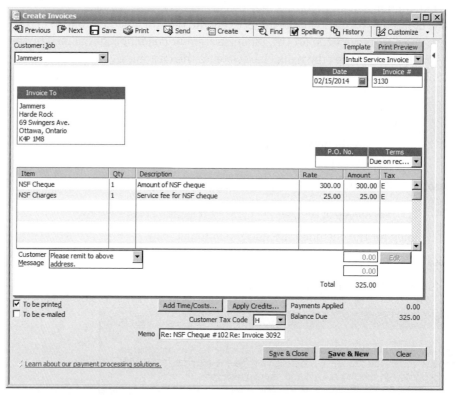

Figure 6-52

<table>
<tr><td>17.</td><td>**Click**</td><td>**Save & New**. The following message appears:</td></tr>
</table>

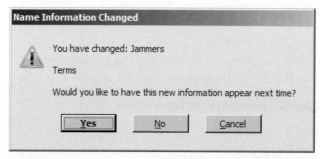

Figure 6-53

Because we changed the customer's default terms on this invoice, QuickBooks allows us to update the terms in the customer record with the terms entered on this invoice. When an NSF cheque is received from a customer, Malin requires the customer to pay immediately for all future services. The method of payment may also be changed, so that cheques are no longer accepted from this customer. We want to change the terms.

18. Click   **Yes** to save the invoice and update the terms in the customer record

Reviewing the Transaction

Let's review the journal entry for the NSF transaction.

With a blank Create Invoices form displayed on the screen:

1. Click   the **Previous button** [◀ Previous] to view the invoice we just entered

2. Press   `ctrl` + **Y** to view the Transaction Journal report:

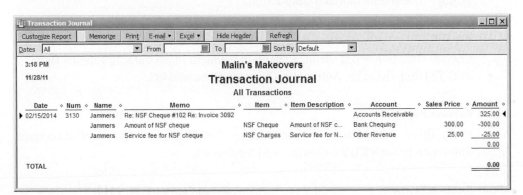

Figure 6-54

You can see that this transaction reverses the original customer payment. The *Accounts Receivable* account has increased by the amount of the original customer cheque and the NSF charges. The *Bank Chequing* account has decreased by the amount of the NSF cheque and the NSF charges have been credited to the *Other Revenue* account. These are the default accounts assigned to the Other Charge items.

3. Close   the **Transaction Journal report**

4. Click   **No** to memorize the report if you made any changes to it

5. Click   **Save & New** to save the invoice and display a blank invoice form ready for the next sale

Source Documents

Now that you have learned more of the new concepts introduced in this chapter, continue to develop your skills by entering the following source documents in QuickBooks. Use the information in this chapter as a guide if necessary.

SD27: Invoice   **Dated February 15, 2014**

Invoice #3131 to Skin Deep Inc. (set up the new customer), makeup consultations for new models.

10	Makeup consultations	$120.00 each	$1,200.00
	HST	13%	156.00
	Invoice total		$1,356.00

Terms: Net 15 days.

Memorize the transaction with weekly reminders because the consultations will be repeated for different models each week beginning February 22nd.

Notes
Use the *Computer Equipment:Other* account for this transaction.

SD28: Bill   Dated February 18, 2014

Bill #OO-904 received from Office Outfitters, $320.00 plus $41.60 HST for new scanner to use with computer. The bill totals $361.60. Terms: Net 20 days.

SD29: Bill   Dated February 19, 2014

Bill #KC-811 received from Keep It Clean, $150.00 plus $19.50 HST for weekly cleaning of salon. The bill totals $169.50. Terms: Net 15 days. Use the memorized transaction.

SD30: Invoice   Dated February 19, 2014

Invoice #3132 to ODSB, $185.00 plus $24.05 HST for a one hour customized seminar for school staff on dress code policy. Invoice totals $209.05. Terms: Net 15 days. Use the memorized transaction.

SD31: Pay Bill   Dated February 19, 2014

Cheque #392 to Keep It Clean, $339.00 in payment of account. Reference Bills #KC-724 and #KC-779. Automatically assign Cheque #392.

SD32: Receive Payment   Dated February19, 2014

From Amore Bridal Party, Cheque #532 for $500.00 in partial payment of account. Reference Invoice #3126. Cheque held for deposit.

SD33: Receive Payment   Dated February 20, 2014

From ODSB, Cheque #12103 for $209.05 in payment of account. Reference Invoice #3127. Cheque held for deposit.

SD34: Sales Receipt #7   Dated February 20, 2014

To Cash Sales customers. Salon visits were a popular Valentine's Day gift.
Payment Method: Cash

10	Hair consultations	$150.00 each	$1,500.00
8	Makeup consultations	120.00 each	960.00
3	Clothing style consultations	190.00 each	570.00
4	Makeovers	390.00 each	1,560.00
10	Reports	90.00 each	900.00
	HST	13%	713.70
	Sales Receipt total cash held for deposit		$6,203.70

Use the memorized transaction and edit the amounts.

SD35: Memo #6   Dated February 20, 2014

From Partners: Deposit all cheques and cash held for weekly deposit to the *Bank Chequing* account. Total deposit is $6,912.75.

SD36: Write Cheque   **Dated February 21, 2014**

Paid cash for purchase received with Bill #P-450 from Perfect Publicity (use Quick Add to add the new vendor) for $2,400.00 plus $312.00 HST for series of poster ads to run for next 12 weeks. The bill total of $2,712.00 is paid in full with Cheque #393. Create new Other Current Asset account: *Prepaid Advertising*.

SD37: Invoice   **Dated February 22, 2014**

Invoice #3133 to Skin Deep Inc., makeup consultations for new models.

10	Makeup consultations	120.00 each	$1,200.00
	HST	13%	156.00
	Invoice total		$1,356.00

Terms: Net 15 days. Use the memorized the transaction.

SD38: Invoice   **Dated February 26, 2014**

Invoice #3134 to ODSB, $185.00 plus $24.05 HST for a one hour customized seminar for school staff on dress code policy. Invoice totals $209.05. Terms: Net 15 days. Use the memorized transaction.

SD39: Receive Payment   **Dated February 26, 2014**

From OTV News, Cheque #4969 for $881.40 in payment of account. Reference Invoice #3129. Cheque held for deposit.

SD40: Invoice   **Dated February 26, 2014**

Invoice #3135 to Sci-Tek, Inc. (use Quick Add to add the new customer), $390.00 plus $50.70 HST for a complete makeover consultation for members of the executive team in a growing company. The team wants to take on a more professional image for presentations and meetings. Invoice totals $440.70. Terms: Net 15 days. Memorize the transaction with weekly reminders beginning March 5, 2014, because consultations will be repeated for a different member of the executive team each week.

SD41: Bill   **Dated February 26, 2014**

Bill #KC-848 from Keep It Clean, $150.00 plus $19.50 GST for weekly cleaning of the salon. The bill totals $169.50. Terms: Net 15 days. Use the memorized transaction.

SD42: Pay Bill   **Dated February 26, 2014**

To Office Outfitters, $203.40 in payment of account. Reference Invoice #OO-692. Automatically assign Cheque #394.

SD43: Sales Receipt #8   **Dated February 27, 2014**

   To Cash Sales customers.

   Payment Method: Cash

4	Hair consultations	$150.00 each	$ 600.00
2	Makeup consultations	120.00 each	240.00
2	Clothing style consultations	190.00 each	380.00
1	Makeover	390.00 each	390.00
6	Reports	90.00 each	540.00
	HST	13%	279.50
	Sales Receipt total held for deposit		$2,429.50

Use the memorized transaction and edit the amounts.

SD44: Memo #7   **Dated February 27, 2014**

From Partners: Deposit all cheques and cash held for weekly deposit to the *Bank Chequing* account. Total deposit is $3,310.90.

SD45: Write Cheque   **Dated February 28, 2014**

Pay cash for purchase received with Bill #CWC-216 from Crystal Wireless Communications, $180.00 plus $23.40 HST for telephone, cell phone, and Internet service for one month. The bill totals $203.40. Write Cheque #395 to pay the bill in full.

📄 **Notes**
Use the General Journal for the adjusting entries.
   The depreciation amounts are the capital cost allowance amounts for the year divided by 12 to arrive at the amount for one month.

SD46: Memo #8   **Dated February 28, 2014**

From Partners: Complete adjusting entries for one month of depreciation:

Computer equipment	$300.00
Salon	750.00
Salon equipment	20.00
Salon furniture	150.00

SD47: Memo #9   **Dated February 28, 2014**

From Partners: Complete adjusting entries for supplies used during February.

Cosmetics supplies	$220.00
Hair care supplies	90.00
Office and computer supplies	70.00

SD48: Memo #10   **Dated February 28, 2014**

From Partners: Complete adjusting entry for prepaid expenses expired.

Insurance	$2,100.00

SD49: Bank Debit Memo DM-56621   **Dated February 28, 2014**

From Capital Bank: Authorized withdrawals from *Bank Chequing* account for service charges and loan payments. Create a new Expense account: *Bank Charges*.

Monthly bank service charges	$ 35.00
Mortgage ($1,000.00 principal; $200.00 interest)	1,200.00
Bank loan ($160.00 principal; $40.00 interest)	200.00
Long term loan ($780.00 principal; $220.00 interest)	1,000.00

SD50: Memo #11   **Dated February 28, 2014**

From Partners: Write Cheques #396, #397, and #398 to the partners for drawings and travel expenses for February. Use Quick Add to add each partner's names on the Name list and choose Other as the name type.

Partner	Cheque No.	Drawings	Travel	Total
Malin Andersson	396	$2,000.00	$120.00	$2,120.00
Kiera O'Sullivan	397	2,000.00	335.00	2,335.00
Dhaibhen Mehta	398	2,000.00	180.00	2,180.00

SD51: Bank Credit Memo CM-89211   **Dated February 28, 2014**

From Capital Bank: Interest earned on bank deposits.

Chequing account	$12.00
Savings account	35.00

Customers & Receivables Reports

You can access customer reports and graphs from the Reports menu or from the Report Centre. You can modify each report by adding or removing columns; by sorting and filtering to select only parts of the data for the report; and by changing headers, footers, fonts, and number formats. The principles for modifying and customizing customer reports are the same as they are for the reports discussed in previous chapters. After modifying reports, you can memorize, rename, and add them to your list of memorized reports.

We will print reports from the Report Centre rather than selecting them from the Reports menu.

Notes
Refer to page 121 to review modifying reports.

1. **Click**   the **Reports icon** on the Icon bar

2. **Click**   the **Customers & Receivables heading** on the left-hand side of the screen

3. **Click**   the **List View icon**  to view the list of Customers & Receivables reports:

Notes
Customer reports are very similar to vendor reports. The same options for modifying, displaying, and drilling down to more detail are also available on customer reports.

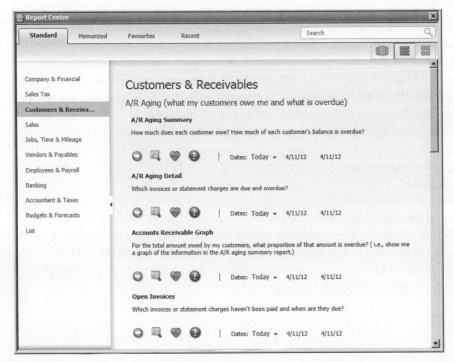

Figure 6-55

Accounts Receivable Aging Reports

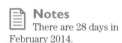 **Notes**
To access the report from the Reports menu:

- Choose the Reports menu, then choose Customers & Receivables, and click A/R Aging Summary to open the report
- Enter 02/28/14 in the Date field
- Press (tab) or click the Refresh button to update the report

The Accounts Receivable Aging reports show the outstanding amounts your customers owe aged according to current and previous billing periods. The default is to display the report in 30-day intervals. You can view the report in Summary form, with only the total amount owed by each customer in each period, or in Detail form, showing the transaction details for each outstanding invoice in each billing period. From these reports, you can see if any invoices are overdue.

The Accounts Receivable Aging Summary Report

1. **Click**   the **Run icon** [Run] under the A/R Aging Summary report to open the report

2. **Double click**   in the **date field**

3. **Type**   **02/28/14**

4. **Click**   the **Refresh button** or **press** (tab) to update the report:

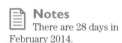 **Notes**
There are 28 days in February 2014.

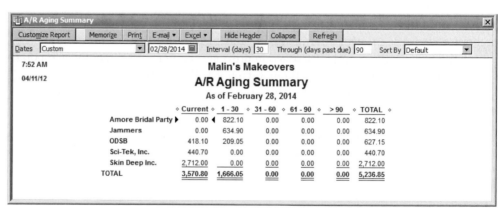

Figure 6-56

The A/R Aging Summary report shows the total amount that each customer owes. The columns on the report include how much each customer owes in the current billing period and how much they owe from previous billing periods. For example, all current invoices dated within the last 30 days are displayed in the current column and amounts that are between 31 and 60 days overdue are displayed in the 31-60 column, amounts that are between 61 and 90 days overdue are displayed in the 61-90 column, etc. By default, customers with zero balances are included in the report.

You can sort the report by total amount or customer (the default) from the Sort By field list. By default the report shows overdue billing periods to 90 days, but you can include more periods (columns) by entering a different number in the Through (days past due) field. For example, if some of your accounts are more than 120 days overdue, you can extend the reporting detail to show the overdue balances that are beyond 120 days by entering 120 in the Through (days past due) field. To change the length of the billing periods in the column heading, enter a different number in the Interval (days) field. We will modify the report to show 15-day billing periods because the terms for Malin's Makeovers are net 15 days.

5.	Double click	**30** in the **Interval (days) field**
6.	Type	**15**
7.	Click	the **Refresh button** to update the report with Current, 1–15, 16–30, 31–45, etc., as the column headings

You can also drill down on the report to view more transaction details.

8.	Double click	the **total for an aging period** to view the A/R Aging QuickZoom report which displays the transactions that make up the total amount
9.	Double click	a **transaction** to drill down to it
10.	Close	the **transaction** when you have finished viewing it
11.	Close	the **A/R Aging QuickZoom report** when you have finished viewing it
12.	Close	the **A/R Aging Summary report** when finished, unless you want to print it first
13.	Click	**No** to indicate that you do not want to memorize the report (this message is displayed because you changed the default report settings)

The Accounts Receivable Aging Detail Report

1.	Click	the **Run icon** ⟳ under the A/R Aging Detail report to open the report
2.	Double click	in the **date field**
3.	Type	**02/28/14**
4.	Click	the **Refresh button** or **press** ⌶tab⌷ to update the report:

Notes
To access the report from the Reports menu:
- Choose the Reports menu, then choose Customers & Receivables, and click A/R Aging Detail
- Enter 02/28/14 in the Date field
- Press ⌶tab⌷ or click the Refresh button to update the report

A/R Aging Detail

Customize Report | Memorize | Print | E-mail ▼ | Excel ▼ | Hide Header | Refresh

Dates | Custom | ▼ | 02/28/2014 | Interval (days) | 30 | Through (days past due) | 90 | Sort By | Default | ▼

7:57 AM
04/11/12

Malin's Makeovers
A/R Aging Detail
As of February 28, 2014

Type	Date	Num	P. O. #	Name	Terms	Due Date	Aging	Open Balance
Current								
Invoice	02/15/2014	3131		Skin Deep Inc.	Net 15	03/02/2014		1,356.00 ◀
Invoice	02/19/2014	3132		ODSB	Net 15	03/06/2014		209.05
Invoice	02/22/2014	3133		Skin Deep Inc.	Net 15	03/09/2014		1,356.00
Invoice	02/26/2014	3134		ODSB	Net 15	03/13/2014		209.05
Invoice	02/26/2014	3135		Sci-Tek, Inc.	Net 15	03/13/2014		440.70
Total Current								3,570.80
1 - 30								
Invoice	01/19/2014	3092		Jammers	Net 15	02/03/2014	25	309.90
Invoice	02/15/2014	3130		Jammers	Due on ...	02/15/2014	13	325.00
Invoice	02/03/2014	3126		Amore Bridal Party	Net 15	02/18/2014	10	822.10
Invoice	02/12/2014	3128		ODSB	Net 15	02/27/2014	1	209.05
Total 1 - 30								1,666.05
31 - 60								
Total 31 - 60								
61 - 90								
Total 61 - 90								
> 90								
Total > 90								
TOTAL								5,236.85

Figure 6-57

The detail report has a separate line for each transaction for each customer within each period, and the due date is displayed for each invoice. You can modify the detail report as you can the summary report. You can change the aging intervals, change the reporting through period, and drill down to view more detail. You can sort by any of the column headings — Type, Date, Number, P.O. #, Name, Terms, Due Date, Aging (age of invoice), and Opening Balance — in either ascending or descending order.

Double click a transaction line to drill down to the transaction. Double click a total for an aging period to display the Custom Transaction Detail report for the amount.

Notes
Double clicking a detail line in the A/R Aging Detail report will open the individual transaction.

5. **Double click** a **transaction line** to drill down to the transaction

6. **Close** the **transaction** when you're finished viewing it

7. **Close** the **report** when finished, unless you want to print it first

8. **Click** **No** to indicate that you do not want to memorize the report if you changed the default report settings

The Customer Balance Reports

The Customer Balance reports show the amount each customer currently owes. The summary report shows only the total amount while the detail report shows individual transactions, both invoices and payments.

The Customer Balance Summary Report

Notes
To access the report from the Reports menu:
- Choose the Reports menu, then choose Customers & Receivables, and click Customer Balance Summary
- Enter 02/01/14 in the From date field
- Enter 02/28/14 in the To date field
- Press (tab) or click the Refresh button to update the report

1. **Click** the **Run icon** [Run] under the Customer Balance Summary report to open the report

2. **Type** **02/01/14** in the **From date field**

3. **Press** (tab) to advance to the To date field

4. **Type** **02/28/14** and **press** (tab) to display the report:

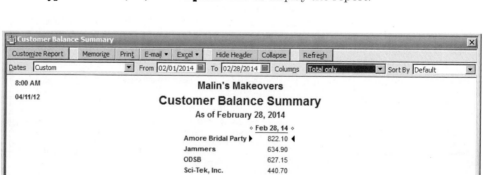

Figure 6-58

The date for this report is entered automatically by the program as the date of the latest transaction. Totals for each customer are shown as the default, but you can add columns for different intervals, such as weeks or months, by choosing from the Columns drop-down list. You can sort the report by total amount or by customer (the default).

Double click an amount or total for a customer to view the invoices and payments that make up that amount on the Customer Balance Detail report. Double click a transaction on the Customer Balance Detail report to drill down to the transaction.

Double click the report total on the Customer Balance Summary report to drill down to the Customer Balance Detail report that lists all the customer transactions that make up the report total.

5. **Close**   the **report** when finished

6. **Click**   **No** to indicate that you do not want to memorize the report if you changed the default report settings

The Customer Balance Detail Report

1. **Click**   the **Run icon** [Run] under the Customer Balance Detail report to open the report

2. **Type**   **02/01/14** in the **From date field**

3. **Press**   (tab) to advance to the To date field

4. **Type**   **02/28/14**

5. The Customer Balance Detail report will be displayed for February as shown:

📝 **Notes**
   To access the report from the Reports menu:
   • Choose the Reports menu, then choose Customers & Receivables, and click Customer Balance Detail
   • Type 02/01/14 in the From date field
   • Type 02/28/14 in the To date field
   • Press (tab) or click the Refresh button to update the report

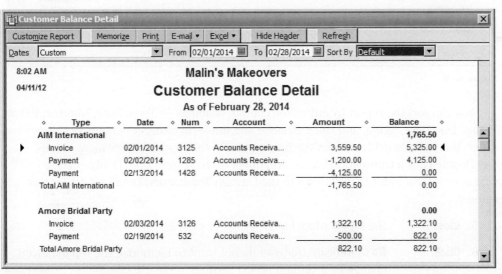

Figure 6-59

The report is organized by customer with a line for each invoice and payment.

You can sort the report by any of the column headings — Type, Date, Number, Account, and Amount — in either ascending or descending order.

Double click a transaction line to drill down to the transaction. Double click a customer total amount to drill down to the Custom Transaction Detail report for that amount.

6. **Close**   the **report** when finished

7. **Click**   **No** to indicate that you do not want to memorize the report if you changed the default report settings

The Open Invoices Report

Notes

To access the report from the Reports menu:

- Choose the Reports menu, then choose Customers & Receivables, and click Open Invoices
- Enter 02/28/14 in the Date field
- Press (tab) or click the Refresh button to update the report

The Open Invoices report shows which invoices have not been paid as at a specific date and when invoices are due. The Aging column provides the number of days since the invoice was created. Individual transactions are listed.

1. **Click** the **Run icon** [Run] under the Open Invoices report to open the report

2. **Double click** the **Date field**

3. **Type** 02/28/14

4. The Open Invoices report will be displayed for February as shown:

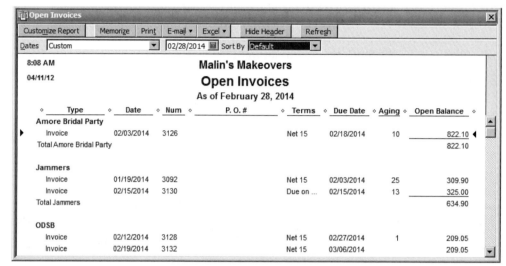

Figure 6-60

You can sort the report by any of the column headings — Type, Date, Number, P.O. #, Terms, Due Date, Aging, and Open Balance amount — in either ascending or descending order. You can also drill down on the information in the report to view more details.

Double click a transaction line to drill down to the transaction. Double click a customer total amount to drill down to the Custom Transaction Detail report for that amount.

5. **Close** the **report** when finished

6. **Click** **No** to indicate that you do not want to memorize the report, if you changed the default report settings

The Collections Report

The Collections report shows invoices that have not been paid and are overdue as at a specific date. The contact name and phone number are provided so that the customers can be contacted from these reports. Individual overdue transactions are listed. You can narrow the report further by providing a different past due interval. For example, you may want to phone accounts that are at least 30 days overdue. The default entered in the past due field is 1; therefore any invoice at least one day overdue is included on the report by default.

1. **Click**   the **Run icon** 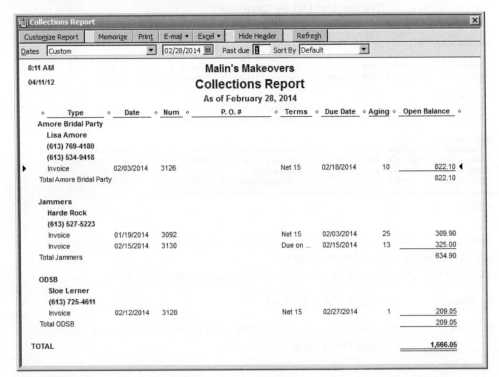 under the Collections report to open the report

2. **Type**   **02/28/14** in the **Date field**

3. **Click**   the **Refresh button** or **press** (tab) to update the report:

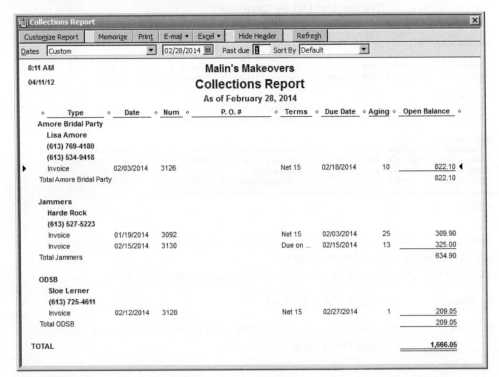

Figure 6-61

Notes
To access the report from the Reports menu:
- Choose the Reports menu, then choose Customers & Receivables, and click Collections report
- Enter 02/28/14 in the date field
- Press (tab) or click the Refresh button to update the report

You can sort the report by any of the column headings — Type, Date, Number, P.O. #, Terms, Due Date, Aging, and Open Balance amount — in either ascending or descending order. You can also drill down on a transaction to view more detail.

4. **Double click**   a **transaction line** to drill down to the original transaction. **Double click** a **total amount** to drill down to the Custom Transaction Detail report for that amount

5. **Close**   the **report** when finished

6. **Click**   **No** to indicate that you do not want to memorize the report if you changed the default report settings

Transaction List by Customer Report

This report shows all individual transactions for all customers for the selected report period.

1. **Click**   the **Run icon** 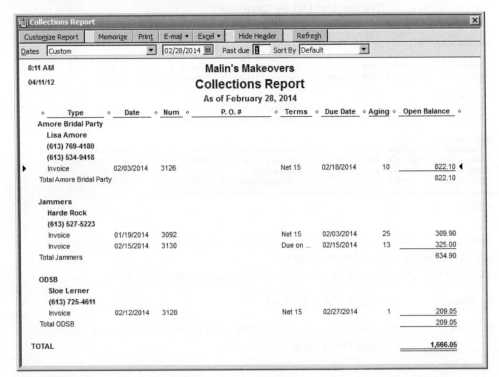 under the Transaction List by Customer report

2. **Double click**   the **From date field**

3. **Type**   **02/01/14**

4. **Press**   (tab) to advance to the To date field

5. **Type**   **02/28/14**

Notes
To access the report from the Reports menu:
- Choose the Reports menu, then choose Customers & Receivables, and click Transaction List by Customer
- Enter 02/01/14 in the From date field
- Enter 02/28/14 in the To date field
- Press (tab) or click the Refresh button to update the report

6. Press ⌨tab⌨ or **click** the **Refresh button** to update the report:

Figure 6-62

You can sort this report by any of the column headings and you can show the transactions in ascending or descending order.

Double click a transaction line to view the original transaction.

7. Close the **report** when finished

8. Click **No** to indicate that you do not want to memorize the report, if you changed the default report settings

Customer Lists

QuickBooks offers two lists for customers: the phone list and the contact list. You can use filters to select a specific group of customers on both of these lists that can be used to contact all or some customers or to check for missing data.

The Customer Phone List

The Customer phone list includes only the customer's name and phone number.

📄 **Notes**
To access the report from the Reports menu:
- Choose the Reports menu, then choose Customers & Receivables, and click Customer Phone List; or
- Choose the Reports menu, then choose List, and click Customer Phone List

1. Click the **Run icon** 🔵Run under the Customer Phone List to open the report:

Figure 6-63

You can sort the list by customer name or by phone number. Sorting by phone number allows you to display all customers within the same area code.

Double click a customer in the report to open the customer record. You can edit the information in the customer record if necessary.

2. Close   the **report** when finished

3. Click   **No** to indicate that you do not want to memorize the report, if you changed the default report settings

The Customer Contact List

1. Click   the **Run icon** under the Customer Contact List to open the report:

Notes
To access the report from the Reports menu:
- Choose the Reports menu, then choose Customers & Receivables, and click Customer Contact List; or
- Choose the Reports menu, then choose List, and click Customer Contact List

Figure 6-64

By default, the Customer Contact List contains the customer's name, invoice address, contact name, phone number, fax number, and balance total as of the latest transaction date. You can sort this report by any of the column headings and show the transactions in ascending or descending order. You can also modify the report to add additional customer details.

Double click a customer in the report to open the customer record. You can edit the information in the customer record if necessary.

2. Close   the **report** when finished

3. Click   **No** to indicate that you do not want to memorize the report if you changed the default report settings

Item Price Lists

The item price list contains the item name, description, preferred vendor, and price for each item.

1. Click   the **Run icon** under the Item Price List to open the report:

Notes
To access the report from the Reports menu:
- Choose the Reports menu, then choose Customers & Receivables, and click Item Price List; or
- Choose the Reports menu, then choose List, and click Item Price List

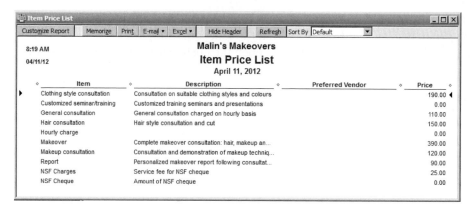

Figure 6-65

You can sort this report by any of the column headings and show the items in ascending or descending order, and you can modify the report to add additional details.

Double click an item to view the item record. You can edit the information in the item record if necessary.

2. Close   the **report** when finished

3. Click   **No** to indicate that you do not want to memorize the report if you changed the default report settings

Accounts Receivable Graphs

The final report for customers is presented as a graph. It displays aging information, as well as the total amount owed by individual customers.

📄 **Notes**

To access the graph from the Reports menu:
- Choose the Reports menu, then choose Customers & Receivables, and click Accounts Receivable Graph
- Click the Dates button
- Enter 02/28/14 in the Show Aging as of date field
- Click OK to display the graph

1. Click   the **Run icon** Run under the Accounts Receivable Graph

2. Click   the **Dates button** in the top left-hand corner of the screen

3. Type   **02/28/14** in the **Show Aging as of field**

4. Click   **OK** to display the graph:

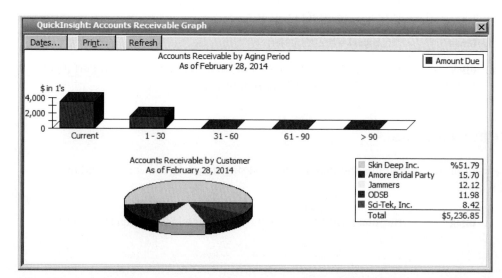

Figure 6-66

The graph has two sections: a bar graph in the upper section that shows the total amount owing for each aging interval and a pie chart in the lower section that shows the total owed by each customer. You can drill down to several other reports and graphs from both sections of the graph.

Double click a bar in the bar chart in the upper section of the Accounts Receivable Graph to view the pie chart breakdown of customer amounts that make up its total. Then, double click a section of this pie chart to view the A/R Aging QuickZoom report for the customer selected. Double click a transaction listed in the A/R Aging QuickZoom report to drill down to the transaction.

Double click a pie section in the pie chart in the lower section of the Accounts Receivable Graph to view an aging bar chart for that customer with separate bars for the total in each aging period. Then, double click a bar in this chart to view the A/R Aging QuickZoom report for the customer selected. Double click a transaction listed in the A/R Aging QuickZoom report to drill down to the transaction.

5. **Close**   the **report** when finished

6. **Click**   **No** to indicate that you do not want to memorize the report if you changed the default report settings

Sales Reports

In addition to the Customers & Receivables reports, there are several Sales reports that include customer information. Some of them display information similar to the customer reports, but they are organized by item instead of by customer.

Sales reports are accessed from the Sales heading in the Report Centre.

To access the Sales reports from the Report Centre:

1. **Click**   the **Sales heading** on the left-hand side of the screen

2. **Click**   the **List View icon**   if it is not already selected to view the list of Sales reports in list view:

Notes
The Sales by Rep reports and the Pending Sales report will be covered in a later chapter. There is no data for these reports for Malin's Makeovers.

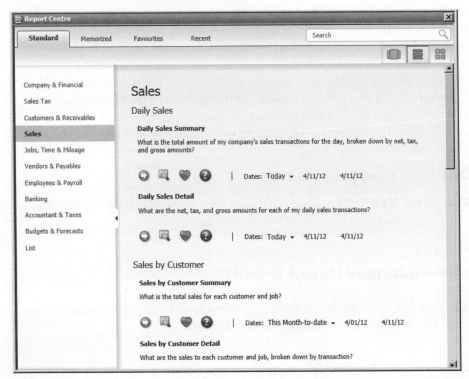

Figure 6-67

Sales by Customer Summary Report

This report also shows the total sales for each customer during the selected period.

Notes
To access the report from the Reports menu:
- Choose the Reports menu, then choose Sales, and click Sales by Customer Summary
- Enter 02/01/14 in the From date field
- Enter 02/28/14 in the To date field
- Press *tab* or click the Refresh button to update the report

1. **Click** the **Run icon** under the Sales by Customer Summary report under the Sales by Customer heading

2. **Double click** the **date** in the **From field**

3. **Type** **02/01/14**

4. **Press** *tab* to advance to the To date field

5. **Type** **02/28/14**

6. **Press** *tab* or **click** the **Refresh button** to update the report:

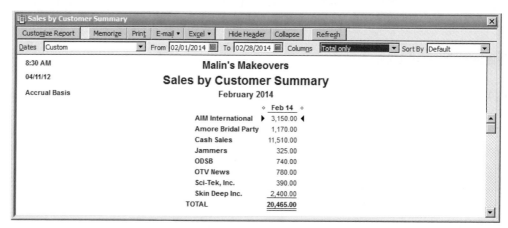

Figure 6-68

Totals for each customer are displayed as the default, but you can add columns for different intervals, such as weeks or months or other details, by selecting a different option from the Columns drop-down list. By default, this report is sorted by customer; however, you can also choose to sort it by total.

Double click an individual transaction line to drill down to the transaction. Double click a customer total to drill down to the Custom Transaction Detail report to view the details that make up the total for that customer, or double click the report total to drill down to the Custom Transaction Detail report to view the details that make up the total for all customers.

7. **Close** the **report** when finished

8. **Click** **No** to indicate that you do not want to memorize the report if you changed the default report settings

Notes
To access the report from the Reports menu:
- Choose the Reports menu, then choose Sales, and click Sales by Customer Detail
- Enter 02/01/14 in the From date field
- Enter 02/28/14 in the To date field
- Press *tab* or click the Refresh button to update the report

Sales by Customer Detail Report

This detail version of the Sales by Customer Summary report displays individual sales transactions for each customer during the selected period.

1. **Click** the **Run icon** under the Sales by Customer Detail report under the Sales by Customer heading

2. **Double click**   the **date** in the **From field**

3. **Type**   02/01/14

4. **Press**   (tab) to advance to the To date field

5. **Type**   02/28/14

6. **Press**   (tab) or **click** the **Refresh button** to update the report:

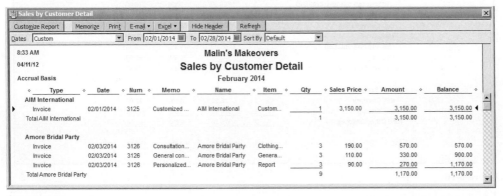

Figure 6-69

You can sort this report by any of the report column headings — Type, Date, Number, Memo, Name, Item, Quantity, Sales Price, and Amount — in either ascending or descending order.

Double click an individual transaction line to drill down to the transaction. Double click a customer total to drill down to the Custom Transaction Detail report to view the details that make up the total for that customer, or double click the report total to drill down to the Custom Transaction Detail report to view the details that make up the total for all customers.

7. **Close**   the **report** when finished

8. **Click**   **No** to indicate that you do not want to memorize the report if you changed the default report settings

Sales by Item Summary Report

This report shows how many of each item or service has been sold during the selected period and displays the percentage of total sales for each item or service. The average price for each item is also displayed on this report.

1. **Click**   the **Run icon** 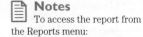 under the Sales by Item Summary report to open the report

2. **Double click**   the **From date field**

3. **Type**   02/01/14

4. **Press**   (tab) to advance to the To date field

5. **Type**   02/28/14

6. **Press**   (tab) or **click** the **Refresh button** to update the report:

📄 **Notes**
To access the report from the Reports menu:
- Choose the Reports menu, then choose Sales, and click Sales by Item Summary
- Enter 02/01/14 in the From date field
- Enter 02/28/14 in the To date field
- Press (tab) or click the Refresh button to update the report

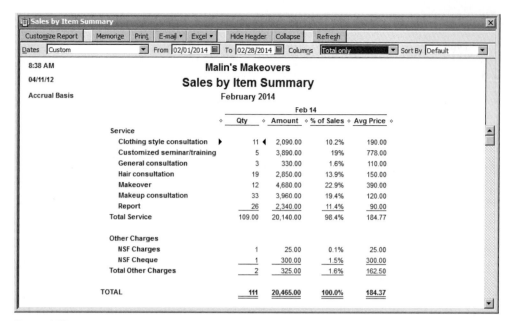

Figure 6-70

Items of the same type are grouped together in the report. For example, in Figure 6-70, you can see that Service items and Other Charges are grouped together. You can sort this report by total or by item type, the default.

Double click an item amount to view the Sales by Item Detail report that lists the individual transactions that make up the total amount for that item. Double click an individual transaction line on the Sales by Item Detail report to drill down to the transaction. Double click the report total on the Sales by Item Summary report to view the Sales by Item Detail Report that displays all of the transactions that make up the total amount of the report.

7. Close   the **report** when finished

8. Click   **No** to indicate that you do not want to memorize the report if you changed the default report settings

Sales by Item Detail Report

The Sales by Item Detail report shows the total sales of each item by transaction.

1. Click   the **Run icon** [Run] under the Sales by Item Detail report

2. Double click the **From date field**

3. Type   **02/01/14**

4. Press   (tab) to advance to the To date field

5. Type   **02/28/14**

6. Press   (tab) or **click** the **Refresh button** to view the report:

📝 **Notes**
To access the report from the Reports menu:
- Choose the Reports menu, then choose Sales, and click Sales by Item Detail
- Enter 02/01/14 in the From date field
- Enter 02/28/14 in the To date field
- Press (tab) or click the Refresh button to update the report

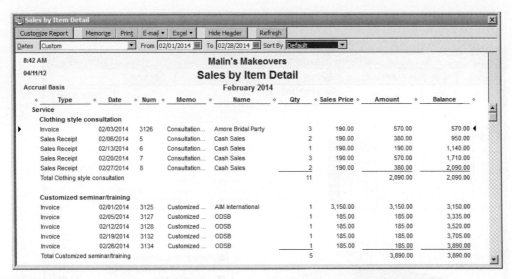

Figure 6-71

You can sort this report by any of the report column headings — Type, Date, Number, Memo, Name, Quantity, Sales Price, and Amount — in either ascending or descending order.

Double click an individual transaction to drill down to the transaction. Double click an item total to view the Custom Transaction Detail report that shows the transactions that make up the total amount for the item.

7. **Close**	the **report** when finished
8. **Click**	**No** to indicate that you do not want to memorize the report, if you changed the default report settings

Sales Graph

The final sales report is presented in a Sales Graph. It shows aging information, as well as the total amount owing to individual customers.

1. **Click**	the **Run icon** 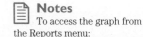 under the Sales Graph to open the graph
2. **Click**	the **Dates button**
3. **Double click**	the **From date field**
4. **Type**	**02/01/14**
5. **Press**	(tab) to advance to the To date field
6. **Type**	**02/28/14**

Notes
To access the graph from the Reports menu:
- Choose the Reports menu, then choose Sales, and click Sales Graph
- Click the Dates button
- Enter 02/01/14 in the From date field
- Enter 02/28/14 in the To date field
- Click OK to update the graph

7. Click   **OK** to view the graph:

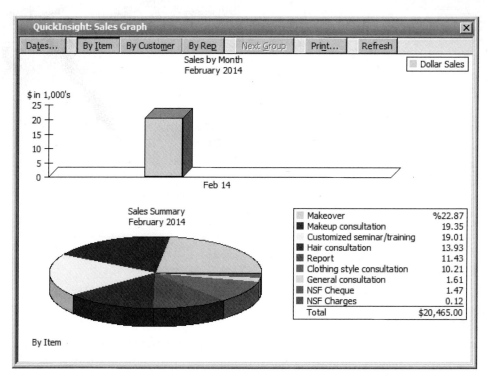

Figure 6-72

The graph has two sections: a bar graph in the upper section that shows the total amount sold in the selected period and a pie chart in the lower section that shows the total sold to each customer. You can drill down to several other reports and graphs from both sections of the graph.

Double click a bar in the bar chart in the upper section of the graph to view the pie chart breakdown of items that make up its total. Then, double click a section of this pie chart to view the item in dollars in a bar graph. Double click the bar graph to view the Custom Transaction Detail report that shows the individual transactions that make up the total for the item. Double click a transaction line to drill down to the transaction.

Double click a pie section in the pie chart in the lower section of the graph to view a bar chart for that item. Then, double click a bar in this chart to view the detail report with individual transactions for the item selected. Double click a transaction line in this detail report to view the original transaction.

8. Close   the **report** when finished

9. Click   **No** to indicate that you do not want to memorize the report if you changed the default report settings

Finishing Your Session

1. Back up   the **company data file**

2. Close   the **company file**

3. Close   the **QuickBooks program**

Objectives

After completing this chapter, you should be able to:

- **apply** sales discounts to receipts from customers
- **apply** purchase discounts to payments
- **apply** sales and purchase credits and deposits
- **prepare** sales estimates for customers
- **enter** sales orders for customers
- **customize** estimate and order forms for customers
- **enter** purchase orders
- **enter** deposits from customers
- **enter** prepayments to vendors
- **enter** credit card sales
- **enter** memorized transactions
- **enter** bills for received items
- **enter** sales invoices from orders and estimates
- **fill** purchase orders

Company Information

Company Profile

Terrific Tours in Calgary, Alberta, is owned and operated by Icharus Mannitoula. His wife, Serena, is employed by the business. Serena was working as a flight attendant and Icharus was employed in a travel agency when they met. Several years later, Icharus started his own travel agency, and his wife resigned from her job and is now employed by her husband. Planning trips for others did not fulfill their own desire to travel so Icharus

 Notes
Terrific Tours
550 Journeys Rd.
Calgary SW, AB T2P 4N9
Tel: (403) 719-8029
Fax: (403) 719-7333
E-mail: info@terrifictours.com
Web: www.terrifictours.com
Business No.: 643 653 843

and Serena decided to add hosted tours to the business a few years ago. They took additional travel and hospitality courses offered by the community college to help them prepare for the tour business. The tour business has grown steadily and now employs their sons.

Because of the Mannitoulas' personal interest in education and the arts, they organize all-inclusive guided tours for school groups and seniors with themes like art, architecture, or gardens. They arrange air, hotel, meals, local transportation, local guides, and admission to local attractions to fit the tour's theme. Most tours occur throughout the school year, September to June, to avoid the peak prices and summer holiday crowds. During the summers the Mannitoulas plan the tours for the coming year.

One family member accompanies each tour as a concierge and makes local arrangements, such as paying the hotel, restaurant, and admission bills; arranging emergency medical care; and troubleshooting to help trips run smoothly. All student groups travel with adult chaperones.

Theme tours are also available to individual clients — often well-educated professionals with flexible schedules that allow them to travel off-season. These customers may join in the full tour or buy only the air travel portion of the trip and make their own arrangements for hotel and local sightseeing.

Prices vary with the tour length and location, and with the variety of planned events. A 5 percent discount for groups of more than 10 allows the group chaperones to travel for half price. Individual customers pay full price for all tours. Schools and groups who have accounts with Terrific Tours receive an additional 1 percent discount if they settle their accounts within 10 days of the booking date. Deposits are requested at the time of booking because the airlines and hotels used by Terrific Tours also require deposits. Individual customers usually pay by credit card, while account customers pay by cheque. Athabaska Alumni Association, an account customer, has just confirmed a tour to Prague for the month of October and has paid the deposit.

Terrific Tours always gives their clients travel accessories as a gift: waist or neck wallets or a small carry-on tote bag. The business places special orders for these promotional items that are printed with the company name and logo, and it keeps inventory of these items on hand.

Terrific Tours has accounts with major airlines and hotel chains. Because of the volume of business, the company receives preferential prices from these vendors as well as discounts for early account settlement. Some vendors request prepayments or deposits from the tour company. Most accounts are paid by cheque but some smaller purchases are paid by credit card. Credit cards are also used for incidental expenses incurred during the tours.

Customers pay 5 percent GST on the airfare component of the tour packages. The tour component is not taxable because it occurs outside of Canada. Terrific Tours pays GST on business-related purchases. Provincial sales taxes are not levied in Alberta.

At the end of September 2014, two months into a new fiscal year, Terrific Tours converted their accounting records to QuickBooks by using the following:

- Chart of Accounts
- Trial Balance
- Vendor Information
- Customer Information
- Item List
- Accounting Procedures

Terrific Tours

ASSETS

Bank
- Bank Chequing
- Bank Savings
- Bank Visa

Accounts Receivable
- Accounts Receivable

Other Current Assets
- Brochures
- Office & Computer Supplies
- Prepaid Insurance
- Travel Accessories

Fixed Assets
- Business Vehicle:Cost
- Business Vehicle:Depreciation
- Computer Equipment:Cost

Computer Equipment:Depreciation
Office:Cost
Office:Depreciation
Office Furniture:Cost
Office Furniture:Depreciation

LIABILITIES

Accounts Payable
- Accounts Payable

Credit Card
- Credit Card Payable

Other Current Liabilities
- Bank Loan
- GST/HST Payable

Long Term Liabilities
- Long Term Loan
- Mortgage Payable

EQUITY
- Capital, Icharus Mannitoula
- Drawings, Icharus Mannitoula
- Retained Earnings

INCOME
- Revenue from Interest
- Revenue from Tours
- Sales Credits & Allowances
- Sales Discounts

EXPENSE

Cost of Goods Sold
- Cost of Tours:
  - Air Travel Expenses
  - Hotel Expenses
  - Local Tours & Admissions
  - Miscellaneous Expenses

Expense
- Advertising & Promotion
- Depreciation Expense
- Insurance Expense
- Interest Expense
- Maintenance & Cleaning
- Purchase Discounts
- Research Expenses
- Supplies Used
- Telephone Expense
- Travel Accessories Issued
- Travel Brochures Used
- Vehicle Expenses

NON-POSTING
- Estimates
- Purchase Orders
- Sales Orders

Trial Balance

Terrific Tours

AS AT SEPTEMBER 30, 2014

	Debits	Credits		Debits	Credits
Bank Chequing	$ 49,895.00		Capital, Icharus Mannitoula		$102,019.40
Bank Savings	38,490.00		Drawings, Icharus Mannitoula	$ 8,600.00	
Bank Visa	3,850.00		Revenue from Interest		1,400.00
Accounts Receivable	41,940.00		Revenue from Tours		165,000.00
Brochures	4,680.00		Sales Credits & Allowances	500.00	
Office & Computer Supplies	740.00		Sales Discounts	4,500.00	
Prepaid Insurance	12,000.00		Cost of Tours:		
Travel Accessories	2,690.00		Air Travel Expenses	47,520.00	
Business Vehicle:Cost	24,000.00		Hotel Expenses	41,360.00	
Business Vehicle:Depreciation		$ 7,200.00	Local Tours & Admissions	8,910.00	
Computer Equipment:Cost	5,000.00		Miscellaneous Expenses	5,220.00	
Computer Equipment:Depreciation		750.00	Advertising & Promotion	8,900.00	
Office:Cost	120,000.00		Depreciation Expense	2,160.00	
Office:Depreciation		11,700.00	Insurance Expense	12,000.00	
Office Furniture:Cost	4,000.00		Interest Expense	1,535.00	
Office Furniture:Depreciation		1,120.00	Maintenance & Cleaning	1,440.00	
Accounts Payable		27,905.60	Purchase Discounts		3,210.00
Credit Card Payable		1,510.00	Research Expenses	620.00	
Bank Loan		40,000.00	Supplies Used	120.00	
GST/HST Payable		1,720.00	Telephone Expense	420.00	
Long Term Loan		30,000.00	Travel Accessories Issued	1,120.00	
Mortgage Payable		60,000.00	Travel Brochures Used	885.00	
			Vehicle Expenses	440.00	
				$453,535.00	$453,535.00

Terrific Tours

Vendor Name (Contact)	Address	Phone No. / Fax No.	E-mail / Business No.	Terms / Credit Limit
Air Europe (Ava Winger)	334 Aviation Circle Toronto, ON M8J 2X4	Tel: (416) 238-4181 Fax: (416) 238-2619 Alt. tel: (877) 238-4000	a.winger@aireurope.com 249 498 587	net 20 $50,000.00
Capital Tours (Ona Coach)	314 Journeys Rd. Toronto, ON M2C 4F3	Tel: (800) 285-2355 Fax: (416) 285-3186	ona@capitaltours.com	1/10, n/30 $25,000.00
Foothills Communications (Ken Tellus)	44 Static St. Calgary NW, AB T5H 8P9	Tel: (403) 654-2355	tellus@foothills.com	net 10 $500.00
Heritage Hotels (Reste Fulle)	20 Rue Accommodation Montreal, QC H2J 7C5	Tel: (877) 377-1900 Fax: (514) 377-2728	rf@heritagehotels.com	1/10, n/30 $25,000.00
Parry's Printing House (Parry Papers)	109 Scanner St. Calgary NW, AB T4C 4F4	Tel: (403) 723-2302	parry@PPH.com 283 283 197	2/10, n/30 $2,000.00
Receiver General	875 Heron Rd. Ottawa, ON K2C 8G4	Tel: (800) 633-1020		quarterly remittances
Travel Totes (Fanny Packes)	900 Denier Ave. Calgary SW, AB T9N 8C9	Tel: (403) 274-8125 Fax: (403) 274-1288	fp@traveltotes.com 201 501 601	2/5, n/30 $3,000.00
Universal Theatre Bookings (Plaice Booker)	133 Showcase Rd. Toronto, ON M5B 3Y4	Tel: (800) 233-SHOW Fax: (416) 233-4990	booker@universal.com	2/5, n/30 $15,000.00

Terrific Tours

Vendor Name	Date	Terms	Due Date	Cheque No.	Amount
Air Europe	Sep. 30/14	net 20	Oct. 20/14	AE-4897	$11,663.00
Foothills Communications	Sep. 21/14	net 10	Oct. 1/14	FC-10982	$128.40
Heritage Hotels	Sep. 25/14	1/10, n/30	Oct. 25/14	HH-2099	$13,910.00
Parry's Printing House	Sep. 25/14	2/10, n/30	Oct. 25/14	PPH-1800	$952.30
Travel Totes	Sep. 28/14	2/5, n/30	Oct. 28/14	TT-5001	$1,251.90
				Grand Total	$27,905.60

Terrific Tours

Customer Name (Contact)	Address	Phone No. / Fax No.	E-mail / Business No.	Terms / Credit Limit
Athabaska Alumni Association (Olda Grads)	75 Olde Thyme Cres. Calgary, AB T3E 5R4	Tel: (403) 228-6532 Fax: (403) 229-3915	OG@athagrads.org	1/10, n/30 $50,000.00
Calgary District School Board (Zolof Tutor)	100 Highroads Ave. Calgary, AB T4G 2L9	Tel: (403) 621-6299 Fax: (403) 628-6381	ZTutor@cdsb.ab.ca 399 722 532	1/10, n/30 $50,000.00
Calgary Region Catholic School Bd. (Vader Priestly)	200 Lowrodes Ave. Calgary, AB T6V 4S3	Tel: (403) 255-7734 Fax: (403) 255-2524	VPriestly@crcsb.ab.ca 444 576 511	1/10, n/30 $50,000.00
Cash Sales				due on receipt

Terrific Tours

Customer Name (Contact)	Address	Phone No. Fax No.	E-mail Business No.	Terms Credit Limit
Foothills Academy of Art (Emmy Oscar)	45 Stage Dr. Calgary, AB T3P 7V7	Tel: (403) 754-2910 Fax: (403) 754-3926	oscar@faa.ca	1/10, n/30 $50,000.00
Rocky Mtn School for the Performing Arts	699 Limelight Cr. Calgary, AB T2H 4C8	Tel: (403) 681-6296 Fax: (403) 688-4361	499 510 294	1/10, n/30 $50.000.00
UpperCrust School for Boys (Rex Masters)	RR #1 Bragg Creek, AB T3K 4H8	Tel: (403) 733-5188 Fax: (403) 732-6994	RM@ucsb.ca 502 638 566	1/10, n/30 $50,000.00

Outstanding Customer Transactions

Terrific Tours

Customer Name	Date	Terms	Due Date	Invoice No./ Cheque No.	Amount	Balance Owing
Athabaska Alumni Association	Sep. 24/14	1/10, n/30	Oct. 24/14	208	$17,120.00	
	Sep. 26/14	1/10, n/30		210	$38,520.00	
	Sep. 26/14	deposit cheque		Chq 3990	−$26,000.00	$29,640.00
Foothills Academy of Art	Sep. 1/14	1/10, n/30	Oct. 1/14	199	$18,300.00	
	Sep. 1/14	deposit cheque		Chq 487	−$9,000.00	$9,300.00
UpperCrust School for Boys	Sep. 18/14	1/10, n/30	Oct. 18/14	204	$3,000.00	$3,000.00
					Grand Total	$41,940.00

Item List

Terrific Tours

Item	Description	Account	Tax Code
Service Items			
Air Travel	Airfare component of tour	Revenue from Tours	G
Tour	Accommodation and local travel component of tour	Revenue from Tours	E
Non-Inventory Items			
Brochures & Books	Travel information booklets	Brochures	G
Local Tours & Events	Tour components arranged locally	Local Tours & Admissions	E
Travel Accessories		Travel Accessories	G

Accounting Procedures

Taxes: GST and PST

Terrific Tours pays GST on goods and services that it buys in Canada and charges GST on airfare. It uses the regular method for remittance of the Goods and Services Tax. GST collected from customers is recorded as a liability in the *GST/HST Payable* account. GST paid to vendors is recorded in the *GST/HST Payable* account as a decrease in liability to the Canada Revenue Agency. The report is filed with the Receiver General for Canada by the last day of the month for the previous quarter, either including the balance owing or requesting a refund.

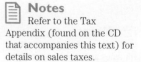

Notes
Refer to the Tax Appendix (found on the CD that accompanies this text) for details on sales taxes.

Notes
We have simplified the tax structure for this application. For example, several other taxes apply to airfares and some components of the tours may be subject to taxes as well.

No taxes apply to services consumed outside of Canada — hotel, tours, event admissions, and local travel. The tax exempt code is used for these parts of the tour. Local taxes are included in the prices for these services, but these taxes are not recorded separately because they are not refundable and therefore are not tracked. Because airfares are taxable, they are priced separately and listed as separate items.

Alberta does not charge PST on any goods or services.

Account Terms

Organized groups set up accounts with Terrific Tours and receive a 1 percent discount if they settle their accounts within 10 days of confirming a tour. The full balance is required within 30 days of booking the tour or before the tour starts, whichever comes first. Most tours are booked at least six weeks in advance of the departure date.

Individual customers who join a pre-packaged tour do not receive discounts and must settle the account in full within 10 days of booking, or before travel, whichever comes first. Most of these customers pay by Visa.

Some vendors offer discounts for early payment.

Bank Deposits and Cheques

All cheques and credit card payments are deposited immediately; they are not held for later deposit. Cheques are manually prepared at the time of the transaction.

Estimates, Orders, and Deposits

Terrific Tours provides estimates for customers who request them. Terrific Tours uses purchase orders for their custom-made inventory. They also place purchase orders for the tour components that involve admissions to local events and local travel arrangements.

Customers pay 50 percent of the price of tour packages as a deposit to confirm the bookings when they accept the estimate. Some vendors also require deposits.

Drawings

The owner withdraws money from the business as needed in lieu of receiving a salary.

Instructions

1. Using the Chart of Accounts, the Trial Balance, and other information, you will record entries for source documents for October 2014 by using QuickBooks. You will find the source documents marked with an SD beside them and listed as you work through the chapter. The procedures for entering each new type of transaction introduced in this chapter are outlined in step-by-step instructions. Additional source documents will be provided, allowing you to have more practice entering transactions. If you have used this textbook in the past and would prefer to skip the step-by-step instructions and work only with a list of source documents, refer to the CD in the back of the textbook for the list of source documents for this chapter.

Notes
Instructions for reports for sales and purchase orders begin on page 394.

2. After you have finished making your entries, print the reports and graphs for October 2014 as indicated on the following printing form:

REPORTS FOR OCTOBER 2014		
Lists	☐ Transaction List by Date	**Customer**
☐ Account Listing	☐ Transaction Detail by Account	☑ A/R Aging Detail at Oct. 31
☐ Customer Phone List	**Other**	☐ Customer Balance
☐ Customer Contact List	☐ Custom Summary Report	☑ Open Invoices at Oct. 31
☐ Vendor Phone List	☐ Custom Transaction Detail Report	☐ Collections Report
☐ Vendor Contact List	☐ Transaction History	☑ Transaction List by Customer from Oct. 1 to Oct. 31
☐ Item Listing	☐ Transaction Journal	**Sales**
☐ Item Price List	**Vendor**	☑ Sales by Customer from Oct. 1 to Oct. 31
Company & Financial	☑ A/P Aging Detail at Oct. 31	☐ Sales by Item
☑ Balance Sheet Standard at Oct. 31	☐ Vendor Balance	☑ Open Sales Orders by Customer
☑ Profit & Loss Standard from Oct. 1 to Oct. 31	☑ Unpaid Bills at Oct. 31	**GRAPHS**
☐ Expenses by Vendor	☐ Transaction List by Vendor	☐ Income and Expense
☐ Income by Customer	**Purchases**	☐ Net Worth
Accountant & Taxes	☐ Purchases by Vendor	☐ Accounts Payable
☑ Trial Balance at Oct. 31	☐ Purchases by Item	☐ Accounts Receivable
☐ General Ledger	☑ Transaction List by Vendor from Oct. 1 to Oct. 31	☐ Sales
☑ Journal from Oct. 1 to Oct. 31	☑ Open Purchase Orders by Vendor	

3. Open the tours.qbw file for Terrific Tours.

Applying Credits to Customer Accounts

Businesses frequently ask customers to pay a deposit when they make a purchase on account. Prepayments can serve several purposes: they allow the business to order and pay for items required for a job for that customer; they help to ensure that a customer will proceed with the purchase; they reduce the final amount owing by the customer so that the customer will not exceed the credit limit; and so on. The deposit creates a credit balance in the customer's receivables account. When a sales invoice is recorded, the initial credit balance reduces the amount owing from the invoice.

Notes
Accounts Receivable normally has a debit balance because the customer owes money to the business. When there is a credit balance, the business owes something to the customer, usually some goods or services.

Terrific Tours requires a deposit of about 50 percent of the total tour package price when a customer confirms a tour, accepts a sales estimate, or places an order. After the money is received and an invoice is prepared, the deposit must be applied to the balance owing by the customer.

The first transaction that we will enter is a deposit that needs to be applied to recorded sales invoices for Athabaska Alumni Association. The deposit has already been received and entered in QuickBooks. Refer to the following source document as we work through the steps to enter it:

SD1: Memo #1 **Dated October 1, 2014**

Apply the deposit Cheque #487 of $26,000.00 received and entered into QuickBooks on September 26, 2014, to the balance owing from Athabaska Alumni Association. Apply $8,000.00 to Invoice #208 and $18,000.00 to Invoice #210.

Source Docs
Refer to the following source document and then follow the step-by-step instructions to enter it.

1. The QuickBooks Home page should be displayed on the screen

Customer deposits are applied to invoices on the Receive Payments form. To open the form:

a) **Click** the **Receive Payments icon** in the Customers section of the Home page; or
b) **Choose** the **Customers menu** and then **click Receive Payments**

Notes
Remember that you can add icons to the Icon bar for any of the forms required for these transactions. Refer to page 67 for more information.

Receive
Payments

2. **Click** the **Receive Payments icon** in the Customers section of the Home page or **choose** the **Customers menu** and **click Receive Payments** to open the Receive Payment form

3. **Click** the **drop-down arrow** in the **Received From field** and **choose Athabaska Alumni Association** to view the outstanding invoices for the customer:

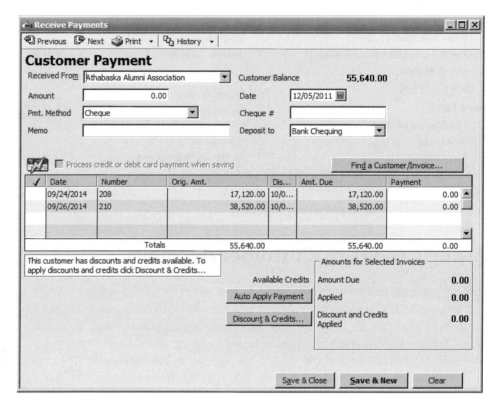

Figure 7-1

4. **Read** the **information** displayed in the bottom left-hand corner of the screen:

This customer has discounts and credits available. To apply discounts and credits click Discount & Credits...

Figure 7-2

The information in the bottom left-hand corner of the form indicates that this customer has discounts and credits available. To view the discounts and credits available, you must click on the Discount and Credits button.

5. **Click** the **Discount & Credits button** Discount & Credits... to open the Discount and Credits screen:

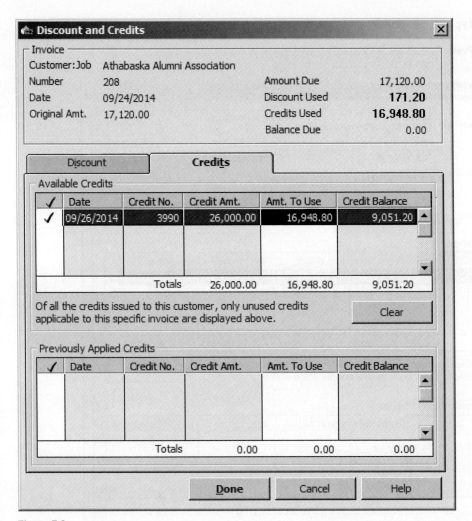

Figure 7-3

Notice that the customer has a total credit amount of $26,000.00 that can be applied to invoices. When you click the Discount and Credits button, the first invoice displayed on the Receive Payments form is selected by default. The credits applicable to that invoice are displayed on the Discount and Credits screen. We need to apply the credit so that approximately 50 percent of each invoice owed by the customer is covered by the deposit so we will not be accepting the distribution of the credits as shown on this screen.

6. **Click**   **Cancel** to close the Discount and Credits screen

On the Receive Payments form, choose the invoices to apply the credit to. To select an invoice, click anywhere on the line except in the Applied To ✓ (checkmark) column.

7. **Click**   **208** the invoice number in the **Number field** (or any invoice detail on that line) to select the first invoice if it is not already selected

8. **Click**   the **Discount and Credits button** to access the Discount and Credits screen

The Credits tab is selected. Notice that the date in the Date column of the Credits tab is the date of the deposit cheque, September 26, 2014. The default is to apply the entire credit or the full amount of the invoice, whichever is less. In this case, the credit is greater than the balance owing on the invoice, so there would be a credit balance remaining. However, we want to apply only $8,000.00 to this invoice.

9. **Double click**   **16,948.80** in the Amt. To Use column to select the amount

10. Type   **8000**

11. Press   ⌨tab to update the Credit Balance as shown:

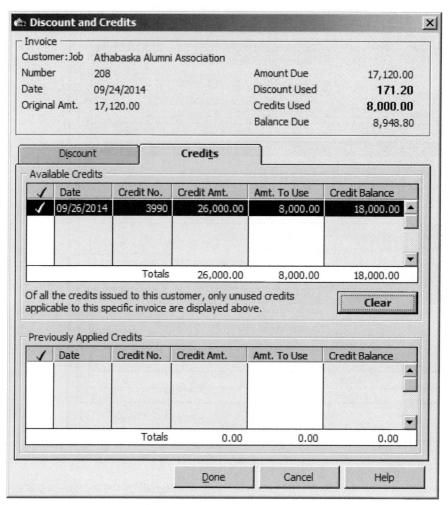

Figure 7-4

Notice the remaining credit balance is $18,000.00.

12. Click   **Done** because we have finished working with the first invoice and the following warning message will be displayed:

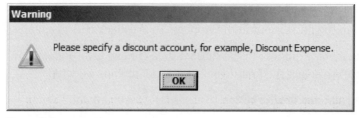

Figure 7-5

This message indicates that QuickBooks has determined that a discount is available for this invoice based on the 1 percent within 10 days, net 30 days terms (abbreviated 1/10, n/30) that have been associated with this invoice and that a discount account is not available to which to post the discount. The invoice date is September 24th, and the date of this deposit is September 26th; therefore, QuickBooks has determined that a discount is due. However, discounts are not given on deposits.

13. Click   **OK** and the Discount tab is displayed

14. Highlight   the **amount** in the **Amount of Discount field** and **press** ⌨del

15. The completed Discount tab should be displayed as shown:

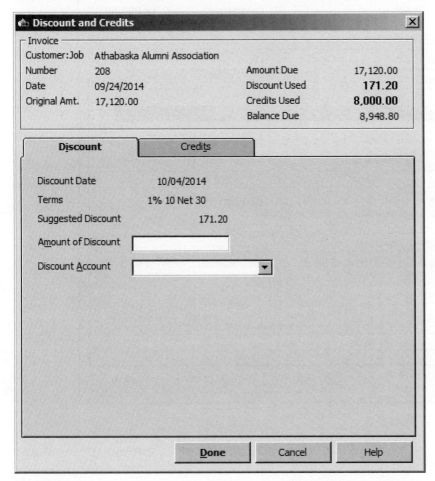

Figure 7-6

16. Click   **Done**

You will be returned to the Receive Payments window. Notice that $8,000.00 now appears in the Credits column for Invoice #208. We can now apply the remaining credit to the second invoice. The first invoice line should still be selected.

17. Click   the **second invoice line**

18. Click   the **Discount and Credits button** again to view the updated Discount and Credits screen:

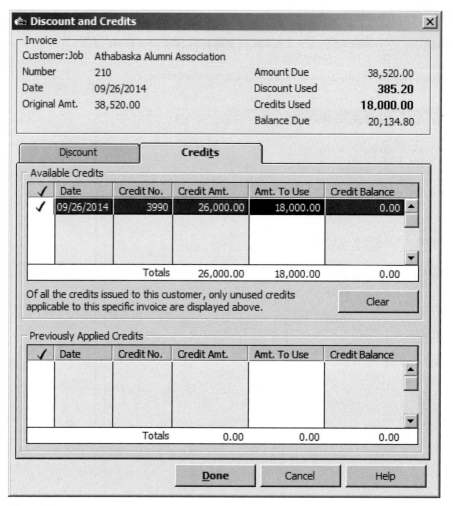

Figure 7-7

This time, the default amount in the Amt. To Use column is correct — the remaining amount of $18,000.00 is applied to Invoice #210.

19. **Click**   **Done**

20. **Click**   **OK** to accept the warning that you must specify a discount account

21. **Highlight**   the **amount** in the **Amount of Discount field** and **press** ⌫del

22. **Click**   **Done** to return to the Receive Payments form

Notice that $18,000.00 now appears in the Credits column for Invoice #210.

The current computer date may still be displayed in the date field. We need to change this date to reflect the transaction date, and we should add a memo to indicate the source of the transaction.

23. **Type**   **10/01/14** in the **Date field**

24. **Click**   the **Memo field**

25. **Type**   **Memo 1 - apply outstanding credit to invoices**

The transaction is now complete.

26. Your completed Receive Payments form should look like the one shown here:

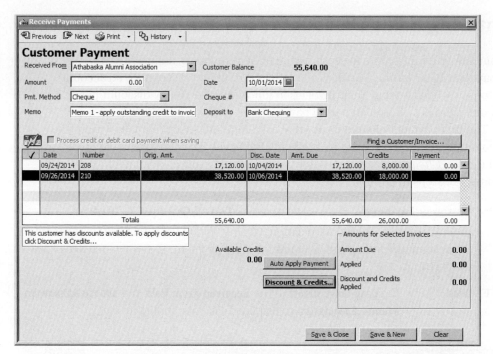

Figure 7-8

Notice that the information in the bottom left-hand corner of the screen that previously indicated that this customer had discounts and credits available has been updated to indicate that this customer only has discounts available.

27. Click   the **Save & New button** so we can apply the next credit

No journal entry results from applying the credits to the customer invoices. When the deposit or prepayment cheque was originally entered, it generated a normal journal entry that debited *Bank Chequing* and credited *Accounts Receivable*. When the deposit is distributed, no journal entries are created; however, the customer's account is updated — the amounts owing for the invoices are reduced and no unused credits remain.

Source Document

Now that you have learned how to apply a customer deposit to an invoice, enter the deposit received from Foothills Academy of Art against a recorded sales invoice. The deposit has already been received and entered into QuickBooks. The source document is as follows:

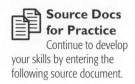

Source Docs for Practice
Continue to develop your skills by entering the following source document.

SD2:   Memo #2   **Dated October 1, 2014**

Apply the $9,000.00 deposit from Foothills Academy of Art to the balance owing on Invoice #199.

Entering Sales Discounts

Businesses offer discounts for early payment of accounts as an incentive for customers to pay their bills on time. Terrific Tours offers a 1 percent discount to all account customers when they pay their invoices in full within the 10-day discount period. Discounts are not offered on partial payments.

The first payment cheque from Athabaska Alumni Association falls within the discount period and both invoices are being fully paid. The cheque should be deposited to the *Bank Chequing* account. Refer to the following source document as we work through the steps to enter it:

SD3:   **Customer Payment**   **Dated October 2, 2014**

From Athabaska Alumni Association, Cheque #4038 for $29,083.60 in payment of the account, including the discount for early payment. Reference Invoices #208 and #210.

1. Click   the **drop-down arrow** in the **Received From field** and **choose Athabaska Alumni Association** to display their outstanding invoices:

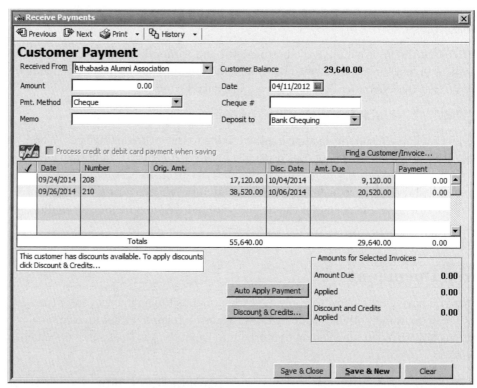

Figure 7-9

2. Press   ⌨ to advance to the Date field and **enter 10/02/14**

Notice that the amounts in the Amt. Due column have been reduced to reflect the applied credits. Discounts are applied like credits — select an invoice, click the Discount & Credits button, accept or enter the discount for the invoice, select the next invoice that is paid by the same cheque, click the Discount & Credits button, accept or enter the discount, and so on.

3. **Click**	**208** to select the number of the first invoice, or anywhere on the line to select the invoice (do not click in the box to the left of the invoice)
4. **Click**	the **Discount & Credits button** to open the Discount and Credits screen:

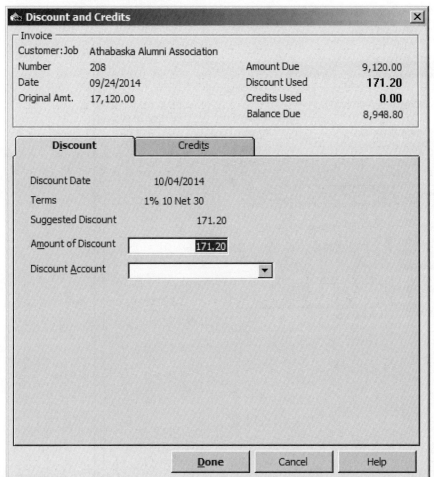

Notes
If the discount does not show in the Discount and Credits window, check that you have entered the correct date for the payment.

Figure 7-10

The Discount tab should be displayed. The full discount amount, the suggested discount according to the payment terms, is entered in the Amount of Discount field — $171.20, which is 1 percent of the full invoice amount $17,120.00. You can change the amount to provide a different discount amount if you want. The original customer, number, date, and amount are all displayed for reference. In addition, the amount due, discount used, credits used, and balance due are also displayed. The discount date is the last date on which the discount is available, based on the terms. If the cheque date is later than the discount date, the suggested discount is removed (set at zero).

The discount amount entered by default is correct so you should accept it. We also need to select the account that the sales discount will be allocated to.

5. **Click**	the **drop-down arrow** in the **Discount Account field**
6. **Click**	**Sales Discounts**
7. **Click**	**Done** to return to the Receive Payments form

Before applying the discount to the second invoice, we will change the transaction date to view the effect this will have.

Notes
Sales Discounts is a contra-revenue account that normally has a debit balance and reduces total income.

8. **Double click**   the **Date field**

9. **Type**   **10/10/14**

10. **Click**   **210** the number of the second invoice, or anywhere on the line to select the invoice (do not click in the box to the left of the invoice)

11. **Click**   the **Discount & Credits button** to open the Discount and Credits screen:

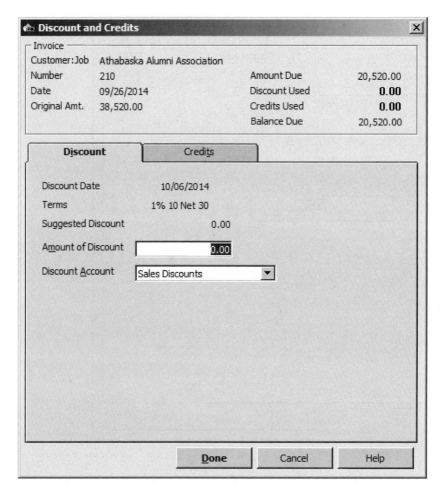

Figure 7-11

Notice that the amount in the Amount of Discount field is zero because the discount period expires on October 6, 2014. If you recall, we changed the payment date to 10/10/14, and, therefore, a discount amount is not available according to the date.

12. **Click**   **Cancel** to return to the Receive Payments form so you can change the date back to October 2, 2014

13. **Double click**   the **Date field**

14. **Type**   **10/02/14**

15. Invoice #210 should still be selected

16. **Click**   the **Discount & Credits button** to open the Discount and Credits screen:

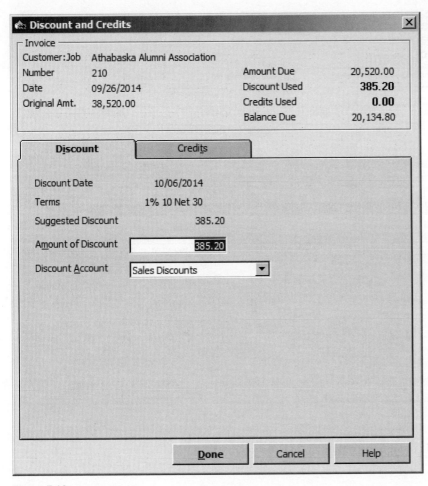

Figure 7-12

Notice that the suggested discount has been restored to $385.20, that is, 1 percent of the original invoice total amount. The discount account should be entered from the previous invoice discount. If it is not, select *Sales Discounts* in the Discount Account field.

17. Click   **Done** to return to the Receive Payments form

We still need to add the cheque amount, include the cheque number for reference, and select the invoices for payment. You can enter a comment in the Memo field if you want.

The total in the Payment column should now match the cheque amount of $29,083.60 because the customer is paying the account in full.

18. Double click   **0.00** in the **Amount field**

19. Type   **29083.60**

20. Press   tab

Notice that the invoices have been selected for payment based on the cheque amount.

21. Press   tab to advance to the Cheque # field

22. Type   **4038**

23. Select   the **Bank Chequing** account in the **Deposit to field** if this is not the account selected already

24. Check   your **work** carefully. The completed payment entry should look like the one shown here:

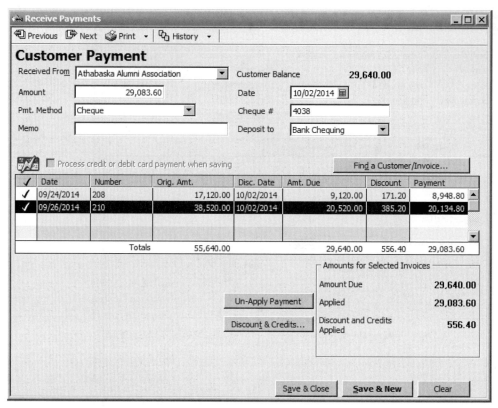

Figure 7-13

You should correct any errors before recording the payment.

CORRECTING DISCOUNTED CUSTOMER PAYMENTS

Click the field that contains the error. You can press (tab) to move forward from one field to the next. Highlight the incorrect information and type the correct information in the field. Press (tab) if necessary to update the information.

To correct a discount, select the invoice line and then click the Discount & Credits button to open the Discount & Credits screen. Edit the information as needed and click Done. Edit any other details of the customer payment that are incorrect just as you would correct regular customer payments (see page 280).

You can also start again by clicking the Clear button.

We want to review the Journal Transaction created from the payment transaction so we need to save the payment and keep the Receive Payments form open.

25. Click   **Save & New** to record the payment

Reviewing the Transaction

With a blank Receive Payments form displayed on the screen:

1. Click   the **Previous button** 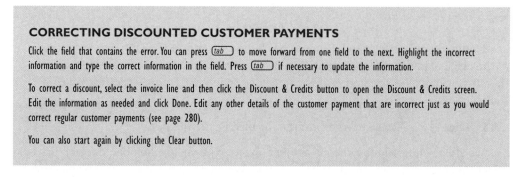 or **press** (alt) + **P** to view the payment we just entered from Athabaska Alumni Association

2. Press   (ctrl) + **Y** to view the Transaction Journal report:

Notes
We have removed
columns from this report
before displaying it here.

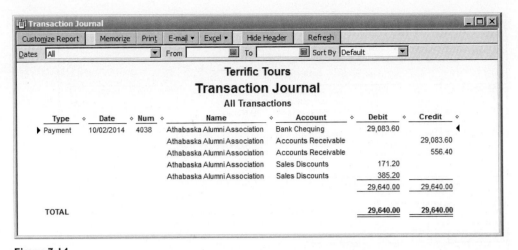

Figure 7-14

You can see that QuickBooks has debited (increased) the *Bank Chequing* account for the net amount of the cheque, after taking the discount. The discount amount is debited to the *Sales Discounts* account, a contra-revenue account that reduces total income. The *Accounts Receivable* account has been credited (reduced for both the amount of the cheque and the amount of the sales discount). As usual, the customer record is updated, and the amount owing is reduced by the full amount of the cheque and discount.

Notes
Revenue accounts usually
have a credit balance.

3. **Close**   the **Transaction Journal report**

4. **Close**   the **Receive Payments form**

Entering Purchase Discounts

The next transaction that we need to enter is a cheque to Travel Totes in payment of account. The payment is made before the early period discount date so it includes a discount. Refer to the following source document as we walk through the steps to enter it:

SD4: Pay Bill   **Dated October 2, 2014**

Cheque #480 to Travel Totes, $1,226.86 in payment of account, including a 2 percent discount for early payment. Reference Bill #TT-5001.

Source Docs
Refer to the following
source document and then
follow the step-by-step
instructions to enter it.

1. **Click**   the **Pay Bills icon** [Pay Bills] in the Vendors section of the Home page to open the Pay Bills form:

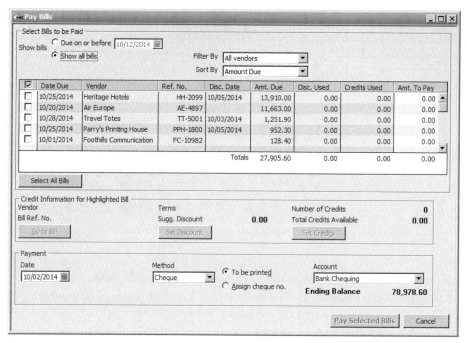

Figure 7-15

The Show all bills option under the Select Bills to be Paid heading should be selected. By default the bills are filtered by vendor and sorted by amount due.

Notice that the Disc. Date column shows the last date that the discount will be available. No discount amounts are entered yet.

2. **Enter**   10/02/14 in the **Payment Date field** (if it is not already entered as the date)

3. **Click**   the **pay column** — the ✓ (checkmark) column — beside invoice TT-5001 from Travel Totes

4. The Pay Bills form is updated as shown:

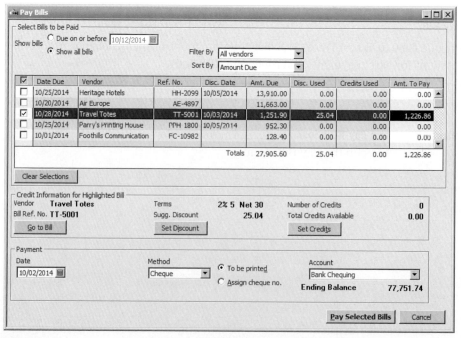

Figure 7-16

Notice that a discount amount is suggested for the selected bill and the Set Discount button is available. An amount appears in the Disc. Used column because the preferences to apply credits and discounts automatically for bill payments have been selected for this company file and because the payment date is within the discount period. We can enter the credits and discounts the way we did for customer payments. If you need to edit a discount or credit amount for the bill to which it is applied, you must choose the Set Discount or Set Credits button to access the relevant screen.

5. **Click** the **Set Discount button** 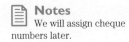 to access the Discount and Credits screen:

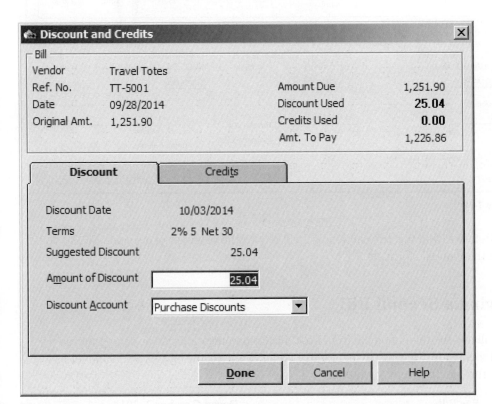

Notes
If the discount is not displayed on the Discount tab, check that you have entered the correct date for the payment.

Figure 7-17

The Discount tab is displayed. As for customer discounts, if the date is beyond the last discount date, the suggested discount amount will be zero. If a discount amount is not displayed in the Amount of Discount field, check the date entered for the payment.

All the details are correct. The suggested discount is the correct discount amount and the *Purchase Discounts* account is the correct Discount Account. You can change the discount amount and the account if necessary. The discount will be credited to this contra-expense account — the discount reduces the total expenses in the Income (Profit & Loss) Statement.

6. **Click** **Done** to return to the Pay Bills window

7. **Click** **Assign cheque no.** to complete the Bill Payment

The Pay Bills form should now look like the one shown here:

Notes
We will assign cheque numbers later.

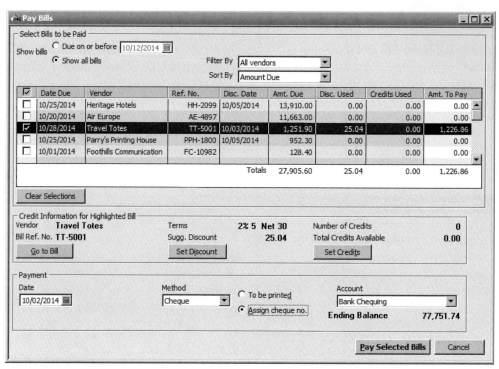

Figure 7-18

Before saving this transaction, we will record the payment of a second bill, so do not close the Pay Bills form yet.

Paying a Second Bill

We will pay the telephone bill from Foothills Communications at the same time, so we need to include it in this payment entry. Refer to the following source document as we work through the steps to enter it:

Source Docs
Refer to the following source document and then follow the step-by-step instructions to enter it.

SD5: Pay Bill   Dated October 2, 2014

Cheque #481 to Foothills Communication, $128.40 in full payment of account. Reference Bill #FC-10982.

1. **Click**   the ✓ **(checkmark) column** beside the bill from Foothills Communications to pay this bill together with the bill from Travel Totes

Notice that this bill does not have a discount associated with it. A date is not displayed in the Disc. Date field and an amount is not displayed in the Disc. Used field.

2. **Click**   the **Pay Selected Bills button** ⟨Pay Selected Bills⟩ to open the Assign Cheque Numbers dialogue box:

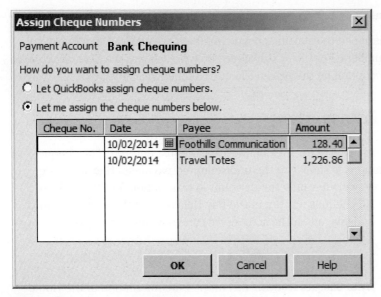

Figure 7-19

The *Let me assign the cheque numbers below* option should be selected. Both cheques are listed so we can assign cheque numbers to both.

3. Click   the **Cheque No.** column beside the bill paid to Travel Totes (the second transaction line)

4. Type   **480**

5. Click   ↑ to move up beside the bill paid to Foothills Communications

6. Type   **481**

7. Click   **OK** to complete the payment

8. The Payment Summary screen is displayed:

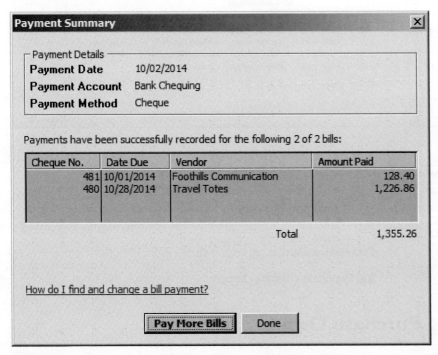

Figure 7-20

9. Click   **Done**

Now that we have assigned the starting cheque numbers, we can let QuickBooks automatically assign these numbers. For the next cheque you write, choose the *Let QuickBooks assign cheque numbers* option on the Assign Cheque Numbers dialogue box.

Reviewing the Transaction

We can now view the journal entry for the cheques that we just entered. The cheque for Foothills Communications is similar to the undiscounted payments that we made in previous chapters so we will view only the discounted transaction for Travel Totes. Remember that we view all cheques written in the Pay Bills form in the Write Cheques form. When the cheque is displayed on the screen, we can view the journal entry.

1. Click the **Write Cheques icon** 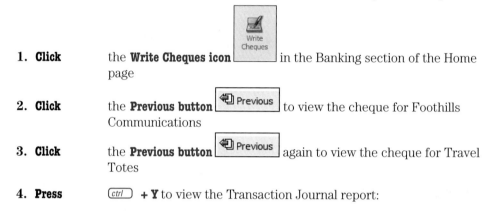 in the Banking section of the Home page

2. Click the **Previous button** to view the cheque for Foothills Communications

3. Click the **Previous button** again to view the cheque for Travel Totes

4. Press `ctrl` **+ Y** to view the Transaction Journal report:

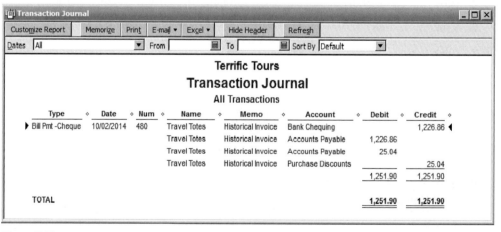

Terrific Tours
Transaction Journal
All Transactions

Type	Date	Num	Name	Memo	Account	Debit	Credit
▶ Bill Pmt -Cheque	10/02/2014	480	Travel Totes	Historical Invoice	Bank Chequing		1,226.86 ◀
			Travel Totes	Historical Invoice	Accounts Payable	1,226.86	
			Travel Totes	Historical Invoice	Accounts Payable	25.04	
			Travel Totes	Historical Invoice	Purchase Discounts		25.04
						1,251.90	1,251.90
TOTAL						1,251.90	1,251.90

Figure 7-21

Notice that *Bank Chequing* is credited for the net amount of the cheque, after taking the discount. The remainder of the original invoice amount is credited to *Purchase Discounts*, the contra-expense account. *Accounts Payable* is debited, or reduced, by the full invoice amount — the amount of the cheque plus the amount of the discount.

5. Close the **Transaction Journal report** to return to the cheque

6. Close the **Bill Payments (Cheque) form**

Entering Purchase Orders

Purchase orders are used to request items from vendors for later delivery. For internal control, some businesses require authorized purchase orders for all purchases that exceed a certain dollar amount. In the next transaction, we will enter a purchase order for Travel Totes. Refer to the following source document as we work through the steps to enter it:

SD6:   Purchase Order   **Dated October 2, 2014**

Create Purchase Order #30 to Travel Totes, $900.00 plus GST for 100 tote bags and passport wallets printed with the company logo. Purchase order totals $945.00. A deposit of 50 percent is requested to confirm the order. (We will enter the purchase order now and enter the deposit a little later in the chapter.)

Source Docs
Refer to the following source document and then follow the step-by-step instructions to enter it.

Purchase orders are entered on the Create purchase orders form. The workflow that contains the purchases orders icon can be found in the Vendors section of the Home page as shown here:

Notes
Notice the flow or sequence of icons in the Vendors section of the Home page.

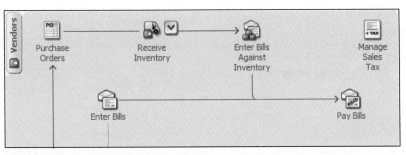

Figure 7-22

1. Click   the **Purchase Orders icon** in the Vendors section of the Home page, or **choose** the **Vendors menu** and **click Create Purchase Orders** to open the Create Purchase Orders form:

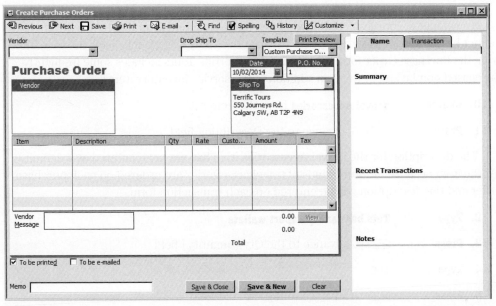

Figure 7-23

Notes
We will close the history tab before taking most transaction print screens in this textbook. You can close the history tab by clicking the Hide history arrow in the top left-hand corner of the history tab.

If you want to open the history tab after closing it, click the Show history arrow in the top right-hand corner of the transaction screen.

Entering a purchase order is similar to entering a bill, and the form is also similar. Just as on the Enter Bills form, the tab displayed to the right of the Purchase Orders form displays vendor and transaction information for the vendor when one is selected for the transaction. This tab can be closed by clicking on the Hide history arrow in the top left-hand corner of the tab.

Notes

Notice that when you press (tab) to accept the vendor on the purchase order, the information on the Vendor tab to the right of the purchase order is updated.

2. Click   the **drop-down arrow** in the **Vendor field**

3. Choose   **Travel Totes**

4. Press   (tab) to advance to the Date field

5. Enter   **10/02/14** as the order Date if necessary

6. Press   (tab) to advance to the P.O. No. field

Purchase orders are numbered just like most other company forms. Number 1 is entered as the default because we have not entered any purchase orders yet. Terrific Tours uses pre-numbered order forms, and the next number is 30.

7. Type   **30**

8. Press   (tab) to the Item field on the first detail line

9. Click   the **drop-down arrow** to view the list of items:

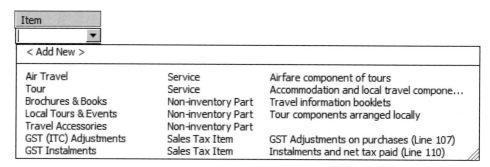

Figure 7-24

To complete a purchase order, you must choose an item from the item list. Expenses cannot be entered on purchase orders because the Chart of Accounts list is not accessible from the Purchase Order form. The item list for Terrific Tours includes some frequently purchased non-inventory items in addition to the service inventory items.

10. Choose   **Travel Accessories** from the Item list

11. Press   (tab) to advance to the Description field

The description for the Travel Accessories item has not been entered as a default for the item because different kinds of travel accessories are ordered on each purchase order and the description will be entered on each transaction form.

12. Type   **Tote bags and passport wallets**

13. Press   (tab) to advance to the Qty (quantity) field

14. Type   **100**

15. Press   (tab) to advance to the Amount field

16. Type   **900**

17. Press   (tab) to update the unit rate, taxes, and the total

18. Click   the **To be printed** option to remove the ✓. We do not want to include the purchase order in a print batch (the purchase order is selected for batch printing by default)

Notes

Normally, a business would print all estimates and purchase orders but you may not want to print all the documents. To print the purchase order immediately, click the Print button to open the Print One Purchase Order dialogue box. To print the purchase order later in a batch, choose the File menu, then choose Print Forms, and click Purchase Orders.

19. Your purchase order is now complete, as shown below:

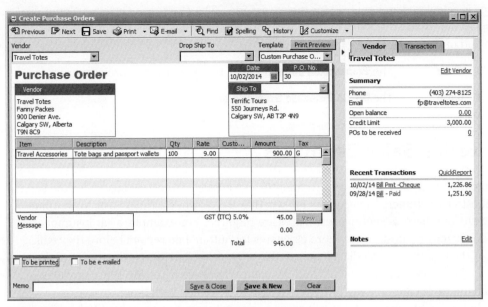

Figure 7-25

Check your work carefully and make corrections if necessary. You can make corrections to purchase orders just as you make corrections to regular vendor bills.

20. Click   **Save & New** to save the order and leave the form open to review it

Reviewing the Purchase Order

Although the purchase order does not create debit and credit entries, it does generate a transaction entry that we can review.

With a blank Purchase Order form displayed on the screen:

1. Click   the **Previous button** [Previous] to view the purchase order to Travel Totes that we just entered

2. Press   [ctrl] + **Y** to view the Transaction Journal report:

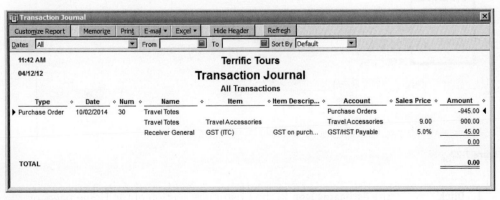

Figure 7-26

Notes
We have removed columns from this report to display it in the textbook.

This entry is the same as a regular vendor bill except that the *Purchase Orders* account is used instead of the *Accounts Payable* account. Notice too that a unit or sales price is calculated and entered for the accessories. The *Purchase Orders* account, like the *Estimates* and the *Sales Orders* accounts, is a non-postable account that appears at the end of the Chart of Accounts.

3. **Close**   the **Transaction Journal report** to return to the purchase order

4. **Close**   the **Create Purchase Orders form**

Entering Sales Estimates

Companies that provide services frequently give customers cost estimates for the service requested. Customers then can decide whether to get other estimates, or to continue with the purchase. Sometimes estimates are required. For example, a car insurance company may request one or more estimates for automobile repairs before they will cover the repair costs. Medical insurers also often ask for written estimates from doctors before procedures are completed and payment is approved. Terrific Tours provides estimates on request for any group interested in travelling with them.

In the next transaction, we will enter a sales estimate to UpperCrust School for Boys. Refer to the following source document as we work through the steps to enter it:

SD7: Estimate #21   **Dated October 2, 2014**

To UpperCrust School for Boys, $16,020.00 plus GST for airfare and $28,800.00 for tour component of complete tour package for 18 senior students and adults. The price of the nine-day tour includes airfare and accommodation and will cover major galleries and museums in European capital cities. Total cost of the tour including taxes is $45,621.00.

Estimates are entered on the Create Estimates form. The workflow that contains the Estimates icon can be found in the Customers section of the Home page as shown here:

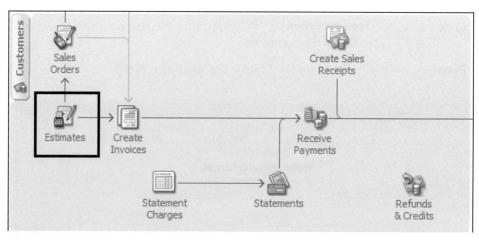

Figure 7-27

1. **Click**   the **Estimates icon** in the Customers section of the Home page, or **choose** the **Customers menu** and **click Create Estimates** to open the Create Estimates form:

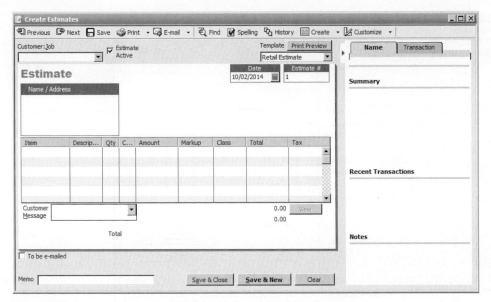

Figure 7-28

📄 **Notes**

Estimates can be entered only if Estimates have been turned on in QuickBooks preferences. To turn the preference on, choose Edit from the menu, select Preferences, click the Jobs & Estimates heading, click the Company Preferences tab, and select Yes in the *Do you Create Estimates* field.

The Create Estimates form is almost the same as the Create Invoices form, and entering estimates is similar to entering invoices. However, some columns on the Create Estimates form are not suitable for Terrific Tours, so we will first customize the form by removing the columns that do not suit our needs.

2. Click the **Customize icon** [📝 Customize ▾] to open the Basic Customization form

3. Click the **Additional Customization button** [Additional Customization...] on the bottom of the form

4. The following message will be displayed:

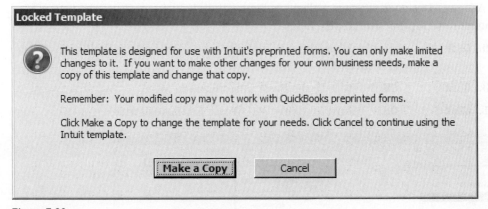

Figure 7-29

This message indicates that this template has been designed for use with Intuit's pre-printed forms and cannot be modified. In order to make modifications to this template, you must make a copy of the template and then modify the copy.

5. Click the **Make a Copy button** [Make a Copy]

6. Click the **Columns tab** to open the list of columns:

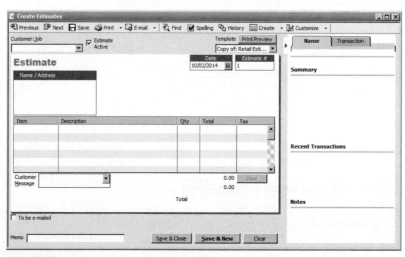

Figure 7-30

All items with a ✓ under the Screen column indicate that the field is displayed on the Create Estimates form. All items with a ✓ under the Print column indicate that the field is displayed on the printed estimate form. You can select which fields will be displayed on the form and which ones will be printed for the customer. You can also change the order of the items displayed in the columns and change the title for each column.

We will remove the Markup and the Cost columns on the Create Estimates form. UpperCrust school, however, requires individual cost estimates, so we will leave the Cost column on the printed copy. Accept any Layout Designer messages that you receive.

7. Click   the **check box for Markup** to remove the ✓ under the Screen column

8. Click   the **check box for Cost** to remove the ✓ under the Screen column

A Layout Designer message is displayed indicating that you must use the Layout Designer to reposition overlapping fields.

9. Click   the **check box** in the Do not display this message in the future option and **click OK**

10. Click   **OK** to return to the Basic Customization form

11. Click   **OK** to return to the revised Create Estimates form:

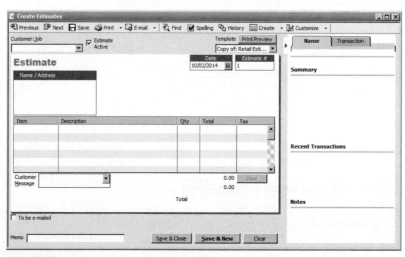

Figure 7-31

Just as on the Create Invoices form, the tab displayed to the right of the estimates form displays customer and transaction information for the customer when one is selected for the transaction. This tab can be closed by clicking on the Hide history arrow in the top left-hand corner of the tab.

Notes
Notice that when you press (tab) to accept the customer on the sales estimate, the information on the Customer tab to the right of the sales estimate is updated.

12.	**Choose**	**UpperCrust School for Boys** in the **Customer:Job field**
13.	**Enter**	**10/02/14** in the **Date field** if this is not the date displayed on your screen
14.	**Choose**	**Air Travel** as the first item on the estimate
15.	**Press**	(tab) to advance to the Qty (quantity) field

We will enter the total cost of the tours for all 18 travellers.

16.	**Type**	**18**
17.	**Press**	(tab) to advance to the Total field
18.	**Type**	**16020**
19.	**Press**	(tab) and the taxes are added to the estimate total
20.	**Press**	(tab) again to advance to the second line on the estimate
21.	**Choose**	**Tour** as the second item on the estimate
22.	**Press**	(tab) twice to advance to the Qty (quantity) field
23.	**Type**	**18**
24.	**Press**	(tab) to advance to the Total field
25.	**Type**	**28800**
26.	**Press**	(tab) to update the estimate total. Taxes are not charged for this item
27.	**Choose**	**We'll take care of you.** as the message in the **Customer Message field**

Estimates are prepared on pre-numbered forms, and the program updates these numbers automatically. The default Estimate number is 1 because Terrific Tours has not entered estimates yet.

28.	**Double click**	**1** in the **Estimate # field** beside the Date field
29.	**Type**	**21**
30.		The estimate is now complete as shown here:

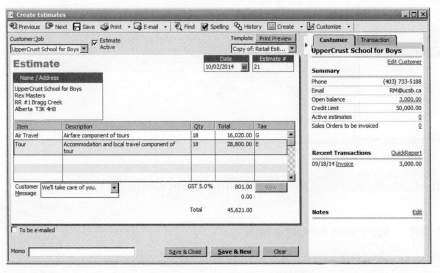

Figure 7-32

31. Review   the **estimate** and **make** any **corrections** before saving it

---

CORRECTING CUSTOMER ESTIMATES

Correcting an estimate is just like correcting a sales invoice. See page 275 if you need any further assistance.

Click the field that contains the error. You can press ⸤tab⸥ to move forward from one field to the next. Highlight the incorrect information and type the correct information in the field. Press ⸤tab⸥ if necessary to update the information.

If you choose a different item, you must re-enter the quantity and total amount. Press ⸤tab⸥ to update the totals.

You can also start again by clicking the Clear button.

CORRECTING CUSTOMER ESTIMATES AFTER RECORDING

After saving the estimate, you can review it and make corrections. Open the Create Estimates form. Click the Previous button until you see the estimate you need, or use the Find button to locate the estimate. Edit the estimate as described above and save the revised form. Click Yes when prompted to save the changes.

---

32. Click   **Save & Close** to record the estimate and close the Create Estimates form

Reviewing the Estimate

Although QuickBooks tracks estimates, it does not create a journal entry for them because no financial transactions have occurred. You can see which customers have estimates on the Customers & Jobs list in the Customer Centre. From the list you can view the report for the estimate.

1. Click   the **Customers icon** on the Icon bar

When you click on a customer, all transactions for that customer are displayed based on the date and filters selected.

2. Highlight   **UpperCrust School for Boys** in the Customers & Jobs list:

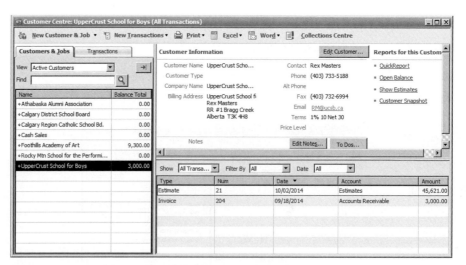

Figure 7-33

Notice the Estimate that we just entered is displayed in the transaction section of the screen.

3. Right-click   **UpperCrust School for Boys**

4. Select   **Show Estimates** to display the Estimates by Job report for the customer as shown:

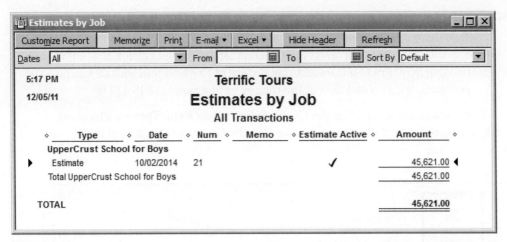

Figure 7-34

The report lists all estimates for the customer, with the estimate number and total amount. *Estimates* is a non-postable account that appears in the Chart of Accounts.

5. Close   the **Estimates by Job report**

6. Click   the **Transactions tab** and **click Estimates**:

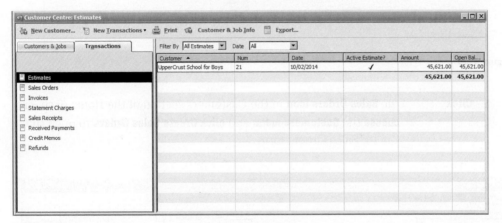

Figure 7-35

This tab displays all transactions for the selected transaction type for all customers based on the filters and dates selected. The Estimate that we entered for UpperCrust School for Boys is also displayed on this screen.

Double clicking the estimate displayed on the Customers & Jobs tab or the Transactions tab will open the original estimate where you can edit it or use it to create an invoice.

7. Click   ☒ to exit the Customer Centre

Entering Sales Orders

Sales orders differ from estimates in that they originate with the customer. Frequently, after a company provides an estimate, the customer will place an order for the items or services in the estimate. Estimates precede the decision to buy and often influence the decision to buy. Sales orders come after the customer has decided to proceed with a purchase. Terrific Tours prepares sales orders when customers place a firm order.

In the next transaction, we will enter a sales order to Calgary District School Board. Refer to the following source document as we work through the steps to enter it:

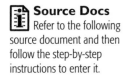

Source Docs
Refer to the following source document and then follow the step-by-step instructions to enter it.

SD8: Sales Order #6   **Dated October 3, 2014**

To Calgary District School Board, $16,280.00 plus GST for the airfare and $28,380.00 for the tour to create the complete tour package for 20 students and two teachers. Price of the eight-day history of England tour includes airfare and accommodation. Total cost of the tour including taxes is $45,474.00.

Sales orders are entered on the Create Sales Orders form. The workflow that contains the Sales Orders icon can be found in the Customers section of the Home page, as shown here:

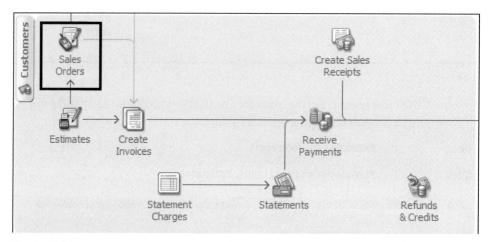

Figure 7-36

1. **Click**   the **Sales Orders icon** in the Customers section of the Home page, or **choose** the **Customers menu** and **click Create Sales Orders** to open the Create Sales Orders form:

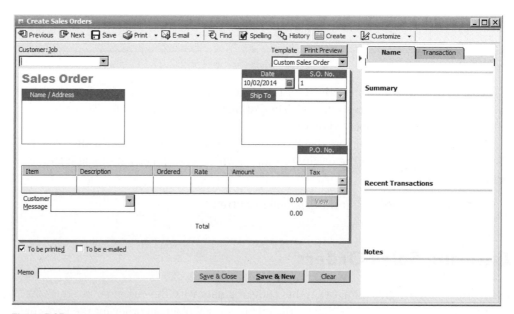

Figure 7-37

The Create Sales Order form is similar to the Create Estimates and Create Invoices form, and entering sales orders is similar to entering estimates or invoices. The Ship To fields are added because items on sales orders are frequently shipped to customers. The purchase order number (P.O. No.) is the number on the purchase order received from the customer that links to this sales order. Again, some of the columns on the form are not suitable for Terrific Tours, so we will begin by customizing the form. Accept any Layout Designer messages that you receive.

Notes
The sales order for a business is the customer's purchase order. Similarly, a purchase order for a business becomes a sales order for the vendor who receives the order.

2. **Click**   the **Customize button** Customize ▾ to open the Basic Customization form

3. **Click**   the **Additional Customization button** Additional Customization... on the bottom of the form

4. **Click**   the **Columns tab** to open the list of columns:

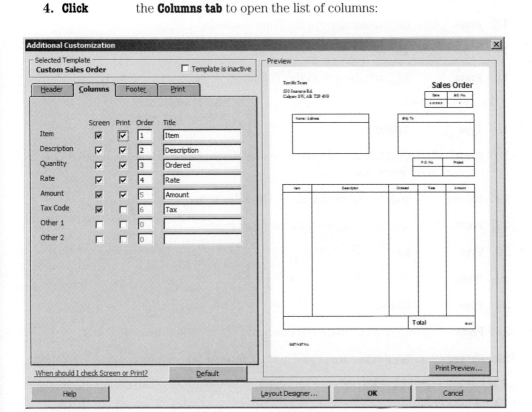

Figure 7-38

All items with a checkmark under the Screen column indicate that the field is displayed on the Create Sales Orders form. All items with a checkmark under the Print column indicate that the field is displayed on the printed sales order form. You can select which fields will be displayed on the form and which ones will be printed for the customer.

We will remove the Rate column, and change the Quantity column title to Number and the Amount column title to Total.

5. **Click**   **both check boxes** for Rate to remove the ✓

6. **Click**   **OK** if you receive the Layout Designer message

7. **Double click**   **Ordered** in the **Quantity Title field**

8. **Type**   **Number**

9. **Double click**   **Amount** in the **Amount Title field**

10.	**Type**	**Total**
11.	**Click**	**OK** to return to the Basic Customization screen
12.	**Click**	**OK** to return to the revised form
13.	**Choose**	**Calgary District School Board** as the Customer:Job for this sales order

Notice that the tab displayed to the right of the Sales Order form displays the customer summary information as soon as the customer is selected for the transaction. This information can be closed by clicking on the Hide history arrow in the top left-hand corner of the tab.

14.	**Enter**	**10/03/14** as the date
15.	**Choose**	**Air Travel** as the first item on the sales order
16.	**Press**	(tab) to advance to the Number field
17.	**Type**	**22**
18.	**Press**	(tab) to advance to the Total field

We will enter the total cost of the tour for all 22 travellers.

19.	**Type**	**16280**
20.	**Press**	(tab) to calculate the taxes for the item and advance to the second detail line
21.	**Choose**	**Tour** as the next item on the sales order
22.	**Press**	(tab) to advance to the Number field
23.	**Type**	**22**
24.	**Press**	(tab) to advance to the Total field
25.	**Type**	**28380**
26.	**Press**	(tab) to calculate the taxes and update the sales order total
27.	**Choose**	**We'll take care of you.** in the **Customer Message field**

The program updates the sales order numbers automatically. The default initial sales order number is 1.

28.	**Double click**	**1** in the **S.O. No. field** beside the date
29.	**Type**	**6**
30.	**Click**	the **To be printed option** to remove the ✓

We do not want to include the sales order in a batch of sales orders to be printed at a later time.

31. The sales order is now complete as shown here:

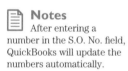
Notes
After entering a number in the S.O. No. field, QuickBooks will update the numbers automatically.

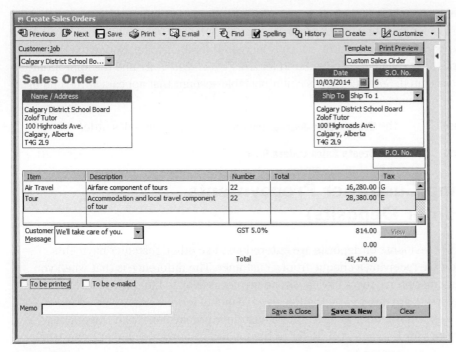

Figure 7-39

32. **Review**   the **Sales Order** and **make** any **corrections** before saving it

> **CORRECTING CUSTOMER SALES ORDERS**
>
> Correcting a sales order is just like correcting an estimate. See page 360 if you need any further assistance.

33. **Click**   **Save & New** to record the sales order and leave the form open to review it

34. **Click**   **No** if you receive a warning that you have changed the tax code for the customer

Reviewing the Sales Order

Although the order does not create debit and credit entries, it does generate a transaction entry that we can review, just as we review any other transaction.

With a blank Sales Order form displayed on the screen:

1. **Click**   the **Previous button** [⬅ Previous] to view the sales order that we just entered for the Calgary District School Board

2. **Press**   *ctrl* **+ Y** to view the Transaction Journal report:

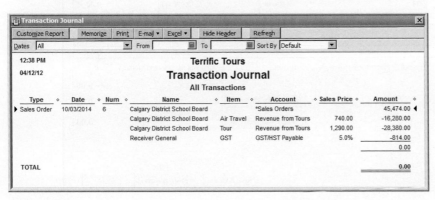

Figure 7-40

Notes
We have removed columns from the report to display it in the textbook.

The journal entry created for a sales order is the same as the journal entry created for an invoice except that the *Sales Orders* account, is increased for a sales order instead of the *Accounts Receivable* account, which is increased for an invoice. Notice too that unit or sales prices are calculated and entered for *Air Travel and Tour* and the appropriate taxes are calculated. *Sales Orders* is a non-postable account that appears at the end of the Chart of Accounts.

3. Close   the **Transaction Journal report** to return to the sales order

4. Close   the **Create Sales Orders form**

Entering Customer Prepayments (Customer Deposits)

Customer prepayments or deposits are entered just like other customer payments because you are receiving a cheque from a customer. The difference is that when you enter a customer prepayment or deposit, no invoice is selected for payment.

Prepayments are entered on the Receive Payments form.

In the next transaction, we will enter a customer prepayment from UpperCrust School for Boys for Estimate #21. Refer to the following source document as we work through the steps to enter it:

Source Docs
Refer to the following source document and then follow the step-by-step instructions to enter it.

SD9:   **Customer Payment**   **Dated October 3, 2014**

From UpperCrust School for Boys, Cheque #698 for $25,000.00 as prepayment to accept Estimate #21 and confirm the tour.

Notes
You can also access the Receive Payments form from the Customers menu.

1. Click   the **Receive Payment button** [Receive Payments] in the Customers section of the Home page to open the Receive Payments form

2. Choose   **UpperCrust School for Boys** as the customer for this prepayment:

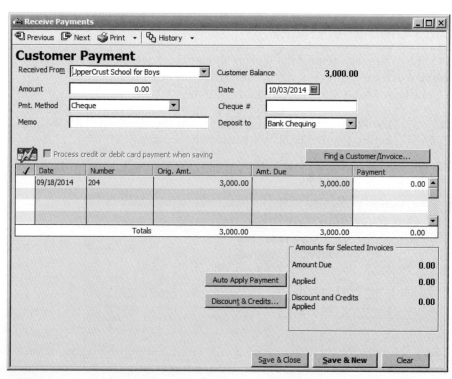

Figure 7-41

Notice there is one outstanding invoice for this customer. The customer prepayment we are about to enter will not be applied against this outstanding invoice.

3. **Press**   (tab) to advance to the Amount field

4. **Type**   **25000** and **press** (tab) to advance to the Date field

5. **Enter**   **10/03/14** as the date if necessary

6. **Click**   the **drop-down arrow** in the **Pmt. Method field** and **click Cheque**

7. **Press**   (tab) to the Cheque # field

8. **Type**   **698**

Notice that QuickBooks automatically applied the payment to the outstanding invoice. Any excess amount not needed to cover the invoice is entered as an overpayment. However, this payment is a prepayment for Estimate #21. The invoice for this estimate will be issued later. We must remove the ✓ beside Invoice #204. We should also add a memo to link the deposit with the estimate.

9. **Click**   the **Un-Apply Payment button** or **click** the ✓ beside Invoice #204 to remove the ✓

10. **Click**   the **Memo field**

11. **Type**   **Prepayment re: Estimate #21**

12. **Confirm**   that the **Bank Chequing account** is selected in the **Deposit to field** (select it if necessary)

13. The payment is now complete as shown:

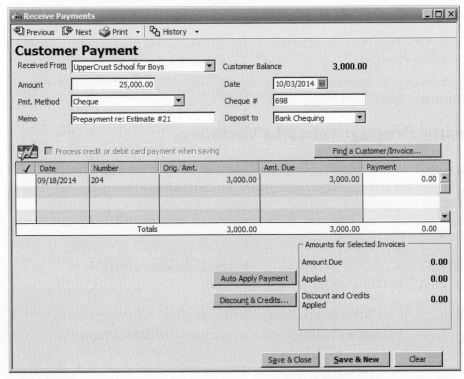

Figure 7-42

Because the payment was not applied to the outstanding invoice, the entire cheque amount is an overpayment. The transaction creates a credit balance in the customer's account.

| 14. **Check** | your **work** and **make** any necessary **corrections** |

15. **Click** Save & New to record the payment and leave the form open for the next receipt. The following message will be displayed:

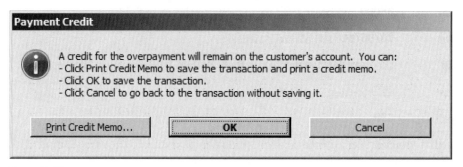

Figure 7-43

You now have the choice of printing a credit memo for the customer overpayment or saving the transaction as an overpayment. Because payments are usually applied to invoices, QuickBooks issues this warning so you can correct the transaction if necessary. In this case, the transaction is correct.

After you record the prepayment and until you apply the credit to an invoice, the overpayment will appear as a credit when entering payments for this customer.

16. **Click** OK to proceed with recording the payment and return to the Receive Payments form

📑 **Source Docs for Practice**
Continue to develop your skills by entering the following source document.

Source Document

Now that you have learned some of the new concepts introduced in this chapter, continue to develop your skills by entering the following source document in QuickBooks. Use the information in this chapter as a guide if necessary.

📝 **Notes**
Because there are no outstanding invoices for Calgary District School Board, the total cheque amount is entered immediately as an overpayment.

SD10: Customer Payment　　　　　　　　　　**Dated October 3, 2014**

From Calgary District School Board, Cheque #3902 for $22,000.00 as prepayment to confirm Sales Order #6.

Entering Prepayments to Vendors

Entering prepayments to vendors is just like making a cash purchase, i.e., writing a cheque, but without selecting an item or expense account for the transaction.

In the next transaction, we will enter a prepayment to our vendor Travel Totes as prepayment for Purchase Order #30. Refer to the following source document as we work through the steps to enter it:

📑 **Source Docs**
Refer to the following source document and then follow the step-by-step instructions to enter it.

SD11: Pay Bill　　　　　　　　　　**Dated October 4, 2014**

Cheque #482 to Travel Totes, $500.00 as prepayment to confirm Purchase Order #30.

1. **Open** the **Write Cheques form** by using one of the following methods:

   a) **Choose Banking** from the menu and **click Write Cheques**; or

   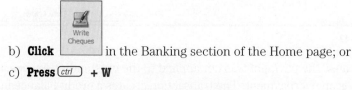

   b) **Click** [ ] in the Banking section of the Home page; or

   c) **Press** ⌈ctrl⌉ **+ W**

2. **Choose** **Travel Totes** in the **Pay to the Order of field**

3. The following message will be displayed:

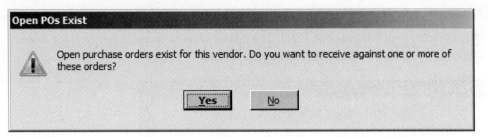

Open POs Exist

⚠ Open purchase orders exist for this vendor. Do you want to receive against one or more of these orders?

[Yes]   [No]

Figure 7-44

> **📄 Notes**
> If you want to fill the purchase order, the rest of the cheque will be completed automatically based on the purchase order information when you choose Yes on this screen.

QuickBooks recognizes that there is an outstanding purchase order for this vendor and offers you the chance to fill the purchase order immediately. However, we have not yet received the items on this purchase order so we are not filling it yet.

4.	**Click**	**No** to return to the Write Cheques form
5.	**Press**	⌨ (tab) to advance to the $ field
6.	**Type**	**500**
7.	**Click**	the **drop-down arrow** in the **Account field** on the Expenses tab
8.	**Scroll up**	the **account list** and choose Accounts Payable
9.	**Click**	the **To be printed option** to remove the ✓
10.	**Click**	the **Memo field**
11.	**Type**	**Deposit for PO #30**
12.	**Double click**	the **date** to select it
13.	**Type**	**10/04/14**
14.	**Type**	**481** in the **No. field**

> **📄 Notes**
> You will replace the *Uncategorized Expense* account on this bill.

15. Your completed cheque should look like this:

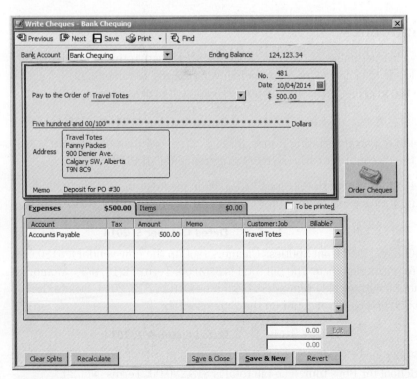

Figure 7-45

16. **Check**   your **work** carefully and **make corrections** if necessary

17. **Click**   **Save & Close**

Notes
The cheque sequence should be incorrect because we entered Cheque #481 as the first cheque number on the list and #480 as the second cheque number (on page 351).

The default cheque number is 481. If you do not change this number, you will see the following warning when you try to save the cheque:

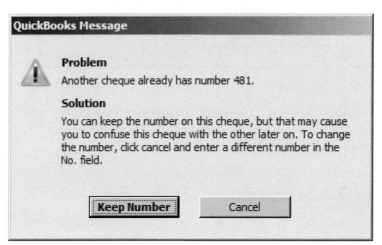

Figure 7-46

QuickBooks does not use duplicate cheque numbers without warning you first. We chose this setting as a preference for the company file.

If you see this message:

18. **Click**   **Cancel** to return to the cheque so you can change the number

19. **Double click**   **481** in the **No. field** to select it

20. **Type**   **482**

21. **Click**   **Save & Close**

Source Documents

Now that you have learned more of the new concepts introduced in this chapter, continue to develop your skills by entering the following source documents in QuickBooks. Use the information in this chapter as a guide if necessary.

SD12: Pay Bills   **Dated October 5, 2014**

     Cheque #483 to Parry's Printing House, for $933.25 in payment of account, including the discount for early payment. Reference Bill #PPH-1800.

     Cheque #484 to Heritage Hotels, for $13,770.90 in payment of account, including the discount for early payment. Reference Bill #HH-2099.

Notes
Spotless Cleaners
(Les Spotts)
420 Vacuum Cr.
Calgary, AB T3C 8H9
Tel: (403) 388-2886
E-mail: less@spotless.com
Terms: 2/10, n/30
Credit limit: $1,000.00
Business No.: 388 477 562

SD13: Bill   **Dated October 5, 2014**

     Bill #SC-1008 received from Spotless Cleaners (set up the new vendor), $180.00 plus GST for cleaning office. The bill total is $189.00. Terms: 2/10, n/30. Memorize the transaction with weekly reminders beginning October 12, 2014. Delete the *Uncategorized Expense* account on the Expenses tab.

SD14: Bill   **Dated October 5, 2014**

     Bill #AE-5992 received from Air Europe, $12,600.00 plus GST for airfare for UpperCrust School for Boys tour. The bill total is $13,230.00. Terms: Net 20.

SD15: Bill   **Dated October 6, 2014**

Bill #HH-3956 received from Heritage Hotels, $16,300.00 including all local taxes for double hotel accommodation for 18 adults for eight nights. No Canadian taxes apply because the hotels are not in Canada. (Tax Exempt is the tax code.) Terms: 1/10, n/30. Delete the *Uncategorized Expense* account from the Expenses tab.

Receiving Items from a Purchase Order

When you receive merchandise that has been entered on a purchase order, you must fill the order. Items may be shipped with the invoice, or the invoice may be mailed separately. In this example, the items arrive before the invoice so we will enter the received items first.

In the next transaction, we will receive items from Purchase Order #30 from Travel Totes. Refer to the following source document as we work through the steps to enter it:

SD16: Received Items: Shipment #45590   **Dated October 6, 2014**

Source Docs
Refer to the following source document and then follow the step-by-step instructions to enter it.

Fill Purchase Order #30 from Travel Totes. Received 100 tote bags and wallets for $900.00 plus $45.00 GST. Bill totals $945.00. All items were received and the bill will follow. Terms: 2/5, n/30.

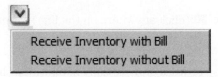

Received items are entered from the Receive Inventory icon found in the Vendors section of the Home page. When you click the Receive Inventory icon or click on the drop-down arrow beside it, you select whether you are receiving the inventory with a bill or receiving items without a bill:

Receive Inventory with Bill

Receive Inventory without Bill

QuickBooks has separate forms for these options. You cannot enter the bill before receiving the inventory; however, you can receive the inventory before entering the bill.

1. Click   the **Receive Inventory icon** and **click Receive Inventory without Bill**

The screen is clearly marked as an item receipt only. However, clicking the check box beside Bill Received in the upper right-hand corner of the form will change the form to an Enter Bills form. Make sure the Bill Received option is not selected for this source document.

2. Choose   **Travel Totes** in the **Vendor field**

3. The following message is displayed:

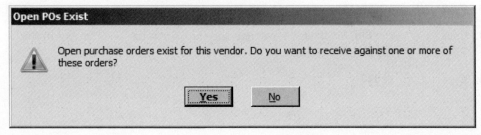

Open POs Exist

Open purchase orders exist for this vendor. Do you want to receive against one or more of these orders?

[Yes]   [No]

Figure 7-47

Because we have previously placed a purchase order with Travel Totes, QuickBooks displays this message allowing us to receive items against previously entered purchase orders. We will receive items against a previously entered purchase order for this source document.

4. Click   **Yes** to view the list of Open purchase orders placed with Travel Totes:

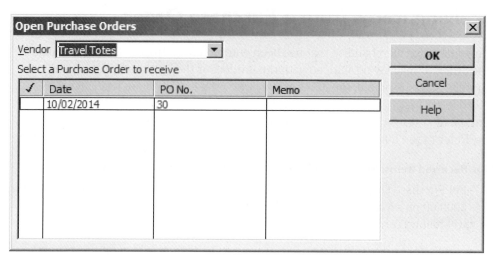

Figure 7-48

You can select purchase orders for other vendors on this screen by clicking the drop-down arrow in the Vendor field and selecting a different vendor.

The Open Purchase Orders screen displays only the single purchase order that we entered previously for Travel Totes.

5. Click   **PO No. 30** (click anywhere on the line) to select it

6. Click   **OK** to add the ordered items to the form

Sometimes, a purchase order is only partially filled with a single shipment. It is important to verify that the shipped items match the number and description on the original purchase order. The purchase order will remain open until all items are marked as received.

If the bill has been received with the items, you can mark the Bill Received check box at the top of the screen so you don't have to enter the bill separately.

If a partial shipment is received, you can change the quantity on the Item Receipt form and then record the receipt. When the rest of the items on the purchase order arrive, you can enter another Item Receipt to record them. The quantity on the purchase order will reflect only the outstanding items.

All items have been received in this shipment and the date should be correct.

7. Press   ⌨ *tab* to advance to the Date field

8. Type   **10/06/14**

9. Click   the **Ref. No. field**. We will add the shipping reference number in this field

10. Type   **45590**

11. The completed Create Item Receipts form should be displayed as shown:

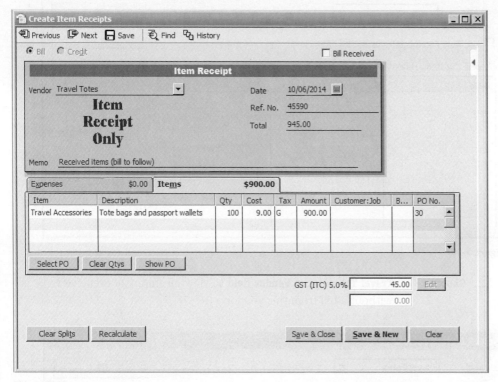

Figure 7-49

12. Check your **work** carefully and **make** any necessary **corrections**

13. Click **Save & Close**

Entering a Bill for Received Items

When a bill arrives for items that have already been received and entered on the Create Item Receipts form, it is entered by selecting the Enter Bills Against Inventory icon in the Vendors section of the Home page.

In the next transaction, we will receive a bill from Travel Totes for shipment #45590. Refer to the following source document as we work through the steps to enter it:

SD17: Bill   **Dated October 6, 2014**

Bill #TT-5987 received from Travel Totes for $900.00 plus $45.00 GST. The bill totals $945.00. Terms: 2/5, n/30.

Source Docs
Refer to the following source document and then follow the step-by-step instructions to enter it.

1. Click the **Enter Bills Against Inventory icon** to open the Select Item Receipt screen:

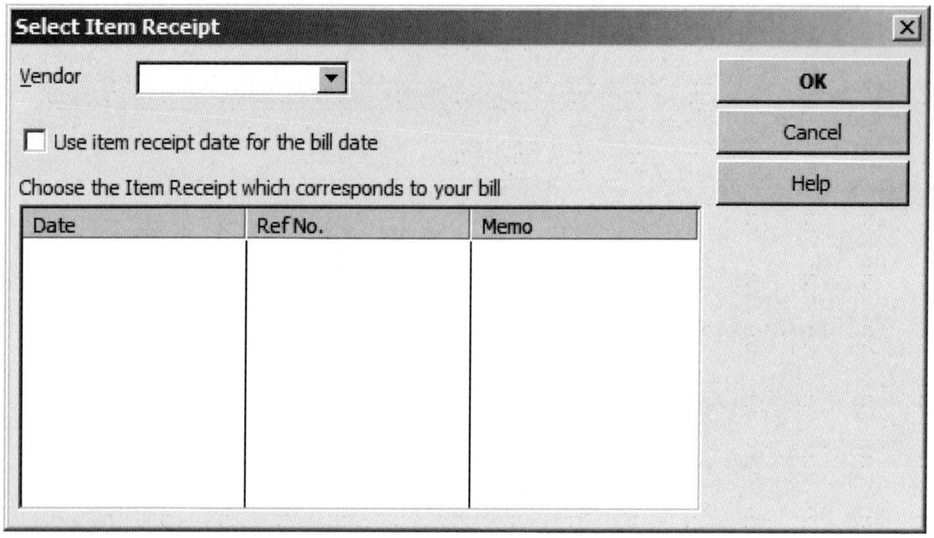

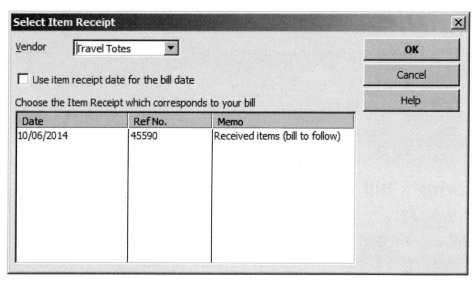

Figure 7-50

2. **Choose**   **Travel Totes** in the **Vendor field** to view all shipments received without a bill from this vendor:

Figure 7-51

The item receipt that we entered in the previous exercise is displayed on the Select Item Receipt screen.

3. **Click**   the **Item Receipt** dated 10/06/14, Ref. No. 45590

4. **Click**   **OK** to select the Item Receipt that corresponds to the bill

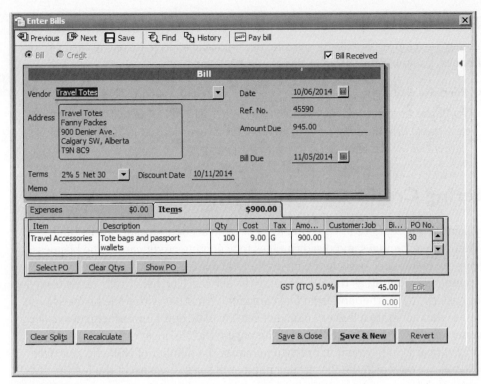

Figure 7-52

The items that were entered on the Item Receipt are automatically displayed on the Enter Bills form.

You can use the buttons on this form to select a purchase order, clear the quantities (edit the bill), or show the original purchase order.

Choosing Revert on the Enter Bills form will open the related Create Item Receipts form.

The form is almost complete. We should add the invoice number in the Ref. No. field and change the date if necessary. We will save the shipment reference number as well by adding it in the Memo field.

5. **Double click** the **date** and **type 10/06/14** if necessary

6. **Press** ⟨tab⟩ to advance to the Ref. No. field

7. **Type** **TT-5987**

8. **Click** the **Memo field** and **type Ref: Shipment #45590**

9. **Check** your **work** carefully and **make corrections** if necessary

10. **Click** **Save & Close** to view the warning:

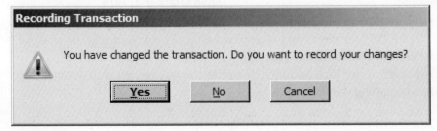

Figure 7-53

📄 **Notes**
The Recording Transaction message is displayed because we changed the reference number.

11. **Click** **Yes** to record the changes and save the bill

Source Documents

Continue to develop your skills by entering the following source document in QuickBooks. Use the information in this chapter as a guide if necessary.

Source Docs for Practice
Continue to develop your skills by entering the following source document.

SD18: Purchase Order   **Dated October 6, 2014**

Purchase Order #31 to Parry's Printing House, $1,400.00 plus GST for printing new travel brochures to give to clients. Purchase order totals $1,470.00. A 25 percent deposit is requested to confirm the order.

Entering Credit Card Sales

Most businesses accept credit cards in payment of an account, usually at the time of a sale. There are advantages and disadvantages to accepting credit cards. The business must pay the credit card provider company a merchant fee, usually a small percentage of each transaction amount, as the cost of using the service. The fee or rate varies from one type of business to another and from one company to another within the business type. Businesses that generate a higher volume of sales usually pay a lower fee than smaller businesses with lower sales volumes. Despite paying the fee, most companies prefer to accept credit cards in payment in order to minimize the number of NSF cheques. One NSF cheque can outweigh the fees from a number of sales. Because of the fees involved, companies that have a very small profit margin may decide not to accept credit cards, or they may accept credit cards only for sales above a specified dollar amount.

Credit card sales are entered like other cash sales because the customer pays in full at the time of the sale. The only difference is the selection of the type of payment — a credit card instead of cash or a cheque. Credit card receipts are usually deposited directly if the business has a direct terminal connection with the credit card bank account. If the business uses manual transaction charge plate slips, the receipts are held and deposited later. The card processing fee, a percentage of the sale amount, may be taken at the time of the deposit or entered as service charges on the monthly statement, depending on the arrangements with the credit card company.

QuickBooks allows a business to set up direct access to the related bank account for immediate processing of credit card receipts at the time of the transaction. In this text, the fees will be entered manually at the time of reconciling the account. This procedure is covered in Chapter 8, along with bank and account reconciliation. Terrific Tours deposits credit card receipts directly, so these receipts are not held for later deposit.

We have created a customer record named Cash Sales to enter the credit card sales in order to avoid creating a large number of individual invoices.

In the next transaction, we will enter a credit card sale from individual cash sales customers. Refer to the following source document as we work through the steps to enter it:

Source Docs
Refer to the following source document and then follow the step-by-step instructions to enter it.

SD19: Sales Receipt   **Dated October 7, 2014**

Enter Sales Receipt #24 to record cash sales from individual cash customers, $4,200.00 plus GST for flights and $3,100.00 for tours booked during the week. The total sales of $7,510.00 was paid by Visa. Visa credit card receipts are deposited to the *Bank Visa* account. Memorize the transaction with weekly reminders beginning October 14, 2014.

1. **Click**   the **Create Sales Receipts icon** in the Customers section of the Home page to open the Enter Sales Receipt form

2. **Choose**   **Cash Sales** as the customer for the transaction

We have selected Visa as the preferred or default payment method in the Cash Sales customer record so it is entered automatically when we choose Cash Sales. You can select a different payment method in the Enter Sales Receipts form if the customer pays differently for the purchase. The rest of the information is entered the same way as other sales receipts.

3.	**Enter**	**10/07/14** as the transaction date
4.	**Press**	⌨ tab to advance to the Sale No. field
5.	**Type**	**24**
6.	**Choose**	**Air Travel** as the first item for the sale
7.	**Enter**	**4200** as the amount for the item. The G tax code is correct
8.	**Choose**	**Tour** as the second item for the sale
9.	**Enter**	**3100** as the amount for the item. The E tax code is correct
10.	**Click**	the **drop-down arrow** in the **Deposit To field**
11.	**Click**	**OK** if you receive the price levels message
12.	**Choose**	**Bank Visa** from the account list
13.	**Click**	the **Memo field**
14.	**Type**	**Weekly sales summary**
15.	**Click**	the **To be printed** option to remove the ✓ (checkmark) in the box so the form will not be selected for batch printing

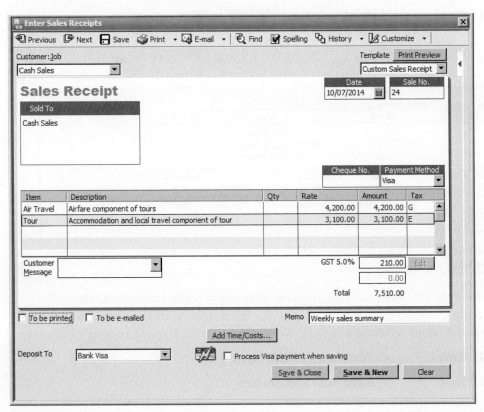

📄 **Notes**
Bank Chequing is set up as the default account for deposits so we need to change the account selection each time we enter a Visa sales receipt.

We do not need to choose a message because this is not a customer copy of the receipt. The form is complete as shown:

Figure 7-54

| 16. | **Check** | your **work** carefully and **make corrections** if needed, just as you would correct any other sales receipt |

If this sales receipt was for a customer, and the customer was in the store, you could print the receipt immediately by clicking the Print button on the form.

We can memorize the transaction so that we won't need to enter all the details each time the weekly sales summary is entered.

Memorizing the Transaction

With the sales receipt still displayed on the screen:

1. **Right-click** and **select Memorize Sales Receipt** to open the Memorize Transaction screen

2. **Select** **Add to my Reminders List** (this should be selected as the default)

3. **Choose** **Weekly** as the reminder frequency in the **How Often field**

4. **Enter** **10/14/14** as the next reminder date

5. **Click** **OK** to save the memorized transaction details

6. **Click** **Save & New** to leave the Enter Sales Receipt window open so we can view the journal entry that was just created from the cash sales transaction

7. **Click** **No** on the message asking if you want to update the Sales Tax Code in the customer record

Reviewing the Transaction

1. **Click** the **Previous button** [Previous] to display the cash sales receipt that we just entered

2. **Press** (ctrl) **+ Y** to display the Transaction Journal report:

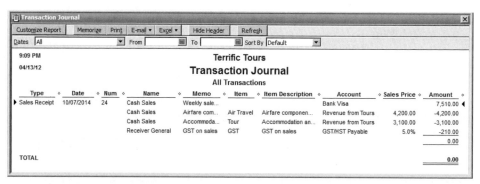

Figure 7-55

The only difference between this and other sales receipt transactions that we've entered previously is that the *Bank Visa* account is debited for the deposit instead of the *Bank Chequing* account because we selected it in the Deposit To field.

3. **Close** the **Transaction Journal report**

4. **Close** the **Enter Sales Receipts form**

Creating Invoices from Estimates

Once a customer accepts an estimate, you can use that estimate to create the invoice.

Estimates are converted to invoices from the Invoices icon. You can see that the Create Invoices icon follows the Estimates icon in the workflow in the Customers section of the Home page:

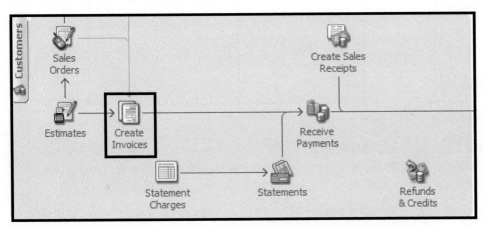

Figure 7-56

When you open the Create Invoices form and select a customer for whom an estimate has been entered, an Available Estimates screen will be displayed. From this screen, you select the estimate that you want to use for the invoice and the invoice will be created automatically from the information on the estimate.

You can also create invoices directly from the estimates form. Open the Create Estimates form, find the estimate that is being invoiced, and click the drop-down arrow beside the Create button on the form and select Invoice. A message will be displayed indicating that the entire estimate has been copied to the invoice. When you click OK, the Create Estimates form will close and the Create Invoices form will open containing the estimate details where you can add, modify, or delete information on the invoice.

In the next transaction, we will create an invoice from an estimate. Refer to the following source document as we work through the steps to enter it:

SD20: Invoice   **Dated October 9, 2014**

> Invoice #212 to UpperCrust School for Boys, based on Estimate #21, $16,020.00 plus 5% GST for the airfare and $28,800.00 for the tour component in the European capital cities tour. Total cost of the tour including taxes is $45,621.00. Terms: 1/10, n/30.

Source Docs
Refer to the following source document and then follow the step-by-step instructions to enter it.

1. **Click**   the **Create Invoices icon** or **press** (ctrl) **+ I** to open the Create Invoices form

2. **Choose**   **UpperCrust School for Boys** in the **Customer:Job field**. A list of estimates available for this customer is displayed on the Available Estimates screen:

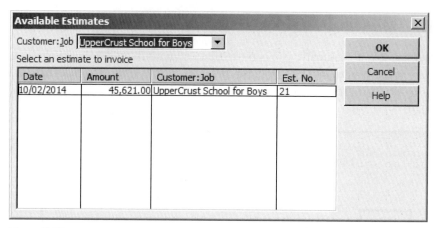

Figure 7-57

The single estimate we entered for this customer is listed. From this screen we can choose an estimate so that the invoice will be created immediately based on the estimate.

3. **Click**   **Estimate number 21** to select it. You can click anywhere on the line

4. **Click**   **OK** to continue and display the related invoice:

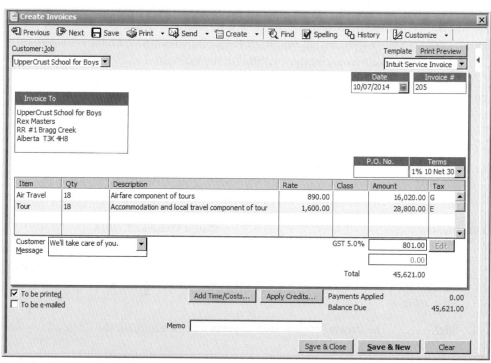

Figure 7-58

5. **Enter**   **10/09/14** as the transaction date

6. **Enter**   **212** in the **Invoice # field**

7. **Enter**   **Ref: Estimate #21** in the **Memo field** to complete the invoice

8. **Click**   **Save & Close** to close the Create Invoices form

9. The following message is displayed:

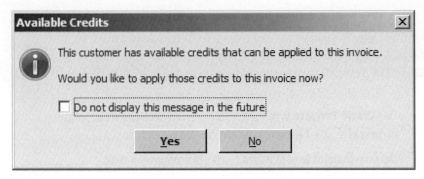

Figure 7-59

This message indicates that the customer has available credits and asks if you would like to apply them to this invoice. We will not apply the credit to this invoice.

10. **Click**   **No**

Source Documents

Source Docs for Practice
Continue to develop your skills by entering the following source documents.

Continue to develop your skills by entering the following source documents in QuickBooks. Use the information in this chapter as a guide if necessary:

SD21: Pay Bill   **Dated October 9, 2014**

Cheque #485 to Parry's Printing House, $375.00 as prepayment to confirm Purchase Order #31. Delete the *Uncategorized Expense* account on the Expenses tab of the bill.

SD22: Bill   **Dated October 9, 2014**

Bill #CT-59927 received from Capital Tours, $8,400.00 for special local tours arranged for Athabaska Alumni Association. Terms: 1/10, n/30.

SD23: Pay Bill   **Dated October 11, 2014**

Cheque #486 to Travel Totes, $427.00 in payment of account, including the credit and discount for early payment. Reference Bill #TT-5987.

SD24: Estimate   **Dated October 12, 2014**

Estimate #22 to Rocky Mountain School for the Performing Arts, $14,450.00 plus GST for the airfare and $20,060.00 for the tour component of the complete tour package for 15 students and two teachers. Price of the eight-day tour to Russia includes airfare and accommodation, and attendance at several ballet and other dance performances. Total cost of the tour including taxes is $35,232.50.

SD25: Bill   **Dated October 12, 2014**

Bill #SC-1128 received from Spotless Cleaners, $180.00 plus GST for cleaning office. The bill totals $189.00. Terms: 2/10, n/30. Use the memorized transaction.

SD26: Purchase Order   **Dated October 13, 2014**

Purchase Order #32 to Universal Theatre Bookings, $3,810.00 to arrange admissions for several tour groups. No Canadian taxes apply. Deposit requested.

Creating Invoices from Sales Orders

When a sales order is filled, you can create the invoice from the sales order directly.

In the next transaction, we will create an invoice from a sales order. Refer to the following source document as we work through the steps to enter it:

SD27: Invoice   **Dated October 14, 2014**

Invoice #213 to Calgary District School Board, based on Sales Order #6, $16,280.00 plus 5% GST for airfare and $28,380.00 for the tour in the England tour package. Total cost of the tour including taxes is $45,474.00. Terms: 1/10, n/30.

1. Click   the **Create Invoices icon** in the Customers section of the Home page or **press** ⌨ctrl + **I** to open the Create Invoices form

2. Choose   **Calgary District School Board** in the **Customer:Job field**

3. A list of available sales orders for this customer is displayed:

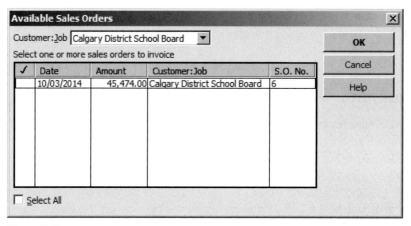

Figure 7-60

The single sales order that we entered previously is displayed on the Available Sales Orders screen. From this screen we can choose a sales order so that the invoice will be created immediately based on that sales order.

4. Click   **Sales Order 6** to select it. You can click anywhere on the line

5. Click   **OK**

6. The Create Invoice Based on Sales Order(s) screen is displayed:

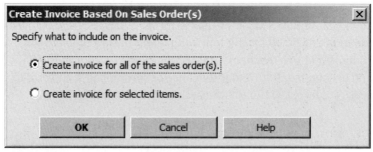

Figure 7-61

From this screen, you can select to create the invoice for all the sales order(s) selected or to create the invoice for selected items. If you select to create the invoice for all the sales orders (this is the option selected by default), all the items on the sales order will be transferred to the invoice. If you select to create the invoice for selected items, a screen will be displayed listing all the items on the sales order where you can enter the quantity that you will ship on the invoice.

7. Click   the **Create invoice for selected items option**

8. Click   **OK** to view the Specify Invoice Quantities for Items on Sales Order(s) screen:

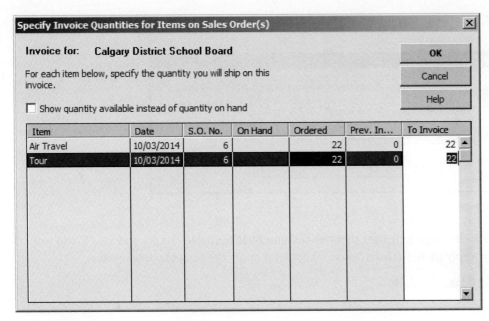

Figure 7-62

Use this screen to change the item quantities for the invoice. When you enter smaller quantities than the quantities ordered, the sales order will remain open until the complete sales order is filled. In this case, we want to fill the complete sales order so we don't need to change the quantities.

9. Click   **OK** to accept the quantities and view the invoice

10. Enter   **10/14/14** as the invoice date

The sales order number is entered automatically for reference in the S.O. No. field and the invoice number is updated with the next available invoice number, so the form is complete as shown:

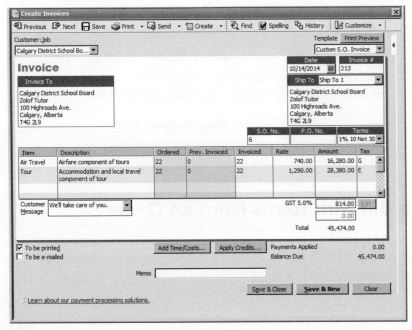

Figure 7-63

Notes
We have closed the Customer and Transaction information on the right-hand side of the screen before taking this print screen.

11. Click   **Save & Close**

12. The following message is displayed:

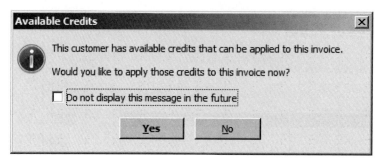

Figure 7-64

This message indicates that the customer has available credits and asks if you would like to apply them to this invoice. We will not apply the credit to this invoice.

13. Click　　**No**

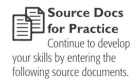

Source Docs for Practice
Continue to develop your skills by entering the following source documents.

Source Documents

Continue to develop your skills by entering the following source documents in QuickBooks. Use the information in this chapter as a guide if necessary:

SD28: Purchase Order　　　　　　　　　　　**Dated October 14, 2014**

> Purchase Order #33 to Universal Theatre Bookings, $3,600.00 for admission to ballet and dance performances for members of the tour. No Canadian taxes apply. A deposit is requested to confirm order.

SD29: Sales Receipt　　　　　　　　　　　**Dated October 14, 2014**

> Enter Sales Receipt #25 to record cash sales from individual cash customers, $3,600.00 plus GST for flights and $1,740.00 for tours booked during the week. Total sales of $5,520.00 were paid by Visa and deposited directly to the *Bank Visa* account. Use the memorized transaction and edit the amounts.

Notes
Remember to select *Bank Visa* as the account for the deposit.

SD30: Pay Bill　　　　　　　　　　　**Dated October 15, 2014**

> Cheque #487 to Spotless Cleaners, $370.80 in payment of account, including the discount for early payment. Reference Bills #SC-1008 and #SC-1128.

SD31: Purchase Order　　　　　　　　　　　**Dated October 15, 2014**

> Purchase Order #34 to Travel Totes, $100.00 plus GST for luggage tags printed with Terrific Tours logo. Purchase Order totals $105.00.

Receiving a Bill with Items from an Order

When ordered items arrive with the invoice, you can complete two steps at the same time — enter the items and the bill. The procedure is almost the same as filling the order without the bill, except that the starting point is different.

In the next transaction, we will receive the bill at the same time we receive the items. Refer to the following source document as we work through the steps to enter it:

SD32: Bill   **Dated October 16, 2014**

Received Bill #PPH-2675 to fill Purchase Order #31 from Parry's Printing House, $1,400.00 plus GST for printing travel brochures. The bill totals $1,470.00. Terms: 2/10, n/30. All items received with bill.

To receive the items from Purchase Order #31 from Parry's Printing House and enter the invoice at the same time, we will use the Receive Inventory with Bill option from the Receive Inventory icon in the Vendors section of the Home page.

Source Docs
Refer to the following source document and then follow the step-by-step instructions to enter it.

1. Click   the **Receive Inventory icon** in the Vendors section of the Home page

2. Click   the **Receive Inventory with Bill option** as shown:

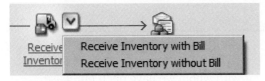

Receive Inventory with Bill
Receive Inventory without Bill

Figure 7-65

3. The Enter Bills form will be displayed as shown:

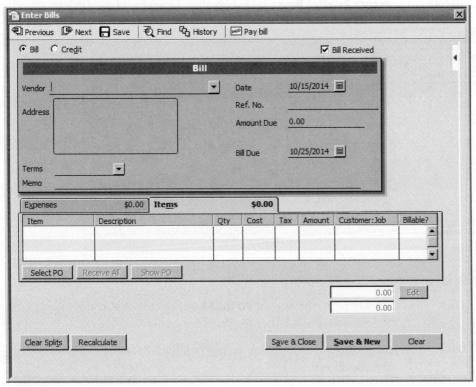

Figure 7-66

Notes
Notice the Bill Received option in the top right-hand corner of the screen is selected automatically. When you select the Receive Inventory with Bill option from the Receive Inventory icon, QuickBooks knows that the bill was received with the items. If you selected this option by mistake, you can uncheck the Bill Received option to display the Create Item Receipts form.

We can use the same approach we used earlier: select the vendor, receive the message that there are open purchase orders, and create the invoice from those purchase orders. However, in this example we will select the purchase orders directly before selecting the vendor.

4. Click   the **Select PO button** 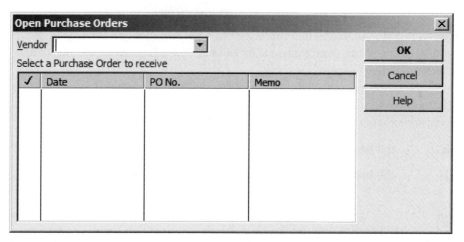 to access the Open Purchase Orders window:

Figure 7-67

From this screen, we can select any vendor with whom we have open purchase orders.

5. Click   the **drop-down arrow** in the **Vendor field**

6. Choose   **Parry's Printing House** to display their Open Purchase Orders:

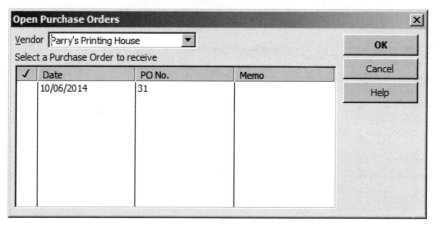

Figure 7-68

Only one purchase order is displayed in the list but we still need to select it.

7. Click   anywhere on the line for **PO No. 31** to select it. A ✓ is displayed in the column to the left of the purchase order

8. Click   **OK** to add the information on the purchase order to the Enter Bills form as shown:

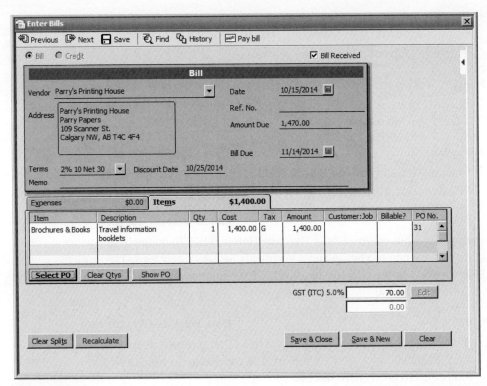

Figure 7-69

By default, the entire quantity ordered is entered on the Enter Bills form. If only a partial shipment is received, change the quantity on the bill. The purchase order will remain open until the order is completely filled.

To complete the entry, we need to change the date, add the invoice reference number, and add a Memo that links the invoice to the purchase order.

9.	**Enter**	**10/16/14** in the Date field
10.	**Click**	the **Ref. No. field**
11.	**Type**	**PPH-2675**
12.	**Click**	the **Memo field**
13.	**Type**	**Fill PO #31**
14.	**Check**	your **work** and **make** any necessary **corrections** as you would correct any other bill
15.	**Click**	**Save & Close** to save the bill and close the form

Source Documents

Continue to develop your skills by entering the following source documents in QuickBooks. Use the information in this chapter as a guide if necessary.

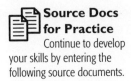

Source Docs for Practice
Continue to develop your skills by entering the following source documents.

SD33: Sales Order   **Dated October 16, 2014**

Sales Order #7 to Calgary Region Catholic School Board, $8,400.00 plus GST for the airfare and $16,200.00 for the tour component of the complete tour package for 10 students and two teachers. Price of the nine-day tour to Tokyo includes airfare and accommodation, and attendance at local cultural events. Total cost of the tour including taxes is $25,020.00.

SD34: Pay Bill   **Dated October 16, 2014**

Cheque #488 to Universal Theatre Bookings, $3,500.00 as prepayment to confirm Purchase Orders #32 and #33.

SD35: Bill   **Dated October 16, 2014**

Bill #AE-8120 received from Air Europe, $12,040.00 plus GST for airfare for 22 adults. The bill totals $12,642.00. Terms: net 20.

SD36: Pay Bill   **Dated October 16, 2014**

Cheque #489 to Heritage Hotels, $16,137.00 in payment of account, including discount for early payment. Reference Bill #HH-3956.

SD37: Bill   **Dated October 16, 2014**

Bill #HH-5993 received from Heritage Hotels, $12,770.00, including all local taxes for hotel accommodation and some meals for seven-day tour. The students will share hotel rooms and the two adults have single rooms. No Canadian taxes apply. Terms: 1/10, n/30.

📄 **Notes**
BroadCast
Communications
(Spinne Docktor)
65 Spammer Rd.
Calgary, AB T5C 7N9
E-mail: sd@bcc.com
Terms: net 20
Credit limit: $3,000.00
Business No.: 529 733 922

SD38: Bill   **Dated October 17, 2014**

Bill #BCC-5664 received from BroadCast Communications (set up the new vendor), $1,920.00 plus GST for advertising campaign for upcoming tours. The bill totals $2,016.00. Terms: net 20.

SD39: Pay Bill   **Dated October 19, 2014**

Cheque #490 to Capital Tours, $8,316.00 in payment of account, including the discount for early payment. Reference Bill #CT-59927.

SD40: Bill   **Dated October 19, 2014**

Bill #SC-1212 received from Spotless Cleaners, $180.00 plus GST for cleaning the office. The bill totals $189.00. Terms: 2/10, n/30. Use the memorized transaction.

SD41: Pay Bill   **Dated October 19, 2014**

Cheque #491 to Air Europe, $11,663.00 in payment of account. Reference Bill #AE-4897.

📄 **Notes**
Enter the bill from
Universal Theatre Bookings
as a Bill with Items Received.

SD42: Bill   **Dated October 20, 2014**

Bill #UTB-390 received from Universal Theatre Bookings, to fill Purchase Order #32, $3,810.00 to arrange admissions for several tour groups. No Canadian taxes apply. Terms: 2/5, n/30. Delete the *Accounts Payable* account from the Expenses tab on this bill. This account was entered on the previous bill from this vendor.

SD43: Estimate   **Dated October 20, 2014**

Estimate #23 to Foothills Academy of Art, $9,900.00 plus GST for the airfare and $18,000.00 for the tour component of the complete tour package for 22 students and two teachers. Price of the five-day tour to New Orleans includes airfare and accommodation, and attendance at Mardi Gras events. Total cost of the tour including taxes is $28,395.00.

SD44: Bill   **Dated October 20, 2014**

Bill #FC-14336 received from Foothills Communication, $120.00 plus GST for monthly telephone charges. The bill totals $126.00. Terms: Net 10. Delete the *Uncategorized Expense* account from the Expenses tab on this bill.

SD45: Sales Receipt   **Dated October 21, 2014**

Enter Sales Receipt #26 to record cash sales from individual cash customers, $4,500.00 plus GST for flights and $1,360.00 for tours booked during the week. Sales invoices total $6,085.00 paid by Visa and deposited to the *Bank Visa* account. Use the memorized transaction and edit the amounts.

Notes
Remember to select *Bank Visa* as the account for the deposit.

SD46: Bill   **Dated October 22, 2014**

Bill #CT-68342 received from Capital Tours, $4,980.00 for special local tours arranged for UpperCrust School for Boys. Terms: 1/10, n/30.

SD47: Pay Bill   **Dated October 23, 2014**

Cheque #492 to Universal Theatre Bookings, $1,933.80 in payment of account. Reference Bill #UTB-390. Apply $1,800.00 of the outstanding credits to this bill.

Notes
To change the credits applied, choose the bill from Universal Theatre Bookings and click the Set Credits button. Enter 1800 as the Amount to Use to replace the default amount.

SD48: Customer Payment   **Dated October 23, 2014**

From Calgary District School Board, Cheque #4988 for $23,027.40 in full payment of account, including the discount for early payment. Reference Invoice #213. Apply the unused credits and discount, and then apply the cheque in payment.

SD49: Purchase Order   **Dated October 24, 2014**

Purchase Order #35 to Capital Tours, $6,000.00 for bus and admissions to museums and galleries for all members of the tour group. No Canadian taxes apply. Twenty-five percent deposit was requested to confirm order.

SD50: Pay Bill   **Dated October 25, 2014**

Cheque #493 to Capital Tours, $1,500.00 as prepayment to confirm Purchase Order #35.

SD51: Pay Bill   **Dated October 25, 2014**

Cheque #494 to Air Europe for $13,230.00 in payment of account. Reference Bill #AE-5992.

SD52: Pay Bill   **Dated October 25, 2014**

Cheque #495 to Parry's Printing House for $1,067.00 in payment of account, including the credits and discount for early payment. Reference Bill #PPH-2675.

SD53: Customer Payment   **Dated October 25, 2014**

From Rocky Mountain School for the Performing Arts, Cheque #1993 for $16,500.00 as prepayment to accept Estimate #22 and confirm the tour.

SD54: Invoice   **Dated October 25, 2014**

Invoice #214 to Rocky Mountain School for the Performing Arts, based on Estimate #22, $14,450.00 plus GST for airfare and $20,060.00 for the Russia tour component. Total cost of the tour including taxes is $35,232.50. Terms: 1/10, n/30.

SD55: Bill   **Dated October 25, 2014**

Invoice #214 to Air Europe, $14,150.00 plus GST for the airfare for the tour to Russia. The bill totals $14,857.50. Terms: net 20.

SD56: Bill   **Dated October 25, 2014**

Bill #HH-6986 received from Heritage Hotels, $11,720.00 including all local taxes for hotel accommodation with breakfast for the tour group. No Canadian taxes apply. Terms: 1/10, n/30.

SD57: Pay Bill   **Dated October 25, 2014**

Cheque #496 to Heritage Hotels, $12,642.30 in payment of account, including the discount for early payment. Reference Bill #HH-5993.

SD58: Bill   **Dated October 26, 2014**

Bill #SC-1311 received from Spotless Cleaners, $180.00 plus GST for cleaning the office. The bill totals $189.00. Terms: 2/10, n/30. Use the memorized transaction.

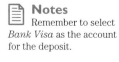 **Notes**
Remember to select *Bank Visa* as the account for the deposit.

SD59: Sales Receipt   **Dated October 28, 2014**

Enter Sales Receipt #27 to record cash sales from individual cash customers, $4,900.00 plus GST for flights and $1,210.00 for tours booked during the week. Total sales of $6,355.00 paid by Visa and deposited to the *Bank Visa* account. Use the memorized transaction and edit the amounts.

SD60: Customer Payment   **Dated October 29, 2014**

From Calgary Region Catholic School Board, Cheque #801 for $12,500.00 as prepayment to accept Sales Order #7 and confirm the tour.

SD61: Customer Payment   **Dated October 29, 2014**

From Foothills Academy of Art, Cheque #546 for $14,000.00 as prepayment to accept Estimate #23 and confirm the tour. Do not apply this payment to the outstanding invoice.

SD62: Sales Order   **Dated October 29, 2014**

Sales Order #8 to Athabaska Alumni Association, $14,700.00 plus GST for the airfare and $28,700.00 for the tour component of the complete tour package for 14 adults. Price of the eight-day tour to Athens includes airfare and accommodation, admission to museums and galleries, and local transportation. Total cost of the tour including taxes is $44,135.00.

 Notes
Matheson College
(SooLing Lee)
500 Classic Ave.
Calgary, AB T4T 8N9
Tel: (403) 588-1020
Fax: (403) 589-4198
E-mail: SL.Lee@
matheson.ca
Terms: 1/10, n/30
Credit Limit: $40,000.00
Payment: By cheque

SD63: Sales Order   **Dated October 29, 2014**

Sales Order #9 to Matheson College (set up the new customer), $8,690.00 plus GST for the airfare and $24,200.00 for the tour component of the complete tour package for 10 students and one adult. Price of the 12-day tour to France includes airfare and accommodation, admission to museums and galleries, and local transportation. Total cost of the tour including taxes is $33,324.50.

SD64: Bank Debit Memo #DM-31188   **Dated October 29, 2014**

> From West Hills Premium Bank: Preauthorized withdrawals were made from the *Bank Chequing* account. Create a new Expense account: *Bank Charges*.
>
> | | |
> |---|---:|
> | Mortgage ($390.00 interest and $120.00 principal) | $510.00 |
> | Bank loan ($210.00 interest and $560.00 principal) | 770.00 |
> | Long term loan ($140.00 interest and $130.00 principal) | 270.00 |
> | Bank service charges | 25.00 |

SD65: Pay Bill   **Dated October 30, 2014**

> Cheque #497 to Icharus Mannitoula, $10,190.50 to reimburse the owner for expenses incurred for business and charged to personal credit card. Receipts were provided for all expenses.
>
> | | |
> |---|---|
> | Vehicle expenses | $ 210.00 plus GST |
> | Research for upcoming tours | $3,800.00 plus GST |
> | Miscellaneous expenses incurred on tours | $5,980.00 |

Notes
Choose Other as the type of payee when you add the new record for Mannitoula. Accept the default tax codes.

SD66: Memo #3   **Dated October 31, 2014**

> From Owner: Apply unused credits for Rocky Mountain School for the Performing Arts to Invoice #214.

Making Estimates Inactive

When we use an estimate to create an invoice, the estimate is still available for future use. If the estimate will not be needed again, we should make it inactive so it does not continue to pop up each time we choose that customer.

In the next transaction, we will review active estimates and make two of them inactive. Refer to the following source document as we work through the steps to enter it:

SD67: Memo #4   **Dated October 31, 2014**

> From Owner: Make Estimates #21 and #22 inactive. They have been invoiced and should not appear on customer lists.

Before we make the estimates inactive, let's view the active customer estimates:

1. **Click**   the **Customers icon** on the Icon bar to open the Customer Centre

2. **Click**   the **Transactions tab**

Source Docs
Refer to the following source document and then follow the step-by-step instructions to enter it.

3. Click   the **Estimates heading** on the left-hand side of the screen to view all open estimates:

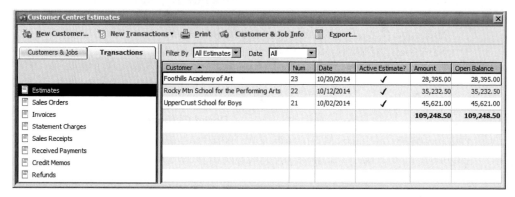

Figure 7-70

The estimates for Foothills Academy of Art, UpperCrust School for Boys, and Rocky Mountain School for the Performing Arts are still listed even though they have already been used to create invoices.

The ✓ (checkmark) under the Active Estimate? column indicates whether an estimate is active. As long as an estimate is active, it will be available for use when we create invoices for those customers with active estimates.

We want to make Estimates #21 and # 22 inactive. We can make them inactive from this screen.

4. Double click   Estimate #21 to open it on the screen as shown:

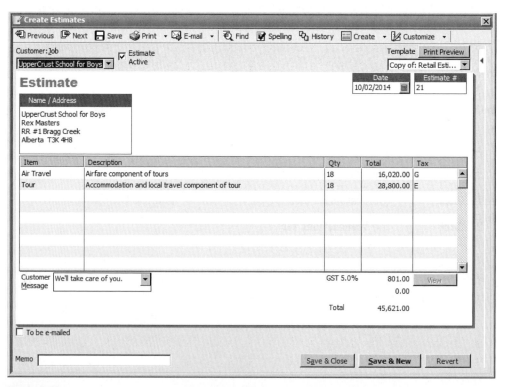

Figure 7-71

The estimate is marked as active. There is a ✓ in the Estimate Active check box ☑ Estimate Active in the upper left-hand corner of the form. Click the Estimate Active check box to remove the ✓ and make the Estimate inactive.

| 5. **Click** | **Save & Close** to save the changes to Estimate #21. You will be asked if you want to record your changes: |

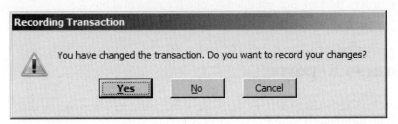

Figure 7-72

6. **Click**	**Yes** to save the changes
7. **Open**	**Estimate #22**
8. **Click**	the **Estimate Active** check box to remove the ✓
9. **Click**	**Save & Close**
10. **Click**	**Yes** to save the changes and close the Create Estimates form

You will be returned to the transaction tab in the Customer Centre with the Estimates heading selected.

The inactive estimates no longer have a ✓ under the Active Estimate? column, and they will not be available for selection when we enter invoices for the customers associated with them.

To use the estimates again for future invoices, change the status back to active by clicking the Estimate Active check box.

Source Documents

Continue to develop your skills by entering the following source documents in QuickBooks. Use the information in this chapter as a guide if necessary.

SD68: Memo #5   **Dated October 31, 2014**

From Owner: Complete adjusting entries for supplies and prepaid expenses used during month.

Travel brochures and magazines	$2,040.00
Travel accessories	1,990.00
Office and computer supplies	380.00
Prepaid insurance	6,000.00

SD69: Memo #6   **Dated October 31, 2014**

From Owner: Complete adjusting entries for depreciation.

Computer equipment	$160.00
Office furniture	50.00
Business vehicle	425.00
Office	450.00

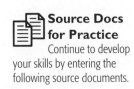

Source Docs for Practice
Continue to develop your skills by entering the following source documents.

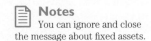

Notes
You can ignore and close the message about fixed assets.

Open Order Reports

Two reports show the orders that are not yet filled — one for sales and one for purchases.

Open Sales Orders Reports

The Open Sales Orders by Customer report shows a list of all customer sales orders that are not completed, filled, or invoiced as of the latest transaction date.

Notes
You can also choose the Reports menu, click Sales, and then click Open Sales Orders by Customer to access the report.

1. **Open**   the **Report Centre**

2. **Choose**   the **Sales heading** on the left-hand side of the screen

3. **Scroll down**   the **screen** to view the Open Sales Orders by Customer report

4. **Click**   the **Run icon** under the Open Sales Orders by Customer report to view the report on the screen:

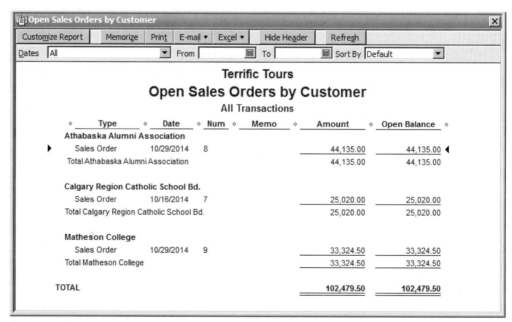

Figure 7-73

Sales orders are listed by customer as the default and include the date of the sales order, the number, a memo, and the amount. You can see that it would be helpful to have the date that the order is to be filled, or, for Terrific Tours, the date of the tour. This information can be added in the Memo field on the sales order so that it would be included on this report.

You can sort the report by any of the column headings on the report in ascending or descending order.

Double click a sales order on the report to drill down to the original sales order. Double click a customer total or the report total to view the Custom Transaction Detail report for that amount.

5. **Close**   the **report** when you have finished

Open Purchase Orders Reports

The Open Purchase Orders report shows a list of all purchase orders that are not completely filled as of the latest transaction date.

1. **Open**   the **Report Centre** if it is not already open from the previous exercise

2. **Choose**   the **Purchases heading** on the left-hand side of the screen

3. **Click**   the **Run icon** [Run] under the Open Purchase Orders report to view the report on the screen:

Notes
You can also choose the Reports menu, click Purchases, and then click Open Purchase Orders to access the report.

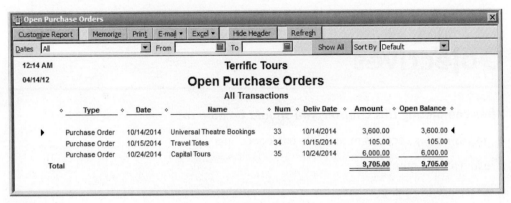

Figure 7-74

Purchase orders are listed by order date, but they can be sorted by any of the column headings on the report in ascending or descending order. By default, the order date is entered as the delivery date.

Double click a purchase order on the report to drill down to the original purchase order. Double click a vendor total or the report total to view the Custom Transaction Detail report for that amount.

4. **Close**   the **report** when you have finished

Sales Orders, Purchase Orders, and Estimates in Other Reports

Two other reports include sales orders, purchase orders, and estimates. The Transaction List by Customer report (found in the Customers & Receivables heading) includes a separate line for each estimate and sales order. The Transaction List by Vendor Report (found in the Vendors & Payables heading) includes a separate line for each purchase order.

Finishing Your Session

1. **Back up**   the **company data file**

2. **Close**   the **company file**

3. **Close**   the **QuickBooks program**

Objectives

After completing this chapter, you should be able to:

- **deposit** sales receipts in multiple bank accounts
- **use** account numbers
- **enter** credit card purchases
- **pay** credit card accounts
- **remit** sales taxes
- **assess** finance charges
- **transfer** funds between bank accounts
- **reconcile** bank and credit card accounts
- **make** end-of-period adjusting journal entries
- **close** the books at the end of a fiscal year
- **display** and **print** banking and tax reports
- **enter** closing date passwords
- **enter** transactions for a previous fiscal period

Company Information

Notes
Curly's Cabinets
46 Maple Cres.
Lindsay, ON K9V 2P3
Tel: (705) 618-7200
Fax: (705) 618-7281
E-mail: curly@
curlyscabinets.com
Web: www.curlyscabinets
.com
Business No.: 844 759 309

Company Profile

Curly's Cabinets in Lindsay, Ontario, is owned and operated by Charles (Curly) Cutter in the garage attached to his home, which he converted into a spacious shop. Curly builds custom-made wooden furniture: cabinets, bedroom suites, wall units, book shelves, plate rails, wainscotting, dressers, tables, and chairs. For new homes, he also designs built-in cabinets and shelves. He sells some smaller pieces at craft shows in Toronto. These shows provide an opportunity to promote his craftsmanship to new customers.

Woodworking was Curly's hobby in high school, and he completed a program in carpentry and small business at a community college. After a two-year apprenticeship, he started his own business. In his spare time, he volunteers at a seniors' residence, doing small repair jobs and supervising and teaching in the woodworking shop.

Curly accepts cash, cheques, and Visa for his furniture. For all his products, he uses fine wood that he buys when a customer places an order. Customer deposits pay for these purchases. All customers pay 13 percent HST on purchases.

For some business purchases, Curly uses a credit card. He also has accounts set up with local lumber supply stores. Other supplies that he purchases regularly include nails, screws, sandpaper of all grades, stains, finishing varnishes, and oils. His tools include small manual woodworking tools, as well as a variety of power saws, drills, and routers. Curly's Cabinets pays HST on all business-related purchases and on items that are not used directly to make furniture.

At the end of September 2014, Curly is ready to enter the last month of transactions for his fiscal year and close the books. He converted his accounting records to QuickBooks by using the following:

- Chart of Accounts
- Trial Balance
- Vendor Information
- Customer Information
- Item List
- Accounting Procedures

Chart of Accounts

Curly's Cabinets

ASSETS

Bank
- 1020 Bank Chequing
- 1040 Bank Savings
- 1060 Bank Visa
- 1100 Petty Cash

Accounts Receivable
- 1200 Accounts Receivable

Other Current Assets
- 1210 Undeposited Funds
- 1260 Prepaid Insurance
- 1280 Prepaid Taxes
- 1300 Office & Computer Supplies
- 1320 Carpentry Supplies
- 1340 Lumber Inventory

Fixed Assets
- 1500 Business Truck:
- 1520 Cost
- 1540 Depreciation

- 1560 Computer Equipment:
- 1580 Cost
- 1600 Depreciation
- 1620 Carpentry Tools & Equipment:
- 1640 Cost
- 1660 Depreciation
- 1680 Shop:
- 1700 Cost
- 1720 Depreciation

LIABILITIES

Accounts Payable
- 2100 Accounts Payable

Credit Card
- 2200 Visa Payable

Other Current Liabilities
- 2260 Bank Loan
- 2300 GST/HST Payable

Long Term Liabilities
- 2720 Long Term Loan
- 2740 Mortgage Payable

EQUITY
- 3220 Capital, Charles Cutter
- 3260 Drawings, Charles Cutter

INCOME
- 4100 Revenue from Sales
- 4140 Sales Credits and Allowances
- 4160 Sales Discounts
- 4180 Freight Revenue
- 4200 Revenue from Interest
- 4250 Sales Tax Compensation

EXPENSE

Cost of Goods Sold
- 5040 Lumber Used
- 5060 Carpentry Supplies Used

Expense
- 5120 Advertising and Promotion
- 5140 Purchase Discounts
- 5180 Office & Computer Supplies Used
- 5200 Depreciation Expense
- 5220 Maintenance Expenses
- 5240 Insurance Expense
- 5260 Interest Expense
- 5280 Property Tax Expense
- 5340 Hydro Expense
- 5360 Telephone Expense
- 5380 Truck Expenses

Curly's Cabinets

AS AT SEPTEMBER 30, 2014

	Debits	Credits		Debits	Credits
1020 Bank Chequing	$23,540.00		2720 Long Term Loan		$ 25,000.00
1040 Bank Savings	42,180.00		2740 Mortgage Payable		30,000.00
1060 Bank Visa	4,385.00		3220 Capital, Charles Cutter		117,203.00
1100 Petty Cash	460.00		3260 Drawings, Charles Cutter	$ 22,000.00	
1200 Accounts Receivable	4,730.00		4100 Revenue from Sales		81,410.00
1210 Undeposited Funds	14,280.00		4140 Sales Credits and Allowances	660.00	
1260 Prepaid Insurance	2,400.00		4160 Sales Discounts	720.00	
1280 Prepaid Taxes	1,260.00		4180 Freight Revenue		750.00
1300 Office & Computer Supplies	685.00		4200 Revenue from Interest		710.00
1320 Carpentry Supplies	620.00		4250 Sales Tax Compensation		320.00
1340 Lumber Inventory	1,290.00		5040 Lumber Used	3,890.00	
1520 Business Truck:Cost	18,000.00		5060 Carpentry Supplies Used	465.00	
1540 Business Truck:Depreciation		$ 5,400.00	5120 Advertising and Promotion	1,295.00	
1580 Computer Equipment:Cost	6,000.00		5140 Purchase Discounts		495.00
1600 Computer Equipment:Depreciation		1,800.00	5180 Office & Computer Supplies Used	370.00	
1640 Carpentry Tools & Equipment:Cost	30,000.00		5200 Depreciation Expense	17,200.00	
1660 Carpentry Tools & Equipment: Depreciation		6,000.00	5220 Maintenance Expenses	420.00	
1700 Shop:Cost	80,000.00		5240 Insurance Expense	6,600.00	
1720 Shop:Depreciation		4,000.00	5260 Interest Expense	4,520.00	
2100 Accounts Payable		6,420.00	5280 Property Tax Expense	880.00	
2200 Visa Payable		445.00	5340 Hydro Expense	1,320.00	
2260 Bank Loan		12,000.00	5360 Telephone Expense	1,650.00	
2300 GST/HST Payable		2,247.00	5380 Truck Expenses	2,380.00	
				$294,200.00	$294,200.00

Vendor Information

Curly's Cabinets

Vendor Name (Contact)	Address	Phone No. Fax No.	E-mail Business No.	Terms Credit Limit
Hydro Two (N. Power)	45 Turbine St. Lindsay, ON K9F 7J9	Tel: (705) 478-2300	npower@hydro2.ca	net 10 $500.00
Kawartha Building Supplies (Markus Sanderling or Nabir)	200 Sylvan Cres. Peterborough, ON K7G 4F5	Tel: (705) 556-0987 Alt: (705) 556-3821 Fax: (705) 556-7743	msanderling@kbs.com 369 466 509	1/10, n/30 $10,000.00
Kawartha Lumber (Freya Pine)	600 Cherry St. Lindsay, ON K9C 5S8	Tel: (705) 676-2929 Alt: (705) 877-3009 Fax: (705) 676-3388	sales@kawarthalumber.com 321 354 812	net 30 $10,000.00
Lindsay's Hardware & Paint (Lindsay Painter or Joel)	155 Millwood Rd. Lindsay, ON K9F 4B9	Tel: (705) 699-8191 Fax: (705) 698-3882	lindsays@shaw.com 125 843 782	1/10, n/30 $3,000.00
Northern Telecom (Bea Hurd)	5 Digital Circle Lindsay, ON K9F 4D6	Tel: (705) 510-2355		net 15 $500.00
Otto's Autos (Otto Ford)	45 Driver Route Lindsay, ON K9B 3G9	Tel: (705) 677-4821		due on receipt
Receiver General				quarterly remittance

Curly's Cabinets

Vendor Name	Date	Terms	Due Date	Invoice No./ Cheque No.	Amount
Kawartha Lumber	Sep. 12/14	net 30	Oct. 12/14	KL-2339	$4,280.00
Lindsay's Hardware & Paint	Sep. 24/14	1/10, n/30	Oct. 24/14	LHP-3011	$2,140.00
				Grand Total	$6,420.00

Customer Information

Curly's Cabinets

Customer Name (Contact)	Address	Phone No. Fax No.	E-mail Preferred Payment Method	Terms Credit Limit
Bayler, Lucas (Lucas Bayler)	11 Router Ave. Lindsay, ON K9P 4D6	Tel: (705) 678-1391	bayler_23@hotmail.com Cheque	1/5, n/30 $5,000.00
Cash Sales			Cash	due on receipt
Doze, Conn (Conn Doze)	88 Walnut Grove Lindsay, ON K9N 4F7	Tel: (705) 659-3773	condoze@istar.com Cheque	1/5, n/30 $5,000.00
Flatte, R. Rapindra or Jason Flatte	499 Oakwood Ave. Lindsay, ON K9G 4D2	Tel: (705) 688-7191 Fax: (705) 688-7191	rflatte@sympatico.ca Cheque	1/5, n/30 $5,000.00
Frame, Alva (Alva Frame)	22 Elm St. Lindsay, ON K9N 4N4	Tel: (705) 678-3298	Aframe@inet.com Cheque	1/5, n/30 $5,000.00
House, M. T. M. T. or Alan House	12 Pinecrest Dr., Lindsay, ON K9T 2B6	Tel: (705) 664-8921 Alt: (905) 884-8200	mthouse@hotmail.com Visa	due on receipt $5,000.00
Nailer, Benchley (Benchley Nailer)	25A Beech St. Lindsay, ON K9T 4D2	Tel: (705) 566-4577	bnailer@interlog.com Visa	due on receipt $5,000.00

Outstanding Customer Transactions

Curly's Cabinets

Customer Name	Date	Terms	Type	Number	Amount	Balance Owing
Cash Sales	Sep. 28/14	due on receipt	Cash sale	184	$230.00	$ 0.00
Lucas Bayler	Sep. 18/14	1/5, n/30	Invoice	448	$3,600.00	3,600.00
Conn Doze	Sep. 30/14		Deposit cheque	510	$3,000.00	−3,000.00
R. Flatte	Sep. 29/14		Deposit cheque	349	$2,000.00	
	Sep. 29/14	1/5, n/30	Invoice	456	$4,830.00	2,830.00
Alva Frame	Sep. 28/14		Deposit cheque	195	$1,000.00	
	Sep. 29/14	1/5, n/30	Invoice	457	$2,300.00	1,300.00
M. T. House	Sep. 30/14	due on receipt	Credit card sale	182	$4,600.00	0.00
Benchley Nailer	Sep. 30/14	due on receipt	Credit card sale	183	$3,450.00	0.00
			Grand Total			$4,730.00

Curly's Cabinets

Item	Description	Price	Tax Code	Account
NON-INVENTORY:				
Furniture	Custom-made wood furniture		H	4100 Revenue from Sales
Lumber	Raw lumber inventory		H	1320 Carpentry Supplies (raw materials)
Hardware	Carpentry and woodworking supplies		H	1340 Lumber Inventory (raw materials)
Advertising material			H	5120 Advertising and Promotion
OTHER CHARGES:				
Delivery	Delivery charge	$75.00	H	4180 Freight Revenue
Finance Charges	Finance Charges on Overdue Balance	18%	E	4200 Revenue from Interest
	(18% > 30 days, min. charge $25.00, grace period 5 days)			

Accounting Procedures

Taxes: HST

Notes
Refer to the Tax Appendix (found on the CD that accompanies this text) for details on sales taxes.

Curly's Cabinets pays 13 percent HST on all goods and services that it buys and charges 13 percent HST on all sales. It uses the regular method for remittance of the HST. The HST collected from customers is recorded as a liability in the *GST/HST Payable* account. The HST paid to vendors is recorded in the *GST/HST Payable* account as a decrease in liability to the Canada Revenue Agency. The sales tax is filed with the Receiver General for Canada by the last day of the month for the previous quarter, either including the balance owing or requesting a refund.

Account Terms

Account customers who pay by cheque receive a 1 percent discount if they settle their account within five days after completion of the work. The full balance is required within 30 days of the sale or completion of work. Finance charges at 18 percent per year are assessed when accounts are more than 30 days overdue, with a minimum charge of $25.00 and a five-day grace period. This revenue is credited to the *Revenue from Interest* account. No discount is available for credit card sales because of the fee attached to cards. Some vendors offer discounts for early payment.

Bank Deposits and Cheques

All cheques, credit card payments, and cash are held for weekly deposit. Cheques are manually prepared at the time of the transaction.

Estimates, Orders, and Deposits

Curly provides estimates on request. When customers decide to order furniture based on the estimate, they pay a 25 percent deposit so that Curly can buy the lumber needed to make the furniture. Some vendors also require deposits.

Delivery Charges

Customers can pay a flat rate of $75.00 plus HST to have their furniture delivered. Not all customers choose the delivery service. Delivery is set up as a sales item and is entered on invoices, estimates, and sales receipts just like any other item.

Supplies

At the end of each month, Curly counts the supplies left in his shop and completes adjusting entries for the cost of lumber and other supplies used. Depreciation is entered at the end of each month.

Instructions

1. Using the Chart of Accounts, the Trial Balance, and other information, you will record entries for source documents for October 2014 by using QuickBooks. You will find the source documents marked with an SD beside them and listed as you work through the chapter. The procedures for entering each new type of transaction introduced in this chapter are outlined in step-by-step instructions. Additional source documents will be provided, allowing you to have more practice entering transactions. If you have used this textbook in the past and would prefer to skip the step-by-step instructions and work only with a list of source documents, refer to the CD in the back of the textbook for the list of source documents for this chapter.

2. After you have finished making your entries, print the reports and graphs for October 2014 as indicated on the following printing form:

Notes
Instructions for banking reports begin on page 450.

REPORTS FOR OCTOBER 2014

Lists
- ☐ Account Listing
- ☐ Customer Phone List
- ☐ Customer Contact List
- ☐ Vendor Phone List
- ☐ Vendor Contact List
- ☐ Item Listing
- ☐ Item Price List

Company & Financial
- ☑ Balance Sheet Standard at Oct. 31 and Nov. 01
- ☑ Profit & Loss Standard from Oct. 01 to Oct. 31
- ☐ Expenses by Vendor
- ☐ Income by Customer

Accountant & Taxes
- ☑ Trial Balance at Oct. 31 and Nov. 01
- ☐ General Ledger
- ☑ Journal from Oct. 01 to Oct. 31
- ☐ Transaction List by Date
- ☐ Transaction Detail by Account

Other
- ☐ Custom Summary Report
- ☐ Custom Transaction Detail Report
- ☐ Transaction History
- ☐ Transaction Journal

Vendor
- ☑ A/P Aging Detail at Oct. 31
- ☐ Vendor Balance
- ☐ Unpaid Bills
- ☐ Transaction List by Vendor

Purchases
- ☐ Purchases by Vendor
- ☐ Purchases by Item
- ☐ Transaction List by Vendor
- ☐ Open Purchase Orders by Vendor

Customer
- ☑ A/R Aging Detail at Oct. 31
- ☐ Customer Balance
- ☐ Open Invoices
- ☐ Collections Report
- ☐ Transaction List by Customer

Sales
- ☐ Sales by Customer
- ☐ Sales by Item
- ☐ Open Sales Orders by Customer

Banking
- ☑ Deposit Detail from Oct. 01 to Oct. 31
- ☑ Cheque Detail from Oct. 01 to Oct. 31 for 1020
- ☑ Missing Cheques for 1020
- ☐ Reconcile Discrepancy
- ☑ Previous Reconciliation for accounts 1020 and 2200

GRAPHS
- ☐ Income and Expense
- ☐ Net Worth
- ☐ Accounts Payable
- ☐ Accounts Receivable
- ☐ Sales

3. Open the curly.qbw file for Curly's Cabinets.

Making Deposits to Multiple Bank Accounts

Curly's Cabinets holds all cheques, cash, and credit card receipts from customers for later deposit. Because two bank accounts are used, you must make a separate deposit for each bank account and choose the items to be deposited to each bank account. Other than choosing the bank account, the deposit procedure is the same as the one described in Chapter 6 for a single account (see page 301).

The first transaction that we will enter is a deposit to the *Bank Chequing* account. Refer to the following source document as we work through the steps to enter it:

SD1:   Memo #1   **Dated October 1, 2014**

Deposit the following undeposited cash and cheques to *Bank Chequing* account.

Cash from cash sale	$ 230.00
Cheque from Doze	3,000.00
Cheque from Flatte	2,000.00
Cheque from Frame	1,000.00
Total deposit	6,230.00
Owner withdraws cash for personal use	200.00
Net deposit	$6,030.00

You can enter deposits by selecting the Record Deposits icon in the Banking section of the Home page, or by choosing the Banking menu and then clicking Make Deposits.

1. **Click**   the **Record Deposits icon**   in the Banking section of the Home page to open the Payments to Deposit window:

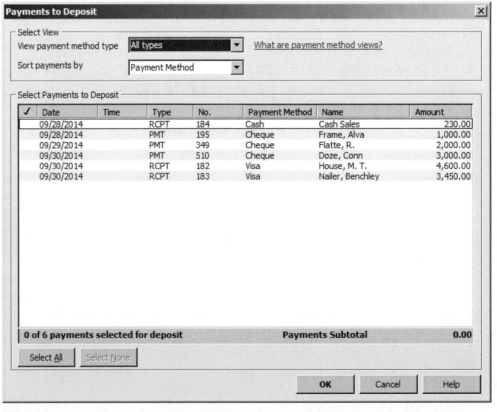

Figure 8-1

Six payments are ready to be deposited. This list makes it easy to select the payments that should be deposited to each account when the business has more than one bank account. Initially, all types of payments are on the same list, but we can choose specific types of payments for the list. We will deposit the cheques and cash to the *Bank Chequing* account and the Visa payments to the *Bank Visa* account. First, we will record the *Bank Chequing* account deposits, so we will select the cheques and cash. You can click the individual items for the deposit from this all-inclusive list or choose to show only one type of payment.

2. **Click**   the **drop-down arrow** in the **View payment method type field** to view the payment methods that can be selected:

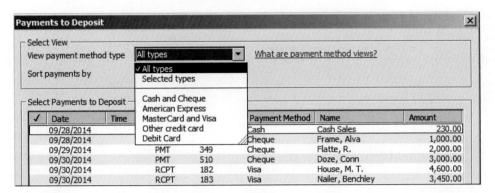

Figure 8-2

Notice that cash and cheques are combined on this list because most businesses use their primary chequing account for depositing both.

3. **Click**   **Cash and Cheque** as the payment method to refine the list:

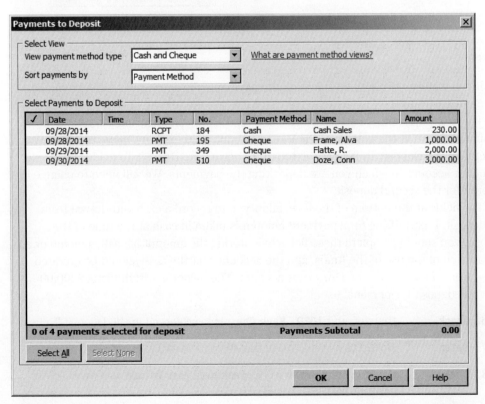

Figure 8-3

You can select the individual items to be deposited by clicking anywhere on a transaction line, or you can select all the items at once. We want to include all items.

4. Click the **Select All button**. Checkmarks appear beside each item in the ✓ column

5. Click **OK** to advance to the next screen:

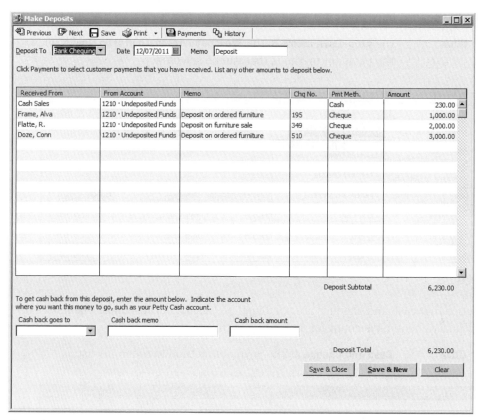

Figure 8-4

If you made an error when selecting the payments for deposit, click the Payments button to return to the Payments to Deposit form and modify the payments selected.

The four payments we selected are listed on the deposit form and the total deposit amount is shown at the bottom of the form. Account 1020 - *Bank Chequing* should be selected in the Deposit To field at the top of the form. The Deposit To field is used to select the account to which you are depositing the payments. We will need to change the account for the second deposit.

The fields at the bottom of the form allow you to record a cash withdrawal from the deposit. If part of the total payment amount is taken in cash at the time of the deposit, you should complete these fields by entering the amount of cash, a memo or an explanation of the use of the funds, and the account that the cash should be credited to — often a *Petty Cash* or a *Drawings* account. The owner is withdrawing $200.00 from this deposit for personal use.

6. Check that account **1020 - Bank Chequing** is selected in the Deposit To field

7. Enter **10/01/14** as the date of the deposit

8. Click the **drop-down arrow** in the **Cash back goes to field** to view the account list:

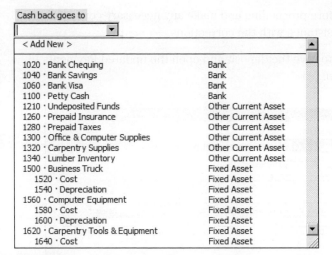

Figure 8-5

Accounts are listed in numerical order as follows for Curly's Cabinets:

- 1000 Assets
- 2000 Liabilities
- 3000 Equity
- 4000 Revenue
- 5000 Expense

> **Notes**
> You can use any numbering system that you want in QuickBooks. We will use the same numbering system for all company files in this text.

9. **Scroll down** the **list of accounts** and **select** account **3260 - Drawings, Charles Cutter**

10. **Press** ⟨tab⟩ to advance to the Cash back memo field

11. **Type** **Owner, personal use**

12. **Press** ⟨tab⟩ to advance to the Cash back amount field

13. **Type** **200**

14. **Press** ⟨tab⟩ to update the Deposit Total and complete the form as shown:

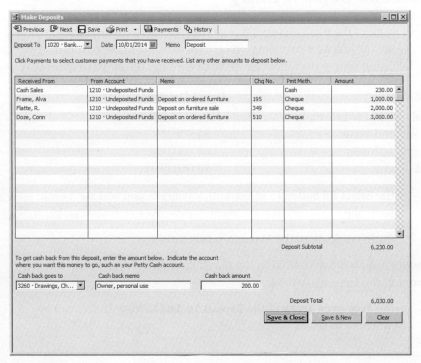

Figure 8-6

Check the form carefully before proceeding and make any necessary corrections. Refer to page 304 if you need assistance with the corrections.

15. Click   **Save & New** to save the deposit and open the updated Payments to Deposit form:

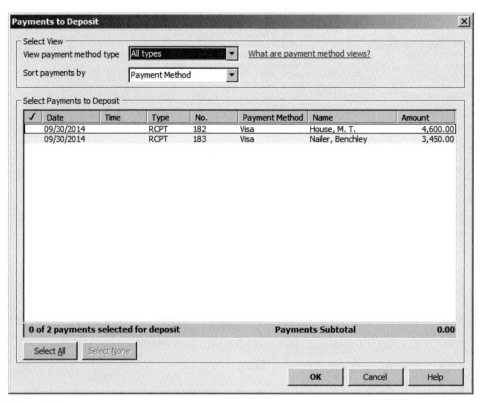

Figure 8-7

Making a Second Deposit Entry

The second deposit includes the two Visa receipts, and they should be deposited to the *Bank Visa* account. These are the only two payments left on the Payments to Deposit form.

Refer to the following source document as we work through the steps to enter it:

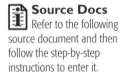

Source Docs
Refer to the following source document and then follow the step-by-step instructions to enter it.

SD2:   Memo #2   **Dated October 1, 2014**

Deposit all credit card receipts to the *Bank Visa* account.

Visa sale to House	$4,600.00
Visa sale to Nailer	3,450.00
Total deposit	$8,050.00

1. Click   the **Select All button** to select both payments and add a ✓ beside each one

2. Click   **OK** to continue to the Make Deposits form

These payments need to be deposited to the *Bank Visa* account so we need to change the account in the Deposit To field.

3. Click   the **drop-down arrow** in the **Deposit To field** to view the accounts available to select:

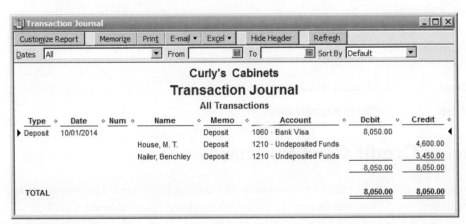

Figure 8-8

4. **Click**   **1060 - Bank Visa** to select the correct bank account

The date should be 10/01/14 from the previous deposit and no cash is taken back so the transaction is complete.

5. **Click**   **Save & New** to save the deposit and leave the Make Deposits form open

The Payments to Deposit form does not open after saving the deposit because all the payments have now been deposited. Before entering the next transaction, we will look at the journal entries that were created from the deposits.

Reviewing the Journal Entry

Let's take a look at the journal entries that we have created from the two deposits. We will review the journal entry for the Visa deposit first.

1. **Click**   the **Previous button**   Previous   to view the deposit made to the *Bank Visa* account

2. **Press**   ctrl + **Y** to view the Transaction Journal report:

Notes
We have removed columns from the report to display it in the textbook.

Curly's Cabinets
Transaction Journal
All Transactions

Type	Date	Num	Name	Memo	Account	Debit	Credit
▶ Deposit	10/01/2014			Deposit	1060 · Bank Visa	8,050.00	
			House, M. T.	Deposit	1210 · Undeposited Funds		4,600.00
			Nailer, Benchley	Deposit	1210 · Undeposited Funds		3,450.00
						8,050.00	8,050.00
TOTAL						8,050.00	8,050.00

Figure 8-9

The journal entry shows the transfer of funds. QuickBooks has debited the *Bank Visa* account for the full amount of the deposit. The entries for the *Undeposited Funds* account are credits to clear the amounts from the account — the original entries were debits to the *Undeposited Funds* account (the holding account). Customer names are also included so that the journal record for the deposit is complete.

3. **Close**   the **Transaction Journal report** to return to the Make Deposits form

Let's look at the Transaction Journal report for the first deposit that we made. When you use the Previous and Next buttons on the Make Deposits form, you scroll through transactions entered for the account in the Deposit To field. To view the first deposit that we made, we need to select the *Bank Chequing* account in the Deposit To field before using the Previous button.

4. **Click**   the **Save & New button**

5. **Click**   the **drop-down arrow** in the **Deposit To field**

6. **Choose**   **1020 - Bank Chequing**

7. **Click**   the **Previous button** 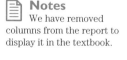 to view the deposit made to the *Bank Chequing* account

8. **Press**   *ctrl* + **Y** to view the Transaction Journal report:

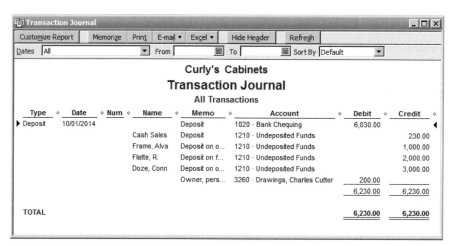

Figure 8-10

The journal entry shows that the bank account has been debited for the full amount of the deposit, and *Drawings, Charles Cutter* has been debited for the amount of cash held back. The entries for the *Undeposited Funds* account are credits to clear the amounts from the account — the original entries were debits to the *Undeposited Funds* account (the holding account). Customer names are also included so that the journal record for the deposit is complete.

9. **Close**   the **Transaction Journal report**

10. **Close**   the **Make Deposits form**

Entering Credit Card Purchases

Many businesses use credit cards for some of their business purchases. This has at least two advantages: short-term credit is available without setting up an account with a vendor because the payment for the purchase can be made later, and the buyer does not need to carry cash. When the credit card bill arrives, it provides a concise summary of business transactions. For most cards, if the balance is paid in full before the due date, no additional charges are incurred. Thus, the credit card provides an interest-free short-term loan. Additional credit cards may be obtained on the same account for employees as well, making it easy for employees to cover legitimate business expenses without the need for personal reimbursement.

Credit card purchases are like cash purchases (writing cheques) because the payment is made at the time of the purchase. Credit card transactions are entered on the Enter Credit Card Charges form.

The next transaction that we will enter is a credit card purchase. Refer to the following source document as we work through the steps to enter it:

Source Docs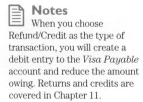
Refer to the following
source document and then
follow the step-by-step
instructions to enter it.

Credit Card payment of Bill #OA-4550 from Otto's Autos, $180.00 plus $23.40
HST for gasoline, oil change, and minor repairs. Invoice totalling $203.40 was
paid in full by Visa.

1. Click   the **Enter Credit Card Charges icon** [Enter Credit Card Charges] from the Banking
section of the Home page to open the Credit Card Charges form:

Notes
You can also open the
Credit Card Charges form by
choosing the Banking menu
and then Enter Credit Card
Charges.

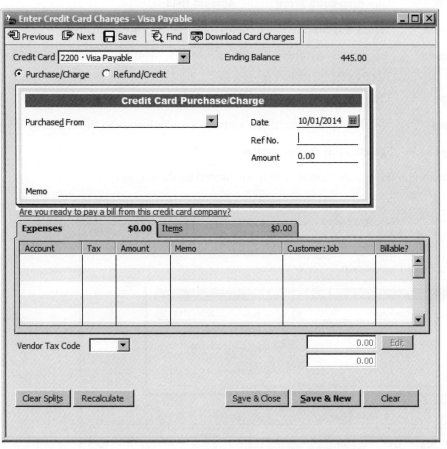

Figure 8-11

Curly's Cabinets uses only one credit card for business purchases, the Visa card, so this
account is the default for credit card charges. As you add different types of credit cards,
they will be available for selection from the Credit Card drop-down list, and you can add a
new card from this field as well. The balance owing on the card is shown for reference.

Each type of credit card should be linked to a different liability account. The account
for Visa, *Visa Payable*, is added to the title bar of the Enter Credit Card Charges form.

The form also includes the option to enter the transaction as a Purchase/Charge or
a Refund/Credit. When entering Visa purchases, select the Purchase/Charge option and
when entering returns or allowances, select the Refund/Credit option.

This form is the same as the Write Cheques form and the transactions are entered
the same way.

Notes
When you choose
Refund/Credit as the type of
transaction, you will create a
debit entry to the *Visa Payable*
account and reduce the amount
owing. Returns and credits are
covered in Chapter 11.

2. Click   the **drop-down arrow** in the **Purchased From field**

Notice that this list includes all customers and vendors, just as the Pay to the Order
of field does in the Write Cheques form. Both customers and vendors are listed because
payments can be made to both customers and vendors.

3. **Choose**   **Otto's Autos**

We will add the bill number as the reference number.

4. **Press**   (tab) to advance to the Date field

5. **Type**   **10/01/14** if necessary

6. **Press**   (tab) to the Ref No. field

7. **Type**   **OA-4550**

8. **Click**   the **drop-down arrow** in the **Account field**

9. **Choose**   **Truck Expenses** as the expense account for the transaction

10. **Press**   (tab) twice to advance to the Amount field and skip the tax code (H should be displayed)

11. **Type**   **180**

12. **Press**   (tab) to update the taxes and totals and advance to the Memo field

13. **Type**   **gasoline, oil change, repairs**

14. The completed transaction should be displayed as shown here:

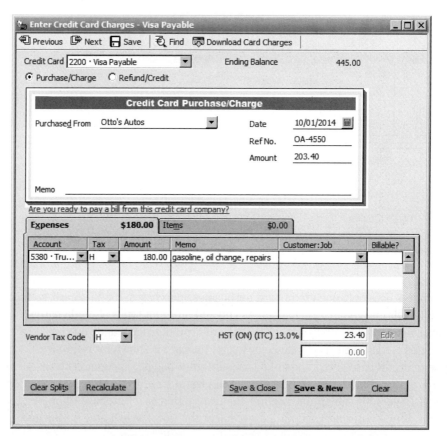

Figure 8-12

15. **Check**   your **work** and **make corrections** if necessary, just as you would correct any other cheque or cash purchase (see page 57).

16. **Click**   **Save & New**

17. **Click**   the **Previous button** [Previous] to display the transaction again

18. Press $\boxed{ctrl}$ **+ Y** to view the Transaction Journal report:

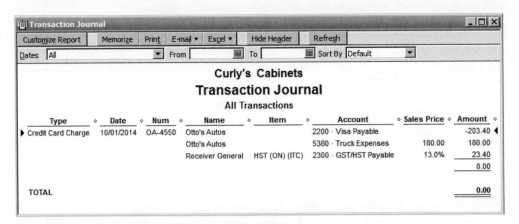

Figure 8-13

Notice that the *Visa Payable* account is credited for the total amount of the credit card charge instead of the bank account. The *Truck Expenses* account and the *GST/HST Payable* account are debited just as they would be in a cash purchase.

19. Close   the **Transaction Journal report**

20. Close   the **Enter Credit Card Charges form**

Paying a Credit Card Bill

When a credit card bill arrives, it should be reconciled and paid. The amounts on the credit card bill may be different from the amount in the account's register in QuickBooks. The credit card bill amount may be higher — it may include interest charges assessed on previous purchases that were not fully paid before the due date, interest charges for cash advances, or monthly or annual fees associated with the credit card. None of these amounts is known until the credit card bill is received. The bill amount can also be lower if purchases were made after the credit card's billing date. These purchases will appear on the next statement. Curly's Cabinets' bill from Visa includes an amount for interest charges for a cash advance from the previous month. The single purchase we entered was made after the credit card billing date, so it is not included in the current amount owing.

Credit card bills are paid as part of the reconciliation process. The Reconcile icon found in the Banking section of the Home page will open the Begin Reconciliation form.

The next transaction that we will enter is a credit card bill payment. Refer to the following source document as we work through the steps to enter it:

SD4: Reconcile and pay Credit Card   **Dated October 1, 2014**

To Kawartha Bank Visa (use Quick Add to add a new Other payee), $451.00 in payment of account, including $445.00 for purchases before September 30 and $6.00 interest charges for cash advances. The credit card bill is paid in full with Cheque #502. Create a new Expense account: *5130 Credit Card Fees*.

1. Click   the **Reconcile icon**   to open the Begin Reconciliation form shown here:

Notes
We have removed the Trans # and Class columns from the report to display it in the textbook.

Source Docs
Refer to the following source document and then follow the step-by-step instructions to enter it.

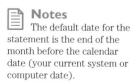
Notes
The default date for the statement is the end of the month before the calendar date (your current system or computer date).

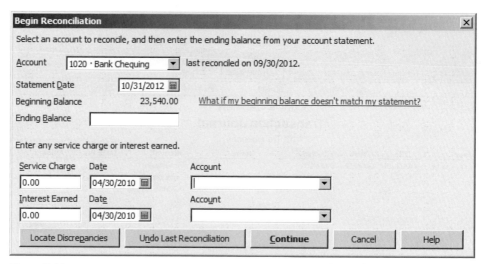

Figure 8-14

The first bank account is shown as the default account in the Account field. Fields for interest and expenses normally associated with a bank account are displayed on the form. The opening account balance is also shown in the beginning balance field. If you were reconciling a bank statement, it would list the information required for the fields on this form. Since we are reconciling a credit card statement, we need to select the *Visa Payable* account from the account list.

2. Click   the **drop-down arrow** in the **Account field**

3. Click   **2200 - Visa Payable**

4. The fields displayed on the form are modified for the credit card account as shown:

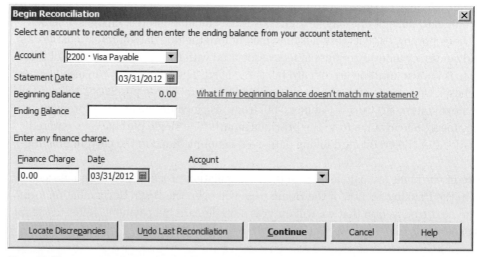

Figure 8-15

The reconciliation form for a credit card account includes only the expense portion. The information required to complete this form is available from the credit card statement.

5. Press   `tab` to advance to the Statement Date field

6. Type   **10/01/14**

7. Press   `tab` to advance to the Ending Balance field

Enter the amount currently due according to the credit card statement in the Ending Balance field.

8. **Type**	**451**	
9. **Press**	(tab) to advance to the Finance Charge field	

Notes
The ending balance is $451.00 — this is $445.00 for previous purchases (the opening balance for the account) plus $6.00 in additional charges.

Credit card fees may be associated with using the credit card and will vary from one credit card company or type of credit card to another. Some credit cards have no fees. Charges may also arise from interest owing on unpaid account balances or on cash advances. Curly's Cabinets has incurred an interest charge of $6.00 for a cash advance in the previous month. We need to create a new account for these charges. We can create it on the fly as we do in other forms.

10. **Type**	**6**	
11. **Press**	(tab) to advance to the Date field	
12. **Type**	**10/01/14**	
13. **Press**	(tab) to advance to Account field	
14. **Type**	**5130**	
15. **Press**	(tab) to view the Account Not Found message:	

Notes
You can add a new account on the fly from any account field in QuickBooks.

Account Not Found

? 5130 is not in the Account list.

[Set Up]   [Cancel]

Figure 8-16

16. **Click**   **Set Up** to add the new account:

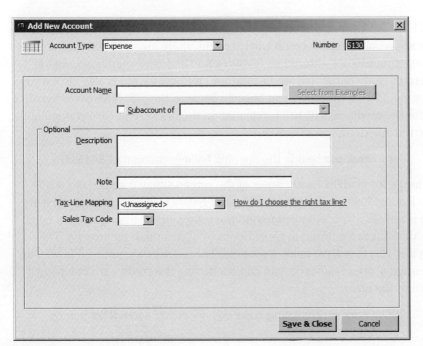

Figure 8-17

Notice that the Add New Account form has fields for an account number and account name. The account type is correctly selected as Expense so we do not need to change it. The account number is also entered because we entered it in the Account field on the Begin Reconciliation form. We need to add the account name.

17. Click	the **Account Name field**
18. Type	**Credit Card Fees**
19. Click	**Save & Close** to save the account and return to the Begin Reconciliation form with the account information entered
20. Click	**Continue** to advance to the Reconcile Credit Card screen:

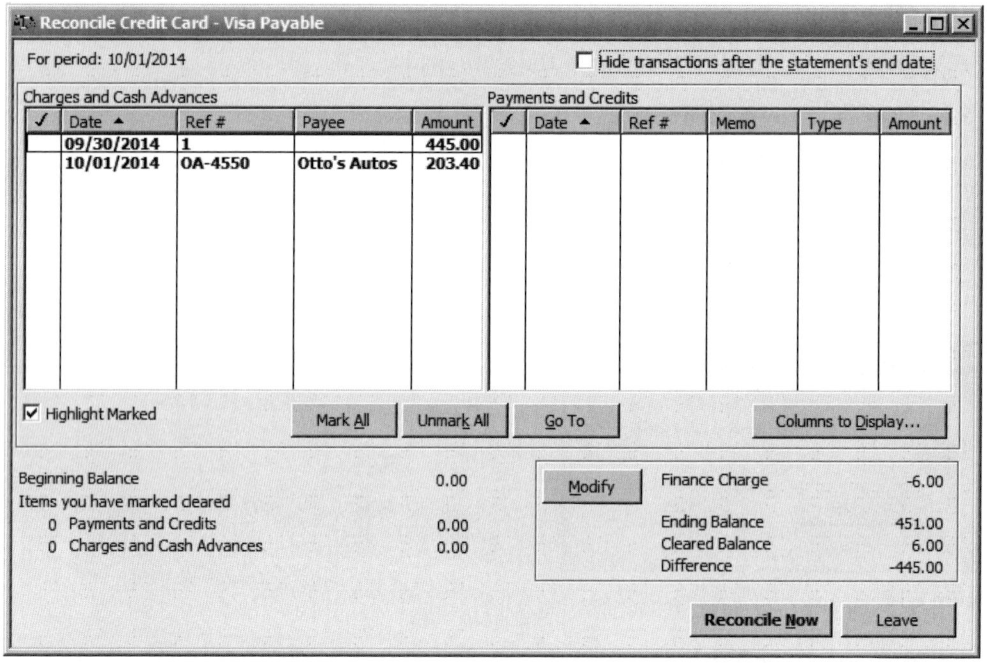

Reconcile Credit Card - Visa Payable
For period: 10/01/2014
Hide transactions after the statement's end date
Charges and Cash Advances
✓ Date Ref # Payee Amount
09/30/2014 1 445.00
10/01/2014 OA-4550 Otto's Autos 203.40
Payments and Credits
✓ Date Ref # Memo Type Amount
Highlight Marked
Mark All
Unmark All
Go To
Columns to Display...
Beginning Balance 0.00
Items you have marked cleared
0 Payments and Credits 0.00
0 Charges and Cash Advances 0.00
Modify
Finance Charge -6.00
Ending Balance 451.00
Cleared Balance 6.00
Difference -445.00
Reconcile Now
Leave

Figure 8-18

Notes
Click Leave in the Reconcile window to save the reconciliation before finishing. This allows you to return to the reconciliation where you left off and to make changes and corrections later.

Because we have not yet completed many transactions in QuickBooks, and this is the first time we are reconciling the credit card account, there are only two transactions on the list. The opening balance entered on 09/30/14 for the *Visa Payable* account is displayed. The credit card charge that we just entered for Otto's Auto is also displayed; however, it is not included in the statement balance because the purchase occurred after the billing date for the credit card. It will be cleared on the next credit card statement so you should leave it unchecked.

21. Click	the **check box** beside the opening balance amount of $445.00

The details in the lower right-hand corner of the screen summarize the reconciliation. We have an Ending Balance equal to the Cleared Balance and a Difference of zero. If the difference is not zero, you will need to find the source of the discrepancy. It could be that a transaction was not entered in QuickBooks or was entered incorrectly. The credit card company also may have made a mistake. These errors should be followed up by checking the original credit card receipts and contacting the credit card company if necessary to correct the error.

22. Check	your **work** carefully and **make** any necessary **corrections** before continuing

CORRECTING THE RECONCILIATION

To correct a date, an amount, or an account, click the Modify button beside the reconciliation summary information in the lower right-hand corner of the form to return to the Begin Reconciliation form. Press ⌐tab⌐ to move forward from one field to the next. Highlight the incorrect information and type the correct information. Press ⌐tab⌐ if necessary to update the information.

If you do not want to complete the reconciliation, click the Leave button at any time. Any information you entered in the reconciliation will be saved and you will be able to make changes later.

WARNING!
You cannot make changes to the reconciliation after you click the Reconcile Now button, so check your work carefully before completing this step. You may want to make a backup copy of the file before starting the reconciliation procedure. This way, you can restore the backup file if you have made a mistake, such as clearing a transaction in error.

It is important to note, that you can undo the last reconciliation if necessary by selecting the Undo Last Reconciliation button on the Begin Reconciliation form.

23. Click   **Reconcile Now** to view the Make Payment screen:

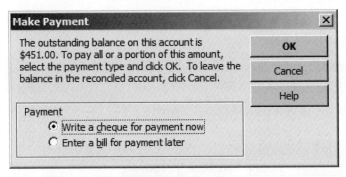

Figure 8-19

You can write a cheque immediately to pay the bill or to enter the payment due as a bill and pay it later. The choice you make will determine which screen you see next. We want to write a cheque for payment now so the default selection is correct.

24. Click   **OK**

25. If you see a message about online banking, **click OK** to continue

26. The Select Reconciliation Report screen is displayed:

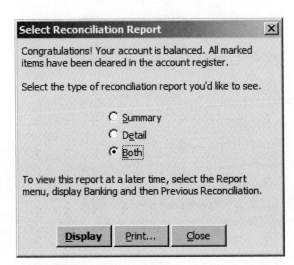

Figure 8-20

Now you should choose what kind of report you want and whether you want to display or print it. You can choose the summary or the detail report or both. Both is selected as the default. We will display the Detail Report.

27. Click   **Detail** to change the report selection

28. Click   the **Display button**

29. The following status message is displayed:

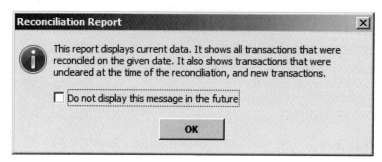

Reconciliation Report [X]

ⓘ This report displays current data. It shows all transactions that were reconciled on the given date. It also shows transactions that were uncleared at the time of the reconciliation, and new transactions.

☐ Do not display this message in the future

OK

Figure 8-21

This status message lets you know what information will be provided in the report.

30. Click   the **box** beside Do not display this message in the future option to bypass this message in the future

31. Click   **OK** to view the Reconciliation Detail report:

Reconciliation Detail   _ □ X

| Customize Report | Memorize | Print | E-mail ▾ | Excel ▾ | Hide Header | Refresh |

7:43 AM

12/08/11

Curly's Cabinets

Reconciliation Detail

2200 · Visa Payable, Period Ending 10/01/2014

Type	Date	Num	Name	Clr	Amount	Balance
Beginning Balance						0.00
Cleared Transactions						
Charges and Cash Advances - 2 items						
▶ General Journal	09/30/2014	1		✓	-445.00	-445.00 ◀
Credit Card Char...	10/01/2014			✓	-6.00	-451.00
Total Charges and Cash Advances					-451.00	-451.00
Total Cleared Transactions					-451.00	-451.00
Cleared Balance					451.00	451.00
Uncleared Transactions						
Charges and Cash Advances - 1 item						
Credit Card Char...	10/01/2014	OA-4...	Otto's Autos		-203.40	-203.40
Total Charges and Cash Advances					-203.40	-203.40
Total Uncleared Transactions					-203.40	-203.40
Register Balance as of 10/01/2014					654.40	654.40
Ending Balance					654.40	654.40

Figure 8-22

Notes
The Ending Balance amount for the Register is the balance before making the payment and includes the finance charge.

The report includes all cleared transactions — in this case, the finance charges, any uncleared transaction amounts, and the ending register balance as of 10/01/2014. Notice that the finance charges are included in the register balance. The credit card charge entered to pay Otto's Auto Bill #OA-4550 is shown as an uncleared transaction on the report. It will be cleared in the next reconciliation performed for the *Visa Payable* account.

The next step is to write the cheque to pay the bill.

32. Click   [X] to exit the Reconciliation Detail report

33. The Write Cheques form will be displayed:

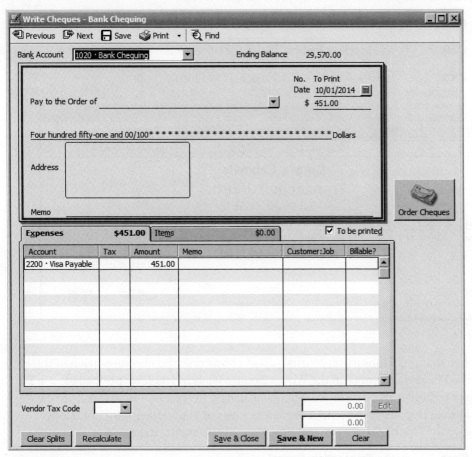

Figure 8-23

The cheque has been partially completed with the information that is already available — the date, amount, and account. You can change the date or amount. QuickBooks assumes that you are paying the full amount that is due. Because this is the first reconciliation, some details are still missing. The Visa bank is not yet on the list of payees so we need to add it. We also need to add the cheque number to start the correct cheque sequence number for cheques in this company data file.

34.	**Click**	the **Pay to the Order of field**
35.	**Type**	**Kawartha Bank Visa**
36.	**Press**	`tab`
37.	**Choose**	**Quick Add** to add the name to the payee list
38.	**Choose**	**Other** to indicate that this is not a vendor, a customer, or an employee
39.	**Click**	**OK** to return to the cheque
40.	**Click**	the **check box** beside To be printed to turn this option off
41.	**Click**	the **No. field**
42.	**Type**	**502**

If you are making a partial payment, edit the amount in the Amount field and click the Recalculate button to update the amount in the cheque portion of the form.

When you pay a partial amount, the ending balance on the next month's statement will include any unpaid amounts from previous statements.

43. Click   **Save & New** to record the payment

44. Click   the **Previous button** [⬛ Previous] to view the cheque again

45. Press   (ctrl) + **Y** to view the Transaction Journal report:

Notes
We have removed columns from the report to display it in the textbook.

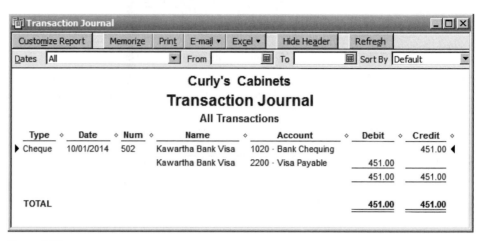

Figure 8-24

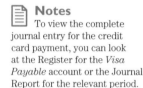
Notes
To view the complete journal entry for the credit card payment, you can look at the Register for the *Visa Payable* account or the Journal Report for the relevant period.

Notice that this Transaction Journal report shows only the cheque portion of the transaction because we were in the Write Cheques window when we pressed (ctrl) + **Y**. The finance charges were recorded when you clicked Reconcile Now and will appear in the Journal Report for the period they were entered and in the register and ledger reports for the *Credit Card Fees* and *Visa Payable* accounts, the relevant accounts.

46. Close   the **Transaction Journal** window

47. Close   the **Write Cheques** window

Source Documents

Now that you have learned some of the new concepts introduced in this chapter, enter the following source documents. You may need to refer to previous chapters for additional information:

October 3 – October 7, 2014

Notes
Group all receipts in the *Undeposited Funds* account and hold for weekly deposit.

SD5: Sales Receipt   **Dated October 3, 2014**

Sales Receipt #185 to M. T. House, $1,450.00 plus $188.50 HST for a pine table and a deacon's bench. Invoice totalling $1,638.50 was paid in full by Visa and held for deposit.

SD6: Bill   **Dated October 4, 2014**

Received Bill #NT-582 from Northern Telecom, $88.00 plus $11.44 HST for one month of telephone and Internet service. The bill totals $99.44. Terms: Net 15 days.

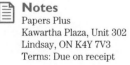
Notes
Papers Plus
Kawartha Plaza, Unit 302
Lindsay, ON K4Y 7V3
Terms: Due on receipt

SD7: Credit Card Charge   **Dated October 4, 2014**

Credit Card payment of Bill #P-7530 from Papers Plus (set up new vendor), $145.00 plus $18.85 HST for office and computer supplies. Invoice totalling $163.85 was paid in full by credit card.

SD8: Customer Payment   **Dated October 4, 2014**

From Alva Frame, Cheque #215 for $1,277.00 in payment of account, including the discount for early payment. Apply credits, discount, and payment to Invoice #457.

SD9: Customer Payment   **Dated October 4, 2014**

From R. Flatte, Cheque #364 for $2,781.70 in payment of account, including the discount for early payment. Apply credits, discount, and payment to Invoice #456.

SD10: Pay Bill   **Dated October 4, 2014**

Cheque #503 paid to Lindsay's Hardware & Paint, $2,118.60 in payment of account, including the discount for early payment. Reference Bill #LHP-3011.

Notes
Do not print cheques. You can automatically assign cheque numbers or enter them yourself.

SD11: Bill   **Dated October 5, 2014**

Bill #KL-4811 received from Kawartha Lumber, $945.00 plus $122.85 HST for cherry lumber to build a bookcase and dressers. The bill totals $1,067.85. Terms: Net 30. Delete the *Uncategorized Expense* account on the Expenses tab.

SD12: Invoice   **Dated October 6, 2014**

Invoice #461 sent to Conn Doze, $7,900.00 plus $1,027.00 HST for a maple dining room table, chairs, a buffet, and a hutch. Delivery charge is $75.00 plus HST. Invoice totals $9,011.75. Terms: 1/5, n/30. Allow customer to exceed credit limit.

Notes
Customer tax codes are not used. Customers are listed in alphabetic order by last name. Remember to reset the invoice number to start at 461.

SD13: Estimate   **Dated October 6, 2014**

Estimate #35 to M. T. House, $3,470.00 plus $451.10 HST for a custom-built walnut bedroom set, including night tables and a headboard. Estimate totals $3,921.10. A 25 percent deposit is required on acceptance of estimate.

SD14: Customer Prepayment   **Dated October 6, 2014**

From M. T. House, $1,000.00 as deposit on Sales Estimate #35, paid by credit card.

SD15: Credit Card Charge   **Dated October 6, 2014**

Bill #OA-6110 received from Otto's Autos, $50.00 plus $6.50 HST for gasoline for truck. The bill totalling $56.50 was paid in full by Visa. Memorize the transaction with weekly reminders starting 10/13/14.

SD16: Sales Receipt   **Dated October 7, 2014**

Sales Receipt #186 to Mina Staples (set up the new customer), $1,800.00 plus $234.00 HST for a cherry bookcase. Delivery charge is $75.00 plus HST. Invoice totalling $2,118.75 was paid in full by Visa.

Notes
Mina Staples
33 Maple St.
Lindsay, ON K5F 7C5
Tel: (705) 798-1290
Alt: (705) 798-1220
Terms: 1/5, n/30
Credit limit: $4,000.00
Preferred payment: Visa

SD17: Sales Receipt   **Dated October 7, 2014**

Sales Receipt #187 from cash sales customers, $540.00 plus $70.20 HST for a set of nesting tables. Invoice totalling $610.20 was paid in full by cash.

October 8 – October 14, 2014

Notes
If your deposit amounts do not match the ones we show, check that you chose the correct method of payment for all receipts.

SD18: Memo #3   **Dated October 8, 2014**

From Owner: Deposit all cash and cheques to *Bank Chequing* account and deposit all credit card receipts to the *Bank Visa* account. Total deposits:

Bank Chequing	$4,668.90
Bank Visa	4,757.25

SD19: Purchase Order   **Dated October 9, 2014**

Purchase Order #18 sent to Papers Plus, $170.00 plus $22.10 HST for business cards and promotional flyers to distribute at the craft show. Invoice totals $192.10. Choose *Advertising Material* as the item.

SD20: Estimate   **Dated October 10, 2014**

Estimate #36 to Mina Staples, $2,600.00 plus $338.00 HST for matching cherry chests of drawers. Delivery charge is $75.00 plus HST. Estimate totals $3,022.75. A 25 percent deposit is required on acceptance of estimate.

SD21: Bill   **Dated October 11, 2014**

Bill #LHP-3864 received from Lindsay's Hardware & Paint, $205.00 plus $26.65 HST for carpentry supplies including stains, polishes, and paints. The bill totals $231.65. Terms: 1/10, n/30. Delete the *Uncategorized Expense* account from the Expenses tab.

Notes
Remember to select the method of payment for all cash sales.

SD22: Customer Payment   **Dated October 11, 2014**

From Mina Staples, Cheque #147 for $800.00 as the deposit on Sales Estimate #36.

SD23: Customer Payment   **Dated October 11, 2014**

From Conn Doze, Cheque #583 for $5,932.00 in payment of account, including the discount for early payment. Apply credits, discount, and payment to Invoice #461.

SD24: Bill   **Dated October 12, 2014**

Bill #KL-5922 received from Kawartha Lumber, $1,300.00 plus $169.00 HST for lumber to build various furniture pieces. The bill totals $1,469.00. Terms: Net 30.

SD25: Credit Card Charge   **Dated October 12, 2014**

Bill #OA-7103 received from Otto's Autos, $230.00 plus $29.90 HST for truck tune-up. The bill totalling $259.90 was paid in full by Visa.

SD26: Bill   **Dated October 12, 2014**

Bill #SFE-4550 received from Something for Everyone (use Quick Add to add the new vendor), $1,300.00 plus $169.00 HST for rental of a craft show booth. The bill totals $1,469.00. Terms: Net 10. Create a new expense account: 5300 *Rental Expense* (tax code H).

SD27: Pay Bill   **Dated October 12, 2014**

Cheque #504 paid to Kawartha Lumber, $4,280.00 in payment of account. Reference Bill #KL-2339.

SD28: Credit Card Charge   **Dated October 13, 2014**

Bill #OA-7218 received from Otto's Autos, $50.00 plus $6.50 HST for gasoline. The bill totalling $56.50 was paid in full by Visa. Use the memorized transaction.

SD29: Sales Receipt   **Dated October 14, 2014**

Sales Receipt #188 received from a cash sales customer, $470.00 plus $61.10 HST for a pair of end tables. Invoice totalling $531.10 was paid in full by cash.

SD30: Sales Receipt   **Dated October 14, 2014**

Sales Receipt #189 received from a cash sales customer, $275.00 plus $35.75 HST for a pair of night tables. Invoice totalling $310.75 was paid in full by Visa.

SD31: Bill   **Dated October 14, 2014**

Bill #KBS-1003 received from Kawartha Building Supplies, $550.00 for lumber and $90.00 for hardware plus $83.20 HST to build an entertainment wall unit. The bill totals $723.20. Terms: 1/10, n/30.

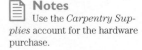

Notes
Use the *Carpentry Supplies* account for the hardware purchase.

October 15 – October 21, 2014

SD32: Memo #4   **Dated October 15, 2014**

From Owner: Deposit all cash and cheques to the *Bank Chequing* account and deposit all credit card receipts to the *Bank Visa* account. Total deposits:

Bank Chequing	$7,263.10
Bank Visa	310.75

SD33: Purchase Order   **Dated October 16, 2014**

Purchase Order #19 to Kawartha Building Supplies, $1,200.00 plus $156.00 HST for a special order of lumber. Order totals $1,356.00.

SD34: Invoice   **Dated October 16, 2014**

Invoice #462 to M. T. House, to fill Sales Estimate #35, $3,470.00 plus $451.10 HST for a custom-built walnut bedroom set including night tables and headboard. Invoice totals $3,921.10. Terms: 1/5, n/30. Change the customer's terms but do not save the changes (the new terms should not appear next time).

SD35: Credit Card Charge   **Dated October 18, 2014**

Credit card payment of Bill #P-9321 from Papers Plus, to fill Purchase Order #18, $170.00 plus $22.10 HST for business cards and promotional flyers to distribute at the craft show. Invoice totalling $192.10 was paid in full by Visa.

SD36: Bill   **Dated October 18, 2014**

Bill #HT-49901 received from Hydro Two, $120.00 plus $15.60 HST for hydro service for the shop for two months. The bill totals $135.60. Terms: Net 10.

SD37: **Customer Payment**   Dated October 19, 2014

From M. T. House, Cheque #92 for $2,886.40, including the discount for early payment. Apply credits, discount, and payment to Invoice #462. Remember to change the payment method.

SD38: **Pay Bill**   Dated October 19, 2014

Cheque #505 paid to Lindsay's Hardware & Paint, $229.60 in payment of account, Including the discount for early payment. Reference Bill #LHP-3864.

SD39: **Pay Bill**   Dated October 19, 2014

Cheque #506 paid to Northern Telecom, $99.44 in payment of account. Reference Invoice #NT-582.

SD40: **Sales Receipt**   Dated October 20, 2014

Sales Receipt #190 from a cash sales customer, $510.00 plus $66.30 HST for small bookshelves. Invoice totalling $576.30 was paid in full by Visa.

SD41: **Credit Card Charge**   Dated October 20, 2014

Bill #OA-7840 received from Otto's Autos, $50.00 plus $6.50 HST for gasoline. The bill totalling $56.50 was paid in full by Visa. Use the memorized transaction.

SD42: **Invoice**   Dated October 21, 2014

Invoice #463 to Mina Staples, to fill Sales Estimate #36, $2,600.00 plus $338.00 HST for a set of cherry chests of drawers. Delivery charge is $75.00 plus HST. Invoice totals $3,022.75. Terms: 1/5, n/30.

October 22 – October 28, 2014

SD43: **Memo #5**   Dated October 22, 2014

From Owner: Deposit all cash and cheques to the *Bank Chequing* account and deposit all credit card receipts to the *Bank Visa* account. Total deposit:

Bank Chequing	$2,886.40
Bank Visa	576.30

SD44: **Bill**   Dated October 22, 2014

Bill #KBS-2191 received from Kawartha Building Supplies, to fill Purchase Order #19, $1,200.00 plus $156.00 HST for lumber. The bill totals $1,356.00. Terms: 1/10, n/30.

SD45: **Pay Bill**   Dated October 22, 2014

Cheque #507 paid to Something for Everyone, $1,469.00 in payment of the account. Reference Bill #SFE-4550.

SD46: **Pay Bill**   Dated October 23, 2014

Cheque #508 paid to Kawartha Building Supplies, $716.80 in payment of the account, including the discount for early payment. Reference Bill #KBS-1003.

SD47: Pay Bill   **Dated October 24, 2014**

Cheque #509 paid to Hydro Two, $135.60 in payment of the account. Reference Bill #HT-49901.

SD48: Customer Payment   **Dated October 24, 2014**

From Mina Staples, Cheque #159 for $2,196.00 in payment of the account, including the discount for early payment. Apply credits, discount, and payment to Invoice #463. Remember to change the payment method.

SD49: Sales Receipts   **Dated October 25, 2014**

Sales Receipts #191–193 received from cash sales customers at the craft show for pre-made furniture items.

> File cabinet: $410.00 plus $53.30 HST. Invoice totals $463.30.
> Wall unit: $3,100.00 plus $403.00 HST. Invoice totals $3,503.00.
> Book shelves: $1,650.00 plus $214.50 HST. Invoice totals $1,864.50.

All sales paid by Visa.

📄 **Notes**
Enter the three credit card sales receipts as separate sales.

SD50: Sales Receipts   **Dated October 25, 2014**

Sales Receipts 194–196 received from cash sales customers at the craft show for pre-made furniture items.

> Coffee table: $400.00 plus $52.00 HST. Invoice totals $452.00.
> End table: $90.00 plus $11.70 HST. Invoice totals $101.70.
> TV stand: $250.00 plus $32.50 HST. Invoice totals $282.50.

All sales paid by cash.

📄 **Notes**
Enter the three cash sales receipts as separate sales.

SD51: Credit Card Charge   **Dated October 27, 2014**

Bill #OA-8223 received from Otto's Autos, $50.00 plus $6.50 HST for gasoline. The bill totalling $56.50 was paid in full by Visa. Use the memorized transaction.

SD52: Credit Card Charge   **Dated October 28, 2014**

Bill #OA-8229 received from Otto's Autos, $70.00 for emergency towing and $600.00 for truck battery plus $87.10 HST. The bill totalling $757.10 was paid in full by Visa.

October 29 – October 30, 2014

SD53: Memo #6   **Dated October 30, 2014**

From Owner: Deposit all cash and cheques to the *Bank Chequing* account and deposit all credit card receipts to the *Bank Visa* account. Total deposits:

Bank Chequing	$3,032.20
Owner withdraws Petty Cash for postage	50.00
Net deposit to Bank Chequing	$2,982.20
Bank Visa	$5,830.80

SD54: Pay Bill   **Dated October 30, 2014**

Cheque #510 paid to Kawartha Building Supplies, $1,344.00 in payment of account, including discount for early payment. Reference Bill #KBS-2191.

SD55: Bank Debit Memo #DM-31188   **Dated October 30, 2014**

From Woodworkers Credit Union, preauthorized withdrawals were made for:

Mortgage ($45.00 principal and $205.00 interest)	$250.00
Bank loan ($140.00 principal and $90.00 interest)	230.00
Long term loan ($225.00 principal and $180.00 interest)	405.00

SD56: Memo #7   **Dated October 30, 2014**

From Owner: Complete adjusting entries for depreciation for October.

Business truck	$ 315.00
Computer equipment	105.00
Carpentry tools & equipment	400.00
Shop	315.00

SD57: Memo #8   **Dated October 30, 2014**

From Owner: Complete adjusting entries for supplies used during month.

Office and computer supplies	$ 140.00
Carpentry supplies	505.00
Lumber	2,800.00

Assessing Finance Charges

Notes
The Collections report, Open Invoices report, and A/R Aging reports will all show overdue accounts.

When customers fail to pay their accounts within the due date period, they may be charged interest on the overdue amounts. Curly's Cabinets charges 18 percent interest per year on accounts over 35 days. Interest charges are calculated on the invoice date. To see how the finance charge is set up, select Edit from the menu and then Preferences. Select Finance Charges on the left-hand side of the screen and click on the Company Preferences tab. Interest charges are assessed at the end of each month at Curly's Cabinets. Lucas Bayler has an outstanding overdue balance so we need to charge him interest.

Although you can display or print various reports to find the overdue accounts, you can use the Finance Charges feature in QuickBooks to find overdue accounts directly.

The next transaction that we will enter is a finance charge on an overdue account. Refer to the following source document as we work through the steps to enter it:

Source Docs
Refer to the following source document and then follow the step-by-step instructions to enter it.

SD58: Memo #9   **Dated October 31, 2014**

From Owner, assess finance charges on Bayler's overdue account.

Interest on overdue accounts is entered from the Finance Charges icon in the Customer section of the Home page.

Notes
Overdue accounts are charged 18 percent interest, assessed from the invoice date. A minimum charge of $25.00 is applied to cover administrative costs.

Curly's Cabinets allows a five-day grace period after the due date before charging interest. This is entered as 35 days in the Finance Charges settings to allow the grace period to pass the original due date by five days.

1. **Click**   the **Finance Charges icon** to open the Assess Finance Charges form:

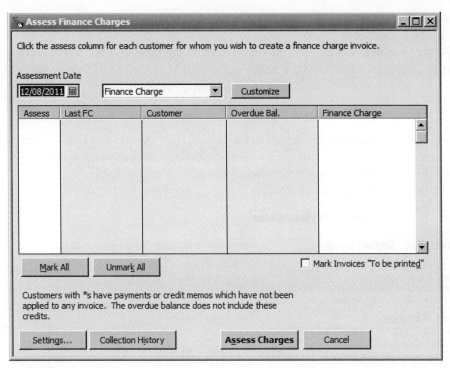

Figure 8-25

Notes
Like most dates in transactions, the date displayed will be your current computer date, so your date will not be the same as the one shown in the textbook.

If the date displayed in the Assessment Date field is earlier than the due date for all invoices, then there will be no invoices subject to finance charges displayed on the form. We'll change the date for this transaction.

2. Type   **10/31/14**

3. Press   _tab_ to refresh the information on the form

The finance charge of $76.34 on an overdue balance of $3,600.00 for Bayler is displayed on the form:

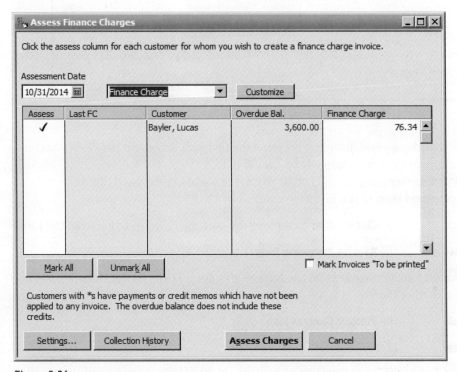

Figure 8-26

You can change the finance amount that was automatically calculated based on the customers overdue balance.

Practise entering different dates to view the effect on the finance charge. Try entering October 20, 2014, and October 24, 2014, as the assessment date. Press ⌈tab⌋ after entering a new date to update the calculations. Enter October 31, 2014, again before continuing.

4. Click the **Assess Charges button** to complete the finance charge

The form will close and you will return to the Home page. QuickBooks has created an invoice for the finance charge and the amount is added to the customer's account. To view the effect of assessing the finance charges, you can look at the customer's outstanding invoices in the Receive Payments window.

5. Click the **Receive Payments icon**

6. Choose **Bayler, Lucas** to view the customer's outstanding invoices:

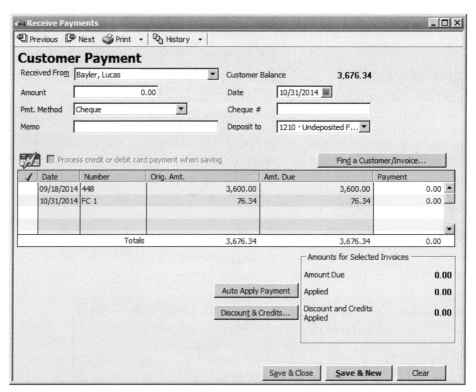

Figure 8-27

Notice that the second invoice represents the finance charge and has been given an invoice number of FC 1 automatically by QuickBooks.

When a customer pays their account, payments should be credited first to the finance charge and then to the invoice balance.

7. Click the **Clear button** to remove the customer's information from the form

8. Close the **Receive Payments form**

Let's take a look at the effect on the finance charges if Lucas Baylor does not pay his account for another month.

9. Click the **Finance Charges icon** again

10. Enter **11/30/14** as the date

11. Press ⌈tab⌋ to update the information in the Access Finance Charges form:

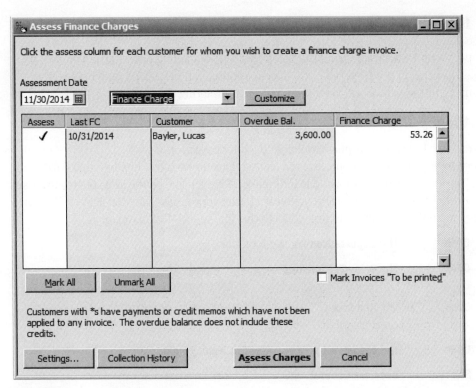

Figure 8-28

A finance charge for the current month is calculated for Lucas Bayler and added to his account. The date of the previous finance charge is displayed in the Last FC column. Curly's Cabinets does not assess interest charges on the previous interest charges; however, that is an option that can be set in the Finance Charge preferences.

12. Click   **Cancel** to close the Access Finance Charges form

Making Tax Remittances

After a business registers to collect taxes from customers, it must report on and remit these collections to the government on a regular basis. Depending on the size of the business, the reports may be required monthly, quarterly, or annually. With annual reporting, quarterly installments may be required as well. Curly's Cabinets files federal HST tax returns quarterly with the Receiver General of Canada.

You cannot return to the tax remittance forms after filing the tax return; however, you can undo the previous return and do it over again. It is a good idea to make a backup copy of your company file before starting your tax remittance. You can make corrections in the registers for the relevant accounts if necessary and adjust later tax returns if errors are made when filing previous tax returns.

Next, we will prepare the HST return. Refer to the following source document as we work through the steps to enter it:

SD59: Memo #10   **Dated October 31, 2014**

Prepare the HST return and write Cheque #511 in remittance to the Receiver General for HST payable as of October 31, 2014.

1. Back up   your **company data file**

2. Print   the **General Ledger report** for the GST/HST Payable account for the remittance period for reference purposes

📄 **Notes**
For further information on sales taxes, refer to the Appendix document "Tax" found on the CD accompanying this text. You should also always consult the latest federal and provincial regulations about taxes in your region.

📑 **Source Docs**
Refer to the following source document and then follow the step-by-step instructions to enter it.

📄 **Notes**
Refer to page 131 for assistance with displaying and printing the General Ledger report.

Tax Reports

Tax reports can be accessed from the Sales Tax report heading or from the Vendors & Payables heading in the Report Centre. These reports can be viewed only before the taxes are remitted, so we will view them before completing the returns.

Tax Agency Reports

There are two tax agency reports available in QuickBooks.

The Tax Agency Detail report lists the transactions for each box number on the sales tax return. The Tax Agency report lists the information for each line on the sales tax return. Use this report to help you file your sales tax return to the appropriate sales tax agency. You can click any amount in this report to drill down to the Tax Agency Detail report.

1.	**Click**	the **Reports icon** on the Icon bar
2.	**Click**	the **Sales Tax heading** on the left-hand side of the screen
3.	**Click**	the **Run icon** under the Tax Agency report to display the report on the screen
4.	**Click**	the **drop-down arrow** in the **Tax Agency field**
5.	**Select**	**Receiver General**
6.	**Enter**	**08/01/14** in the **From date field**
7.	**Enter**	**10/31/14** in the **To date field**
8.	**Press**	⌨ *tab* or **click Refresh** to update the report:

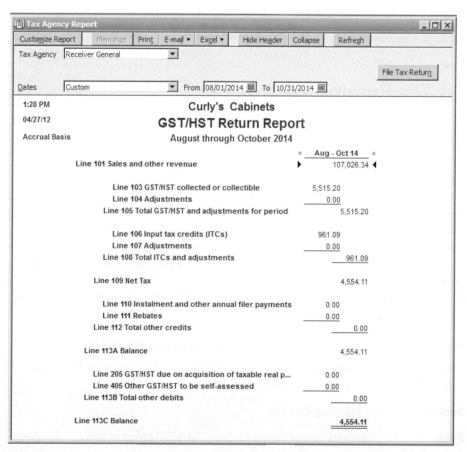

Figure 8-29

You can double click an amount to view the individual amounts that make up that total. These amounts will be displayed on the Tax Agency Detail report. Then double click an amount on the Tax Agency Detail report to view the original transaction.

9. **Double click** the **amount** for Line 103 GST/HST collected or collectible to drill down to the details that make up the amount on the Tax Agency Detail report

Notes
The Tax Agency Detail report can also be selected directly from the Sales Tax heading in the Report Centre or from the Manage Sales Tax window.

10. **Double click** an **amount** on the Tax Agency Detail report to drill down to the original transaction

11. **Close** the **report** when you have finished viewing it

Making an HST Remittance

QuickBooks automatically creates a vendor record for the Receiver General when you set up the company files. The completion of the HST tax return is largely automatic and based on the transactions for the relevant period. Taxes are filed from the Manage Sales Tax window, which can be opened by using one of the following methods:

a) **Click** the **Manage Sales Tax icon** in the Vendors section of the Home page; or

b) **Click Sales Tax** from the menu and then **click Manage Sales Tax**

1. **Open** the **Manage Sales Tax window** by using one of the methods listed above:

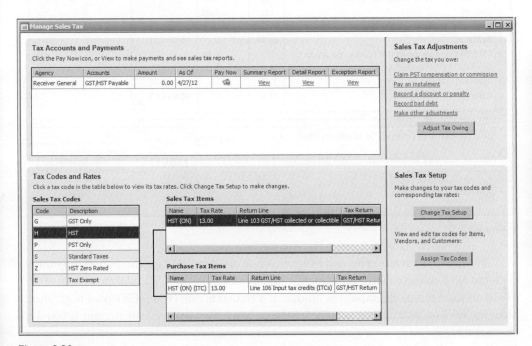

Figure 8-30

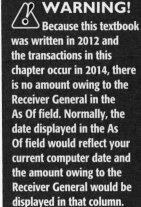

WARNING!
Because this textbook was written in 2012 and the transactions in this chapter occur in 2014, there is no amount owing to the Receiver General in the As Of field. Normally, the date displayed in the As Of field would reflect your current computer date and the amount owing to the Receiver General would be displayed in that column.

Click the Pay Now icon to file the HST Sales Tax return, click the View link under the Summary Report heading to view the Tax Agency report, and click the View link under the Detail Report heading to view the Tax Agency Detail report.

2. Click the **Pay Now icon** beside the Receiver General to open the File Sales Tax form

Notes
Curly's pays HST on a quarterly basis. The current quarter is August through October, 2014.

The Receiver General should already be selected in the Tax Agency field. Curly's pays HST on a quarterly basis. The current quarter is between August 1, 2014, and October 31, 2014. We need to change the dates to reflect our remittance period.

3. Type **08/01/14** in the **From date field**

4. Type **10/31/14** in the **To date field**

5. Press ⌨ tab ⌨ to update the File Sales Tax form:

Notes
After you update the dates to include the date of the transactions entered in the textbook, the amount owing to the Receiver General is displayed.
You can see that for the period of 08/01/14–10/31/14, the amount you owe to the Receiver General is $4,554.11.

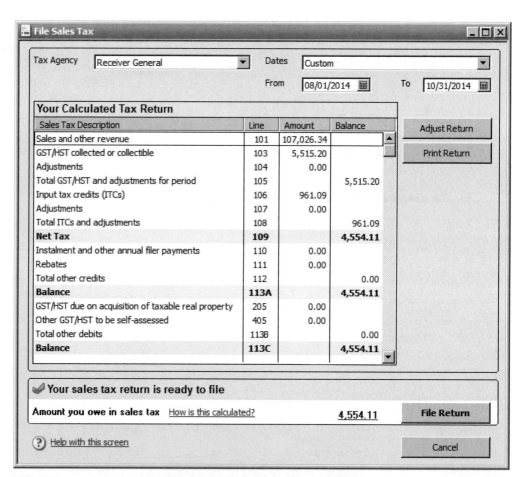

Figure 8-31

The amounts for the sales and other revenue are displayed for the period, together with the HST collected, any adjustments, and input tax credits. The Balance equals the HST collected minus the input tax credits. If a refund is due (when HST paid is greater than the HST collected), the balance will be in brackets; otherwise an amount is owed to the tax agency.

You can drill down on any of the balances that are displayed on the Sales Tax form and continue to drill down until the original transaction is displayed.

You can make Sales Tax Adjustments from this window by clicking on the Adjust Return button.

6. Click the **Adjust Return** button to display the Sales Tax Adjustment form:

Figure 8-32

Use the Sales Tax Adjustment form to enter an adjustment to your sales tax liability if necessary. Adjustments may be required for sales returns, credits, discounts, or bad debts for which tax was not recorded. Sales credits will reduce the tax owing, so a negative amount will be entered. Purchase credits will increase the tax owing. Adjustment accounts can be created at this point if you do not already have them. QuickBooks will create a General Journal entry from the adjustment you enter here.

7. Click **Cancel** to return to the File Sales Tax form

Use the Print Return button to print the GST/HST Return report before filing the return.

QuickBooks completes the return based on the journal transaction details.

To make corrections later, you must make a journal entry for the adjustment. If you have not yet made a backup of the file, you should click Cancel and make the backup before proceeding.

For Curly's Cabinets, the amounts entered on the Files Sales Tax form are correct so we can accept them and continue.

8. Click the **File Return button** when you are ready to file the return

9. The following message will be displayed:

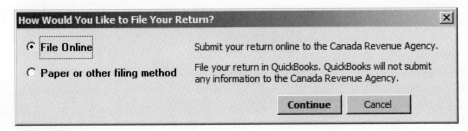

Figure 8-33

> ⚠️ **WARNING!**
> You cannot return to the tax remittance forms after filing the tax return, so make a backup copy of your company file before starting and proceed carefully. It is possible to undo the last reconciliation if necessary by selecting the Undo Last Reconciliation button on the Begin Reconciliation form.

QuickBooks allows you to file your return online or manually.

10. Click the **Paper or other filing method option** to file the return manually

11. Click   **Continue**

12. The following message will be displayed:

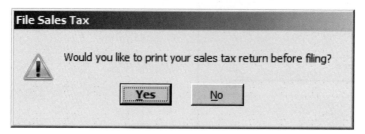

Figure 8-34

Notes
   A business should print their sales tax return before filing. We have selected no here; however, you may want to print the sales tax return if you have access to a printer.

13. Click   **No**. The following message will be displayed:

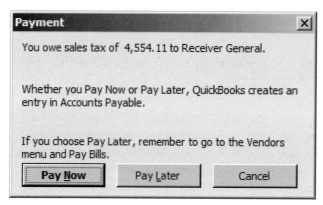

Figure 8-35

This message indicates that you owe the Receiver General $4,554.11. If you select Pay Now, a General Journal entry will automatically be created and the Pay Bills form will automatically be displayed, allowing you to make the payment to the Receiver General in the Pay Bills form. If you select Pay Later, a journal entry will automatically be created and you will have to pay the bill at a later time. If you click Cancel, the return will not be filed and you will be returned to the File Sales Tax form.

14. Select   **Pay Now** and the following message will be displayed:

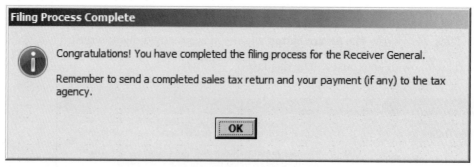

Figure 8-36

15. Click   **OK** and the Pay Bills form will be displayed:

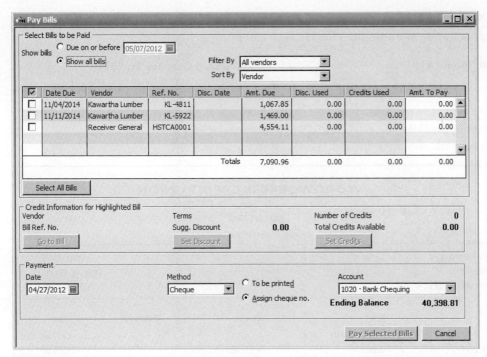

Figure 8-37

Notice that because you selected the Pay Now option, the bill has already been created and all you have to do is select it for payment in the Enter Bills form.

16. Click   the **check box** beside the Receiver General

Most of the default selections on the Enter Bills form are correct because they have been set for the other cheques we wrote. The default bank account is correct and cheque is correct as the method of payment. In addition, we want to assign the cheque number and prepare the cheque manually, so this selection is also correct.

17. Click   the **Payment Date field**

18. Type   **10/31/14** if necessary

19. Click   the **Pay Selected Bills button**

20. Type   **511** in the **Cheque field**

21. Click   **OK**

22. Click   **Done** in the Payment Summary window

23. Close   the **Manage Sales Tax screen**

Reconciling a Bank Account

Reconciling a bank account statement against the computer files is an important step in verifying the accuracy of your records. The bank statement may be different from the ledger for the bank account in QuickBooks for many reasons: cheques written on the account may not have been cashed; a deposit may not be recorded if it was made at the end of the banking day before the statement was prepared; bank charges and interest paid appear on the bank statement but not in the ledger record; and deposits or cheques may have been recorded incorrectly by you or by the bank. Reconciliation is the process of resolving, or accounting for, all these differences between two sets of records.

Next, we will reconcile the *Bank Chequing* account. Refer to the following source document as we work through the steps to enter it:

Source Docs
Refer to the following source document and then follow the step-by-step instructions to enter it.

SD60: Memo #11   **Dated October 31, 2014**

Use the following bank statement to reconcile the *Bank Chequing* account.

To begin the reconciliation, you should compare the bank statement with the bank register in QuickBooks.

The bank statement follows:

WOODWORKERS CREDIT UNION
500 Millionaire's Rd. Lindsay, ON K7G 4D5
(705) 664-7400
www.woodworkerscu.com

Curly's Cabinets
46 Maple Cres.
Lindsay, ON K9V 2P3

October 31/14
Chequing Account
42045 774990

Date	Item	Deposits	Withdrawals	Balance
	Balance Forward			23,540.00
10/01/2014	Deposit	6,030.00		29,570.00
10/04/2014	502		451.00	29,119.00
10/05/2014	503		2,118.60	27,000.40
10/08/2014	Deposit	4,668.90		31,669.30
10/14/2014	504		4,280.00	27,389.30
10/15/2014	Deposit	7,263.10		34,652.40
10/20/2014	505		229.60	34,422.80
	506		99.44	34,323.36
10/22/2014	Deposit	2,886.40		37,209.76
10/23/2014	507		1,469.00	35,740.76
10/23/2014	508		716.80	35,023.96
10/24/2014	509		135.60	34,888.36
10/28/2014	510		1,344.00	33,544.36
10/30/2014	Debit Memo: mortgage		250.00	33,294.36
	Debit Memo: loan		230.00	33,064.36
	Debit Memo: loan		405.00	32,659.36
10/30/2014	Deposit	2,982.20		35,641.56
	Interest	25.00		35,666.56
	Service fee		35.00	35,631.56
	Closing Balance			35,631.56
		Total Deposits: 6		23,830.60
		Total Withdrawals: 9		11,729.04

Next, you should print the ledger record for the bank account for reference. You can use the General Ledger report or the Custom Transaction Detail report. The General Ledger report includes all accounts, so you should modify it and apply Account as the filter. The Custom Transaction Detail report must also be filtered for the account we want.

Notes
To print the transaction report, choose the Reports menu and click Custom Transaction Detail report. Enter 9/30/14 and 10/31/14 as the report dates in the Modify Report window.

Or, to print the General Ledger report, choose the Reports menu, then choose Accountant & Taxes, and click General Ledger. Enter 10/1/14 and 10/31/14 as the report dates. Press [tab] and click Modify Report.

For either report, click the Modify Report button, then the Filters tab, and select Account as the filter. Choose the *Bank Chequing* account from the list of accounts. Click OK to return to the report. Click the Print button.

Close the report window. Refer to page 122 for assistance with filtering reports.

1. **Click**   the **Report Centre icon** from the Icon bar

2. **Click**   the **Accountant & Taxes heading** on the left-hand side of the screen

3. **Click**   the **General Ledger link**

4. **Type**   **10/01/14** in the **From date field**

5. **Type** **10/31/14** in the **To date field**

6. The report will be displayed for the *Bank Chequing* account as shown:

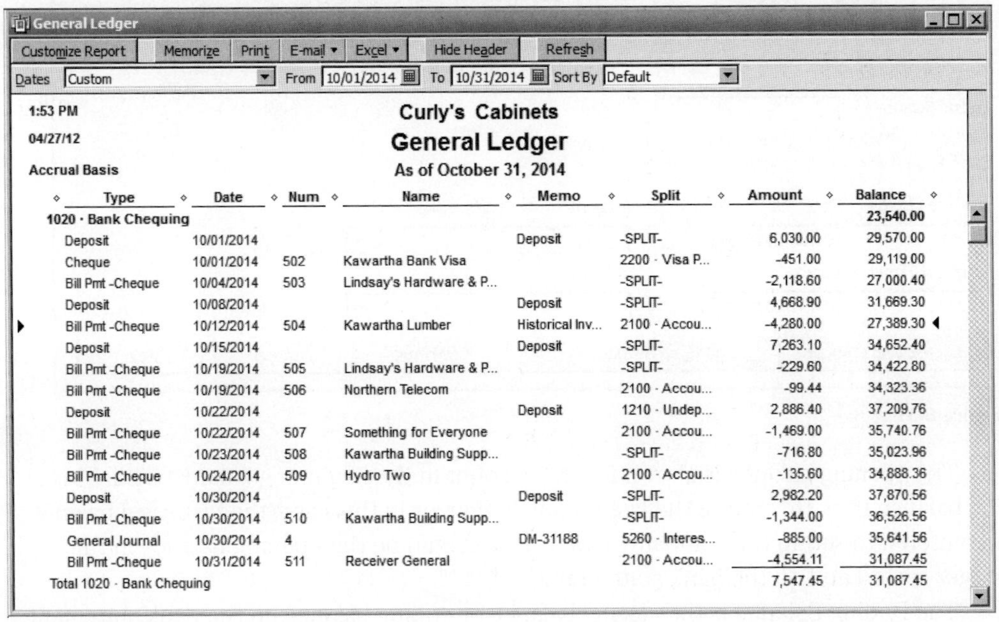

Type	Date	Num	Name	Memo	Split	Amount	Balance
1020 · Bank Chequing							**23,540.00**
Deposit	10/01/2014			Deposit	-SPLIT-	6,030.00	29,570.00
Cheque	10/01/2014	502	Kawartha Bank Visa		2200 · Visa P...	-451.00	29,119.00
Bill Pmt -Cheque	10/04/2014	503	Lindsay's Hardware & P...		-SPLIT-	-2,118.60	27,000.40
Deposit	10/08/2014			Deposit	-SPLIT-	4,668.90	31,669.30
Bill Pmt -Cheque	10/12/2014	504	Kawartha Lumber	Historical Inv...	2100 · Accou...	-4,280.00	27,389.30
Deposit	10/15/2014			Deposit	-SPLIT-	7,263.10	34,652.40
Bill Pmt -Cheque	10/19/2014	505	Lindsay's Hardware & P...		-SPLIT-	-229.60	34,422.80
Bill Pmt -Cheque	10/19/2014	506	Northern Telecom		2100 · Accou...	-99.44	34,323.36
Deposit	10/22/2014			Deposit	1210 · Undep...	2,886.40	37,209.76
Bill Pmt -Cheque	10/22/2014	507	Something for Everyone		2100 · Accou...	-1,469.00	35,740.76
Bill Pmt -Cheque	10/23/2014	508	Kawartha Building Supp...		-SPLIT-	-716.80	35,023.96
Bill Pmt -Cheque	10/24/2014	509	Hydro Two		2100 · Accou...	-135.60	34,888.36
Deposit	10/30/2014			Deposit	-SPLIT-	2,982.20	37,870.56
Bill Pmt -Cheque	10/30/2014	510	Kawartha Building Supp...		-SPLIT-	-1,344.00	36,526.56
General Journal	10/30/2014	4		DM-31188	5260 · Interes...	-885.00	35,641.56
Bill Pmt -Cheque	10/31/2014	511	Receiver General		2100 · Accou...	-4,554.11	31,087.45
Total 1020 · Bank Chequing						7,547.45	31,087.45

Figure 8-38

Notice the differences between the account register and the bank statement:

- a cheque written on October 31 does not appear on the bank statement
- the mortgage payable, bank loan, and interest expenses are posted in detail on the bank statement; however, they are lumped together as one payment of $885.00 in the QuickBooks ledger
- interest income and service charges appear on the bank statement but not in the ledger report
- the dates for the cheques and deposits do not match the dates in the ledger report

We are now ready to reconcile the bank account so that the two reports match.

1. **Click** the **Reconcile icon** on the Banking section of the Home page to open the Begin Reconciliation form

> **Notes**
> If you closed the Curly data file after reconciling the *Visa Payable* account, the *Bank Chequing* account will be displayed in the Account field.

This is the same screen we used earlier to reconcile the *Visa Payable* account, and *Visa Payable* is still selected because it was the account we last reconciled. We need to select the *Bank Chequing* account.

2. **Click** the **drop-down arrow** in the **Account field** and **select Bank Chequing** to open the Begin Reconciliation form for this account as shown:

> **Notes**
> All Balance Sheet accounts are available for selection in the Account field on the Begin Reconciliation form. In theory, you could receive statements for any asset, liability, or equity account for reconciliation.

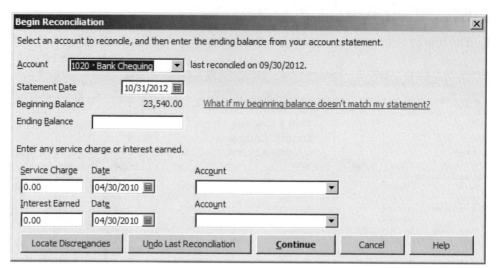

Begin Reconciliation

Select an account to reconcile, and then enter the ending balance from your account statement.

Account [1020 · Bank Chequing ▼] last reconciled on 09/30/2012.

Statement Date [10/31/2012 ▦]

Beginning Balance 23,540.00 <u>What if my beginning balance doesn't match my statement?</u>

Ending Balance [   ]

Enter any service charge or interest earned.

Service Charge Date Account
[0.00] [04/30/2010 ▦] [▼]

Interest Earned Date Account
[0.00] [04/30/2010 ▦] [▼]

[Locate Discrepancies] [Undo Last Reconciliation] [**Continue**] [Cancel] [Help]

Figure 8-39

The opening balance is shown for the account in the beginning balance field. This is the balance from the end of the last reconciliation, or in this case, the historical balance we entered to set up the company data files. It should be the opening balance in the ledger record and on the bank statement.

The Ending Balance is the closing balance or ending balance on the bank statement.

Notes
The default Statement Date is the last day of the month before your current calendar month (according to your computer system date).

3. Type   **10/31/14** in the **Statement Date field**

4. Press   ⌨tab to advance to the Ending Balance field

5. Type   **35631.56**

6. Press   ⌨tab to advance to the Service Charge field.

This field is used for any fees that the bank has charged, including monthly service fees, NSF fees, and so on. You can add all the fees together and enter a single amount.

A single entry appears on the statement for fees, the entry on October 31st for $35.00.

Notes
If you want to enter different kinds of charges for different accounts, you should make individual General Journal entries for them on the dates they occurred and then clear them with the other transactions in the next step.

7. Type   **35**

8. Press   ⌨tab to advance to the Date field

As elsewhere, the calendar date appears as the default date.

9. Type   **10/31/14**

10. Press   ⌨tab to advance to the Account field

When you click on the drop-down arrow in the Account field, you will see that you do not have an account called *Bank Charges*, so it needs to be created.

11. Type   **5080**

12. Press   ⌨tab to display the Account Not Found message

13. Click   **Set Up**

Notice the expense account type has automatically been selected for this account.

14. Click   the **Account Name field**

15. Type   **Bank Charges**

16. **Click**   **Save & Close** to return to the Begin Reconciliation form

The cursor is now in the Interest Earned field.

17. **Type**   **25**

18. **Press**   ⌷tab⌷ to move to the Date field

19. **Type**   **10/31/14**

20. **Press**   ⌷tab⌷

21. **Click**   the **drop-down arrow** in the **Account field**

22. **Choose**   **4200 - Revenue from Interest**

23. The Begin Reconciliation form is now complete as shown:

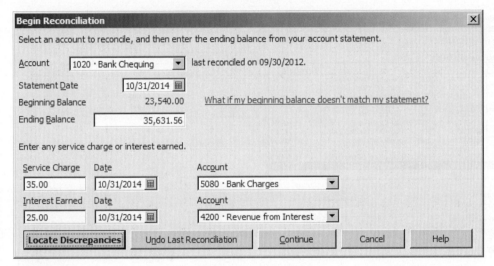

Figure 8-40

24. **Check**   your **work** and **make** any necessary **corrections**

25. **Click**   the **Continue button** to proceed to the next screen:

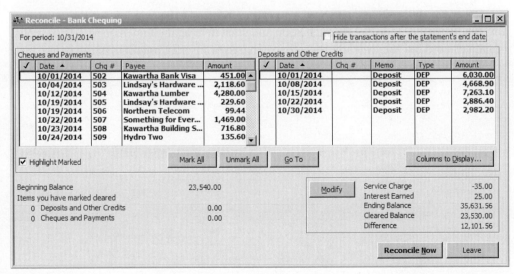

Figure 8-41

Notes
If you are reconciling for more than one month at a time, you may want to show the transactions before the statement date (click the check box at the top of the Reconcile window beside the Hide transactions after the statement's end date option) so that only the transactions that will be cleared from that statement are displayed on the screen.

This screen shows all transactions for the account for the relevant period. Most of these transactions also appear on the bank statement. We need to indicate which of these transactions have been cleared on the bank statement. The ✓ column is used to mark the cleared transactions. We can mark each transaction individually, or mark them all and deselect the ones that do not appear on the statement. Most of the transactions have cleared the bank so we will mark all of them first, then unmark the last cheque that has not cleared the bank.

26. Click the **Mark All button**

A checkmark is displayed in the ✓ column for all transactions.

Notes
You can click on any part of a transaction to add a ✓ or to remove a ✓.

27. Click the ✓ **column** for Receiver General, Cheque #511 to remove the ✓

The Difference amount should be zero because we have accounted for all the differences already. Your complete Reconcile form should look like the following:

Notes
If the difference is not zero when you click Reconcile Now, QuickBooks will ask you if you want to return to the Reconcile window (now or later) to make corrections or allow QuickBooks to make an adjustment for the difference. If you allow QuickBooks to make an adjustment, the adjusting journal entry will be made to the bank and capital accounts.

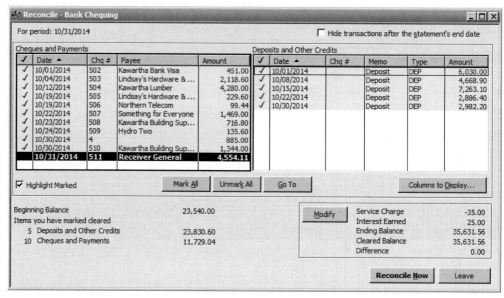

Figure 8-42

28. Check your **work** carefully and **make corrections** before proceeding

Once you choose Reconcile Now, you cannot return to this window for these dates. You can, however, undo the reconciliation and start over again if necessary. Transactions remain cleared but you can edit the service charge or interest amounts in the bank account's register.

Once you are sure that the information is correct, you can save the reconciliation.

29. Click   **Reconcile Now** to open the report screen

30. Click   **Display or Print** to view the Reconciliation Summary report:

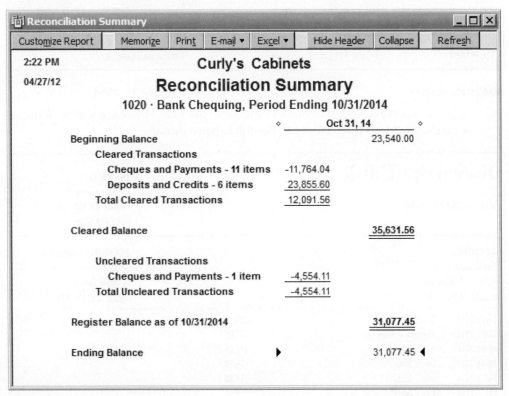

Figure 8-43

Source Documents

Now that you have learned some of the new concepts introduced in this chapter, enter the following source documents. Refer to the information in this chapter for help if necessary.

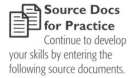

Source Docs for Practice

Continue to develop your skills by entering the following source documents.

Notes

The transaction fees are 2.3 percent of the total sales amount. Enter this charge as a Service Charge. Choose *Credit Card Fees* as the account for the charge.

SD61: Memo #12 **Dated October 31, 2014**

Use the following bank statement to reconcile the *Bank Visa* account.

Kawartha Bank

www.kbfg.ca
29 Moneysworth St.
Lindsay, ON K6B 5F9
(705) 644-8409

ACCOUNT			**ACCOUNT HOLDER**
Visa Deposit Account			Curly's Cabinets
3499 6003340			46 Maple Cres.
October 31/14			Lindsay, ON K9V 2P3

	Balance Forward			$ 4,385.00
10/01/14	Deposit	$8,050.00		12,435.00
10/08/14	Deposit	4,757.25		17,192.25
10/15/14	Deposit	310.75		17,503.00
10/22/14	Deposit	576.30		18,079.30
10/30/14	Deposit	5,830.80		23,910.10
10/30/14	Transaction Fees		$640.50	23,269.60
10/31/14	Closing Balance			$23,269.60

SUMMARY	Deposits $19,525.10	Withdrawals $640.50

SD62: Memo #13 **Dated October 31, 2014**

Use the following bank statement to reconcile the *Visa Payable* account. Write Cheque #512 for $1,060.25 to pay the full balance owing.

Kawartha Bank

Visa Statement

www.kbfg.ca
29 Moneysworth St.
Lindsay, ON K6B 5F9
(705) 644-8409

ACCOUNT		**ACCOUNT HOLDER**
Visa Account		Curly's Cabinets
4505 7499 6558 6443		46 Maple Cres.
October 31/14		Lindsay, ON K9V 2P3

10/01/2014	Otto's Autos	$203.40
10/02/2014	Payment - thank you	−451.00
10/04/2014	Papers Plus	163.85
10/06/2014	Otto's Autos	56.50
10/12/2014	Otto's Autos	259.90
10/13/2014	Otto's Autos	56.50
10/18/2014	Papers Plus	192.10
10/20/2014	Otto's Autos	56.50
10/27/2014	Otto's Autos	56.50
10/29/2014	Annual Fee	15.00

STATEMENT SUMMARY

	Previous Balance	$ 451.00	
	New Charges	1,060.25	
	Total Credits	451.00	
	Balance Owing	1,060.25	
	Minimum Payment	$110.00	by Nov 12, 2014

440 Chapter 8

Transferring Funds between Bank Accounts

Companies frequently need to transfer funds from one account to another to cover cheques or to move excess funds to a savings or investment account that earns a higher rate of interest. Curly's Cabinets does not need to keep a large balance in the *Bank Visa* account because this account is not used to write cheques.

The next transaction that we will enter is a transfer of funds from the *Bank Visa* to the *Bank Savings* account. Refer to the following source document as we work through the steps to enter it:

SD63: Memo #14   **Dated October 31, 2014**

Transfer $15,000.00 from the *Bank Visa* account to the *Bank Savings* account.

Source Docs
Refer to the following source document and then follow the step-by-step instructions to enter it.

1. Choose   the **Banking menu** and **click Transfer Funds** to open the Transfer Funds Between Accounts form:

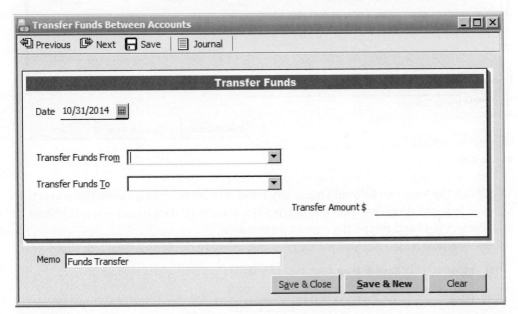

Figure 8-44

This form is very easy to use. All you need to do is choose the two bank accounts involved in the transfer and enter the date and amount of the transfer. The *Bank Chequing* account is selected as the default, so we need to change it. The current account balance for the *Bank Chequing* account is displayed on the form. The date should be correct from previous entries.

2. Type   **10/31/14** as the date if necessary

3. Click   the **drop-down arrow** in the **Transfer Funds From field**

4. Choose   **1060 - Bank Visa**. The *Bank Visa* account balance replaces the *Bank Chequing* balance

5. Click   the **drop-down arrow** in the **Transfer Funds To field**

6. Choose   **1040 - Bank Savings**. The *Bank Savings* account balance is displayed

7. Press   tab to advance to the Transfer Amount field

8. **Type**   **15000**

9. **Press**   (tab) to advance to the Memo field

"Funds Transfer" is entered in the memo field as the default memo, and we will accept the default memo. The account balances will be updated when we save the transfer so the form is complete as shown:

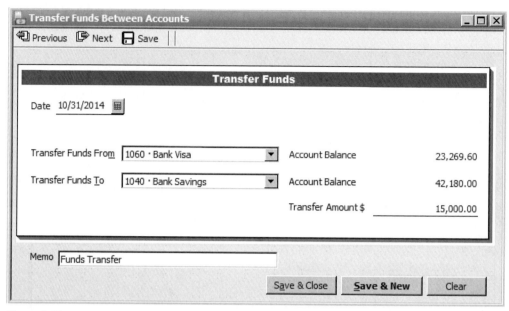

Figure 8-45

Check the form carefully and make any necessary corrections. Choose the correct account from the drop-down list and correct the amount or date if necessary. Highlight an incorrect field and retype the correct information.

We can now review the journal entry, so we will save the form without closing.

10. **Click**   **Save & New**

11. **Click**   the **Previous button** ⏮ Previous to view the transfer you just entered

Notice that the account balances have now been updated by the transferred amount.

12. **Press**   (ctrl) + **Y** to display the Transaction Journal report:

📄 **Notes**
We have removed columns from the report to display it in the textbook.

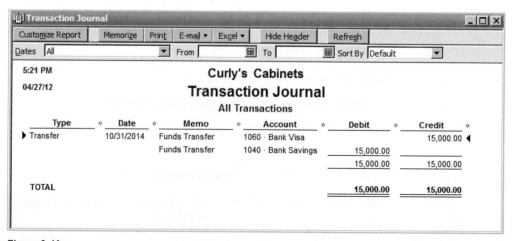

Figure 8-46

The entry shows a credit to the *Bank Visa* account and a debit entry to the *Bank Savings* account, just as it would if we had used the General Journal to complete the transaction.

13. **Close**   the **Transaction Journal report**

14. **Close**   the **Transfer Funds Between Accounts form**

Ending a Fiscal Year

At the end of a fiscal year, a business normally closes its books. In accrual-based accounting, this procedure involves completing all adjusting entries so that all revenue and expenses have been recorded for the appropriate period. Income and expense accounts are then closed to the appropriate capital accounts so that the next year can begin with zero balances for these accounts. We have already completed the adjustments for depreciation, supplies used, and expired prepaid expenses. Except for these adjusting entries, QuickBooks completes most of the closing steps automatically when you define the end date for a fiscal period.

Next, we will work through the necessary steps to close the books as of October 31, 2014. Refer to the following source document as we work through the steps to close the books:

SD64: Memo #15   **Dated October 31, 2014**

Close the books as of October 31, 2014. Transfer the *Retained Earnings* balance to the *Capital, Charles Cutter* account.

Source Docs
Refer to the following source document and then follow the step-by-step instructions to enter it.

Defining the Fiscal Year End Date

The first step in closing the books is the selection of a date for closing the books that will define the end of the fiscal year. Normally a business will choose one year as its fiscal period, but shorter periods may also be used.

However, before we close the books, we should make a backup copy of the data file so that we can return to the pre-closing period if necessary.

1. **Back up**   the **data file** to a new CD or other backup medium

2. **Label**   the **CD** "Pre-closing Data for Curly" and **store** the **CD** in a safe place

Now we will select a closing date for the fiscal period.

3. **Choose**   the **Edit menu** and **click Preferences**

4. **Click**   the **Accounting heading** on the left-hand side of the screen

Notes
Remember, only the Administrator of the company file or a user set up as an External Accountant can change the preferences on the Company tab.

5. **Click** the **Company Preferences tab**:

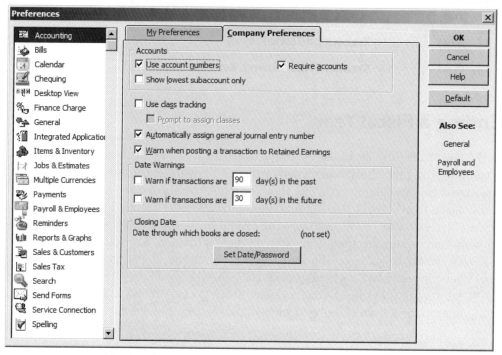

Figure 8-47

6. **Click** the **Set Date/Password button** on the bottom of the screen to open the Set Closing Date and Password form

7. **Click** the **Closing Date field** (the Date through which the books are closed)

8. **Type** **10/31/14**

9. **Press** ⌨tab to advance to the Closing Date Password field

The closing date password you set here applies only to transactions dated on or before the closing date: October 31, 2014. Although you can enter this password at any time, it is advised to set it at the time of setting the closing date.

This password will prevent unauthorized access to the transactions dated on or before the closing date. For security purposes, in an ongoing business, you should set a password after setting the closing date. The password will also help ensure that transaction dates for the previous fiscal period are not entered in error.

For practice, choose a password that is easy to remember, such as your first name. In an ongoing business, you should choose a password that is easy for you to remember but unknown to anyone else (and cannot be guessed). The cursor is in the Password field. You must enter the same code twice. This ensures you typed the password that you intended, without making a mistake that you cannot duplicate later.

10. **Type** **curly** in the **Closing Date Password field**

11. **Press** ⌨tab to advance to the Confirm Password field

For added security, the characters you type do not appear on the screen.

12. **Type** **curly** in the **Confirm Password field**

13. The completed Set Closing Date and Password form is displayed as shown:

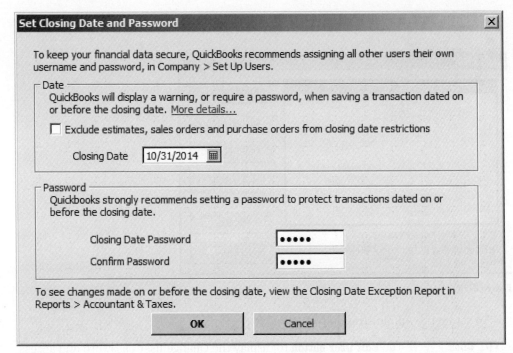

Figure 8-48

While working in QuickBooks, if you try to save a transaction dated October 31, 2014, or earlier, you will be prompted for the closing password. If the transaction date is correct, and it should be completed, enter the password to continue with the transaction. Otherwise, choose Cancel and correct the transaction date.

14. Click   **OK** to continue

15. The following message will be displayed:

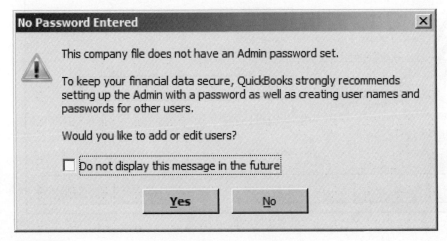

Figure 8-49

In an ongoing company, it is important to set an administration password and select a challenge question that no one can guess. This will protect your QuickBooks company file from being viewed by people who should not be able to view it.

16. Click   the **box** beside the Do not display this message in the future option

17. Click   **Yes**

18. The User List is displayed:

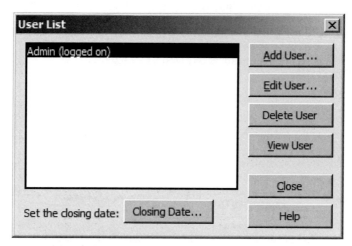

Figure 8-50

To set up the Administration password:

19. Click   the **Edit User button** to display the Change user password and access form as shown:

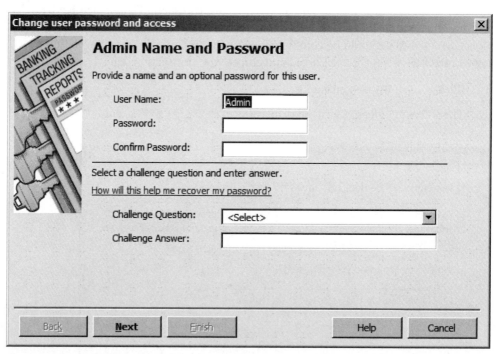

Figure 8-51

20. Press   tab to advance to the Password field

Type a password that no one can guess. For this company file, we will use "curly" as the password.

21. Type   **curly**

22. Press   tab to advance to the Confirm Password field

23. Type   **curly**

24. **Click**   the **drop-down list** in the **Challenge Question field**

25. **Select**   a **Challenge Question** that no one will guess

26. **Press**   ⬚tab⬚ to advance to the Challenge Answer field

27. Type the **answer** to your challenge question

If you forget the company file password and can answer your challenge question, you will be able to re-set your password for the company file.

28. **Click**   **Next** to display the following message:

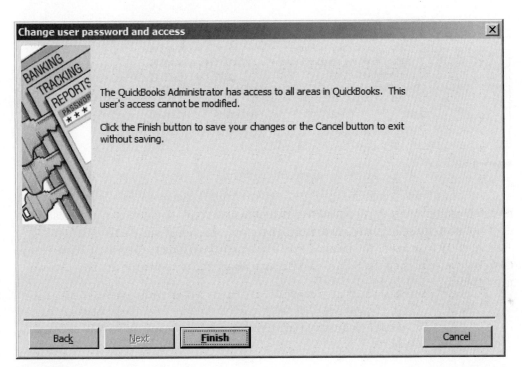

Figure 8-52

29. **Click**   **Finish**

30. **Close**   the **User List**

31. **Close**   the **Preferences screen**

From now on, when you open the Curly company data file, you will have to enter the admin password.

Closing the Books

When you enter a date in QuickBooks within the new year (after the closing date you set in QuickBooks), QuickBooks automatically transfers the income and expense balances to the *Retained Earnings* account. Income and expense account balances are reset to zero to begin a new fiscal period.

We can see the effect of entering a date in the new year (after the set closing date) when we examine the equity section of the Balance Sheet for the last day of the previous fiscal year and the first day of the current year.

Notes
To show the comparative Balance Sheet:
- Open the Report Centre
- Choose the Company & Financial heading on the left-hand side of the screen
- Click the Run icon under the Balance Sheet Standard report under the Balance Sheet and Net Worth heading
- Enter 11/01/14 as the date for the statement
- Press ⌨ or click the Refresh button
- Click the Customize Report button
- Click Previous Period in the Add subcolumns for section
- Click OK

The equity section of the comparative statement is shown here:

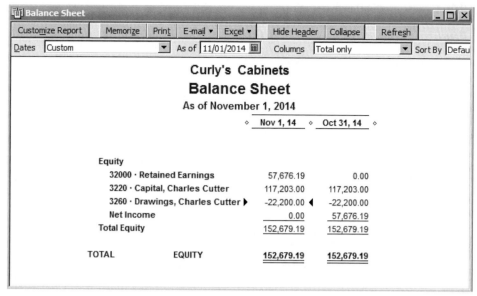

Figure 8-53

Some businesses maintain the *Retained Earnings* balance separately from the invested capital. Many small businesses do not maintain this distinction. Curly's Cabinets does not keep these balances separately. Therefore, we should make a final General Journal entry to transfer the balance from *Retained Earnings* to *Capital, Charles Cutter* to finish closing the books. The Balance Sheet above shows the amount that we must transfer, $57,676.19.

1. **Make** the **General Journal entry** to debit (reduce) *Retained Earnings* and credit (increase) *Capital, Charles Cutter* for $57,676.19 as shown here:

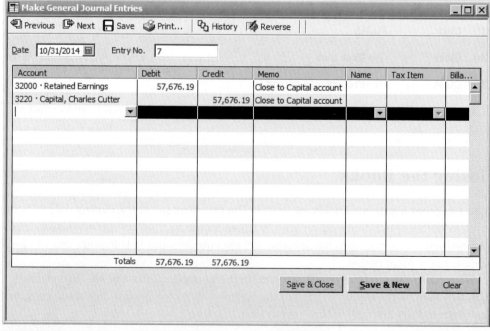

Figure 8-54

2. **Click**   **Save & Close** to display the screen that requires the closing date
password before proceeding with the transaction:

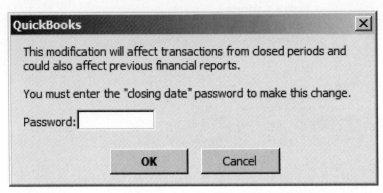

Figure 8-55

Normally, once you have closed the books, you won't make entries to the previous
period. Sometimes, you need to make entries after closing the books because the
information for the adjusting entries isn't available until after the closing date. As long
as you set the closing date and password, this screen will be displayed requesting the
closing date password in order to allow you to save the transaction.

3. **Type**   **curly**

4. **Click**   **OK**

If you enter a closing date but do not enter a closing date password, the following
warning will be displayed when you try to save a transaction dated on or before the
closing date:

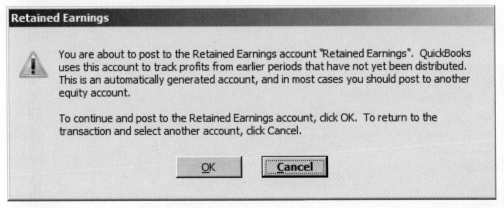

Figure 8-56

5. **Click**   **OK** to continue

When you review the equity section of the Balance Sheet for November 1 after
transferring the balance from *Retained Earnings* to *Capital, Charles Cutter* you will
see that the entry for *Retained Earnings* has been removed and *Capital, Charles
Cutter* has been increased as shown here:

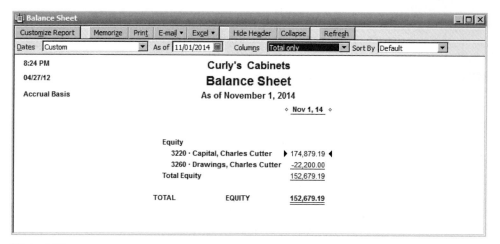

Figure 8-57

Banking Reports

The banking reports show detailed records of cheques, deposits, and reconciliations. You can view these reports from the Reports menu or from the Report Centre. We will view the reports from the Report Centre as we have in previous chapters.

1. **Click**   the **Reports icon** from the Icon bar

2. **Click**   the **Banking heading** on the left-hand side of the screen

3. **Click**   the **List View icon** to view the reports in list view:

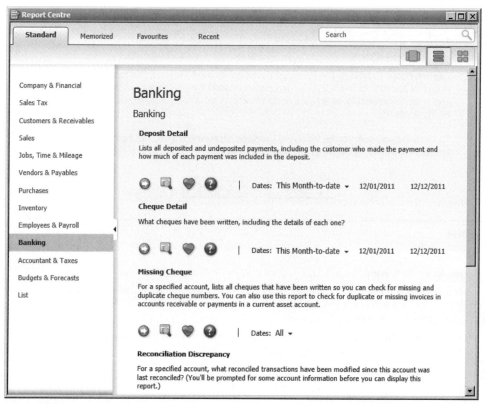

Figure 8-58

The Deposit Detail Report

The Deposit Detail report includes a list of all deposits to all accounts that have been used in a Deposit To field in the journals and the customers who made the payments.

1. **Click**   the **Run icon** under the Deposit Detail report

2. **Type**   **10/01/14** in the **From date field**

3. **Type**   **10/31/14** in the **To date field**

4. **Press**   `tab` or **click** the **Refresh button** to update the report:

Notes

To access the report from the Reports menu:
- Choose the Reports menu, then choose Banking, and click Deposit Detail to open the report
- Enter 10/01/14 as the From date
- Enter 10/31/14 as the To date
- Press `tab` or click the Refresh button to update the report

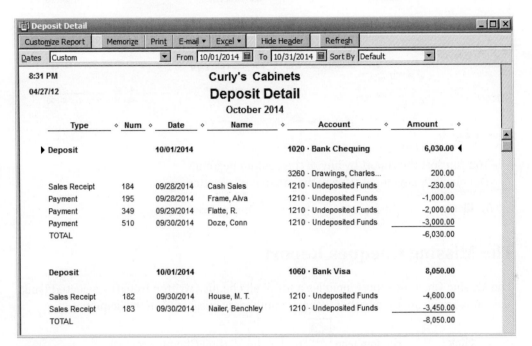

Figure 8-59

Each deposit shows the individual receipts that were part of that deposit. Undeposited receipts, if there are any, will be shown separately in the report. The report can be sorted by any of the column headings.

5. **Double click**   **any detail** to view the original transaction

6. **Close**   the **report** when you have finished viewing it

The Cheque Detail Report

The Cheque Detail report includes a list of all cheques written from bank accounts during the selected period and the vendors and accounts involved in the payment. General Journal transactions that involve the Bank accounts are also listed.

1. **Click**   the **Run icon** under the Cheque Detail report under the Banking heading

2. **Type**   **10/01/14** in the **From date field**

3. **Type**   **10/31/14** in the **To date field**

4. **Press**   `tab` or **click** the **Refresh button** to view the report:

Notes

To access the report from the Reports menu:
- Choose the Reports menu, then choose Banking and click Cheque Detail to open the report
- Enter 10/01/14 in the From date
- Enter 10/31/14 in the To date
- Press `tab` or click the Refresh button to update the report

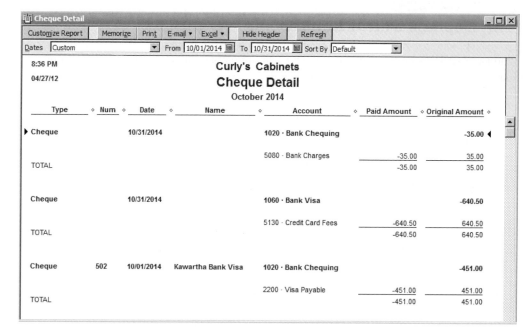

Figure 8-60

You can sort the report by any of the column headings. Double click any detail to view the original transaction.

5. Close the **report** when you have finished viewing it

The Missing Cheques Report

The Missing Cheques report includes a list of all cheques written from the selected bank account so you can see whether a cheque number is missing from the sequence.

1. Click the **Run icon** ⟳ under the Missing Cheques report

2. Click the **drop-down arrow** beside the **Specify Account field** to view the accounts available for selection:

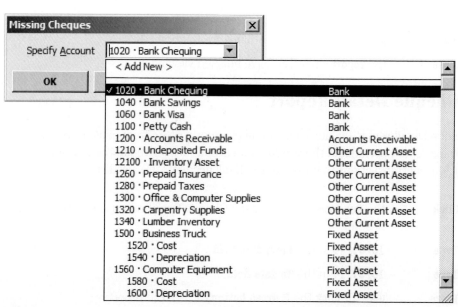

Notes
To access the report from the Reports menu:
• Choose the Reports menu, then choose Banking, and click Missing Cheques
• Select the account from the drop-down list and click OK

Figure 8-61

All bank and asset accounts are available for selection.

Reports are created for each account separately because each account has its own numbering sequence. Select the account from the drop-down list for which you want to view the report. The account we want — *1020 - Bank Chequing* — is already selected so we can continue.

3. Click   **1020 - Bank Chequing**

4. Click   **OK** to view the report:

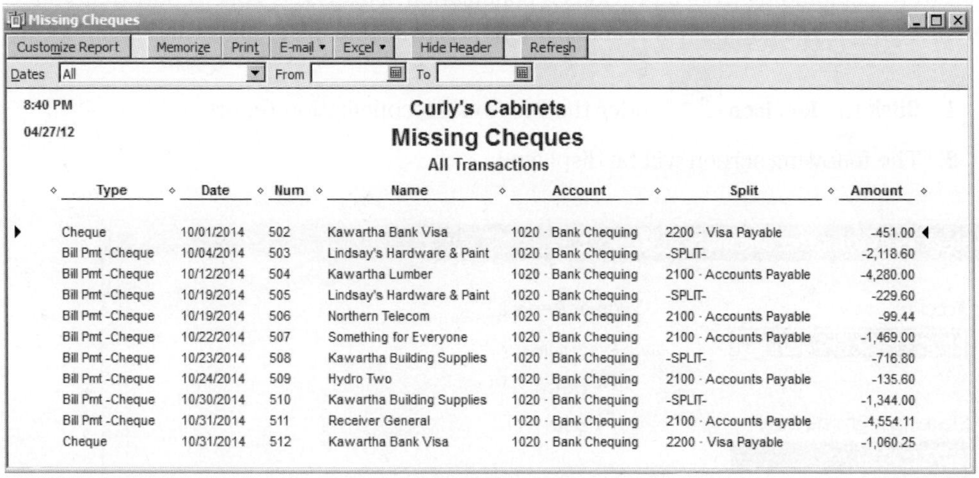

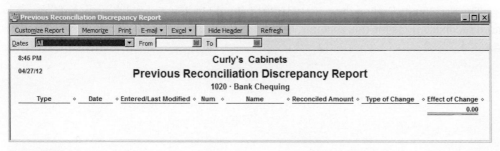

Figure 8-62

All the details you need to trace a cheque are included on the Missing Cheques report: type of transaction, date, cheque number, payee, invoice number (provided you entered the invoice number in the memo field on the payment form), account, other accounts involved, and the cheque amount. If more than one account was involved with the transaction, SPLIT appears in the Split column.

5. Double click   any **detail line** to drill down to the original transaction

6. Close   the **report** when you have finished viewing it

The Reconcile Discrepancy Report

The Reconcile Discrepancy report lists reconciled transactions that have been modified since the account was last reconciled.

1. Click   the **Run icon** [Run] under the Reconciliation Discrepancy report

2. Select   **1020 - Bank Chequing** and **click OK**

3. The Previous Reconciliation Discrepancy report will be displayed as shown:

Notes
To access the report from the Reports menu:
• Choose the Reports menu, then choose Banking and click Reconciliation Discrepancy to open the account selection window

Notes
You can enter a range of dates for the report or you can choose to show modified transactions for all periods.

Figure 8-63

The report has no data because no changes were made to reconciled transactions. The column headings give you a good idea of the report's purpose.

4. Close the **report window** when you have finished viewing it

The Previous Reconciliation Report

The Previous Reconciliation report shows you what transactions were cleared or which ones were outstanding from a previous reconciliation. This is the same report that you can print when you complete a reconciliation. It is available in summary and detail form.

📄 **Notes**
To access the report from the Reports menu:
 • Choose the Reports menu, then choose Banking, and click Previous Reconciliation to open the account selection window

1. Click the **Run icon** ⊙ Run under the Previous Reconciliation report

2. The following screen will be displayed:

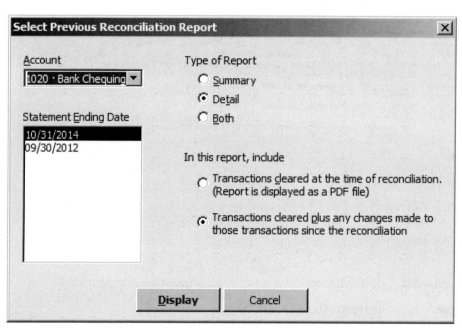

Figure 8-64

For each account selected, you can choose to print the summary or detail report or both. You can include only the transactions that were cleared at the time of reconciliation or include transactions cleared at the time of reconciliation plus any changes made to those transactions since the reconciliation (the default selection).

3. Choose **1020 - Bank Chequing** in the **Account field**

4. Choose **Summary** as the type of report and leave the final selection to include transactions and changes

The Statement Ending date of 10/31/2014 should be highlighted. As you perform more reconciliations for this account, they will also be available for selection.

5. **Click**   **Display** to continue

6. **Click**   **OK** to close the Reconciliation Report window after reading it to
                 display the Reconciliation Summary report:

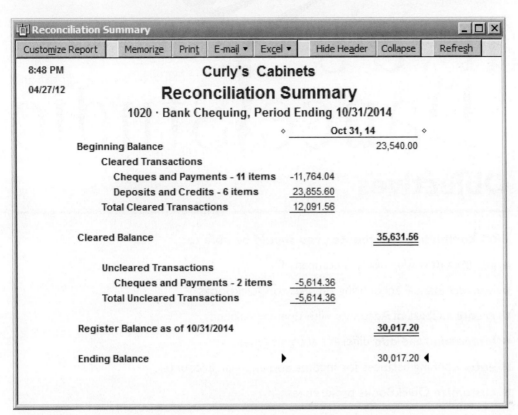

Figure 8-65

The Summary report shows the total amount of cleared transactions for both
cheques and deposits, the total of uncleared transactions, and the ending balance.

The Reconciliation Detail report shows the individual transactions that make up the
totals on the Summary report.

7. **Double click**   the **ending balance amount** on the Summary report to drill down to
                      the Detail report

8. **Double click**   **any detail on the Detail report** to drill down to the original transaction

9. **Close**   all **open reports** when you have finished viewing them

Finishing Your Session

1. **Back up**   the **company data file**

2. **Close**   the **Company file**

3. **Close**   the **QuickBooks program**

CHAPTER NINE

Darya's Dance Studio

Objectives

After completing this chapter, you should be able to:

- **set up** a new QuickBooks company file
- **convert** manual accounting records to QuickBooks
- **create** a Chart of Accounts with opening balances
- **understand** and **add** different account types
- **enter** opening balances for income and expense accounts
- **customize** QuickBooks preferences
- **create** customer records with opening balances
- **create** vendor records with opening balances
- **understand** and **add** different types of items
- **set up** and **edit** terms for vendors and customers
- **set up** finance charges for customers

Company Information

Company Profile

Notes
Darya's Dance Studio
11 Nutcracker St.
Regina, SK S3G 2P6
Tel: (306) 224-8632
Fax: (306) 224-3918
E-mail: lessons@
daryasdance.com
Web: www.daryasdance.
com
Business No.: 577 499 299

Darya's Dance Studio in Regina, Saskatchewan, is owned and operated by Darya Danovich. Darya retired from professional dancing several years ago and has been teaching ever since. Now she runs a variety of dance classes for all ages, as well as general stretch and conditioning classes. Darya offers classical ballroom, basic ballet, and jazz dance classes, so they attract single adults, couples, and children. Sometimes entire families enroll for the different classes.

Most students enroll in 15-week program sessions, and many attend more than one class per week. The stretch and conditioning classes are available on a drop-in or pay-as-you-go basis. Those students who register and pay for three classes per week may attend as many additional classes as they want.

Members of a family who enroll for several sessions can set up accounts with Darya's Studio. Groups requesting custom-designed programs can also set up accounts. For example, Darya taught dance routines to gymnastics students and provided coordination and balance training to Olympic athletes to promote teamwork. She also designs special short programs for schools.

The Studio accepts cash, cheques, and credit cards in payment. For purchases, Darya has a business credit card and accounts set up with some vendors.

Darya owns a studio, piano, and sound system. Her studio consists of two classrooms and two change rooms with washrooms — one for men and one for women. The instructors are paid monthly by cheque according to their contracts for the number of classes they teach. They are not on payroll so there are no payroll deductions. The pianist is also paid on a contractual basis. Most classes use live music to teach the basic dance steps but also rely on recordings for longer routines and some performances. Darya herself withdraws money from the business periodically in lieu of a regular salary.

Customers pay 5 percent GST for all classes, but PST is not applied to the services offered by the Studio. Darya's Dance Studio pays both PST and GST on all business-related purchases.

No classes are held in August, though some students have already enrolled for the session beginning in September. August is used to plan for the coming year and to close the business records for the previous fiscal period. At the end of August 2014, the following information is available for converting the accounting records to QuickBooks:

- Chart of Accounts
- Trial Balance
- Vendor Information
- Customer Information
- Item List
- Accounting Procedures

Notes
The *Undeposited Funds* account is automatically created by QuickBooks the first time you enter a customer payment or sales receipt.

Notes
The *Retained Earnings* account will be created by QuickBooks at the beginning of the next fiscal year, when QuickBooks automatically transfers income and expense account balances into the *Retained Earnings* account.

Notes
The *Estimates* and *Purchase Orders* accounts are holding accounts that are automatically created by QuickBooks the first time you enter an estimate or a purchase order, respectively.

Chart of Accounts

Darya's Dance Studio

ASSETS
Bank
  1050 Bank - Chequing
  1080 Bank - Savings
  1100 Bank - Credit Card
Accounts Receivable
  1200 Accounts Receivable
Other Current Assets
  1260 Music Inventory
  1280 Prepaid Insurance
  1300 Office & Computer Supplies
  1450 Undeposited Funds
Fixed Assets
  1500 Computers [P]
  1520 Computers:Cost [S]
  1540 Computers:Depreciation [S]
  1560 Piano [P]
  1580 Piano:Cost [S]
  1600 Piano:Depreciation [S]

  1620 Stereo Equipment [P]
  1640 Stereo Equipment:Cost [S]
  1660 Stereo Equipment:
    Depreciation [S]
  1700 Studio [P]
  1720 Studio:Cost [S]
  1740 Studio:Depreciation [S]
  1760 Vehicle [P]
  1780 Vehicle:Cost [S]
  1800 Vehicle:Depreciation [S]

LIABILITIES
Accounts Payable
  2100 Accounts Payable
Credit Card
  2150 Visa Payable
Other Current Liabilities
  2260 Bank Loan
  2460 GST/HST Payable

Long Term Liabilities
  2720 Long Term Loan
  2740 Mortgage Payable

EQUITY
  3200 Capital, Darya Danovich
  3260 Drawings, Darya Danovich
  3400 Retained Earnings

INCOME
  4100 Revenue from Lessons
  4160 Sales Discounts
  4200 Revenue from Interest
  4250 Other Revenue

EXPENSE
  5020 Advertising & Promotion
  5060 Office & Computer Supplies
    Used
  5080 Music Inventory Expenses

  5100 Depreciation Expense
  5120 Maintenance Expenses
  5140 Insurance Expense
  5160 Interest Expense
  5180 Printing & Copying
  5200 Property Tax Expense
  5220 Purchase Discounts
  5240 Hydro Expense
  5260 Telephone Expense
  5280 Vehicle Expenses
  5300 Wages Expenses
Non-posting Accounts
  6000 Estimates
  6050 Purchase Orders

[P] Parent account
[S] Subaccount

Darya's Dance Studio

AS AT AUGUST 31, 2014

	Debits	Credits			Debits	Credits
1050 Bank - Chequing	$ 8,860.00			2720 Long Term Loan		$ 22,000.00
1080 Bank - Savings	14,900.00			2740 Mortgage Payable		30,000.00
1100 Bank - Credit Card	6,400.00			3200 Capital, Darya Danovich		96,165.00
1200 Accounts Receivable	1,445.00			3260 Drawings, Darya Danovich	$ 7,400.00	
1260 Music Inventory	1,460.00			4100 Revenue from Lessons		3,800.00
1280 Prepaid Insurance	4,500.00			4160 Sales Discounts	30.00	
1300 Office & Computer Supplies	480.00			4200 Revenue from Interest		20.00
1520 Computers:Cost	4,500.00			5020 Advertising & Promotion	2,100.00	
1540 Computers:Depreciation		$ 1,820.00		5060 Office & Computer Supplies Used	185.00	
1580 Piano:Cost	10,000.00			5080 Music Inventory Expenses	45.00	
1600 Piano:Depreciation		1,450.00		5100 Depreciation Expense	1,000.00	
1640 Stereo Equipment:Cost	6,000.00			5120 Maintenance Expenses	220.00	
1660 Stereo Equipment:Depreciation		2,430.00		5140 Insurance Expense	3,250.00	
1720 Studio:Cost	90,000.00			5160 Interest Expense	420.00	
1740 Studio:Depreciation		6,000.00		5180 Printing & Copying	560.00	
1780 Vehicle:Cost	24,000.00			5200 Property Tax Expense	120.00	
1800 Vehicle:Depreciation		9,720.00		5220 Purchase Discounts		95.00
2100 Accounts Payable		1,455.00		5240 Hydro Expense	85.00	
2150 Visa Payable		875.00		5260 Telephone Expense	120.00	
2260 Bank Loan		11,500.00		5280 Vehicle Expenses	240.00	
2460 GST/HST Payable		990.00			$188,320.00	$188,320.00

Darya's Dance Studio

Vendor Name (Contact or Alternate)	Address	Phone No. Fax No.	E-mail Business No.	Terms Credit Limit
Foley's (Jane Foley or Robin)	122 Baryshnikov St. Regina, SK S3P 7N5	Tel: (306) 224-4632 Fax: (306) 225-6722	JF @ foleys.com 398446722	1/5 n/30 $300.00
Fox Trotte, Instructor T4A eligible	18 Tango Circle Regina, SK S3K 4T2	Tel: (306) 238-4916	FTrotte @ hotmail.com	due on receipt
Mimi Pascoe, Pianist T4A eligible	88 Keyes Blvd. Regina, SK S4N 2H5	Tel: (306) 296-2991	mpascoe @ yahoo.ca	due on receipt
Prairie Energy Corp. (Business Accounts Dept.)	55 Windmill Rd. Regina, SK S3V 4C2	Tel: (306) 229-5166 Fax: (306) 229-6019	accounts @ pec.sk.ca	net 10 $500.00
Prime Contacts (Tokk Toomee)	200 Cellular Way Regina, SK S2S 4G4	Tel: (306) 278-7835 Fax: (306) 278-2815	toomee @ prime.ca	net 15 $500.00
Receiver General	4 Legislate Dr. Regina, SK S4B 3P5	Tel: (800) 959-2019		quarterly reports
Sounds Inc. (Dylan or Bob)	69 Acoustic Rd. Regina, SK S2R 1B7	Tel: (306) 257-4994 Fax: (306) 257-5181	dylan @ sounds.com 277344598	2/10, n/30 $1,000.00
Treble & Bass (Ken Fiddler)	5 Kettledrum Way Regina, SK S3F 6K8	Tel: (306) 256-6388 Fax: (306) 255-7188	fiddler @ treble&bass.com 471639672	1/10, n/30 $5,000.00
Wendy Groen, RMT	100 Healer St. Regina, SK S3K 7C5	Tel: (306) 277-3997	w.groen @ sympatico.ca	net 10 $500.00

Vendor Opening Balances

Darya's Dance Studio

Vendor Name	Ref #	Date	Terms	Due Date	Opening Balance
Foley's	F-445	Aug. 28/14	1/5, n/10	Sep. 9/14	$115.00
Sounds Inc.	SI-390	Aug. 24/14	2/10, n/30	Sep. 23/14	$510.00
Treble & Bass	TB-2918	Aug. 29/14	1/10, n/30	Sep. 28/14	$380.00
Wendy Groen, RMT	WG-103	Aug. 25/14	net 10	Sep. 4/14	$450.00
				Grand Total	$1,455.00

Customer Information

Darya's Dance Studio

Customer Name (Contact)	Address	Phone No. Fax No.	E-mail Preferred Payment Method	Terms Credit Limit
Canadian Sledders (Pers Johansson)	189 Bobsled Hill Rd. Regina, SK S3T 7E8	Tel: (306) 299-8644 Fax: (306) 298-6219	thefastest@yahoo.ca Cheque	1/10, n/30 $2,000.00
Minuet Family (Ron or Lynda)	2 Steppe Rd. Regina, SK S3R 3W1	Tel: (306) 246-5643	r.minuet@shaw.ca Cheque	1/10, n/30 $2,000.00
Saskie Gliders (Korinne)	42 Skaters Ave. Regina, SK S4B 2C8	Tel: (306) 341-7299 Fax: (306) 342-2915	korinne@gliders.com Cheque	1/10, n/30 $8,000.00
Waltzer Family (Lee)	3 Fourtime Cr. Regina, SK S3M 4B9	Tel: (306) 284-3882 Fax: (306) 284-4290	lee.w.57@hotmail.com Cheque	1/10, n/30 $2,000.00
Wheatfields Academy (F. Astaire)	90 Granery Rd. Regina, SK S4C 5F7	Tel: (306) 248-1920 Fax: (306) 246-4837	fastaire@wheatfields.ca Cheque	1/10, n/30 $9,000.00
Cash Sales			Cash	due on receipt
Visa Sales			Visa	due on receipt

Customer Opening Balances

Darya's Dance Studio

Customer Name	Ref #	Date	Terms	Due Date	Opening Balance
Canadian Sledders	—	Aug. 10/14	1/10, n/30	Sep. 20/14	$400.00
Minuet Family	Inv#92	Aug. 5/14	1/10, n/30	Sep. 4/14	$310.00
Saskie Gliders	Inv#102	Aug. 29/14	1/10, n/30	Sep. 28/14	$735.00
				Grand Total	$1,445.00

Darya's Dance Studio

Item	Description	Price	Tax Code	Account
Service Items				
Class - Single	Single dance or exercise class	$ 25.00	G	4100 Revenue from Lessons
Classes - Month	One month of classes	75.00	G	4100 Revenue from Lessons
Classes - Session	Four month seasonal session	220.00	G	4100 Revenue from Lessons
Non-inventory Part Items				
Music Inventory	CDs and sheet music	varies	S	1260 Music Inventory
Supplies	Office and computer supplies	varies	S	1300 Office & Computer Supplies
Other Charge Items				
Admin Charge	Handling charge for NSF cheque	$30.00		4250 Other Revenue
NSF Cheque	Amount of NSF Cheque	varies		1050 Bank - Chequing
Finance Charge	Interest Charges on Overdue Balance	15%		4200 Revenue from Interest
(enter from Preferences)	over 30 days, 5 days' grace, $10.00 minimum			

Accounting Procedures

Taxes: GST and PST

Notes
Refer to the Tax Appendix (found on the CD that accompanies this text) for details on sales taxes.

Darya's Dance Studio pays 5 percent GST and 5 percent PST on all goods and services that it buys, and charges GST on all lessons. PST is not charged on any of the lessons offered by Darya's Dance Studio. The business uses the regular method for remittance of the Goods and Services Tax. GST collected from customers is recorded as a liability in the *GST/HST Payable* account. GST paid to vendors is recorded in the *GST/HST Payable* account as a decrease in liability to the Canada Revenue Agency. The report is filed with the Receiver General for Canada by the last day of the month for the previous quarter, either including the balance owing or requesting a refund.

Account Terms

Notes
A five-day grace period becomes 35 days past the invoice date before charges are assessed.

Account customers (families and groups) receive a discount of 1 percent if they settle their accounts within 10 days after signing up for classes. The full balance is required within 30 days of the start of classes. Individual students pay in full at the start of a session or individual class. Finance charges are applied to overdue accounts at 15 percent per year starting after the due date, but there is a five-day grace period before interest charges are applied. A minimum charge of $10.00 applies to overdue accounts to cover administration costs. Some vendors also offer discounts for early payment.

Deposits and Cheques

All cheques, credit card payments, and cash are held for deposit. Cheques are hand printed at the time of the transaction.

Estimates, Orders, and Prepayments

Estimates are provided for custom-designed programs. When customers decide to proceed with these classes, they pay a 50 percent deposit. Darya's Dance Studio also places purchase orders with regular suppliers who may require deposits.

Account Numbers

Darya's Dance Studio uses account numbers for all accounts.

Instructions

1. Using the Chart of Accounts, the Trial Balance, and other information, set up the company files for Darya's Dance Studio. Detailed keystroke instructions for the setup follow.

2. After completing the setup, record entries for the source documents for September 2014 in QuickBooks. The source documents begin on page 517, following the instructions for setup.

3. After you have finished making your entries, print the reports and graphs for September 2014 indicated on the following printing form:

REPORTS FOR SEPTEMBER 2014

Lists
- ☐ Account Listing
- ☐ Customer Phone List
- ☐ Customer Contact List
- ☐ Vendor Phone List
- ☐ Vendor Contact List
- ☐ Item Listing
- ☐ Item Price List
- ☐ Tax Code
- ☐ Terms List

Company & Financial
- ☑ Balance Sheet Standard at Sep. 30
- ☑ Profit & Loss Standard from Sep. 01 to Sep. 30
- ☐ Expenses by Vendor
- ☐ Income by Customer

Accountant & Taxes
- ☑ Trial Balance at Sep. 30
- ☐ General Ledger
- ☑ Journal from Sep. 01 to Sep. 30

- ☐ Transaction List by Date
- ☐ Transaction Detail by Account

Other
- ☐ Custom Summary Report
- ☐ Custom Transaction Detail Report
- ☐ Transaction History
- ☐ Transaction Journal

Vendor
- ☑ A/P Aging Detail at Sep. 30
- ☐ Vendor Balance
- ☐ Unpaid Bills
- ☐ Transaction List by Vendor

Purchases
- ☐ Purchases by Vendor
- ☐ Purchases by Item
- ☐ Transaction List by Vendor
- ☐ Open Purchase Orders by Vendor

Customer
- ☑ A/R Aging Detail at Sep 30
- ☐ Customer Balance

- ☐ Open Invoices
- ☐ Collections Report
- ☐ Transaction List by Customer

Sales
- ☐ Sales by Customer
- ☐ Sales by Item
- ☐ Open Sales Orders by Customer

Banking
- ☐ Deposit Detail
- ☐ Cheque Detail
- ☑ Missing Cheques for 1050
- ☐ Reconcile Discrepancy
- ☐ Previous Reconciliation

GRAPHS
- ☐ Income and Expense
- ☐ Net Worth
- ☐ Accounts Payable
- ☐ Accounts Receivable
- ☐ Sales

Creating a New Company

We will create a set of files from scratch for Darya's Dance Studio rather than use the EasyStep Interview. We will review the setup steps from Chapter 4 as we use them in the setup and provide complete detail for any aspects that are new.

Refer to the setup instructions in Chapter 4 for more details and to review any of the setup steps.

If you would prefer to skip the setup of this company file and work through the source documents only, open the Darya file in the Setup folder on the CD. The source documents begin on page 517.

1. **Start** the **QuickBooks program**

2. **Choose** the **File menu** and **click Close Company**

The files you worked with most recently are displayed in the **No Company Open window**. We need to select the option to create a new company.

3. **Click**   the **Create a new company button** or **choose** the **File menu** and **click New Company**

The QuickBooks Setup screen appears:

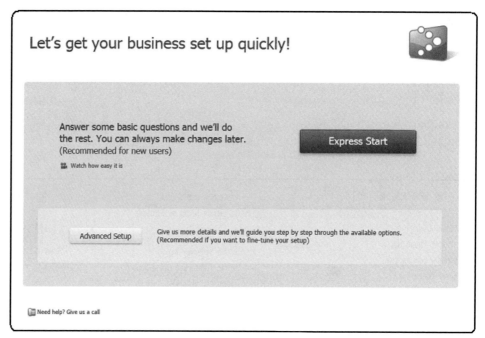

Let's get your business set up quickly!

Answer some basic questions and we'll do the rest. You can always make changes later. (Recommended for new users)

Watch how easy it is

Express Start

Advanced Setup   Give us more details and we'll guide you step by step through the available options. (Recommended if you want to fine-tune your setup)

Need help? Give us a call

Figure 9-1

We will select the Express Start button to create our company file and enter the information required to create our company. After we create the company file, we will begin the manual setup process.

4. **Click**   **Express Start** to begin the setup of the company file and to open the Company Information window

The cursor is in the Company Name field.

5. **Type**   **Darya's Dance Studio**

6. **Press**   ⟨tab⟩ to advance to the Industry field

7. **Click**   the **Help me choose link** to the right of the Industry field

8. **Select**   **Other/None** as the industry (you will have to scroll down to the bottom of the list)

9. **Click**   **OK**

10. **Press**   ⟨tab⟩ to advance to the Company Type field

11. **Click**   the **drop-down arrow** in the field

12. **Select**   **Sole Proprietorship**

13. The completed screen should be displayed as shown here:

WARNING! You cannot change the type of industry so you must choose carefully.

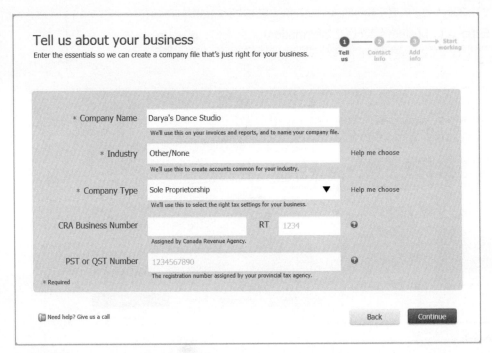

Tell us about your business
Enter the essentials so we can create a company file that's just right for your business.

① — ② — ③ — → Start
Tell   Contact   Add   working
us   info   info

* Company Name	Darya's Dance Studio
	We'll use this on your invoices and reports, and to name your company file.
* Industry	Other/None Help me choose
	We'll use this to create accounts common for your industry.
* Company Type	Sole Proprietorship ▼ Help me choose
	We'll use this to select the right tax settings for your business.
CRA Business Number	RT 1234 ⊘
	Assigned by Canada Revenue Agency.
PST or QST Number	1234567890 ⊘
	The registration number assigned by your provincial tax agency.

* Required

🖳 Need help? Give us a call   Back   Continue

Figure 9-2

14. Click   **Continue** to advance to the next screen

The name entered in the Company Name field on the previous screen has automatically been entered in the Legal Name field. We will accept the name entered as the legal name for the company.

15. Press   `tab` to advance to the first line of the Address field

16. Type   **11 Nutcracker St.**

17. Press   `tab` to advance to the City field

18. Type   **Regina**

19. Press   `tab` to advance to the Province field

20. Click   on the **drop-down arrow** in the **Province field** and **select SK**

21. Press   `tab` to advance to the Postal Code field and **type S3G 2P6**

22. Press   `tab` to advance to the Country field and **accept Canada**

23. Press   `tab` to advance to the Phone field and **type (306) 224-8632**

24. Press   `tab` to advance to the Email address field

25. Type   **lessons@daryasdance.com**

26. Press   `tab` to advance to the Website field

27. Type   **www.daryasdance.com**

28. The completed screen should be displayed as shown here:

> **Notes**
> You can also enter or edit company information after creating the company file by choosing the Company menu and clicking Company Information.

> **Notes**
> You must format the phone and fax numbers in these fields the way you want them to appear in QuickBooks.

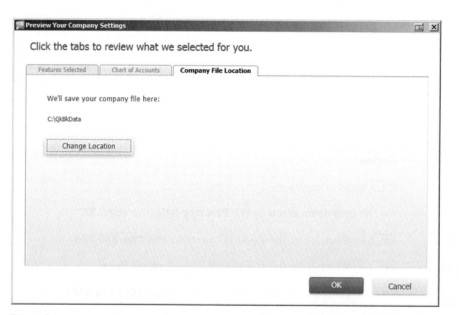

Enter your business contact information

Once you enter your contact information, you're ready to create your company file.

| ① Tell us | — ② Contact info | — ③ Add info | ⋯→ Start working |

Legal Name Darya's Dance Studio   ❷

Address 11 Nutracker St.

City Regina

* Province SK ▼   Postal Code S3G 2P6

Country Canada ▼

Phone (306) 224-8632

Email lessons@daryasdance.com

Website www.daryasdance.com

* Required

Enter basic contact information so you can instantly print and email invoices and other forms to your customers and vendors.

[Back]   [Preview Your Settings]   [Create Company File]

Figure 9-3

29. Click the **Preview Your Settings button** on the bottom of the screen

30. Click the **Company File Location tab** to display it on the screen

Preview Your Company Settings   ▫ ✕

Click the tabs to review what we selected for you.

| Features Selected | Chart of Accounts | **Company File Location** |

We'll save your company file here:

C:\QkBkData

[Change Location]

[OK]   [Cancel]

Figure 9-4

This tab displays the drive and folder where the company file will be saved when you create the company file. The file selected on your screen will likely be different than the one displayed on the print screen. If you want to save the file to a different location, click the Change Location button and select the appropriate drive and folder.

31. Click **OK** when you have selected the appropriate drive and folder

32. Click the **Create Company File**

A QuickBooks Setup screen is displayed with access to various functions in QuickBooks. We will use the menus to enter our information so you will close this screen.

33. Click the **Start Working button**

34. Click to close the Quick Start Centre

35. The Home page is displayed, and the Live Community and Help tab opens by default

QuickBooks has created the new company file with some default settings that control how the program works; a preliminary set of taxes and codes for the province you selected for the business; and a set of payment terms, payment methods, and messages. The Chart of Accounts includes only some basic QuickBooks accounts. We will modify these defaults or preferences to suit Darya's Dance Studio. Then we will create the Chart of Accounts, the vendor and customer records, and the list of items. We also need to add historical information for accounts, customers, and vendors to create the opening balances for accounts and the outstanding balances for vendors and customers.

Setting Preferences

One of the first steps in setting up a new company file is the creation of new accounts. However, before we can create the new accounts, we should select some preferences that will influence how the accounts are set up.

Other preferences include choosing default accounts, such as the accounts used for writing cheques or entering discounts and finance charges. We will set these preferences after creating the Chart of Accounts.

Refer to the sections in Chapter 4 beginning on pages 151, 175, and 196 to review QuickBooks Preferences.

1. Choose the **Edit menu** and **click Preferences**

2. Click the **Help button** to update the information displayed in the Help tab

By default, the Preferences window opens at the My Preferences tab for General Preferences the first time you open it.

The General Preferences do not affect the financial aspects of the program, so you should decide how you want to interact with the program by choosing your settings. In our data files we have used the default settings for all QuickBooks preferences except the beep for entering transactions. We have turned that preference off so your computer doesn't beep every time a transaction is recorded.

3. Click the **Company Preferences tab** (for the General Preferences)

The preferences on this tab affect the date and time formats used in the company file. You can accept the default settings for dates. You can also decide whether changes you make to customer or vendor information in transactions will update the customer or vendor records permanently, and whether transactions should be saved before they are printed.

We will accept the default settings for the preferences on this tab.

4. Click the **Desktop View preferences** to view the Desktop View preferences

The settings on the Company Preferences tab allow you to select which features you use in QuickBooks. Depending on the features you select, the icons will be displayed on the Home page.

5. Click the **My Preferences tab**

You may select your own preferences to control the appearance of open windows in QuickBooks.

6. Click the **Payroll & Employees heading** to view the Payroll preferences

7. Click the **Company Preferences tab**

The preferences on the Company Preferences tab allow you to turn payroll on or off (assuming you have subscribed to QuickBooks payroll), and then set various payroll

Notes
Remember that most preference settings can be changed at any time.

With the Preferences screen displayed, click Help to view explanations of each set of preferences.

You can leave the Help tab open until you have finished setting all preferences. Just click Help again after you choose a different preference heading to update the information on the Help tab.

⚠ WARNING!
Do not turn off the Warn when deleting a transaction or unused list item preference.

Notes
If you make changes to any of the QuickBooks preferences, you will be prompted to save your changes when you move to the next preference heading.

preferences. The QuickBooks student software includes payroll, so we will turn it off for this company file.

8.	**Select**	**No payroll**
9.	**Click**	the **Reminders preference heading** to view the Reminders preferences
10.	**Click**	**Yes** to save the Payroll & Employees preferences
11.	**Click**	**OK** when prompted with the message that QuickBooks must close all its open windows to change this preference

On the My Preferences tab in the Reminders preferences, you can select to show the Reminders List when opening the company file.

12.	**Click**	the **Company Preferences tab**

If you use reminders in the program, you should choose to show them and then indicate how you want to show them and how many days before the item is due that the reminder should be displayed on the Reminders List. We have not changed these settings for any of our data files. Use the Help button to provide more detail if needed.

13.	**Click**	the **Reports & Graphs heading** to view the Reports & Graphs preferences
14.	**Click**	**Yes** if you made any changes to the Reminders preferences and want to save them

The Company Preferences tab should be displayed.

15.	**Click**	the **Age From Transaction Date** under the Aging Reports heading to select it
16.	**Click**	the **My Preferences tab**
17.	**Choose**	the **Reports & Graphs options** you want for your data file on this tab
18.	**Click**	the **Spelling preference heading** to view the Spelling preferences
19.	**Click**	**Yes** to save the changes you made to the Reports & Graphs preferences

The My Preferences tab should be displayed.

20.	**Choose**	the **Spelling options** you want for your company data file

Before we create the accounts for the data file, we should define the accounting preference settings.

Changing Accounting Preferences

Preferences on the Company Preferences tab for all QuickBooks preferences can only be changed by the Administrator of the company file or by a user set up as an External Accountant. Other users cannot change these settings. If the file has only one user, then that user is the Administrator.

Most of the Accounting preferences are found on the Company Preferences tab for the Accounting preference, which means that only the Administrator or a user set up as an External Accountant can change the accounting preferences.

1.	**Click**	the **Accounting heading** to view the Accounting preferences
2.	**Click**	**Yes** to save any changes you made to the Spelling preferences

On the My Preferences tab, you can select to autofill the memo field in general journal entries. This means that when you enter general journal entries, the memo that you enter on the first line of the transaction will automatically be displayed for all other transaction lines in the journal entry.

3.	**Click**	the **Company Preferences tab**:

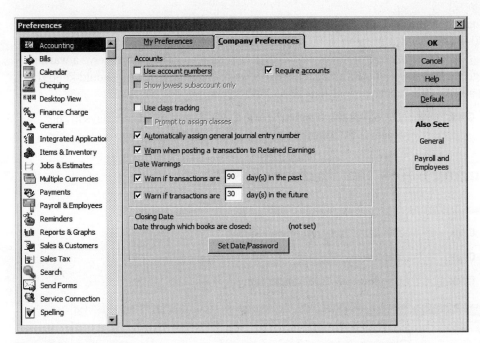

Figure 9-5

One preference that affects accounts is the option to use account numbers. In some of our earlier applications, we did not use account numbers and accounts were listed in alphabetic order within their account type. When account numbers are used, the accounts are listed in numerical order within their account type. Although you can use any numbering system you want, it is best to use a logical sequence of account numbers. We will use the following numbering sequence for accounts:

- 1000–1999 Assets
- 2000–2999 Liabilities
- 3000–3999 Equity
- 4000–4999 Income
- 5000–5999 Expense

Notes
This numbering sequence is consistent with the GIFI codes used by CRA for online tax reporting by companies.

The default account setting is not to use account numbers, but Darya's Dance Studio uses account numbers. By changing this setting before we create accounts, we can add numbers at the start instead of editing all accounts later to add the numbers.

4. Click   Use account numbers

We will show all accounts — parent accounts as well as subaccounts — so that we can easily select the correct account when names are similar; therefore, we want to leave the Show lowest subaccount only preference turned off. For example, *Depreciation* applies to more than one fixed asset account. When we display a depreciation account, we want to see which fixed asset account it belongs to. The only way to see this is to leave the Show lowest subaccount only option turned off. If we turn this option on, we would only see the depreciation account and may select the wrong one.

We will leave the Require accounts preference selected so that a transaction won't be recorded unless it has been assigned to an account. If we turn this preference off and do not enter an account during transaction entry, QuickBooks will automatically assign the transactions to the *Uncategorized Income* account or the *Uncategorized Expense* account.

QuickBooks will automatically assign numbers to journal entries. You have the option to be warned when we post transactions to the *Retained Earnings* account and when transactions are entered 90 days in the past or 30 days in the future. The number of days entered in these fields can also be modified. When we are ready to close the books, we can add the closing date and password. The password for this field prevents unauthorized changes to historical records.

Notes
Journal entry numbers are not assigned to other types of transactions.

Since the transactions in this textbook are in the year 2014 and are likely more than 30 days in the future in relation to your current computer date, we will turn off the *Warn if transactions are 30 days in the future* option so we do not receive a warning message each time we enter a transaction. In a work environment, you should keep this option selected to ensure proper dates are entered on your transactions.

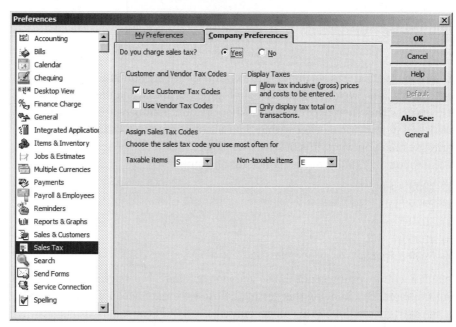

Figure 9-6

Most of the default settings are already correct. Darya's is registered for GST, so we must indicate that we charge sales taxes. The default selection for the Do you charge sales tax? preference should be set to "yes."

In the next section, you indicate whether you want to use customer and vendor tax codes. If you choose to use customer or vendor tax codes, a field will be available in each customer and vendor record, allowing you to select a tax code. If selected, QuickBooks will use the customer and vendor tax codes during transaction entry and they will override item tax codes. Tax codes can always be changed during transaction entry. Although we won't be using customer and vendor tax codes, we will leave the Use Customer Tax Codes preference selected so you can see the tax code field when setting up customers.

Customers pay GST on lessons, but no taxes on finance or NSF charges. In this scenario, it would be best to turn off the Use Customer Tax Codes preference and use the taxes assigned to items and not customers, since all items use the same tax code. However, we will leave the Use Customer Tax Codes preference selected so you can view the tax code field displayed in the customer records.

Under the Assign Sales Tax Codes heading, you enter the tax codes that you use most often for taxable and non-taxable items. These tax codes will be used as the default

Notes

If you are using this text in 2014 or later, turn off the Warn if transactions are 90 days in the past option.

5. **Click**   the **check box** beside the Warn if transactions are 30 days in the future preference to turn this preference off

Changing Sales Tax Preferences

Sales tax preferences are located on the Sales Tax Preferences screen.

1. **Click**   the **Sales Tax preference heading**

2. **Click**   **Yes** to save the Accounting Preferences changes

3. **Click**   the **Company Preferences tab**:

Notes

You might choose to apply customer tax codes for customers who are exempt from some taxes. Then the customer code will serve as the default instead of the item's code. You can always change the tax code selection on the invoice.

when setting up items and services. Taxable items are charged GST only and non-taxable items are tax exempt.

4. Leave the **checkmark** in the Use Customer Tax Codes box displayed in order to leave this preference selected

Although we won't be using customer sales tax codes, leave this preference selected to view the sales tax code field displayed in customer records.

5. Click the **drop-down arrow** in the **Taxable items field**

6. Click **G - GST Only** from the tax code list

For non-taxable items, E - Exempt is already selected and this is the tax code that we want to use by default for non-taxable items.

7. Click **OK** to save the changes

A grey screen should currently be displayed. This screen is displayed because while you changed preference settings, a message appeared indicating that QuickBooks must close all open QuickBooks windows. When you click OK to save and exit your preference changes, no QuickBooks windows are open and a grey screen is displayed.

8. Click the **Home icon** on the Icon bar to display the QuickBooks Home page

Notes
The next time you open the Preferences window, it will open on the tab of the preference heading that was displayed when you closed the Preferences window.

Entering the Company Business Number and Fiscal Year

The Company business number and fiscal year are entered on the Company Information screen.

1. Choose **Company** from the menu and **click Company Information**:

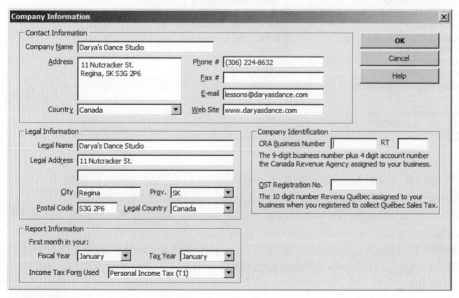

Figure 9-7

You can make the necessary changes to the information on this screen.

2. Click the **CRA Business Number field**

3. Type **577499299**

4. Click the **drop-down arrow** in the **Fiscal Year field**

5. Select **August**

6. Click the **drop-down arrow** in the **Tax Year field**

7. **Select**   **August**

8. **Click**   **OK** to accept the changes

9. **Click**   the **Continue Anyway button** when the Invalid Business Number message is displayed

Creating the Chart of Accounts

It is not necessary to enter all the required accounts in the Chart of Accounts before using QuickBooks on a daily basis because they can be created from any account field on the fly; however, we will create them first so that we can choose the default accounts for the other setup steps as they are needed. We can also monitor the creation of the accounts in a logical order when we set them up first.

In this chapter, we will show the New Account screens for the types of accounts and features that were not covered in Chapter 4. For a review of how to create new accounts, refer to page 158.

New accounts are created from the Chart of Accounts list.

1. **Click**   the **Chart of Accounts icon** in the Company section of the Home page to open the Chart of Accounts:

Figure 9-8

As you can see, some accounts are set up in the Chart of Accounts by default even though we selected Other/None as the industry during QuickBooks setup. We will use some of these default accounts, rename others, and delete or make other accounts inactive.

Also notice that each default account has been given an account number. These numbers do not match the account numbering system that we are using, so they will have to be modified.

2. **Click**   the **Account button** to view the list menu and **click New**, or **press** *ctrl* **+ N**

When you create accounts directly from the Chart of Accounts list, the account type for the new account is blank.

Entering Bank Accounts

1. **Select**   **Bank** as the account type and **click Continue** to display the Add New Account form:

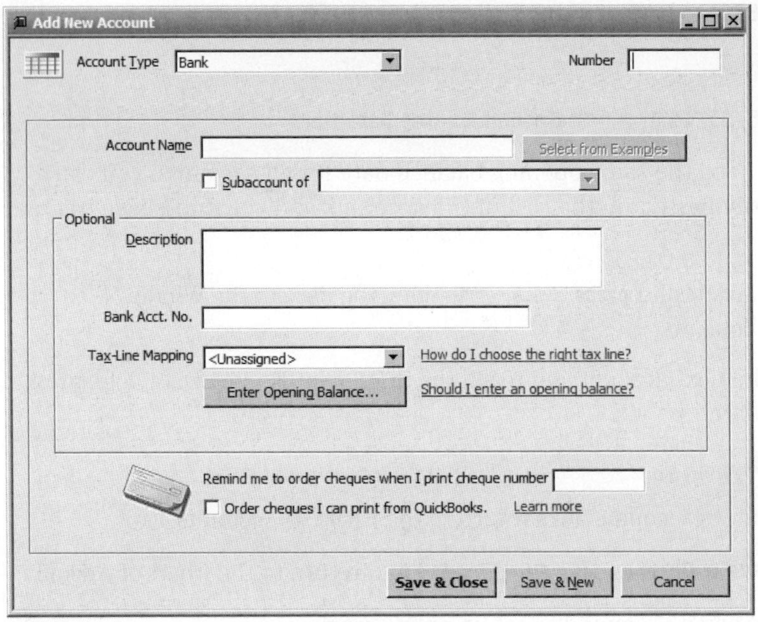

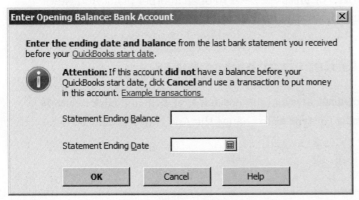

Figure 9-9

Because we chose to use account numbers, a Number field is added to all Account forms. The bank account is not a subaccount. We are not using online banking so we don't need to add the name of the bank and account number. We also are not using pre-printed cheques so we can leave those fields blank as well.

We need to add the opening account balance. We will enter the balance as of August 31, 2014, the day before we begin to use the program for current transactions. By using this opening date, we can produce complete reports for current entries beginning in September without including the historical transactions.

We need to enter three bank accounts:

Number	Name	Opening Balance	Date
1050	Bank - Chequing	$ 8,860.00	August 31/14
1080	Bank - Savings	14,900.00	August 31/14
1100	Bank - Credit Card	6,400.00	August 31/14

2. **Press**   (tab) or **click** the **Number field**

3. **Type**   **1050**

4. **Press**   (tab) to advance to the Account Name field

5. **Type**   **Bank - Chequing**

6. **Click**   the **Enter Opening Balance button** to display the Enter Opening Balance screen:

Notes
Remember that we cannot use colons in account names. Colons are reserved for subaccounts and are added automatically by the program.

Figure 9-10

7. **Type**   **8860** in the **Statement Ending Balance field**

8. **Press**   ⌊tab⌋

9. **Type**   **08/31/14** in the **Statement Ending Date field**

Because you will need the same opening balance date for all accounts, you can copy it so you can easily paste it in the rest of the accounts and you don't have to type it each time.

10. **Double click**   the **date** and **press** ⌊ctrl⌋ **+ C** to copy the date to the Windows Clipboard

When you enter the next account and reach the Statement Ending Date field, **press** ⌊ctrl⌋ **+ V** to paste the date.

11. **Click**   **OK**

Before we create more accounts, let's return to the Chart of Accounts.

12. **Click**   **Save & Close** to save the account and return to the Chart of Accounts

13. **Click**   **No** when prompted to set up online services

Notice that QuickBooks has created an *Opening Balance Equity* account. The account currently has a credit balance of $8,860.00 — the same amount as the *Bank Chequing* account. The *Opening Balance Equity* account is used as the offsetting account when setting up opening balances. We will rename this account later and make adjustments to the amount as needed.

We will continue adding the rest of the accounts in the Chart of Accounts.

14. **Press**   ⌊ctrl⌋ **+ N** to open the Add New Account form

If a message is displayed about pre-printed cheques, click Do not display this message in the future and click No (we are not using pre-printed cheques).

15. **Create**   the **Bank - Savings account.** Refer to the list on page 471.

16. **Click**   **Save & New** or **press** ⌊alt⌋ **+ N** to save the account and open a blank Add New Account form

The *Bank - Credit Card* account, used for deposits from customer credit card receipts, is also a bank account. Do not select the Credit Card account type for this account. The Credit Card account type applies to credit cards used by the business and creates a credit card payable account, a liability account. The Credit Card account type cannot be used for credit cards accepted in payment from customers.

17. **Enter**   the **Bank - Credit Card account.** Refer to the list on page 471.

18. **Click**   **Save & New** or **press** ⌊alt⌋ **+ N** to open another blank Add New Account form

Entering Accounts Receivable Accounts

📄 **Notes**
When you type a or A in the Type field, Accounts Receivable will be selected as the type because it is the next account type in the list whose initial letter is A. Accounts Payable appears later in the list so it would not be selected. If you type A again, or type A from an Accounts Receivable form, Accounts Payable will be displayed because it is the next type in the list that begins with the letter A.

Keyboard shortcuts are not case sensitive so you can type A or a.

1. **Click**   the **drop-down arrow** in the **Account Type field** and **click Accounts Receivable** (or **type a**) to change the Add New Account form:

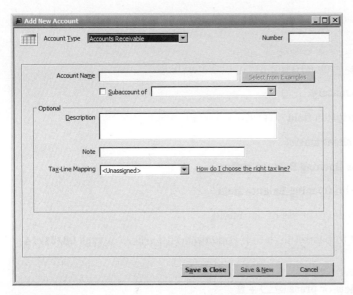

Figure 9-11

Notice that fields that apply to bank accounts are not displayed when Accounts Receivable is selected as the account type. The form does not have an Enter Opening Balance button because its balance is created automatically by QuickBooks as the sum of all amounts owed by customers. The balance is increased from the invoices and opening balances you enter for customers. Customer payments reduce the *Accounts Receivable* balance. We will enter these amounts when we create the customer records.

2. **Press**   `tab` to advance to the Number field

3. **Type**   **1200**. Press `tab` to advance to the Account Name field

4. **Type**   **Accounts Receivable**

5. **Click**   **Save & New** or **press** `alt` **+ N** to save the account and open a blank Add New Account form

Entering Other Current Asset Accounts

The next accounts are also current assets but they are neither bank nor accounts receivable accounts. This group is called Other Current Assets. When you clicked Save & New to open an Add New Account form, the previous account type you used remains selected as the default.

6. **Click**   the **drop-down arrow** in the **Account Type field** and **select Other Current Asset** as the account type (or **type o**) to change the Add New Account form

Fields that apply only to bank accounts are not included on the form when you select Other Current Asset as the account type, but the Enter Opening Balance button is available. The bank account number field remains because assets like treasury bills or investments are current assets that may be linked to a bank account.

For this group of accounts you must enter the account number, account name, opening balance, and date. The remaining fields, including the description, are optional.

The three other current asset accounts are listed here, with the descriptions in brackets:

Number	Name	Opening Balance	Date
1260	Music Inventory (CDs and sheet music)	$1,460.00	08/31/14
1280	Prepaid Insurance	4,500.00	08/31/14
1300	Office & Computer Supplies	480.00	08/31/14

> **Notes**
> Typing o will advance to the next account type on the list that begins with the letter o. In this case, if you start from Accounts Receivable, you will advance to Other Current Asset.

	7.	**Press**	(tab) to advance to the Number field
	8.	**Type**	**1260**
	9.	**Press**	(tab) to advance to the Account Name field
	10.	**Type**	**Music Inventory**
	11.	**Click**	the **Description field**
	12.	**Type**	**CDs and sheet music**
	13.	**Click**	the **Enter Opening Balance button**
	14.	**Type**	**1460** in the **Opening Balance field**
	15.	**Press**	(tab) to select the As of date field
	16.	**Press**	(ctrl) + **V** to paste the date if you copied it earlier (or **type 08/31/14**)
	17.	**Click**	**OK**
	18.	**Click**	**Save & New** or **press** (alt) + **N**

Enter the two Other Current Asset accounts and then click Save & New to open a blank Add New Account form.

Entering Fixed Asset Accounts

Darya's Dance Studio's fixed assets are grouped into parent (heading) and subaccounts for each type of asset. This structure allows us to view the net asset value or subaccount total (cost minus accumulated depreciation) in the parent account balance.

Other Current Asset is still selected as the type.

	1.	**Click**	the **drop-down arrow** in the **Account Type field** and **select Fixed Asset** as the account type (or **type f**) to change the Add New Account form

Fixed asset account forms also allow you to add a note.

For parent accounts, you must enter the account number and account name. For subaccounts you must enter the number, name, opening balance, and date; indicate that the account is a subaccount; and choose the parent account from the list. The other fields are optional. For parent accounts, the balance is calculated automatically by the program as the sum of its subaccount balances.

Depreciation accounts are contra-asset accounts. Their credit balances are entered as negative amounts, so they reduce the total asset value.

The complete list of fixed assets is displayed in the following chart:

No.	Name	Subaccount of	Description	Opening Balance	Date
1500	Computers	[Parent account]			
1520	Cost	1500 Computers	Original cost of computers	$4,500.00	08/31/14
1540	Depreciation	1500 Computers	Accum deprec on computers	−1,820.00	08/31/14
1560	Piano	[Parent account]			
1580	Cost	1560 Piano	Original cost of piano	$10,000.00	08/31/14
1600	Depreciation	1560 Piano	Accum deprec on piano	−1,450.00	08/31/14
1620	Stereo Equipment	[Parent account]			
1640	Cost	1620 Stereo Equipment	Original cost of stereo equip	$6,000.00	08/31/14
1660	Depreciation	1620 Stereo Equipment	Accum deprec on stereo equip	−2,430.00	08/31/14
1700	Studio	[Parent account]			
1720	Cost	1700 Studio	Original cost of studio	$90,000.00	08/31/14
1740	Depreciation	1700 Studio	Accum deprec on studio	−6,000.00	08/31/14
1760	Vehicle	[Parent account]			
1780	Cost	1760 Vehicle	Original cost of vehicle	$24,000.00	08/31/14
1800	Depreciation	1760 Vehicle	Accum deprec on vehicle	−9,720.00	08/31/14

Notes

You can also create items for fixed assets and enter the purchase date and cost to help track these assets. You can enter these special items when you purchase or order fixed assets.

Notes

The account type for a subaccount must be the same as the account type for its parent account.

2.	**Press**	(tab) to advance to the Number field
3.	**Type**	**1500**
4.	**Press**	(tab) to advance to the Account Name field
5.	**Type**	**Computers**

You do not need to define an account as a parent account. QuickBooks defines a parent account automatically when you identify a subaccount for it. QuickBooks also calculates its opening balance as the sum of all its subaccount balances.

6.	**Click**	**Save & New or press** (alt) **+ N**
7.	**Press**	(tab) to advance to the Number field
8.	**Type**	**1520**
9.	**Press**	(tab) to advance to the Account Name field
10.	**Type**	**Cost**
11.	**Click**	the **box** beside the Subaccount of field to display a ✓ in the box
12.	**Press**	(tab)
13.	**Click**	the **drop-down arrow** in the **Subaccount name field**
14.	**Choose**	account **1500 - Computers**
15.	**Press**	(tab) to advance to the Description field
16.	**Type**	**Original cost of computers**
17.	**Click**	the **Enter Opening Balance button**
18.	**Type**	**4500** in the **Opening Balance field**
19.	**Press**	(tab) to advance to the as of field
20.	**Press**	(ctrl) **+ V** to paste the date (or **type 08/31/14**)
21.	**Click**	**Save & New or press** (alt) **+ N**
22.	**Enter**	the **remaining Fixed Asset accounts** in the chart on page 474

Notes
QuickBooks has some helpful shortcuts on the Add New Account form. From the Name field, press (tab) to advance to the Subaccount field. Press the Space bar to select the subaccount option. The space bar will also toggle the subaccount option off. Press (tab) to move to the Subaccount name field. Type c — the first letter in the Computers account name and press (tab) to continue. Computers is the first account on the Chart of Accounts beginning with the letter c, so it is entered as the default. If it was not the first account on the Chart of Accounts beginning with the letter c, all accounts beginning with the letter c would be displayed where you can then highlight the account you want to use.

Depreciation accounts are contra-asset accounts with a credit balance that reduces the total asset value on the Balance Sheet. Therefore, you must enter negative opening balance amounts (add a minus sign) for these accounts.

Notes
Enter negative amounts for depreciation accounts by adding a minus sign in the Opening Balance field.

| 23. | **Click** | **Save & Close or press** (alt) **+ a** after adding account 1800 to save and close the Add New Accounts form and return to the Chart of Accounts |

We have now completed entering all of the assets accounts for Darya's Dance Studio.

Entering Liability Accounts

Liability accounts are the next group of accounts that we will enter. As with assets, there are several types of liability accounts. *Accounts Payable* is the first type of QuickBooks liability account — it appears before other liability accounts on the Balance Sheet; however, it was automatically entered when we created the company file. We do not have to enter the *Accounts Payable* account; however, we do need to change the account number assigned automatically by QuickBooks.

| 1. | **Right-click** | the **Accounts Payable account** |
| 2. | **Click** | **Edit Account** |

Your cursor should be in the Number field. Notice the number automatically assigned by QuickBooks to this account is 20000. This number does not fit in with our account numbers so we will have to change it.

3. Type   2100

The *Accounts Payable* account has no opening balance because the balance is created automatically by the program as the sum of all amounts owing to vendors. The balance is updated each time you enter a bill or an opening balance amount for a vendor.

4. Click   Save & Close to save the account and return to the Chart of Accounts list

Entering Credit Card Accounts

Credit Card accounts appear next in order on the Balance Sheet. This account type is reserved for credit cards that the business uses for purchases. Darya's uses one credit card for business and has a single account for it.

1. Press   _ctrl_ + N to open the Add New Account form

2. Choose   Credit Card as the account type and **click Continue** to display the updated Add New Account screen:

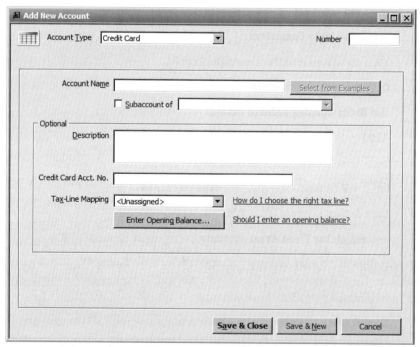

Figure 9-12

The Credit Card form has a field for the credit card number. This field is optional. For security reasons, you may not want to include the card number in your data files.

3. Type   2150 in the **Number field**

4. Press   _tab_ to advance to the Account Name field

5. Type   Visa Payable

6. Click   the Enter Opening Balance button

7. Type   875 in the **Statement Ending Balance field**

8. Press   _tab_ to advance to the Statement Ending Date

9. Press   _ctrl_ + V to paste the date (or **type 08/31/14**)

10. **Click**   **OK**

11. **Click**   **Save & New** or **press** (alt) + **N** to open a new blank Add New Account form

Entering Other Current Liability Accounts

The next group of liability accounts are other current liabilities. QuickBooks has already created four accounts in this group — *GST/HST Payable, GST/QST Payable, Payroll Liabilities,* and *PST Payable (SK)*. We need to add one other current liability account type, the *Bank Loan* account.

1. **Choose**   **Other Current Liability** in the **Account Type field** (or **type o**)

This form has the same fields as accounts with the Other Current Asset account type selected. Refer to page 473 for assistance if needed.

2. **Enter**   the **account number**, **name**, **opening balance**, and **date** for the Bank Loan account

Number	Name	Opening Balance	Date
2260	Bank Loan	$11,500.00	08/31/14

3. **Click**   **Save & New** or **press** (alt) + **N** to open a blank Add New Account form

Entering Long Term Liability Accounts

Long Term Liabilities form the final group of liability accounts. They are not due within the next year and therefore appear after Current Liabilities on the Balance Sheet.

1. **Choose**   **Long Term Liability** in the **Account type field** (or **type l**) to enter the next group of accounts

This form has the same fields as accounts with the Other Current Assets account type and Other Current Liabilities Account Type selected (see page 473).

2. **Add**   the **two long term liability accounts** by entering the account number, name, opening balance, and date:

Number	Name	Opening Balance	Date
2720	Long Term Loan	$22,000.00	08/31/14
2740	Mortgage Payable	$30,000.00	08/31/14

3. **Click**   **Save & New** or **press** (ctrl) + **N** to save the account and open a blank Add New Account form

Entering Equity Accounts

QuickBooks has already created three equity accounts: *Opening Balance Equity, Owners Draw,* and *Owners Equity.* We will modify these accounts. The *Opening Balance Equity* account will be renamed *Capital, Darya Danovich.* The *Owners Equity* account will be deleted and the *Owners Draw* account will be renamed *Drawings, Darya Danovich.* We will edit the accounts later in the Deleting and Making Accounts Inactive and the Editing Accounts section to match the Equity section in our Chart of Accounts shown on page 457.

Entering Income Accounts

After adding all the Balance Sheet accounts, we must create Income Statement accounts. Darya's Dance Studio has only regular income accounts.

1. Choose   **Income** in the **Account type field** (or **type i**) to change the Add New Account form

The balance for income accounts is generated automatically from transactions that use the account. We will add the year-to-date income balances in a general journal entry for the *Opening Balance Equity* account (decreasing equity balance) after creating all accounts.

2. Create   the **following income accounts**. **Enter account numbers** and **names**:

Number	Name
4100	Revenue from Lessons
4160	Sales Discounts
4200	Revenue from Interest
4250	Other Revenue

3. Click   **Save & New** or **press** `ctrl` **+ N** to save the account and open a blank Add New Account form

Entering Expense Accounts

QuickBooks has two types of expense accounts: *Cost of Goods Sold* to calculate Gross Profit, and *Other Expense* to determine Net Income. Service businesses like Darya's have no Cost of Goods Sold accounts so we will only enter expense accounts.

1. Choose   **Expense** as the Account type (or **type e**) to change the Add New Account form

Notes
If Bank is selected as the account type, type e to select Equity and then type e again to select Expense.

Like income accounts, the expense account balance is generated by the program from transactions that use the account. We will make the adjusting entry for the opening balance (year-to-date expenses) later.

Expense accounts are listed in the following chart:

Number	Name	Tax Code	Number	Name	Tax Code
5020	Advertising & Promotion	S	5180	Printing & Copying	S
5060	Office & Computer Supplies Used		5200	Property Tax Expense	
5080	Music Inventory Expenses		5220	Purchase Discounts	
5100	Depreciation Expense		5240	Hydro Expense	G
5120	Maintenance Expenses	G	5260	Telephone Expense	S
5140	Insurance Expense	P	5280	Vehicle Expenses	S
5160	Interest Expense		5300	Wages Expenses	

Notes
Two other account types are not used by Darya's. These are the *Other Income* and *Other Expense* account types. These accounts would be used for one-time events in the business, such as losses or gains from the sale of assets.

2. Create   the **expense accounts**. For each account, **enter** the **account number**, **name**, and **tax code**, if there is one

3. Click   **Save & Close** instead of Save & New to save the account and close the Add New Account form after adding the *Wages Expenses* account

You will be returned to the Chart of Accounts. You should notice several changes. All the new accounts you created have been added with balances, if you entered them. The following accounts need some adjustments:

a) The *GST/HST Payable* account needs to be renumbered and it does not have a balance yet. The balance will be entered when the historical invoices, which include GST, are entered

b) The *GST/QST Payable* account is not needed and needs to be removed. This account is associated with a sales tax agency vendor, so we will make both the *GST/QST Payable* account and the associated sales tax agency inactive.

c) The *PST Payable (SK)* account is not needed. This account is associated with a sales tax agency vendor, so we will make both the *PST Payable (SK)* account and the associated sales tax agency inactive.

d) The *Opening Balance Equity* account balance has changed. Every time you entered an account balance, the program added an offsetting amount to the *Opening Balance Equity* account. If the account you created had a debit balance, the *Opening Balance Equity* account was credited by the same amount. If you added a credit balance, a debit amount was entered for the *Opening Balance Equity* account. This ensures that the Trial Balance remains balanced. We will renumber and rename this account to *3200 - Capital, Darya Danovich* and correct the balance by adding outstanding historical income and expense amounts.

e) The *Owners Draw* account needs to be renumbered and renamed to *3260 - Drawings, Darya Danovich*.

f) The *Owners Equity* account is not needed and needs to be removed.

g) The *Uncategorized Expenses* account is not needed and needs to be removed.

h) The *Payroll Liabilities* and *Payroll Expenses* accounts are not needed. These accounts are used in payroll items that have been set up by default; therefore, they cannot be deleted so we'll make these accounts inactive.

> ⚠ **WARNING!**
> The Opening Balance Equity amount may still be incorrect if you entered an incorrect amount for any account or you omitted an account balance.

Always check the account balances with the amounts in the reports used to enter the setup information.

4. Compare the **Chart of Accounts** on the screen with the information on page 457, and **mark** the **accounts** that require corrections.

We will now make the necessary corrections to the Chart of Accounts.

Deleting and Making Accounts Inactive

QuickBooks automatically creates accounts when you create a new company. You may want to delete some of those accounts to match your own Chart of Accounts. Accounts with a balance, linked to other items in QuickBooks, or that have been used in transactions, cannot be deleted.

If an account cannot be deleted, you can make it inactive to remove it from the Chart of Accounts. For example, you will see that some of the accounts in this exercise cannot be deleted from the Chart of Accounts because they are linked to other QuickBooks items. You will have to make them inactive in order to remove them from the Chart of Accounts.

The Chart of Accounts includes six accounts that are not needed for this company: *GST/QST Payable, PST Payable (SK), Owners Equity, Uncategorized Expenses, Payroll Liabilities*, and *Payroll Expenses*. The Chart of Accounts should still be open.

1. **Highlight**   the **GST/QST Payable account**

2. **Press**   *ctrl* **+ D** to delete the account and the following warning will be displayed:

Figure 9-13

The warning indicates that you cannot delete this account because it is associated with a sales tax agency, the Ministère du Revenu. We will make the account and the sales tax agency inactive.

First, we will make the *GST/QST Payable* account inactive.

3. **Click**   **OK** to close the warning

4. **Right-click**   the **GST/QST Payable account**

5. **Select**   **Make Account Inactive**

Notice that the *GST/QST Payable* account is removed from the Chart of Accounts.

Next, we will remove the sales tax agency, the Ministère du Revenu, from the Vendors list.

6. **Click**   the **Vendors icon** on the Icon bar

7. **Highlight**   the **Ministère du Revenu**

8. **Press**   *ctrl* **+ D**

9. The following warning will be displayed:

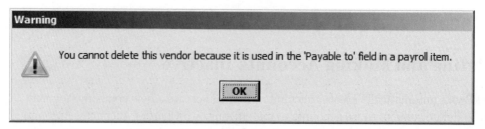

Figure 9-14

The warning indicates that you cannot delete this vendor because it is used in the "Payable to" field in a payroll item. We will make the sales tax agency inactive.

10. **Click**   **OK** to close the warning

11. **Right-click**   on **Ministère du Revenu**

12. **Select**   **Make Vendor Inactive**

The vendor's name is no longer displayed by default on the Vendors list and cannot be selected from Vendor fields in QuickBooks forms.

You can restore a vendor record (make it active) at any time. Click the drop-down arrow in the View field and select All Vendors. All active and inactive vendors will be displayed in the Vendors list. The inactive vendors will be marked with an X displayed in the column to the left. To make an inactive vendor active, right-click an inactive vendor and choose Make Vendor Active. You can also click the X displayed in the column to the left, which will remove the X and automatically make the vendor active.

Notice the Ministère du Revenu is removed from the Vendors list.

13.	**Close**	the **Vendor Centre**
14.	**Return**	to the **Chart of Accounts**
15.	**Highlight**	the **PST Payable (SK) account**
16.	**Press**	(ctrl) + **D**
17.	**Click**	**OK** to accept the warning that this account cannot be deleted

📄 **Notes**
Follow the same steps used to make the *GST/QST Payable* account and the Ministère du Revenu sales tax agency inactive.

Just like the *GST/QST Payable* account, you receive a warning that the *PST Payable (SK)* account cannot be deleted because it is associated with the Saskatchewan Finance sales tax agency. We need to make the account and the sales tax agency inactive.

18.	**Make**	the **PST Payable (SK) account** inactive
19.	**Make**	the **Saskatchewan Finance sales tax agency** inactive
20.	**Return**	to the **Chart of Accounts**

We will now delete the *Owners Equity* account.

21.	**Right-click**	the **Owners Equity account**
22.	**Click**	**Delete Account**
23.	The following message will be displayed:	

Figure 9-15

This message is displayed if the account can be deleted from the Chart of Accounts.

24.	**Click**	**OK** to delete the account

We will now delete the *Uncategorized Expenses* account.

25.	**Highlight**	the **Uncategorized Expenses account**
26.	**Press**	(ctrl) + **D**
27.	**Click**	**OK** to delete the account

We will remove the *Payroll Liabilities* and *Payroll Expenses* accounts.

28. **Highlight**	the **Payroll Liabilities account**
29. **Press**	`ctrl` + **D** to delete the account and the following warning will be displayed:

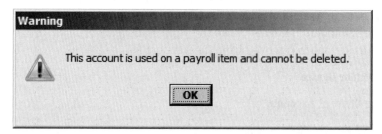

Figure 9-16

This warning indicates that the account is used on a payroll item and cannot be deleted. We will make the account inactive.

30. **Click**	**OK** to close the warning
31. **Right-click**	the **Payroll Liabilities account**
32. **Click**	**Make Account Inactive**

The *Payroll Liabilities* account is now removed from the Chart of Accounts.

33. **Right-click**	the **Payroll Expenses account**
34. **Click**	**Delete Account**

Just like with the *Payroll Liabilities* account, you receive a warning that the account cannot be deleted because it is used on a payroll item. We need to make the account inactive.

35. **Click**	**OK** to close the warning
36. **Right-click**	the **Payroll Expenses account**
37. **Click**	**Make Account Inactive**

The *Payroll Expenses* account is now removed from the Chart of Accounts.

Editing Accounts

When you review the Chart of Accounts, you may find that some of the accounts were entered incorrectly. You can easily correct an account number or name at this stage by opening the account record. To correct an opening balance or date, you must change the amount in the ledger for the account. As soon as you save a new account, the Opening Balance field is no longer available in the record.

Editing Account Names and Numbers

The accounts created by QuickBooks do not match the accounts on our Chart of Accounts so we need to edit them. We need to edit the *GST/HST Payable* account and the equity accounts. The *GST/HST Payable* account number is incorrect, and the equity account names and numbers require the changes shown in the following chart:

Number	Name	Changes to	Number	Name
25500	GST/HST Payable		2460	
30000	Opening Balance Equity		3200	Capital, Darya Danovich
30800	Owners Draw		3260	Drawings, Darya Danovich

Notes
You can also edit an account by choosing the Edit menu and clicking Edit Account when the account is highlighted.

1. **Open**   the **Chart of Accounts**

2. **Click**   **25500 - GST/HST Payable**

3. **Press**   ⌷ctrl⌷ + **E**, or **choose** the **Account button** and **click Edit Account**

The Edit Account form appears for the selected account:

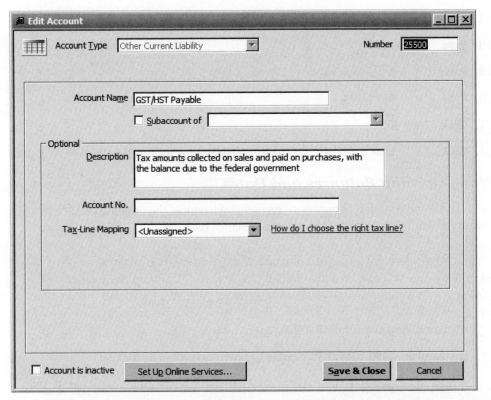

Figure 9-17

Notice that the Enter Opening Balance button has been removed for this account. The account type is dimmed. Some account types cannot be changed. (Refer to page 486 for assistance with correcting account types.) The *GST/HST Payable* account is linked to the GST tax setup so its type cannot be changed. The *Opening Balance Equity* account is also a special linked account, so its type cannot be changed. To edit an account balance, we need to edit the ledger for the account. The account number is highlighted so we can change it.

4. **Type**   **2460** to replace the account number

5. **Click**   **Save & Close** to save the change and return to the Chart of Accounts

6. **Highlight**   **30000 - Opening Balance Equity**

7. **Press**   ⌷ctrl⌷ + **E**

8. **Type**   **3200** to replace the account number

9. **Press**	(tab) to advance to the account name
10. **Type**	**Capital, Darya Danovich**
11. **Click**	**Save & Close** to save the changes and return to the Chart of Accounts
12. **Highlight**	**30800 - Owners Draw**
13. **Press**	(ctrl) + **E**
14. **Type**	**3260** to replace the account number
15. **Press**	(tab) to advance to the account name
16. **Type**	**Drawings, Darya Danovich**
17. **Click**	**Enter Opening Balance button**
18. **Type**	**-7400**
19. **Press**	(tab) to advance to the As of field
20. **Type**	**08/31/14**
21. **Click**	**OK**
22. **Click**	**Save & Close** to save the changes and return to the Chart of Accounts

Editing Opening Balances and Dates

As soon as you save a new account with its opening balance, the opening balance field is closed. To edit the balance, or the opening balance date, you must edit the account register.

We need to add $990.00 as the opening balance for *GST/HST Payable* on Aug. 31, 2014. The balance will also be added to *Capital, Darya Danovich*. Because the opening balance field is not available, we have to create a journal entry to add the account balance.

The Chart of Accounts should still be open.

1. **Double click 2460 - GST/HST Payable** to open the account's register:

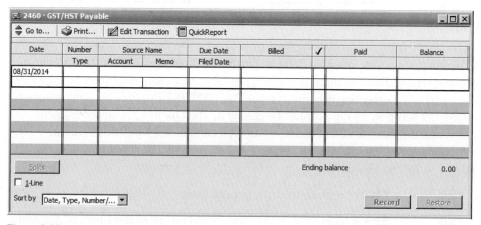

Figure 9-18

The last date you used for opening balances should be entered. However, when you try to enter information in any of the fields, you will find that the fields are locked. We need to enter the opening balance as a General Journal entry.

2. **Double click** the **date** or **double click any field** in the first line of the register to view the message that QuickBooks automatically assigns numbers to journal entries

3. **Click** the **Do not display this message in the future option** and then **click OK** to close the message

4. The Make General Journal Entries form is displayed

The *GST/HST Payable* account is different from other General Ledger accounts because of its link to the tax report. The journal entry form has an extra Tax Item column for this account. In this column, you must choose the tax item that the amount is associated with. To connect the *GST/HST Payable* opening balance to the correct lines on the GST return, we will enter the GST on purchases separately from the GST collected on sales. That is, we will enter two separate detail lines on the journal entry so that we can select the correct tax item for each line. The *Capital, Darya Danovich* account will be used as the offsetting account. For Darya's Dance Studio, these tax amounts are shown below:

Tax Account	GST Paid on Purchases	GST Collected on Sales	GST/HST Payable
2460 GST/HST Payable	$640.00	$1,630.00	$990.00

Notes
As a liability account, *GST/HST Payable* normally has a credit entry. GST collected on sales increases the liability so a credit amount is entered. GST paid on purchases reduces the liability so it requires a debit entry. Refer to the document entitled "Tax" in the Appendix (found on the CD that accompanies this text) for additional information on GST.

5. **Enter** 08/31/14 as the date if this is not the date shown for the entry

6. **Click** the **Debit field** on the first line of the journal entry

7. **Type** 640

8. **Press** (tab) to advance to the Memo field

9. **Type** **Opening account balance**

10. **Press** (tab) to advance to the Tax Item field

11. **Click** the **drop-down arrow** in the field to view the tax items available:

Tax Item		
▼		
< Add New >		
GST	Sales Tax Item	GST on sales
GST (ITC)	Sales Tax Item	GST on purchases (Input Tax Credit)
GST (ITC) Adjustments	Sales Tax Item	GST Adjustments on purchases (Input Ta...
GST (ITC) Zero Rated	Sales Tax Item	GST on Zero Rated purchases (Input Tax...
GST Adjustments	Sales Tax Item	GST Adjustments on sales
GST Instalments	Sales Tax Item	GST Instalments and net tax paid
GST Zero Rated	Sales Tax Item	GST on Zero Rated sales

Figure 9-19

12. **Click** **GST (ITC) - GST on purchases (Input Tax Credit)**

13. **Press** (tab) to advance to the second line on the journal entry

14. **Click** the **drop-down arrow** in the **Account field**

15. **Choose** **2460 - GST/HST Payable** from the account list

16. **Click** the **Credit field**

17. **Type** 1630

18. **Press** (tab) to advance to the Tax Item field

19. **Click** the **drop-down arrow** in the field

Notes
Typing a negative amount in the Debit field also generates a credit entry.

20.	Click	GST - GST on sales
21.	Press	<kbd>tab</kbd> to advance to the third line on the journal entry
22.	Click	the **drop-down arrow** in the **Account field**
23.	Choose	**3200 - Capital, Darya Danovich**

The offsetting debit entry of $990.00 is correct for the *Capital, Darya Danovich* account.

24. The completed journal entry should be displayed as shown:

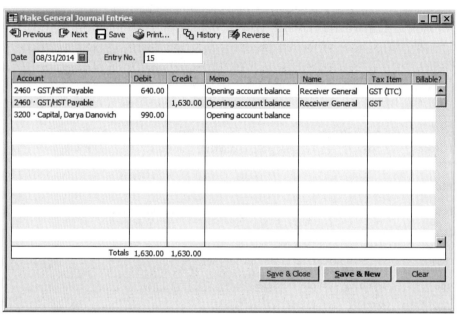

Figure 9-20

| 25. | Click | **Save & Close** to save the transaction and return to the *GST/HST Payable* Register |

Both entries to the *GST/HST Payable* account have been added to the register, and the final balance of $990.00 as shown in the bottom right-hand corner of the register is correct.

| 26. | Close | the **GST/HST Payable register** to return to the Chart of Accounts |

The *GST/HST Payable* balance is now displayed in the Chart of Accounts

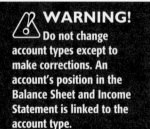

WARNING!
Do not change account types except to make corrections. An account's position in the Balance Sheet and Income Statement is linked to the account type.

CORRECTING BALANCE SHEET ACCOUNT OPENING BALANCES

To edit other amounts or dates for other Balance Sheet accounts, open the Chart of Accounts. Double click an account name to open the account register. Highlight the date or amount that is incorrect. Type the correction. Click Record and then click Yes to confirm the change.

CORRECTING AN ACCOUNT TYPE

To edit the account type, click the account type list and select the correct type. However, some account types cannot be changed; you cannot change an account type to or from *Accounts Receivable* or *Accounts Payable*, and parent and subaccounts must be of the same type. QuickBooks will display a warning message when you try to make one of these changes. If the account type is dimmed, as it is for the *GST/HST Payable* account and the *Capital, Darya Danovich* account, you cannot change the account type.

If you cannot change the account type, you must delete the account. If the account has been used in journal entries, you must delete the journal entry (the opening balance) before you can delete the account. Entering an opening balance creates a journal entry. To delete an opening balance, open the account register and highlight the journal entry. Choose the Edit menu and click Delete Journal. Click Yes to confirm. Close the register and then delete the account (press <kbd>ctrl</kbd> + D). Click Yes to confirm. Create the account again and choose the account type carefully.

Entering Opening Income and Expense Account Balances

The ideal time for a business to convert its accounting records to QuickBooks is after closing the books or at the start of a new fiscal year. At that time, all the income and expense accounts have zero balances. But you can convert the files after the start of the fiscal year. You have two options at this point: to add all the transactions for the fiscal year up to the date you start using QuickBooks, or to enter historical outstanding amounts as summaries.

When adding income and expense accounts, the Add New Account form does not include the Enter Opening Balance button, which allows the opening balance to be entered for an account. Assuming that you do not want to enter all the transactions for the fiscal year up to the date you start using QuickBooks, the opening balances for income and expense accounts can be entered either as journal entries on the Make General Journal Entries form or as transactions in the offsetting account register — the capital account. We will enter one transaction for income and one transaction for expenses in the capital account register. We cannot access the registers for income or expense accounts, which is why we must add the appropriate amounts for these accounts to the *Capital, Darya Danovich* account.

Notes
You can access revenue and income accounts from the Make General Journal Entries form, but the account registers are not available for these accounts.

1. **Double click** the **Capital, Darya Danovich account** to open the account register:

Notes
You could also make a General Journal entry as we did for *GST/HST Payable*.

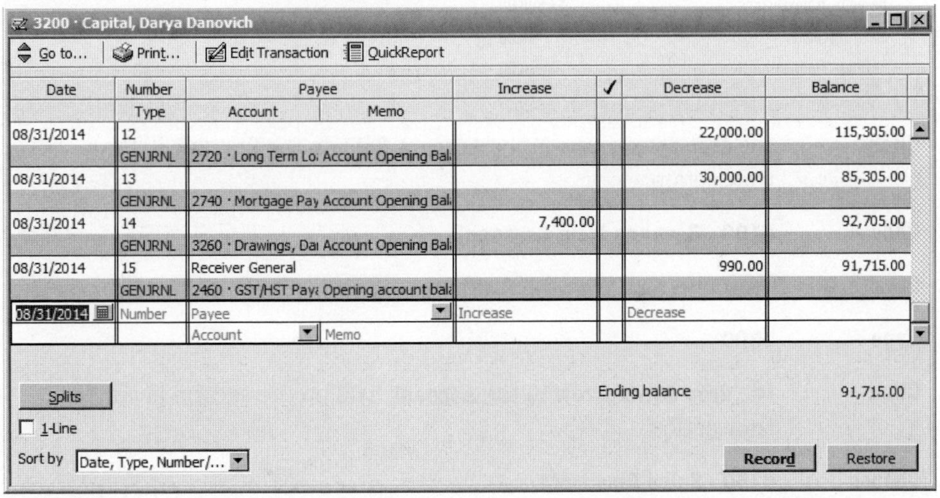

3200 · Capital, Darya Danovich
Go to... Print... Edit Transaction QuickReport
Date | Number Type | Payee Account Memo | Increase | ✓ | Decrease | Balance
08/31/2014 | 12 GENJRNL | 2720 · Long Term Lo: Account Opening Bal | | | 22,000.00 | 115,305.00
08/31/2014 | 13 GENJRNL | 2740 · Mortgage Pay Account Opening Bal | | | 30,000.00 | 85,305.00
08/31/2014 | 14 GENJRNL | 3260 · Drawings, Da Account Opening Bal | 7,400.00 | | | 92,705.00
08/31/2014 | 15 GENJRNL | Receiver General 2460 · GST/HST Pay Opening account bal | | | 990.00 | 91,715.00
08/31/2014 Number Payee Account Memo Increase Decrease
Splits
Ending balance 91,715.00
1-Line
Sort by Date, Type, Number/...
Record Restore

Figure 9-21

Notice that each opening balance appears as an individual entry in the register. We could enter the historical income and expense amounts individually as well but it is faster to enter them together as a split transaction. A split transaction indicates that the transaction is split across different accounts.

The date is correct — 08/31/2014. This date is entered because our General Preferences included the option to use the last transaction date as the default, and we used this date for the *GST/HST Payable* entry.

2. **Click** the **Splits button** Splits in the lower left-hand corner of the screen

A warning will be displayed indicating that you cannot use registers to enter transactions with sales taxes.

3. **Click** the **box** beside Do not display this message in the future
4. **Click** **OK** to accept the warning

5. The split area is displayed as shown here:

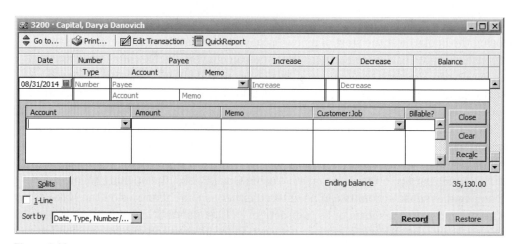

Figure 9-22

Notes
Sales Discounts is a contra-revenue account. Since this balance reduces the total revenue, you must enter it as a negative amount.

The income amounts we need to add are summarized in the following chart:

Number	Name	Amount
4100	Revenue from Lessons	$3,800.00
4160	Sales Discounts	−30.00
4200	Revenue from Interest	20.00

6. Click   the **drop-down arrow** in the **Account field** on the first line in the transaction

7. Choose   **4100 - Revenue from Lessons**

8. Press   ⎡tab⎤ to advance to the Amount field

9. Type   **3800**

10. Click   the **drop-down arrow** in the **Account field** on the second line in the transaction

11. Choose   **4160 - Sales Discounts**

12. Press   ⎡tab⎤ to advance to the Amount field

13. Type   **−30**

14. Click   the **drop-down arrow** in the **Account field** on the third line in the transaction

15. Choose   **4200 - Revenue from Interest**

16. Press   ⎡tab⎤

17. Type   **20**

18. Click   the **Memo field** beside **-split-** in the Ledger section of the transaction

19. Type   **Opening income balance**

Notice that QuickBooks enters the total income amount of $3,790.00 automatically in the Decrease column in the *Capital, Darya Danovich* account register.

20. Check   the **amounts** carefully and **make corrections** if necessary

21. The completed transaction should look like the one below:

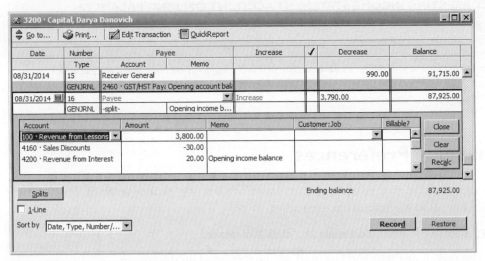

Figure 9-23

22. Click   **Record** to save the transaction and update the Capital, Darya Danovich account balance

23. Click   the **Splits button** again to prepare for entering the expense balances

24. The expense amounts we need to add are summarized in the following chart:

Number	Name	Amount	Number	Name	Amount
5020	Advertising & Promotion	$2,100.00	5180	Printing & Copying	$560.00
5060	Office & Computer Supplies Used	185.00	5200	Property Tax Expense	120.00
5080	Music Inventory Expenses	45.00	5220	Purchase Discounts	−95.00
5100	Depreciation Expense	1,000.00	5240	Hydro Expense	85.00
5120	Maintenance Expenses	220.00	5260	Telephone Expense	120.00
5140	Insurance Expense	3,250.00	5280	Vehicle Expenses	240.00
5160	Interest Expense	420.00			

Notes

Purchase Discounts is a contra-expense account. It normally has a credit balance and reduces the total expenses. Enter its balance as a negative amount.

25. Enter   the **expense accounts and balances**

26. Click   the **Memo field** beside **-split-** in the Ledger section of the transaction

27. Type   **Opening expenses balance**

28. Check   the **amounts** carefully and **make corrections** if necessary

29. Click   **Record** to save the entry

30. Click   **Record** to save the transaction and update the *Capital, Darya Danovich* account balance

31. Close   the **Capital, Darya Danovich register** and return to the Chart of Accounts

32. Close   the **Chart of Accounts**

Changing Preferences

Now that we have created all the accounts, we are ready to change some of the preferences that we did not change earlier.

1. **Choose** the **Edit menu** and **click Preferences**

The preference that you last used will be displayed on the screen.

Changing Preferences for Chequing

Notes
Refer to pages 196–198 for more information on chequing preferences.

1. **Click** the **Chequing heading** on the left-hand side of the screen

2. **Click** the **My Preferences tab** if it is not already selected

On this tab you can enter the default account for writing cheques, paying bills, and making deposits. Darya's uses the *Bank - Chequing* account as the default account for all these QuickBooks transactions.

3. **Click** the **check box** beside Open the Write Cheques preference to add a ✓

4. **Choose** **1050 Bank - Chequing** in the Account field

Notes
You can also type 1050, the account number, in the Account field to choose the account.

5. **Click** the **check box** for Open the Pay Bills and Open the Make Deposits preferences and **choose 1050 Bank - Chequing** as the default account for both types of transactions

Changing Company Preferences for Chequing

1. **Click** the **Company Preferences tab**

The company preferences affect all users and can only be changed by the Administrator of the company file or by a user set up as an External Accountant.

The warning about duplicate cheque numbers is on by default and you should leave it on. We are not using payroll so we don't need to select accounts for any of the payroll options. Do not select the option to change cheque dates when cheques are printed. This will ensure that the transactions you enter will match the exercises in the textbook. For the other settings you can choose your own preferences.

Changing Company Preferences for Finance Charges

QuickBooks will create an item record named Fin Chg automatically when you add details about the finance charges in the Preference settings.

1. **Click** the **Finance Charge heading** on the left-hand side of the screen

2. Click   **Yes** to save the Chequing preferences

3. Click   the **Company Preferences tab** if necessary:

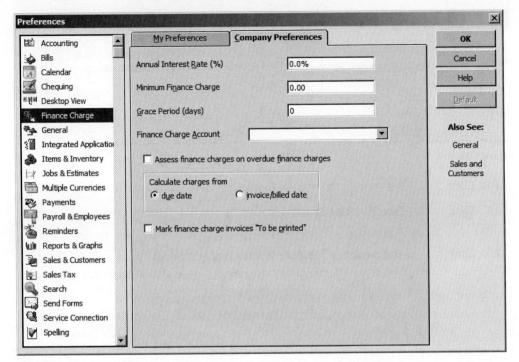

Figure 9-24

Use the options on this tab to define the interest charges on overdue customer accounts. Darya charges 15 percent interest on accounts after the 30-day account period. A minimum charge of $10.00 is applied as an administrative fee and charges are cumulative — that is, interest is charged on previous overdue interest amounts. Darya's allows a five-day grace period after the 30 days before charging interest. That means interest charges are assessed starting 35 days after the transaction date. The overdue period is assessed from the invoice or billing date rather than the due date. Interest revenue is credited to the *Revenue from Interest* account.

The default settings are set to charge no interest. Zero is entered in the default Annual Interest Rate field.

4. Press   ⟨tab⟩ to highlight 0.0% in the Annual Interest Rate field

5. Type   **15**

6. Press   ⟨tab⟩ to advance to the Minimum Finance Charge field

7. Type   **10**

8. Press   ⟨tab⟩ to advance to the Grace Period (days) field

9. Type   **35**

10. Press   ⟨tab⟩ to advance to the Finance Charge Account field

11. Type   **4200**

12. Press   ⟨tab⟩ to advance to the Assess finance charges on overdue finance charges field

13. Press the **Space bar** or **click** in the **check box** to select this preference and see the warning:

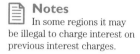
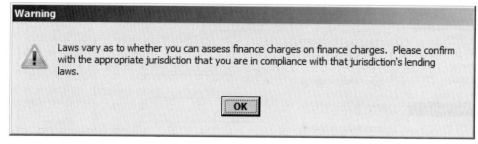

Figure 9-25

14. Click **OK** to indicate that we can legally select this option

15. Click **invoice/billed date** to change the starting date from which the finance charges are calculated

16. Click the **check box** for **Mark finance charge invoices "To be printed"** if you want the finance charge invoices to be available for batch printing

There are no personal preferences for finance charges.

Once you have set up preferences for finance charges, an item called Fin Chg is automatically added to the Item list. You can edit finance charges either from the Finance Charge preferences, or by editing the Fin Chg item on the Item List. Depending on the changes you need to make, you may need to make the changes to the item in the Item list or in the Finance Charge preferences.

Changing Company Preferences for Jobs & Estimates

1. Click the **Jobs & Estimates heading** on the left-hand side of the screen

2. Click **Yes** to save the changes made to the Finance Charges preferences

3. Click the **Company Preferences tab** if necessary:

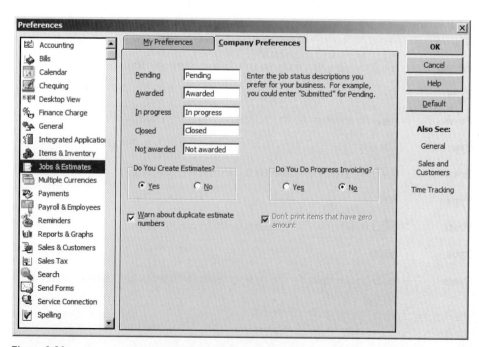

Figure 9-26

Use the preferences on this tab to indicate whether the business uses estimates for customer jobs or services and to assign names to the different stages of a job in progress. Progress invoicing is also enabled from this tab. Progress invoicing allows you to invoice customers regularly for work in progress. Again, a warning about duplicate estimate numbers is switched on as the default, and you should leave this warning turned on.

All the default settings for Jobs & Estimates are correct for Darya's: estimates are used and progress invoicing is not, so we do not need to make any changes to these preferences.

There are no personal preferences for jobs and estimates.

Changing Company Preferences for Items & Inventory

1. **Click**   the **Items & Inventory heading** on the left-hand side of the screen

2. **Click**   the **Company Preferences tab** if necessary:

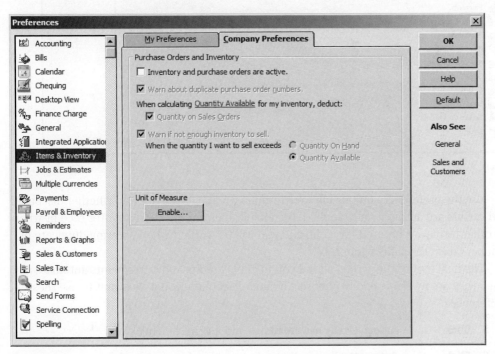

Figure 9-27

Many of the preferences on this tab apply to inventory and Darya's does not use inventory. However, inventory and purchase orders are activated together and Darya's does use purchase orders.

3. **Click**   the **box** beside Inventory and purchase orders are active to select this preference

By selecting this preference, the Purchase Orders icon will be displayed in the Vendors section of the Home page and all the related menu options will be available from the Vendors menu. The warning about duplicate purchase order numbers should remain selected. The next two options are related to inventory so we can ignore these settings.

Changing Company Preferences for Bills

1. **Click**   the **Bills heading** on the left-hand side of the screen

2. **Click**   **Yes** to save the changes made to the Items & Inventory preferences

3.	**Click**	**OK** when prompted with the warning that QuickBooks must close all its open windows to change this preference
4.	**Click**	the **Company Preferences tab** if necessary:

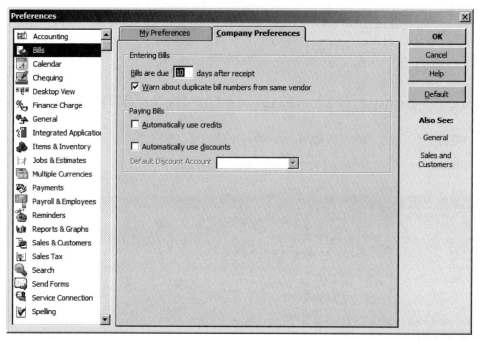

Figure 9-28

Use the preferences on this tab to determine when bills are due and whether discounts and credits are automatically applied. By default, bills are due 10 days after receipt when no other terms are entered for a bill, and you will be warned when entering duplicate bill numbers from the same vendor.

The final part of the screen allows you to apply credits and/or discounts automatically when they are available and to choose a default discount account. We want to use these preferences.

5.	**Click**	**Automatically use credits** to add a ✓ in the check box
6.	**Click**	**Automatically use discounts** to add a ✓ in the check box
7.	**Click**	the **drop-down arrow** in the **Default Discount Account field**
8.	**Choose**	**5220 - Purchase Discounts** as the default account

There are no personal preferences for Bills.

Changing Company Preferences for Reports & Graphs

1.	**Click**	the **Reports & Graphs heading** on the left-hand side of the screen
2.	**Click**	**Yes** to save the changes made to the Bills preferences
3.	**Click**	on the **Company Preferences tab** if necessary:

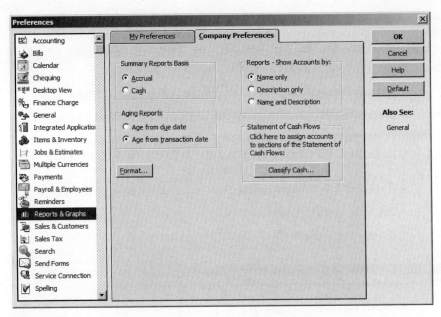

Figure 9-29

Darya's uses the accrual basis so the setting for the Summary Reports Basis is correct. We want to use account names only in reports because we have not used descriptions for all accounts. If you want, you can add both names and descriptions to reports. We want aging periods in reports to be based on the transaction date rather than the due date so the Aging Reports setting is correct.

The format button allows you to choose a standard format for reports — what headings to include, date format, fonts, etc. The Classify Cash button allows you to decide how accounts should be classified for cash flow reports.

You may want to change the standard format for reports. For example, you can add your name as a report footer to make it easier to identify your work.

4. **Click**   the **Format button** and review the formatting settings that you can modify for reports and **make** any **changes** you want for your reports

5. **Click**   **OK** to save any changes that you made

6. **Click**   the **My Preferences tab**:

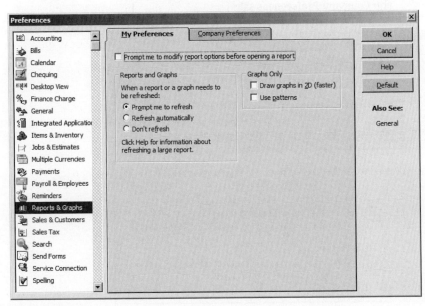

Figure 9-30

From this tab, you can decide whether to display the Modify Report window automatically when you select a report. You can also choose whether reports should be refreshed automatically when you make a change to any of the settings or data. Graphs can be drawn in two or three dimensions and with or without patterns.

7. Click   **Refresh Automatically** under the Reports & Graphs heading

8. Change   **other settings** to suit the way you want to work with the program

Changing Company Preferences for Sales & Customers

1. Click   the **Sales & Customers heading** on the left-hand side of the screen

2. Click   **Yes** to save the changes made to the Reports & Graphs preferences

3. Click   the **My Preferences tab** if it isn't already selected:

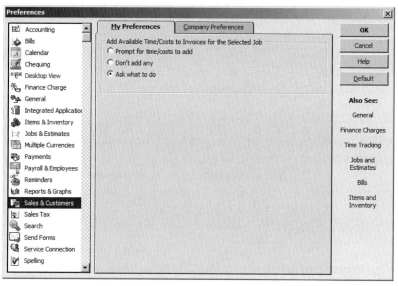

Figure 9-31

If you record billable time and costs that will be charged to customers, use this tab to determine how the costs are added to customer invoices.

4. Click   the **Company Preferences tab**:

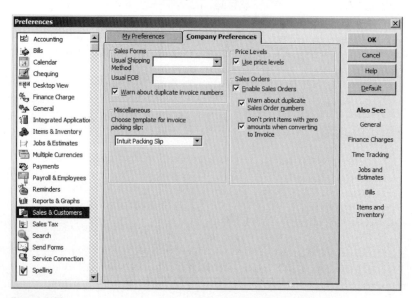

Figure 9-32

Many of these preferences refer to businesses that sell inventory. These fields can be skipped for Darya's. Shipping does not apply to Darya's and neither does markup or pricing levels. Duplicate invoice numbers should prompt a warning, Sales Orders should be enabled, and items with zero amounts should not be printed when converting sales orders to invoices. These default settings are correct.

5. **Click**	**Use price levels** to remove the ✓ in the check box

Changing Company Preferences for Payments

1. **Click**	the **Payments heading** on the left-hand side of the screen
2. **Click**	**Yes** to save the changes made to the Sales & Customers preferences
3. **Click**	the **Company Preferences tab** if it isn't already selected:

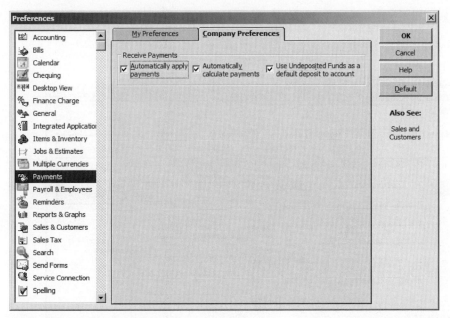

Figure 9-33

We want QuickBooks to automatically apply customer payments to invoices when we enter customer payments, so we leave the Automatically Apply Payments preference selected. We also want QuickBooks to automatically enter the amount in the Amount Received field as we select customer invoices that have been paid so we will leave the Calculate Payments preference selected. Darya's holds all cheques and deposits before taking them to the bank, so we will leave the Use Undeposited Funds as a default deposit to account preference selected.

4. **Click**	**OK** to save the final preference changes to the preferences
5. **Click**	the **Home icon** on the Icon bar to return to the Home page

Creating Customer Accounts

As we have seen in earlier chapters, customer records can be entered from any customer field in a QuickBooks form. Although we can add customers on the fly as needed, it is more efficient to start with a list of existing customers. As with many other activities in QuickBooks, customers can be added in many ways. Other than starting in a Customer:Job field on a form, all methods begin from the Customer:Job list. This list can only be accessed from the Customer Centre.

Notes
Depending on the changes made to the preferences, QuickBooks may need to close all open windows before the changes are accepted. Once this is completed, a blank screen will be displayed. Click the Home icon on the Icon bar to return to the Home page.

To access the Customer Centre:

a. **Click**   the **Customers icon** on the Icon bar; or

b. **Choose** **Customers** from the menu and **click Customer Centre**; or

c. **Click**   the **Customers button** in the Customers section of the Home page; or

d. **Press**   ⎡ctrl⎤ **+ J**

1. Open   the **Customer Centre** using one of the methods described above

2. Open   the **New Customer form** by performing one of the following options:
   a) **Right-click** in the **Customers & Jobs list** and **select New Customer**; or
   b) **Click** the **New Customer & Job button** and **click New Customer**; or
   c) **Choose Edit** from the menu and **click New Customer:Job**; or
   d) **Press** ⎡ctrl⎤ **+ N**

3. Click   ☒ to close the Add/Edit Multiple List Entries screen

4. The New Customer form will be displayed:

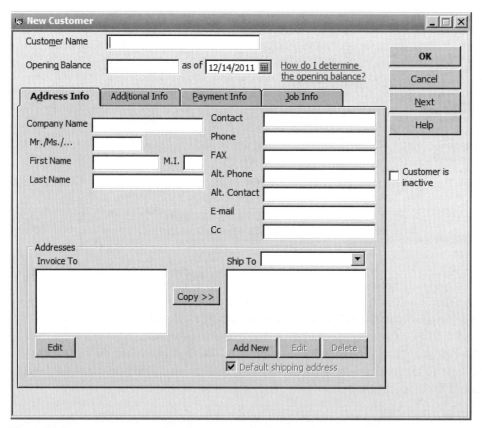

Figure 9-34

This is the same record form we used earlier when we added customer records from the Customer:Job field for River Run and Malin's Makeovers. This time we will add the opening balances for customers — the invoice amounts that are outstanding before the date we started to use QuickBooks.

Use the customer information chart on page 459 to create customer records.

5. Type   **Canadian Sledders**

6. Press   ⎡tab⎤ to advance to the Opening Balance field

Notes

Pressing ⎡ctrl⎤ + N will add a new record of any type once a list is displayed on the screen. Other keyboard shortcuts are also the same from one list to another. To edit a record, click ⎡ctrl⎤ + E and to delete a record, click ⎡ctrl⎤ + D.

| 7. **Type** | 400 |
| 8. **Press** | (tab) to advance to the Date field |

The date applies to the invoice date. Entering this date correctly will allow the correct calculation of discounts, due dates, and finance charges.

9. **Type**	08/10/14
10. **Press**	(tab) to advance to the Company Name field
11. **Type**	**Canadian Sledders**
12. **Press**	(tab) twice to move to the First Name field
13. **Type**	**Pers**
14. **Press**	(tab) twice to move to the Last Name field
15. **Type**	**Johansson**
16. **Press**	(tab)

The company name and contact appear in the Address text area, and the name we entered is added to the Contact field. You can enter a different name in the Contact field if this is appropriate. The cursor is in the Address text box beside the contact.

17. **Press**	(enter) to move to the next line in the Addresses Invoice To text box
18. **Type**	**189 Bobsled Hill Rd.**
19. **Press**	(enter)
20. **Type**	**Regina, Saskatchewan**
21. **Press**	(enter)
22. **Type**	**S3T 7E8**
23. **Click**	the **Edit button** to check the information and add the Country
24. **Correct**	the **address details** if needed
25. **Click**	the **Country/Region field**
26. **Type**	**Canada**
27. **Click**	**OK** to return to the Customer Record

> **Notes**
> Information entered in the Note field on the Edit Address Information screen will appear in the Address field on invoices and forms for the customer.

If the customer has merchandise shipped, you should enter the shipping address by clicking the Copy button and entering a ship to address in the Add Shipping Address Information screen. Both addresses will appear on invoices if the invoice template includes the shipping address. The shipping address is not used by Darya's Dance Studio because no items are shipped to customers.

28. **Click**	the **Phone field**
29. **Type**	**(306) 299-8644**
30. **Press**	(tab) to advance to the FAX field
31. **Type**	**(306) 298-6219**

There is no alternate phone number or alternate contact so we can skip these fields.

| 32. **Click** | the **E-mail address field** |
| 33. **Type** | **thefastest@yahoo.ca** |

34. Click   the **Additional Info tab**:

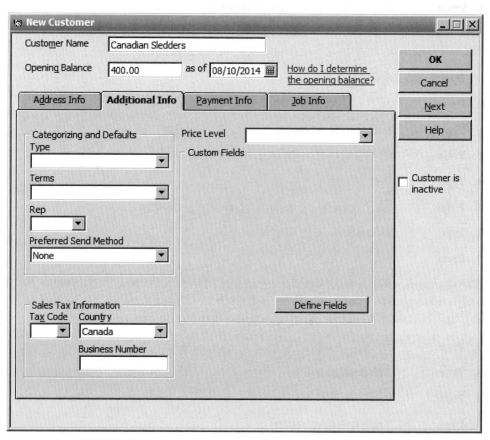

Figure 9-35

Darya's Dance Studio does not use customer types and sales reps are not used. A number of payment terms are set up automatically by QuickBooks, and we can add more if needed. We will edit the list of terms later.

The Tax Code field is displayed only because we chose to leave the Use Customer Tax Codes option selected in the Sales Tax preferences. If a sales tax code is entered in this field in the customer record, it will be used when entering sales taxes on sales transactions for the customer and it will override item tax codes. Darya's does not use customer tax codes, which means that the item tax codes will be used as the default tax codes on sales transactions. The sales tax codes are correct for all customers. The tax codes can be changed on invoices for individual invoice items if needed.

Notes
The customer tax code field will appear in the customer record only if the Use Customer Tax Codes option was selected in the Sales Tax Preferences.

35. Click   the **drop-down arrow** in the **Terms field** to view the payment terms set up by default

36. Click   **1% 10 Net 30** to add the terms to the customer record

37. Click   the **Payment Info tab**:

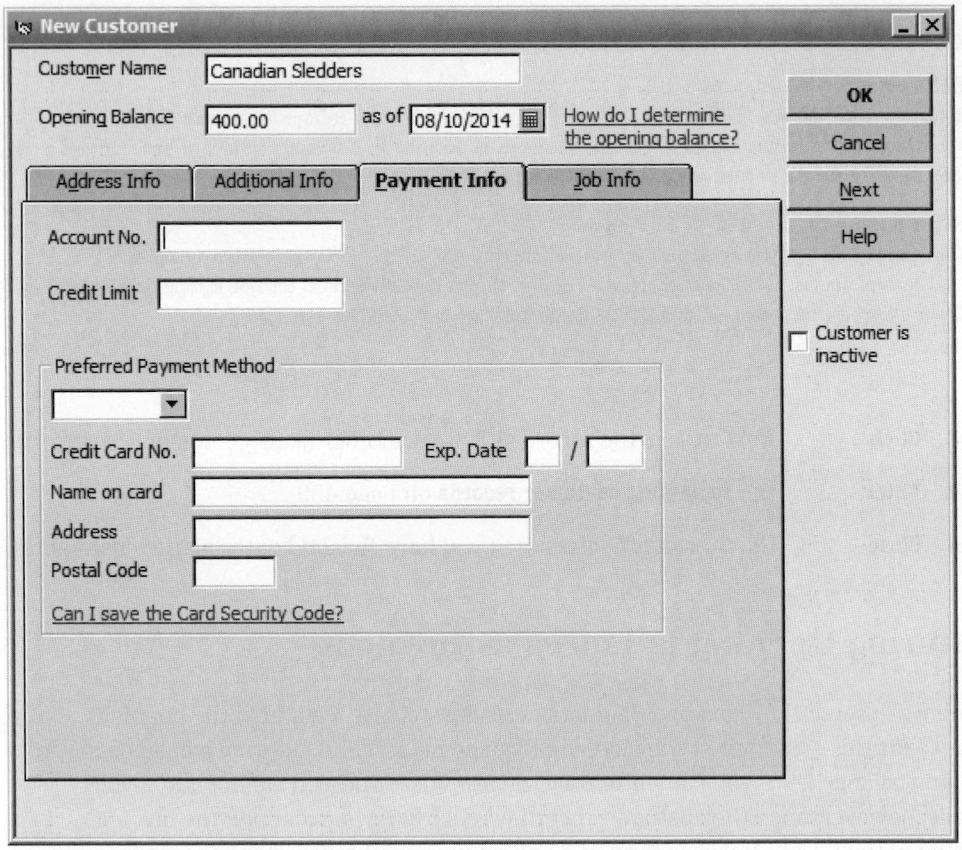

Figure 9-36

Most businesses place limits on the amount a customer is allowed to purchase on credit. Once the credit limit is reached, the customer may be asked for a down payment or may be granted a limit increase. Customer credit limits should be reviewed regularly with reference to a customer's buying and payment patterns to determine whether the limits should be raised or lowered for individual customers. As we saw on page 276, QuickBooks warns when a credit limit is exceeded by a sale; however, QuickBooks does not prevent a transaction to be posted if the customer is over their credit limit. The limit for Canadian Sledders is $2,000.00.

38. **Click**	the **Credit Limit field**
39. **Type**	**2000**
40. **Click**	the **drop-down arrow** in the Preferred Payment Method list to view the options available for selection

These payment methods were created automatically by QuickBooks. We will edit the list later. The Sledding team pays by cheque.

41. **Click**	**Cheque**

The fourth tab, the Job Info tab, allows you to organize the work done for customers according to specific jobs. This allows you to track the work done for customers in a more detailed way. When jobs are set up, you can choose the Customer and Job from the customer name lists. Customer jobs do not apply to Darya's Dance Studio.

42. **Check**	your **work** carefully before **saving** the **customer record**

CORRECTING CUSTOMER RECORDS

Before Saving the Record

To correct a record while you are creating it, just return to the field that has the error and type the correction. Click the Address Info, Additional Info, or Payment Info tab to return to those screens to check your work. To change the terms or payment method, select the correct terms or payment method from the drop-down list.

After Saving the Record

If you need to make corrections or changes later, open the Customer Centre to access the Customers & Jobs list. Right-click a customer name, then click Edit Customer:Job (or press ⌐ctrl⌐ + E). With the customer record displayed, highlight the incorrect details, and type the correction. Click OK to save the changes and return to the Customers & Jobs list.

43. **Click**   **Next** to save the record and open another blank customer record form

44. **Enter**   the **remaining customer records** on page 459

45. **Close**   the **Customer Centre** when you have finished entering the customers

Entering Opening Balances as Invoices

When we entered the Canadian Sledders customer record, we added the opening balance for this customer in the Opening Balance field. When entering a balance in the opening balance field, you can enter only the as of date and you cannot add invoice details; however, once the customer record is recorded, you can open the invoice created in the Create Invoices form and add an invoice number giving the transaction more detail. If you use the opening balance field, only one invoice is created for the customer.

If your customers have multiple outstanding invoices, you can add opening balances for customers and vendors as ordinary invoices in the same way you would enter a current invoice. This allows you to track more information for the sales, such as the invoice number, customer's cheque number for prepayments, and so on.

Sometimes a customer has more than one outstanding invoice. The sales probably occurred on different dates and therefore have different due dates. Entering them as a single opening balance with one date will make it impossible to apply discounts correctly for early payments. If there is more than one outstanding invoice for a customer, and you want to track each invoice separately, you must add them as separate invoices. This method will allow you to record payments and apply discounts to specific invoices.

Notes
When we used this approach in earlier chapters, we created a special item called History and used it when entering the historical invoices. The History item was linked to the *Uncategorized Income* account.

Creating Vendor Records

As we have seen in earlier chapters, vendor records can be entered from any vendor field in a QuickBooks forms.

Although we can add vendors on the fly as needed, it is more efficient to start with a list of existing vendors. As with many other activities in QuickBooks, vendors can be added in many ways. Other than starting in a Vendor field on a form, all methods begin from the Vendors List. This list can only be accessed from the Vendor Centre.

To access the Vendor Centre:

a. **Click** the **Vendors icon** on the Icon bar; or

b. **Choose Vendors** from the menu and **click Vendor Centre**; or

c. **Click** the **Vendors button** in the Vendors section of the Home page

1. **Open** the **Vendor Centre** using one of the methods described above

2. **Open** the **New Vendor form** by performing one of the following options:

   a) **Right-click** in the **Vendors list** and **select New Vendor**; or
   b) **Click** the **New Vendor button** and **select New Vendor**; or
   c) **Choose Edit** from the menu and **select New Vendor**; or
   d) **Press** (ctrl) **+ N**

3. **Click** ☒ to close the Add/Edit Multiple List Entries screen

4. The New Vendor form will be displayed:

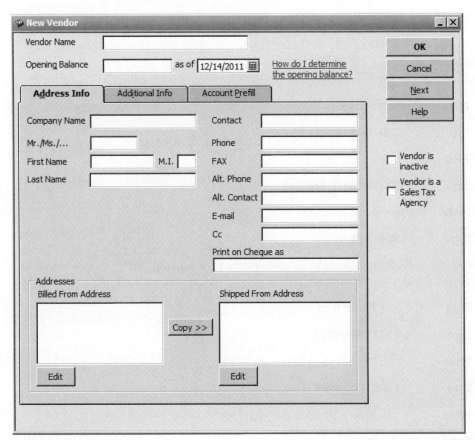

Figure 9-37

QuickBooks has automatically created vendor records for the Receiver General and Saskatchewan Finance, the tax agencies for the collection of sales taxes. You cannot remove these records even if you do not collect taxes. We will edit the record for the Receiver General to add the address details, and we will make the Saskatchewan Finance record inactive so it will not appear on our lists.

This is the same New Vendor form we used earlier when we added complete vendor records. This time, we will add opening invoice balance amounts for the new vendors.

5. **Type** **Foley's** in the **Vendor Name field**

6. **Press** (tab) to move to the Opening Balance field

7. **Type** **115**

8. **Press** (tab) to move to the As of date field

The date applies to the invoice date. Entering this date correctly will allow the correct calculation of discounts and due dates.

9.	Type	08/28/14
10.	Press	⌨ tab ⌨ to advance to the Company Name field
11.	Type	Foley's
12.	Press	⌨ tab ⌨ twice to move to the First Name field
13.	Type	Jane
14.	Press	⌨ tab ⌨ twice to move to the Last Name field
15.	Type	Foley
16.	Press	⌨ tab ⌨

The company name and contact appear in the Address text area, and the name we entered is added to the Contact field. You can enter a different name in the Contact field if this is appropriate. The cursor is in the Billed From Address text box.

17.	Press	⌨ enter ⌨ to move the next blank line in the Billed From Address text box
18.	Type	122 Baryshnikov St.
19.	Press	⌨ enter ⌨
20.	Type	Regina, Saskatchewan
21.	Press	⌨ enter ⌨
22.	Type	S3P 7N5

There are no more lines for address information. We will complete the fields on this screen before adding address details. The vendor has only one phone number.

23.	Click	the **Phone field**
24.	Type	(306) 224-4632
25.	Press	⌨ tab ⌨ to advance to the FAX field
26.	Type	(306) 225-6722
27.	Press	⌨ tab ⌨ twice to advance to the Alt. Contact field
28.	Type	Robin
29.	Press	⌨ tab ⌨ to advance to the E-mail address field
30.	Type	jf@foleys.com

The company name is entered by default as the name that should appear on the cheque. You can edit this name if necessary.

31.	Click	the **Edit button** to open the Edit Address Information window

This screen has the address fields separated for easier editing. If you need to make changes to the address details later, it is easier to do so from this screen. The address information has been entered in the correct fields already but the country is missing.

32.	Click	the **Country/Region field**
33.	Type	Canada
34.	Click	**OK** to return to the New Vendor form. This tab is now complete

35. Click the **Additional Info tab**:

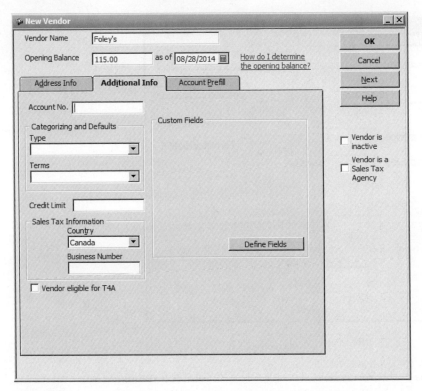

Figure 9-38

Companies can assign unique vendor numbers to each vendor to make it easier to organize the vendor records in reports. Vendors can also be grouped by types, such as region or type of business for targeted business contacts. For example, information about items needed for special contracts may be sent only to the businesses that supply those kinds of products. Vendor account numbers and vendor types are not used by Darya's vendors so we can skip these fields.

Most vendors place limits on the amount that a customer is allowed to purchase on credit. Once the credit limit is reached, the customer may be asked for a down payment or may be granted a credit limit increase. The program warns when a credit limit is exceeded by a purchase; Darya's is allowed to carry an account balance of $300.00 with Foley's.

Business numbers are also frequently added to invoices for tax purposes when taxes are charged by a business. The T4A field will be checked for vendors who provide subcontracted labour and need the T4A income tax form. Both the pianist and the instructor who work with Darya's need T4A forms.

36. Click the **drop-down arrow** in the **Terms field** to view the terms set up by default. **Add** the **term 1% 5 Net 30** for Foley's

37. Click **<Add New>** at the top of the terms list as shown:

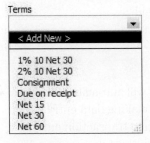

Figure 9-39

38. The New Terms form opens:

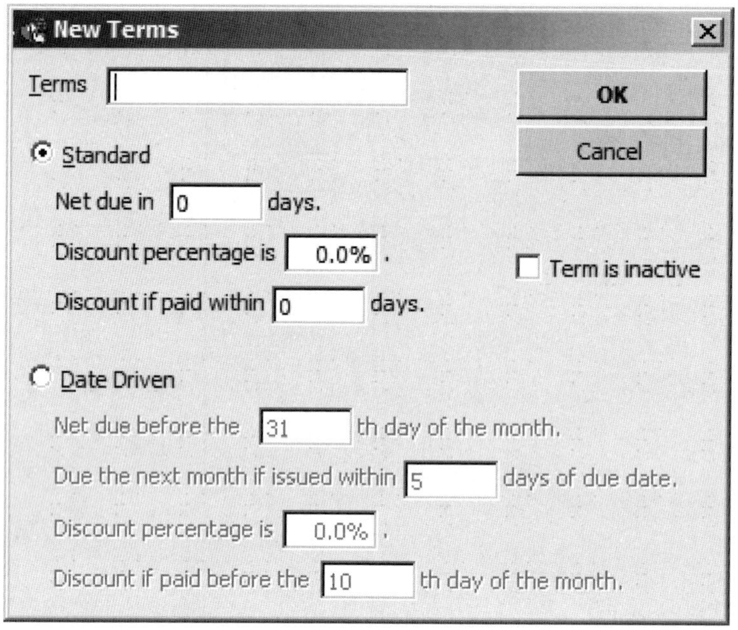

New Terms form:

Terms [ ]

OK
Cancel

☉ Standard

Net due in [0] days.

Discount percentage is [0.0%] .

☐ Term is inactive

Discount if paid within [0] days.

○ Date Driven

Net due before the [31] th day of the month.

Due the next month if issued within [5] days of due date.

Discount percentage is [0.0%] .

Discount if paid before the [10] th day of the month.

Figure 9-40

The cursor is in the Terms field. The 1% 5 Net 30 term is a standard term rather than a Date Driven term. Payments due at the end of a month or on the 15th of each month are Date Driven terms.

39. Type	1% 5 Net 30 in the **Terms field**
40. Double click	the **Net due in ___ days field**
41. Type	30
42. Press	⌨ tab to advance to the Discount Percentage is field
43. Type	1
44. Press	⌨ tab to advance to the Discount if paid within __ days field
45. Type	5
46. Click	**OK** to return to the Additional Info tab of the New Vendor form

The new terms code is automatically displayed in the Terms field for the current vendor.

47. Click	the **Credit Limit field**
48. Type	300
49. Press	⌨ tab to advance to the Business Number field
50. Type	398446722
51. Click	the **Account Prefill tab**

This tab is used to enter up to three expense accounts that will automatically be entered when you create a bill or write a cheque to the vendor, making data entry easier to accurately track expenses. The accounts can be changed during transaction entry.

Darya's will not be entering expense accounts for vendors on this tab.

52. Click	**Next** to save the vendor record and open a blank New Vendor form
53. Enter	the **remaining vendor records** on pages 458–459
54. Click	**OK** to save the last vendor and return to the Vendors list in the Vendor Centre (**Click Cancel** if you have a blank vendor form open on the screen)

Editing Vendor Records

1. Highlight	the **Receiver General** on the Vendors list
2. Press	⌃ctrl + **E** to open the incomplete vendor record
3. Complete	the **record** by entering the address and phone number shown on page 458
4. Click	**OK** to save the changes and return to the Vendor Centre
5. Close	the **Vendor Centre**

Notes
You can also edit a selected vendor by right-clicking in the Vendors list and choosing Edit Vendor from the menu, or choosing the Edit menu and clicking Edit Vendor.

Creating Items

We have seen that QuickBooks processes all sales, estimates, and orders by selling items. Revenue accounts are linked to items. Therefore you must create items to use the program. You cannot access revenue accounts from any of the customer sales forms.

Perhaps because items are central to the way the program operates, you can add records for items from many different places. Just as you can add other types of records on the fly during transaction entry from their respective fields in the forms, you can add items on the fly from any Item field in any form in QuickBooks. You can also set up records for items from the Item List, and you can access this list in several ways.

Notes
Any account can be linked to any item but normally a revenue account is selected for items and services you sell. For merchandise you purchase, you would normally use an asset account.

1. **Open**   the **Item List** using one of the following methods:

a)   **Click** the **Items & Services icon** found in the Company section of the Home page; or

b)   **Click Lists** from the menu and **select Item List;** or

c)   **Click Sales Tax** from the menu and **select Item List**; or

d)   **Click Customers** from the menu and **select Item List**; or

e)   **Click Vendors** from the menu and **select Item List**

2. The Item List is displayed as shown:

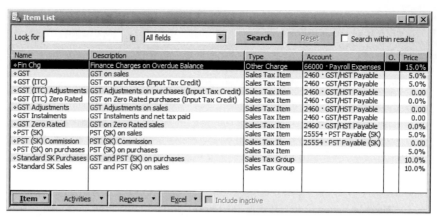

Figure 9-41

The item list includes taxes that are automatically set up for the province selected during QuickBooks setup and the item QuickBooks created for finance charges, based on the preference setting we entered.

3. Press   `ctrl` **+ N** to create a new item

4. Click   ☒ to close the Add/Edit Multiple List Entries window and open a New Item form:

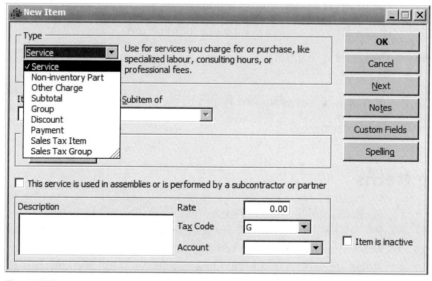

Figure 9-42

Creating Service Items

> **Notes**
> You cannot use colons in item names because colons are used to identify subitem relationships.

The drop-down list in the Type field is displayed with Service selected as the default type, and it is the one we will use first. The dance and exercise classes offered by Darya's Dance Studio are service items. They are associated only with an income account for tracking purposes. For each service item, you can indicate the item name and/or number, whether the account is a subitem of another item, whether the service is performed by a subcontractor, the item description, a default rate, the tax code, and the account. You can change the tax code and rate for individual sales at any time during transaction entry, but you cannot change the income account associated with the item.

Darya does not use item numbers or subitems, and no services are provided by subcontractors. By default, the items in the item list will appear in alphabetical order when selected in forms, so we will have to keep that in mind when entering item names.

The first service item we will enter is Class - Single, first on the Item list on page 460.

5.	**Press**	(tab) to select Service and advance to the Item Name/Number field
6.	**Type**	**Class - Single**
7.	**Click**	the **Description field**
8.	**Type**	**Single dance or exercise class**
9.	**Press**	(tab) to advance to the Rate field
10.	**Type**	**25**
11.	**Press**	(tab) to advance to the Tax Code field

Services are subject to GST but not to PST, so the correct code is G. This sales tax code charges GST only at 5%.

12.	**Accept**	**G** as the sales tax code

G should already be displayed as the sales tax code because it was selected as the sales tax code used most often for taxable items in the Sales Tax preferences.

13.	**Press**	(tab) to advance to the Account field
14.	**Click**	the **drop-down arrow** in the **Account field** to view the Chart of Accounts
15.	**Select**	**4100 - Revenue from Lessons**

If the account you need is not displayed on the Chart of Accounts, type the account number in the account field and press (tab) to add the account. Click Set Up to open the Add New Account form. Income will be selected correctly as the account type for the new account.

CORRECTING ITEM RECORDS

To correct an item record while you are creating it, return to the field that has the error, highlight the incorrect details, and type the correction. To correct the item type, tax code, or account, select the correct type, tax code, or account from the drop-down lists.

If you need to make corrections or changes later, after saving the item record, refer to page 512.

16.	**Click**	**Next** to save the item and open a blank New Item form

Notice that the default tax code and account number from the previous item are still displayed.

17.	**Enter**	the **remaining service items** on page 460.
18.	**Click**	**Next** after entering the last service item to leave a blank New Item form displayed on the screen

Creating Non-inventory Part Items

In addition to services, Darya's will create items for some assets it buys or places on purchase orders because purchase orders require you to select an item. The type most appropriate for these purchases is Non-inventory Part. The Non-inventory Part type is used for items, such as supplies or materials, for specific customer jobs that are later charged to a customer.

1.	**Click**	the **drop-down arrow** in the **Type field**
2.	**Click**	**Non-inventory Part** to change the account type and the New Item form

📄 **Notes**
In previous chapters, we selected Non-inventory Part for items sold to customers that were not tracked as inventory.

Notice that the default tax code and account number from the previous entry are still displayed, even though the account type is different. A new Manufacturer's Part Number field is displayed for Non-inventory Part items. Refer to the list on page 460.

3. **Press** $\boxed{tab}$ to advance to the Item Name/Number field

4. **Type**   **Music Inventory**

5. **Click**   the **Description field**

6. **Type**   **CDs and sheet music**

Do not enter a price because prices will change with each purchase or order.

7. **Click**   the **drop-down arrow** in the **Tax Code field**

8. **Choose**   **S** which will calculate both GST and PST at 5%

9. **Click**   the **drop-down arrow** in the **Account field**

10. **Choose**   **1260 - Music Inventory**

11. **Click**   **Next**

12. **Enter**   **Supplies**, the second Non-inventory Part item as shown on page 460

13. **Click**   **Next** after entering the last Non-inventory Part item to leave a blank New Item form displayed on the screen

Creating Other Charge Items

Darya's also requires items for charges relating to NSF cheques. We used these items to record NSF charges for Terrific Tours' customers. Items of this type are entered as Other Charges in QuickBooks. The Fin Chg (finance charge) item is already entered. Again, refer to the list on page 460.

1. **Click**   the **drop-down arrow** in the **Type field**

2. **Click**   **Other Charge** to change the account type and the New Item form:

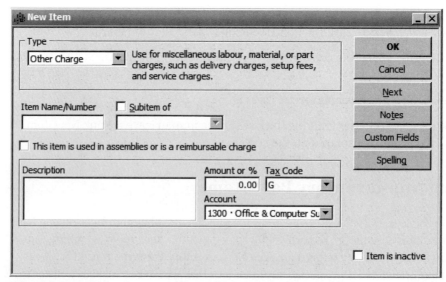

Figure 9-43

Read the description displayed for this type of item.

Notice that the default tax code and account number from the previous entry are displayed, even though the account type is different.

3.	**Press**	(tab) to advance to the Item Name/Number field
4.	**Type**	**Admin Charge**
5.	**Click**	the **Description field**
6.	**Type**	**Handling charge for NSF cheque**
7.	**Press**	(tab) to advance to the Amount or % field
8.	**Type**	**30**
9.	**Press**	(tab) to advance to the Sales Tax Code field
10.	**Press**	(del) to remove the sales tax code. Sales taxes do not apply on NSF charges
11.	**Press**	(tab) to advance to the Account field
12.	**Choose**	**4250 - Other Revenue** as the account
13.	**Click**	**Next**
14.	**Enter**	**NSF Cheque** as the final Other Charge. Refer to page 460
15.	**Click**	**OK** to save the item and return to the Item List
16.	Notice that the Item List now includes all the items we have created	

Editing the Finance Charge Item

We will now edit the item for finance charges created when we set up the Finance Charge preferences to match our item list. We will change the name and terms of the finance charge. Darya has decided not to charge interest on previous interest amounts. The Item List should still be open.

Notes
You can edit only some of the finance charge settings from the Item List — the name, description, rate (amount), tax code, and account. To change the annual interest rate, minimum finance charge, grace period, finance charge account, or to determine how finance charges are calculated, you must access the Finance Charge preferences.

1. **Double click** **Fin Chg** to open the item record:

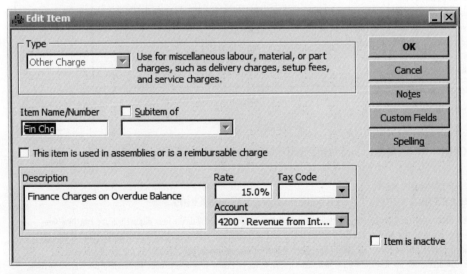

Figure 9-44

2. **Type** **Interest Charge** to replace the default name of Fin Chg

3. **Double click** **Finance** in the **Description field** (select only the single word)

4. **Type** **Interest**

5.	**Click**	the **drop-down arrow** in the **Account field**
6.	**Accept**	**4200 - Revenue from Interest**
7.	**Click**	**OK** to save the changes and close the item record

We must return to the Finance Charge preferences screen to change the assessment of finance charges on overdue finance charges. Darya's does not assess finance charges on previous assessed finance charges.

8.	**Choose**	the **Edit menu** and **click Preferences**
9.	**Click**	the **Finance Charge heading** on the left-hand side of the screen
10.	**Click**	the **Company Preferences tab**
11.	**Click**	**Assess finance charges on overdue finance charges** to remove the ✓
12.	The completed Finance Charge preference screen should be displayed as shown:	

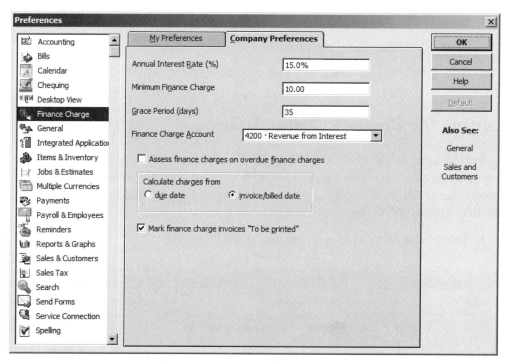

Figure 9-45

13.	**Click**	**OK** to save the changes

CORRECTING ITEMS AFTER THEY HAVE BEEN SAVED

To correct items, open the Item List. Double click the item that you want to edit. With the item displayed in the Edit Item form, highlight the text that you want to change and type the correct information to replace it. Select a different tax code or account from the drop-down list for those fields. When you select a different account for an item, QuickBooks will ask if you want all previous transactions for the item to use the new account. Choose Yes to change prior transactions, No to leave the previous account, or click Cancel to return to the item record.

You cannot change the item type, even if you haven't used the item in transactions. To change the item type for a service item, you must create a new item. If the incorrect item has not been used in transactions, you can delete it. You can change subitem links after creating an item. You can change the item type to Service from Non-inventory Part or from Other Charge, but these changes cannot be reversed.

You cannot use the same item name for different items, even if their types are different.

Adjusting Opening Balances

Now that we have entered opening balances for all customers and vendors, the *Accounts Payable* and *Accounts Receivable* balances should be correct. All vendor balances have been debited to the *Uncategorized Expense* account — the account QuickBooks created for this purpose. All customer balances have been credited to the *Uncategorized Income* account — the account QuickBooks created for this purpose. QuickBooks created these accounts automatically when we entered an amount in the Opening Balance field in customer and vendor records. When an opening balance is entered for a vendor, a bill is created in the vendor record for the opening balance amount. When an opening balance is entered for a customer, an invoice is created in the customer record for the opening balance amount. If the *Accounts Receivable* and *Accounts Payable* amounts do not match the balances shown in the Trial Balance on page 458, one or more of the entries may be incorrect, and they can be edited just as any other bill or invoice would be edited.

1. **Print**   the **A/R Aging Detail Report** and the **A/P Aging Detail Report at August 31, 2014** to check the opening balance entries for customers and vendors

2. **Compare**   these **reports** with the charts on page 459

3. **Make**   **corrections** if necessary using the information in the Correcting Opening Balances paragraph below before completing the next step

---

CORRECTING OPENING BALANCES

A bill is automatically created for a vendor if an opening balance is entered when setting up the vendor record. These vendor bills can be corrected from the Enter Bills form. With the Enter Bills form open, find the bill by using the Find tool or by clicking the Previous and Next buttons to review the entries and locate the error. Refer to page 242 for assistance if needed.

An invoice is automatically created for a customer if an opening balance is entered when setting up the customer record. These customer invoices can be corrected from the Create Invoices form. With the Create Invoices form open, use the Find tool or click the Previous and Next buttons to review the entries and locate the error. Refer to page 297 for assistance if needed.

After making all the corrections to the customer and vendor opening balances, the final adjustment that remains is to transfer the amounts in the *Uncategorized Expense* and *Uncategorized Income* accounts to the *Capital, Darya Danovich* account, the equity account. We need to complete this step because these amounts have been entered twice — once in the original expense and revenue entries (page 487) and once in the opening balances for vendors and customers. We need to add back the revenue to the capital account and subtract the expenses. Originally, we created the opening revenue balances by subtracting them from capital because they are still part of current income.

First, we will record the adjustment for the revenue amount entered from the customer opening balances.

Notes
You can access revenue accounts from the General Journal but you cannot open the register for revenue accounts.

1. **Open**   the **Chart of Accounts**

2. **Double click** the **Capital, Darya Danovich account** to open the account register

3. **Enter**   **08/31/14** as the date for the transaction

4. **Choose**   **49900 - Uncategorized Income** as the account in the Account field

5. **Type**   **Adjust opening income** in the **Memo field**

6. **Enter**   **1445** (the amount of the customer opening balances) as the amount in the Increase column

7. **Click**   **Record** to record the transaction and update the account register

Next, we will record the adjustment for the expense amount entered from the vendor opening balances.

8.	**Accept**	the **date** of 08/31/14 for the next transaction
9.	**Choose**	**69800 - Uncategorized Expenses** as the account in the Account field
10.	**Type**	**Adjust opening expenses** in the **Memo field**
11.	**Enter**	**1455** (the amount of the vendor opening balances) as the amount in the Decrease column
12.	**Click**	**Record** to record the transaction and update the account register:

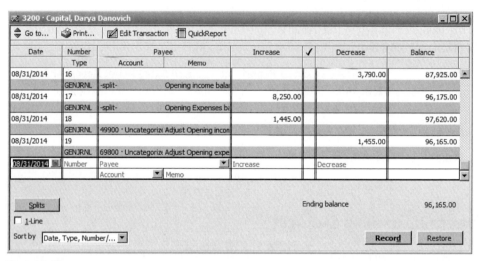

Figure 9-46

13.	**Close**	the **register** to return to the Chart of Accounts

Making Accounts Inactive

Now that we have entered our customer and vendor opening balances and transferred the amounts in the *Uncategorized Income* and *Uncategorized Expenses* accounts, we no longer need these accounts. We cannot delete them because they were used in transactions; however, we can make them inactive so they are not displayed in account lists and accidentally used in transactions.

1.	**Click**	the **Uncategorized Income account** to select it
2.	**Click**	the **Account button** and then **click Make Account Inactive**
3.	**Click**	the **Uncategorized Expense account** to select it
4.	**Click**	the **Account button** and then **click Make Account Inactive**

These two accounts are now inactive and are not displayed in the Chart of Accounts. You can restore these accounts (make them active) at any time. Choose the Account button and click Show Inactive Accounts. The inactive accounts will be marked with an X displayed in the column to the left. Click the account you want to change. Choose the Account button and click Make Account Active to make the account active.

5.	**Close**	the **Chart of Accounts**

Notes
To make a selected account inactive, you can also right-click in the Chart of Accounts window and choose Make Account Inactive from the menu, or choose the Edit menu and click Make Account Inactive.

Editing Lists

When we chose terms and payment methods for vendors and customers, we saw that QuickBooks created a number of terms automatically. We don't need all these terms so we should delete the ones that we won't be using.

Editing Terms

1. **Choose**   the **Lists menu**, then **choose Customer & Vendor Profile Lists** and **click Terms List** to open the Terms List:

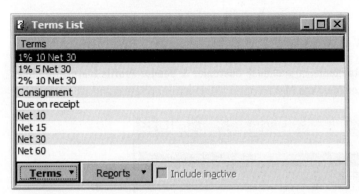

Figure 9-47

The Terms List is just like any other list in QuickBooks. From this window, you can create new terms, edit or delete terms, make terms inactive, display a number of reports, and so on. The keyboard shortcut commands are the same as the commands for other lists.

Although we are not using all these terms, we can retain most of them in case we need them later. We will delete the Net 60 days term.

2. **Click**   **Net 60**

3. **Click**   the **Terms button** and **click Delete Terms** or **press** `ctrl` **+ D** to view the warning message

4. **Click**   **OK** to delete the terms code

5. **Close**   the **Terms List**

Editing Payment Methods

1. **Choose**   the **Lists menu**, then **choose Customer & Vendor Profile Lists**, and **click Payment Method List** to open the Payment Method List:

Figure 9-48

We can delete most of the payment methods on the list. Darya's Dance Studio accepts cash, cheques, and Visa for payment so we will keep these payment methods.

2. **Click**   **American Express**

3. **Click**   the **Payment Method button** and **click Delete Payment Method** or **press** (ctrl) **+ D** to view the warning message

4. **Click**   **OK** to delete the payment method

5. **Repeat**   the **above steps** to **delete MasterCard**, **Direct Payment**, and **Interac Debit**

6. **Close**   the **Payment Method List**

Editing Customer Messages

1. **Choose**   the **Lists menu**, then **choose Customer & Vendor Profile Lists**, and **click Customer Message List** to open the Customer Message List:

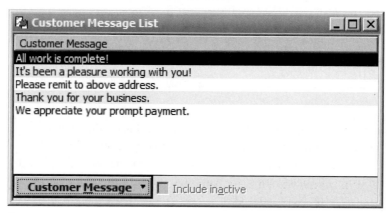

Figure 9-49

We can keep most of the customer messages on the list. We don't need the first customer message because it applies to customized service or contract work that is not applicable to Darya's.

2. **Click**   the **All work is complete!** customer message

3. **Click**   the **Customer Message button** and **click Delete Customer Message** or **press** (ctrl) **+ D** to view the warning message

4. **Click**   **OK** to delete the customer message

5. **Close**   the **Customer Message List**

Checking the Setup

Notes
To add columns of additional information on reports, display the report, and click the Modify Report button. Click the Display tab. Then click each field that you want to add to the list. Click OK to return to the revised list.

You should check all the information you entered to verify the accuracy of your work. Although you can make corrections at any time, you should attempt to have a data file that is error free before entering current year transactions. To check your work,

1. **Print**   or **display** the **following reports**:

   a) Trial Balance as of August 31, 2014
   b) Customer Contact List: **Add columns** for Terms, E-mail, and Credit Limit to the list

c) Vendor Contact List: **Add columns** for Terms, E-mail, Credit Limit, and Business Number to the list

d) A/R Aging Detail Report as of August 31, 2014

e) A/P Aging Detail Report as of August 31, 2014

f) Item Price List: **Add columns** for Account and Sales Tax Code

Source Documents

Now that you have set up the company file, enter the following source documents. You may need to refer to previous chapters for additional information.

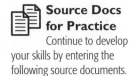

Source Docs for Practice
Continue to develop your skills by entering the following source documents.

September 1 – September 7, 2014

SD1: **Invoice**   **Dated September 1, 2014**

Invoice #115 to Waltzer Family, two classes per week for three family members for a 15-week session (6 sessions of classes) at $220.00 each plus GST. Invoice totals $1,386.00. Terms: 1/10, n/30.

SD2: **Credit Card Charge**   **Dated September 1, 2014**

Bill #GP-30012 received from The Grand Papery (set up the new vendor), $130.00 plus $6.50 GST and $6.50 PST for copying dance class schedules and pamphlets for a new session. The bill totalling $143.00 was paid in full by Visa.

Notes
The Grand Papery (Greeting Card)
33 Woodpulp St.
Regina, SK S3V 6F6
Terms: Due on receipt
Credit Limit: $1,000.00

SD3: **Pay Bill**   **Dated September 2, 2014**

Cheque #591 paid to Foley's, $113.85 in payment of account, including the discount for early payment. Reference Bill #F-445.

SD4: **Pay Bill**   **Dated September 3, 2014**

Cheque #592 paid to Sounds Inc., $499.80 in payment of account, including the discount for early payment. Reference Bill #SI-390.

SD5: **Credit Card Charge**   **Dated September 3, 2014**

Bill #WG-209 received from Wendy Groen, RMT, $85.00 plus $4.25 GST for a weekly one-hour massage. Invoice totalling $89.25 was paid in full by Visa. Create a new expense account: 5170 - *Massage Therapy Expense* (tax code G, GST only). Memorize the transaction with weekly reminders beginning Sep. 10, 2014.

Notes
Close the message about outstanding invoices.
Enter Wendy Groen, RMT as the name for the memorized transaction if necessary.

SD6: **Customer Payment**   **Dated September 4, 2014**

From Minuet Family, Cheque #204 for $310.00 in payment of account. Reference Invoice #92. Group all deposits with other undeposited funds.

Notes
The first time you enter a sales receipt or receive a customer payment in QuickBooks, an *Undeposited Funds* account is automatically created in the Chart of Accounts. Renumber it to account number 1450.

SD7: **Pay Bill**   **Dated September 4, 2014**

Cheque #593 paid to Wendy Groen, RMT, $450.00 in payment of account. Reference Bill #WG-103.

SD8: **Credit Card Charge**   **Dated September 5, 2014**

Bill #P-7107 received from Petra's Petrol (use Quick Add to add the new vendor), $30.00 plus $1.50 GST and $1.50 PST for the weekly gasoline purchase for the business vehicle. Invoice totalling $33.00 was paid in full by Visa. Memorize the transaction with weekly reminders beginning Sep. 12, 2014.

SD9: **Customer Payment**   **Dated September 6, 2014**

From Saskie Gliders, Cheque #1098 for $727.65 in payment of account, including the discount for early payment. Reference Invoice #102.

SD10: **Bill**   **Dated September 6, 2014**

Bill #LT-199 received from Les Toyle (use Quick Add to add the new vendor), $220.00 plus $11.00 GST for the weekly cleaning bill. The bill totals $231.00. Terms: Net 15. Memorize the transaction with weekly reminders beginning Sep. 13, 2014. Save the new terms.

📄 **Notes**
  A non-posting *Estimates* account is automatically added to the Chart of Accounts the first time you enter an estimate in QuickBooks. This non-posting account does not affect your Balance Sheet or Income Statement. Change its account number to 6000.

SD11: **Estimate**   **Dated September 6, 2014**

Estimate #11 to Saskie Gliders, $220.00 each plus GST for teaching a dance routine to the eight-member skating team. Classes to begin in two weeks. Estimate totals $1,848.00. Deposit of 50 percent required on acceptance of the estimate.

    Create new Service item (price varies; do not enter an item price):

Item Name:	Customized Program
Description:	Classes created for customer
Tax code:	G
Account:	*4100 - Revenue from Lessons*

📄 **Notes**
  To create the new item, choose the Add New option from the drop-down list in the Item field to open the New Item form.

SD12: **Memo #1**   **Dated September 6, 2014**

From Owner: Customize the Estimates form by removing the Markup column.

SD13: **Visa Sales Receipt Summary #420**   **Dated September 6, 2014**

To Visa Sales customers:

100	Classes - Session	$220.00 each	$22,000.00
12	Classes - Month	75.00 each	900.00
12	Classes - Single	25.00 each	300.00
	GST	5%	1,160.00
	Total receipts held for deposit:		$24,360.00

Memorize the transaction with weekly reminders to begin Sep. 13, 2014.

SD14: Cash Sales Receipt Summary #421   **Dated September 7, 2014**

To Cash Sales customers

1	Classes - Session	$220.00 each	$ 220.00
8	Classes - Month	75.00 each	600.00
10	Classes - Single	25.00 each	250.00
	GST	5%	53.50
	Total cash receipts held for deposit		$1,123.50

Memorize the transaction with weekly reminders to begin Sep. 14, 2014.

SD15: Memo #2   **Dated September 7, 2014**

From Owner: Deposit $2,161.15 to the *Bank - Chequing* account and $24,360.00 to the *Bank - Credit Card* account.

SD16: Pay Bill   **Dated September 7, 2014**

Paid Cheque #594 to Treble & Bass, $376.20 in payment of account, including the discount for early payment. Reference Bill #TB-2918.

Notes
If some payments do not show in the Cash and Cheque list, select items for deposit individually from the list of all Payments to Deposit.

September 8 – September 14, 2014

SD17: Invoice   **Dated September 8, 2014**

Invoice #116 to Minuet Family, two classes per week for three children and two adults for a 15-week session (10 sessions of classes) at $220.00 each plus GST. Invoice totals $2,310.00. Terms: 1/10, n/30. Allow customer to exceed their credit limit.

SD18: Bank Debit Memo #29901   **Dated September 8, 2014**

Cheque #204 from Minuet Family for $310.00 in payment of Invoice #92 was returned as NSF. Create Invoice #117 to charge the $310.00 NSF cheque amount to the Minuet Family and add the $30.00 Admin Charges. No taxes apply to these amounts. Invoice totals $340.00. Terms: Due on receipt. Do not save the new terms.

SD19: Credit Card Charge   **Dated September 9, 2014**

Bill #GP-30891 received from The Grand Papery, $75.00 plus $3.75 GST and $3.75 PST for computer and office supplies. Invoice totalling $82.50 was paid in full by Visa.

SD20: Customer Payment   **Dated September 9, 2014**

From Saskie Gliders, Cheque #1203 for $900.00 as a deposit on Estimate #11.

SD21: Customer Payment   **Dated September 9, 2014**

From Waltzer Family, Cheque #235 for $1,372.80 in payment of account, including the discount for early payment. Taxes are not included in the discount. Reference Invoice #115.

SD22: Customer Payment   **Dated September 10, 2014**

From Minuet Family, certified Cheque #RB-204 for $340.00 in full payment of account. Reference Invoice #117.

SD23: Credit Card Charge   **Dated September 10, 2014**

Bill #WG-264 received from Wendy Groen, RMT, $85.00 plus $4.25 GST for the weekly one-hour massage. Invoice totalling $89.25 was paid in full by Visa. Use the memorized transaction.

Notes
A non-posting *Purchase Orders* account is automatically added to the Chart of Accounts the first time you enter a purchase order in QuickBooks. This non-posting account does not affect your Balance Sheet or Income Statement. Change its account number to 6050.

SD24: Purchase Order   **Dated September 10, 2014**

Purchase Order #102 to Sounds Inc., $900.00 plus $45.00 GST and $45.00 PST for specialized choreography software. Invoice totals $990.00. Change the *Purchase Orders* account number to 6050.

SD25: Bill   **Dated September 11, 2014**

Bill #PC-4911 received from Prime Contacts, $245.00 plus $12.25 GST and $12.25 PST for business telephone service. The bill totals $269.50. Terms: Net 15 days.

SD26: Estimate   **Dated September 11, 2014**

Estimate #12 to Canadian Sledders, $220.00 each plus GST for specialized rhythm and stretch classes for the six-member bobsled team (6 sessions of classes). Estimate totals $1,386.00. A 50 percent deposit is required on accepting the estimate.

SD27: Credit Card Charge   **Dated September 12, 2014**

Bill #P-7865 received from Petra's Petrol, $30.00 plus $1.50 GST and $1.50 PST for the weekly gasoline purchase for the business vehicle. Invoice totalling $33.00 was paid in full by Visa. Use the memorized transaction.

Notes
Do not apply the receipt from Canadian Sledders to the outstanding invoice.

SD28: Customer Payment   **Dated September 13, 2014**

From Canadian Sledders, Cheque #85 for $700.00 as deposit on Estimate #12.

SD29: Bill   **Dated September 13, 2014**

Bill #LT-235 received from Les Toyle, $220.00 plus $11.00 GST for the weekly cleaning bill. The bill totals $231.00. Terms: Net 15. Use the memorized transaction.

SD30: Invoice   **Dated September 13, 2014**

Invoice #118 to Polka Family (use Quick Add to create the new customer), three classes per week for two children for the entire 15-week session (6 sessions of classes) at $220.00 each plus GST. Invoice totals $1,386.00. Terms: 1/10, n/30. Save the new terms.

SD31: Visa Sales Receipt Summary #422   **Dated September 13, 2014**

To Visa Sales customers:

80 Classes - Session	$220.00 each	$17,600.00
19 Classes - Month	75.00 each	1,425.00
8 Classes - Single	25.00 each	200.00
GST	5%	961.25
Total receipts held for deposit:		$20,186.25

Use the memorized transaction and edit the quantities.

SD32: Cash Sales Receipt Summary #423   **Dated September 14, 2014**

To Cash Sales customers:

2 Classes - Session	$220.00 each	$ 440.00
4 Classes - Month	75.00 each	300.00
11 Classes - Single	25.00 each	275.00
GST	5%	50.75
Total cash receipts held for deposit:		$1,065.75

Use the memorized transaction and edit the quantities.

SD33: Estimate   **Dated September 14, 2014**

Estimate #13 to Wheatfields Academy, $220.00 each plus GST for special classes in ballroom dancing to prepare for the New Year's Eve dance gala. Classes will be open to 30 students in total. Estimate totals $6,930.00. Classes will be offered only if fully enrolled.

SD34: Memo #3   **Dated September 14, 2014**

From Owner: Deposit $4,378.55 to chequing and $20,186.25 to the *Bank - Credit Card* account.

September 15 – September 21, 2014

SD35: Purchase Order   **Dated September 17, 2014**

Purchase Order #103 to The Grand Papery, $210.00 plus $10.50 GST and $10.50 PST for printing customized receipt forms and invoices. Invoice totals $231.00.

SD36: Credit Card Charge   **Dated September 17, 2014**

Bill #WG-291 received from Wendy Groen, RMT, $85.00 plus $4.25 GST for the weekly one-hour massage. Invoice totalling $89.25 was paid in full by Visa. Use the memorized transaction.

SD37: Invoice   **Dated September 18, 2014**

Invoice #119 to Canadian Sledders, to fill Estimate #12, $220.00 each plus GST for specialized rhythm and stretch classes for the six-member bobsled team (6 sessions of classes). Invoice totals $1,386.00. Terms: 1/10, n/30.

SD38: Bill   **Dated September 18, 2014**

Bill #PEC-9182 received from Prairie Energy Corp., $80.00 plus $4.00 GST for one month of hydro service for studio. The bill totals $84.00. Terms: Net 10.

SD39: Credit Card Charge   **Dated September 19, 2014**

Bill #P-8120 received from Petra's Petrol, $30.00 plus $1.50 GST and $1.50 PST for weekly gasoline purchase for business vehicle. Invoice totalling $33.00 was paid in full by Visa. Use the memorized transaction.

SD40: Invoice   **Dated September 19, 2014**

Invoice #120 to Wheatfields Academy, to fill Estimate #13, $220.00 each plus GST for special classes in ballroom dancing to prepare for the New Year's Eve dance gala. 30 students enrolled. Invoice totals $6,930.00. Terms: 1/10, n/30.

SD41: Bill   **Dated September 20, 2014**

📄 **Notes**
Do not create a fixed asset item for the piano. Enter *1580 - Piano:Cost* account.
Allow the purchase from Treble & Bass to exceed the credit limit.

Bill #TB-3449 received from Treble & Bass, $8,500.00 plus $425.00 GST and $425.00 PST for upright grand Yamaha piano. The bill totals $9,350.00. Terms: 1/10, n/30.

SD42: Visa Sales Receipt Summary #424   **Dated September 20, 2014**

To Visa Sales customers:

6 Classes - Session	$220.00 each	$1,320.00
6 Classes - Month	75.00 each	450.00
9 Classes - Single	25.00 each	225.00
GST	5%	99.75
Total receipts held for deposit:		$2,094.75

Use the memorized transaction and edit the quantities.

SD43: Bill   **Dated September 20, 2014**

Bill #LT-259 received from Les Toyle, $220.00 plus $11.00 GST for the weekly cleaning bill. The bill totals $231.00. Terms: Net 15. Use the memorized transaction.

SD44: Invoice   **Dated September 21, 2014**

Invoice #121 to Saskie Gliders, to fill Estimate #11, $220.00 each plus GST for teaching dance routine to the eight-member skating team. Invoice totals $1,848.00. Terms: 1/10, n/30.

SD45: Pay Bill   **Dated September 21, 2014**

Paid Cheque #595 to Les Toyle, $462.00 in payment of account. Reference Bills #LT-199 and #LT-235.

SD46: Write Cheque   **Dated September 21, 2014**

Bill #GP-37212 received from The Grand Papery, to fill Purchase Order #103, $210.00 plus $10.50 GST and $10.50 PST for printing customized receipt forms and invoices. The bill totalling $231.00 is paid by Cheque #596.

SD47: Cash Sales Receipt Summary #425   **Dated September 21, 2014**

To Cash Sales customers:

6	Classes - Session	$220.00 each	$1 320.00
2	Classes - Month	75.00 each	150.00
20	Classes - Single	25.00 each	500.00
	GST	5%	98.50
	Total cash receipts held for deposit:		$2,068.50

Use the memorized transaction and edit the quantities.

SD48: Memo #4   **Dated September 21, 2014**

From Owner: Deposit $1,868.50 to chequing and $2,094.75 to the *Visa* account. Owner held back $200.00 cash from the *Bank Chequing* deposit for personal use.

September 22 – September 30, 2014

SD49: Estimate   **Dated September 22, 2014**

Estimate #14 to Wheatfields Academy, $1,500.00 flat rate plus GST for special dance instruction for a performance in a school fundraising event. Estimate totals $1,575.00. A deposit of $500.00 is required on acceptance of the estimate.

SD50: Credit Card Charge   **Dated September 24, 2014**

Bill #WG-325 received from Wendy Groen, RMT, $85.00 plus $4.25 GST for the weekly one-hour massage. Invoice totalling $89.25 was paid in full by Visa. Use the memorized transaction.

SD51: Credit Card Charge   **Dated September 26, 2014**

Bill #P-8921 received from Petra's Petrol, $30.00 plus $1.50 GST and $1.50 PST for the weekly gasoline purchase for the business vehicle. Invoice totalling $33.00 was paid in full by Visa. Use the memorized transaction.

SD52: Customer Payment   **Dated September 26, 2014**

From Wheatfields Academy, Cheque #277 for $500.00 in acceptance of Estimate #14.

Notes
Do not apply the receipt from Wheatfields to the outstanding invoice.

SD53: Bill   **Dated September 26, 2014**

Bill #S-3002 received from Sounds Inc., to fill Purchase Order #102, $900.00 plus $45.00 GST and $45.00 PST for specialized choreography software. Invoice totals $990.00. Terms: 2/10, n/30.

SD54: Pay Bill   **Dated September 26, 2014**

Paid Cheque #597 to Prime Contacts, $269.50 in payment of account. Reference Bill #PC-4911.

SD55: Pay Bill   **Dated September 26, 2014**

Paid Cheque #598 to Prairie Energy Corp, $84.00 in payment of account. Reference Invoice #PEC-9182.

SD56: Customer Payment Dated September 26, 2014

From Wheatfields Academy, Cheque #276 for $6,864.00 in payment of account, including the discount for early payment. Taxes are not included in the discount. Reference Invoice #120. Do not apply used credits.

SD57: Bill Dated September 27, 2014

Bill #LT-274 received from Les Toyle, $220.00 plus $11.00 GST for the weekly cleaning bill. The bill totals $231.00. Terms: Net 15. Use the memorized transaction.

SD58: Visa Sales Receipt Summary #426 Dated September 27, 2014

To Visa Sales customers:

4 Classes - Session	$220.00 each	$ 880.00
10 Classes - Month	75.00 each	750.00
10 Classes - Single	25.00 each	250.00
GST	5%	94.00
Total receipts held for deposit:		$1,974.00

Use the memorized transaction and edit the quantities.

SD59: Cash Sales Receipt Summary #427 Dated September 28, 2014

To Cash Sales customers:

3 Classes - Session	$220.00 each	$ 660.00
6 Classes - Month	75.00 each	450.00
8 Classes - Single	25.00 each	200.00
GST	5%	65.50
Total cash receipts held for deposit:		$1,375.50

Use the memorized transaction and edit the quantities.

SD60: Pay Bill Dated September 28, 2014

Paid Cheque #599 to Treble & Bass, $9,265.00 in payment of account, including the discount for early payment. Reference Bill #TB-3449.

SD61: Customer Payment Dated September 28, 2014

From Saskie Gliders, Cheque #1401 for $930.40 in payment of account. Reference Invoice #121. Apply credits, discount, and payment.

SD62: Memo #5 Dated September 28, 2014

From Owner: Deposit $9,669.90 to chequing and $1,974.00 to *Bank - Credit Card* account.

SD63: Write Cheque Dated September 29, 2014

To pay cash for Bill #MP-39 received from Mimi Pascoe, Pianist, $2,000.00 fee for accompanying dance classes for four weeks, as per contract. Bill total is paid by Cheque #600.

SD64: Write Cheque   **Dated September 29, 2014**

To pay cash for Bill #FT-9-4 received from Fox Trotte, Instructor, $1,500.00 fee for instructing dance classes for four weeks, as per contract. Invoice total was paid by Cheque #601.

SD65: Memo #6   **Dated September 30, 2014**

From Owner: Transfer funds to cover scheduled end-of-month payments. Transfer $15,000.00 from *Bank - Credit Card* to *Bank - Chequing*. Transfer $30,000.00 from *Bank - Credit Card* to *Bank - Savings*.

SD66: Memo #7   **Dated September 30, 2014**

Pay GST owing as of September 30, 2014. Write Cheque #602 for $3,725.25 in payment.

SD67: Bank Debit Memo #38103   **Dated September 30, 2014**

From Mid-Prairies Trust, preauthorized withdrawals from chequing account for September:

Bank loan ($690.00 principal and $110.00 interest)	$800.00
Mortgage ($120.00 principal and $180.00 interest)	300.00
Long term loan ($180.00 principal and $130.00 interest)	310.00

SD68: Visa Payment   **Dated September 30, 2014**

Reconcile the *Visa Payable* account. The following transactions appeared on the statement:

Date	Transaction Details	Amount
Sep. 27	Ending balance	$1,484.25
Aug. 31	Balance forward from previous statement	875.00
Sep. 1	The Grand Papery	143.00
Sep. 3	Wendy Groen, RMT	89.25
Sep. 5	Petra's Petrol	33.00
Sep. 9	The Grand Papery	82.50
Sep. 10	Wendy Groen, RMT	89.25
Sep. 12	Petra's Petrol	33.00
Sep. 17	Wendy Groen, RMT	89.25
Sep. 19	Petra's Petrol	33.00
Sep. 27	Interest charges	17.00

Create a new Expense account for the interest charge: *5010 - Credit Card Expenses*.
Write Cheque #603 for $1,484.25 in full payment, payable to Artists' Credit Union Visa (use Quick Add to add the new Other payee).

SD69: Memo #8   **Dated September 30, 2014**

Assess finance charges for overdue accounts.

SD70: Memo #9   **Dated September 30, 2014**

    Prepare adjusting entries for supplies and prepaid expenses for September:

Office & computer supplies	$ 155.00
CDs and sheet music damaged	90.00
Prepaid insurance expired	3,250.00

SD71: Memo #10   **Dated September 30, 2014**

    From Owner: Enter depreciation for the month of September as follows:

Computers	$ 65.00
Piano	140.00
Stereo equipment	90.00
Studio	345.00
Vehicle	360.00

Finishing Your Session

1. **Back up**   your **company data file**

2. **Close**   the **company file**

3. **Close**   the **QuickBooks program**

CHAPTER TEN

Landscaping and Interior Design

Scotts' Total Concept

Objectives

After completing this chapter, you should be able to:

- **prepare** pay cheques for hourly and salaried employees
- **enter** time taken for employee sick leave
- **release** accrued vacation pay and time
- **pay** and **recover** advances to employees
- **pay** payroll liabilities
- **edit** and **review** payroll transactions
- **record** sales reps on invoices to track commissions
- **correct** payroll journal entries after saving
- **understand** automatic payroll deductions
- **pay** sales commissions to employees
- **display** and **print** payroll reports

Company Information

Company Profile

Scotts' Total Concept in Victoria, British Columbia, is owned and operated by Jennifer and Heather Scott. After completing their degrees in interior design and landscape architecture, respectively, the sisters started their business together. They offer complete interior home and garden design work, from concept design to completed project. Although some customers use only one part of the business, either interior design or landscaping, many, especially buyers of new homes, take advantage of both services Scotts' can provide.

Scotts' interior design work might include consulting on fabric colour and design, regular indoor painting or murals, choosing and hanging wallpaper, reupholstering furniture, and making drapes. Scotts' can also design complete period restorations.

Notes
Scotts' Total Concept
28 Artistic Cres.
Victoria, BC V9V 1K7
Tel: (250) 484-9026
Fax: (250) 484-2991
E-mail: scott@
totalconcept.ca
Web: www.totalconcept.com
Business No.: 247 561 550

Scotts' landscape design work often includes installing stone work; selecting and planting trees, shrubs, and perennials; and designing and building waterfalls and ponds. By emphasizing native plants, Scotts' often creates lower-maintenance gardens.

The sisters have recently purchased office and work space, but they still use their own garages to store the two vans and most of the landscaping equipment. Most of the landscaping tools are stored in the vans.

The moderate Victoria climate makes it possible to continue outdoor garden work into late fall. Scotts' business late in the year is a bit slower than during the spring and summer months, so employees take most of their vacation time in late fall and winter. No employees have taken vacation time yet this year.

Scotts' Total Concept accepts cash, cheques, and Visa in payment, with discounts for early payment and finance charges for overdue accounts. Accounts set up with regular vendors often have favourable payment terms because of the volume of business supplied by Scotts'. A credit card is used for some business purchases.

Customers pay 12 percent HST on all purchases and Scotts' pays HST on all business-related purchases.

At the end of September 2014, Scotts' is ready to enter transactions in QuickBooks after using the following information to convert their manual accounting records:

- Chart of Accounts
- Trial Balance
- Vendor Information
- Customer Information
- Item List
- Employee Information
- Accounting Procedures

NOTE: We are using a QuickBooks sample file while working in this chapter in order to keep the payroll taxes the same no matter what year you are working with this file. The sample file uses default dates in the year 2007. You will be changing that as you work through the lesson; however, some reports will still show dates in 2007.

📄 Notes
While using the sample file, you will see dates in the year 2007. This year is displayed only because this is a sample file. You will change the dates appropriately for each transaction.

Chart of Accounts

Scotts' Total Concept

ASSETS

Bank
- 1020 Bank Chequing
- 1040 Bank Savings
- 1060 Bank Visa

Accounts Receivable
- 1200 Accounts Receivable

Other Current Assets
- 1210 Undeposited Funds
- 1220 Employee Advances
- 1260 Prepaid Insurance
- 1280 Prepaid Taxes
- 1300 Office & Computer Supplies
- 1320 Decorating Supplies & Material
- 1350 Landscaping Supplies & Material
- 1380 Lawn Signs

Fixed Assets
- 1520 Design Software
- 1580 Computer Equipment
- 1640 Sewing Machines & Sergers
- 1660 Landscaping Tools
- 1680 Landscaping Equipment
- 1700 Vans
- 1740 Office

LIABILITIES

Accounts Payable
- 2100 Accounts Payable

Credit Card
- 2200 Visa Payable

Other Current Liabilities
- 2260 Bank Loan
- 2300 GST/HST Payable
- 2400 Payroll Liabilities

Long Term Liabilities
- 2720 Long Term Loan
- 2740 Mortgage Payable

EQUITY
- 3220 Capital, Jennifer Scott
- 3240 Capital, Heather Scott
- 3260 Drawings, Jennifer Scott
- 3280 Drawings, Heather Scott
- 3600 Retained Earnings

INCOME
- 4100 Revenue from Design
- 4120 Revenue from Landscaping
- 4160 Sales Discounts
- 4200 Revenue from Interest
- 4300 Other Revenue

EXPENSE

Cost of Goods Sold
- 5040 Decorating Materials Used

- 5050 Decorating Supplies Used
- 5060 Landscaping Material Used

Expense
- 5080 Bank Service Charges
- 5100 Credit Card Fees
- 5120 Advertising & Promotion
- 5140 Purchase Discounts
- 5180 Office & Computer Supplies Used
- 5220 Maintenance Expenses
- 5240 Insurance Expense
- 5260 Interest Expense
- 5280 Property Tax Expense
- 5340 Hydro Expense
- 5360 Telephone Expense
- 5380 Vehicle Operating Expenses
- 5510 Payroll Expenses

Scotts' Total Concept

AS AT SEPTEMBER 30, 2014

	Debits	Credits		Debits	Credits
1020 Bank Chequing	$ 28,320.00		3220 Capital, Jennifer Scott		39,171.68
1040 Bank Savings	55,450.00		3240 Capital, Heather Scott		39,171.68
1060 Bank Visa	3,680.00		3260 Drawings, Jennifer Scott	7,000.00	
1200 Accounts Receivable	29,556.00		3280 Drawings, Heather Scott	7,000.00	
1210 Undeposited Funds	8,000.00		4100 Revenue from Design		308,500.00
1260 Prepaid Insurance	2,940.00		4120 Revenue from Landscaping		270,000.00
1280 Prepaid Taxes	810.00		4160 Sales Discounts	4,200.00	
1300 Office & Computer Supplies	370.00		4200 Revenue from Interest		510.00
1320 Decorating Supplies & Material	1,650.00		4300 Other Revenue		50.00
1350 Landscaping Supplies & Material	2,120.00		5040 Decorating Materials Used	74,000.00	
1380 Lawn Signs	890.00		5050 Decorating Supplies Used	4,900.00	
1520 Design Software	8,500.00		5060 Landscaping Material Used	80,000.00	
1580 Computer Equipment	9,800.00		5080 Bank Service Charges	380.00	
1640 Sewing Machines & Sergers	3,100.00		5100 Credit Card Fees	285.00	
1660 Landscaping Tools	2,200.00		5120 Advertising & Promotion	9,900.00	
1680 Landscaping Equipment	24,500.00		5140 Purchase Discounts		1,400.00
1700 Vans	41,000.00		5180 Office & Computer Supplies Used	290.00	
1740 Office	160,000.00		5220 Maintenance Expenses	10,600.00	
2100 Accounts Payable		$ 11,363.00	5240 Insurance Expense	8,700.00	
2200 Visa Payable		390.00	5260 Interest Expense	5,340.00	
2260 Bank Loan		12,000.00	5280 Property Tax Expense	3,200.00	
2300 GST/HST Payable		3,500.00	5340 Hydro Expense	950.00	
2400 Payroll Liabilities		17,770.19	5360 Telephone Expense	1,830.00	
2720 Long Term Loan		40,000.00	5380 Vehicle Operating Expenses	6,500.00	
2740 Mortgage Payable		80,000.00	5510 Payroll Expenses	215,865.55	
				$823,826.55	$823,826.55

Vendor Information

Scotts' Total Concept

Vendor Name (Contact)	Address	Phone No. / Fax No.	E-mail / Business No.	Terms / Credit Limit
BC Energy Group (Mo Turbine)	500 Generator St. Victoria, BC V6D 3L9	Tel: (250) 487-2100	m.turbine@bceg.com	net 10 $500.00
Celine's Service Centre (Celine)	48 Motor Way Victoria, BC V5D 3P8	Tel: (250) 337-2819 Fax: (250) 339-2016		net 20 $2,000.00
Freya's Home Interiors (Freya Brocade, or Belle Chintz)	188 Silkworm Rd. Victoria, BC V6G 3P5	Tel: (250) 866-8201 Fax: (250) 866-1010	freya@freyas.com 364 577 409	2/5, n/30 $10,000.00
Groen's Greens (Sherri Groen)	386 Blooming Way Victoria, BC V8T 3R5	Tel: (250) 484-1726	sherri@groensgreens.com 478 265 253	1/15, n/30 $10,000.00
Haida Investments Inc. (Penny Money)	200 Totem Cres. Victoria, BC V7E 3F5	Tel: (250) 778-2983 Alt: (800) 498-2314 Fax: (250) 778-4821	money@haida.inv.com	end-of-month
Minister of Finance (BC)	100 Legislature Rd. Vancouver, BC V2D 8J9	Tel: (800) 288-6217		end-of-month

Vendor Information Continued

Scotts' Total Concept

Vendor Name (Contact)	Address	Phone No. / Fax No.	E-mail / Business No.	Terms / Credit Limit
Primus Communications (Dyal Tone)	33 Synergic Rd. Victoria, BC V3B 2J8	Tel: (250) 508-7108	accounts@primus.ca	net 15 $500.00
Receiver General	1050 Federal Lane Vancouver, BC V2P 7E8	Tel: (800) 926-3917		end-of-month
Stonewall Inc. (Rocky Plaices)	79 Flagstone Ave. Victoria, BC V6D 2L9	Tel: (250) 481-4956 Fax: (250) 488-1927	Rocky@stonewall.ca 289 367 455	1/10, n/30 $9,000.00
Workers' Compensation Board of BC	10 Protectorate Cres. Vancouver, BC V1B 5G5	Tel: (604) 526-3828 Alt: (800) 466-1927		end-of-month

Outstanding Vendor Transactions

Scotts' Total Concept

Vendor Name	Date	Terms	Due Date	Invoice No./ Cheque No.	Amount
Celine's Service Centre	Sep. 15/14	net 20	Oct. 5/14	CSC-3324	$286.00
Freya's Home Interiors	Sep. 28/14	2/5, n/30	Oct. 28/14	FHI-4801	$2,675.00
Groen's Greens	Sep. 22/14	1/15, n/30	Oct. 22/14	GG-559	$912.00
Stonewall Inc.	Sep. 23/14	1/10, n/30	Oct. 23/14	SI-3981	$4,280.00
	Sep. 26/14	1/10, n/30	Oct. 26/14	SI-3998	$3,210.00
				Balance Owing	$7,490.00
				Grand Total	$11,363.00

Customer Information

Scotts' Total Concept

Customer Name (Contact)	Address	Phone No. / Fax No.	E-mail / Preferred Payment Method	Terms / Credit Limit
Everwood, Ashby	114 Bluegrass Rd. Victoria, BC V7N 4B1	Tel: (250) 489-1514	everwoods@shaw.ca Cheque	1/5, n/30 $25,000.00
Planter, Flora	67 Peony Rd. Victoria, BC V6N 9J7	Tel: (250) 487-6673	flora67@yahoo.ca Cheque	1/5, n/30 $25,000.00
Schleger, Marie Rose	200 Fescue St. Victoria, BC V8G 5G2	Tel: (250) 904-6229 Fax: (250) 905-2619	marie.rose@sympatico.ca Cheque	1/5, n/30 $25,000.00
Toussieng, Nina	711 Oceanview Rd. Victoria, BC V8T 4B9	Tel: (250) 766-4928	nina9@hotmail.com Cheque	1/5, n/30 $25,000.00
Woodslea, Nedaa	528 Hedgerow Blvd. Victoria, BC V7T 2M5	Tel: (250) 779-2561 Alt: (250) 720-8380	Woodslea@firstcontact.ca Cheque	1/5, n/30 $25,000.00

Scotts' Total Concept

Customer Name	Date	Terms	Type	Invoice No./ Cheque No.	Amount	Balance Owing
Ashby Everwood	Sep. 22/14	1/5, n/30	Invoice	351	$9,160.00	
	Sep. 24/14		Cheque	128	$3,000.00	$6,160.00
Flora Planter	Sep. 14/14	1/5, n/30	Invoice	345	$16,946.00	
	Sep. 21/14		Cheque	1888	$5,000.00	$11,946.00
Marie Rose Schleger	Sep. 28/14	1/5, n/30	Invoice	359	$11,450.00	$11,450.00
			Grand Total			$29,556.00

Item List

Scotts' Total Concept

Item	Description	Price	Tax Code	Account
SERVICES				
Design	Interior design and decorating		H	4100 Revenue from Design
Landscaping	Garden landscaping		H	4120 Revenue from Landscaping
OTHER CHARGES				
Finance Charges	Finance Charges on Overdue Balance	18%	not used	4200 Revenue from Interest
	18% > 30 days, $25.00 min., 5-day grace period			
NSF Cheque	Amount of NSF cheque from customer		not used	1020 Bank Chequing
NSF Fee	Administrative charge for NSF cheque	$25.00	not used	4300 Other Revenue
NON-INVENTORY				
Decorating Material	Paint, paper, etc.		H	1320 Decorating Supplies & Material
Decorating Supplies	Paintbrushes, cleaning products, etc.		H	1320 Decorating Supplies & Material
Landscaping Material	Stones, tiles, plants, soil		H	1350 Landscaping Supplies & Material
Landscaping Tools	Shovels, hoes, rakes, etc.		H	1660 Landscaping Tools

Employee Information

Scotts' Total Concept

Employee	Dee Zijner	Vijay Gardner	Stone Kutter	Nicolai Digger	Mita Paynter	Serge Draper
Position	Interior Designer	Landscaper	Stoneworker	Gardener	Decorator	Upholsterer
Address	55 Windswept Pl.	350 Treeline Ave.	498 Marble Court	1040 Paradise Rd.	18 Chartreuse Cr.	299 Velveteen Dr.
	Victoria, BC	Victoria, BC	Victoria, BC	Victoria, BC	Victoria, BC	Victoria, BC
	V3Y 9K9	V6S 2D1	V5P 1B1	V4R 1J2	V7M 3B3	V6B 3W8
Telephone	(250) 455-7162	(250) 728-2910	(250) 522-3954	(250) 613-7029	(250) 279-9115	(250) 274-3714
Alt. Telephone	(250) 587-7399		(250) 633-1098		(250) 832-8711	(250) 485-8109
SIN	129 632 774	428 161 020	563 444 868	931 216 550	148 196 835	406 529 420
Employee Number	1177	1389	1328	1499	1023	1239
Date of Birth (mm-dd-yy)	07-13-78	12-16-69	04-29-63	09-19-79	02-27-72	10-31-74
Date of Hire (mm-dd-yy)	05-01-02	06-15-04	01-01-04	04-01-05	03-01-00	10-15-03
Earnings						
Regular Wage Rate			$24.00/hour	$14.00/hour	$18.00/hour	$14.00/hour
Overtime Wage Rate			$36.00/hour	$21.00/hour	$27.00/hour	$21.00/hour
Regular Annual Salary	$42,600.00	$42,600.00	—	—	—	—
Commission	2%	2%	—	—	—	—
	(design revenue)	(landscaping revenue)				

Scotts' Total Concept

Employee	Dee Zijner	Vijay Gardner	Stone Kutter	Nicolai Digger	Mita Paynter	Serge Draper
Pay Period	monthly	monthly	semi-monthly	weekly	semi-monthly	weekly
Hours per Period	160	160	80	40	80	40
WCB Rate	6.94%	4.7%	4.7%	3.07%	6.94%	6.94%
Deductions each pay period						
Medical - Employee (limit)	$48.00 (576)	$27.00 (324)	$13.50 (324)	$6.25 (324)	$27.00 (648)	$6.25 (324)
RRSP	$400.00	$200.00	$150.00	$25.00	$150.00	$25.00
CSB	$200.00	$200.00	$50.00	–	$50.00	–
Income Tax, EI, and CPP	Amounts and calculations built in to QuickBooks program					
Federal (BC) Claim - TD1						
Personal	$10,382.00 (11,000.00)	$10,382.00 (11,000.00)	$10,382.00 (11,000.00)	$10,382.00 (11,000.00)	$10,382.00 (11,000.00)	$10,382.00 (11,000.00)
Spousal/Equivalent	$10,382.00 (9,653.00)	–	–	–	$10,382.00 (9,653.00)	–
Education	–	–	–	$ 2,850.00 (2,250.00)	–	–
Other (Age)	–	–	–	–	$ 4,223.00 (4,118.00)	–
Total Claim	$20,764.00 (20,653.00)	$10,382.00 (11,000.00)	$10,382.00 (11,000.00)	$13,332.00 (13,250.00)	$24,987.00 (24,771.00)	$10,382.00 (11,000.00)
Vacation	4 weeks	4 weeks	8% retained	6% retained	8% retained	6% retained
Sick Pay Rate	same as regular hourly or salary rate					
Accrued Vacation	$3,550.00	$3,550.00	$3,075.84	$1,506.96	$2,350.08	$1,408.68
Accrued Sick Leave Time	80 hours	70 hours	80 hours	40 hours	80 hours	40 hours

PAYROLL LIABILITY	AMOUNT	PAYABLE TO
Medical - Employee	$ 206.00	Minister of Finance
Medical - Company	206.00	Minister of Finance
RRSP	1,400.00	Haida Investments Inc.
CSB Plan	600.00	Haida Investments Inc.
Income Tax	3,167.39	Receiver General
EI - Employee	391.64	Receiver General
EI - Company	548.32	Receiver General
CPP - Employee	894.73	Receiver General
CPP - Company	894.73	Receiver General
WCB	1,119.82	Workers' Compensation Board of BC
Total	$9,428.63	

Employee Profiles and TD1 Information

All employees receive vacation and sick leave benefits. Gardner and Zijner, the salaried employees, are allowed four weeks' vacation each year. Kutter and Paynter, the senior employees, receive 8 percent of their pay as vacation pay (about four weeks), and this amount is retained until they take their time off. Digger and Draper, the junior employees, receive 6 percent vacation pay (about three weeks) and this amount is also retained. Employees are encouraged to take their time off during the late fall and winter months because the company is less busy at this time of year. No employee has taken vacation time yet this year. All employees are entitled to 10 days' leave per year for illness and can carry forward two extra days.

Gardner and Zijner are set up as sales representatives so the program will track their sales for the purpose of calculating sales commissions.

Occasionally, the Scotts will grant employees small advances on future pay cheques. These amounts are paid back from future pay cheques at an agreed rate.

Through an investment company, Scotts' allows payroll deductions for Canada Savings Bond (CSB) purchases and contributions to Registered Retirement Savings Plans (RRSPs).

As required, Scotts' pays 50 percent of the provincial medical premiums for employees and the compulsory contributions for Employment Insurance (EI), Canada Pension Plan (CPP), and Workers' Compensation Board (WCB).

Dee Zijner is the head designer and sales rep for all design projects. She works with Jenn Scott to design interiors and supervise the completion of tasks by Paynter and Draper. She earns a monthly salary of $3,550.00, or $42,600.00 per year, plus a sales commission of 2 percent of the revenue from design. She fully supports her spouse who is a full-time student, and therefore claims the spousal amount for tax purposes and pays the provincial medical insurance for a couple. She has elected to purchase a CSB and contribute to her RRSP through regular salary deductions.

Vijay Gardner is the head landscaper and the sales rep for all landscaping projects. He works with Heather Scott to plan the garden projects, supervise Kutter and Digger, and order materials. His annual salary of $42,600.00 per year is paid monthly at the rate of $3,550.00. He also earns a sales commission of 2 percent of the revenue from landscaping work. Gardner is single, so he claims the single tax amount and pays the single medical premium. He also contributes to both his RRSP and his CSB plan.

Stone Kutter works on the landscaping tasks and specializes in cutting and laying stones and tiles. He is paid twice per month at a rate of $24.00 per hour for 40 hours per week. He earns $36.00 per hour for any overtime hours. As a single individual, he claims the single tax amounts and pays single medical premiums. Kutter has elected to participate in both the CSB purchase and the RRSP.

Nicolai Digger performs a variety of gardening and landscaping tasks under Kutter's supervision. He receives his pay every week at a rate of $14.00 per hour for the first 40 hours and $21.00 per hour for additional time worked beyond 40 hours. As a part-time student, Digger has a tax claim amount for education and tuition in addition to the single claim amount. His medical premiums are also deducted at the single rate. Part of his weekly pay is withheld as an RRSP contribution.

Mita Paynter works under the direction of Zijner on the interior decorating parts of the projects. A skilled decorator herself, she can work independently at the customer's home as needed. Paynter is paid twice each month at a rate of $18.00 per hour for a 40-hour week and $27.00 per hour for additional time worked. As a single parent who supports her elderly infirm mother, Paynter is allowed to claim the spousal equivalent and caregiver amounts for income tax purposes. She pays the family rate for medical premiums and participates in both RRSP and CSB programs.

Serge Draper performs a variety of decorating tasks under Paynter's supervision. He receives his weekly pay at a rate of $14.00 per hour for 40 hours and $21.00 per hour for additional time worked. He is single and therefore claims the single amount for income tax purposes and pays the single rate for medical premiums. He makes regular RRSP contributions through payroll but does not participate in the CSB purchase.

Accounting Procedures

Taxes: HST

Scotts' Total Concept pays HST on all goods and services that it buys and charges HST on all services. HST collected from customers is recorded as a liability in the *GST/HST Payable* account. HST paid to vendors is recorded in the *GST/HST Payable* account as a decrease in liability to the Canada Revenue Agency. The report is filed with the Receiver General for Canada by the last day of each month for the previous month, either including the balance owing or requesting a refund.

Scotts' Total Concept pays 12 percent HST on all taxable purchases.

Account Terms

All customers receive a 1 percent discount if they settle their account within five days after completion of the work. The full balance is required within 30 days of completion of the work. Customers with small jobs often pay by credit card and receive no discount.

For overdue accounts, customers pay finance charges of 18 percent per year after 30 days from the invoice date and a minimum charge of $25.00 for administration expenses. A five-day grace period results in charges being applied 35 days after the invoice date and credited to the *Revenue from Interest* account.

Customers whose cheques are returned as NSF are notified of their outstanding account balance and are assessed a handling charge of $25.00 to cover the fee charged by the bank.

Some vendors offer discounts for early payment.

Deposits and Cheques

All cheques, credit card payments, and cash are held for deposit. Cheques are hand printed at the time of the transaction.

Estimates, Orders, and Deposits

Scotts' Total Concept prepares estimates on request. When customers decide to proceed with a project, they pay a deposit of 25 percent so that Scotts' can buy the materials or items needed for the project.

Scotts' Total Concept also places purchase orders with regular suppliers and some-times pays a deposit on these orders.

Supplies

At the end of each month, Scotts' counts supplies and materials remaining to determine costs and prepare adjusting entries for these and other prepaid expenses. Depreciation will be entered at the end of the fiscal year.

Instructions

1. Using the Chart of Accounts, the Trial Balance, and other information, you will record entries for source documents marked with an SD beside them for October 2014, using QuickBooks. You will find the source documents listed as you work through the chapter. The procedures for entering each new type of transaction introduced in this chapter are outlined in step-by-step instructions. Additional source documents will be provided, allowing you to have more practice entering transactions. If you have used this textbook in the past and would prefer to skip the step-by-step instructions and work only with a list of source documents, refer to the CD in the back of the textbook for the list of source documents for this chapter.

Notes
Instructions for payroll reports begin on page 571.

2. After you have finished making your entries, print the **reports and graphs** for October 2014 as indicated on the following printing form:

REPORTS FOR OCTOBER 2014

Lists
- ☐ Account Listing
- ☐ Customer Phone List
- ☐ Customer Contact List
- ☐ Vendor Phone List
- ☐ Vendor Contact List
- ☐ Employee Contact List
- ☐ Item Listing
- ☐ Item Price List
- ☐ Payroll Item List

Company & Financial
- ☑ Balance Sheet Standard at Oct. 31
- ☑ Profit & Loss Standard from Oct. 1 to Oct. 31
- ☐ Expenses by Vendor
- ☐ Income by Customer

Accountant & Taxes
- ☑ Trial Balance at Oct. 31
- ☐ General Ledger
- ☑ Journal from Oct. 1 to Oct. 31
- ☐ Transaction List by Date
- ☐ Transaction Detail by Account

Other
- ☐ Custom Summary Report
- ☐ Custom Transaction Detail Report
- ☐ Transaction History
- ☐ Transaction Journal

Vendor
- ☑ A/P Aging Detail at Oct. 31
- ☐ Vendor Balance
- ☐ Unpaid Bills
- ☐ Transaction List by Vendor

Purchases
- ☐ Purchases by Vendor
- ☐ Purchases by Item
- ☐ Transaction List by Vendor
- ☐ Open Purchase Orders by Vendor

Customer
- ☑ A/R Aging Detail at Oct. 31
- ☐ Customer Balance
- ☐ Open Invoices
- ☐ Collections Report
- ☐ Transaction List by Customer

Sales
- ☐ Sales by Customer
- ☐ Sales by Item
- ☐ Open Sales Orders by Customer
- ☑ Sales by Rep from Oct. 1 to Oct. 31

Employees & Payroll
- ☑ Payroll Summary from Oct. 1 to Oct. 31
- ☐ Payroll Item Detail from Oct. 1 to Oct. 31
- ☐ Payroll Detail Review
- ☑ Employee Earnings Summary from Oct. 1 to Oct. 31

- ☑ Payroll Transactions by Payee from Oct. 1 to Oct. 31
- ☐ Payroll Transaction Detail
- ☐ Payroll Liability Balances
- ☐ Employee Withholding
- ☐ TD1 Review List
- ☐ T4 Summary
- ☐ PD7A Summary
- ☐ Record of Employment

Banking
- ☐ Deposit Detail
- ☑ Cheque Detail from Oct. 1 to Oct. 31
- ☐ Missing Cheques
- ☐ Reconcile Discrepancy
- ☐ Previous Reconciliation

GRAPHS
- ☐ Income and Expense
- ☐ Net Worth
- ☐ Accounts Payable
- ☐ Accounts Receivable
- ☐ Sales

---

3. Open the Scott.qbw file for Scotts Total Concept

Paying Hourly Wage Employees

Preparing pay cheques in QuickBooks is similar to entering other transactions — we enter the information on forms that look like payroll cheques and stubs.

> **IMPORTANT:** The QuickBooks company file for Scotts' Total Concept has been converted to a Sample file so that you can enter payroll information for dates outside the current payroll tax table period. This is important for learning purposes. No matter what QuickBooks tax table you have installed, the payroll information in the print screens in the textbook will be the same as yours as long as you use the sample file. The sample data file is set up so that December 15, 2007, is the current date displayed when entering forms. You will change the dates, using the year 2014, as you work through the textbook.

1. The following message will be displayed when you open the Scott.qbw file in QuickBooks:

📄 Notes
The payroll information and calculations in this chapter do not reflect current payroll information. Do not use the figures calculated in this payroll in your company file.

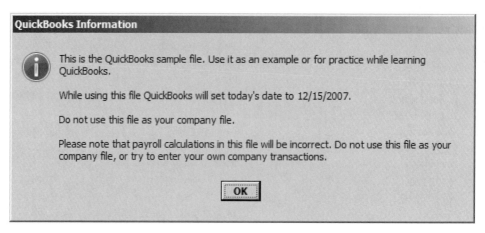

QuickBooks Information

This is the QuickBooks sample file. Use it as an example or for practice while learning QuickBooks.

While using this file QuickBooks will set today's date to 12/15/2007.

Do not use this file as your company file.

Please note that payroll calculations in this file will be incorrect. Do not use this file as your company file, or try to enter your own company transactions.

OK

Figure 10-1

2. Click **OK** to continue

The first transaction that we will enter is a payroll for two hourly employees. Refer to the following source document as we work through the steps to enter it:

Source Docs
Refer to the following source document and then follow the step-by-step instructions to enter it.

SD1:

EMPLOYEE TIME SUMMARY SHEET #1

Date: October 1, 2014 (for the pay period ending September 27, 2014)

Name of Employee	Regular Hours	Overtime Hours	Sick Leave Hours	Vacation Pay	Advances Received/ Advances Repaid
Nicolai Digger	40	2	—	—	—
Serge Draper	32	4	8	—	$200

a. Using Employee Time Summary Sheet #1 and the Employee Information Sheet, complete payroll for weekly paid employees
b. Issue a $200.00 advance to Serge Draper and recover $50.00 from each of the following four pay cheques
c. Manually prepare cheques #521 and #522 (do not use computer generated cheques)

Payroll functions are performed from the Payroll Centre.

3. Open the **Payroll Centre** by using one of the following methods:

Payroll Centre

a) **Click** the **Payroll Centre icon** in the Employees section of the Home page; or
b) **Choose Employees** from the menu and **click Payroll Centre**

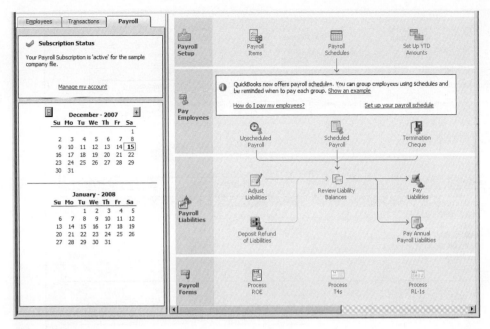

Figure 10-2

The Payroll Centre is part of the Employee Centre. Notice the tab currently displayed is the Payroll tab. All activities connected with payroll can be accessed from the Payroll tab: paying employees, submitting payroll liabilities, preparing Records of Employment (ROEs) and T4s (or RL-1s for Quebec), and managing payroll items.

The Employees tab contains the Employees list, which includes contact information and payroll transactions for each of your employees, and the transactions tab allows you to view all payroll transactions.

Payroll Dates

Because this is a specially prepared file, you are allowed to enter dates outside of the dates covered by the current tax tables. In other company files, you must work with dates that fall within the range of the current tax tables. Most tables allow you to go back a few months, but you cannot go forward into the next calendar year. To see the tax table expiry date for your program, choose the Help menu and click My Licence Information.

To pay employees, you select either the Unscheduled Payroll icon or the Scheduled Payroll icon in the Pay Employees section of the Payroll Centre. A scheduled payroll is a payroll that has been set up to occur on a regular frequency, and an unscheduled payroll can be run at any time. You don't need to set up a scheduled payroll in order to pay your employees. We will be using the unscheduled payroll option.

4. **Click**   the **Unscheduled Payroll icon** [Unscheduled Payroll] or **choose** the **Employees menu, click Pay Employees**, and then **click Unscheduled Payroll**:

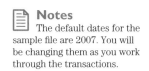

Notes
The default dates for the
sample file are 2007. You will
be changing them as you work
through the transactions.

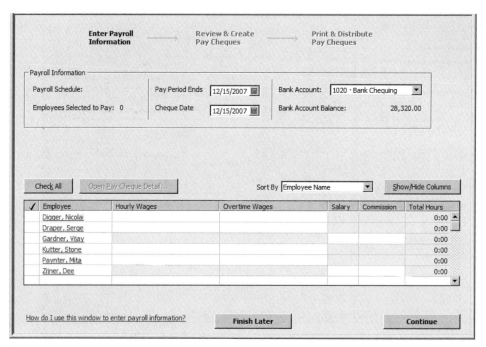

Figure 10-3

All employees are listed. Two dates appear on the form: the date that defines the
end of the pay period and the cheque date. Often these dates are different. Hourly
paid employees must usually complete their work period before the number of hours is
known, so the pay period date usually precedes the cheque date. Salaried employees are
paid on a schedule that is not based on hours worked so their pay period end dates often
match and may even follow the cheque date. Cheques are manually prepared.

You can select one or more employees from the list for each payroll run. We are paying the two weekly paid hourly employees for the week ended September 27th.

5. **Click**	the ✓ **(pay) column** for **Digger** to add a ✓ beside his name
6. **Click**	the ✓ **(pay) column** for **Draper** to add a ✓ beside his name
7. **Double click**	the **Pay Period Ends field**
8. **Type**	**09/27/14** (12/15/07 is displayed as the current date in the sample file)
9. **Press**	⌈*tab*⌋ to advance to the Cheque Date field
10. **Type**	**10/01/14** (12/15/2007 is displayed as the current date in the sample file)
11. **Click**	the **drop-down arrow** in the **Bank Account field** to view the accounts available
12. **Click**	**1020 - Bank Chequing**

If all amounts are the same from one pay period to the next, you can create the
cheque directly, but previewing the cheque gives you a chance to verify the amounts
before printing.

13. **Click**	the **Open Pay Cheque Detail button** to open the Review Or Change Pay Cheque window for the first employee:

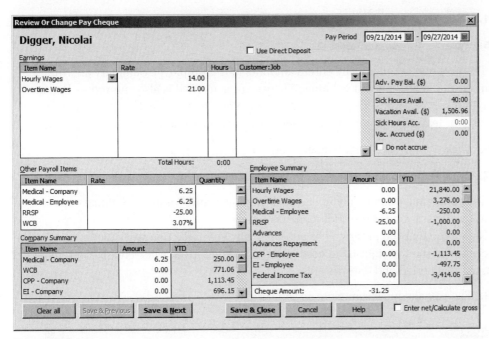

Figure 10-4

Just as sales in QuickBooks are based on selecting items from the item list, all payroll amounts are entered by selecting payroll items. Each payroll item is set up with a number of defaults, including a linked account. Payroll items displayed on an employee's pay cheque have already been entered in the employee record as defaults. Some of these payroll items have an amount or rate predefined and some do not. Each type of income is defined as a payroll item. Thus we have payroll items for hourly wages, overtime wages, salary, sick leave, vacation, and so on.

For hourly employees, we need to enter the number of hours worked so that QuickBooks can calculate the total wages and deduction amounts based on wages: federal income tax, CPP, EI, WCB premiums, and so on. Both employee and employer contributions are calculated and displayed on an employee's pay cheque. Other deductions, such as medical premiums or contributions to a savings plan, may be fixed amounts per pay period. Payroll items are also created for these deductions.

The employer's contribution to EI is 1.4 times the amount of an employee's contribution. The employer's contribution to CPP equals the employee's contribution. WCB is paid entirely by the employer, and the rate is based on the type of work and the industry's safety record. Medical premiums in BC are divided equally between employer and employee. Some deductions, such as RRSP and income tax, are paid only by the employee. Employer contributions are entered as *Payroll Expenses* and increase *Payroll Liabilities*. Employee deductions also increase *Payroll Liabilities* and reduce the net pay amount taken from the *Bank Chequing* account.

QuickBooks also tracks and reports on year-to-date amounts for the employee. Opening values are entered for the employee, and the amounts are updated with each pay cheque. Some items have annual amount limits, so QuickBooks will stop taking deductions when the limit is reached.

Accumulated sick leave and vacation pay are also reported on the Review Or Change Pay Cheques screen. These are shown in Sick Hours Avail. and Vacation Avail. When an employee takes sick leave or vacation, these amounts will be reduced.

For Digger, we need to enter only the number of regular and overtime wage hours worked during the week. The cursor should be in the Hours column for the hourly wages.

Notes
Limits for EI and CPP are built into the tax tables. Other items may have limits defined by the employer, such as advances, or by the employee, such as RRSP contributions.

14. Click the **Hours column** beside Hourly Wages if necessary

15. Type **40** and **press** (tab)

The program automatically enters amounts in the Employee Summary and the Company Summary Amount columns. The vacation accrued is also entered — Digger receives 6 percent of his wages as vacation pay. This amount is held until he takes vacation time or leaves the company, at which time the accrued amount will be released.

16. Click the **Hours column** beside Overtime Wages

17. Type **2** and **press** (tab) to update the totals and deductions

The program automatically updates all Employee and Company Summary amounts and accrued vacation for the additional income.

Notice too that the program has automatically entered a one-week pay period for the pay cheque in the top right-hand corner of the screen for the week ending September 27th, the pay period end date we entered.

18. The pay cheque is complete as shown:

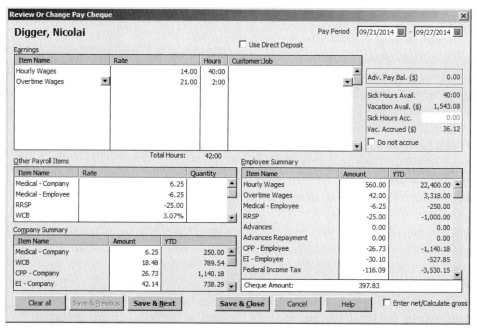

Figure 10-5

⚠ **WARNING!**
Remember that the tax amounts (Federal Income Tax, EI, and CPP) are not correct for Sample files.

19. Check your **work** carefully

CORRECTING A PAY CHEQUE

Return to the field you need to change. To correct a date or amount, double click the current entry to select it, highlight the amount or date, and type the correct information. Press (tab) to update the wage and deduction amounts.

If you have selected the wrong employee, or do not want to complete the pay cheque, click Cancel to begin again.

20. Click **Save & Next** to record the pay cheque and open the preview screen for Draper, the second employee we selected for payment

We will need to work through the following three topics: entering other payroll items, entering sick leave taken, and entering payroll advances, in order to enter the information for Draper's pay cheque.

Entering Other Payroll Items

Pay cheques are often different from one period to the next. Employees may work a different number of hours or take time off for vacation or illness. Some employers offer coverage for illness, payroll advances, or other benefits, such as payment of tuition fees. You would set up items for each of these.

Draper received a payroll advance with this cheque, and he took one day of sick leave (8 hours). We will enter these other payroll items on his pay cheque. First, we will add the regular and overtime hours as we did for Digger's pay cheque.

1. **Click** the **Hours field** beside Hourly Wages

2. **Type** 32

3. **Press** ⊥ to place the cursor in the Overtime Hours field

4. **Type** 4

5. **Press** (tab) to update the amounts

Entering Sick Leave Taken

We are now ready to enter the information for sick leave and advances. Digger has 40 hours of sick leave available to him. He has taken one day off this week and a normal work day is 8 hours. The Scotts pay their employees the regular wage rate when they are ill, to a maximum of 10 days per year. Thus, sick leave is entered as an income item to which regular taxes and deductions apply.

6. **Click** the **line** below Overtime Wages in the Item Name field under the Earnings heading to display the drop-down arrow

7. **Click** the **drop-down arrow** to view the income items available:

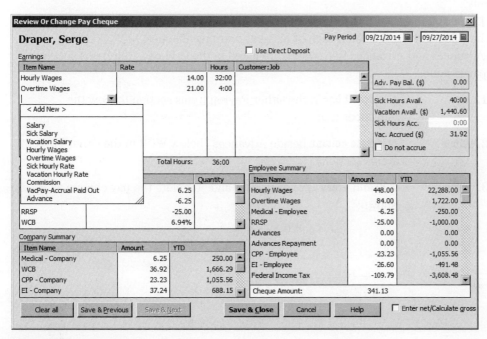

Figure 10-6

Notice that the items for sick leave and vacation are separated for hourly and salaried workers, because the pay base is different for these employees. Hourly workers are paid hourly wages for sick leave time. Salaried workers have their regular work hours

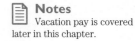
Notes
Vacation pay is covered later in this chapter.

reduced for the month, that is, some of their regular salary is assigned to sick leave instead of working hours but total pay is not affected by the number of hours.

We need to select the item and then enter the number of hours taken.

Notes
You can edit the rate for sick leave, but permanent changes should be entered in the employee record.

8. Click   **Sick Hourly Rate** to select the item. The regular hourly rate has automatically been entered for the item

9. Press   ⌷*tab*⌷ **twice** to advance to the Hours field

10. Type   **8** and **press** ⌷*tab*⌷ to update the pay cheque amounts and deductions

The number in the Sick Hours Avail. field displayed on the right-hand side of the screen has been reduced from 40 to 32. All regular taxes and deductions apply to this amount. These defaults are set up for the sick hourly rate item. The actual amount paid for sick leave is recorded separately from wages in the Employee Summary.

Entering Payroll Advances

Payroll advances may be issued to an employee occasionally for personal reasons. These amounts are given at the owners' discretion and limits may be set on the amount advanced at one time, for the entire year, or for the employee's entire term of employment. Frequent requests for advances may suggest that financial counselling is advisable. Employees pay back the advance over a prearranged number of pay cheques.

Two items are created for advances, one for the advance and one for the repayment. The advance — a short-term interest-free loan — is an addition to payroll, while the repayment — a repayment of the loan — is a deduction. Both items are linked to the *Employee Advances* account, an asset account. Advances and repayments are not taxable items — they do not affect income tax or other deduction amounts.

Advances are added as default items for all employees but no amounts are entered as defaults. When the item is not part of the employee record, QuickBooks will ask if you want to make it a regular payroll item for this employee, that is, add it to the record as a default.

Draper has been authorized to receive an advance of $200.00 with this pay cheque, and he will pay back $50.00 on each of his next four pay cheques.

Advances and Advances Repayment are listed in the Other Payroll Items section of the pay cheque.

1. Use   the **scroll bar** in the Other Payroll Items section to view the Advances item

2. Click   the **Rate column** beside Advances (below WCB in the Other Payroll Items section)

3. Type   **200** and **press** ⌷*tab*⌷ to update and complete the pay cheque as shown:

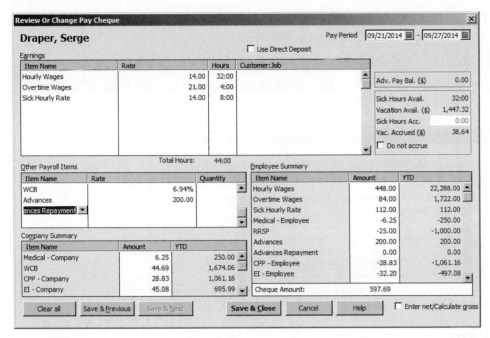

Figure 10-7

Notice that the advance is entered separately in the Employee Summary section. The Cheque Amount below the Employee Summary section is updated, and the tax amounts did not change when the Advance was added to the pay cheque.

Notes
To see that the taxes and deduction amounts have not changed, you can observe the summary amounts carefully as you make changes. Delete the amount for advances and press ⟨*tab*⟩. Then enter the amount again and press ⟨*tab*⟩.

4. **Check** your **work** carefully and **make corrections** before you record the pay cheque

5. **Click** **Save & Close** to save the pay cheque and return to the Enter Payroll Information screen:

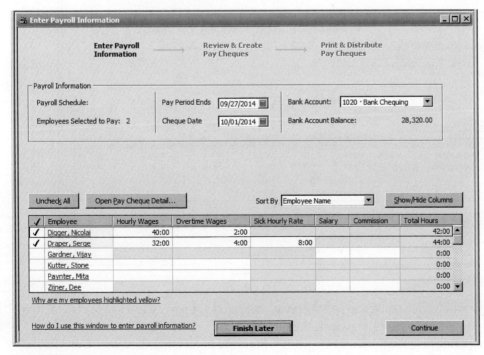

Figure 10-8

The list now includes the employees included in the payroll and the number of hours entered for each payroll item has been updated.

6. Click   **Continue**

7. The following message will be displayed because we are using a QuickBooks Sample file:

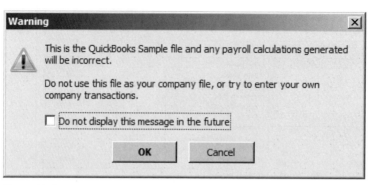

Figure 10-9

8. Read   the **Warning**

9. Click   the **box** beside the Do not display this message in the future option

10. Click   **OK**

11. The Review and Create Pay Cheques window is updated with the payroll information as shown:

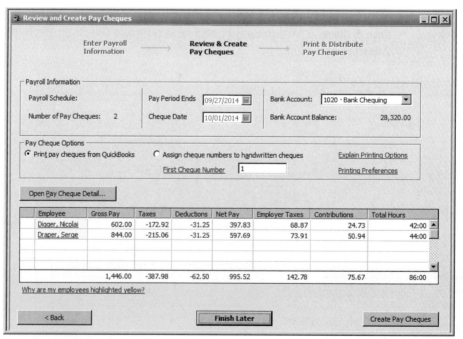

Figure 10-10

Because you can prepare pay cheques for several employees in a single session, the first cheque number for the payroll cheque run is entered. This is the first cheque we are preparing in QuickBooks, so we need to start the numbering sequence. QuickBooks updates this number sequentially once you enter the first number.

12. Click   the **radio button** beside the Assign cheque numbers to handwritten cheques option

13. **Double click**   1 in the **First Cheque Number field**

14. **Type**   **521**

15. **Click**   the **Create Pay Cheques button** to display the Confirmation and Next Steps window:

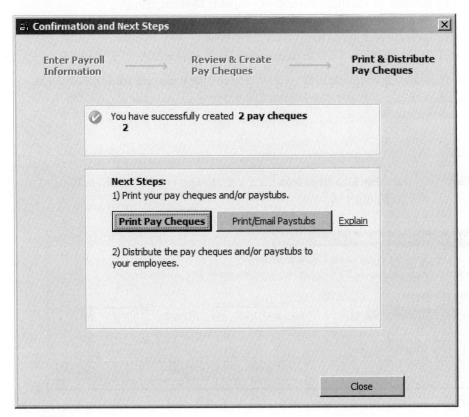

Figure 10-11

From this screen, you can print the pay cheques or print and e-mail the paystubs. We will not be printing the pay cheques at this time. Ask your instructor if you are required to print them.

16. **Click**   **Close**

Paying Payroll Liabilities

Most businesses with employees have payroll liabilities with a number of different agencies and organizations. The business withholds taxes from employees and also contributes taxes. Payroll taxes remitted to the Receiver General consist of income tax, EI premiums, and CPP premiums withheld from employee income, as well as the employer's contribution to EI and CPP. The federal government collects both provincial and federal income taxes in all provinces except Quebec. Employer expenses for WCB are submitted to the provincial Workers' Compensation Board, and medical premiums or taxes are sent to the provincial Minister of Finance. In addition, there may be company-specific payroll benefits and plans that employees and employers pay into, such as union dues, insurance plans, and savings plans.

QuickBooks tracks all these payroll taxes and liabilities, just as it tracks sales taxes and summarizes them to make remittances easier.

In the next transactions, we will pay all payroll liabilities. Refer to the following source document as we work through the steps to enter it:

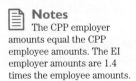
Notes
The CPP employer amounts equal the CPP employee amounts. The EI employer amounts are 1.4 times the employee amounts.

Source Docs

Refer to the following source document and then follow the step-by-step instructions to enter it.

SD2: Memo #10-1   **Dated October 2, 2014**

From Owners: Pay all payroll liabilities outstanding from January 1 to September 30.

To Receiver General: Federal Income Tax, EI - Company, EI - Employee, CPP - Company, CPP - Employee

To Minister of Finance: Medical - Company, Medical - Employee

To Workers' Compensation Board: WCB

To Haida Investments Inc.: CSB Plan, RRSP

Issue Cheques #523 to #526 to these agencies in payment.

The Payroll Centre should still be open. Payroll liabilities are paid by selecting the Pay Liabilities icon in the Payroll Liabilities section on the Payroll tab in the Payroll Centre.

Notes

QuickBooks uses a single default account for all payroll liabilities but tracks the amounts for each payroll item separately.

1. **Click**   the **Pay Liabilities icon** [Pay Liabilities] to open the Select Date Range for Liabilities window:

Notes

Remember, the default year in the sample company is 2007. It is displayed by default on all transactions and all reports.

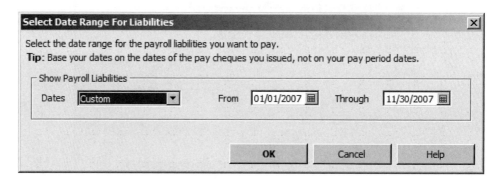

Figure 10-12

The date range for the liabilities is usually the oldest date on record for outstanding amounts to the end of the month before the current month. The default year in the sample company is 2007.

The Scotts have paid the liabilities from the beginning of the year through to August 31. The balances remaining for September have been entered as historical amounts. Custom is selected as the type of date range. We need to enter our own date range, so Custom is the correct selection.

From the drop-down list in the Dates field, you can choose a time interval, such as month, week, quarter, and so on. QuickBooks will enter the corresponding date range.

Notes

Year-to-date payroll liabilities were entered as total amounts for each item for January 1 to September 30. Year-to-date payments were entered as total payments for each item on August 31.

2. **Press**   (tab) to advance to the From date field

3. **Type**   **01/01/14**

4. **Press**   (tab) to advance to the Through date field

5. **Type**   **09/30/14**

6. **Click**   **OK** to advance to the Pay Liabilities window:

Notes

Notice that the default date in the Through field is November 30, the end of the month before December 15, the Sample file's preset current date.

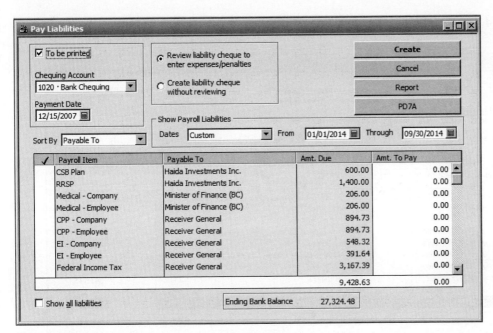

Figure 10-13

Outstanding amounts for all liabilities are entered. For each, the agency that collects the money is listed along with the total amount owing. You may choose to pay the total or some lesser amount. We will pay all outstanding amounts to all agencies. The Sample file date (December 15, 2007) is entered as the default payment date, so we need to change it. Also, we are not printing cheques so we will deselect this option.

7. Click   the **To be printed option** to remove the ✓

We want to preview all cheques before sending them, and this option is correctly selected by default.

8. Double click   the **Payment Date field**

9. Type   **10/02/14**

Now we need to select the items we are paying. When you click in the pay column to the left of an item, a checkmark will be displayed indicating that it has been selected for payment.

10. Click   the **column** to the left of the CSB Plan item to add a ✓ beside it

The amount in the Amt. Due column is added to the Amt. To Pay column. You can change this amount in order to pay more or less than the amount due. Usually, the full amount is paid because the date range selected is for the current amount due.

11. Click   the **column** to the left of the RRSP item to add a ✓ beside it

12. Click   the **column** to the left of the other items to add a ✓ beside them (you may have to scroll down the screen to select all items)

When you click beside CPP - Company, all the items payable to the Receiver General are selected at the same time.

Check your work carefully before proceeding — you cannot go back to these amounts or this screen once you choose Create.

13. To remove an item from the pay column, **click** the ✓ in the column to remove it

14. Your completed Pay Liabilities screen should be displayed as shown here:

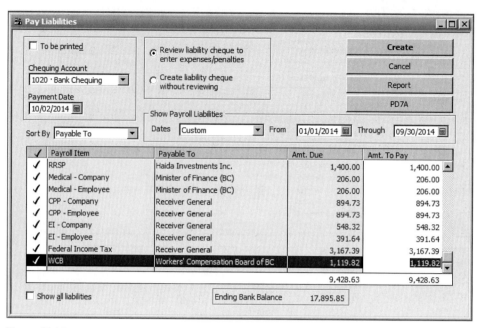

Figure 10-14

15. Click **Create** to continue to review the cheque for the first payee:

WARNING!
As soon as you choose Create, the amounts are recorded in journal entries, so check your work carefully before continuing.

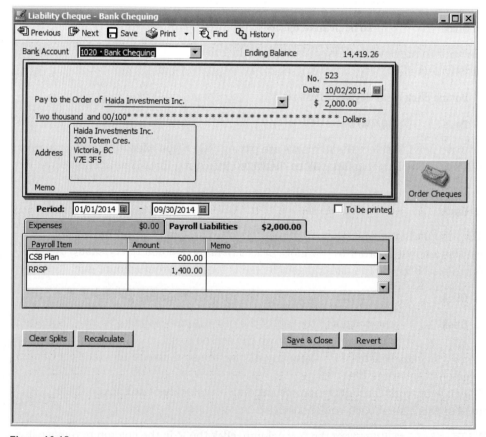

Figure 10-15

Notice that the cheque number follows our last payroll cheque number.

16. **Press** ⌂ **+ Y** to view the journal entry created from this cheque:

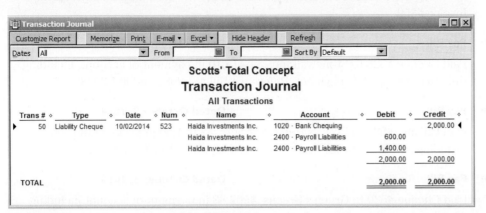

Trans # ◇	Type	◇ Date	◇ Num ◇	Name	◇ Account	◇	Debit	◇	Credit	◇
▶ 50	Liability Cheque	10/02/2014	523	Haida Investments Inc.	1020 · Bank Chequing				2,000.00	◀
				Haida Investments Inc.	2400 · Payroll Liabilities		600.00			
				Haida Investments Inc.	2400 · Payroll Liabilities		1,400.00			
							2,000.00		2,000.00	
TOTAL							**2,000.00**		**2,000.00**	

Figure 10-16

17. **Close**   the **Transaction Journal report** when you're finished viewing it

18. **Click**   the **Next button** 🖘 Next to review or edit the next payment. The cheque for the Minister of Finance should be displayed on the screen

19. **Click**   **Yes** to save the changes

20. **Click**   the **Next button** 🖘 Next again to view the cheque issued to the Receiver General

21. **Click**   the **Next button** 🖘 Next again to view the final payment to the Workers' Compensation Board

There are times when you may need to edit a cheque. For example, you may need to add an amount for a late payment or an interest penalty. You can edit a liability cheque just like any other cheque. When you save the cheque, click Yes when asked to save the changes.

22. **Close**   the **Liability Cheque window** when you have finished viewing the cheques

Source Documents

Enter the following source documents for this company. You may need to refer to previous chapters for additional information:

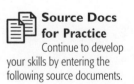

📄 **Source Docs for Practice**
Continue to develop your skills by entering the following source documents.

SD3: Memo #10-2   **Dated October 2, 2014**

From Owners: Deposit $8,000.00 in outstanding receipts to chequing account.

SD4: Estimate   **Dated October 2, 2014**

Estimate #38 to Nedaa Woodslea, $6,900.00 plus $828.00 HST for redecorating living room, including painting, reupholstering furniture, and balloon-style valance with drapes. Estimate totals $7,728.00.

SD5: Reconcile and pay Credit Card   **Dated October 2, 2014**

To Pacific Coast Visa (use Quick Add to add the new Other payee), $500.00 in payment of account, including $390.00 for purchases before September 25 and a $110.00 annual card fee. Reconcile and pay credit card bill in full with Cheque #527.

SD6: **Customer Payment** **Dated October 2, 2014**

From Marie Rose Schleger, Cheque #206 for $11,335.50 in payment of account, including the discount for early payment. Apply the discount and payment to Invoice #359.

SD7: **Pay Bill** **Dated October 2, 2014**

Paid Cheque #528 to Stonewall Inc., $7,415.10 in payment of account, including the discount for early payment. Reference Bill #SI-3981 and #SI-3998.

SD8: **Pay Bill** **Dated October 2, 2014**

Paid Cheque #529 to Freya's Home Interiors, $2,621.50 in payment of account, including the discount for early payment. Reference Bill #FHI-4801.

SD9: **Pay Bill** **Dated October 3, 2014**

Paid Cheque #530 to Groen's Greens, $902.88 in payment of account including discount for early payment. Reference Bill #GG-559.

Reviewing and Correcting Payroll Entries

There is no Previous button on the payroll forms. We can review and correct pay cheques written to employees from the Write Cheques form.

In the next transaction, we will correct the pay cheque created for Draper. Refer to the following source document as we work through the steps to correct it:

Source Docs
Refer to the following source document and then follow the step-by-step instructions to enter it.

SD10: Memo #10-3 **Dated October 3, 2014**

From Owners: Correct the pay cheque for Draper. It should have included 7.5 hours overtime. Draper has returned the incorrect Cheque #522.

1. **Click** the **Write Cheques icon** in the Banking section of the Home page to open the Write Cheques form

2. **Press** `ctrl` + **F** to open the Find Cheques window

3. **Choose** **Draper** from the Payee list

4. **Click** the **Find button** to view the pay cheque for Draper:

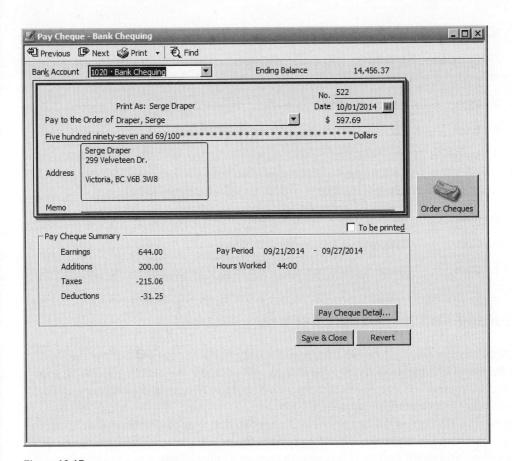

Figure 10-17

The cheque shows a summary of the items entered on the pay cheque.

We can edit the pay cheque just as we edit other transactions after saving them.

The Pay Cheque Detail button allows you to access the Preview screen that includes all payroll items entered on the pay cheque. We will use this screen to correct the pay cheque.

5. Click the **Pay Cheque Detail button** to open the Review Pay Cheque window:

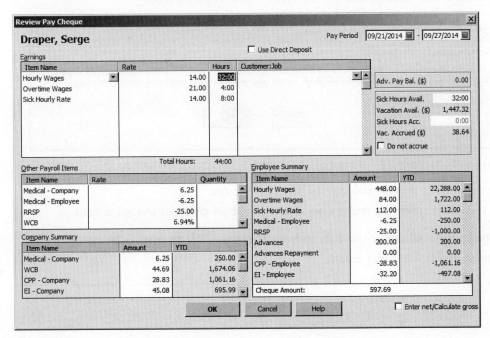

Figure 10-18

Notes (margin): Notice that the name of the form has changed to Pay Cheque to reflect the way the cheque was created.

Notes (margin): Note the change in title for the screen from Review Or Change Pay Cheque to Review Pay Cheque.

6. **Double click** **4:00** in the Hours column beside Overtime Wages

You can enter fractions for hours as decimals or as the number of hours and minutes separated by a colon.

Notes
Formats for entering and displaying time are set up on the Company Preferences tab for the General preferences.

7. **Type** **7.5** or **type 7:30**

8. **Press** ⌨tab to update all totals and deductions

If you typed 7.5, the program changes this entry to 7:30. We indicated in the General preferences that this is how we want portions of an hour to be entered and displayed.

You can edit the cheque number if you are using pre-printed forms.

9. **Click** **OK** to return to the cheque form

10. **Click** **Save & Close** to save the changes

11. **Click** **Yes** to confirm that you want to save the changes

Voiding and Deleting Cheques

Notes
If the incorrect cheque is not returned, remember to notify the bank to cancel the cheque.

If your cheques are pre-printed, you cannot use the same cheque number for the replacement cheque. In this case, you should void or delete the old cheque and issue a new one. Voiding a pay cheque will keep a record of the cheque in the register but mark it as void. All payroll information for the employee is retained. A new cheque can be issued with the corrections for the same amount so that year-to-date payroll information will be correct, but it may be difficult to correct the year-to-date information afterwards. Therefore, you might choose this option to correct a cheque date or an incorrectly spelled name when none of the payroll amounts on the revised cheque were changed.

INSTRUCTIONS FOR VOIDING CHEQUES

1. Display a **pay cheque** on the screen

2. Choose the **Edit** menu and **click Void Pay Cheque.** You will see a warning message:

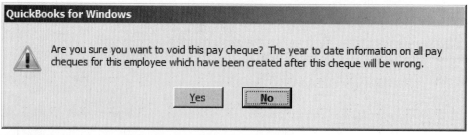

Figure 10-19

The message warns about the implications for employee history data.

3. Click Yes to confirm your decision if you want to void the pay cheque and **click No** to cancel

Deleting a cheque will undo or remove the entire payroll transaction from the record, so this option is preferred when you need to revise payroll amounts.

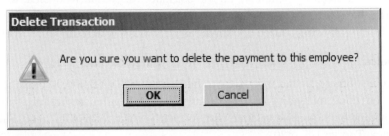
Source Documents

Enter the following source documents for this company. You may need to refer to previous chapters for additional information:

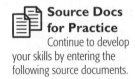

Source Docs for Practice
Continue to develop your skills by entering the following source documents.

SD11: Estimate   **Dated October 4, 2014**

Estimate #39 to Nina Toussieng, $15,900.00 plus $1,908.00 HST for terracing and landscaping a ravine lot with stone retaining walls and appropriate shrubs and groundcover plants. Estimate totals $17,808.00.

SD12: Customer Payment   **Dated October 4, 2014**

From Nedaa Woodslea, Cheque #376 for $2,000.00 as prepayment for acceptance of Estimate #38.

SD13: Estimate   **Dated October 4, 2014**

Estimate #40 to Casa Blanca Estates (set up the new customer), $15,500.00 for design work plus $3,900.00 for landscaping plus $2,328.00 HST on model suite in new condo. Project includes designing and furnishing the suite, laying terrazzo tiles, and arranging plants and small shrubs on the balcony. Estimate totals $21,728.00.

Notes
Casa Blanca Estates
Contact: Whipple Peduto
49 Wildginger Way
Victoria, BC V8T 4D7
Tel: (250) 488-7383
Terms: 1/5, n/30
Payment: Cheque
Credit Limit: $25,000.00

SD14: Bill   **Dated October 5, 2014**

Bill #P-699 received from Primus Communications, $210.00 plus $25.20 HST for one month of telephone, pager, cell phone, and Internet service. Bill totals $235.20. Terms: Net 15 days.

SD15: Customer Payment   **Dated October 5, 2014**

From Nina Toussieng, Cheque #48 for $4,500.00 as prepayment for acceptance of Estimate #39.

Entering Sales Reps on Invoices

Gardner and Zijner are paid commissions on sales. If we enter their names on invoices, the program will track their sales in order to calculate commissions. Any employee can be identified as a sales representative, and sales reps can be added in the REP field on invoices. When we fill the estimate for Nedaa Woodslea, we will add Zijner as the sales rep.

Refer to the following source document as we work through the steps to enter it:

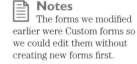
SD16: Invoice   **Dated October 5, 2014**

Invoice #362 to Nedaa Woodslea, to fill Estimate #38, $6,900.00 plus $828.00 HST for redecorating living room, including painting, reupholstering furniture, and providing balloon-style valance with drapes. Invoice totals $7,728.00. Sales Rep: Zijner. Terms: 1/5, n/30.

1. Open   the **Create Invoices form**

The service invoice does not include a field for Sales Rep so we will customize the form template before filling the estimate. The Intuit Service Invoice should be selected as the template for this invoice. If it isn't, click the drop-down arrow in the template field and select it.

2. Click   the **Customize icon** on the form Icon bar

The Basic Customization screen opens. We need to create a new template because we cannot add a field to the Intuit Service Invoice form.

3. Click   the **Manage Templates button**

4. Highlight   the **Intuit Service Invoice** if necessary in the Select Template list

5. Click   **Copy**

A new template called Copy of: Intuit Service Invoice is now displayed and highlighted in the Select Template list.

We need to name the new invoice template.

6. Highlight   the **name** in the **Template Name field** on the right-hand side of the screen

7. Type   **Scotts**

8. Click   **OK** to return to the Basic Customization screen

9. Click   the **Additional Customization button**

10. Click   the ✓ **box** under the Screen column for the REP field to add a ✓ to complete the customization as shown:

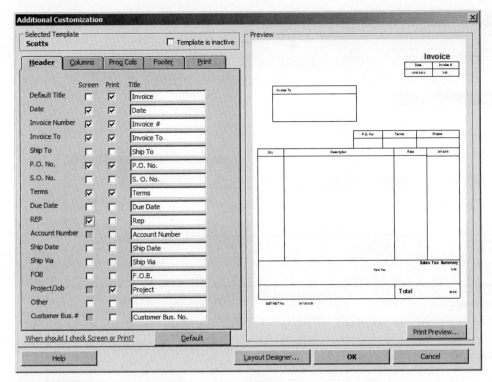

Figure 10-21

11. Click   **OK**

12. The following message will be displayed:

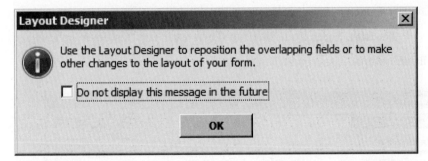

Figure 10-22

This message indicates that you may have to use the Layout Designer to reposition the new field we added to the invoice template.

13. Click   the **box** beside Do not display this message in the future

14. Click   **OK**

15. Click   **OK** to return to the Basic Customization screen

16. Click   **OK** to return to the revised invoice:

Notes

Remember, the default date for the Sample file is 12/15/2007.

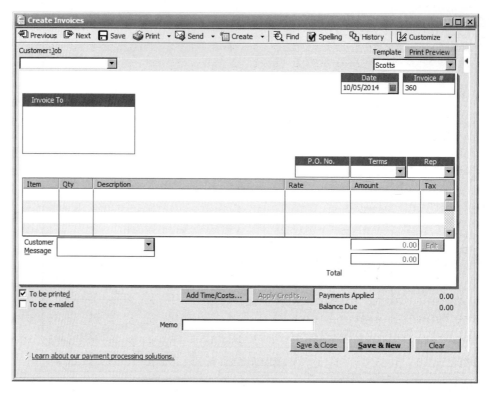

Figure 10-23

"Scotts" now appears in the Template field and a Rep field is now displayed beside the Terms field on the invoice. Once we save the invoice, this template will open as the default invoice. It will also appear on the drop-down list in the Template field so you can select it later if another invoice template becomes the default.

17. Choose   **Woodslea, Nedaa** from the drop-down list in the Customer: Job field

18.   The Available Estimates screen is displayed:

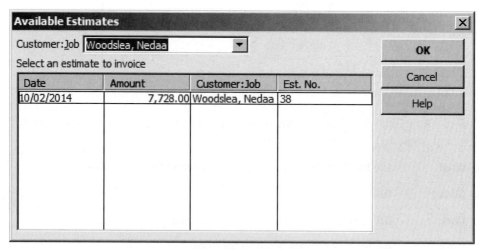

Figure 10-24

19. Click   **Estimate number 38** to select it

20. Click   **OK** to add the estimate details to the invoice

21. Enter   **10/05/14** as the date if necessary

22. **Enter**   **362** as the Invoice Number

23. **Click**   the **drop-down arrow** in the **REP field** to view the two employees designated as sales reps:

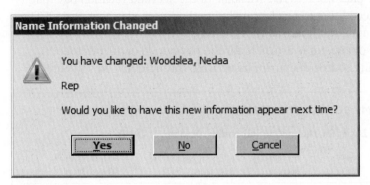

< Add New >		
DZ	Zijner, Dee	Employee
VG	Gardner, Vijay	Employee

Figure 10-25

24. **Click**   **DZ-Zijner, Dee** to add her name as the sales rep to the invoice

25. **Click**   **Save & Close** to record the invoice. The following message will be displayed:

Name Information Changed

⚠ You have changed: Woodslea, Nedaa

Rep

Would you like to have this new information appear next time?

[**Yes**]   [**No**]   [**Cancel**]

Figure 10-26

Scotts' customers frequently work with both sales reps so we do not want a default name attached to this customer.

26. **Click**   **No** to continue

27. **Click**   **No** when prompted that the customer has available credits that can be applied to the invoice

Source Documents

Enter the following source documents for this company. You may need to refer to previous chapters for additional information:

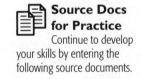

Source Docs for Practice
Continue to develop your skills by entering the following source documents.

SD17: Credit Card Charge   **Dated October 5, 2014**

   Credit card payment of Bill #CSC-4530 from Celine's Service Centre, $120.00 plus $14.40 HST for gasoline for the business vans and gas-powered landscaping equipment. The bill totalling $134.40 was paid in full by credit card. Memorize the transaction to recur every two weeks beginning October 19, 2014.

SD18: Bill   **Dated October 5, 2014**

   Bill #FHI-5628 received from Freya's Home Interiors, $1,050.00 plus $126.00 HST for upholstery and drapery fabrics and notions. The bill totals $1,176.00. Terms: 2/5, n/30.

SD19: Bill   **Dated October 6, 2014**

   Bill #SI-4811 received from Stonewall Inc., $2,100.00 plus $252.00 HST for tiles, paving stones, sand, and screening for garden and patio area. The bill totals $2,352.00. Terms: 1/10, n/30.

SD20: Bill   **Dated October 6, 2014**

   Bill #GG-692 received from Groen's Greens, $1,800.00 plus $216.00 HST for perennials, shrubs, and soil for a garden project. The bill totals $2,016.00. Terms: 1/15, n/30.

SD21: Invoice   **Dated October 6, 2014**

> Invoice #363 to Nina Toussieng, to fill Estimate #39, $15,900.00 plus $1,908.00 HST for terracing and landscaping a ravine lot with stone retaining walls and appropriate shrubs and groundcover plants. Invoice totals $17,808.00. Sales Rep: Gardner. Terms: 1/5, n/30.

Paying Vacation Pay

Vacation items are also separated for hourly and salaried workers because vacation pay is allotted and paid out differently. Salaried workers receive regular pay during their vacation — their usual hours are allocated to vacation time instead of salary but the total pay is unchanged. Hourly paid workers receive some of the accrued vacation pay that has been held for them in addition to pay for any hours they worked in that period. They can receive the regular number of hours as vacation pay.

The following source document is available for the pay period ending October 4, 2014. Refer to the following source document as we walk through the steps to enter it:

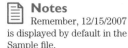
Source Docs
Refer to the following source document and then follow the step-by-step instructions to enter it.

SD22:

EMPLOYEE TIME SUMMARY SHEET #2

Date: October 8, 2014 (for the pay period ending October 4, 2014)

Name of Employee	Regular Hours	Overtime Hours	Sick Leave Hours	Vacation Hours	Advances Received/ Advances Repaid
Nicolai Digger	40	8	—	—	$100.00
Serge Draper	8	—	—	32	–$ 50.00

a. Using Employee Time Summary Sheet #2 and the Employee Information Sheet, complete payroll for weekly paid employees

b. Recover $50.00 advance from Serge Draper

c. Draper will take one week of vacation. Pay Draper four days of vacation pay. He worked one day before starting his vacation

d. Manually prepare Cheques #531 and #532

---

1. **Open**   the **Payroll Centre** and **click** the **Unscheduled Payroll icon**, or **choose** the **Employees** menu and **click Pay Employees, Unscheduled Payroll**

2. October 4 should be displayed in the Pay Period Ends field by default (enter 10/4/14 if it is not displayed in the Pay Period Ends field)

3. **Enter**   **October 8, 2014** as the Cheque date

4. **Select**   **Digger** and **Draper** for payment in this period

The Enter Payroll Information screen displays the hours from the previous period entered by default.

5. **Click**   **Continue** to display the Review and Create Pay Cheques form

The Review and Create Pay Cheques form shows the calculated payroll based on the hours from the previous period. If the payroll is correct, you can click the Create Pay Cheques button to create the pay cheques. If you need to make any changes, you must click on the Open Pay Cheque Detail button to access each individual pay cheque.

6. **Click**   the **Open Pay Cheque Detail button** to display the payroll for Digger

7. **Edit**   the **Hours for Overtime Wages** (**enter 8**) and **enter 100.00** for Advances in the Other Payroll Items section

Notes
Remember, 12/15/2007 is displayed by default in the Sample file.

Notes
Entering the hours from the previous period is a company preference that can be set in the Payroll & Employees preferences.

8. Click   **Save & Next** to record Digger's pay cheque and display Draper's pay cheque

9. The Review Or Change Pay Cheque screen for Draper should now be displayed on the screen:

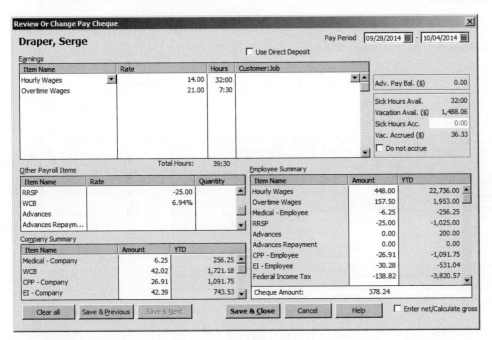

Figure 10-27

The hours worked from the previous period are entered by default. Notice that only the regular and overtime hours are entered; previous amounts for sickness or advances are not considered as regular occurrences and are not set up as defaults for the employee.

10. Type   **8** in the Hours column beside Hourly Wages

11. Press   ⬇ to advance to the Hours column beside Overtime Wages

12. Press   *del* to delete the number of hours currently displayed in the field

13. Press   *tab* to update all amounts

14. Click   the **field** below Overtime Wages to display the drop-down arrow

15. **Click** the **drop-down arrow** to view the Earnings that can be added to the pay cheque:

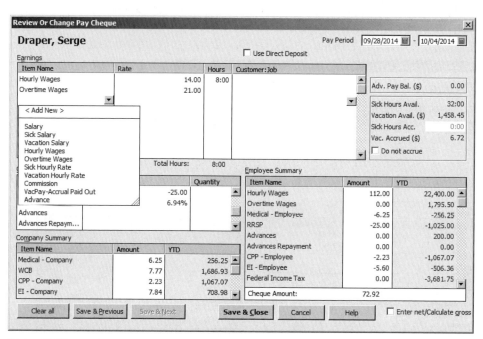

Figure 10-28

Notes The rate of vacation pay for the weekly paid employees is 6 percent of wages earned, or about three weeks of regular pay.

Two items on the list relate to vacation pay paid to hourly employees. If the entire amount of vacation accrued is paid out, you can choose VacPay-Accrual Paid Out and enter the amount in the Rate field. The accrued vacation pay available is shown in the summary area in the upper-right corner of the screen. If the employee receives regular hourly pay while on vacation, you can choose Vacation Hourly Rate and enter the number of vacation hours for the pay period. Both entries will reduce the amount of vacation pay available. Draper worked for 8 hours and took 4 days (32 hours) of vacation time. He will be on vacation next week as well. We will enter these hours.

Notes Because vacation pay is also paid on overtime wages, 6 percent vacation pay may be more than three weeks of regular wages. There may be an accrued vacation amount remaining at the end of the year.

16. **Click**   **Vacation Hourly Rate**

The regular hourly wage rate is entered automatically.

17. **Press**   (tab) twice to advance to the Hours field

18. **Type**   **32**

19. **Press**   (tab) to update the totals and taxes

The Vacation Avail. ($) amount field shown in the top right-hand corner of the screen is reduced by $448.00. Now we need to enter the first repayment of the advance received on a previous pay cheque.

Notes Because the Other Payroll Items section is too small to display all the items, you can press (tab) repeatedly from the Advances item to advance to the next item in this section or to a blank field with a drop-down arrow. Or you can press the down arrow (↓) to move to the next field in the Item Name column.

20. **Click**   **Advances** in the Other Payroll Items section (Item Name column)

21. **Press**   (↓) to select the Advances Repayment item

22. **Press**   (tab) to advance to the Rate field

23. **Type**   **50**

24. **Press**   (tab) to update the totals as shown:

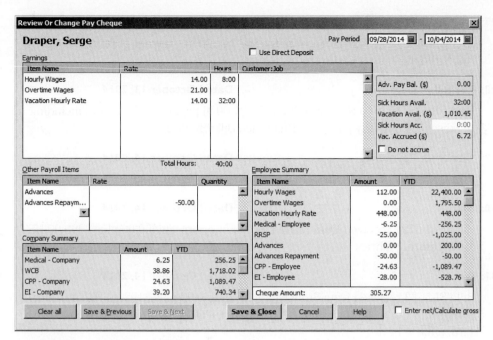

Figure 10-29

The Advances payroll item is set up as an Addition item, so the amount is added to the net pay amount. The Advances Repayment payroll item is set up as a Deduction item so its amount is deducted from net pay. No taxes or other deductions apply to either amount. The Employee Summary section tracks the amount still owing on the advance.

25. **Click**   **Save & Close**

26. **Check**   your **work** carefully before creating the pay cheques

27. **Click**   **Create Pay Cheques** to create the pay cheques for Digger and Draper

28. **Click**   **Close** to close the Confirmation and Next Steps window

📄 **Notes**
You can click on the Open Pay Cheque Detail button to review the pay cheques.

Source Documents
Enter the following source documents for this company. You may need to refer to previous chapters for additional information:

📑 **Source Docs for Practice**
Continue to develop your skills by entering the following source documents.

SD23: Memo #10-4   **Dated October 8, 2014**

From Owners: Deposit $17,835.50 in outstanding receipts to chequing account.

SD24: Customer Payment   **Dated October 10, 2014**

From Casa Blanca Estates, Cheque #1998 for $5,000.00 as prepayment for acceptance of Estimate #40.

SD25: Pay Bill   **Dated October 10, 2014**

Paid Cheque #533 to Celine's Service Centre, $286.00 in payment of account. Reference Bill #CSC-3324.

SD26: Pay Bill   **Dated October 10, 2014**

Paid Cheque #534 to Freya's Home Interiors, $1,155.00 in payment of account, including the discount for early payment. Reference Bill #FHI-5628.

SD27: Customer Payment   **Dated October 11, 2014**

From Nina Toussieng, Cheque #59 for $13,149.00 in payment of Invoice #363. Apply the discount and the credit.

SD28: Pay Bill   **Dated October 13, 2014**

Paid Cheque #535 to Stonewall Inc., $2,331.00 in payment of account, including the discount for early payment. Reference Bill #SI-4811.

SD29: Customer Payment   **Dated October 14, 2014**

From Flora Planter, Cheque #1925 for $11,946.00 in payment of Invoice #345.

SD30: Bill   **Dated October 14, 2014**

Bill #FHI-6721 received from Freya's Home Interiors, $3,250.00 plus $390.00 HST for decorating fabrics and notions. The bill totals $3,640.00. Terms: 2/5, n/30.

SD31: Bill   **Dated October 14, 2014**

Bill #SI-5622 received from Stonewall Inc., $1,600.00 plus $192.00 HST for tiles and paving stones for a garden and patio area. The bill totals $1,792.00. Terms: 1/10, n/30.

SD32:

EMPLOYEE TIME SUMMARY SHEET #3

Date: October 15, 2014 (for the pay period ending October 13, 2014)

Name of Employee	Regular Hours	Overtime Hours	Sick Leave Hours	Vacation Hours	Advances Received/ Advances Repaid
Nicolai Digger	36	–	4	–	–$25.00
Serge Draper	–	–	–	40	–$50.00
Stone Kutter	40	–	–	40	–
Mita Paynter	80	4	–	–	–

a. Using Employee Time Summary Sheet #3 and the Employee Information Sheet, complete payroll for weekly paid and semi-monthly paid employees

b. Recover $25.00 advance from Digger and $50.00 advance from Draper

c. Release 40 hours vacation pay for Draper. He is taking his second week of vacation

d. Release 40 hours of accrued vacation pay for Kutter

e. Manually prepare Cheques #536 through #539

SD33: Memo #10-5   **Dated October 15, 2014**

From Owners: Deposit $30,095.00 in outstanding receipts to the chequing account.

SD34: Bill   **Dated October 15, 2014**

Bill #GG-801 received from Groen's Greens, $1,200.00 plus $144.00 HST for perennials and shrubs for a garden project. The bill totals $1,344.00. Terms: 1/15, n/30.

SD35: Bill   **Dated October 15, 2014**

Bill #VG-1100 received from Village Galleries (set up new vendor), $5,800.00 plus $696.00 HST for a living room suite for Casa Blanca Estates project. The bill totals $6,496.00. Terms: 2/10, n/30.

📝 **Notes**
Village Galleries
455 Divan Rd.
Victoria, BC V5E 2D6
Terms: 2% 10, Net 30
Credit Limit: $10,000.00

SD36: Estimate Dated October 15, 2014

Estimate #41 to Dawn Knight (set up new customer), $7,800.00 for interior design and $17,000.00 for landscaping plus $2,976.00 HST for consultation and period restoration of living room, dining room, and garden. Estimate totals $27,776.00. Allow the customer to go over their credit limit.

SD37: Bank Debit Memo #PC-63392 Dated October 16, 2014

From Pacific Coast Bank: Cheque #1925 for $11,946.00 from Flora Planter in payment of Invoice #345 was returned as NSF. Create Invoice #364 to record the returned cheque and NSF charges. Invoice totals $11,971.00. Terms: Due on receipt.

SD38: Pay Bill Dated October 16, 2014

Paid Cheque #540 to Primus Communications, $235.20 in full payment of account. Reference Bill #P-699.

SD39: Customer Payment Dated October 16, 2014

From Dawn Knight, Cheque #108 for $6,000.00 as prepayment for acceptance of Estimate #44.

📄 **Notes**
Dawn Knight
198 Crestview Blvd.
Victoria, BC V6B 2C9
Tel: (250) 399-2019
Terms: 1% 10, Net 30
Credit Limit: $25,000.00
Payment: By cheque

Creating Two Invoices from One Estimate

Some estimates include both design and landscaping projects. However, the invoice form allows for only one sales rep. Because these two types of work are connected with different sales reps, we need to fill the estimate as two separate invoices. The invoice for Casa Blanca Estates needs to be separated in this way.

Refer to the following source document as we work through the steps to enter it:

SD40: Invoices Dated October 16, 2014

Invoice #365 and #366 to Casa Blanca Estates, to fill Estimate #40, $15,500.00 for design work plus $3,900.00 for landscaping work plus $2,328.00 HST on model suite and balcony in new condo building. Invoice totals $21,728.00. Sales Reps: Zijner for design project and Gardner for landscaping work. Terms: 1/5, n/30.

1. **Open**   the **Create Invoices form** and **choose Casa Blanca Estates** as the customer

2. **Choose**   **Estimate #40** and **click OK** to add the details to the invoice

3. **Click**   **Landscaping** on the second line of the invoice

4. **Choose**   the **Edit menu** and **click Delete Line** or **press** ⌨️ **ctrl** + **D**

5. **Choose**   **DZ - Zijner, Dee** as the sales rep

6. **Enter**   **10/16/14** in the **Date field** if necessary

7. **Click**   **Save & New** to save the invoice

8. **Click**   **No** so you do not save this employee as the customer's sales rep

📇 **Source Docs**
Refer to the following source document and then follow the step-by-step instructions to enter it.

📄 **Notes**
The "Scotts" template should be displayed in the Template field. Select it if it isn't displayed by default.

9. The Available Credits screen is displayed. **Click No** when prompted to apply the customer's credits to the invoice

10. **Choose**   **Casa Blanca Estates** as the customer for the next invoice

11. **Choose**   **Estimate #40** and **click OK** to add the details of the estimate to the invoice

12. **Select**   **Design** on the first line of the invoice

13. **Choose**   the **Edit menu** and **click Delete Line** or **press** ⌃ctrl + **D**

14. **Choose**   **VG-Gardner, Vijay** as the sales rep

15. **Click**   **Save & Close** to save the invoice

16. **Click**   **No** so you do not save this employee as the customer's sales rep

Source Docs for Practice

Continue to develop your skills by entering the following source documents.

Notes

Digby Shack
200 Pacific Blvd.
Victoria, BC V8M 3C4
Tel: (250) 488-4660
Terms: 1% 10, Net 30
Credit Limit: $25,000.00
Payment: By cheque

Source Documents

Enter the following source documents for this company. You may need to refer to previous chapters for additional information:

SD41: Estimate   Dated October 17, 2014

Estimate #42 to Digby Shack (set up new customer), $12,000.00 plus $1,440.00 HST for designing and painting murals in nursery and family rooms. Estimate totals $13,440.00.

SD42: Pay Bill   Dated October 18, 2014

Paid Cheque #541 to Groen's Greens, $1,998.00 in payment of account, including the discount for early payment. Reference Bill #GG-692.

SD43: Customer Payment   Dated October 18, 2014

From Digby Shack, Cheque #544 for $3,000.00 as prepayment for acceptance of Estimate #42.

SD44: Credit Card Charge   Dated October 19, 2014

Credit card payment of Bill #CSC-6993 from Celine's Service Centre, $120.00 plus $14.40 HST for gasoline for vans and gas-powered landscaping equipment. The bill totalling $134.40 was paid in full by credit card. Use the memorized transaction.

SD45: Credit Card Charge   Dated October 19, 2014

Credit card payment of Bill #OS-2113 from Office Suppliers (use Quick Add to add the new vendor), $220.00 plus $26.40 HST for pre-printed forms. The bill totalling $246.40 was paid in full by credit card.

SD46: Customer Payment   Dated October 19, 2014

From Flora Planter, certified Cheque #31 for $11,971.00 in payment of Invoice #364.

SD47: Pay Bill   Dated October 19, 2014

Paid Cheque #542 to Freya's Home Interiors, $3,575.00 in payment of account, including the discount for early payment. Reference Bill #FHI-6721.

SD48: Pay Bill   **Dated October 20, 2014**

Paid Cheque #543 to Village Galleries, $6,380.00 in payment of account, including the discount for early payment. Reference Bill #VG-1100.

SD49: Estimate   **Dated October 21, 2014**

Estimate #43 to Siobhan Marble (set up the new customer), $15,400.00 plus $1,848.00 HST for consultation and landscaping of a front garden and creation of a new backyard design with swimming pool. Estimate totals $17,248.00.

SD50: Invoice   **Dated October 21, 2014**

Invoice #367 to Digby Shack to fill Estimate #42, $12,000.00 plus $1,440.00 HST for murals in nursery and family rooms. Invoice totals $13,440.00. Sales Rep: Zijner. Terms: 1/5, n/30.

Notes
Siobhan Marble
122 Glistening Way
Victoria, BC V7V 3E3
Tel: (250) 498-1920
Terms: 1% 10, Net 30
Credit Limit: $25,000.00
Payment: By cheque

SD51:

EMPLOYEE TIME SUMMARY SHEET #4

Date: October 22, 2014 (for the pay period ending October 18, 2014)

Name of Employee	Regular Hours	Overtime Hours	Sick Leave	Vacation Hours	Advances Received/ Advances Repaid
Nicolai Digger	40	2	–	–	–$25.00
Serge Draper	40	4	–	–	–$50.00

a. Using Employee Time Summary Sheet #4 and the Employee Information Sheet, complete payroll for weekly paid employees
b. Recover $25.00 advance from Digger and $50.00 advance from Draper
c. Manually prepare Cheques #544 and #545

SD52: Memo #10-6   **Dated October 22, 2014**

From Owners: Deposit $20,971.00 in outstanding receipts to chequing account.

SD53: Pay Bill   **Dated October 23, 2014**

Paid Cheque #546 to Stonewall Inc., $1,776.00 in payment of account, including the discount for early payment. Reference Bill #SI-5622.

SD54: Bill   **Dated October 25, 2014**

Bill #FHI-8102 received from Freya's Home Interiors, $2,800.00 plus $336.00 HST for upholstery and drapery fabrics and notions. The bill totals $3,136.00. Terms: 2/5, n/30.

SD55: Bill   **Dated October 25, 2014**

Bill #SI-7006 received from Stonewall Inc., $1,920.00 plus $230.40 HST for large rocks and interlocking paving stones for garden area. Purchase invoice totals $2,150.40. Terms: 1/10, n/30.

SD56: Bill   **Dated October 25, 2014**

Bill #GG-831 received from Groen's Greens, $840.00 plus $100.80 HST for flowers and shrubs for a garden project. Purchase invoice totals $940.80. Terms: 1/15, n/30.

SD57: Invoices   **Dated October 28, 2014**

Invoice #368 and #369 to Dawn Knight, to fill Estimate #41, $7,800.00 for design and $17,000.00 for landscape work plus $2,976.00 HST for period restoration. Invoice totals $27,776.00. Sales Reps: Zijner for design and Gardner for landscaping work. Terms: 1/5, n/30.

SD58: Pay Bill   **Dated October 28, 2014**

Paid Cheque #547 to Freya's Home Interiors, $3,080.00 in payment of account, including the discount for early payment. Reference Bill #FHI-8102.

SD59: Customer Payment   **Dated October 28, 2014**

From Siobhan Marble, Cheque #236 for $4,000.00 as prepayment for acceptance of Estimate #43.

SD60:

EMPLOYEE TIME SUMMARY SHEET #5

Date: October 29, 2014 (for the pay period ending October 25, 2014)

Name of Employee	Regular Hours	Overtime Hours	Sick Leave	Vacation Hours	Advances Received/ Advances Repaid
Nicolai Digger	40	2	—	—	−$25.00
Serge Draper	40	4	—	—	−$50.00

a. Using Employee Time Summary Sheet #5 and the Employee Information Sheet, complete payroll for weekly paid employees
b. Recover $25.00 advance from Digger and $50.00 advance from Draper
c. Manually prepare Cheques #548 and #549

SD61: Memo #10-7   **Dated October 29, 2014**

From Owners: Deposit $4,000.00 in outstanding receipts to chequing account.

SD62: Invoice   **Dated October 30, 2014**

Invoice #370 to Siobhan Marble to fill Estimate #43, $15,400.00 plus $1,848.00 HST for garden landscaping. Invoice totals $17,248.00. Sales Rep: Gardner. Terms: 1/5, n/30.

Paying Salaried Employees

The procedure for paying salaried employees is similar to that for hourly employees. Although you select different items, you still enter the number of hours for each item. Scotts' pays salaried employees a commission based on sales. Before creating the pay cheque, we need to find the sales amounts on which the commissions are based. We can find these amounts in the Sales by Rep Summary Report for the pay period. You cannot display this report while creating the pay cheque so we will review the report first.

Refer to the following source document as we work through the steps to enter it:

EMPLOYEE TIME SUMMARY SHEET #6

Date: October 31, 2014 (for the pay period ending October 29, 2014)

Name of Employee	Regular Hours	Overtime Hours	Sick Leave	Vacation Hours	Advances Received/ Advances Repaid
Vijay Gardner	112	–	8	40 hours	–
Stone Kutter	80	6	–	–	–
Mita Paynter	40	–	–	40 hours	–
Dee Zijner	144	–	–	16 hours	–

a. Using Employee Time Summary Sheet #6 and the Employee Information Sheet, complete payroll for semi-monthly paid and salaried employees
b. Record vacations for this month. Gardner has taken one week of vacation and Zijner has taken two days of vacation
c. Release 40 hours of vacation pay for Paynter
d. Include commissions for Gardner (2% of landscaping revenue) and Zijner (2% design revenue). Display Profit & Loss Standard or the Sales by Rep Summary Report for October 1 to October 31 to determine the revenue amounts needed to calculate the commissions
e. Manually prepare Cheques #550 through #553

Source Docs
Refer to the following source document and then follow the step-by-step instructions to enter it.

Displaying the Sales by Rep Summary Report

1. Choose the **Reports menu**, then **click Sales** and **choose Sales by Rep Summary**

2. Enter **10/01/14** in the **From date field** and **10/31/14** in the **To date field**

3. Click the **Refresh button** to update the report:

Notes
You can also find the revenue amounts in the Profit & Loss Standard Report from October 1 to October 31, 2014.

Notes
The Sales Rep by Detail report shows all transactions that make up the total sales amount in the Summary report.

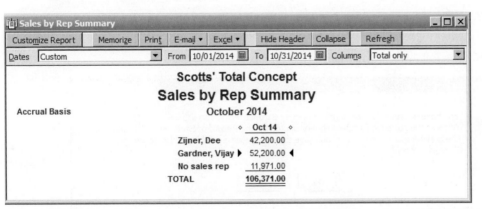

Figure 10-30

Notes
The amount beside No sales rep represents the NSF cheque and NSF fee to Flora Planter.

4. Write down the **sales amounts** for Zijner and Gardner

5. Close the **report**. Do not save the changes

Entering the Hours Worked

1. Open the **Payroll Centre**

2. Click the **Unscheduled Payroll icon** or **choose** the **Employees menu**, **click Pay Employees**, and **click Unscheduled Payroll**

3. Enter **10/29/14** in the **Pay Period Ends field** if necessary

4. Enter **10/31/14** in the **Cheque Date field**

5. Select the **four employees** who are being paid (refer to SD63 above)

6. Click   **Continue** to open the Review and Create Pay Cheques screen:

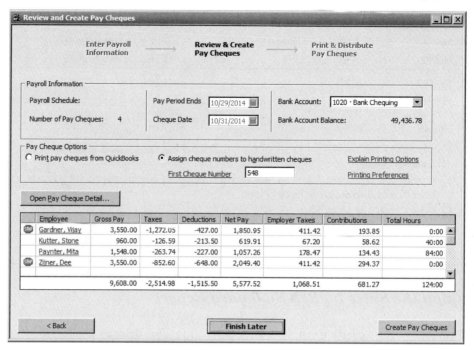

Figure 10-31

A Stop button is displayed beside Gardner and Zinger. This indicates that there is a problem with their payroll information.

7. Click   the **Open Pay Cheque Detail button** to open the Review and Create Pay Cheques screen for Gardner

8. The following warning message is displayed:

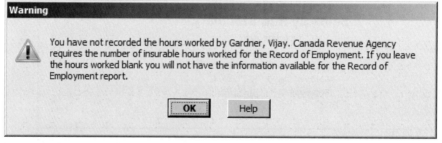

Figure 10-32

This warning indicates that we have not recorded the hours worked for Gardner and Vijay. Canada Revenue Agency requires the number of insurable hours worked for the Record of Employment.

9. Click   **OK** to close the warning and display the Review and Create Pay Cheques form for Gardner

One notable difference between the Review and Create Pay Cheques form for the salaried employees and the hourly employees is the addition of a Quantity column. This column is used to enter a base for the calculation of a commission, either a revenue amount or the number of items sold, depending on how the payroll item is calculated.

Gardner has taken one week's vacation and one day's sick leave this month. We need to enter the hours for each of these items as well as the number of regular hours worked and the revenue amount that forms the basis for the 2 percent commission. The number of hours is used to determine eligibility for EI benefits, not to calculate pay. The pay amount is fixed for the month.

First we will enter the number of hours for each item.

10. Click   the **Hours column** beside Salary if necessary

11. Type   **112** and **press** (tab)

Notice that the Salary amount in the Employee Summary section does not change.

12. Click   the **Item Name field** below Commission to display the drop-down arrow

For salaried workers, we must choose the sick leave payroll item created for them.

13. Choose   **Sick Salary** from the drop-down list

14. Press   (tab) twice to advance to the Hours field

15. Type   **8**

16. Press   (tab) to update the form

Notes
The payroll item for sick leave for salaried workers is different from the one for hourly employees.
The payroll item for vacation pay leave for salaried workers is also different from the one for hourly employees.

Notice that the amount in the Rate field for Salary has decreased proportionately so that eight hours' worth of the regular salary amount is allocated to sick leave. The number of hours of sick leave available is reduced by eight hours in the summary information on the right-hand side of the screen.

Paying Vacation Pay to Salaried Employees

For salaried workers, we choose a different payroll item for vacation than the one used for hourly employees.

17. Press   (tab) again to advance to the Item Name field

18. Choose   **Vacation Salary** from the drop-down list

19. Press   (tab) twice to advance to the Hours field

20. Type   **40**

21. Press   (tab) to update the amounts

The regular total salary amount is now divided among salary, sick leave, and vacation in proportion to the number of hours for each, as shown:

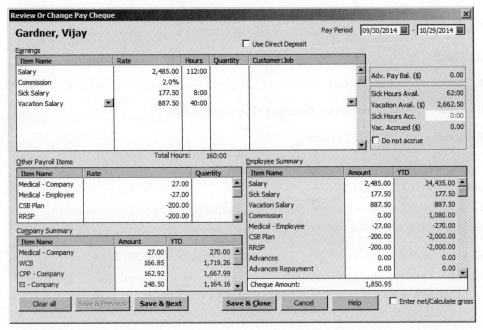

Figure 10-33

The Vacation Available amount has decreased as shown in the right-hand corner of the screen by the vacation amount taken. Gardner has about three weeks' vacation remaining. Again, net pay has not changed.

Paying Sales Commissions

We are now ready to enter the commission. The rate is entered as 2 percent, the default set up for the employee. We need to enter the revenue amount that this rate is based on.

1. **Click**   the **Quantity field** for Commission

2. **Type**   **52200**

3. **Press**   (tab) to update and complete the pay cheque:

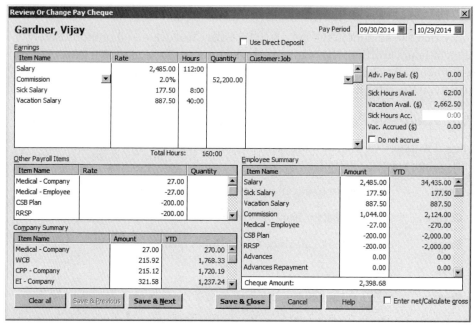

Figure 10-34

The commission amount is entered in the Employee Summary section and added to the gross pay amount. The commission is fully taxable so all tax amounts are increased.

4. **Check**   your **work** carefully and **make corrections** before continuing

5. **Click**   **Save & Next** to save the pay cheque and open the next pay cheque

6. **Enter**   the **remaining three pay cheques** in SD63

7. **Create**   the **Pay Cheques**

Source Docs for Practice
Continue to develop your skills by entering the following source documents.

Source Documents

Enter the following source documents for this company. You may need to refer to previous chapters for additional information:

SD64: Memo #10-8   **Dated October 31, 2014**

Assess finance charges on Ashby Everwood's overdue account. Apply the unused credits to the invoice before assessing interest charges.

SD65: Bank Debit Memo #42291 **Dated October 31, 2014**

From Pacific Bank, preauthorized bank service charges and loan and mortgage payments were taken from the chequing account as follows:

Bank service charges	$ 55.00
Mortgage ($350.00 interest and $100.00 principal)	$450.00
Bank loan ($60.00 interest and $880.00 principal)	$940.00
Long term loan ($180.00 interest and $540.00 principal)	$720.00

SD66: Memo #10-9 **Dated October 31, 2014**

From Owners: Pay all payroll liabilities outstanding from October 1 to October 31. Issue Cheques #554 to #557 in payment.

> To Receiver General: Federal Income Tax, EI - Company, EI - Employee, CPP - Company, CPP - Employee
>
> To Minister of Finance: Medical - Company, Medical - Employee
>
> To Workers' Compensation Board: WCB
>
> To Haida Investments Inc.: CSB Plan, RRSP

SD67: Memo #10-10 **Dated October 31, 2014**

Make remittance to the Receiver General for HST payable as of October 31. Issue Cheque #558 in payment.

SD68: Memo #10-11 **Dated October 31, 2014**

From Owner: Complete adjusting entries for supplies and inventory used in October and for prepaid expenses expired.

Decorating supplies	$ 1,200.00
Decorating materials	$13,400.00
Landscaping materials	$11,350.00
Office & computer supplies	$305.00
Prepaid insurance	$970.00
Prepaid taxes	$270.00

SD69: Reconcile and pay Credit Card **Dated October 31, 2014**

To Pacific Coast Visa, $515.20 in full payment of account for purchases before October 25. Reconcile and pay credit card bill in full with Cheque #559. The statement included the following entries:

Date	Description	Amount
Oct. 2/14	Payment Received	$–500.00
Oct. 5/14	Celine's Service Centre	$134.40
Oct. 19/14	Celine's Service Centre	$134.40
Oct. 19/14	Office Suppliers Inc.	$246.40
Oct. 25/14	Ending Balance (Total owing)	$515.20

Payroll Reports

Like other reports, the group of payroll reports can be displayed from the Report Centre or the Reports menu. We'll use the Report Centre to view the payroll reports.

1. **Click** the **Reports icon** on the Icon bar

Notes
The procedures for sorting, filtering, and customizing the reports are the same as for other reports.

2. **Click**   the **Employees & Payroll heading** on the left-hand side of the screen

3. **Click**   the **List View icon** to view the reports in list view that are available under this heading:

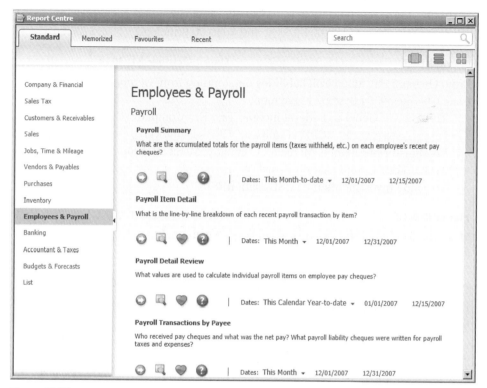

Figure 10-35

When we are displaying the payroll reports in this chapter, it is assumed that you are beginning from the Report Centre in List view with the Employees & Payroll heading selected. You may have to scroll down the list of reports to find the one you want to display on the screen.

The Payroll Summary Report

The Payroll Summary Report shows the total for each payroll item for each employee for any period you select.

1. **Click**   the **Run icon** under the Payroll Summary report

2. **Double click**   the **date** in the **From date field**

3. **Type**   **10/01/14**

4. **Press**   (tab) to advance the To date field

5. **Type**   **10/31/14**

6. **Press**   (tab) or **click** the **Refresh button** to update the report:

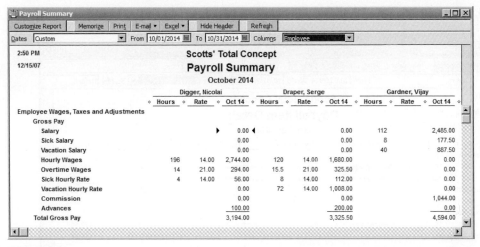

Figure 10-36

Each payroll item — earnings items, additions to income, deductions, and accruals — is listed separately and the number of hours for each type of income is included. Gross and net pay amounts are also provided on the reports.

You can add several columns to the report — different payroll details and different time intervals — by selecting from the Columns drop-down list.

Double click an amount to see the transactions by payroll item report. Double click any transaction detail to see the original pay cheque.

7. Close   the **Payroll Summary report** when you have finished viewing it. Choose not to memorize the changes if you made any

The Payroll Item Detail Report

This report organizes payroll details by item. A line is added for each payroll transaction that uses the item, along with the totals for each item in the selected period.

1. Click   the **Run icon** under the Payroll Item Detail report

2. Double click   the **date** in the **From date field**

3. Type   **10/01/14**

4. Press   ⟨tab⟩ to advance the To date field

5. Type   **10/31/14**

📄 **Notes**
To access the report from the Reports menu:
- Choose the Reports menu, then choose Employees & Payroll, and click Payroll Item Detail to open the report
- Enter 10/01/14 in the From date field
- Enter 10/31/14 in the To date field
- Press ⟨tab⟩ or click the Refresh button to update the report

6. Press (tab) or **click** the **Refresh button** to update the report:

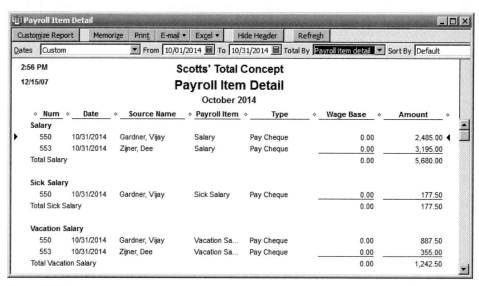

Figure 10-37

You can sort the report by any of the column headings. You can organize the report to show total amounts differently by selecting a different total from the Total By drop-down list. For example, you can show totals by account instead of the default, by Payroll item detail.

Double click any transaction detail to view the original pay cheque.

7. Close the **Payroll Item Detail** report when you have finished viewing it. Choose not to memorize the changes if you made any

The Payroll Detail Review Report

The Payroll Detail Review Report provides a detailed listing of each item and amount that was used to calculate the payroll cheques. It also has an "audit" column indicating whether the transaction was modified after the original entry. The default dates are for year-to-date amounts so that all transactions for each item are listed for each employee.

Notes
To access the report from the Reports menu:
- Choose the Reports menu, then choose Employees & Payroll, and click Payroll Detail Review to open the report
- Enter 10/01/14 in the From date field
- Enter 10/31/14 in the To date field
- Press (tab) or click the Refresh button to update the report

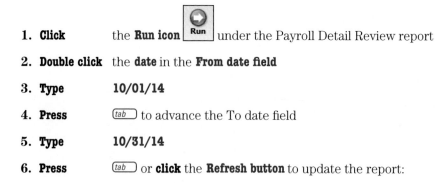

1. Click the **Run icon** [Run] under the Payroll Detail Review report

2. Double click the **date** in the **From date field**

3. Type **10/01/14**

4. Press (tab) to advance the To date field

5. Type **10/31/14**

6. Press (tab) or **click** the **Refresh button** to update the report:

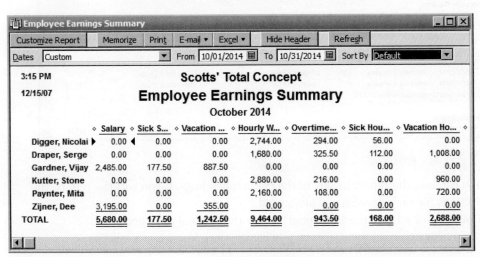

Figure 10-38

You can sort the report by date, the date/time the transaction was entered or last modified, or by the transaction number. Double click any transaction detail to view the original pay cheque.

7. **Close**   the **Payroll Detail Review report** when you have finished viewing it. Choose not to memorize the changes if you made any

The Employee Earnings Summary Report

The Employee Earnings Summary report shows the total for each payroll item for each employee for the selected period. Totals for each item for all employees are included.

Notes
To access the report from the Reports menu:
- Choose the Reports menu, then choose Employees & Payroll, and click Employee Earnings Summary to open the report
- Enter 10/01/14 in the From date field
- Enter 10/31/14 in the To date field
- Press (tab) or click the Refresh button to update the report

1. **Click**   the **Run icon** [Run] under the Employee Earnings Summary report

2. **Double click**   the **date** in the **From date field**

3. **Type**   **10/01/14**

4. **Press**   (tab) to advance the To date field

5. **Type**   **10/31/14**

6. **Press**   (tab) or **click** the **Refresh button** to update the report:

Employee Earnings Summary

3:15 PM
12/15/07

Scotts' Total Concept
Employee Earnings Summary
October 2014

	Salary	Sick S...	Vacation ...	Hourly W...	Overtime...	Sick Hou...	Vacation Ho...
Digger, Nicolai	0.00	0.00	0.00	2,744.00	294.00	56.00	0.00
Draper, Serge	0.00	0.00	0.00	1,680.00	325.50	112.00	1,008.00
Gardner, Vijay	2,485.00	177.50	887.50	0.00	0.00	0.00	0.00
Kutter, Stone	0.00	0.00	0.00	2,880.00	216.00	0.00	960.00
Paynter, Mita	0.00	0.00	0.00	2,160.00	108.00	0.00	720.00
Zijner, Dee	3,195.00	0.00	355.00	0.00	0.00	0.00	0.00
TOTAL	5,680.00	177.50	1,242.50	9,464.00	943.50	168.00	2,688.00

Figure 10-39

By default the report is sorted by employee; however you can choose to sort the report by total by selecting it in the Sort By field.

Double click any amount to view the individual transactions that formed that total. Double click any of these transaction details to view the original pay cheque.

7. Close   the **Employee Earnings Summary report** when you have finished viewing it. Choose not to memorize the changes if you made any

The Payroll Transactions by Payee Report

The Payroll Transactions by Payee report lists all payees who received payroll-related cheques — employees as well as agencies to whom payroll liability remittances were made. For each payee, the total amount of each cheque is provided.

Notes
To access the report from the Reports menu:
- Choose the Reports menu, then choose Employees & Payroll, and click Payroll Transactions by Payee to open the report
- Enter 10/01/14 in the From date field
- Enter 10/31/14 in the To date field
- Press (tab) or click the Refresh button to update the report

1. Click   the **Run icon** [Run] under the Payroll Transactions by Payee report

2. Double click the **date** in the **From date field**

3. Type   **10/01/14**

4. Press   (tab) to advance the To date field

5. Type   **10/31/14**

6. Press   (tab) or **click** the **Refresh button** to update the report:

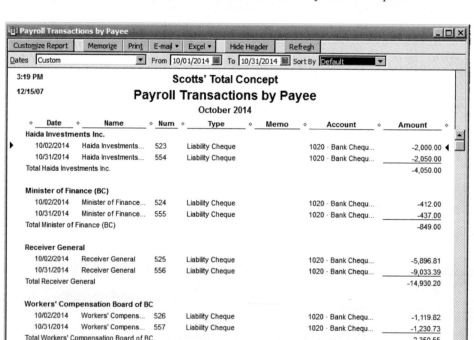

Figure 10-40

You can sort the report by any of the column headings. If you sort the report, the transactions for each payee name are sorted.

Double click any transaction detail to view the original pay cheque.

7. Close   the **Payroll Transactions by Payee report** when you have finished viewing it. Choose not to memorize the changes if you made any

The Payroll Transaction Detail Report

The Payroll Transaction Detail report shows the item amounts that make up each payroll transaction. Both liability payments and employee pay cheques are included.

1. **Click** the **Run icon** under the Payroll Transactions Detail report

2. **Double click** the **date** in the **From date field**

3. **Type** 10/01/14

4. **Press** (tab) to advance the To date field

5. **Type** 10/31/14

6. **Press** (tab) or **click** the **Refresh button** to update the report:

Notes
To access the report from the Reports menu:
- Choose the Reports menu, then choose Employees & Payroll, and click Payroll Transaction Detail to open the report
- Enter 10/01/14 in the From date field
- Enter 10/31/14 in the To date field
- Press (tab) or click the Refresh button to update the report

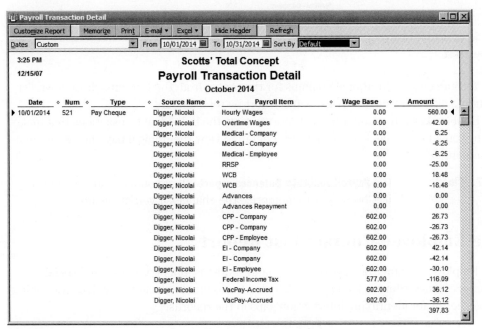

Figure 10-41

You can sort the report by any of the column headings.
Double click any transaction detail to view the original pay cheque or liability cheque.

7. **Close** the **Payroll Transaction Detail report** when you have finished viewing it. Choose not to memorize the changes if you made any

The Payroll Liability Balances Report

The Payroll Liability Balances report shows the monthly totals owing for each payroll item.

1. **Click** the **Run icon** under the Payroll Liability Balances report

2. **Double click** the **date** in the **From date field**

3. **Type** 10/01/14

4. **Press** (tab) to advance the To date field

Notes
To access the report from the Reports menu:
- Choose the Reports menu, then choose Employees & Payroll, and click Payroll Liability Balances to open the report
- Enter 10/01/14 in the From date field
- Enter 10/31/14 in the To date field
- Press (tab) or click the Refresh button to update the report

5. **Type**   **10/31/14**

6. **Press**   ⌨ *tab* or **click** the **Refresh button** to update the report:

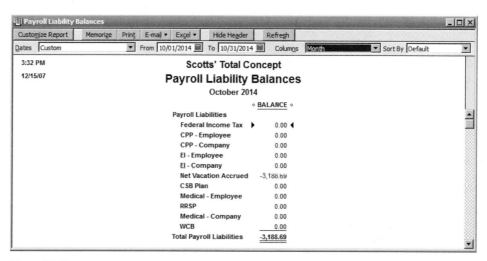

Figure 10-42

You can choose additional columns for the report from the Columns drop-down list, including different time intervals. You can sort by total amount.

   Double click any amount in the report to view the individual transactions that make up the total. Double click any transaction detail to view the original pay cheque or liability screen.

7. **Close**   the **Payroll Liability Balances report** when you have finished viewing it. Choose not to memorize the changes if you made any

The Employee Contact List Report

The Employee Contact List provides the name, address, phone number, and social insurance number for each employee. The list forms an easy base for mailing or phoning employees or for identifying information gaps in the records.

1. **Click**   the **Run icon**  under the Employee Contact List report:

Figure 10-43

You can sort the list by any of the column headings.

Double click any employee to open the employee record for editing.

2. **Close**   the **Employee Contact List report** when you have finished viewing it. Choose not to memorize the changes if you made any

The Employee Withholding Report

The Employee Withholding report shows the TD1 federal tax claim amounts and the EI factor for each employee. The employee's social insurance number and date of birth and whether the employee pays income tax are also in the report.

1. Click the **Run icon** [Run] under the Employee Withholding report

Scotts' Total Concept
Employee Withholding

3:43 PM
12/15/07

Employee	SIN	Payroll Province	Birth Date	Fed TD1	EI Factor	Fed. In...
Digger, Nicolai	931 216 550	BC	09/19/1979	13,332.00	1.4	Yes
Draper, Serge	406 529 420	BC	10/31/1974	10,382.00	1.4	Yes
Gardner, Vijay	428 161 020	BC	12/16/1969	10,382.00	1.4	Yes
Kutter, Stone	563 444 868	BC	04/29/1963	10,382.00	1.4	Yes
Paynter, Mita	148 196 835	BC	02/27/1972	24,987.00	1.4	Yes
Zijner, Dee	129 632 774	BC	07/13/1978	20,764.00	1.4	Yes

Figure 10-44

Notes
An EI factor of 1.4 means that the employer's share of EI premiums is 1.4 times the amount of the employee's share.

You can sort the report by any of the column headings.
Double click any employee to open the employee record for editing.

2. Close the **Employee Withholding report** when you have finished viewing it. Choose not to memorize the changes if you made any

The Payroll Item Listing Report

The Payroll Item Listing report shows the item record details: item type, Record of Employment information, default amounts and limits, default accounts, and the box used for the item on T4s.

1. Click the **Run icon** [Run] under the Payroll Item Listing report:

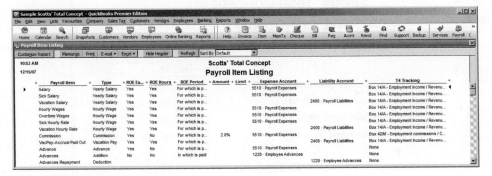

Figure 10-45

Notes
To access the report from the Reports menu:
- Choose the Reports menu, then choose Employees & Payroll, and click Payroll Item Listing to open the report; or
- Choose the Reports menu, then choose List, and click Payroll Item Listing to open the report

You can sort the report by any of the column headings.
Double click any item detail to open the wizard for editing the item.

2. Close the **Payroll Item Listing report** when you have finished viewng it. Choose not to memorize the changes if you made any

The Employee TD1 Review List Report

The Employee TD1 Review List report shows the province of taxation and federal and provincial TD1 amounts for each employee. This report also shows whether the employee's claim amounts are base amounts or include claims for other deductions (custom amounts).

Notes
To access the report from the Reports menu:
- Choose the Reports menu, then choose Employees & Payroll, and click TD1 Review List to open the report

1. Click the **Run icon** 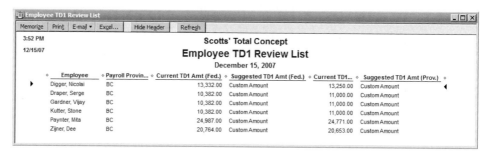 under the TD1 Review List report:

Figure 10-46

Notes
The default date for the Employee TD1 Review List report is your current computer date. You are working in a sample file, so the current date is 12/15/2007.

You cannot sort or modify this list.

2. Close the **Employee TD1 Review List report** when you have finished viewing it

The T4 Summary Report

Notes
T4 slips are usually prepared at the beginning of a new year in preparation for employees filing their personal income tax returns before April 30th.

The T4 Summary report shows the totals for all employees in the company for the items on T4s for the current year. The number of T4 slips already printed for this tax year is included.

1. Click the **Run icon** 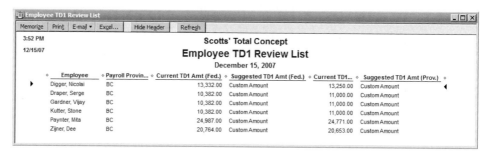 under the T4 Summary report:

Notes
To access the report from the Reports menu:
- Choose the Reports menu, then choose Employees & Payroll, and click T4 Summary to open the report

Notes
You can select this calendar year or the last calendar year for this report. The current year in the sample company file is 2007, even though our transactions have been entered in 2014. You cannot change the date to 2014; in the sample file, therefore, this report is blank because there were no payroll transactions in 2007.

Figure 10-47

Refer to the note in the left margin of the previous page which explains why this report is blank. This report cannot be sorted or modified.

2. **Close**   the **T4 Summary report** when you have finished viewing it

The PD7A Summary Report

The PD7A report shows the total monthly payroll tax liabilities for federal taxes (income tax, CPP, and EI employer and employee amounts).

1. **Click**   the **Run icon** 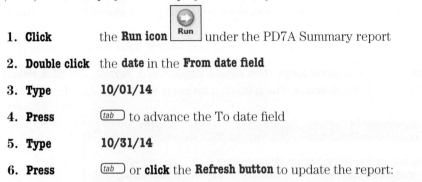 under the PD7A Summary report

2. **Double click**   the **date** in the **From date field**

3. **Type**   **10/01/14**

4. **Press**   (tab) to advance the To date field

5. **Type**   **10/31/14**

6. **Press**   (tab) or **click** the **Refresh button** to update the report:

Notes
To access the report from the Reports menu:
- Choose the Reports menu, then choose Employees & Payroll, and click PD7A Report to open the report
- Enter 10/01/14 in the From date field
- Enter 10/31/14 in the To date field
- Press (tab) or click the Refresh button to update the report

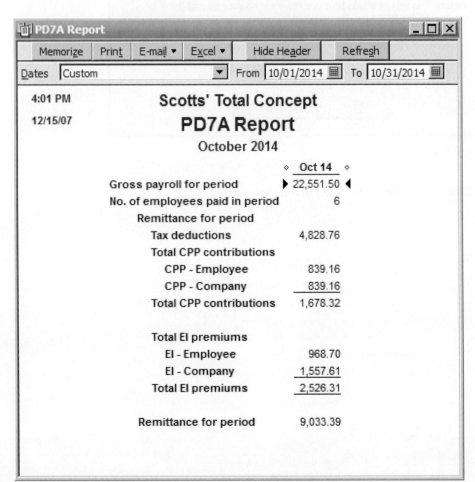

Figure 10-48

You cannot sort or modify this report, though you can change the date range from the date fields inside the report window. The report always shows the totals for the selected period.

7. Close   the **PD7A report** when you have finished viewing it

The Record of Employment Report

📄 **Notes**
You cannot display a record of employment unless an employee has left the company.

The Record of Employment report is prepared for employees who have terminated their employment with the company. It shows the number of hours worked, the date of hire, the date of termination, and the reason for termination (to assess the employee's eligibility for EI benefits).

The Record of Employment report can be displayed only from the Reports menu.

1. Choose   the **Reports menu**, then **choose Employees & Payroll**, and **click Record of Employment**. The following message will be displayed:

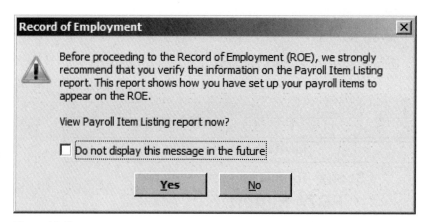

Record of Employment   ⊠

⚠ Before proceeding to the Record of Employment (ROE), we strongly recommend that you verify the information on the Payroll Item Listing report. This report shows how you have set up your payroll items to appear on the ROE.

View Payroll Item Listing report now?

☐ Do not display this message in the future

Yes   No

Figure 10-49

2. Click   **No** to skip the Payroll Item Listing report

The Payroll Item Listing report shows the Record of Employment status for each payroll item. The following screen will be displayed where you select the employee for whom you want to generate a Record of Employment:

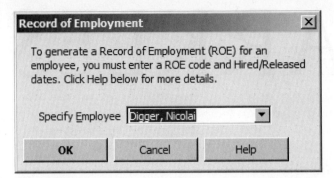

Figure 10-50

Before you can generate the report, the date of hire, termination date, and reason for leaving work must be entered in the employee record.

3. **Choose**   the **employee** who has left the company

4. **Click**   **OK** to view the report

5. **Close**   the **Record of Employment report** when you have finished viewing it

Finishing Your Session

1. **Back up**   your **company data file**

2. **Close**   the **Company file**

3. **Close**   the **QuickBooks program**

CHAPTER ELEVEN

SPARKLES

Objectives

After completing this chapter, you should be able to:

- **sell** inventory items

- **purchase** and **order** inventory items

- **enter** sales returns and credits

- **enter** purchase returns and credits

- **enter** returns for credit card sales and purchases

- **adjust** inventory for losses

- **assemble** inventory items

- **apply** discounts to invoice subtotal amounts

- **handle** transactions for insufficient inventory

- **display** and print inventory reports

Company Information

Company Profile

Notes
Sparkles
55 Glittering Way
Toronto, ON M3T 5F9
Tel: (416) 889-3918
Fax: (416) 887-4112
E-mail: sales@sparkles.com
Web: www.sparkles.com
Business No.: 233 495 851

Sparkles, located in Toronto, Ontario, is owned and run by Rubie Dimond. The jewellery store sells diamond jewellery in unique gold settings and also makes customized settings for the precious gem.

As a child, Dimond experimented with many media. She created original and interesting jewellery with ceramics and modelling clay. But the sparkle of diamonds always held the most interest for her, so she completed a jewellery making and design program at community college. There she learned how to work with gems and to make original gold settings. She makes many of the pieces she sells now, but she also carries a number of standard chains and bracelets to which she can attach her custom-designed pendants.

Dimond employs two assistants — one works exclusively on sales and one assists with making jewellery and sales. Dimond herself also works in the store regularly because she enjoys interacting with customers, and learning more about their tastes and preferences helps her plan her future designs.

The store accepts cash, cheques, and Visa in payment and has a credit card for some business purchases. Many customers have also set up accounts and these customers receive a discount for early payment as well as a volume sales discount of 10 percent when they buy multiple pieces of jewellery. For custom-designed pieces, customers pay a deposit on accepting an estimate or placing an order. Dimond has also arranged discounts with some of her vendors and has accounts set up for regular purchases.

Customers pay 13 percent HST on all purchases. Sparkles pays HST on all business-related non-inventory purchases.

Dimond will use the inventory features of QuickBooks to help track inventory costs and sales. At the beginning of January 2014, she is ready to enter the first month of transactions in QuickBooks after closing the books at the end of 2013 and submitting all payroll and tax liabilities. Her sales assistant converted the accounting records to QuickBooks by using the following:

- Chart of Accounts
- Post-closing Trial Balance
- Vendor Information
- Customer Information
- Item Lists
- Employee Information
- Accounting Procedures

NOTE: We are using a QuickBooks sample file while working in this chapter in order to keep the payroll taxes the same no matter what year you are working with this file. The sample file uses default dates in the year 2007. You will be changing that as you work through the lesson; however, some reports will still show dates in 2007.

Chart of Accounts

Sparkles

ASSETS

Bank
- 1020 Bank Chequing
- 1040 Bank Savings
- 1060 Bank Visa

Accounts Receivable
- 1200 Accounts Receivable

Other Current Assets
- 1220 Employee Advances
- 1300 Jewellery Boxes & Bags
- 1320 Jewellery Parts Inventory
- 1340 Office & Computer Supplies
- 1360 Other Supplies
- 1400 Inventory [Parent account]
- 1410 Bracelets
- 1420 Diamonds
- 1430 Earrings
- 1440 Necklaces
- 1450 Pendants
- 1460 Rings

Fixed Assets
- 1520 Computer Equipment
- 1540 Display Cabinets & Fixtures
- 1550 Equipment & Tools
- 1560 Safe
- 1580 Store

LIABILITIES

Accounts Payable
- 2100 Accounts Payable

Credit Card
- 2200 Visa Payable

Other Current Liabilities
- 2260 Bank Loan
- 2300 GST/HST Payable
- 2360 Payroll Liabilities

Long Term Liabilities
- 2740 Mortgage Payable

Equity
- 3220 Capital, Rubie Dimond
- 3260 Drawings, Rubie Dimond
- 3600 Retained Earnings

INCOME
- 4100 Revenue from Sales
- 4120 Revenue from Services
- 4140 Sales Discounts
- 4200 Revenue from Interest
- 4250 Sales Tax Compensation
- 4300 Other Revenue

EXPENSE

Cost of Goods Sold
- 5040 Cost of Inventory Sold
- 5060 Jewellery Parts Used

Expense
- 5120 Advertising & Promotion
- 5130 Bank Charges
- 5140 Credit Card Fees
- 5160 Purchase Discounts
- 5170 Boxes & Bags Used
- 5180 Office & Computer Supplies Used
- 5190 Other Supplies Used
- 5220 Maintenance Expenses
- 5240 Insurance Expense
- 5260 Interest Expense
- 5280 Property Tax Expense
- 5340 Hydro Expense
- 5360 Telephone Expense
- 5600 Payroll Expenses

Post-closing Trial Balance

Sparkles

AS AT JANUARY 1, 2014

	Debits	Credits		Debits	Credits
1020 Bank Chequing	$ 33,460.00		1520 Computer Equipment	$ 9,400.00	
1040 Bank Savings	60,000.00		1540 Display Cabinets & Fixtures	18,000.00	
1060 Bank Visa	2,180.00		1550 Equipment & Tools	12,000.00	
1200 Accounts Receivable	9,350.00		1560 Safe	6,500.00	
1300 Jewellery Boxes & Bags	3,400.00		1580 Store	160,000.00	
1320 Jewellery Parts Inventory	4,900.00		2100 Accounts Payable		$ 10,700.00
1340 Office & Computer Supplies	585.00		2200 Visa Payable		210.00
1360 Other Supplies	280.00		2260 Bank Loan		25,000.00
1400 Inventory: 1410 Bracelets	8,775.00		2300 GST/HST Payable		210.00
1400 Inventory: 1420 Diamonds	42,800.00		2740 Mortgage Payable		95,000.00
1400 Inventory: 1430 Earrings	2,100.00		3220 Capital, Rubie Dimond		337,920.00
1400 Inventory: 1440 Necklaces	26,270.00		3260 Drawings, Rubie Dimond	8,400.00	
1400 Inventory: 1450 Pendants	6,360.00			$469,040.00	$469,040.00
1400 Inventory: 1460 Rings	54,280.00				

Vendor Information

Sparkles

Vendor Name (Contact)	Address	Phone No. Fax No.	E-mail Business No.	Terms Credit Limit
Faithful Insurers				monthly
Goldcrest Inc. (Troy Waytes)	200 Crystal Cres. Markham, ON L4G 4F5	Tel: (905) 388-2819 Alt: (905) 769-2928	twaytes@goldcrest.com	1/10, n/30 $15,000.00
Hydro One (N. U. Kleer)	50 Bloor St. W. Toronto, ON M5K 2B4	Tel: (416) 524-2345	nukleer@hydroone.ca	net 10 $500.00
Kimberley Mines (Silver Minor)	600 Starlight Rd. North York, ON M4C 8B2	Tel: (416) 292-4910 Fax: (416) 292-3991	minor@kimberleymines.com	net 30 $20,000.00
Ministry of Finance				
Sprint Canada (Ena Tellus)	5 Satellite Circle Toronto, ON M2M 5C3	Tel: (416) 2SP-RINT		net 15 $500.00
Trevor's Treasures (Trevor)	45 Findings Lane Oakville, ON L9M 3G9	Tel: (905) 687-9812		2/10, n/30 $5,000.00
Receiver General				monthly
Workplace Safety and Insurance Board				monthly

Outstanding Vendor Transactions

Sparkles

Vendor Name	Date	Terms	Due Date	Invoice No./ Cheque No.	Amount
Goldcrest Inc.	Dec. 27/13	1/10, n/30	Jan. 26/14	GI-2018	$6,420.00
Trevor's Treasures	Dec. 29/13	2/10, n/30	Jan. 28/14	TT-3170	$4,280.00
				Grand Total	$10,700.00

Customer Information

Sparkles

Customer Name (Contact)	Address	Phone No. Fax No.	E-mail Preferred Payment Method	Terms Credit Limit
Cash Sales			Visa	due on receipt
Carat, Goldie	103 Sheen Ave. Toronto, ON M9T 4D2	Tel: (905) 498-1820	gcarat@sympatico.ca Cheque	1/5, n/30 $10,000.00
Glitters, Jem	12 Opal Ave. Toronto, ON M4V 5C2	Tel: (416) 893-1021 Alt: (416) 884-4991	jglitters@google.ca Cheque	1/5, n/30 $10,000.00
Goldwyn, William	33 Nugget Court Oak Ridges, ON L3B 7N9	Tel: (905) 372-3001	goldwyn7@rogers.ca Cheque	1/5, n/30 $10,000.00
Perley, Bess	23 Tinsel Grove Toronto, ON M4J 4J3	Tel: (416) 387-1098	bperley@yahoo.ca Cheque	1/5, n/30 $10,000.00
Saffire, Wanda	499 Cluster Ave. Burlington, ON L9G 4D2	Tel: (905) 458-7331 Fax: (905) 458-4301	wsaffire@sympatico.ca Cheque	1/5, n/30 $10,000.00

Outstanding Customer Transactions

Sparkles

Customer Name	Date	Terms	Type	Invoice No./ Cheque No.	Amount	Balance Owing
Glitters, Jem	Dec. 10/13		Deposit cheque	192	−$1,000.00	
	Dec. 16/13	1/5, n/30	Invoice	278	$3,450.00	$2,450.00
Goldwyn, William	Dec. 24/13	1/5, n/30	Invoice	297	$4,600.00	$4,600.00
Perley, Bess	Dec. 30/13	1/5, n/30	Invoice	315	$2,300.00	$2,300.00
			Grand Total			$9,350.00

Non-inventory Item List

Sparkles

Item	Description	Price	Tax Code	Account
NON-INVENTORY PARTS				
Gold	Gold used to make and repair jewellery	$604.00/ounce	H	1320 Jewellery Parts Inventory
Jewellery Parts	Repair parts, findings, etc.	Variable	H	1320 Jewellery Parts Inventory
OTHER CHARGES				
Finance Charges	Finance Charges on Overdue Balance (18% > 30 days, min. charge $30.00, grace period 5 days)	18%		4200 Revenue from Interest
NSF Cheque	Amount of NSF Cheque	Variable		1020 Bank Chequing
NSF Fees	NSF cheque handling charge	$30.00		1020 Bank Chequing
SUBTOTALS				
Subtotal - pretax	Invoice subtotal for discount application			
DISCOUNTS				
Discount	Sales discount on pretax subtotal	10%	H	4140 Sales Discounts

Sparkles

Item Name/Number	Description	Selling Price	Sales Tax Code	Purchase Tax Code	Reorder Point	Number on Hand	Total Value
INVENTORY PARTS							
BRACELETS (Revenue Account: 4100 Revenue from Sales; Asset Account: 1410 Bracelets; Cost of Goods Sold Account: 5040 Cost of Inventory Sold)							
B101 Bracelet	14 Kt bangle plain	$590.00	H	H	3	6	$1,770.00
B102 Bracelet	14 Kt bangle solitaire setting	510.00	H	H	3	6	1,530.00
B103 Bracelet	14 Kt bangle 3 stone setting	625.00	H	H	3	6	1,875.00
B104 Bracelet	14 Kt link plain	400.00	H	H	3	6	1,200.00
B105 Bracelet	14 Kt link solitaire setting	370.00	H	H	3	6	1,110.00
B106 Bracelet	14 Kt link 3 stone setting	430.00	H	H	3	6	1,290.00
					Total		$8,775.00
DIAMONDS (Revenue Account: 4100 Revenue from Sales; Asset Account: 1420 Diamonds; Cost of Goods Sold Account: 5040 Cost of Inventory Sold)							
D101 Diamond	0.10 ct diamond	$ 400.00	H	H	50	60	$12,000.00
D102 Diamond	0.25 ct diamond	1,000.00	H	H	10	14	7,000.00
D103 Diamond	0.50 ct diamond	2,500.00	H	H	4	8	10,000.00
D104 Diamond	1.0 ct diamond	6,900.00	H	H	2	4	13,800.00
					Total		$42,800.00
EARRINGS (Revenue Account: 4100 Revenue from Sales; Asset Account: 1430 Earrings; Cost of Goods Sold Account: 5040 Cost of Inventory Sold)							
E101 Earrings	18 Kt drop setting	$140.00	H	H	10	14	$ 980.00
E102 Earrings	18 Kt stud setting	80.00	H	H	10	14	560.00
E103 Earrings	18 Kt studs	80.00	H	H	10	14	560.00
					Total		$2,100.00
NECKLACES (Revenue Account: 4100 Revenue from Sales; Asset Account: 1440 Necklaces; Cost of Goods Sold Account: 5040 Cost of Inventory Sold)							
N101 Necklace	16 inch feather chain 18 Kt	$600.00	H	H	10	14	$4,200.00
N102 Necklace	16 inch box chain 18 Kt	550.00	H	H	10	12	3,300.00
N103 Necklace	16 inch wire chain 18 Kt	480.00	H	H	10	16	3,840.00
N104 Necklace	18 inch feather chain 18 Kt	800.00	H	H	10	12	4,800.00
N105 Necklace	18 inch box chain 18 Kt	750.00	H	H	10	14	5,250.00
N106 Necklace	18 inch wire chain 18 Kt	610.00	H	H	10	16	4,880.00
					Total		$26,270.00
PENDANTS (Revenue Account: 4100 Revenue from Sales; Asset Account: 1450 Pendants; Cost of Goods Sold Account: 5040 Cost of Inventory Sold)							
P101 Pendant	18 Kt gold small setting	$110.00	H	H	8	12	$ 660.00
P102 Pendant	18 Kt gold medium setting	320.00	H	H	6	12	1,920.00
P103 Pendant	18 Kt gold large setting	630.00	H	H	4	12	3,780.00
					Total		$6,360.00
RINGS (Revenue Account: 4100 Revenue from Sales; Asset Account: 1460 Rings; Cost of Goods Sold Account: 5040 Cost of Inventory Sold)							
R101 Ring	18 Kt engagement solitaire setting	$1,000.00	H	H	4	8	$ 4,000.00
R102 Ring	18 Kt engagement 3 stone setting	900.00	H	H	4	8	3,600.00
R103 Ring	18 Kt band narrow plain	375.00	H	H	6	8	1,500.00
R104 Ring	18 Kt band wide plain	570.00	H	H	6	8	2,280.00
R105 Ring	18 Kt band narrow 3 stone setting 0.25 ct	1,050.00	H	H	4	8	4,200.00
R106 Ring	18 Kt band wide 3 stone setting 0.25 ct	1,500.00	H	H	3	8	6,000.00
R107 Ring	18 Kt band narrow 5 stone setting 0.65 ct	2,000.00	H	H	3	6	6,000.00
R108 Ring	18 Kt band wide 5 stone setting 0.65 ct	2,500.00	H	H	3	6	7,500.00
R109 Ring	18 Kt diamond band 0.25 ct total	1,200.00	H	H	5	8	4,800.00
R110 Ring	18 Kt diamond band 0.50 ct total	1,900.00	H	H	3	6	5,700.00
R111 Ring	18 Kt diamond band 0.75 ct total	2,900.00	H	H	2	6	8,700.00
					Total		$54,280.00
SERVICES (Revenue Account: 4120 Revenue from Services)							
C101 Design	Custom design and setting	Custom pricing	H				
R100 Repairs	Jewellery repairs	Custom pricing	H				

Sparkles

EMPLOYEE	GARNET Y. AMARALD	JADINE R. AMETHYST
Position	Jeweller	Salesperson
Address	55 Windswept Pl.	350 Treeline Ave.
	Toronto, ON	Toronto, ON
	M3P 4J1	M6S 3H8
Telephone	(416) 461-6125	(416) 300-8210
Alt. Telephone	(416) 529-1725	
SIN	852 364 272	312 589 120
Date of Birth (mm-dd-yy)	12-01-72	03-02-80
Date of Hire (mm-dd-yy)	05-01-04	06-15-05
Earnings		
Regular Wage Rate	–	$16.00/hour
Overtime Wage Rate	–	$24.00/hour
Regular Annual Salary	$48,600.00	–
Commission	0.5% Net Revenue from Sales	0.5% Net Revenue from Sales
	5% Revenue from Services	
Pay Period	semi-monthly	semi-monthly
Hours per Period	85	85
WSIB Rate	2.58%	1.00%
Deductions Each Pay Period		
Group Insurance	$20.00	$10.00
Income Tax, EI, and CPP	Amounts and calculations built into QuickBooks program	
Federal (Ontario) Claim – TD1		
Personal	$10,382.00 (8,943.00)	$10,382.00 (8,943.00)
Spousal/Equivalent	$10,382.00 (7,594.00)	
Education		$ 7,200.00 (7,464.00)
Total Claim	$20,764.00 (16,537.00)	$17,582.00 (16,407.00)
Vacation	3 weeks	6% retained
Sick Pay Rate	same as regular hourly or salary rate	
Accrued Vacation	$2,850.00	$1,920.00
Accrued Sick Leave Time	40 hours	40 hours

Employee Profiles and TD1 Information

Garnet Y. Amarald works as an assistant to Dimond in all aspects of the business, including making and repairing jewellery. Amarald is paid twice every month based on an annual salary of $48,600.00. In addition, he receives a commission of 5 percent of all revenue from services and 0.5 percent of the sales revenue (net of the 10 percent sales discount), and he can take three weeks' vacation each year. He is married and claims the spousal amount for income tax purposes in addition to the base personal claim amount. His only pay cheque deduction in addition to regular taxes is a contribution to a group insurance plan. At the beginning of January, he has 40 hours of sick leave accrued and three weeks of vacation time, the allowances for one year.

Jadine R. Amethyst works primarily as the salesperson, but she also assists with the bookkeeping for the business. She is paid $16.00 per hour for the first 40 hours each week and $24.00 per hour for additional hours. She also earns a sales commission of 0.5 percent of the sales revenue (net of the 10 percent sales discount). As a single part-time student, she is allowed an education deduction in addition to the personal tax claim

Notes
The Workplace Safety and Insurance Board (WSIB) is the name for the Workers' Compensation Board in Ontario.

Organizations in Ontario that have total payroll greater than $400,000.00 must pay EHT (Employer Health Tax) to pay for health insurance coverage for Ontario residents.

When used, EHT is set up as an employer-paid payroll tax, similar to WSIB/WCB.

amount. Her vacation pay is calculated at the rate of 6 percent of her pay and is retained until she takes time off. She also makes contributions to the group insurance plan and has vacation and sick leave entitlements accrued for the coming year.

Accounting Procedures

Taxes: HST

Notes
Refer to the Tax Appendix (found on the CD that accompanies this text) for details on sales taxes.

Sparkles pays HST on all goods and services that it buys and charges HST on all sales. HST collected from customers is recorded as a liability in the *GST/HST Payable* account. HST paid to vendors is recorded in the *GST/HST Payable* account as a decrease in liability to the Canada Revenue Agency. The report is filed with the Receiver General for Canada by the last day of the month for the previous quarter, either including the balance owing or requesting a refund. The next remittance is due at the end of January.

Account Terms

All customers receive a 1 percent discount if they settle their accounts within five days after a purchase. The full balance is required within 30 days of a sale or on completion of a special order. Finance charges of 18 percent per year apply after 30 days from the invoice date, with a minimum charge of $30.00 and a five-day grace period. No discount is allowed on credit card sales because of the fee attached to cards.

Customers receive additional discounts of 10 percent when they purchase more than one piece of jewellery, not counting the diamonds for a setting. The data file includes items to calculate the pretax subtotal and discount in order to include them on invoices.

Some vendors offer discounts for early payment.

Deposits and Cheques

Cheques, credit card receipts, and cash are not held for deposit. Cheques are hand printed at the time of the transaction.

Estimates, Orders, and Deposits

For special orders, Sparkles prepares sales estimates. When customers proceed with an estimate, they pay a deposit of at least 30 percent of the finished jewellery. Some customers also place sales orders with Sparkles. These also require a deposit of about 30 percent.

Sparkles regularly places purchase orders with suppliers of premade jewellery items, special parts, and gold used to make and repair jewellery.

Supplies

At the end of each month the staff assess the quantity of supplies left in the store to determine the cost of the gold and parts used. They then make adjusting entries in QuickBooks for these costs. Depreciation will be entered at the end of each quarter.

Account Numbers

The store assigns account numbers to accounts: 1000s for asset, 2000s for liability, 3000s for equity, 4000s for income, and 5000s for expense accounts. Account numbers are not used for customers, vendors, or employees.

Instructions

1. Using the Chart of Accounts, the Trial Balance, and other information, you will record entries for source documents for January 2014 by using QuickBooks. You will find the source documents marked with an SD beside them and listed as you work through the chapter. The procedures for entering each new type of transaction introduced in this chapter are outlined in step-by-step instructions. Additional source documents will be provided by allowing you to have more practice entering transactions. If you have used this textbook in the past and would prefer to skip the step-by-step instructions and work only with a list of source documents, refer to the CD in the back of the textbook for the list of source documents for this chapter.

2. After you have finished making your entries, print the reports and graphs for January 2014 as indicated on the following printing form:

Notes
Instructions for inventory reports begin on page 637.

REPORTS FOR JANUARY 2014

Lists
- ☐ Account Listing
- ☐ Customer Phone List
- ☐ Customer Contact List
- ☐ Vendor Phone List
- ☐ Vendor Contact List
- ☐ Employee Contact List
- ☑ Item Listing
- ☑ Item Price List
- ☐ Payroll Item List

Company & Financial
- ☑ Balance Sheet Standard at Jan. 31
- ☑ Profit & Loss Standard from Jan. 1 to Jan. 31
- ☐ Expenses by Vendor
- ☐ Income by Customer

Accountant & Taxes
- ☑ Trial Balance at Jan. 31
- ☐ General Ledger
- ☑ Journal from Jan. 1 to Jan. 31
- ☐ Transaction List by Date
- ☐ Transaction Detail by Account

Banking
- ☐ Deposit Detail
- ☐ Cheque Detail
- ☐ Missing Cheques
- ☐ Reconcile Discrepancy
- ☐ Previous Reconciliation

Vendor
- ☑ A/P Aging Detail at Jan. 31
- ☐ Vendor Balance
- ☐ Unpaid Bills
- ☐ Transaction List by Vendor

Purchases
- ☐ Purchases by Vendor
- ☐ Purchases by Item
- ☐ Transaction List by Vendor
- ☐ Open Purchase Orders by Vendor

Customer
- ☑ A/R Aging Detail at Jan. 31
- ☐ Customer Balance
- ☐ Open Invoices
- ☐ Collections Report
- ☐ Transaction List by Customer

Sales
- ☐ Sales by Customer
- ☑ Sales by Item Summary from Jan. 1 to Jan. 31
- ☐ Sales Pending
- ☐ Open Sales Orders by Customer
- ☐ Open Sales Orders by Item
- ☐ Sales by Rep

Employees & Payroll
- ☐ Payroll Summary
- ☐ Payroll Item Detail
- ☐ Payroll Detail Review
- ☑ Employee Earnings Summary from Jan. 1 to Jan. 31

- ☐ Payroll Transactions by Payee
- ☐ Payroll Transaction Detail
- ☐ Payroll Liability Balances
- ☐ Employee Withholding
- ☐ TD1 Review List
- ☐ T4 Summary
- ☐ PD7A Summary
- ☐ Record of Employment

Inventory
- ☐ Inventory Valuation Summary
- ☑ Inventory Valuation Detail from Jan. 1 to Jan. 31
- ☑ Inventory Stock Status by Item at Jan. 31
- ☐ Inventory Stock Status by Vendor
- ☐ Physical Inventory Worksheet
- ☐ Pending Builds

Other
- ☐ Custom Summary Report
- ☐ Custom Transaction Detail Report
- ☐ Transaction History
- ☐ Transaction Journal

GRAPHS
- ☐ Income and Expense
- ☐ Net Worth
- ☐ Accounts Payable
- ☐ Accounts Receivable
- ☑ Sales from Jan. 1 to Jan. 31

Opening the Sample Data File

1. **Start**   **QuickBooks**

2. **Open**   the **Sparkles.qbw file**. You will see the following information screen reminding you that this is the QuickBooks Sample file:

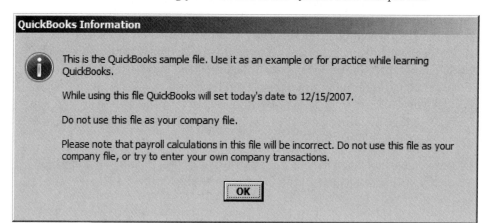

QuickBooks Information

This is the QuickBooks sample file. Use it as an example or for practice while learning QuickBooks.

While using this file QuickBooks will set today's date to 12/15/2007.

Do not use this file as your company file.

Please note that payroll calculations in this file will be incorrect. Do not use this file as your company file, or try to enter your own company transactions.

OK

Figure 11-1

Notes
This message will be displayed each time you open the Sparkles company file and it cannot be turned off.

3. **Click**   **OK** to continue

Notes
The payroll information and calculations in this chapter do not reflect current payroll information. Do not use the figures calculated in this payroll in your company file.

IMPORTANT:

This file has been converted to a Sample file so that you can enter payroll information for dates outside of the current payroll tax table period. This is important for learning purposes. No matter what QuickBooks tax table you have installed, the payroll information in the print screens in the textbook will be the same as yours as long as you use the Sample file. The sample data file is set up so that December 15, 2007 is the current date displayed when entering forms. You will override this date as you're working in the chapter.

Entering Inventory Sales

Inventory sales are not entered differently from other sales in QuickBooks because items are used for all sales transactions. Inventory items have more accounts linked to them, but these items are set up in the item record and are used by the program to create the appropriate journal entries and update the necessary ledger records.

The first transaction that we will enter is a sales invoice that includes a pretax subtotal and a 10 percent discount. Refer to the following source document as we work through the steps to enter it:

Source Docs
Refer to the following source document and then follow the step-by-step instructions to enter it.

SD1: **Invoice**   **Dated January 2, 2014**

Invoice #321 to Wanda Saffire

1	E101 Earrings	18 Kt drop setting	$ 140.00	$ 140.00
1	N101 Necklace	16 inch feather chain 18 Kt	600.00	600.00
1	P102 Pendant	18 Kt gold medium setting	320.00	320.00
2	D101 Diamonds	0.10 ct diamond	400.00 ea.	800.00
1	D103 Diamond	0.50 ct diamond	2,500.00	2 500.00
	Subtotal - pretax			$4,360.00
	Discount		10%	−436.00
	HST		13%	510.12
	Invoice total			$4,434.12

Terms: 1/5, n/30

Notes
All customers are listed alphabetically by last name, e.g., Saffire, Wanda.

1. Click   the **Create Invoices icon** 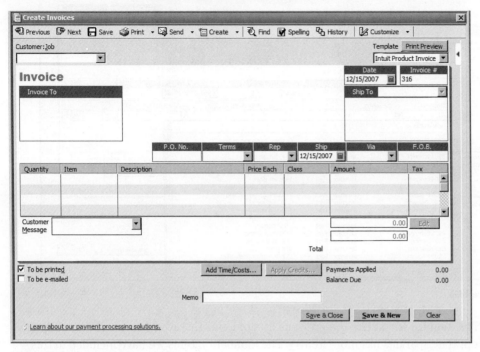 in the Customers section on the Home page or **press** ⌄ctrl⌄ + **I** to open the Create Invoices form:

Figure 11-2

December 15, 2007 is preset as the default date for the Sample file, as it was for Scotts' Total Concept. The product invoice form is similar to ones we used previously, but it includes fields commonly used for inventory items, such as shipping details, sales rep, and purchase order number. The Quantity field comes before the Item field.

2. Choose   **Saffire, Wanda** from the Customer:Job drop-down list

3. Double click   the **Date field**

4. Type   **01/02/14**

5. Press   ⌄tab⌄ to advance to the Invoice # field

6. Type   **321**

7. Click   the **To be printed box** to remove the ✓. We will not print the invoices

8. Click   the **Quantity field** in the first detail line of the invoice

9. Type   **1**

10. Press   ⌄tab⌄ to move to the Item field

11. **Click** the **drop-down arrow** in the **Item field** to view the item list:

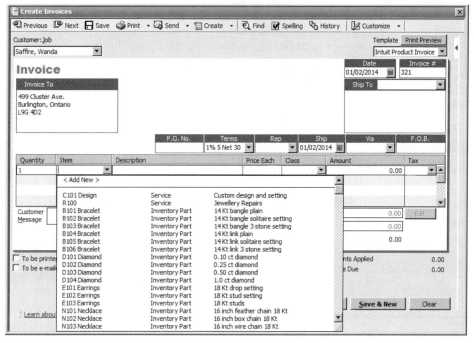

Figure 11-3

The item list is just like the previous lists of items that we've seen in other chapters (except that Sparkles has more items). The number of items we have included in this chapter makes it realistic for a jewellery store.

12. **Click** **E101 Earrings** as the first item

The remaining details for the item are added automatically based on the information in the item record.

You can change any of the default information if necessary. Just select the text you want to change and type the new information. You can change the price or the description, but not the item name or number displayed in the item field.

13. **Click** the **Quantity field** on the second detail line of the invoice

14. **Type** 1

15. **Press** to move to the Item field

16. **Type** n

QuickBooks fills in the name based on what you type. If you keep typing, QuickBooks will continue to match your entry with the items on record. When a mismatch occurs, the program assumes the item is new and will offer you the chance to create it. In this case, we want the first item beginning with *n* so we can accept the default.

17. **Press** *tab* to add the remaining item information

18. **Click** the **Quantity field** on the next detail line

19. **Type** 1

20. **Press** *tab* to move to the Item field

21. **Type** **P102** or **choose P102 Pendant** from the item list

22.	**Click**	the **Quantity field** on the next invoice detail line
23.	**Type**	2
24.	**Press**	<kbd>tab</kbd> to move to the Item field
25.	**Type**	D
26.	**Press**	<kbd>tab</kbd> to enter the remaining item details for D101
27.	**Type**	1 in the **Quantity field** on the next line
28.	**Press**	<kbd>tab</kbd>
29.	**Type**	**D103** or **choose D103 Diamond** from the item list

Notes
As soon as you click a different field, the program fills in the details for the item.

Notes
D101 is the first item starting with D, and it is the item we want so we need to enter only the first letter.

Sparkles gives a 10 percent discount when customers buy more than one item, excluding the diamonds for a setting. Therefore, we need to calculate the amount on which the discount is based. The next two items we will use are special types. The first creates a subtotal amount for the invoice by adding together all amounts above the subtotal line that follow another subtotal item, if there was one. The second item calculates a discount for the amount on the previous line. We want the discount to be calculated on the subtotal amount.

| 30. | **Click** | the **drop-down arrow** in the **Item field** on the next invoice detail line |
| 31. | **Choose** | **Subtotal - pretax** to update the invoice as shown: |

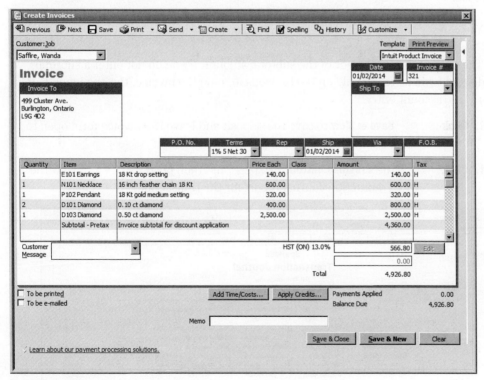

Figure 11-4

A subtotal entry is added in the Amount column. You cannot edit this amount.

32. Choose   **Discount** from the Item field list on the next invoice detail line to add the 10 percent discount and complete the invoice as shown:

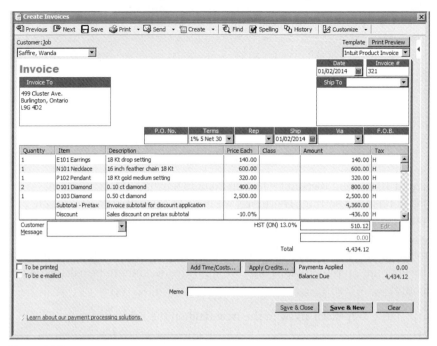

Figure 11-5

 Notes
The discount is taxable so the final taxes will be based on the discounted amount and not on the subtotal before discounts.

You can see the effect of changing the tax code by removing the H tax code beside the Discount item and then re-entering it.

The discount is 10 percent of the subtotal amount. If you do not enter a subtotal, the discount will be taken only on the previous item on the invoice, the one immediately before the discount entry.

Notes
You can create separate discount items for different percentages and apply them to individual items on a line-by-line basis.

33. Click   **Save & New** to save the deposit and leave the Invoice form open to review the journal entry

34. Click   the **Previous button** [Previous] and then **press** *ctrl* **+ Y** to view the Transaction Journal report for the transaction:

Notes
The Trans # and Class columns have been removed from this report.

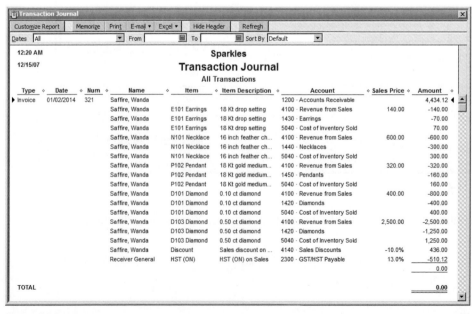

Figure 11-6

When inventory items are tracked, more accounts are involved in transactions because inventory is continually updated. For each item sold, QuickBooks has credited (increased) the *Revenue from Sales* account for the full sales price before discounts; the inventory asset account is credited (decreased) and the *Cost of Inventory Sold* account is debited (increased) for the cost of the item. The discount is debited to *Discounts*, a contra-revenue account that decreases overall revenue. The sales tax liabilities are also updated (increased). And finally, *Accounts Receivable* is debited (increased) by the net sale amount. The inventory records are updated to reduce the quantity on hand, and the customer's outstanding balance is increased.

Notes
In previous chapters, we did not track inventory — a General Journal adjusting entry was made periodically to update the inventory accounts. Even when the program tracks inventory, the business must periodically check the stock on hand against the computer records (see Physical Inventory Worksheet, page 641).

35. Close   the **Transaction Journal report** and then **close** the **Create Invoices form**

Entering Purchase Orders for Inventory Items

The next transaction is the entry of a purchase order for tracked inventory items. Again, the procedure is similar to that for non-inventory transactions. Refer to the following source document as we work through the steps to enter it:

SD2:   **Purchase Order**   **Dated January 3, 2014**

Source Docs
Refer to the following source document and then follow the step-by-step instructions to enter it.

Purchase Order #125 to Goldcrest Inc.

10	N101 Necklaces	16 inch feather chain 18 Kt	$ 3,000.00
10	N102 Necklaces	16 inch box chain 18 Kt	2,750.00
10	N104 Necklaces	18 inch feather chain 18 Kt	4,000.00
10	N105 Necklaces	18 inch box chain 18 Kt	1,750.00
	HST @ 13%		1,495.00
	Purchase Order total		$12,995.00

1. Choose   the **Vendors menu** and **click Create Purchase Orders**:

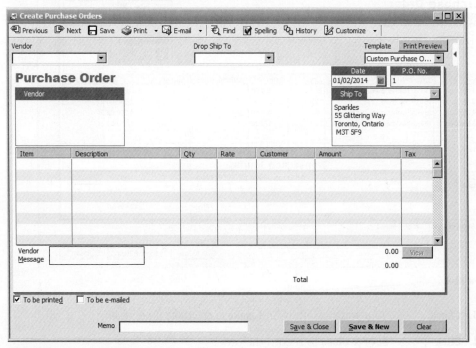

Figure 11-7

The Purchase Order form is unchanged.

2. **Choose**   **Goldcrest Inc.** from the Vendor drop-down list

3. **Enter**   **01/03/14** in the **Order date field**

4. **Enter**   **125** in the **P.O. No. field**

5. **Click**   the ✓ in the To be printed box to remove it. We are not printing purchase orders

6. **Choose**   **N101 Necklace** from the **Item field list** or **type n** and **press** ⌨*tab*

The description, cost (Rate field), and tax code are entered from the item record. The cost is based on previous purchases of the item.

7. **Click**   the **Qty field**

8. **Type**   **10**

9. **Enter**   the **remaining items** on the purchase order as listed in SD2 on page 597

The cost for N105 has changed so we need to edit it.

10. **Double click**   **3750.00** in the Amount column (the total cost for N105)

11. **Type**   **1750**

12. **Press**   ⌨*tab* to complete the order as shown:

Notes
QuickBooks uses the average cost method for inventory valuation so the costs are continually updated with each transaction.

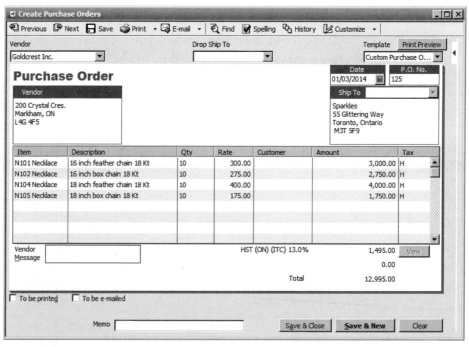

Figure 11-8

13. **Check**   your **work** carefully and **make corrections** if necessary

14. **Click**   **Save & Close** to record the order

Entering Sales Returns

Customers frequently return items because they are not satisfied in some way: the colour or size may be wrong or the wrong item was purchased. Stores vary in their return policies. Some stores do not allow returns, some have time limits, and some charge a handling fee. Like most jewellery stores, Sparkles does not allow earrings to be returned for health reasons, but gives refunds for other items returned within 15 days. Saffire is returning a necklace.

Refer to the following source document as we work through the steps to enter it:

SD3:   Credit Memo   **Dated January 4, 2014**

Wanda Saffire returned the 16 inch necklace (N101) because she wanted a longer chain for her pendant. Create credit memo #321-R to enter the return.

1	N101 Necklace	16 inch feather chain 18 Kt	$600	$600.00
	Discount		10%	−60.00
	HST		13%	70.20
	Sales Credit Total			$610.20

Sales returns are entered as credits for the customer when the invoice has an outstanding balance.

Source Docs
Refer to the following source document and then follow the step-by-step instructions to enter it.

Notes
Cash and credit card refunds are shown later in this chapter on page 610.

Notes
You can also choose the Customers menu and click Create Credit Memos/Refunds to open the Credit Memos form.

Notes
The Use Credit to icon at the top of the screen allows you to change the credit memo into an immediate refund or apply the credit memo to an invoice. See page 611.

1. Click   the **Refunds and Credits icon** 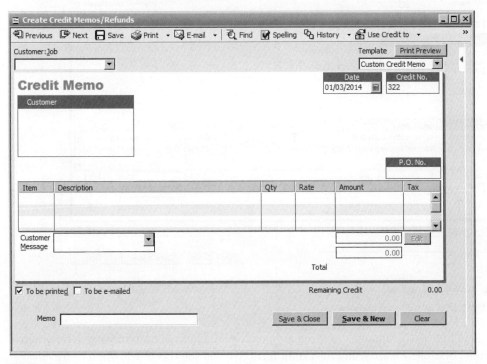 from the Customers section of the Home page to open the Create Credit Memos/Refunds form:

Figure 11-9

This form is like an invoice form, and we complete it in the same way. However, QuickBooks automatically reverses the usual sales journal entry to create the credit.

	2. **Choose**	**Saffire, Wanda** from the Customer:Job field list
	3. **Enter**	**01/04/14** as the **Credit memo date**
	4. **Enter**	**321-R** as the **Credit No.**

Adding *R* to the number will identify the form as a credit instead of an invoice.

	5. **Click**	the **To be printed box** to remove the ✓
	6. **Click**	the **drop-down arrow** in the **Item field**
	7. **Click**	**N101 Necklace** to select the item
	8. **Click**	the **Qty field** so we can enter the number of items
	9. **Type**	1
	10. **Press**	(tab)

We also need to reverse the discount for the item. This time there is only one item line so we do not need to create a subtotal before adding the discount.

	11. **Choose**	**Discount** in the **Item field**
	12. **Press**	(tab) to update and complete the form as shown:

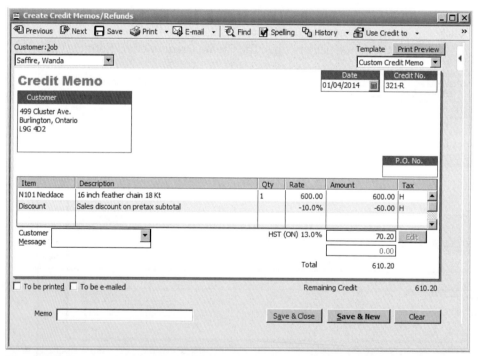

Figure 11-10

Although all the amounts entered are positive, the journal entry reverses the original amounts because we are using the credit form. We will see this effect when we review the journal entry created by this transaction.

	13. **Check**	your **work** carefully and **make corrections** if necessary
	14. **Click**	**Save & New** to record the entry and leave the form open

15. The Available Credit screen is displayed:

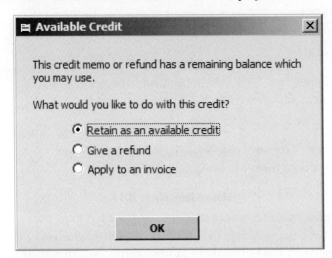

Figure 11-11

Use this screen to indicate what you want to do with the credit memo. You can retain it as an available credit on your customer's account, give your customer a refund, or apply it to an invoice. We will retain it as an available credit.

16. Click   **Retain as an available credit** (this should be selected as the default)

17. Click   **OK**

18. Click   the **Previous button** Previous and then **press** *ctrl* + **Y** to view the Transaction Journal report:

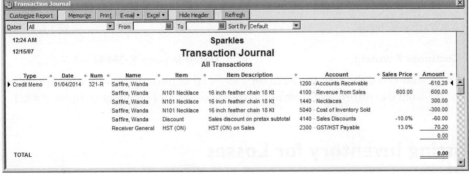

Figure 11-12

Notes
Columns have been removed from this report to display it in the textbook.

You can see that amounts that were positive for the original invoice, *Accounts Receivable*, *Cost of Inventory Sold*, and *Sales Discounts* (see Figure 11-6, page 596), are now negative. Amounts that were negative, *Revenue from Sales*, *Inventory:Necklaces*, and tax amounts, are now positive. The customer has unused credits that can be applied to the outstanding invoice, and the inventory quantity has been restored.

19. Close   the **Transaction Journal report** and the **Create Credit Memos/Refunds form**

Source Documents

Enter the following source documents for this company. You may need to refer to previous chapters for additional information:

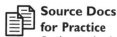

Source Docs for Practice

Continue to develop your skills by entering the following source documents.

Notes

Cash receipts are deposited directly to *Bank Chequing* and are not held for later deposit.

Notes

Choose not to track fixed assets when prompted.

Save the new terms for the vendor.

SD4: **Customer Payment**   **Dated January 4, 2014**

From B. Perley, Cheque #175 for $2,277.00 in payment of account, including the discount for early payment. Reference Invoice #315.

SD5: **Pay Bill**   **Dated January 4, 2014**

Paid Cheque #1124 to Goldcrest Inc., $6,355.80 in payment of account, including the discount for early payment. Reference Bill #GI-2018.

SD6: **Pay Bill**   **Dated January 6, 2014**

Paid Cheque #1125 to Trevor's Treasures, $4,194.40 in payment of account, including the discount for early payment. Reference Bill #TT-3170.

SD7: **Bill**   **Dated January 6, 2014**

Bill #SSS-10082 received from Secure Security Services (use Quick Add to add the new vendor), $2,500.00 for alarm system plus HST and $1,200.00 plus HST for six months of monitoring service. The bill totals $4,181.00. Terms: Net 10. Create the new Fixed Asset account: 1500 - *Alarm System* and the new Other Current Asset account: 1240 - *Prepaid Security Services*.

SD8: **Estimate**   **Dated January 6, 2014**

Estimate #35 to William Goldwyn for engagement ring with matching wedding bands

1	C101 Design	Custom design and setting		$ 3,000.00
6	D102 Diamond	0.25 ct diamond	$1,000.00 ea.	6,000.00
1	D103 Diamond	0.50 ct diamond	2,500.00	2,500.00
	Subtotal - pretax			$11,500.00
	Discount		10%	–1,150.00
	HST		13%	1,345.50
	Estimate total			$11,695.50

SD9: **Customer Payment**   **Dated January 7, 2014**

From Wanda Saffire, Cheque #123 for $3,784.68 in payment of account. Apply the credit from the return and then apply the discount and payment to Invoice #321.

Adjusting Inventory for Losses

Inventory losses can occur when items are stolen by customers or employees, damaged beyond recovery, or just misplaced. The computer records should reflect the actual stock on hand so customers who make inquiries about availability can be given accurate answers. You can make inventory adjustments on an ongoing basis whenever an item is discovered missing or damaged, as well as periodically when complete inventory stock is taken.

Refer to the following source document as we work through the steps to enter it:

From Owner: One 18 inch feather chain 18 Kt necklace (item N104 Necklace) is missing. Adjust inventory for the lost necklace. To record the loss, create a new Expense account: 5200 - *Inventory Losses*. The Adjust Quantity/Value on Hand icon can be accessed from the Inventory Activities icon in the Company section of the Home page.

1. **Click**   the **Inventory Activities icon** in the Company section of the Home page and **click Adjust Quantity/Value on Hand** or **choose** the **Vendors menu**, then **choose Inventory Activities**, and **click Adjust Quantity/Value On Hand**

2. The Adjust Quantity/Value on Hand form will be displayed:

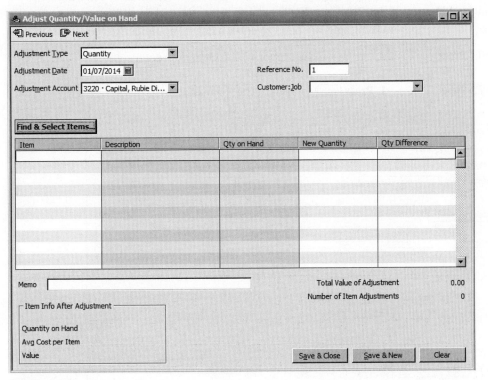

Notes
Inventory revaluation might be done when stock is damaged but can still be sold, or when the stock is out of date and prices must be marked down. Reducing the asset value will split the expenses for the sale between the cost of goods sold accounts and the account for inventory losses.

Figure 11-13

From this form you can make adjustments to one or more inventory items based on known quantities or values.

To change the value of inventory, click the drop-down arrow beside the Adjustment Type field and select Total Value. The default column entries will change to dollar amounts that you can edit.

3. **Click**   the **drop-down arrow** beside the **Adjustment Type field**

4. **Select**   **Quantity** (this should be the default)

5. **Enter**   **01/08/14** as the date

6. **Press**   (tab) to move to the Ref. No. field. We will enter the memo number

7. **Type**   **1-1** and then **press** (tab) to move to the Adjustment Account field

8. **Type**   **5200 - Inventory Losses** and then **press** (tab)

9. **Click**   **Set Up** when the Account Not Found message is displayed

10.	**Click**	the **drop-down arrow** beside the **Account Type field**
11.	**Select**	**Expense**

The rest of the default information is correct.

12.	**Click**	the **Find & Select Items button** to select an item to adjust
13.	**Click**	the **scroll bar** to move down the list until item N104 is displayed on the screen
14.	**Click**	the **check column** beside N104 Necklace to select the item (This will ensure that we are working on the correct line)
15.	**Click**	the **Add Selected Items button** to add the item to the list

📄 **Notes**
If a missing item is later recovered, enter an adjustment with a positive number as the difference. Use the same account.

You can make adjustments by typing the new quantity on hand or by entering the quantity difference if that is known. We know one item is lost so we will enter the difference. Because an item is missing, we need to enter a negative number to reduce inventory.

16.	**Press**	⌨tab to move the cursor to the Qty Difference column
17.	**Type**	**–1**. **Press** ⌨tab to update the form as shown:

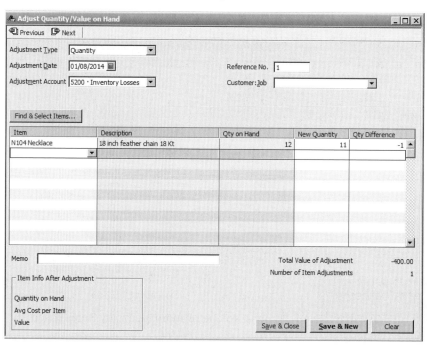

Figure 11-14

The new amount, 11, is now displayed in the New Quantity field.

📄 **Notes**
To make corrections after recording an adjustment, complete another adjustment to reverse the incorrect number and use the same account (e.g., enter 1 in the Qty Different column to reverse this entry).

18.	**Click**	the **Memo field** so we can add an explanation for the adjustment
19.	**Type**	**Item missing**
20.	**Check**	your **work** carefully and **make corrections** if necessary
21.	**Click**	**Save & Close** to record the adjustment

Source Documents

Enter the following source document for this company. You may need to refer to previous chapters for additional information:

SDII: Credit Card Sales Receipt #1001 Dated January 8, 2014

**Source Docs
for Practice**
Continue to develop
your skills by entering the
following source document.

To Cash Sales customers

1	B101 Bracelet	14 Kt bangle plain	$ 590.00	$ 590.00
3	D101 Diamonds	0.10 ct diamond	400.00 ea.	1,200.00
1	E103 Earrings	18 Kt studs	80.00	80.00
2	N101 Necklaces	16 inch feather chain 18 Kt	600.00 ea.	1,200.00
3	P101 Pendants	18 Kt gold small setting	110.00 ea.	330.00
1	R101 Ring	18 Kt engage. solitaire setting	1,000.00	1,000.00
1	R110 Ring	18 Kt diamond band 0.50 ct total	1,900.00	1,900.00
	R100 Repairs	Jewellery repairs		50.00
	HST		13%	825.50

Total deposited to the *Bank Visa* account $7,175.50

Filling a Purchase Order for Inventory Items

When you receive inventory items from a purchase order, you must fill the order in the same way you fill orders for other items.

Refer to the following source document as we work through the steps to enter it:

SD12: Bill Dated January 9, 2014

Source Docs
Refer to the following
source document and then
follow the step-by-step
instructions to enter it.

Bill #GI-2819 received from Goldcrest Inc. to fill Purchase Order #125

10	N101 Necklaces	16 inch feather chain 18 Kt	$ 3,000.00
10	N102 Necklaces	16 inch box chain 18 Kt	2,750.00
10	N104 Necklaces	18 inch feather chain 18 Kt	4,000.00
10	N105 Necklaces	18 inch box chain 18 Kt	1,750.00
	HST @ 13%		1,495.00
	Bill total		$12,995.00

Terms: 1/10, n/30

1. Click the **drop-down arrow** beside the **Receive Inventory Icon** in the Vendors section of the Home page to view the choices available:

Notes
You can also choose Ven-
dors from the menu, and click
Enter Bill for Received Items.

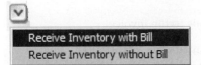

Figure 11-15

2. Click **Receive Inventory with Bill**

3. The Enter Bills form will be displayed:

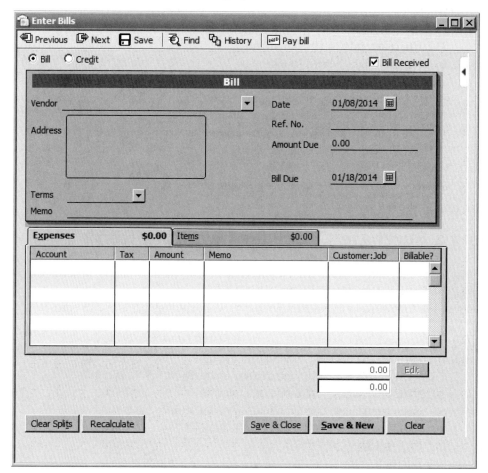

📄 **Notes**
The date on the Enter Bills form will be 01/08/2014 unless you have closed the Company file. If you closed it, the date will be 12/15/2007, the current date in the Sample file.

Figure 11-16

4.	**Choose**	**Goldcrest Inc.** from the Vendor field drop-down list
5.	**Click**	**Yes** on the Open PO's Exist message
6.	**Click**	**PO No. 125** to select it
7.	**Click**	**OK** to add the purchase order details to the invoice

If some of the merchandise has not arrived, you can edit the quantity (Qty field) for the item involved. You can also edit prices if they have changed since the order was placed.

8.	**Press**	[tab] to advance to the Date field
9.	**Type**	**01/09/14**
10.	**Click**	the **Ref. No. field** and **type GI-2819**

11. The vendor bill (purchase invoice) is now complete as shown here:

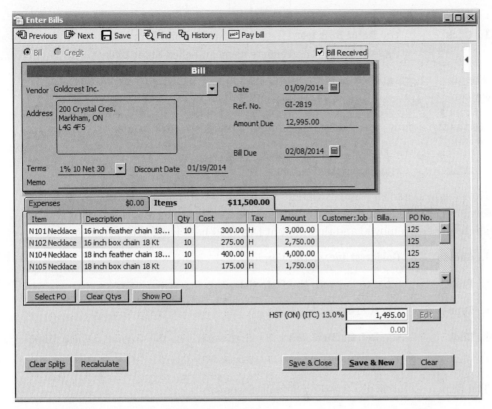

Figure 11-17

12. Check your **work** carefully and **make corrections** if necessary

13. Click **Save & Close** to record the bill

Returning Purchased Inventory

Purchase returns are normal activities for most businesses. Once the bill is entered, you can enter the return as a credit, as we did for sales returns. As for sales returns, using a credit form causes QuickBooks to reverse the normal purchase debit and credit entries.

Refer to the following source document as we work through the steps to enter it:

SD13: Purchase Return #GI-2819-R   **Dated January 10, 2014**

To Goldcrest Inc. 10 Kt chains were delivered instead of 18 Kt chains.

10 N105 Necklaces	18 inch box chain 18 Kt	$1,750.00
HST @ 13%		227.50
Purchase return total credit		$1,977.50

Source Docs
Refer to the following source document and then follow the step-by-step instructions to enter it.

1. **Click** the **Enter Bills icon** in the Vendors section of the Home page or **choose** the **Vendors menu** and **click Enter Bills**

The two buttons at the top of the Enter Bills form (below the tool buttons), as shown here ⊙ Bill ○ Cre_d_it control the option of entering a bill or a credit. Bill is selected as the default, and we used this option previously. Now we need to enter a credit.

2. **Click** the **Credit radio button**

Notice how the form changes when Credit is selected. The heading across the top of the form has changed from Bill to Credit. The Bill Received box and the vendor address section have been removed and the Amount Due field has changed to Credit Amount.

3. **Choose** **Goldcrest Inc.** as the Vendor

4. **Press** (tab) to move to the Date field

5. **Type** **01/10/14**

6. **Click** the **Ref. No. field**. We will link the credit to the original invoice number

7. **Type** **GI-2819-R**

The Expenses tab is displayed by default as shown:

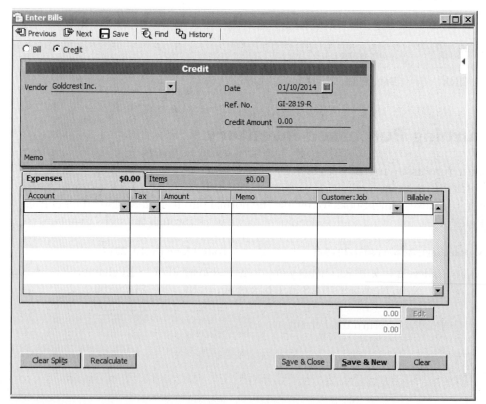

Figure 11-18

The Expenses tab does not allow us to enter inventory items, so we must select the Items tab.

8. Click   the **Items tab** as shown:

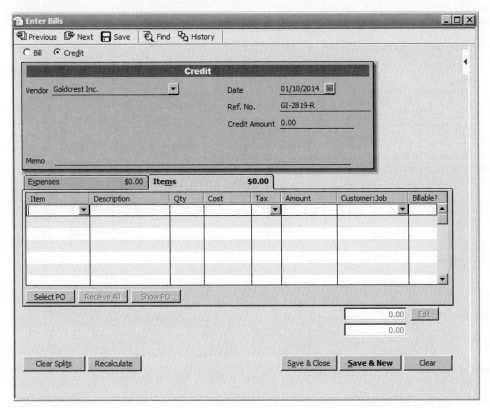

Figure 11-19

Item and Quantity fields are now available. The rest of the transaction is entered the same way as purchase orders and bills are entered.

9. Click   the **drop-down arrow** in the **Item field**

10. Choose   **N105 Necklace** to add the item to the bill

11. Press   *tab* twice to advance to the Qty field

12. Type   **10**

The cost from the item record is entered. It is not the price we paid, so we need to edit it. We will enter the total cost and let QuickBooks calculate the unit cost. Then we will add the reason for the return as a memo.

📝 **Notes**
Because we are using the credit form, we can enter positive quantities for the return.

13. Press   *tab* until you advance to the Amount field and highlight the amount

14. Type   **1750**

15. Press   *tab* to update the taxes and totals

16. Click   the **Memo field**

17. Type   **10 Kt chains delivered in error**

18. This completes the credit as shown:

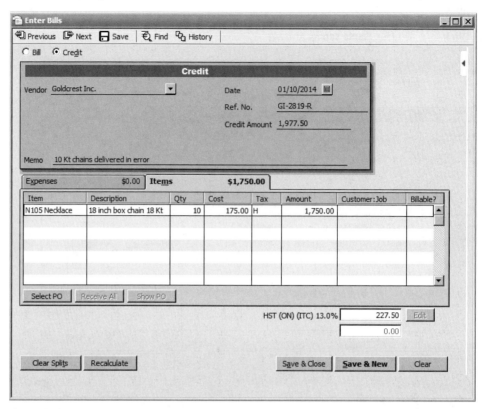

Figure 11-20

Notes
The journal for this transaction will show that the transaction is a reversing entry for the original bill.

Although this looks like an ordinary bill, choosing Credit instead of Bill automatically reverses all amounts.

19. Check your **work** carefully and **make corrections** if necessary

20. Click **Save & Close** to record the credit

Source Docs for Practice
Continue to develop your skills by entering the following source documents.

Source Documents

Enter the following source documents for this company. You may need to refer to previous chapters for additional information.

SD14: Customer Payment   **Dated January 10, 2014**
     From William Goldwyn, Cheque #2003 for $3,500.00 as the deposit to accept Estimate #35 for custom-designed rings. Do not apply to outstanding invoice.

SD15: Credit Card Charge   **Dated January 10, 2014**
     Credit card payment of Bill #S-4253 from Stationers (use Quick Add to add the new vendor), $140.00 plus $18.20 HST for office and computer supplies. The bill totals $158.20 and was paid in full by credit card.

Entering Credit Card Sales Returns

When a customer returns merchandise and receives a refund, the refund uses the same method of payment as the original purchase. Thus, credit notes are issued for invoices, payments by cheque or cash are usually refunded in cash, and credit card sales returns have a credit applied to the credit card. The procedure is similar for all credits, with the added step of issuing cash or a credit card credit for the refund.

Refer to the following source document as we work through the steps to enter it:

SD16: **Credit Card Sales Return #1001-R**   **Dated January 11, 2014**

One Cash Sales customer returned a pendant. Issue a credit card refund.

1	P101 Pendant	18 Kt gold small setting	$110.00	$110.00
1	D101 Diamond	0.10 ct diamond		400.00	400.00
	HST		13%	66.30
	Total credit card refund			$576.30

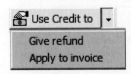

1. Click   the **Refunds & Credits icon** 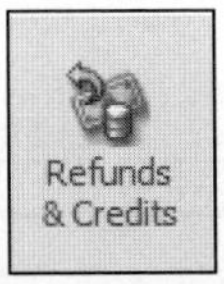 or **choose** the **Customers menu** and **click Create Credit Memos/Refunds**

The Create Credit Memos/Refunds form opens. Refer to Saffire's return (see page 599) for information on entering the credit memo.

2. Choose   **Cash Sales** as the Customer (normally you would enter a customer name on this form)

3. Enter   **01/11/14** as the date

4. Enter   **1001-R** in the **Credit No. field**

5. Choose   **P101 Pendants** as the first item

6. Enter   **1** as the quantity

7. Choose   **D101 Diamond** as the second item

8. Enter   **1** as the quantity

Now we must indicate that we are providing a refund rather than a credit memo. The Use Credit to button **Use Credit to ▾** is located at the right end of the tool bar and is used to determine how we will process the credit.

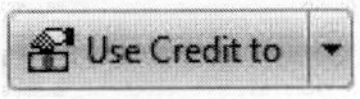

Notes
Maximize the QuickBooks window if your form does not include the Use Credit to button.

9. Click   the **drop-down arrow** beside the **Use Credit to button** to view the choices available:

Use Credit to ▾
Give refund
Apply to invoice

Figure 11-21

10. Click the **Give Refund option** to open the Issue a Refund form:

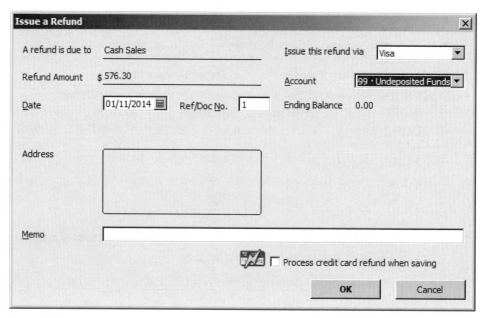

Figure 11-22

The default bank account is selected for the refund cheque. However, we are issuing a credit card refund so we need to select the bank account that credit card receipts are deposited to, *1060 - Bank Visa*. *Accounts Receivable* is entered as the default account that will be debited for the refund. Because the credit memo uses *Accounts Receivable* as the default account as well, we need to reverse that entry (refer to the Journal Report in Figure 11-26 on page 614).

11. Click the **drop-down arrow** in the **Account field**

12. Click **1060 - Bank Visa**

13. Enter **1001-R** as the number in the **Ref/Doc No. field**

14. Enter an **appropriate memo** to complete the transaction as shown:

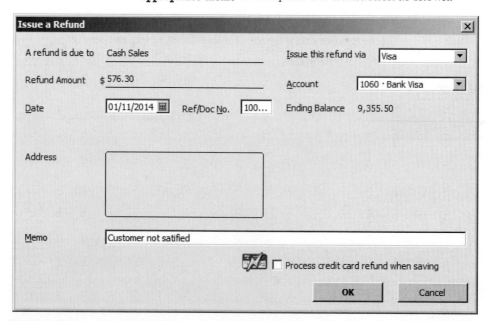

Figure 11-23

15. Check your **work** carefully and **make corrections** if necessary

16. Click **OK** to display the updated Create Credit Memos/Refunds form:

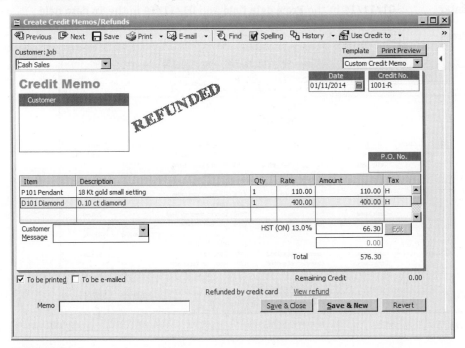

Figure 11-24

Notice that the Credit memo now has "Refunded" stamped across it. To view the refund, click the View Refund link on the bottom right-hand corner of the form.

17. Click **Save & New** to record the refund

18. Click the **Previous button** [Previous] and **display** the **credit memo** we just entered

19. Press (ctrl) **+ Y** to view the Transaction Journal report:

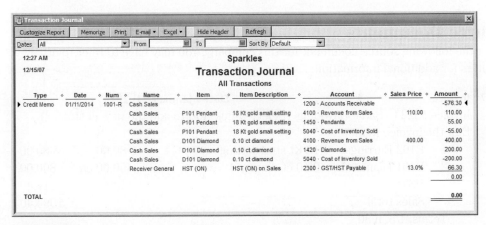

Figure 11-25

This screen shows the journal entry for the credit memo.

20. Close the **Transaction Journal report**

QuickBooks actually created two journal entries. One transaction is created for the credit memo and the other transaction is created for the credit card refund. We will look at the Journal report for January 11, 2014 to view both transactions.

Notes
The Trans # and Class columns have been removed from the report.

<table>
<tr><td></td></tr>
</table>

Notes
You can also view this report in the Report Centre by choosing the Report Centre icon on the Icon bar, clicking the Accountant & Taxes heading on the left-hand side of the screen, and then clicking the Journal report link.

Notes
Columns have been removed from the report.

Notes
Do not save the changes for the Journal report if you made any changes to the report, as we have done in Figure 11-26.

Source Docs for Practice
Continue to develop your skills by entering the following source document.

Notes
You will need to correct the invoice number for the sale. The default number follows the credit return number we used.

21. **Choose** the **Reports menu**, then **choose Accountant & Taxes** and **click Journal** to open the report

22. **Enter** **01/11/14** in the **From date field** and **01/11/14** in the **To date field**

23. **Press** ⟨tab⟩ or **click** the **Refresh button** to view the two entries:

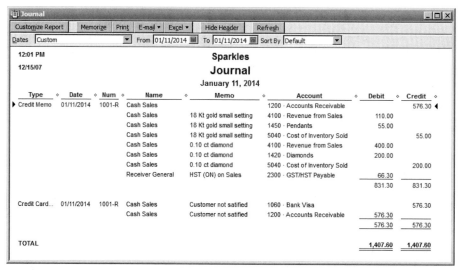

Figure 11-26

In the first entry, created by the credit memo, QuickBooks has credited (decreased) the *Accounts Receivable* account and debited (decreased) the *Revenue from Sales* account to reverse the original sale. The *Cost of Inventory Sold* account is also reduced and the inventory assets accounts (*Pendants* and *Diamonds*) have increased because the inventory was restored. The quantity on hand for these items is also increased. This part of the transaction by itself would leave the *Accounts Receivable* account with a credit balance. The transaction in the second entry, created by the refund, reverses this by debiting *Accounts Receivable* and crediting (reducing) the *Bank Visa* account.

24. **Close** the **Journal report**

Source Documents

Enter the following source document for this company. You may have to refer to other chapters for additional information:

SD17: Invoice   **Dated January 11, 2014**

Invoice #322 to Sadie Hawkings (Select Quick Add to add the new customer). Edit the invoice number.

1	E102 Earrings	18 Kt stud setting	$ 80.00	$ 80.00
2	D101 Diamonds	0.10 ct diamond	400.00 ea.	800.00
	HST		13%	114.40
	Sales total			$994.40

Terms: 1/5, n/30

Entering Credit Card Purchase Returns

Returns of items purchased on a credit card are entered on the credit card charge form, just as returns on account were entered on the Enter Bills form. Refer to the following source document as we work through the steps to enter it:

Source Docs
Refer to the following
source document and then
follow the step-by-step
instructions to enter it.

Return to Stationers, business forms costing $40.00 plus $5.20 HST (the form size does not fit the store printer). Total credit $45.20 applied to credit card.

Enter Credit
Card Charges

1. **Click**   the **Enter Credit Card Charges icon** [Enter Credit Card Charges] in the Banking section of the Home page or **choose** the **Banking menu** and **click Enter Credit Card Charges**

The default setting is to enter a Purchase/Charge, as we have done for all previous credit card transactions. Now we need to enter a credit.

2. The buttons on the Enter Credit Card Charges form, as shown here, will allow us to make this change: ⦿ Purchase/Charge   ○ Refund/Credit

3. **Click**   **Refund/Credit** to change the form

The Refund/Credit radio button is now selected and the heading on the cheque portion of the form has changed colour and has changed from Credit Card Purchase/Charge to Credit Card Refund/Credit. QuickBooks will now reverse all the usual entries when entering a transaction on this form.

4. **Choose**   **Stationers** as the Vendor

5. **Enter**   **01/12/14** as the transaction date

6. **Enter**   **S-4253-R** as the reference number to connect this to the earlier purchase

7. **Choose**   **1340 - Office & Computer Supplies** in the **Account field** (it should already be displayed as the default)

8. **Press**   (tab) to advance to the Tax field

9. **Type**   **H**

10. **Press**   (tab) to advance to the Amount field

11. **Type**   **40**

12. **Click**   the **Memo field** so we can enter the reason for the return

13. **Type**   **Incorrect form size for printer**

14. This completes the credit card purchase return as shown:

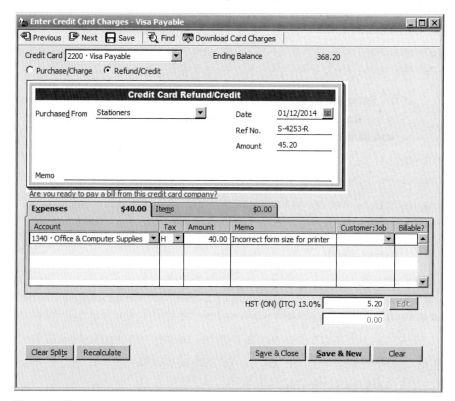

Figure 11-27

15. Check   your **work** carefully and **make corrections** if necessary

16. Click   **Save & New** to record the return and prepare to review the Transaction Journal report

17. Click   the **Previous button** 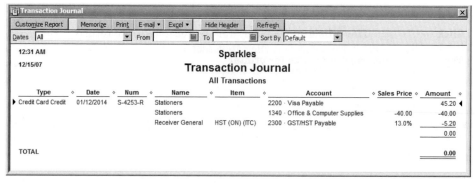 to display the transaction on the screen

18. Press   *ctrl* + **Y** to view the Transaction Journal report:

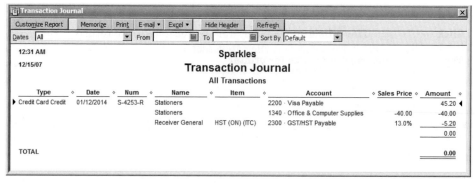

Notes
Columns have been removed from this report.

Figure 11-28

The Transaction Journal report shows that all original amounts have been reversed. The *Visa Payable* account has been debited to reduce the liability, the *GST/HST Payable* account has been credited to increase the liability, and the *Office & Computer Supplies* account has been credited to decrease the asset account balance.

19. Close   the **Transaction Journal report**

20. Close   the **Enter Credit Card Charges form**

Building Inventory Items

The next transaction requires us to create a new inventory item that is made up of other items. Then we can use this definition to build the new item as required. Refer to the following source document as we work through the steps to enter it:

SD19: Assembly #A-01   **Dated January 12, 2014**

The store will sell some items as sets for discounted prices. The sets include a necklace with a diamond pendant and matching diamond earrings. Create new Inventory Assembly item: S101 Gift Sets (Necklace, pendant, and earrings).

3	D102 Diamonds	0.25 ct diamond
1	E102 Earrings	18 Kt stud setting
1	N101 Necklace	16 inch feather chain 18 Kt
1	P102 Pendant	18 Kt gold medium setting

Selling price for the set will be $3,500.00.

Cost of Goods Sold account:	5040 - *Cost of Inventory Sold*
Revenue account:	4100 - *Revenue from Sales*
Sales Tax Code:	H
Asset account:	Create new Other Asset subaccount: 1480 - *Sets*
	(1480 - *Sets* is a subaccount of
	1400 - *Inventory*)
Build point:	0

Assemble two Gift Sets using these component items.

First we must create the new item.

Creating Assembly Items

1. **Click** the **Items & Services icon** [Items & Services] in the Company Section of the Home page to open the Item List

You can also access the Item List in other ways:

   a) **Choose** the **Lists menu** and **click Item List**; or

   b) **Choose** the **Sales Tax menu** and **click Item List**; or

   c) **Choose** the **Customers menu** and **click Item List**; or

   d) **Choose** the **Vendors menu** and **click Item List**

We are now ready to create the new item.

2. **Click** the **Item button** and **click New** or **press** ⌨ctrl + **N**

Source Docs
Refer to the following source document and then follow the step-by-step instructions to enter it.

Notes
Item descriptions are shown in parentheses after the item number and name.

3. The New Item form opens with the item Type list displayed:

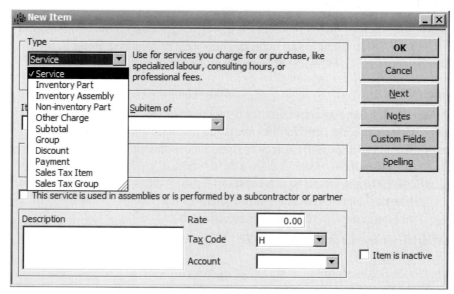

Figure 11-29

Because we have enabled the Inventory and purchase orders are active preference in this company file, the Type list has been expanded from the ones we saw in previous chapters. We are creating an Inventory Assembly item.

4. Click   **Inventory Assembly**

5. The New Item form changes to the one displayed here when this type is selected:

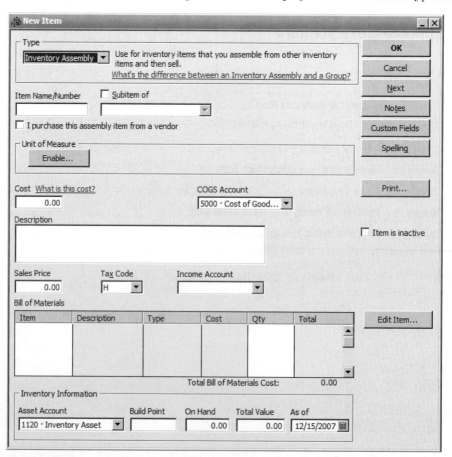

Figure 11-30

On this form we define how we want to create the new item, that is, what components are needed and how many of each. We also designate the default asset and cost of goods sold accounts. QuickBooks has created default accounts already, but we will change them to match our Chart of Accounts.

6.	**Click**	(tab) to advance to the Item Name/Number field
7.	**Type**	**S101 Gift Sets**

The item is not purchased so we should leave the I purchase this assembly item from a vendor option unchecked. We need to enter the COGS (cost of goods sold) Account. This expense account is increased each time we sell the item.

The cost field is used to enter the total cost of the assembly. It can either be the total cost of the components that you enter in the Bill of Materials table, or it can include a mark-up and other costs not listed in the Bill of Materials table. As you enter items in the Bill of Materials table, the total cost of the components will be calculated by QuickBooks. You may want to wait until the amount is calculated before entering the cost in this field. We will leave this field blank for now.

8.	**Click**	the **drop-down arrow** in the **COGS Account field**
9.	**Choose**	**5040 - Cost of Inventory Sold** to add this as the default expense account
10.	**Press**	(tab) to advance to the Description field
11.	**Type**	**Necklace, pendant, and earrings**
12.	**Press**	(tab) to advance to the Sales Price field
13.	**Type**	**3500**
14.	**Press**	(tab) to advance to the Sales Tax Code field
15.	**Type**	**H**
16.	**Press**	(tab) to advance to the Income Account field
17.	**Choose**	**4100 - Revenue from Sales** from the drop-down list
18.	**Press**	(tab) to advance to the Item field in the Bill of Materials section

This section will list the inventory part items that make up the set, along with the number or quantity of each item that is required.

19.	**Click**	the **drop-down arrow** in the **Item field** so we can select the first component item
20.	**Choose**	**D102 Diamond** to add the item to the list
21.	**Press**	(tab) to advance to the Qty field
22.	**Type**	**3**
23.	**Press**	(tab) to advance to the next Item field line
24.	**Choose**	**E102 Earrings**
25.	**Press**	(tab) to advance to the Qty field
26.	**Type**	**1**
27.	**Press**	(tab) to move to the next item line
28.	**Choose**	**N101 Necklace**

Notes

QuickBooks creates the *Cost of Goods Sold* and *Inventory Asset* accounts automatically when we choose Inventory Part or Inventory Assembly as the item type. And it enters these as default accounts for the item, so you need to change the accounts.

You can delete these accounts because they are not used, but QuickBooks will create them again as soon as you create another Inventory item.

29.	Press	(tab) to advance to the Qty field
30.	Type	1
31.	Press	(tab) to advance to the next Item field line
32.	Choose	**P102 Pendant**
33.	Press	(tab) to advance to the Qty field
34.	Type	1

Now we must enter the default asset account. We will create a new account for the items we sell as sets. This asset account is increased when we buy (create) the item and reduced when we sell the item.

35.	Click	the **drop-down arrow** in the **Asset Account field.** Scroll up and **click** the **<Add New> option**
36.		Other Current Asset is correctly selected as the Account Type
37.	Press	(tab) to advance to the Number field
38.	Type	**1480**
39.	Press	(tab) to advance to the Account Name field
40.	Type	**Sets**
41.	Click	the **box** beside the **Subaccount of field** to add a ✓
42.	Choose	**1400 - Inventory** from the account list as the parent account
43.	Click	**Save & Close** to return to the New Item form

The next field, Build Point, defines the minimum quantity for the item. Once the item reaches this level, the program displays a reminder in the Reminders List that we need to build or assemble more items. Inventory reports also flag items that are low in stock. We can assemble these sets at any time so we do not need to keep extra sets on hand.

Notice that the total bill of materials cost is displayed directly below the table. We will enter this amount in the Cost field.

44.	Click	the **Cost field**
45.	Enter	**2000**

The remaining fields will be updated when we build and sell the items, so the form is complete as shown:

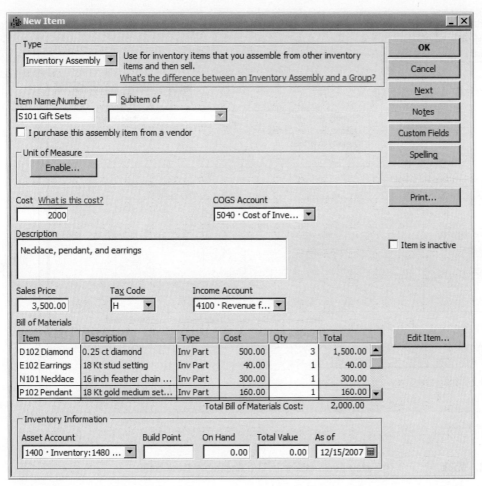

Figure 11-31

We need to complete this definition part of the build process only once for an item.

46. Check   your **work** carefully and **make corrections** if necessary

47. Click   **OK** to save the new inventory assembly item

48. Close   the **Item List**

Building Assembly Items

Once we have defined the assembly item, we can proceed to the build process.

1. Click   the **Inventory Activities icon** [Inventory Activities] in the Company Section of the Home page and **click Build Assemblies** or **choose** the **Vendors menu**, then **choose Inventory Activities** and **click Build Assemblies** to open the Build Assemblies form:

Notes
You can also open the Build Assemblies form from the Item List window. Click the Activities button at the bottom of the Item List window, and then click Build Assemblies.
Or open the Build Assemblies form by choosing Vendors from the menu, clicking Inventory Activities, and then clicking Build Assemblies.

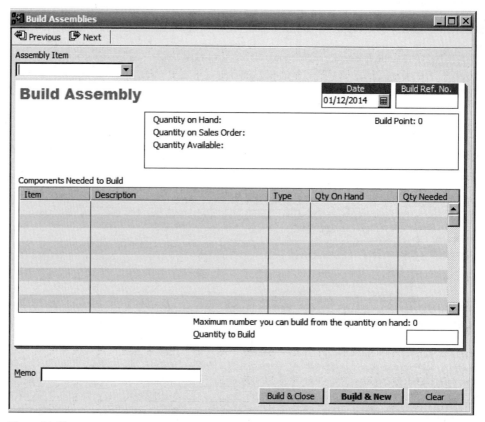

Figure 11-32

2. **Click**   the **drop-down arrow** in the **Assembly Item field**

The Gift Sets Assembly Item we created is displayed on the list.

3. **Click**   **S101 Gift Sets** to add the item to the form

To complete the form, we must define the number of items we are building. We will enter this quantity next.

4. **Click**   in the **Quantity to Build field** below the list of components

5. **Type**   **2**

6. **Press**   ⌨ *tab* to update the form

The quantities for each component have been added to the form based on the amount entered in the Quantity to Build field. The date should be correct from the previous transaction. We will add a reference number and comment (memo) to complete the form.

7. **Enter**   **01/12/14** in the **Date field** if necessary

8. **Click**   the **Build Ref. No**. field

9. **Type**   **A-01**

10. **Press**   ⌨ *tab* to advance to the Memo field

11. **Type**   **Create gift sets**

12. The Build Assemblies form is now complete as shown here:

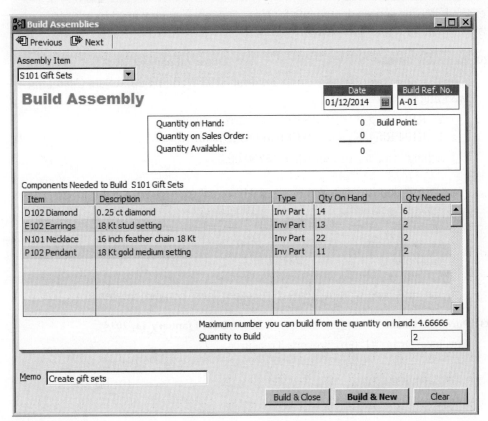

Figure 11-33

13. Check your **work** carefully and **make corrections** if necessary

14. Click **Build & New** to leave the form open on the screen for the next assembly item

Display the Journal report to view how QuickBooks has entered the item assembly transaction. The journal entry is displayed here:

📋 **Notes**
To display this Journal report, choose the Reports menu, then choose Accountant & Taxes, and click Journal. Enter 01/12/14 in the From and To date fields for the report.

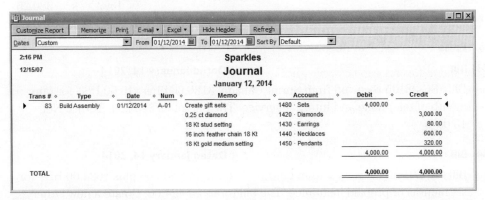

Figure 11-34

The asset values have been transferred from the components to the new item. The inventory quantities have also been updated.

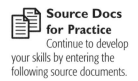

Source Docs for Practice

Continue to develop your skills by entering the following source documents.

Source Documents

Enter the following source documents for this company. You may need to refer to previous chapters for additional information:

SD20: Assembly #A-02   **Dated January 12, 2014**

Create a new Inventory Assembly item for S102 Wedding Band Sets (Matching wedding bands).

1	R103 Ring	18 Kt band narrow plain
1	R104 Ring	18 Kt band wide plain

Selling price for the set will be $750.00.

Cost of Goods Sold account:	5040 - *Cost of Inventory Sold*
Revenue account:	4100 - *Revenue from Sales*
Sales Tax Code:	H
Asset account:	1480 - *Sets*
Build point:	0

Assemble two Wedding Band Sets using these component items.

SD21: Purchase Order   **Dated January 13, 2014**

Purchase Order #126 to Trevor's Treasures

Jewellery Parts	$800.00
HST @ 13%	104.00
Purchase Order total	$904.00

SD22: Invoice   **Dated January 14, 2014**

Invoice #323 to Bess Perley

1	B105 Bracelet	14 Kt link solitaire setting	$ 370.00	$ 370.00
1	N104 Necklace	18 inch feather chain 18 Kt	800.00	800.00
1	E102 Earrings	18 Kt stud setting	80.00	80.00
2	D102 Diamonds	0.25 ct diamond	1,000.00	2,000.00
	Subtotal - pretax			$3,250.00
	Discount		10%	–325.00
	HST		13%	380.25
	Sales total			$3,305.25

Terms: 1/5, n/30

SD23: Bill   **Dated January 14, 2014**

Bill #SC-38105 received from Sprint Canada, $120.00 plus $15.60 HST for one month of telephone and Internet service. The bill totals $135.60. Terms: Net 15 days.

SD24: Bill   **Dated January 14, 2014**

Bill #FI-2014-34 received from Faithful Insurers, $4,800.00 plus $624.00 HST for six months of prepaid insurance. The bill totals $5,424.00. Create a new Other Current Asset account: 1260 - *Prepaid Insurance*. Terms: Net 15 days. Save the new terms.

SD25: Pay Bill   **Dated January 15, 2014**

Paid Cheque #1126 to Secure Security Services, $4,181.00 in payment of Bill #SSS-10082.

SD26:

EMPLOYEE TIME SUMMARY SHEET #2014-1

Date: January 15, 2014 (for the pay period ending January 15, 2014)

Name of Employee	Regular Hours	Overtime Hours	Sick Leave Hours	Vacation Hours	Advances Received/ Advances Repaid
Garnet Y. Amarald	75	–	–	8	–
Jadine R. Amethyst	74	6	8	–	–

a. Using Employee Time Summary Sheet #2014-1 and the Employee Information Sheet, complete payroll for two employees.

b. Amarald took one day of vacation and Amethyst took one day of sick leave.

c. Manually prepare Cheques #1127 and #1128.

SD27: Invoice **Dated January 15, 2014**

Invoice #324 to Goldie Carat

1	R101 Ring	18 Kt engage. solitaire setting	$1,000.00	$1,000.00
1	D104 Diamond	1.0 ct diamond	6,900.00	6,900.00
	HST		13%	1,027.00
	Sales total			$8,927.00

Terms: 1/5, n/30

SD28: Credit Card Sales Receipt #1002 **Dated January 15, 2014**

Notes
Remember to change the default account for the Visa sales deposit.

To Cash Sales customers

1	B106 Bracelet	14 Kt link 3 stone setting	$ 430.00	$ 430.00
6	D101 Diamonds	0.10 ct diamond	400.00 ea.	2,400.00
2	D102 Diamonds	0.25 ct diamond	1,000.00 ea.	2,000.00
1	E101 Earrings	18 Kt drop setting	140.00	140.00
1	E102 Earrings	18 Kt stud setting	80.00	80.00
1	N101 Necklace	16 inch feather chain 18 Kt	600.00	600.00
1	N102 Necklace	16 inch box chain 18 Kt	550.00	550.00
2	P102 Pendants	18 Kt gold medium setting	320.00 ea.	640.00
1	R101 Ring	18 Kt engage. solitaire setting	1,000.00	1,000.00
1	R104 Ring	18 Kt band wide plain	570.00	570.00
1	R105 Ring	18 Kt band narrow 3 st. 0.25 ct	1,050.00	1,050.00
1	S101 Gift Set	Necklace, pendant, and earrings	3,500.00	3,500.00
	R100 Repairs	Jewellery repairs		90.00
	HST		13%	1,696.50

Total deposited to the *Bank Visa* account $14,746.50

SD29: Pay Bill **Dated January 18, 2014**

Paid Cheque #1129 to Goldcrest Inc., $10,920.00 in payment of account, including the discount and credit. Change the discount amount to $97.50. Reference Bill #GI-2819.

Notes
The discount needs to be reduced because of the credit for the return.
Click the Set Discount button and edit the discount amount.

SD30: Purchase Order   **Dated January 18, 2014**

Purchase Order #127 to Goldcrest Inc.

10	E101 Earrings	18 Kt drop setting	$ 700.00
10	E102 Earrings	18 Kt stud setting	400.00
10	E103 Earrings	18 Kt studs	400.00
10	N105 Necklaces	18 inch box chain 18 Kt	3,750.00
	HST @ 13%		682.50
	Purchase Order total		$5,932.50

SD31: Bill   **Dated January 19, 2014**

Bill #TT-4821 received from Trevor's Treasures, to fill Purchase Order #126

Jewellery Parts	$800.00
HST @ 13%	104.00
Bill total	$904.00

Terms: 2/10, n/30

SD32: Credit Card Charge   **Dated January 19, 2014**

Credit card payment of Bill #HSS-8002 from Hardware Surplus Supplies (use Quick Add to add the new vendor), $45.00 plus $5.85 HST for glass and other cleaning products. The bill totalling $50.85 was paid in full by credit card.

SD33: Customer Payment   **Dated January 19, 2014**

From Bess Perley, Cheque #204 for $3,276.00 in payment of account, including the discount for early payment. Reference Invoice #323.

SD34: Customer Payment   **Dated January 20, 2014**

From William Goldwyn, Cheque #2108 for $4,600.00 in payment of Invoice #297.

SD35: Customer Payment   **Dated January 20, 2014**

From Goldie Carat, Cheque #13 for $8,848.00 in payment of account, including the discount for early payment. Reference Invoice #324.

SD36: Sales Order   **Dated January 21, 2014**

Sales Order #25 from Goldie Carat, including customization of some pieces

1	E101 Earrings	18 Kt drop setting	$ 140.00	$ 140.00
2	D102 Diamonds	0.25 ct diamond	1,000.00 ea.	2,000.00
1	D103 Diamond	0.50 ct diamond	2,500.00	2,500.00
1	P102 Pendant	18 Kt gold medium setting	320.00	320.00
1	N101 Necklace	16 inch feather chain 18 Kt	600.00	600.00
	C101 Design	Custom design and setting		500.00
	Subtotal - pretax			$6,060.00
	Discount		10%	−606.00
	HST		13%	709.02
	Sales total			$6,163.02

SD37: Credit Card Sales Receipt #1003   **Dated January 22, 2014**

To Cash Sales customers

1	B104 Bracelet	14 Kt link plain	$ 400.00	$ 400.00
8	D101 Diamonds	0.10 ct diamond	400.00 ea.	3,200.00
2	D102 Diamonds	0.25 ct diamond	1,000.00 ea.	2,000.00
1	E101 Earrings	18 Kt drop setting	140.00	140.00
2	E102 Earrings	18 Kt stud setting	80.00/pr.	160.00
2	N106 Necklaces	18 inch wire chain 18 Kt	610.00 ea.	1,220.00
2	P101 Pendants	18 Kt gold small setting	110.00 ea.	220.00
1	R103 Ring	18 Kt band narrow plain	375.00	375.00
1	R104 Ring	18 Kt band wide plain	570.00	570.00
1	S102 Wed. Bd St	Matching wedding bands	750.00	750.00
	R100 Repairs	Jewellery repairs		50.00
	HST		13%	1,181.05

Total deposited to the *Bank Visa* account $10,266.05

Notes
Remember to change the default account for the Visa sales deposit.

SD38: Memo #1-2   **Dated January 23, 2014**

From Owner: One 18 Kt gold medium setting pendant (item P102 Pendant) was damaged beyond repair. Adjust inventory for the damaged item.

SD39: Credit Card Charge   **Dated January 23, 2014**

Credit card payment of Bill #GE-6161 from Glass Experts (use Quick Add to add the new vendor), $300.00 plus $39.00 HST for replacing display cabinet glass. The bill totalling $339.00 was paid in full by credit card. Use the *Maintenance Expenses* account.

SD40: Pay Bill   **Dated January 24, 2014**

Paid Cheque #1130 to Trevor's Treasures, $888.00 in payment of account, including the discount for early payment. Reference Bill #TT-4821.

SD41: Purchase Order   **Dated January 24, 2014**

Purchase Order #128 to Kimberley Mines

10	D102 Diamonds	0.25 ct diamond	$5,000.00
6 oz	Gold		3,624.00
	HST @ 13%		1,121.12
Purchase Order total			$9,745.12

Handling Out-of-Stock Inventory Items

Sometimes the items needed for a sale are out of stock. When the item your customer wants to buy is out of stock, you can enter a sales order for the customer for the outstanding items. QuickBooks provides a warning like the following whenever you enter a quantity on a sales receipt or invoice that is greater than the amount on hand:

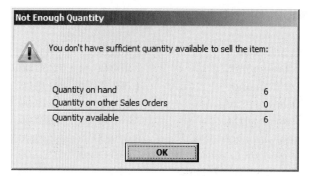

Figure 11-35

The specific wording of the warning will vary with the starting point (the form you are using and the stage in the transaction), as we will see in the following examples.

> **IMPORTANT:**
>
> In QuickBooks Premier, this warning will not stop you from completing the sale and thus entering into negative inventory. Since this is not proper accounting practice, you should review the Inventory Stock Status by Item report and determine how many items you have available to sell before continuing. If you have physically received the inventory, but have not received it in QuickBooks, you should receive it in QuickBooks first before continuing with the sale.

Selling Out-of-Stock Inventory

Refer to the following source document as we work through the steps to enter it:

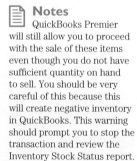

Source Docs
Refer to the following source document and then follow the step-by-step instructions to enter it.

SD42: Invoice   **Dated January 24, 2014**

Invoice #325 to William Goldwyn for a ring set, to partially fill Estimate #35. Some diamonds were out of stock. Create Sales Order #26 for the items not available.

1	C101 Design	Custom design and setting		$ 3,000.00
6	D102 Diamonds	0.25 ct diamond	$1,000.00 ea.	6,000.00
1	D103 Diamond	0.50 ct diamond	2,500.00	2,500.00
	Discount		10%	−1,150.00
	Taxable subtotal			10,350.00
	HST		13%	1,345.50
	Sales total			$11,695.50

Terms: 1/5, n/30

1. **Open**   the **Create Invoices form**
2. **Select**   **William Goldwyn** as the customer
3. **Click**   on **Estimate 35** to bring the items on the estimate into the invoice
4. The following warning is displayed:

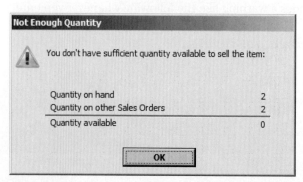

Figure 11-36

Notes
QuickBooks Premier will still allow you to proceed with the sale of these items even though you do not have sufficient quantity on hand to sell. You should be very careful of this because this will create negative inventory in QuickBooks. This warning should prompt you to stop the transaction and review the Inventory Stock Status report.

5. Click   **OK** to continue and the invoice is displayed on the screen with all inventory items (including the one out of stock) invoiced:

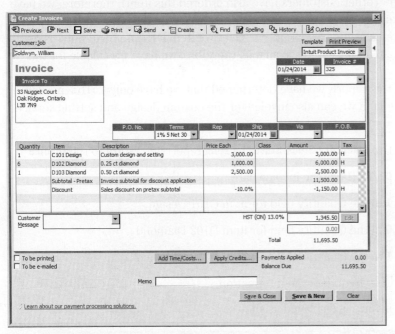

Figure 11-37

Before we enter this item, we will stop and look at the Inventory Stock Status report (which will be reviewed in more detail later in this chapter) to view how many items are actually available for sale. We'll leave the invoice open on the screen while reviewing the report.

6. Choose   **Reports** from the menu

7. Click   **Inventory** and then **click Inventory Stock Status by Item**

The date displayed on the report reflects the current date. Remember, the current date in the sample company is 12/15/2007. We'll change the date to the current date of the invoice so we can see the inventory status as of the day we're entering the invoice.

8. Type   **01/24/14** in the **From field**

9. Press   (tab)

10. Type   **01/24/14** in the **To field**

11. Press   (tab) or **click** the **Refresh button** to update the report:

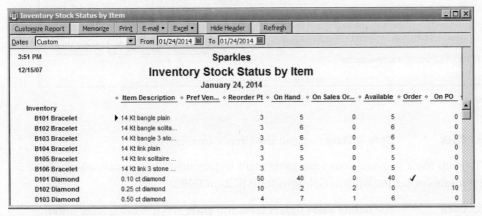

Figure 11-38

If you refer to Figure 11-37, you'll see that the customer has ordered 6 of item D102 and 1 of item D103. In Figure 11-38, you can see that we have 2 of item D102 on hand and, 2 on sales orders (other customers have also ordered this item); therefore, we have 0 available. We can also see that we have 10 on purchase order and are waiting for a shipment of these items from our vendor. We have 7 of item D103 on hand but 1 is on a sales order, making 6 of these items available; therefore, we have 1 available for this invoice.

After reviewing this report, we have determined that we have only 1 D103 available to sell on this invoice, and we can also invoice for the custom design and setting service charge.

12. Close	the **Inventory Stock Status by Item** report and **return** to the **invoice**
13. Type	**01/24/14** as the invoice date
14. Accept	**1** in the Quantity field for item C101 Design
15. Type	**0** in the Quantity field for item D102 Diamond
16. Accept	**1** in the Quantity field for item D103 Diamond
17. Press	(tab) to update the information

18. The updated invoice is displayed as shown:

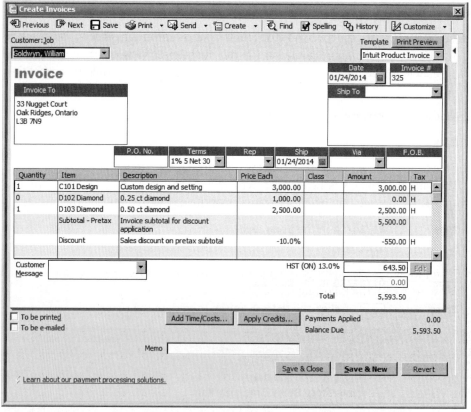

Figure 11-39

19. Click	**Save & Close** to close the Create Invoices form

To keep track of items your customers want to purchase, you create sales orders. Create a sales order for William Goldwyn for 6 of item D102.

20. Open	the **Create Sales Orders form** and **enter** the following **sales order**:

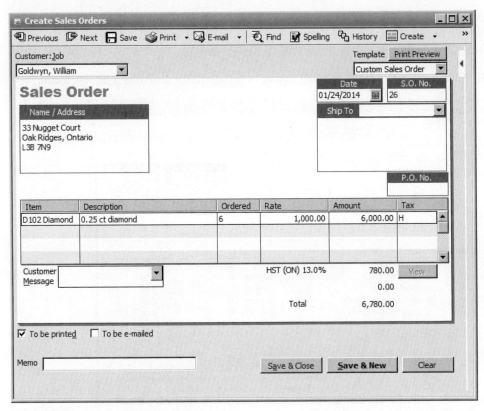

Figure 11-40

21. **Click**   **Save & Close**

Assembling Items with Insufficient Stock

Refer to the following source document as you process the next assembly:

SD43: Assembly #A-03   **Dated January 25, 2014**

Assemble three S101 Gift Sets. Delay assembly because of insufficient stock.

1. **Open** the **Build Assemblies form**

2. **Enter** the **information** for the build as listed in SD43

3. When we enter the quantity to build for the assembly of Gift Sets, we are presented with the following warning:

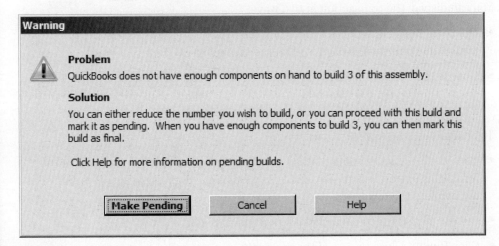

Figure 11-41

> **Source Docs**
> Refer to the following source document and then follow the step-by-step instructions to enter it.

> **Notes**
> The Build Assemblies form window always includes a field to insert the maximum number that you can build from the quantity on hand. Entering a value in this field will also let you know whether you can complete the assembly you want.

Again, QuickBooks recognizes that the items needed are not available. We can cancel and return to the transaction to enter a different quantity, or proceed and mark the build as pending. We will proceed and mark the build as pending.

4. Click the **Make Pending button** to return to the Build Assemblies form:

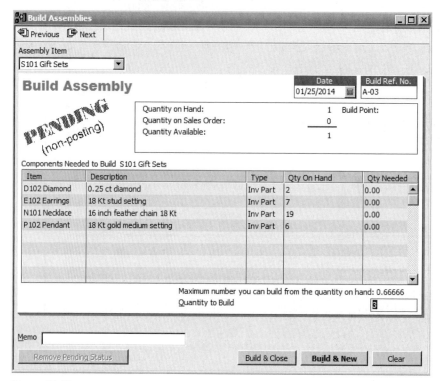

Figure 11-42

The Build Assemblies form is now stamped with the note PENDING (non-posting) to let you know that this transaction is not complete.

5. Click **Build & New** to build the next assembly item

Completing the Pending Assembly

When the inventory required is available to complete the build, you can finish the transaction. Display the Build Assemblies transaction that is pending on the screen and then change its status.

You can display the transaction in two ways:

- Open the Build Assemblies form. Click the Previous button 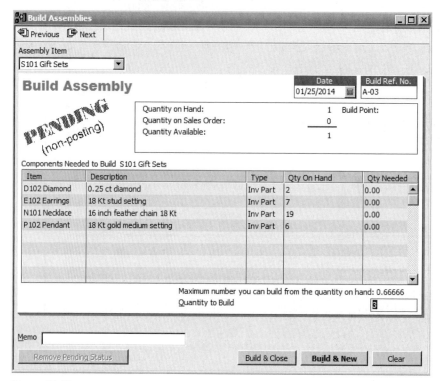 until the transaction you want is displayed on the screen; or

- Choose the Reports menu, then choose Inventory, and click Pending Builds (see page 641). Double click the build you want to complete. This method is preferred if you have recorded many build assembly transactions.

To change the status of the transaction:

- Click the Remove Pending Status button on the bottom left-hand corner of the form. This button becomes available as soon as the quantity available is sufficient to complete the build; or

- Choose the Edit Menu and click Mark Build as Final.

- Click Build & Close to record the assembly.

Source Documents

Enter the following source documents for this company. You may need to refer to previous chapters for additional information:

Source Docs for Practice
Continue to develop your skills by entering the following source documents.

SD44: Assembly #A-04   Dated January 25, 2014

Assemble three S102 Wedding Band Sets by using defined component items.

SD45: Customer Payment   Dated January 25, 2014

From Sadie Hawkings, Cheque #1778 for $994.40 in full payment of Invoice #322.

SD46: Bill   Dated January 25, 2014

Bill #HO-500834 received from Hydro One, $155.00 plus $20.15 HST for one month of hydro and heating service. The bill totals $175.15. Terms: Net 10 days.

SD47: Pay Bill   Dated January 25, 2014

Paid Cheque #1131 to Faithful Insurers, $5,424.00 in payment of Bill #FI-2014-34.

SD48: Pay Bill   Dated January 26, 2014

Paid Cheque #1132 to Sprint Canada, $135.60 in payment of Bill #SC-38105.

SD49: Invoice   Dated January 28, 2014

Invoice #326 to Pearl Black (set up new customer)

1	N104 Necklace	18 inch feather chain 18 Kt	$ 800.00	$ 800.00
1	D102 Diamond	0.25 ct diamond	1,000.00	1,000.00
1	P101 Pendant	18 Kt gold small setting	110.00	110.00
	HST		13%	248.30
	Sales total			$2,158.30

Terms: 1/5, n/30

Notes
Pearl Black
2333 Onyx Rd. #408
Toronto, ON M6D 2L9
Tel: (647) 499-1019
Credit limit: $4,000.00
Terms: 1/5, n/30

SD50: Bank Debit Memo #GT-54328   Dated January 28, 2014

From Golddiggers Trust, Cheque #1778 from Sadie Hawkings for $994.40 was returned as NSF. Create Sales Invoice #327 for the amount of the NSF cheque and the $30.00 administrative charge. Invoice totals $1,024.40. Terms: Due on receipt.

SD51: Bill   Dated January 28, 2014

Bill #GI-3622 received from Goldcrest Inc. to fill Purchase Order #127

10	E101 Earrings	18 Kt drop setting	$ 700.00
10	E102 Earrings	18 Kt stud setting	400.00
10	E103 Earrings	18 Kt studs	400.00
10	N105 Necklaces	18 inch box chain 18 Kt	3,750.00
	HST @ 7%		682.50
	Bill total		$5,932.50

Terms: 1/10, n/30

SD52: Credit Card Sales Receipt #1004   **Dated January 29, 2014**

To Cash Sales customers

1 B103 Bracelet	14 Kt bangle 3 stone setting	$ 625.00	$ 625.00
1 B105 Bracelet	14 Kt link solitaire setting	370.00	370.00
10 D101 Diamonds	0.10 ct diamond	400.00 ea.	4,000.00
4 E101 Earrings	18 Kt drop setting	140.00/pr.	560.00
3 E102 Earrings	18 Kt stud setting	80.00/pr.	240.00
2 N106 Necklaces	18 inch wire chain 18 Kt	610.00 ea.	1,220.00
3 P101 Pendants	18 Kt gold small setting	110.00 ea.	330.00
1 P102 Pendant	18 Kt gold medium setting	320.00	320.00
1 P103 Pendant	18 Kt gold large setting	630.00	630.00
1 R103 Ring	18 Kt band narrow plain	375.00	375.00
1 R104 Ring	18 Kt band wide plain	570.00	570.00
1 R109 Ring	18 Kt diamond band 0.25 ct	1,200.00	1,200.00
1 S101 Gift Set	Necklace, pendant, and earrings	3,500.00	3,500.00
1 S102 Wed. Bd St	Matching wedding bands	750.00	750.00
R100 Repairs	Jewellery repairs		160.00
HST		13%	1,930.50

Total deposited to the *Bank Visa* account $16,780.50

SD53: Pay Bill   **Dated January 29, 2014**

Paid Cheque #1133 to Hydro One, $175.15 in payment of Bill #HO-500834.

SD54: Bank Credit Memo #GT-819788   **Dated January 30, 2014**

From Golddiggers Trust: Preauthorized withdrawals from the chequing account for

Mortgage ($155.00 principal and $405.00 interest)	$560.00
Bank loan ($210.00 principal and $80.00 interest)	290.00

SD55:

EMPLOYEE TIME SUMMARY SHEET #2014-2

Date: January 31, 2014 (for the pay period ending January 31, 2014)

Name of Employee	Regular Hours	Overtime Hours	Sick Leave Hours	Vacation Hours	Advances Received/ Advances Repaid
Garnet Y. Amarald	85	—	—	—	—
Jadine R. Amethyst	85	10	—	—	$200.00

a. Using Employee Time Summary Sheet #2014-2 and the Employee Information Sheet, complete payroll for two employees
b. Amethyst will receive an advance of $200.00 and repay $50.00 over each of the next four pay cheques
c. Pay commissions: 5% of $3,350.00 and 0.5% of $61,424.00 to Amarald and 0.5% of $61,424.00 to Amethyst
d. Manually prepare Cheques #1134 and #1135

Notes
Commissions are calculated as follows: Net Revenue from Sales for January was $61,424.00 (i.e., revenue less 10 percent volume discount = 62,675.00 – 1,251.00).
Revenue from Services for January was $3,350.00.

Notes
Refer to page 335 for assistance with applying unused credits to an invoice.

SD56: Memo #1-3   **Dated January 31, 2014**

From Owner: Assess finance charges on overdue account from Glitters as of January 31, 2014. Apply unused credits before assessing interest charges.

SD57: Memo #1-4　　　　　　　　　　　　**Dated January 31, 2014**

From Owner: Complete adjusting entries for supplies and prepaid expenses for January. Create new Expense account: 5380 - *Security Expenses*.

Prepaid security services	$ 200.00
Prepaid insurance	800.00
Jewellery boxes & bags	120.00
Office & computer supplies	140.00
Jewellery parts and gold	2,390.00

SD58: Memo #1-5　　　　　　　　　　　　**Dated January 31, 2014**

From Owner: Make remittance to the Receiver General for HST Payable as of January 31. Issue Cheque #1136.

SD59: Memo #1-7　　　　　　　　　　　　**Dated January 31, 2014**

From Owner: Pay all payroll liabilities through to January 31, 2014, to the following agencies. Issue Cheques #1137 to #1139.
To Receiver General: EI, CPP, and income tax
To Workplace Safety and Insurance Board: WSIB
To Faithful Insurers: Insurance

SD60: Memo #1-8　　　　　　　　　　　　**Dated January 31, 2014**

Use the following bank statement to reconcile the *Bank Chequing* account.

Notes

Remember to include the NSF Fee with Service Charges as expenses for the reconciliation.

Golddiggers Trust

www.golddiggers.com
200 Spenders Rd.
Toronto, ON M2G 4D5
(416) 464-7111

ACCOUNT	**ACCOUNT HOLDER**
January 31/14	Sparkles
Chequing Account	55 Glittering Way
27765 43100	Toronto, Ontario M3T 5F9

Date	Item	Deposits	Withdrawals	Balance
	Balance Forward			$32,460.00
01/02/2014	Deposit	$ 1,000.00		$33,460.00
01/04/2014	Deposit	2,277.00		35,737.00
01/04/2014	Cheque 1124		6,355.80	29,381.20
01/06/2014	Cheque 1125		4,194.40	25,186.80
01/07/2014	Deposit	3,784.68		28,971.48
01/10/2014	Deposit	3,500.00		32,471.48
01/15/2014	Cheque 1126		4,181.00	28,290.48
01/15/2014	Cheque 1127		1,356.83	26,933.65
01/15/2014	Cheque 1128		1,041.14	25,892.51
01/18/2014	Cheque 1129		10,920.00	14,972.51
01/19/2014	Deposit	3,276.00		18,248.51
01/20/2014	Deposit	4,600.00		22,848.51
01/20/2014	Deposit	8,848.00		31,696.51
01/24/2014	Cheque 1130		888.00	30,808.51
01/25/2014	Deposit	994.40		31,802.91
01/25/2014	Cheque 1131		5,424.00	26,378.91
01/26/2014	Cheque 1132		135.60	26,243.31
01/28/2014	NSF Cheque		994.40	25,248.91
	NSF Fee		30.00	25,218.91
01/30/2014	Debit Memo		850.00	24,368.91
	Service Fee		30.00	24,338.91
	Interest	50.00		24,388.91
	Closing Balance			$24,388.91

Total Deposits: 8		$28,330.08
Total Withdrawals: 13		$36,401.17

SD61: Memo #1-9　　　　　　　　　　　　**Dated January 31, 2014**

Use the following bank statement to reconcile the *Bank Visa* account.

Golddiggers Trust

www.golddiggers.com
200 Spenders Rd.
Toronto, ON M2G 4D5
(416) 464-7111

ACCOUNT	ACCOUNT HOLDER
Visa Deposit Account	Sparkles
January 31/14	55 Glittering Way
27765 89971	Toronto, Ontario M3T 5F9

Date	Item	Deposits	Withdrawals	Balance
	Balance Forward			$ 2,180.00
01/08/2014	Deposit	$ 7,175.50		9,355.50
01/11/2014	Payment		$576.30	8,779.20
01/15/2014	Deposit	14,746.50		23,525.70
01/22/2014	Deposit	10,266.05		33,791.75
01/29/2014	Deposit	16,780.50		50,572.25
01/30/2014	2% transaction fee		967.85	49,604.40
01/31/2014	Closing Balance	$49,604.40		

SUMMARY	5 Deposits	$48,968.55
	2 Withdrawals	$ 1,544.15

SD62: Memo #1-10　　　　　　　　　　　　**Dated January 31, 2014**

Use the following Visa statement to reconcile the *Visa Payable* account. Write Cheque #1140 to Golddiggers Trust Visa (use Quick Add to add the new Other payee) to pay the full balance.

Golddiggers Trust

www.golddiggers.com
200 Spenders Rd.
Toronto, ON M2G 4D5
(416) 464-7111

Visa Statement

ACCOUNT	ACCOUNT HOLDER
Visa Account 4550 3948 7449 7171	Sparkles
January 31/14	55 Glittering Way
27765 89971	Toronto, Ontario M3T 5F9

12/30/2013	Marcie's Gifts (opening balance)	$210.00
01/11/2014	Stationers	158.20
01/13/2014	Stationers (credit)	−45.20
01/20/2014	Hardware Surplus Supplies	50.85
01/23/2014	Glass Experts	339.00
01/29/2014	Annual fee	25.00

STATEMENT SUMMARY

	New Charges	$548.05	
	Credits	$ 45.20	
	Balance Owing	$737.85	
	Minimum Payment	$ 75.00	by Feb. 12, 2014

Notes
The first purchase was made in the previous month and accounts for the opening balance on January 1.

SD63: Memo #1-11　　　　　　　　　　　　**Dated January 31, 2014**

Transfer $45,000.00 from the *Bank Visa* account to the *Bank Savings* account.

Inventory Reports

We saw some reports for inventory items in previous chapters: Sales by Item Summary report, Sales by Item Detail report, Item List, and Item Price. The Sales Graph also provides inventory sales information. Refer to Chapter 6 for a review of these reports. The Inventory Sales reports are reviewed on page 643. The Inventory group of reports provides inventory control information for a company.

As with other groups of reports, you can access inventory reports from the Reports menu or from the Report Centre.

We will continue to use the Report Centre because of its report preview feature. To access the same reports from the Report Centre,

1. **Click**	the **Reports icon** on the Icon bar and **click Inventory** on the left-hand side of the screen
2. **Click**	the **List View icon** [≡] to view the reports that are available under this heading in list view:

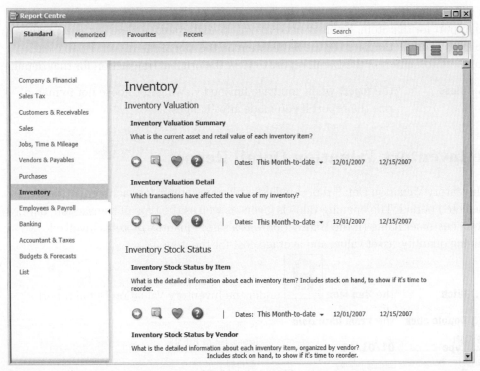

Figure 11-43

The Inventory Valuation Summary Report

The Inventory Valuation Summary report shows the current totals for all Inventory Part and Inventory Assembly items, the items that have costs and asset values. For each item, the quantity on hand, the total asset value, and the retail value based on sales prices are shown. Separate columns show the percentage of the total for each item and value.

1. **Click**	the **Run icon** [Run] under the Inventory Valuation Summary report
2. **Double click**	the **Date field**
3. **Type**	**01/31/14**

Notes

You can filter the report just like any other report and modify the headings, footers, and format.

4. Press ⌨(tab) or **click** the **Refresh button** to update the report:

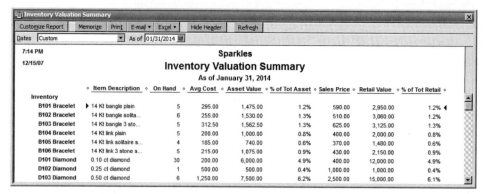

Figure 11-44

The report shows the inventory value on a specific date. You cannot sort this report and the only modification you can make is to select a different date for the valuation. You can also drill down to other reports from this one.

Double click the summary information for any item to view the Inventory Valuation Detail report for that item. You may need to edit the date range for the Detail report if there are no transactions for the individual item on the day of the report. Double click any of the information in the Detail report to view the original transaction for that detail.

5. Close the **report** when you have finished viewing it. Choose not to memorize the report if you made any changes

The Inventory Valuation Detail Report

The Inventory Valuation Detail report includes all transactions for each item during the selected period. The opening value is given, as well as the type of transaction, date, number, customer name (if the transaction was a sale), quantity of items involved, remaining quantity, asset value, and average cost for the item.

Notes

To access the report from the Reports menu:

- Choose the Reports menu, then choose Inventory, and click Inventory Valuation Detail to open the report
- Enter 01/01/14 in the From date field
- Enter 01/31/14 in the To date field
- Press ⌨(tab) or click the Refresh button to update the report

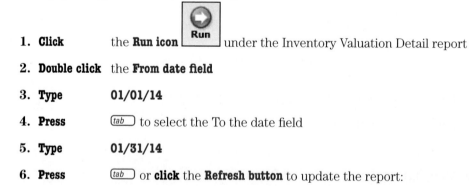

1. Click the **Run icon** [Run] under the Inventory Valuation Detail report

2. Double click the **From date field**

3. Type **01/01/14**

4. Press ⌨(tab) to select the To the date field

5. Type **01/31/14**

6. Press ⌨(tab) or **click** the **Refresh button** to update the report:

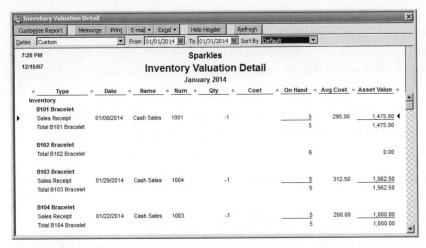

Figure 11-45

You can sort this report by any of the column headings.

You can double click any detail to view the original transaction for that detail.

7. Close the **displayed report** when you have finished viewing it. Choose not to memorize the report if you made any changes

The Inventory Stock Status by Item Report

The Inventory Stock Status by Item report is a quantity report. For each item, you will see the preferred vendor for the item, the reorder point, the number currently on order from customers, the number actually in stock, the number on purchase orders, the order date (delivery date), and the average number sold each week during the selected period. In addition, an Order column shows whether the item needs to be ordered because its stock has fallen below the reorder point, so you could use this report to prepare purchase orders.

1. Click the **Run icon** under the Inventory Stock Status by Item report

2. Double click the **From date field**

3. Type **01/01/14**

4. Press ⓣⓐⓑ to select the To date field

5. Type **01/31/14**

6. Press ⓣⓐⓑ or **click** the **Refresh button** to view the report:

Notes
To access the report from the Reports menu:
- Choose the Reports menu, then choose Inventory, and click Inventory Stock Status by Item to open the report
- Enter 01/01/14 in the From date field
- Enter 01/31/14 in the To date field
- Press ⓣⓐⓑ or click the Refresh button to update the report

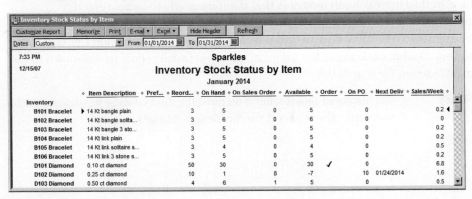

Figure 11-46

The ✓ in the Order column indicates that the item needs to be reordered.

You can modify this report only by entering a different date range.

You can double click any item to drill down to the Inventory Valuation Detail report for that item. Double click any of the information in the Detail report to drill down to the original transaction for that detail.

7. Close   the **displayed report** when you have finished viewing it. Choose not to memorize the report if you made any changes

The Inventory Stock Status by Vendor Report

The Inventory Stock Status by Vendor report is the Inventory Stock Status by Item report organized by preferred vendor. For each vendor, the items are listed with the same details as the Item report. If no vendors are entered, as in our data file, the two reports are the same.

Notes

To access the report from the Reports menu:

- Choose the Reports menu, then choose Inventory, and click Inventory Stock Status by Vendor to open the report
- Enter 01/01/14 in the From date field
- Enter 01/31/14 in the To date field
- Press `tab` or click the Refresh button to update the report

1. Click   the **Run icon** [Run] under the Inventory Stock Status by Vendor report

2. Double click   the **From date field**

3. Type   **01/01/14**

4. Press   `tab` to select the To date field

5. Type   **01/31/14**

6. Press   `tab` or **click** the **Refresh button** to view the report:

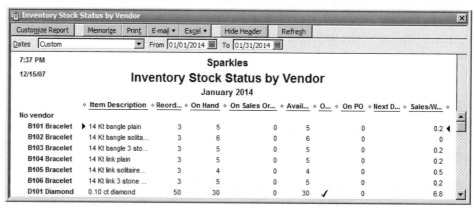

Figure 11-47

The ✓ in the Order column indicates that the item needs to be reordered.

You can modify this report only by entering a different date range.

You can double click any item to drill down to the Inventory Valuation Detail report for that item. Double click any of the information in the Detail report to drill-down to the original transaction for that detail.

7. Close   the **displayed report** when you have finished viewing it. Choose not to memorize the report if you made any changes

The Physical Inventory Worksheet

The Physical Inventory Worksheet is a form that you can use for taking inventory in a business. It includes the quantity on hand for each item and a space for entering the actual number found in stock, based on a physical count, i.e., a worksheet. You can handle discrepancies by adjusting the quantity on hand.

1. **Click** the **Run icon** under the Physical Inventory Worksheet report:

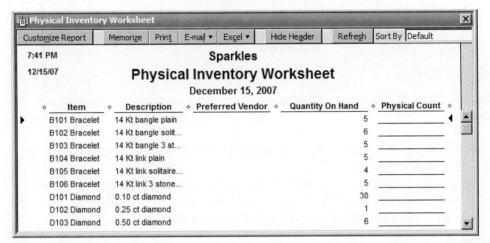

Figure 11-48

Notes

To access the worksheet from the Reports menu:
- Choose the Reports menu, then choose Inventory, and click Physical Inventory Worksheet to open the worksheet; or
- Choose the Vendors menu, and then choose Inventory Activities, and click Physical Inventory Worksheet to open the worksheet

You cannot modify or filter this report.

You can double click any item detail to drill down to the Inventory Valuation Detail report for that item. Double click any of the information in the Detail report to drill down to the original transaction for that detail.

2. **Close** the **report** when you have finished viewing it. Choose not to memorize the report if you made any changes

The Pending Builds Report

The Pending Builds report shows any items that you tried to assemble with insufficient quantities and chose to mark as pending. From the report you can open the form to complete a build.

1. **Click** 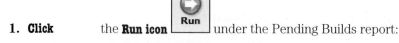 the **Run icon** under the Pending Builds report:

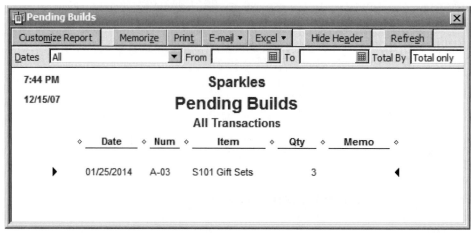

Figure 11-49

You can modify this report only by changing the date range. The default is to show all pending transactions.

You can double click any detail in the report to drill down to the Build Assemblies form for that transaction so that you can complete the build. The form will open with all the information you entered before you marked it as pending.

2. **Close** the **report** when you have finished viewing it. Choose not to memorize the report if you made any changes

Inventory Reminders

The Reminders list can include a reminder to reorder inventory that has fallen below the minimum or reorder point if the preference is selected in the Reminders preferences. The Reminders list is shown here:

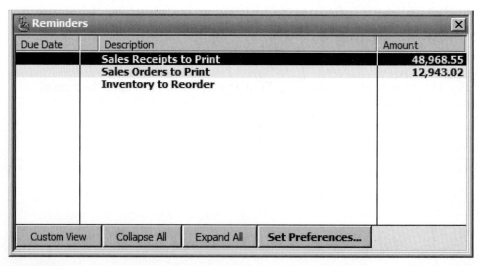

Figure 11-50

1. **Double click** **Inventory to Reorder** to open the list of reminder details:

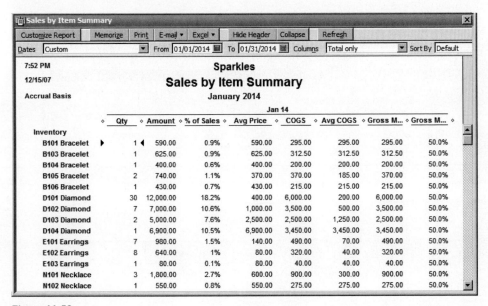

Reminders

Due Date	Description	Amount
	Sales Receipts to Print	**48,968.55**
	Sales Orders to Print	**12,943.02**
	Inventory to Reorder	
	D101 Diamond - 0.10 ct diamond	
	P101 Pendant - 18 Kt gold small setting	
	P102 Pendant - 18 Kt gold medium setting	
	R103 Ring - 18 Kt band narrrow plain	
	R104 Ring - 18 Kt band wide plain	

Custom View	Collapse All	Expand All	Set Preferences...

Figure 11-51

> **Notes**
> The Gift Sets that we need to build do not appear on the Reminders list because the build point was marked as zero.

Assemblies to Build would be added on the Reminders list as a separate line when the build point is greater than zero and the number on hand has fallen below the build point.

Sales Reports for Inventory

When the data file includes inventory (inventory part or assembly items), some sales reports have additional information. The zoom-in reports and modifying and filtering features remain unchanged. Refer to Chapter 6 for more information on sales reports.

Sales by Item Summary Report

The Sales by Item Summary report has different information for different types of items as shown in the following report:

> **Notes**
> To view the report,
> • Open the Report Centre
> • Click the Sales heading on the left-hand side of the screen
> • Click the Run icon under the Sales by Item Summary report
> • Enter 01/01/14 in the From date field
> • Press (tab)
> • Enter 01/31/14 in the To date field

Sales by Item Summary

Customize Report	Memorize	Print	E-mail ▾	Excel ▾	Hide Header	Collapse	Refresh

Dates Custom ▾ From 01/01/2014 To 01/31/2014 Columns Total only ▾ Sort By Default

7:52 PM
12/15/07
Accrual Basis

Sparkles
Sales by Item Summary
January 2014

		Qty	Amount	% of Sales	Avg Price	COGS	Avg COGS	Gross M...	Gross M...
						Jan 14			
Inventory									
B101 Bracelet	▶	1	590.00	0.9%	590.00	295.00	295.00	295.00	50.0%
B103 Bracelet		1	625.00	0.9%	625.00	312.50	312.50	312.50	50.0%
B104 Bracelet		1	400.00	0.6%	400.00	200.00	200.00	200.00	50.0%
B105 Bracelet		2	740.00	1.1%	370.00	370.00	185.00	370.00	50.0%
B106 Bracelet		1	430.00	0.7%	430.00	215.00	215.00	215.00	50.0%
D101 Diamond		30	12,000.00	18.2%	400.00	6,000.00	200.00	6,000.00	50.0%
D102 Diamond		7	7,000.00	10.6%	1,000.00	3,500.00	500.00	3,500.00	50.0%
D103 Diamond		2	5,000.00	7.6%	2,500.00	2,500.00	1,250.00	2,500.00	50.0%
D104 Diamond		1	6,900.00	10.5%	6,900.00	3,450.00	3,450.00	3,450.00	50.0%
E101 Earrings		7	980.00	1.5%	140.00	490.00	70.00	490.00	50.0%
E102 Earrings		8	640.00	1%	80.00	320.00	40.00	320.00	50.0%
E103 Earrings		1	80.00	0.1%	80.00	40.00	40.00	40.00	50.0%
N101 Necklace		3	1,800.00	2.7%	600.00	900.00	300.00	900.00	50.0%
N102 Necklace		1	550.00	0.8%	550.00	275.00	275.00	275.00	50.0%

Figure 11-52

For the Inventory Part and Inventory Assembly items, the cost of goods sold, the average cost of goods sold, the gross margin, and the percentage margin are added to the details provided for other items. For Discount items, only the total and the percentage of total sales is provided.

Pending Sales Report

The Pending Sales report shows the transactions that we marked as pending. In this company file, only one pending build transaction was created. The report is shown here:

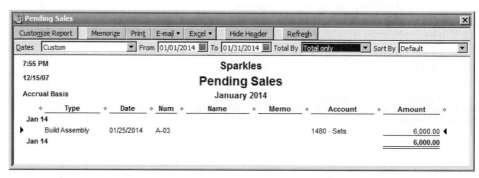

Figure 11-53

You can double click on a pending sale on the report to open the Build Assemblies form and complete the assembly. The Build Assemblies form will open with all the information you entered before you marked it as pending.

Finishing Your Session

1. **Back up**   your **Company data file**

2. **Close**   the **Company file**

3. **Close**   the **QuickBooks program**

Notes
To view the report,
- Open the Report Centre
- Click the Sales heading on the left-hand side of the screen

- Click the Run icon under the Pending Sales report
- Enter 01/01/14 in the From date field
- Press (tab)
- Enter 01/31/14 in the To date field

Chapter 12 Contre Le Vent:
Payroll & Inventory Setup

Chapter 13 Melody's Music Centre:
Practice Application

**Chapter 12 and Chapter 13 can be found on the CD
that accompanies this text.**

INDEX

Note: The chapters found on the CD accompanying this text are indicated as follows:

Chapter 12: Contre le Vent – ClV

Chapter 13: Melody Music Centre – MMC

Tax Appendix - Tax